DATE DUE

GAYLORD			PRINTED IN U.S.A.

Sir Francis Drake

SIR FRANCIS DRAKE

Yale University Press   New Haven and London

HARRY KELSEY

The Queen's Pirate

Frontispiece: *Manuscript World Map on Vellum showing Drake's Route of Circumnavigation* (London, 1587). Yale Center for British Art, Paul Mellon Collection

Publication of this book is supported in part by a grant from the Giles W. and Elise G. Mead Foundation.

Printed in the United States of America.

Library of Congress Cataloging-in-Publication Data
Kelsey, Harry, 1929–
Sir Francis Drake : the queen's pirate / Harry Kelsey.
p. cm.
Includes bibliographical references (p.   ) and index.
ISBN 0-300-07182-5 (cloth : alk. paper)
1. Drake, Francis, Sir, 1540?–1596.   2. Great Britain—History, Naval—Tudors, 1485–1603.   3. Admirals—Great Britain—Biography.   4. Pirates—Great Britain—Biography.   5. Explorers—America—Biography.   I. Title.
DA86.22.D7K45   1998
942.05'5'092—dc21   97-40312
[B]
A catalogue record for this book is available from the British Library.

The paper in this book meets the guidelines for permanence and durability of the Committee on Production Guidelines for Book Longevity of the Council on Library Resources.

10 9 8 7 6 5 4 3 2 1

For Giles Mead,
who tempts life from dirt to wine in a habit of seasons stronger than love

From *The Lord and the General Din of the World*
by Jane Mead

CONTENTS

Illustrations

Maps and Plans

ACKNOWLEDGMENTS

BY SCHOLARLY CUSTOM THE FIRST few pages of a book are used to introduce people who might reasonably be asked to shoulder some of the blame for errors and omissions, perhaps even the whole concept of the work. This is a marvelous tradition, and I intend to honor it to the full. If anyone bears responsibility for the book, it is my friend Giles Mead, who told me to do it. More than that, he encouraged the Giles W. and Elise G. Mead Foundation to provide funding for travel to European and American libraries and archives, and he otherwise supported the preparation of the manuscript.

Other friends also gave their assistance. Martin Ridge, former director of research at the Huntington Library, gave me an office to work in, urged me to complete the study, and waded patiently through the finished manuscript. Paul Hoffman, Geoffrey Parker, Robert Ritchie, Dan Heaton, and Iris Engstrand performed similar services. Each person read the full manuscript, and without exception each one pointed out passages where I had managed to make an exciting story boring, or somehow contrived to get other things wrong. My former professor William B. Faherty, S.J., helped me during several trips to the Vatican Film Collection at Saint Louis University's Pius XII Library and later made useful comments on the completed manuscript.

Staff members at both the Huntington and Pius XII libraries gave their usual courteous assistance, as did the staff of the Bancroft Library, the California State Library, the Folger Shakespeare Library, the John Carter Brown Library, and the Library of Congress (manuscript, map, and rare book departments).

In Spain, I received great assistance at the Archivo General de Indias in Seville, the Archivo Histórico Nacional in Madrid, and the Biblioteca de Francisco Zabálburu in Madrid. Of all the archives in Spain, the one outstanding in my mind is the Archivo General de Simancas, where the staff sets an example of service and assistance that other archives are seldom able to match. A Spanish historian and friend, Marisol Santos Arrebola, copied materials for me at the AGI after I neglected to copy them myself during earlier visits.

The British Library (map and manuscript departments) and the Public Record Office are both blessed with competent staff members who somehow respond promptly to requests from an astonishing horde of researchers. Some smaller English archives do equally well. People at the Lambeth Palace Library, the Canterbury Cathedral Archives, and the Kent Record Office at Maidstone were all extremely helpful in getting me through the relevant materials in their important holdings of ecclesiastical records. Staff members at the Devon Record Office and the West Country Studies Library in Exeter were patient and courteous during my several visits, as were the people in the Plymouth branch of the Devon Record Office, the Plymouth City Museum, the Plymouth Public Library, the Gloucestershire Record Office in Gloucester, and the National Maritime Museum in Greenwich. Library officials at both the Bodleian Library of Oxford University and the Cambridge University Library allowed me to use their manuscript collections. Beyond that, the staff of the Corpus Christi College Parker Library made other manuscript materials available for my use. The officials of the Inner Temple Library in London let me study collections of manuscripts and globes. The Institute of Historical Research at the University of London gave free use of their modern published materials, which are available on open shelves and thus much easier to access than those in the general reading room of the nearby British Library.

The staff of the Bayerische Staatsbibliothek in Munich allowed me to make copies of the Drake materials in that collection and answered my queries by mail when it turned out that I had neglected to check one or two items. The Kartensammlung und Globenmuseum of the Österreichische Nationalbibliothek in Vienna let me spend several days analyzing the Gutiérrez planisphere and other cartographic materials. The Biblioteca Apostolica Vaticana gave me complete access to the manuscript and cartographical collections of that institution, as it does for all scholarly researchers. The Algemeen Rijksarchief and the Koninklijke Bibliotheek, The Hague, proved to me that it is possible for a library to be both modern and scholarly, with fine collections, a helpful staff, and new buildings of great architectural merit.

My son Joseph Kelsey gave me a good deal of practical computer advice, and my son Matthew advised me on the preparation of computer-generated illustrations. My neighbor Steve Bass introduced me to the mysteries of CorelDraw. My daughter Sarah Forrest served as my agent-in-place at the Bancroft Library, copying materials from microfilm and from those books that were not available at the Huntington Library. My wife, Mary Ann Kelsey, helped me copy manuscript materials, and while I was tucked away in reading rooms, she scouted out lectures and historic places that we could visit after the libraries closed.

A few other pieces of self-justification might as well be placed here as anywhere. Most published collections of early manuscripts modernize spelling and grammar and otherwise change the original documents. As a result the exact meaning is often obscured, and writers of little learning or sophistication often appear to be more literate than they really were. I have tried to avoid these problems by consulting the original documents in all cases of any importance. Beyond this, I have rechecked all quotations in the text by comparing them with the original documents. Spellings, accents, and abbreviations have been preserved to the extent that such things are reasonably possible. Because it is not possible to deal this way with translations, I have put the original wording in notes.

There is a related problem with the titles of books and manuscripts cited in the notes and in the list of sources. I have almost invariably used the form followed in the original manuscript or publication. Proper names were also difficult. I prefer to use the form followed in the sixteenth century, but people in those days often used a variety of spellings, even for their own names. As a result, I have followed sixteenth-century usage where it is practical and modern usage in cases where confusion might otherwise result.

Most readers will find their interest waxing and waning as the story proceeds. Drake enthusiasts in the United States will no doubt be more interested in the voyage to California than will readers in England. Those with genealogical interests will want more information about family history than will others. No doubt some parts of the book will appeal only to the author. These are matters of personal preference, and there seems to be no traditional way to spread the blame for them.

Or perhaps there is. While I was trying to write the book, my dog Barney did little but sit at the door and whine. While this was not a major problem, dogs are usually willing to take the blame when things go wrong. No doubt he would do so on this occasion, though it hardly seems fair. Infelicities in style and inadvertent errors are really my fault. I cheerfully take responsibility and ask the reader in advance to accept my apology.

Introduction

FOR FOUR CENTURIES NEW BOOKS about Francis Drake have made a regular appearance in libraries and bookstores. In recent years the rate has been one every year or so, and with good reason. Francis Drake did things that few men have matched. Drake first captured the fancy of the European world with his yearlong raid on Spanish colonial ports and shipping. His subsequent escape took him on a voyage around the globe, an astounding trip of nearly three years. In the process Drake stole so much and traveled so far that no one could remember anything quite like it. Drake was the talk of the capitals of Europe, where people wanted to know exactly what sort of man he was.

That seems to be the problem, getting the story straight. Drake loved to regale his friends with tales—not necessarily factual—of his grand achievements. In this process he did not lack for assistance. The English government put out varying stories about his voyage around the world, while Drake's victims volunteered embellished accounts of his depredations. Chroniclers in England and elsewhere added to the confusion with biographical sketches that were part hearsay and part speculation. Family members, who should have known the facts, contributed to the compilation of mythical details. The Drake that emerged from this material was a man who would have pleased the old pirate: a heroic figure, brave and just, but a bit pompous and preachy, and unbelievably pious. This Drake bears only a passing resemblance to the Devon farmboy who went to sea, became a pirate, and made himself rich, managed to have himself knighted, and became a friend of the queen.

In ordinary times, piracy would not have been much of a stepping-stone to social advancement. But for Devon during the life of Francis Drake these were not ordinary times. Drake was born into a provincial society racked by economic, social, and religious change. The wealth amassed during past centuries by the churches and monasteries of England suddenly became available for secular appropriation. Under government assault, traditional Catholicism was abandoned or suppressed, and there was no re-placement that held any great attraction for the ordinary people.[1] In this atmosphere, a man with no overwhelming attachment to conservative val-ues could hope to better himself, both economically and socially.

The most dramatic social change occurred just a year before Francis Drake was born. It began with a ceremony that took place in the town of Tavistock. On 3 March 1539 the monks of the Abbey of the Blessed Virgin Mary and Saint Rumon sat in their chapter house, where the representative of King Henry VIII waited to read a declaration inscribed on parchment.[2]

The document was written in Latin, but the monks understood the words: "Omnibus Christifidelibus ad quos presentus scriptum pervenerit," began the king's man. "To all faithful Christians to whom these presents shall come, John Peryn, who through the sufferance of God was abbot of the abbey and church of the Blessed Virgin Mary and Saint Rumon of Tavystock in the County of Devon, and of the monastic community of the order of Saint Benedict in the same place, sends eternal greetings in the Lord."

It took about five minutes for the king's representative to read the entire text. By its terms Abbot John Peryn and the other members of the Bene-dictine community at Tavistock surrendered their lands and buildings, along with all their legal and spiritual rights and privileges, to the king. It was an astonishing document, covering enormous clerical privileges, plus thousands of acres of agricultural and grazing land, forests, fisheries, mills, and mines. There were inheritances and annuities, tithes and pensions, and all sorts of ecclesiastical benefices. There were courts and fairs and of-fices and franchises. According to the document the king's man had pre-pared, the assembled monks did it all "by their own free will and consent" and recognized King Henry VIII as "the supreme head on earth of the English church."[3]

The tone of the document was mild, considering the tenor of the times, but the monks were far from willing. Still, no one grumbled aloud, for monks in most other places had been required to sign documents couched in the most humiliating terms.[4] In truth, the king's man expected no dif-ficulties. That had been settled some months before at Tyburn, when stub-

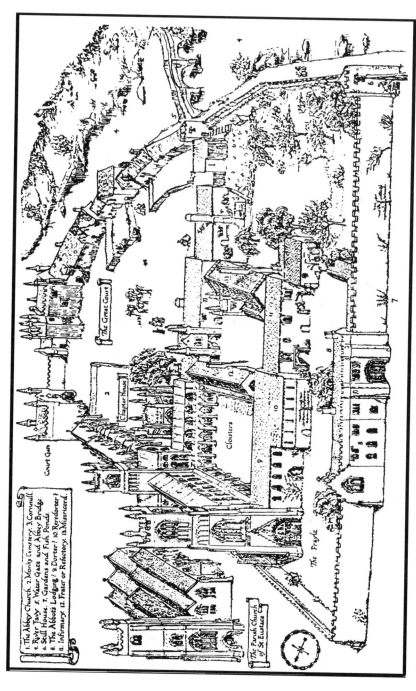

Tavistock Abbey, no doubt falling into decay, was the largest structure in town when Francis Drake was a boy. The parish church, far left, still stands, as does a gateway and some sections of wall, and some other remnants. Adapted from Finberg, Tavistock Abbey, *221.*

born monks who refused to acknowledge the king as head of the church were hanged and quartered. When the reading was over, the abbot signed his name, "per me, Johannem, Abbattem," followed by the prior and then by each monk in order of seniority.[5]

An entire way of life had come to an end, and everyone knew it. Most people could not imagine just how things would change, but some things were already clear. The abbot and the prior received generous pensions, enough to ensure their comfort in a newly secular world. The choir monks, ordained priests, were in a different category. Their pensions were tiny, and if they could not find parish work, most faced a bleak future. Still, these monks from Tavistock were better off than some religious. By a cruel logic, the members of the mendicant orders, who had vowed to live on daily charity, were given nothing. Chantry priests, often hired by religious houses to fill benefices, were forced to fend for themselves when their benefactions were confiscated. Of course, some men could farm or work at family crafts, as they always had, but many priests had no experience in caring for their own needs.[6]

Tavistock laymen had their own problems. Medical care, social life, charity, education, and a good deal of subsistence had come from the monastery. Many farmers held land in some sort of rental arrangement with the abbey, which had actual title to the property. Some of these arrangements had endured for generations, with nearly automatic renewal and reasonable fees. With confiscation of monastic property, everything changed, and not for the better. The land titles seldom went to the local farmers. At Tavistock most of the monastic holdings were quickly given to John, Lord Russell, and his agents began negotiating new leases, collecting substantial fines from those who wanted their leases renewed. One such leaseholder was John Drake, who farmed at Crowndale with his sons, John, Robert, and Edmund.[7]

Sir Francis Drake

I

Loomings

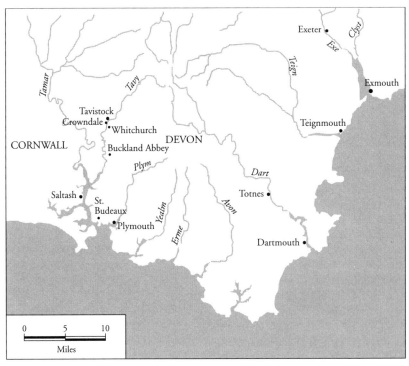

Francis Drake was born in Crowndale, a mile or so south of Tavistock. He was raised in Plymouth with the Hawkins family. In later life he bought the former Buckland Abbey and lived there, still keeping his ties with Plymouth.

I

From Tavistock to Plymouth

No hero ever dies. He lives, instead, in myth and legend. Part of the myth stretches back to include his origins. In the case of Francis Drake his forbears were dimly known and his boyhood obscure. The Drake family was established in Crowndale, Devon, a century or more before his birth. The place was originally part of the demesne land of Tavistock Abbey, but from very early days the fields at Crowndale seem to have been rented to families who had formerly served the abbot of Tavistock and the religious community. Some of their lease arrangements had endured for generations, with reasonable fees and nearly automatic renewal.[1]

Before Francis Drake spread terror through the ports of Spanish America, none of the Crowndale Drakes ever attracted much attention. Precisely when they arrived in Crowndale is unclear. Records of the abbey go back far enough to show that Richard Lamborn held the farm in the middle of the fourteenth century, followed by his son-in-law, William Gylys. By the middle of the fifteenth century Henry Drake, perhaps related by blood or marriage to Lamborn and Gylys, held the Crowndale lease. On 10 September 1481 Simon Drake, who was perhaps the son of Henry Drake, received a forty-year lease on messuages, lands, and tenements in Crowndale, with an annual rent of a little more than four pounds, probably a reasonable sum.[2] The loamy soil at Crowndale was fertile enough to make the Drake family prosperous, and with prosperity came the desire to keep the land in the family.[3] In time Simon Drake passed the lease along to his nephew John Drake, who ultimately gave it to his own son John.[4]

John Drake and his wife Margerie seem to have had three children. John junior was their eldest, followed by Edmund and Robert, along with another son named John, perhaps the child of an earlier marriage. In the

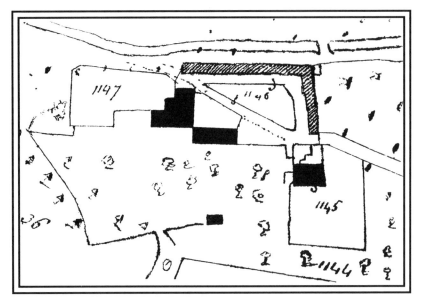

*Crowndale farm, from a 1765 plat of the Bedford Estate drawn by Gilbert Aislabie. The small
dark building in the lower center is the one generally thought to have been the birthplace of
Francis Drake. Reprinted from Aislabie, "Plan of the West Part." See also Alexander,
"Crowndale"; "Early Life of Francis Drake."*

course of time these sons married and had their own families. The records
are scant, but it is clear that Edmund married and became the father of
Francis Drake. Some idea of Drake family wealth can be seen in the Lay
Subsidy Rolls of 1524. Simon Drake had goods valued at £18, while John
had goods with a value of £5.[5] A similar record made nearly twenty years
later shows that John and Margerie Drake had about what Simon Drake
had when the farm was his: their personal holdings were valued at £20 in
1543. Their son Edmund had goods rated at £4, about what his father had
twenty years earlier.[6] The Drake family was well off, much more so than
most of their neighbors.

Crowndale was located a mile or so southwest of the town and abbey of
Tavistock. If the boundaries of the Crowndale farm remained about the
same over the years, then it was a very sizable place for the Drake family. A
description of the farm in the eighteenth century recorded a "Dwelling
House, Barnes, Stables, Brewhouse, pond-house, Sheep-penns & Linnys,

*The house in which Francis Drake lived probably
looked something like this longhouse. The interior was
divided by the chimney, which separated living
quarters from the byre, where the farm animals lived.
Adapted from Mercer,* English Vernacular Houses,
*39–40, original drawing in the collection of the
National Monuments Record; and from Lewis,*
Scenery of the Rivers Tamar and Tavy, *view no. 18.*

with two Gardens and three Orchards."[7] The entire property contained a bit more than 157 acres.[8] Several decades later the buildings were listed as "a Good Farm House, Two Barns, Stable, Beast House and Pigsties," with somewhat more than 191 acres of woods, meadows, pastures, and arable land.[9]

The original dwelling was destroyed in the early 1800s, but a few years earlier a drawing of the place was made by the local vicar.[10] Later the sketch was engraved and published.[11] Still later, in the twentieth century, the ruins of the building were located and marked, and they can still be seen in an enclosure near the present farm buildings.[12]

A good idea of the size of the place can be gained from an eighteenth-century estate map, which shows a stone farmhouse facing a long, narrow courtyard, with another building of stone or wood on the opposite side.[13] Judging from the sketch and the map, the dwelling was a typical sixteenth-century longhouse. In this sort of structure the interior fireplace and chimney served as a dividing wall and supported a stairway to the loft. A passageway on one side of the chimney separated the house from the byre, which usually had a stone floor and center drainage channel to make the job of removing animal waste a bit less messy.[14]

The family occupied both floors of the dwelling, a main room about fifteen feet square on the ground floor, with one or two other rooms in the loft or attic. Heat for the dwelling came from the fireplace, which also served for cooking and baking. Furnishings were plain, and there was no effort to separate sleeping quarters from the living areas.

Life was much simpler then. Most people had but a single change of clothes, and laundry was done only once or twice a month. Bathing was even less frequent. An occasional sponge bath would do for the summer, and no bath at all in the winter, though most people were careful to wash their face and hands and keep their teeth clean.[15]

Food was usually plentiful but not fancy.[16] Bread and beer were staples, along with peas and beans, greens, parsnips, turnips, carrots, and beets. Cows, sheep, and goats provided milk, butter, and cheese, and on rare occasions there was beef, pork, and mutton. There were chickens and eggs, while fruit trees and bushes provided apples, plums, and berries. But elaborate meals were for the wealthy and powerful. Farm families ate in accordance with their station: soup and another dish or two for the main meal; bread, cheese, and possibly fruit at other times. The local Tavistock beer, made with oats, had an unusual taste that some visitors to the region found disgusting.[17]

The Drakes were farmers, but like other farmers in the area, they also worked with cloth and engaged in other trades. At Shillamill, a quarter-mile down the river, an old waterwheel had been converted to power a fulling mill, and on a quiet morning the Drake family at Crowndale could probably hear trip-hammers pounding the locally woven woolen cloth to tighten the weave.[18] One of the earlier John Drakes, perhaps the grandfather of Francis, was a mercer, or dealer in cloth.[19] Edmund Drake, the father of Francis, was a shearman, the most skilled of all the craftsmen, who teased the nap of the cloth and then trimmed the nap with fine shears to make the surface as smooth as possible.[20] As cloth making in Tavistock was not a full-time occupation, Edmund Drake soon took up another occupation: he became a priest.[21]

Very little is known of Edmund's family life or his ecclesiastical connections. The date of his ordination is unclear, as is the date of his marriage. His wife may have been named Anna Myllwaye, though the evidence for this is slim. In any case, they were probably married in 1539, and Francis Drake, by the best estimate, was born in February or March 1540.[22]

The recent sequestration of religious property eliminated many of the ecclesiastical benefices that had once supported secular priests. Either this circumstance or Edmund's recent marriage made it difficult for him to find a living as a priest. It may also explain why he became involved in a dispute in 1548, a dispute so serious that he was forced to leave Tavistock.

As a result of the dispute Edmund Drake and two other men were charged with assault. At least one and perhaps two of the men were priests. The story of the crimes is simple. On 16 April 1548, Edmund Drake and William Master came upon Roger Langiford in Le Cross Lane near Petertavy, just outside Tavistock. First insulting the man, Drake and Master then beat the poor fellow with staves and swords "so . . . that he feared for his life." More than this, they took poor Roger's purse, which held twenty-one shillings and seven pence.

Nine days later Edmund Drake and John Hawking were in Tavistock. Another man, John Harte, came by on his horse, an animal valued at three pounds. Drake and Hawking, threatening Harte with staves, swords, and knives, forced him to give them the horse. Afterward, John Drake, William Master, and John Hawking fled the county.

William Master was a priest, well known in Tavistock, where he sometimes said Mass and read the bederoll.[23] Lacking a regular appointment, he took temporary service wherever he could find priestly work, no doubt supplementing his income with work as a cordiner, or shoemaker.[24] After fleeing the parish in 1548, Master disappeared from the records until 1556, in the reign of Queen Mary. During that year, when the English Church renewed its connection with Rome, William Master once more served in Tavistock parish.[25]

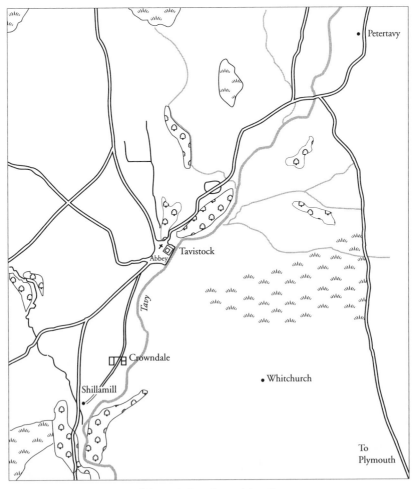

Map of the roads from Crowndale to Petertavy

The identity of John Hawking is a little less certain. He may have been ordained at Exeter Cathedral in 1534, as William Drake had been.[26] The uncle of Edmund Drake, William was ordained in 1530 for the Benedictine Abbey of Buckland.[27] The John Harte whose horse was stolen was also well known in Tavistock. In one document, dated 1543, he referred to himself as *generosus,* a gentleman.[28] Like John Harte, Roger Langiford was a prosperous landowner in the Tavistock vicinity.[29]

When Edmund Drake left town, he did not take his family with him, and his whereabouts for the next few years are unclear.[30] In 1553 he was curate of the parish at Upchurch, Kent, but he was soon forced to leave that post, very likely because of his marriage.[31]

His father's departure probably had no direct effect on the home life of young Francis Drake, as he had already joined a number of other young relatives living with the Hawkins family in Plymouth. This information comes from Edmund Howes, whose 1615 book said that the child was one of "twelve brethren brought up under his kinsman Sir John Hawkins."[32] The "brethren" mentioned by Howes were very likely "cousin-brethren," as John Drake once termed it in a deposition.[33] It was common practice for sixteenth-century parents to send their children to serve in the houses of prosperous relatives or friends and to be educated there.[34] An acknowledged "kinsman" of the Hawkins family, Francis Drake no doubt lived for several years in the house of William Hawkins.[35] The group of cousin-brethren perhaps included his younger brothers John and Joseph Drake, young John Hawkins, and other boys put out by their parents for a period of training and service.[36]

It is possible to make a few guesses about the sort of training that Francis Drake received from his cousin John Hawkins and from John's father, William Hawkins, at the Hawkins family home in Plymouth.[37] Old William Hawkins was from a Tavistock family that had moved to Plymouth around the turn of the century but still retained active connections with people in Tavistock.[38] His father had been a merchant who raised his son for trading and seafaring. On several occasions William took ships to the Guinea coast of Africa and then to Brazil. At an early age he held important political posts in Plymouth and represented the town in Parliament. In 1544, with a letter of marque from the crown, Hawkins raided French and even Spanish ships, serving a term in prison for taking one of the latter. His sons John and William went to sea as boys, as did Francis Drake and other boys in the household. At home they heard talk of politics and religion, trade and foreign affairs. They mingled with people who knew how to live well, dress well, and speak well. At sea they learned that it was possible and profitable to seize foreign ships and cargoes from merchants who were themselves shading the law. They saw that a successful fleet commander with influential friends at court could on occasion commit piracy and suffer little or nothing in consequence.[39]

Flexible in morals, the Hawkins household was flexible in religion as well, though perhaps not in a way that Edmund Drake would have found objectionable. Protestant enough to satisfy the Archbishop of Canterbury in 1559, Edmund Drake had earlier been Catholic enough to please the religious officials in the reign of Queen Mary who made him a curate at Upchurch.[40] Nothing now known about him indicates a burning zeal for either trend in religion. Nor is there any hint of excessive zeal in the religious training of the Hawkins family. William Hawkins was neither a "rigid Catholic" nor an "ardent Protestant," but something in between.[41] His son John Hawkins seems to have been the same. John Hawkins not only attended Mass during trading visits to Spanish Tenerife but did so with an apparent fervor that made his Spanish friends think he was a devout Catholic.[42] This attitude may have been typical of merchant families in the period. Though Catholic in doctrine and ritual, they were probably glad to see papal authority ended and religious property secularized. Growing up in this atmosphere, young Francis Drake very likely adopted the moderate religious practices of the Hawkins family. But he also discovered that there were opposing viewpoints. The boy Francis went with his Hawkins relatives to Dutch, French, and Spanish ports, attending both Catholic and Protestant churches, just as circumstances might dictate.

As a result of all the training they received in the Hawkins household, Francis Drake and the other young men learned to negotiate with foreign merchants and to deal with government officials. They learned to accept a sort of religion that was very different from the one into which they were born. And they learned especially how to handle a ship.

2

Learning to Be a Pirate

THE FEW BRIEF SOURCES FOR the early life of Francis Drake seem confusing in detail, but the general meaning is clear. Drake was a natural sailor—not born to the sea, but raised in a seafaring family and given the opportunity to show his talent at an early age. According to the English chronicler Edmund Howes, Francis Drake was a youth of eighteen years when he sailed as purser on one of the Hawkins ships in the Bay of Biscay. The year was about 1558. In the Howes narrative all of Francis Drake's early voyages were in vessels belonging to the Hawkins family, but little else about these journeys is clear. Corbett thinks the reference to Biscay means a trading visit to the northern coast of Spain, a good possibility, for Spain was a recent ally, and the Hawkins family had commercial ties in that country. More likely, though, this brief reference means that during his middle teens Drake sailed on one of the Hawkins ships that prowled the French coast looking for merchant vessels to pick off.[1] Drake may have served on the *Tiger,* a ship of about 50 tons and one of the few Hawkins raiders from this period identified by name in the records.[2]

Perhaps more important than the name of the ship is the business in which it engaged. Hawkins and the other Devon seamen were merchants, but they also found piracy profitable. Then as now, a pirate was a mariner who robbed from the ship of another mariner. There were varying degrees of piracy, and war could sometimes turn piracy into an act of patriotism, when pirates stole from the ships of the enemy. When pirates stole from one another, whether in war or in peace, the authorities usually looked the other way. The older British historians often used the word *privateer* to describe Hawkins and his associates, but that special term invests these sixteenth-century rascals with more dignity than their contemporaries were usually willing to give them.[3] In reality William Hawkins and his sons were successful merchants who did a pretty good business as part-time pirates. We misjudge them if we call them anything else. Francis Drake grew up in this Devon coast society where piracy was a common calling, not highly respected, but widely tolerated and easily understood.

One additional story about Francis Drake's early development further suggests his maritime destiny. While Francis lived with the Hawkins family in Plymouth, Edmund Drake lived in Upchurch, Kent. The parish of Upchurch consisted of about forty households with 260 communicants. Situated almost on the water, Upchurch was home port for a dozen ships and boats, all small, most less than 8 tons and none more than 14 tons. Fourteen men in the parish made their living from fishing or transportation.[4] With contacts among the boatmen of the Medway, Edmund Drake was able to find a place for his oldest son as apprentice on a small vessel that sailed between the Kentish ports along the Medway and the ports of the French and Dutch coast. The unnamed master of the vessel found in young Francis Drake the son he did not have. When the man died, the boat went to Francis Drake.[5]

This is the story told by William Camden, who no doubt heard it from Drake himself. Even so, we need not think of it as entirely true. As did so many seamen, Drake liked to spin tales about his considerable exploits and his continual triumph over adversity. The great Victorian historian of British sea power, John Knox Laughton, wrote, "The several points of his story, notwithstanding its general acceptance, are inaccurate or absurd."[6] The problem is that Camden heard the tale in the mid 1590s, during the period of Drake's growing estrangement from John Hawkins. Although the details are misleading, as Laughton indicates, "There is no need to doubt the substantial truth of the story told by Camden." Drake did not say so, but the vessel probably belonged to the Hawkins family, perhaps even to John Hawkins, who was himself moving to London and placing his ships in the Medway. The essential truth in Camden's story may be found in the tale told by Howes. Growing up in the Hawkins family, Francis Drake sailed with John Hawkins or some of his captains to the French coast and other parts of Europe in the later 1550s.[7]

This much seems pretty clear. Less certain is the part of the story that says Francis Drake inherited the little boat from the owner and that by selling it Drake "managed to scrape together a little money," then went off to join a Hawkins fleet to the Guinea coast.[8] If Francis Drake did acquire a share in a small vessel, it was probably his share in a prize taken by the Hawkins ships from a luckless French or Spanish merchant. More than a few possibilities appear in the record, especially during the war with France that ended in 1559.[9]

Whatever he did to acquire the money, at the age of twenty, according to Howes, young Drake invested in trade goods and signed on as a seaman with one of the Hawkins ships sailing for the Guinea coast of West Africa.[10] Since the early fifties, over considerable objection from Portugal, English traders including the Hawkins family had visited the Guinea coast and brought home valuable stores of gold, pepper, and ivory. No doubt this trip was one of the numerous unrecorded ventures by John Hawkins into the African trade. Under Queen Mary, English ships were prohibited from going to the Guinea coast, but her own officials allowed the trade to flourish. When Elizabeth came to the throne, she refused to extend Mary's prohibition, contending that the people of Guinea should be allowed to trade with whomever they pleased.[11]

During these early visits John Hawkins established important business connections in the Canary Islands, which he used as a base for his visits to the Guinea coast. A Hawkins relative named John Lovell was for a time the family's resident agent in Tenerife, where the families of Pedro Soler and Pedro de Ponte were the personal friends of John Hawkins. Two other close friends were Catholic priests, Pedro Soler the merchant's son and Mateo de Torres. During the 1560 visit Hawkins sold his shipload of woolens at Santa Cruz de Tenerife and Abona, and probably also at Adeje, Puerto de la Luz, and San Sebastián de la Gomera. Before returning home he stopped again with the family of Pedro Soler and loaded his vessel with sugar from the Soler family mill in Abona.[12]

A few years later Mateo de Torres told a curious story about this visit. He held an ecclesiatical benefice at Santa Cruz, and Padre Pedro Soler was vicar of Tenerife. One day Padre Soler came to see him in Santa Cruz, say-

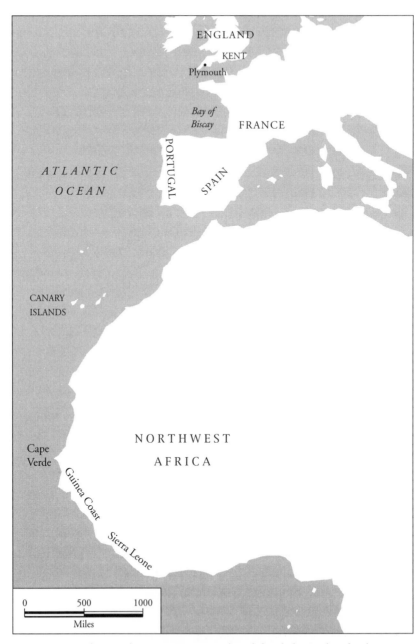

Ports and coasts where young Francis Drake sailed with the Hawkins family

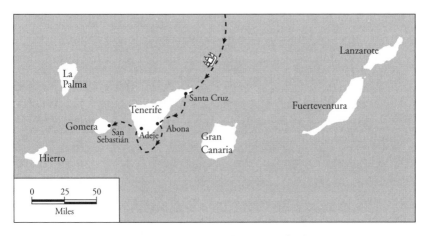

The Hawkins voyages in the Canary Islands

ing that he had come "to charter a boat for some English friends, who wanted to go to Canaria to look for a ship to take them home." He wanted Padre Torres to help him with the charter and assured him that nothing could happen that might be to his disadvantage. The Englishmen wanted only to go to Canaria to "take care of things." Anyway, they had letters of recommendation from the governor of Tenerife, and the governor himself had given them a license to make the trip. So the Englishmen chartered a boat from a local shipmaster, while Padre Soler suggested that they keep everything secret, saying the governor of Canaria did not really need to know about their movements. Some time later, Padre Soler wrote to the other priest and said the Englishmen would arrive that night, which they did, five or six men. They took the chartered boat to Canaria, where they joined several other Englishmen and purchased a ship. Some nights later the English partners quietly drew their ship into the harbor at Santa Cruz. There they climbed aboard another ship that was loaded with goods for the Indies, stole out of the port with it, and set sail for home.[13]

The Spanish biographer of John Hawkins thinks that the somewhat obscure references in the testimony of Padre Torres show conclusively that the pirates came from a ship belonging to John Hawkins. The main English biographer of Hawkins does not think the incident is even worth a mention.[14] Whether John Hawkins was involved or not, young Francis

Drake at least heard about the incident and learned an important lesson. Foreign ships and cargoes could be easily separated from their owners.

Drake saw, too, how religion could be used to seal a friendship. Both priests testified that John Hawkins attended Mass in the islands as though he were a faithful Catholic. As late as 1568, after numerous others had sworn that it was well known that John Hawkins was a *luterano* (as the Spanish called all Protestants), Padre Torres begged to differ. "The other time he was in the Indies, perhaps seven years ago," Padre Torres "saw him hear Mass."[15] Padre Soler said much the same thing. "John Hawkins went to church, and he heard Mass. By his words he seemed to be a Catholic, and he was commonly thought to be one."[16]

During negotiations on these early journeys John Hawkins made plans with his friends in the Canaries to break into the slave trade in Guinea. Pedro de Ponte would help provide the fleet with water and supplies, make necessary arrangements with merchants in the Indies, and find a skilled pilot to handle navigation.[17] Hawkins would provide the ships and the capital. The partners made their plans with such little apparent compunction that historians are sometimes tempted to forget what a nasty business they were undertaking.[18] Condemned by many religious officials as totally inhuman, slavery was tolerated by others on the ground that the slaves would be baptized and therefore eligible for salvation. For Hawkins and his partners the main consideration seemed to be profit. Prices in the Indies were high, forty ducados per slave, and costs in Africa were low.[19] To keep the captives in line and to hold expenses to a minimum, the slaves were crammed into the holds of the ships, provided with the bare minimum of food and water. Sanitation simply did not exist. Profits in the slave trade were enormous, and it was not hard to find financial backing.

From his new base in London, Hawkins made his preparations for the journey. His father-in-law, Benjamin Gonson, was treasurer of the navy and took a major role in the syndicate formed to finance the trip. Among the other partners were William Wynter, surveyor of the navy and master of ordnance, as well as two city magistrates.[20]

The fleet of three or four small ships left Plymouth in October 1562, manned by a hundred sailors of whom one was probably Francis Drake. The largest ship was only 140 tons. Called the *Salomon,* this vessel was owned by the Hawkins brothers and commanded by John Hawkins himself, general of the fleet, as the title was in those days. Another boat belonging to the Hawkinses was the *Swallow,* about 30 tons and commanded by Thomas Hampton. A third boat, the *Jonas,* was rated at 40 tons. The name of the fourth ship is unrecorded.[21]

Leaving Plymouth in October 1562, Hawkins stopped as planned to meet with business contacts at Tenerife. Pedro de Ponte had secured the services of an experienced pilot from Cádiz named Juan Martínez, who knew the routes to the Guinea coast and to the Indies. Martínez joined the fleet in Tenerife while water and supplies were taken on board. No doubt the ships also carried the usual woolens and other trade goods from Devon, plus a supply of beans that would be cooked to feed the captives.[22]

From Tenerife the fleet sailed to Cape Verde and on down the Guinea coast to Sierra Leone. There Hawkins filled the ships with blacks, stealing some from Portuguese traders, capturing others on his own, and finally taking a Portuguese vessel to carry the slaves that could not be crammed into his own holds. The unnamed English ship was sent home with goods, some traded, some acquired "by the sword." This seems to have been the ship on which Francis Drake sailed, as the evidence seems to show that he did not go to the Indies on this occasion.[23]

With the other vessels full of slaves, Hawkins sailed on to the West Indies, selling his cargo at below-market rates to eager Spanish buyers in three ports on La Española, Isabella, Puerto de Plata, and Monte Christi. He was back in Plymouth by September 1563, awash in such stunning profits that the Spanish government joined Portuguese diplomatic officials in attempting to bring an end to this new English adventure.[24]

Was Hawkins a pirate? The government of Portugal plainly thought so, as did Spain, whose ambassador complained about the unauthorized appearance of the Hawkins ships in the Indies.[25] The dispute was not over individual rights but over trade and markets. No matter that the trade involved selling human beings, there was money in it, and by October 1564 Hawkins was ready to go again. The sources are ambiguous at best, but it is

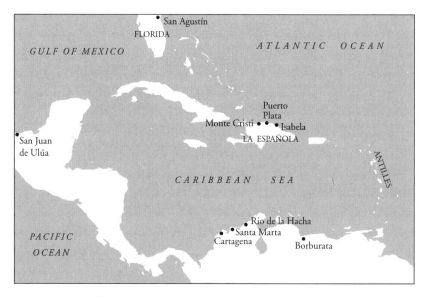

John Hawkins and John Lovell in the West Indies, 1562–68

clear that Francis Drake had more sea experience with the Hawkins family than the three voyages mentioned by Howes. This second slaving voyage for young John Hawkins was likely the first West Indies trip for twenty-two-year-old Francis Drake, sailing again as a simple seaman.[26]

The second Hawkins voyage was very much a repetition of the first. As general of the fleet, Hawkins sailed in the queen's 700-ton *Jesus of Lubeck*, a crumbling crown vessel that Henry VIII had purchased from the Hanseatic League nearly twenty years earlier. Three other ships completed the fleet: the *Salomon,* 140 tons; the *Tiger,* 50 tons; and the *Swallow,* 30 tons. Hawkins stopped on the way at Tenerife, consulting with his friends and taking on supplies. In Sierra Leone he took slaves by force, sometimes from other traders, sometimes by raids on black villages. The slaves and trade goods were soon sold for a profit at stops in the West Indies and on the coast of South America, but delicate negotiations were required. Since the trade was illegal, the Spanish colonists usually insisted that Hawkins first make a show of force, after which they hurried to buy his slaves at a big discount from the usual price.[27]

As was his custom, Hawkins employed pilots who knew the route. In

Guinea, for example, he freed a Spanish merchant from Jamaica who had been captured by the local people during a previous slaving expedition. As it turned out, this man did not recall as much about the Jamaican coast as he thought he would. As a result, the fleet sailed past the island without stopping, then proceeded to repeat the performance along the coast of Cuba. Hawkins thus missed the opportunity to purchase a cargo of hides and replenish his supply of water, while the poor Jamaican merchant ended up going back to England with the rest of the fleet.[28]

Another pilot was more useful. Martin Atinas of Dieppe had previously come to Florida with the expedition of René Laudonnière in 1562. Hawkins secured his services as pilot and was repaid when the man led him directly to the French settlement at Fort Caroline on the Rio de Mayo. Here Hawkins was received like a brother by the Huguenot Laudonnière, and he responded in kind. Seeing that Laudonnière needed a ship, Hawkins sold him the smallest one in his fleet in exchange for four cannon and a supply of powder and shot.[29]

It was a perfect training voyage for young Drake, with attacks by land and sea, intricate navigational problems, and diplomatic and business negotiations of every kind.[30] The extremely cordial relations with Laudonnière's Huguenot colony reflected the growing tendency among the officers of the fleet and the English merchant class in general to align themselves with the liturgical and doctrinal innovations introduced by Queen Elizabeth's new archbishop, Matthew Parker.

This development illuminates one of the major problems of the reformers. While theologians could understand and debate their differences, the doctrinal disputes were often too subtle for less sophisticated people to grasp. Then as now, many people could not appreciate the distinction between the Catholic teaching about transubstantiation and the new Anglican teaching that the bread and wine became the Body and Blood of Christ in a less literal but much more than symbolic way. On the other hand, the evident similarities between the new communion service and the Holy Bread that everyone had formerly received at the end of Mass must have made it easier for some to accept the changes in the liturgy.[31]

Other religious innovations in the Elizabethan era were also less revolutionary than they may seem now. In England the people had for years been accustomed to saying prayers in the vernacular, and they were probably not greatly shocked by the other changes in the liturgy. In many places the rood screens and altars had been removed some years earlier, then replaced, then removed again. The introduction of the liturgical table in place of the altar had great significance for theologians, but ordinary people may have seen it as less than a revolutionary move.[32] A good many people liked the changes, and those who did not probably expected things to change again in a way that was more to their taste. For the most part, the changes in dogma had more appeal for the upper class, offset by a sort of dogged resistance among the ordinary people. So firm was this resistance that the seamen in Hawkins's fleet usually had to be menaced with a whip and threatened with imprisonment before they would attend religious services.[33]

In spite of this resistance, attendance at shipboard services became mandatory during the 1560s, and everybody went, if reluctantly. Two years after this voyage, Father Torres in Tenerife noted a remarkable change in the religious practices of the Hawkins seamen. "Some Englishmen from the crew of his ship came to town to buy fowls and other things that they needed," he said. "One of these men went to Confession, and others heard Mass. The upper class did not, because they were afraid to do so. I heard it said that there are many Lutherans [Protestants] in England and there are also Catholics."[34]

By the time Hawkins and his fleet reached England, both the Portuguese and the Spanish ambassadors were making strenuous objections to his new intrusions in Guinea and the West Indies. It was not that Philip objected so much to the traffic in slaves but rather that he wanted to keep the Indies trade as a special preserve of Spanish merchants. For several months Hawkins negotiated with the queen's representatives and even with the Spanish ambassador, all the while assembling cargo and preparing ships for a new voyage to the Indies.[35] Though pleased with the generous return on their investments, the queen and her counselors were anxious to avoid offending the Spanish king, if this could be done without great expense. As a result Hawkins was required to post a £500 bond, promising not to go to the Indies that year or to send the *Swallow* or any of his other ships. This done, he promptly appointed his kinsman John Lovell to take charge of the fleet and sent him off on a repeat of the previous voyage.[36] Such astonishing behavior surely signifies that Hawkins had at least tacit royal approval for the voyage. And if future diplomatic considerations should require that the bond be forfeit, the amount was small enough to make little difference to the investors who hoped to share his profits.[37]

There were four ships in Lovell's fleet, including the *Salomon*, commanded by James Raunse; the *Paul*, commanded by James Hampton; the *Pascoe*, commanded by Robert Bolton; and the *Swallow*.[38] The *Paul* and the *Salomon* were about the same size, 140 tons or so, depending on the method of measurement.[39] The *Pascoe* was a 40-ton vessel and the newly-built *Swallow* 180 tons.[40]

A relative of John Hawkins, Lovell may have been a relative of Francis Drake as well. In fact, the record seems to show that Hawkins and later Drake commonly appointed family members to fill important command positions in their fleets. Cousin or uncle, whatever he was, John Lovell was an ardent Protestant, and his conduct set an important example for young Francis Drake.

According to later testimony by a seaman called both Miguel Morgan and Morgan Tillert, "They recited psalms in every ship, along with the other things that are specified in . . . the books the Protestants use in England."[41] On the flagship the prayers were read by a merchant, very likely Thomas Hampton, the brother of James Hampton, commander of the *Paul*. Firmly grounded in the new religious practices, Lovell made no effort to accommodate opposing views. While John Hawkins had always taken some pains to conform to the religious practices of the Canary Islands, Lovell did no such thing. In fact, he seems to have gone out of his way to scandalize and offend the local people. Stopping as usual in Tenerife for supplies, Lovell told the alcalde of Garachico that "he had made a vow to God that he would come to these islands, burn the image of Our Lady in Candelaria, and roast a young goat in the coals."[42]

Lovell also made it difficult for the Catholic members of his crew. Recalling the pressure to conform, Morgan Tillert said that he had converted to the Protestant doctrines on this voyage, largely due to a conversation he had had with Francis Drake. As the Spanish notary observed: "Francis Drake, a firm English protestant, came in the ship and converted him to his law." Beyond this, Drake told Tillert that "God would receive the good work that he might perform in either law, that of Rome or that of England, but the true law and the best one was that of England." Tillert said that his conversion came about because of Drake's persistence; on the ship these ideas were "taught and discussed every day."[43] Even so, the religious opinions reported by Tillert must reflect the ideas of many ordinary people in sixteenth-century England, that God could see good in either religious viewpoint, though he no doubt preferred one to the other.

Sailing on to Guinea, Lovell spent two or three months trading, raiding, and gathering slaves. He seized four or five Portuguese ships, with cargoes worth perhaps thirty thousand ducats. Williamson believed that the *Swallow* must have returned to England with most of the ivory, gold, and other goods and that only three ships went on to the Indies. But a Spanish document states clearly that all four of Lovell's ships made the journey.[44]

Not much is known in detail about the voyage. Stopping first at the Caribbean island of Margarita, just off the coast of Venezuela, Lovell may have traded with the inhabitants there. Lacking a report about this from Spanish authorities, it seems more likely that he simply took on wood, water, and food. The next stop was Borburata on the Venezuelan coast, where he established his procedure for the rest of the voyage. Two French pirate fleets had already been on the coast ahead of him, and a third was in the harbor when he arrived. Jean Bontemps was well known to the Hawkins men, and Lovell quickly determined to join him in demanding permission to sell his slaves and merchandise.[45]

Saying that they had come in peace, Lovell and Bontemps anchored in the harbor at Borburata and sent their agents to see Governor Pedro Ponce de León in the nearby port of Coro. They told local officials in Borburata that they planned to give a hundred slaves to the royal treasury and to sell another two hundred to local citizens. Because the governor had given his license the previous year, everyone expected that things would go the same way. But the agents came back in a few days with a firm refusal from the governor.[46] The rebuff prompted the sort of aggressive measures that John Hawkins had used to such good effect in the past.

Landing as though for another negotiating session, Lovell and Bontemps seized two government officials and several other citizens of Borburata, imprisoning them on the ships. Two of the hostages, merchants from Nuevo Reyno de Granada, just happened to be carrying 1,500 pesos in their purses. Lovell and Bontemps took the money, gave the merchant-hostages twenty-six slaves in exchange, and set everyone free. It did not require great intelligence on the part of the local officials to see through this trickery. The slaves were immediately confiscated, and the merchants were required to pay a fine to the crown before the slaves were returned. But the pattern seemed to be set for successful trading in the Spanish colonies: English force, Spanish resistance, and secret negotiations that satisfied both the traders and the colonists. The colonists were determined to trade, whether the royal officials liked it or not. Business negotiations were carried on at night, and when they were questioned, the colonists "covered for one another."[47] For their part, the officials said they hated to make the colonists testify about matters under oath. "We think they only perjure themselves."[48]

A few days later, on 18 May 1567, Lovell and his ships arrived in Rio de la Hacha and again sent an agent ashore, requesting a license to trade. The local commander was Miguel de Castellanos, royal treasurer for the pearl fishery and the business associate of John Hawkins from the year just passed. He replied that trade was now forbidden by the crown.[49]

What happened from this point is a matter of some dispute. Several weeks after the event, Baltasar de Castellanos, brother of the commander, wrote a letter signed by several other citizens. According to his story, Lovell spent six days in port, either coming ashore himself or sending an agent, to ask for permission to trade. Failing this, he unloaded "ninety or ninety-two slaves" on the far side of the river, then sailed away in the middle of the night.[50]

A somewhat different version of events was written by Miguel de Castellanos about six months later. According to Castellanos, Lovell sent a message, threatening to land his forces and lay waste the town with all its inhabitants. Castellanos replied that he would like to see him try.[51]

Lovell immediately brought his ships close to the shore and tried to land his men in the smaller boats. The local people, with only sixty-three able-bodied men at their disposal, were nonetheless able to keep Lovell's party from landing. After a time—and a great deal of gunfire on each side, mostly English cannons and Spanish harquebuses—he gave up the attempt.[52]

The Spanish colonists had only a few days earlier managed to hold off a similar attack by Jean Bontemps, who had told them that Lovell was on the way. Buoyed by success, they were not about to surrender to the less threatening English force. Firing from their prepared fortifications, the Spanish defenders managed to kill or wound a considerable number of Lovell's people, or so they reported. Lovell and his men retreated to the ships and remained there for several days. Finally, late one night, he landed "ninety-six slaves that were old and weak and on the point of dying" and sailed away.[53]

Another letter written by local colonists said that the "ninety-six slaves were so old and weak and sick that they were about to die." Even so, said the colonists, they had worked so hard and so bravely to defend the port that surely the king would want them to keep the slaves as part payment for all their trouble and expense.[54]

All this looks suspiciously like the same sort of arrangement that had been made in Borburata. Official resistance, followed by several days— and nights—of unofficial business dealing. Most merchandise could be hidden away and used as needed, but slaves had to be accounted for in some other way. Very likely there were secret payments, followed by the midnight delivery of the slaves at a place agreed upon across the river.[55]

Lovell lacked the tact and diplomacy of Hawkins. His arrogance with the Spanish authorities almost certainly cost a few English lives, just as the later Spanish reports say. This interpretation of events seems to be confirmed in a passage published by Philip Nichols in 1626, mentioning "the wrongs [Drake] received at Rio de Hacha with Captaine John Lovell . . . not only in the losse of his goods of some value, but also of his kinsmen & friends."[56]

Having concluded his business at Rio de la Hacha, Lovell took his fleet to La Española to sell the remainder of his cargo. We have only the briefest mention of his dealings in La Española. Writing to the king a few months later, several citizens at Rio de la Hacha said, "He then departed and sailed on to the island of Española, where they say he wrought great evil and destruction."[57] Perhaps he managed to take on a load of hides, as Hawkins had tried to do a year earlier. Whatever he accomplished, Lovell's voyage was not a great success, and Hawkins later blamed this on "the simpleness of my [deputies] who knew not how to handle these matters."[58] Francis Drake was only a crewman on this voyage, not one of the "deputies." Nevertheless, he recalled the events with great embarrassment in later years.[59]

Drake arrived in Plymouth in the first part of September 1567, to be greeted by sad but expected news. His father, who had been ill for some time, had died the day after Christmas. Perhaps because of this illness, Drake's youngest brother, Thomas, was being cared for by Thomas Baker of London. Edmund Drake left a brief will that contains a number of hints about the family of Francis Drake.[60]

First, Edmund asked for burial "in Upchurch by my son Edwarde Drake, by the graves of the Bletchendens howsholde." Edmund's son Thomas, though underage, was named executor of the estate, while Thomas Baker was appointed "overseer." Clement Myllwaye and Richard Saywell signed as witnesses. Baker was offered a cock and four hens for his trouble. The two witnesses melded into one in Edmund's failing consciousness, so that "Richard Melwaye" received "my owne chaier with my best cushin." Thomas Drake could select pretty much what he wanted, but particularly "the best fether bedd" and two pillows; two chests of books; a new basin and six platters; four of the best candlesticks; five shirts; a "penner and inke"; in short, "the best [of] evry thynge."[61]

All the rest devolved upon "my true Nurse who hathe kepte me well." There is a clue here to Edmund's final, lingering illness, a digestive disorder that sixteenth-century medicine treated by breast nursing, a completely honorable profession.[62] So zealous was Edmund Drake to reward his nurse that he added a line at the end of his will to spell out her name clearly: "The name of my nurse wich kept me her name is Jone Justis." She was the person Edmund trusted to select the best items from his modest possessions for delivery to his son Thomas.[63] No other record about this nurse has been found, nor has any mention of Edmund's wife, except for one brief sentence in the will.

This unnamed wife may have lived with Edmund at Upchurch in 1553, along with his son Edward.[64] The family may have been elsewhere by the time Thomas was born in 1556. None of this is really clear, because parish records begin in 1560. By then Edmund was a widower, and only Thomas lived with him. The will's brief references to Edmund's wife and his son Edward show that the boy was buried at Upchurch, but she was not.

"Remember my wiffe," Edmund told Thomas, "to be newe sett in the begynning of the Romaynes." The clearest reference in this ambiguous statement is to Saint Paul's epistle to the Romans, considered by Elizabethan churchmen to be the basic statement of Christian belief. In one sense Edmund seems to have intended that Thomas should pray for the unnamed wife (his mother?) so that she might be "redeamed by the bloud of christ," as Edmund had been.[65] This seemingly laudable concern for her spiritual welfare was not the sort of wish an Elizabethan priest ought to have had. A good Protestant should have thought that the lady no longer needed his prayers, but Edmund Drake seemingly still embraced the Catholic belief about praying for the souls of the departed.

A second but less likely interpretation would have Edmund's wife "newe sett in the begynning of the Romaynes" with pen and ink. Among the books that Edmund left to Thomas was a seemingly new copy of the Bible, not yet cut or bound. In the 1562 edition of the English Bible a blank half-column follows the Acts of the Apostles, just before the beginning of the Epistle to the Romans, the only such blank space in the entire volume. Edwin's somewhat confusing admonition to his son may have been a simple request that his son inscribe her name in that blank space in the new book as a testimony of his affection. The condition of the book is clearly stated in Edmund's further advice that Thomas should "trem the bocke and kepe in bosom and fedd a pon"—that is, Thomas should bind the book properly with the edges trimmed, then commit it to memory and draw sustenance from it. The last bit of advice followed William Tyndale's recommendation to the reader of the Epistle to the Romans: "I think it mete that everye Christian manne not only know it by herte and withoute the booke, but also exercise himselfe therein evermore continually, as with the daily bread of the soule."[66]

For good reason Francis, John, and Joseph Drake, Edmund's older sons, went unmentioned in his will. They were already well established, even mildly prosperous. Elizabethan parents of limited means worried mainly about their minor children who were not self-supporting. In many cases poor parents did not even bother to mention the adult children who were already provided for.[67]

Thomas Butler is as mysterious as Clement Myllwaye and Richard Saywell. A man named Thomas Butler lived in Tavistock when Edmund lived there. So did men named Melwaye and Sawell, while others of similar name were well established in Upchurch. Lady Elizabeth Fuller Eliott-Drake, a family historian and collateral descendent who resumed the name, thinks that Thomas Butler headed the stores department in the London navy offices and met Edmund during a visit to the fleet in the Medway, but documentary evidence is not available.[68] We can only guess that Francis assured himself about the arrangements for his brother Thomas. In later life Thomas claimed to have spent his early years sailing with Francis.

When Drake arrived at Plymouth in September 1567, John Hawkins had seven ships ready for a massive effort to open the Spanish Indies to English slave traders. Hawkins intended to lead the fleet himself, taking three Portuguese agents who claimed to know about the location of a rich but secret gold mine on the African coast.[69] The queen furnished two ships, while the usual array of London investors became shareholders. For his flagship, Hawkins took the *Jesus of Lubeck,* with Robert Barrett as master and William Saunders as mate. The second royal vessel was the *Minion,* with John Hampton as captain and master and John Garrett as mate.

Shortly after these two ships arrived at Plymouth, the Portuguese agents fled, claiming that Hawkins had mistreated them. It did not matter. For Hawkins and his investors, black slaves were the real gold of Africa. In proof of this, the queen dispatched new instructions to the fleet to proceed to Guinea, find a cargo of slaves, and sell them in the West Indies.[70]

All this took less than a month. By the first of October 1567 the fleet was ready to sail.[71] Four Hawkins ships joined the two royal vessels. The *William and John,* 150 tons, had Thomas Bolton as captain and master, with James Raunse as mate. The *Swallow,* 180 tons, was nearly new and still in good condition.[72] Quickly refitted, it became part of John Hawkins's new slaving fleet, along with fifty or so slaves that had been brought back in its hold.[73] Two other ships, the *Judith,* 50 tons, and the *Angel,* 33 tons, made up the rest of the fleet, along with a tiny pinnace of 7 tons that was towed by the *Swallow.* This little vessel was lost a few days later in a storm.[74]

If we can believe the report that Miles Phillips wrote some years later, Francis Drake commanded the *Judith.*[75] Other witnesses gave conflicting testimony. Morgan Tillert (Miguel Morgan) sailed aboard the *Jesus of Lubeck* and was later captured by the Spanish authorities. In December 1572 he was forced to testify before the Mexican Inquisition. Under some pressure to implicate the various English officers who had become known to Spanish authorities, Tillert said that "Harry Newman, Francis Drake, and Nicholas Anthony also came on the flagship."[76] But the real subject of his testimony was the religious observances held on the ship, and Tillert may not have meant to say that Drake and the others were part of the flagship's crew.

This is one of the problems in interpreting sixteenth-century records. A Spanish notary was under serious obligation to listen carefully to the witnesses, to summarize their responses in the third person but in their own words, and then to let them read and correct the summaries before signing. Thus the documents often contain the exact words of witnesses, but only to the extent that their testimony pertained to the question at hand.

Another seaman, Job Hortop, wrote an account many years later, giving evidence about the voyage that may have come in part from Drake himself. In the first editions of his memoirs Hortop managed to summarize the voyage without even mentioning Drake. John Hawkins himself did the same. Miles Phillips referred to him only once. Obviously annoyed that none of them had given him credit for what he considered to be his great contributions to the voyage, Drake in early 1593 addressed an open letter to the queen, complaining that his own part in this and other voyages had not been properly acknowledged.[77]

No doubt as a result of this and other complaints, Hortop revised his account, though he still got it wrong, and the revised version did not appear until several years after Drake's death. As Hakluyt published the revised story, Hortop said that Drake's first command was a caravel, possibly a captured Portuguese ship, perhaps the *Swallow* or even the *Judith*.[78] The important point to take from Hortop's confusion and from Phillips's brevity is that Drake commanded one of the small boats, probably the *Judith*, from the very beginning of the voyage.

Four days out of Plymouth, the *Judith* became separated from the other vessels in a storm that lasted for days.[79] The *Angel* managed to rejoin the *Jesus of Lubeck* near Cape Finisterre. Astonished at the extensive damage, Hawkins initially determined to sail for home. When the storm ceased altogether a day later, things looked much better, and Hawkins gave orders to resume the voyage. The *Minion,* the *William and John,* and the *Swallow* also came together and sailed in a group to the Canaries. When the storm began, the *Swallow* had the pinnace in tow, but the line parted in the storm, and the pinnace was lost with its two-man crew. Unable to locate the others, the *Judith* kept sailing alone, also headed for the Canaries. On 11 November, when the *Jesus* and the *Angel* were within sight of Gomera, the *Judith* came sailing up, firing a salute to the flagship.[80]

From Gomera, Hawkins took the three ships to Santa Cruz in Tenerife, where he intended to purchase supplies as usual from his friend Pedro de Ponte and take on a fresh supply of water. This time he found conditions drastically changed. In a number of pointed letters, the authorities in Spain directed local officials to treat Hawkins with circumspection. As soon as his ships came into view, all the local militia units were mobilized. When the harbor officials came aboard the *Jesus of Lubeck,* they saw that it was too heavily armed for any direct attack. Instead they kept the militia drawn up in battle order, just outside the town. Hawkins kept a guard on the alert throughout their stay in Santa Cruz, and only good friends like Pedro de Soler and a few others came out to visit with him.[81]

With no further need for pretense, Hawkins abandoned his former gestures of conformity to local religious practices. Nearly everyone was scandalized that he allowed meat to be eaten on Friday, but Hawkins joked that he had a special papal dispensation for everyone aboard his ships, and he invited the islanders to join him at table.[82]

In this condition of guarded friendship, Hawkins entertained old friends aboard ship with a feast of Canary Island partridge. A quarter-mile away the local militia remained armed and ready, just in case he might decide on sudden hostilities. In this state of tension, discipline suffered on the *Jesus of Lubeck,* and fights broke out among the men who were confined to the ship. Two of them, Edward Dudley and George Fitzwilliam, argued so bitterly that they decided to go ashore for a duel. Hearing of this, Hawkins ordered Fitzwilliam to remain on board and sent word to Dudley that he should return immediately. When Dudley returned, Hawkins gave him a lecture, and Dudley answered with a rude remark. Angered, Hawkins struck the man with his fist, Dudley drew his knife, and Hawkins did the same. Before they could be separated, both men were badly cut. Hawkins then directed that Dudley be placed in irons and brought before him for sentencing. The insult to himself could be forgiven, said Hawkins, but not the insult to the queen, whose ship they were on. Having said this, Hawkins took a loaded harquebus, pointed it at Dudley, and told the man to say his prayers and prepare to die. Dudley begged for mercy, and many of the bystanders also urged Hawkins to forgive the man.[83] Among those asking clemency for the man was the priest Pedro de Soler, who later said that it was entirely through his own efforts that Hawkins decided to pardon Dudley.[84] Whether this is true or not, Hawkins did pardon the man, and young Francis Drake got an additional lesson in the nearly unlimited authority of the commander of a fleet.

While Hawkins kept his seamen busy repairing and resupplying the ships, his main concern was to find the three missing vessels. After a few days he discovered that they were waiting for him at Gomera, though the rendezvous point was Tenerife.[85] As they sailed out of the harbor at Santa Cruz, his ships traded cannon salutes with the local fortress, and one of the guns on the *Jesus of Lubeck* fired a shot into the town. Whether by accident no one could say for certain, but the house of Juan de Valverde was badly damaged. Many people insisted that the only accident was that Hawkins had hit the house instead of the nearby church.[86]

Once arrived at Gomera, Hawkins had his fleet back together for the first time in weeks.[87] Members of the crew were greeted as old friends by the merchants on shore, where they traded freely and refilled the water casks on all the ships. The seamen seem to have enjoyed themselves during the brief stay at Gomera in the ways sailors usually do. A Tenerifan islander later said that he had heard that they burned images of saints in the local church.[88] The English sailors denied that anything of the sort happened.[89] At least one man, the same George Fitzwilliam who had been involved in the argument with Dudley, attended Mass in the local church.[90] Whether Fitzwilliam was really a devout Catholic has always been a matter of great speculation, but the evidence seems to show that his religious convictions probably matched those of John Hawkins.[91]

On 4 November all was finished, and the reunited fleet departed for the coast of Africa. Two weeks of monotonous sailing brought them to Cabo Blanco. In the harbor Hawkins found three ships, fully equipped but completely abandoned by their crews, who had been attacked by French raiders and forced to take refuge in the nearby fort. Hawkins took the best caravel and added it to his fleet. The other two ships Hawkins sold back to their commander after he came down from the fort to investigate.[92]

Coasting south along the African mainland, the ships stopped again at Cabo Verde. Here Hawkins met a fleet of six French merchant ships, two of which may have been involved in the attack on the Portuguese at Cabo Blanco. Four of the Frenchmen convinced him of their good intentions. Hawkins added the other two ships to his fleet, though one of them escaped a few days later.[93] The ship that remained, the *Don de Dieu,* was commanded by Paul Blondel, known in the English accounts as Captain Bland. Blondel served valiantly with Hawkins and Drake in this voyage and was associated with Drake in a later one.[94]

While they were anchored at Cape Verde, Hawkins assembled a shore party to capture slaves. Marching inland a few miles, they attacked a large village but took only a few captives. In the process about twenty-five of the seamen were wounded with poison arrows. They appeared to recover, but several of them later sickened, and seven or eight of them died in great agony, jaws clamped from pain and paralysis.[95]

Many years later Job Hortop, one of the seamen, revised an earlier account to say that here "Francis Drake was made master & captaine of the Caravel." Most writers have interpreted this to mean the French ship. As has been noted earlier, this is most unlikely. A few days later Hortop had Drake commanding the *Swallow* and still later the *Judith,* which was no doubt his ship all along.[96]

From Cabo Verde they headed east to the Guinea Coast, trading on the way with French captains and Portuguese merchants. Slave hunting proved to be a difficult occupation, and in desperation Hawkins finally allied himself with two local kings, Sheri and Yhoma at the Taggarin River in Sierra Leone. Asking for aid against their enemies, kings Sacina and Setecama, the two rulers promised to give the Englishmen an equal share of any prisoners whom they might take.[97] The attack on the enemy village was mounted partly by land and partly with a large English force that came up the river in the smaller vessels, including the one that Francis Drake commanded.[98] Attacking from both sides, they burned the town and took several hundred prisoners, though the kings kept the larger share of slaves and dared Hawkins to do anything about it.[99]

Counting the fifty slaves apparently left over from Lovell's voyage, the Hawkins fleet had managed to round up about five or six hundred miserable souls for transport to America.[100] In the various battles Hawkins probably lost about sixty men killed and many more wounded.[101] Edward Dudley, who fought with Hawkins at Santa Cruz, was wounded at Cabo Verde, but recovered and led a party at Taggarin. He was among those who died on the way to the Indies.[102]

The journey across the Atlantic lasted from early February to the end of March, seven or eight weeks of unbroken ocean travel.[103] But the fleet was well supplied, the cargo of slaves required constant attention, and the men did not lack for diversions of one sort or another. Hawkins insisted on setting a good table, with fine linen and silver, and dishes cooked to his liking. A group of five or six musicians on board the *Jesus of Lubeck* played fiddle music for the enjoyment of the captain and the crew. The leader of the group was a tiny youth named William Low, twenty years old, though he looked like a freckle-faced boy.[104]

In addition to all this, every morning between seven and eight o'clock and again when the watch changed at nightfall, the mate William Saunders gathered all the men before the mainmast and had them kneel to recite Psalms, the Lord's Prayer, and the Creed. On Sunday morning at eight they said the same prayers, and someone who was literate read the Epistle and the Gospel appointed for that day. Saunders, or sometimes Barrett or Hawkins, then gave a homily, reading from the *Paraphrases* of Erasmus, then expanding upon the theme in his own words. The whole observance took forty-five minutes or an hour. The same thing was done on each of the other ships in the fleet, and when time allowed, the Sunday observances were also read during the week.[105]

Attendance was compulsory. When some of the men on the flagship refused to attend services, Thomas Williams, the second mate, was sent with a whip to force them to come on deck and participate in the prayers. Even the slightest hint of "papistry" was forbidden. A man on the *Minion* who blessed himself before taking the helm was roundly excoriated before all the crew. "There are on this voyage such evil papist Christians," said Saunders, "that we cannot avoid having a pestilence visited on this armada."[106]

Certainly, pestilence was a problem, and medical care was important, if rudimentary. Without being aware of germs and viruses, people of the day still understood that disease could be transmitted by personal contact. As a result, anyone who became ill on the flagship was immediately transferred to the *Minion* until he was fully recovered. The reasoning was that the flagship was a floating fortress, and the crew had to be in perfect health, ready for action at any time.[107]

The first landfall after two months at sea was the island of Dominica, where Spanish charts marked a safe passage through the Antilles. Here the fleet took on fresh water but nothing else, for the local Indians had nothing to trade. Turning south, they landed at Margarita. Hawkins immediately dispatched a messenger to tell the local governor that he wished to trade peaceably, restock his ships with food and water, and rest his crew. The response came in unexpectedly cordial terms, so the fleet stayed there for more than a week. When Hawkins departed on 9 April 1568, he left behind a town full of happy colonists who had traded island meat and produce for good Devon cloth at attractive prices. In fact, the islanders could scarcely have refused to trade, since the inhabitants numbered no more than fifty souls, and their town had been very nearly destroyed a few months earlier by French pirates.[108]

The first mainland destination was Borburata, the Spanish pearl fishery where Hawkins had traded profitably on earlier voyages. Arriving on Holy Saturday, 17 April 1568, Hawkins again wrote to the governor, asking permission to trade. The letter is an interesting attempt by Hawkins to provide the local authorities with a rationalization for trading: Hawkins had not really intended to come to the Indies, but since he was there, he needed to sell a few slaves and a small amount of goods to make expenses; surely the Spanish king would have no objection to that.[109]

Several days later, with no response from the governor, Hawkins addressed a similar letter to the bishop, his "right reverend father in God," who encouraged him to stay and trade. Hawkins kept his fleet in the harbor for two months, trying various stratagems to extract a trading license, even sending an armed shore party to seize the town of Valencia. Other trading forays were made by portions of the fleet, sailing to Coro and Curaçao, but with indifferent success.[110] Very likely Drake was in command of the two small vessels sent to Coro. Except for his solitary journey to the Canaries in the *Judith* following the November storm, this may be taken as the first independent command Drake had on this voyage with John Hawkins.

Late in May, just before the entire fleet left Borburata, Hawkins sent Drake with two of the smaller ships, *Judith* and *Angel,* to inspect the port at Rio de la Hacha, the next destination. This is the port where Lovell had created such a ruckus the previous year, trying to force the local people to buy his slaves. Warned in advance by advisories from Borburata, the port commander had built new gun batteries and mobilized a hundred harquebusiers to defend the approaches. When Drake's small ships came into the harbor, the Spanish batteries opened fire, and the two English ships withdrew.[111]

For the next few days the *Judith* and the *Angel* rode just out of cannon range, blockading the port and awaiting the arrival of the fleet. When Hawkins appeared in the harbor on 10 June, he followed his usual practice of sending a messenger to the local commander to request formal approval for a bit of trading. In this case the commander was an old friend and trading partner, Miguel de Castellanos. But things had changed, and the commander was unwilling to break the explicit royal prohibition of trade with the English pirates.[112]

Again, attempting to provide a rationale for trade, Hawkins told Castellanos that the slave cargo sent in 1567 was one that he had supposed Castellanos was willing to receive. He apologized for the rash behavior of Lovell, then repeated his argument to the governor at Borburata: he had really not intended to come to the Indies, but since he was there, he needed only to sell about sixty slaves and some trade goods to pay expenses.[113]

The letter was no more successful at Rio de la Hacha than at Borburata. Consequently, Hawkins landed two hundred armed men, took the town, burned some dwellings, and seized the royal treasury, some storehouses, and a few hostages. As Hawkins reported the events, this had the desired effect on Castellanos, who agreed to let the people trade. The local planters bought 150 to 200 slaves plus other goods of considerable value. As usual, Hawkins distributed gifts to Castellanos and other officials.[114]

Castellanos gave a different account in his report to the king. Hawkins required him to pay a ransom of four thousand pesos for the release of the hostages. He then left a number of slaves on shore to repay the damage done to the dwellings. Castellanos reported that these were mostly children and old people, who were distributed to local planters who provided food and shelter; they were being sold off gradually, he wrote, though the value did not approach the cost of repairing the damage.[115]

Most likely, the truth lies somewhere in between the two accounts. The Spanish colonists no doubt bought a number of slaves while government officials looked the other way. Hawkins then left a few other slaves in the hands of the local treasurer, who could be expected to keep careful sales records on these unfortunates in order to confuse the inevitable government inspectors who would be sent later.[116] The Hawkins trade pattern had become a familiar one: his formal request for a license to trade; a formal refusal by the local officials; a brief battle, with a few men killed and injured on each side; and finally two or three weeks of profitable trade in slaves and merchandise, carried out under the guise of ransom payments on one side and reimbursement for damages on the other.[117]

Finished at Rio de la Hacha, Hawkins took his fleet on to Santa Marta, reaching there about 10 July, and followed the usual pattern of request, refusal, scuffle, and trade. After selling another 114 slaves, Hawkins took his fleet further along the coast to Cartagena. The usual battle ensued, but the Spanish colonists put up a stiff defense, and the English managed only to capture a supply of oil and wine. Moreover, the Spanish commander refused to participate in any negotiations with the pirates, so Hawkins was forced to leave with the loot, as well as the fifty or so slaves and small quantity of trade goods that remained in his ships.[118]

With the hurricane season well advanced, Hawkins decided to abandon one of the vessels seized on the African coast and sail home with a smaller fleet. Leaving the Portuguese ship at anchor in the harbor of Cartagena, the remaining eight ships sailed north about the middle of August. Heading for the Yucatan Channel and the Straits of Florida, the fleet had scarcely rounded Cabo San Antonio when a terrible storm bore down on the ships. The *Jesus* sprung its planks and began to take on water, while the *William and John* disappeared in the storm and made a separate voyage home. Four days later, when the storm blew itself out, the fleet lay hundreds of miles north off the coast of Florida. For two weeks Hawkins searched in vain, hoping to find a port in which to repair his battered vessels. Finally, he decided to sail south for New Spain, where he expected to find a haven. Capturing a Spanish ship along the way, he interrogated the pilot and determined to head for San Juan de Ulúa, the port town for Vera Cruz.[119]

The harbor was broad and open, only slightly sheltered from the weather by the low-lying island of San Juan de Ulúa.[120] With badly faded banners flying from its masts, the *Jesus* led the rest of the fleet into port on 17 September, where they were welcomed by local officials who thought they were the merchant fleet sent each year with an armed escort from Spain. Taking advantage of the confusion, Hawkins seized the island as his headquarters and sent the inhabitants to the mainland. By the following day, when the Spanish fleet arrived, Hawkins was well dug in on shore and able to negotiate from a strong position.[121]

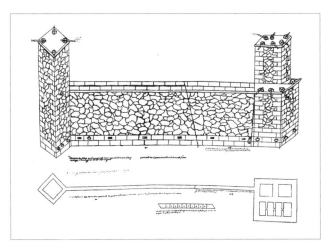

*Drawing by Christobal de Eraso of the fort at San Juan de Ulúa
(c. 1570). The portion left of the diagonal line shows the extent of the
fort in 1568, when Hawkins and Drake occupied the place. From Hans
P. Kraus Collection, Library of Congress.*

Sailing aboard the Spanish flagship was Martín Enríquez, the newly appointed viceroy of New Spain, who faced a difficult decision even before he landed. If he attacked Hawkins, he risked losing his fleet and the ships in the harbor as well. Yet the weather was threatening, and it was necessary to bring the fleet immediately into port. Consequently, Enríquez agreed to let Hawkins remain in control of the island for a brief time, repairing his ships and buying necessary supplies. Hawkins and Enríquez then exchanged hostages as a guarantee of good faith.[122]

In spite of this agreement, three more days passed before the Spanish fleet entered the harbor, during which time both threats and friendly overtures passed back and forth between the two commanders. On 23 September 1568, two days after entering San Juan de Ulúa, the Spanish forces mounted a surprise attack on the Hawkins ships and on his island fortifications. Nothing went according to plan. The Spanish commander gave the signal to attack nearly an hour before the time agreed upon and well before the attacking forces were in position. This allowed Hawkins to cut the cables on the *Jesus of Lubeck* and drift away from his anchorage. A hulk

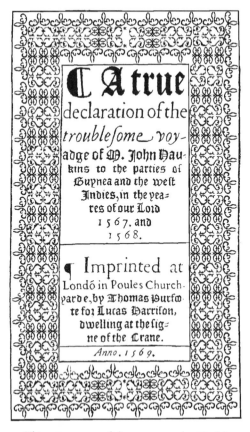

This 1569 account of the voyage says that Drake's
Judith *"forsooke us in our great miserie," a charge of*
desertion that haunted Drake for the rest of his life.
Copy at Huntington Library.

that was supposed to become a fire ship failed to catch fire, and another
had to be prepared. The second fire ship did the trick, bearing down on
the *Jesus of Lubeck* with such unrelenting accuracy that Hawkins abandoned it, barely making his escape aboard the *Minion*.[123]

Drake, who was nearby in the *Judith*, was ordered to come alongside the
Minion to take on some of the extra men and equipment saved from the
Jesus of Lubeck. Job Hortop wrote thirty years later that Drake did exactly
that, though Hawkins himself told a different story, reflecting less credit

on his young colleague. While the *Minion* lay in the lee of the island outside the range of the Spanish guns and loaded with more English survivors
than it could carry, Drake sailed off in the darkness, heading for home.
"The *Judith*," said Hawkins, "forsooke us in our great myserie."[124]

Five English ships were abandoned in the port, four captured, and one
destroyed by the Spanish militia.[125] In fact, these seaworn prizes made it
possible for Hawkins and the others to escape. As soon as the *Minion* and
the *Judith* were out of the harbor, the undisciplined Spanish militiamen
ended their pursuit and spent the rest of the day looting the English ships
and fortifications.[126]

An honored tradition in most maritime communities, this practice of
looting abandoned goods was something of an art at San Juan de Ulúa.
When Hawkins first arrived with his fleet, all the wealthy merchants fled
with whatever they could carry. Townspeople who stayed behind then
helped themselves to what was left. As one man described the scene,
"Those who had little wanted to help those who had something to save it,
so it seems they put it away for themselves."[127]

Drake and his men in the *Judith* also saved themselves, leaving Hawkins
with an overloaded ship at San Juan de Ulúa. The scandal haunted Drake
for the rest of his life, for Hawkins was forced to abandon a hundred of the
men on the Mexican coast, and most of them never saw England again.[128]

Although Drake's failure to stay with Hawkins in his desperate situation
outside San Juan de Ulúa created a serious rift between the two men,
Drake never forgot the lessons learned from his cousin and mentor. The
commander of a pirate fleet traveled in style, with fine food, good clothes,
a richly appointed cabin, and a band of musicians for his entertainment.
Discipline was sure and swift, with no leniency, even in matters of religion. The patterns that came to typify Drake's behavior as a fleet commander are the ones that Hawkins taught him. Even so, there were some
character traits that were his alone. From his earliest days at sea, he preferred to sail alone. He was never comfortable with a large fleet.

3

Raids on the Spanish Main

THE TRIP FROM SAN JUAN de Ulúa to the southeast coast of England usually required no more than four weeks of sailing, but the weather was bad and both ships were in poor repair. John Hawkins, with the overloaded *Minion,* lurked for several days in the islands south of the port, then sailed north toward Panuco, where he stopped for wood and water. About half the men said that they would rather take their chances on the coast of New Spain than risk the return voyage, so Hawkins left them on the coast and sailed for home. It was slow going, but by the middle of November he was in the Bahamas Channel, heading for the open sea. Even then, luck eluded him, and a month later his ship was near the coast of Galicia, blown there by contrary winds.[1]

On the last day of December 1568, Hawkins and the *Minion* anchored at Ponte Vedra, near Vigo. Sending ashore for food, he began to nurse the men back to health. A great number apparently overate and fell violently ill, so with only a few hands to man the ship, Hawkins took the *Minion* into port at Vigo, where some English merchants were docked. From these ships he got supplies and another dozen men and set sail for home. Again unable to reach Plymouth, he docked instead at Mounts Bay in Cornwall, where his brother William sent seamen and supplies to bring the survivors home.[2]

Strangely enough, the *Judith* arrived at Plymouth only three days before Hawkins reached Mounts Bay. Francis Drake, who had abandoned Hawkins and his men at the end of September, seems to have sailed home along an equally circuitous course. Moreover, Drake and his crew were in surprisingly good health, so fit that William Hawkins sent him to London on the very same day to report in person to the government officials and

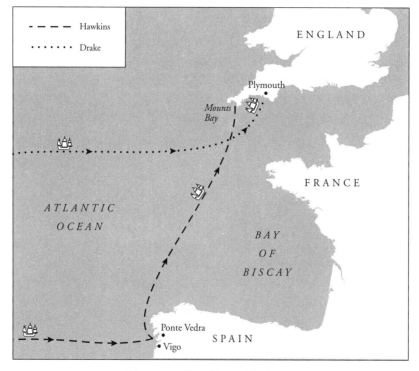

The returns of Hawkins and Drake, 1569

others who had a financial interest in the venture. No doubt the *Judith* had managed to stop somewhere for supplies and recuperation, just as Hawkins had done in the *Minion*.[3]

It is difficult to know whether the voyage was profitable or not. On 22 January, when he thought that Drake's little ship might be the only survivor, William Hawkins estimated that the loss could be as much as £2,000.[4] This soon changed. Early in December a fleet of Spanish ships sailing for the Netherlands with a crown payroll had landed in English ports. Amid considerable diplomatic controversy, the chests of money were confiscated by the English government. And while John Hawkins made his own way to London with four pack horses loaded with gold and silver, and his brother sent an even larger pack train with an armed escort for the rest of the treasure, William also asked the government to reimburse his losses from the Spanish payroll.[5]

Within a few weeks Hawkins was claiming losses of more than £25,000.[6] At the same time, the Spanish ambassador, who originally reported that Hawkins had lost 50 percent of his capital, suddenly wrote to his government that the English pirates had returned with 28,000 pesos in gold, plus a small trunk full of pearls.[7] The gold, he said, was worth about £7,000. This is very nearly the estimate given by a Portuguese seaman named Antonio Texera, who was with Hawkins and said Hawkins had managed to take 40,000 ducados from the *Jesus of Lubeck* before leaving San Juan de Ulúa.[8]

An account written some years later and said to have been approved by Francis Drake made reference to the loss at San Juan de Ulúa. According to this story, Drake suffered "not onely in the losse of his goods of some value, but also of his kinsmen and & friends." So his losses included goods or money and also the great numbers of men killed and wounded in the battle, abandoned later on the coast of New Spain, or buried at sea when they died on the way home. No doubt he was correct in citing the "falsehood of Don Martin Henriques," who had agreed to allow the English to trade without molestation, but this was something of an afterthought.[9] Not trusting the Spanish, John Hawkins had kept his men fortified on the island despite the guarantees.

For the next few years Hawkins worked to secure the return of the captives lost in New Spain, and some of them actually managed to make their way home. The most successful negotiation was that carried out by George Fitzwilliam. Sometimes alone, sometimes with the personal help of Hawkins, Fitzwilliam used his close relationship with the Duke of Feria to negotiate the release of a number of English prisoners who had been transported to Spain. As part of the bargain struck by Fitzwilliam, Hawkins was supposed to help place Mary Stuart on the throne and was to receive a royal pardon and a grant of nobility from the king of Spain. No doubt Hawkins never intended to carry out his part of the bargain, perhaps a fitting repayment for the duplicity of the Spanish viceroy.[10]

What John Hawkins thought of Francis Drake is another matter. Twenty years after Hawkins's accusation that the *Judith* "forsooke us in our great myserie," that version retained wide currency: "Frauncis Drake . . .

demeaned him self towardes his Master and Admyral, Mr John Hawkyns, at the port of St John de Loo in the Weste Indyas, when contrary to his saide Admyrals comaunde he came awaye and left his sayde master in greate extremytie, wheruppon he was forced to set at shoare in that contrye to seek their adventurs 100 of his men; which matter . . . he colde noe wayes exchuse."[11]

Not all the details are known, but it may not have been a clear case of desertion. A good many biographers have excused Drake on the ground that his own ship must have been in great peril and that there was little he could have done for Hawkins anyway.[12] Hawkins clearly did not hold this view, refusing even to mention Drake's name in his own account of the voyage.

According to the account written thirty years later by the Spanish historian Antonio de Herrera, Drake escaped with most of the treasure. Arriving in England, Drake reported that Hawkins was lost and the treasure was gone, distributed by Drake among the seamen. When John Hawkins showed up shortly thereafter, it was clear that Drake had not told the real story. Queen Elizabeth put him in prison for a time, but Drake kept insisting that he had given the treasure away. For three months Drake begged Elizabeth to release him, and finally she relented.[13] No English source confirms this story, though Drake did disappear for a while, just when he should have been in London testifying with the other survivors about the battle at San Juan de Ulúa.[14]

If not in prison, Francis Drake may have made a quick return trip to the Indies, perhaps going on a ship that belonged to William Hawkins. There is nothing more than circumstantial evidence about such a voyage, mostly the information that French and English pirates continued to raid the Spanish Main during the early part of 1569. Not surprisingly, the pirates claimed to be reimbursing themselves for losses suffered in previous encounters.[15] Transparent as this might seem now, the argument convinced many in Spain. The historian Herrera wrote a very labored defense of the Spanish conduct at San Juan de Ulúa. In his version, Viceroy Don Martín Enríquez was not even present when the attack was made. Instead, the decision was made by the field commander, Francisco de Luján, who reasoned that "the Englishmen were pirates, so it was not necessary to abide by the promises that had been made."[16]

Whatever happened, Francis Drake managed to take some time out for romance. On 4 July 1569 he married Mary Newman in Saint Budeaux Parish Church near Plymouth.[17] Nothing at all is known of Mary Newman or her family, but it has become customary to say that her brother was a shipmate of Drake's, perhaps the one named Harry Newman.[18] Some writers speculate that several of the Newmans listed in the parish register at Saint Budeaux were Mary's sisters, but there is no reason to think this is so.[19] John Drake said that Mary Newman's family was from London.[20] This may explain why the Newmans do not appear in parish records before the 1530s. No records have been found to prove any of these suppositions, partly because there were no children from the marriage to remember and record the names of grandparents and other relatives.

The lack of records has not proven an insurmountable obstacle to local historians. During the 1970s an Elizabethan cottage in Saltash was preserved and later restored as the home of Mary Newman, despite the protests of the town clerk, who called it a "historical fraud." Many agreed with the clerk but supported the preservation movement anyway, because the house was the only Elizabethan cottage remaining in Saltash.[21]

Drake's marriage to Mary Newman provides a reason for believing Herrera's assertion that Drake had come home with some of the profits of the voyage. Obviously he was rich enough to take a wife. Beyond that, he could afford to sail again to the Indies, more or less on his own for the first time. The details are skimpy enough, and, as is often the case, the earliest printed information is not entirely correct. In a book assembled in 1626 by Philip Nichols, called *Sir Francis Drake Revived,* a few brief lines say that Drake made two reconnaissance trips to the West Indies "to gaine such intelligences as might further him to get some amends for his losse." The first trip was in 1570, according to Nichols. Drake sailed with two ships that Nichols called the *Dragon* and the *Swan.*"[22]

Spanish and English archives give a little more information to flesh out the spare account assembled by Nichols and to correct some of the details. The voyage began on 25 November 1569 and included three ships owned by William Hawkins. Francis Drake was master of a 50-ton vessel called the *Brave,* carrying goods to the Guinea coast of Africa. Hawkins went as far as Guinea, then returned home, sending Drake to the Indies with the other two ships.[23]

What happened on the voyage is uncertain. The lack of Spanish complaint in 1570 seems to imply a trading voyage with no remarkable incidents.[24] Drake's cargo included woolen cloth from Devon, and no doubt he took on a load of slaves in Guinea.[25] Very likely the venture was a final attempt by the Hawkins brothers to force the Spaniards to concede their right to trade in the West Indies.[26] But the voyage also provided Francis Drake with a chance to learn what the French and English pirates were accomplishing. Whether he became involved in their raids is uncertain, but one source suggests that he intended to do so. A somewhat garbled translation of a commercial newsletter, dated at Seville in December 1569, reported that Drake was on his way to trade in the Indies and possibly to menace the ships coming back from New Spain.[27]

If the report was true, Drake may have changed his mind when he saw the results of a new Spanish maritime policy. In answer to the growing threat from foreign traders and pirates, the Spanish authorities inaugurated the Indies Fleet in 1568 to help defend the Caribbean ports. At the same time, Spain developed a convoy system to protect Spanish trading ships from pirate attacks. The French and English pirates quickly responded with innovations of their own. Using swift, oar-propelled, shallow-draft vessels based on a mother ship, the pirates discovered that they could raid at will, then elude the Spanish galleons sent in pursuit. Local Spanish officials fitted out their own frigates to counter the new threat, but there was no determined Spanish effort to eliminate piracy altogether. Because the pirate raids were localized and sporadic, it was cheaper and easier to follow a policy of containment.[28]

When Drake saw what the pirates were able to accomplish, he determined to return and take a share in the booty. On that second trip, taken in 1571, he came in a tiny vessel of 25 tons, a pinnace called the *Swan,* no doubt the same one that his brother commanded the following year.[29] During the 1571 voyage Drake's ship may have been part of a three-vessel fleet organized by William Wynter and his brother George. In a summary prepared by Spanish authorities several years later, Francis Drake and his brothers, plus William and George Wynter and John and William Hawkins, were listed as the most notorious of the English pirates.[30] It is clear that Drake was not fully independent at this time but worked for another English pirate stationed in a mother ship off Cabo Cativa in Panama.[31] There is some evidence that Drake worked for both the Hawkins and the Wynter brothers, though the voyage no doubt had a number of financial backers.[32] Only one name appears in the record, that of a "merchant of Exeter called Richard Dennys," who apparently went with other merchants in the ship with Drake.[33]

In the early part of February 1571 Drake and his crew joined French pirates in a daring raid up the Rio Chagres, which cuts through the mountains of the Isthmus of Panama. Citizens in the little port of Panama, on the Pacific side of the isthmus, had established a trading post called Venta de Cruces on the banks of the Chagres about five leagues from their city. Literally the Crossroads Warehouse, the building contained forty-seven storerooms where goods were kept during the dry season, when loaded ships could not sail on the Chagres. While stored at Venta de Cruces, the goods were supervised by an alcalde who acted as agent for the Panama merchants, kept accounts, and made periodic reports. The same man also had charge of a similar warehouse called Venta de Chagres, which lay further along the road, six leagues from Panama and twelve from Nombre de Dios, on the Caribbean coast. The road to Nombre de Dios was bad, hazardous at the best of times and nearly impassible during the May to December rainy season. The country was mountainous and broken, full of trees and swamps and thorny underbrush. In addition, there was a constant threat from the *negros cimarrones,* escaped black slaves who would not submit to Spanish authority. The only practical route from the Ventas was by riverboat, a safe, swift, and easy eighteen leagues, except during the dry months, when river craft could not ascend to the warehouse.[34]

Taking advantage of the dry season, Drake and his allies rowed up the shallow river in a *galeota,* a small galley with sixteen oars on each side. Thirty-six of the men were armed with harquebuses, and a black named

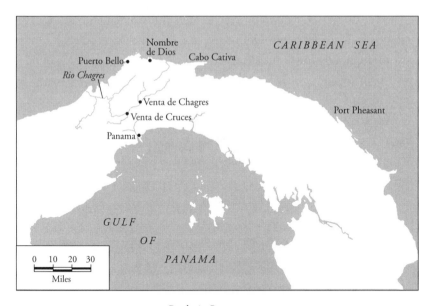

Drake in Panama, 1571

Pedro Mandinga was their guide. About five or six leagues from the Casa de Cruces they discovered a *fragata* belonging to Baltazar de Melo; the small vessel was loaded with goods that belonged to Melo and a merchant named Baltazar Domínguez. Seizing the vessel and its contents, worth perhaps 50,000 pesos, the pirates sailed back down the river, destroying what they could not carry away. Before leaving the place Drake and his associates went around to the other boats that were moored along the river bank and stove in the bottoms so that no one could follow in pursuit. It was too late. Mandinga had already escaped, carrying the news of the raid back to Panama, where word was sent to Diego Flores de Valdés, captain general of the Indies Fleet.[35]

A few days later the pirates were back at the mother ship, at Cabo Cativa near the port of Nombre de Dios, looking for another prize. Finding a Spanish trading frigate at anchor in the outer bay, Drake in his pinnace attempted to board. As he drew alongside, one of his men sounded a trumpet, and the Spanish suddenly realized what was happening. Armed only with swords and stones, the Spanish seamen still managed to drive the pirates back. During the fracas Drake's pirates fired a shower of bullets and arrows at the vessel, wounding several men and women and killing three people. A citizen of Santo Domingo named Diego Azevedo took "an arrow through the brows" and died within the hour. A seaman was wounded with an arrow in the chest and died two days later. A black slave was killed by a culverin ball. Finally, while the pirates were distracted by the arrival of another frigate, someone had the good sense to cut the anchor cable. The frigate then drifted ashore, where the passengers and crew escaped into the mangroves. The pirates immediately looted the ships and left a message for the passengers and crew.[36]

Translated to Spanish and sent along to Spain as an example of the impudence of the pirates, the original message may have been composed by Drake himself. If so, it is the earliest surviving example of his consummate audacity in the face of an enemy:

> Captain and others of this ship.
>
> We are surprised that you ran from us in that fashion and later refused to come to talk to us under our flag of truce, knowing us, and having seen evidence a few days past that we do ill to no one under our flag of truce. We only wished to speak with you. And since you will not come courteously to talk with us, without evil or damage, you will find your frigate spoiled by your own fault. And to any who courteously may come to talk with us, we will do no harm, under our flag. And whoever does not come will bear the blame.
>
> And do not think we were afraid of those ships, nor of others. By the help of God it shall cost them their lives before they prevail over us.
>
> Now you have proof that it would have been better had you come to talk with us, for in the frigate you had not the value of four silver *reales*.
>
> Done by English who are well disposed, if there be no cause to the contrary. If there be cause, we will be devils rather than men.[37]

"Those ships" doubtless were the Indies Fleet of Diego Flores de Valdés, which had pursued the pirate vessels, chasing them into some of the shallow bays and inlets of the isthmus and forcing them to abandon three captured fragatas and about 30,000 pesos' worth of goods. Taking a cue from the pirates, Valdés proceeded to refit these small ships with oars and sails so that he could pursue the pirates into shallow water.[38]

Not the least bit frightened, Drake and the other pirates sailed back to the Rio Chagres. Once more going inland, they attacked the Venta de Cruces and looted the warehouse. Spanish reports, perhaps exaggerated, said that the pirates took clothing and merchandise belonging to Lope Ruiz de Leço and Baltasar Díaz worth 10,000 pesos or more.[39] A few days later in the mouth of the Chagres River they stopped three boats in ballast heading for Nombre de Dios to report the raid. Putting the crews ashore, the pirates beat holes in the bottoms of the boats so that the crews could not sail on to give the alarm.[40]

Three leagues west of Nombre de Dios the passage from the Chagres River ran between the mainland and Bastimentos Island.[41] For several days Drake and his men lay in wait near the island, picking off a dozen or so riverboats loaded with clothing, slaves, and merchandise. The amount of loot was so massive that the pirates could not carry it away in their own ships. Consequently, they loaded the surplus goods and slaves onto the two best of the raided boats and took them also. The owners claimed a loss of 150,000 pesos.[42]

Perhaps the most embarrassing loss for the Spaniards was the fragata from Cartagena, taken off Cabo Cativa about 8 May 1571. This was the mail boat, carrying both personal and official letters from Spain. Finding nothing worth stealing, the pirates dumped all the personal mail into the sea. During the attack the pirates killed several people, including the owner of the ship, a man named Salvatierra, and wounded a number of others. A friar was stripped and taunted, but otherwise unharmed.[43] Staying around for one final assault, the pirate fleet sailed again into the Chagres River and seized riverboats with about 70,000 pesos' worth of merchandise.[44]

With so many bays in which the pirates could hide and so much coastline to cover, there was little the local people could do in their own defense. On three separate occasions the people of Nombre de Dios sent their small fragatas out to look for the pirate ships, each time without success. It is unlikely that they were terribly disappointed, for the major losses were incurred by the merchants of Panama. In any case, it was the job of the government to offer them protection, and they said so in no uncertain terms.[45]

Along with the other pirates, Drake established his headquarters in a small secluded bay on the Acla coast. This was the place he called Port Pheasant, near the mouth of the Rio de Piñas and about fifteen leagues east of Nombre de Dios.[46] Reloading his cargo, Drake sailed for home about the first part of June 1571, returning to England with some three ships crammed full of Spanish goods, coin, and slaves. After he left, some of his Spanish captives made their way back to Nombre de Dios and reported the location of the base, which the Spanish inspected on regular visits thereafter.[47]

Lacking royal authority for the voyage, Drake waited offshore at Plymouth while word went to London reporting on the results of his voyage and ascertaining that the government would not hold the men accountable for the raids.[48] There was little likelihood of punishment: the Spanish claims totaled more than 250,000 pesos. At 8 shillings, 3 pence per peso the total profits must have been close to £100,000, even allowing for exaggeration on the part of the Spanish claimants.[49] What Drake's share might have been is unclear, though it must have been a respectable sum, sufficient to finance Drake as commander of his own small fleet.

Taking a few months of rest, Drake began to plan with English captains for a new voyage to the Indies. The details are unknown, but it is clear that Drake arranged to meet them at Port Pheasant and to use that as a base of operations. The other ship commanders included John Garret and James Raunse, both of whom were companions on previous voyages.[50]

Drake's own fleet was made up of just two ships. The larger, which he called his "Admirall," was the *Pascoe,* the ship that the Hawkins brothers had sent to the Indies with Lovell. Whether Drake owned this ship or whether he sailed it for the Hawkins brothers is not certain. John Hawkins claimed ownership in 1571, but there is evidence that the Drake brothers may have bought it from him before the voyage.[51] It was a small vessel, only 40 tons, but about right for the shallow bays around the isthmus.[52]

The second ship was the *Swan,* the same 25-ton pinnace that he had used in the previous voyages. This was his "Vice-Admirall," commanded by his brother John. Part of the cargo consisted of three other pinnaces, newly built in Plymouth, then knocked down for later assembly at Port Pheasant. The pinnaces, about 10 tons apiece, were named *Lion, Minion,* and *Bear.* Crews for all five vessels were crammed aboard the two small ships. Forty-seven men went in the *Pascoe* and twenty-six in the *Swan.* It was a voyage for young adventurers; except for one fifty-year-old man, all were under the age of thirty.[53] Drake's brother Joseph also went on the voyage, as did John Oxnam, now usually called Oxenham.

Leaving Plymouth on 24 May 1572, the Drake vessels took the usual route through the Canary Islands, which they reached within twelve days. Making such good time, they did not stop in the islands but sailed on to the island of Guadalupe in the West Indies, where they arrived on 28 June. Sailing through the channel between Guadalupe and Dominica, they went ashore on the south side of Dominica, where they rested for three days and took on water.[54]

Crossing to the mainland, the ships passed within a few miles of Santa Marta, but Drake knew that they would be unwelcome and did not stop. These were familiar waters, and Drake had sailed there on earlier occasions with both Lovell and Hawkins. Their destination was Port Pheasant, where Garret expected to meet them. Arriving at Port Pheasant on 12 July 1572, they found the place deserted but discovered a message from Garret incised on a lead plate nailed to the largest tree at the landing place:

> Captaine Drake, if you fortune to come to this Port,
> mak hast away, for the Spaniards which you had with
> you here last yeere have bewrayed this place, and taken
> away all that you left here. I departed from hence, this
> present 7. of July, 1572.
> Your verie loving friend
> John Garret.[55]

Disregarding this warning, Drake decided to stay at Port Pheasant and let his carpenters assemble the three pinnaces. It was a delightful spot. The

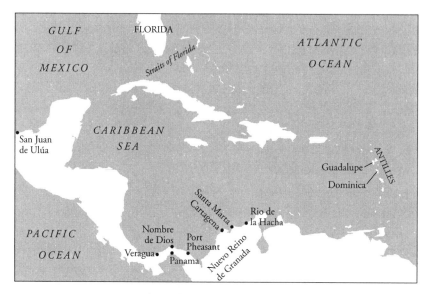

Drake's raids in the Caribbean, 1572–73

bay was full of fish, and the shore teemed with the birds that gave the port its name. In addition, there was a partial clearing of about three-quarters of an acre, where Drake ordered his crew to begin erecting a barrier of logs. If the account written by Nichols can be believed, they had the fort finished within a week, a walled pentagonal enclosure thirty feet high. Built of huge tree trunks wrestled into place with block and tackle, the fort opened onto the water, where a tree trunk was drawn across at night to serve as a gate.[56]

The construction work was aided to a great extent by the arrival next day of Raunse, who had captured the Spanish mail ship from Seville and brought it into port, apparently under the command of John Overy, his master. Raunse and Drake concluded their arrangements for a raid on Nombre de Dios and made an agreement for dividing the spoils of their raids.[57]

In addition to the three pinnaces, Drake had brought a good supply of infantry weapons and explosives, sealed in casks to prevent damage. These included "six Targets, six Firepikes, twelve Pikes, twentie foure Muskets and Callivers, sixteene Bowes, and six Partizans, two Drums, and two

Trumpets." The last two items acknowledged the fact that noise is as important in battle as any other weapon, the principle presumably being that if all else fails it might just be possible to scare someone to death.[58]

Once the construction was finished, Drake and Raunse with their three ships and four pinnaces sailed from Port Pheasant for Nombre de Dios. This was a small town, with no fort, no quay, no permanent military or naval presence. There were a hundred and fifty or two hundred houses, most of them deserted when Drake and his men arrived. Basking in the tropical sun for most of the year, Nombre de Dios became active only during the rainy season and then only when the convoy from Seville was in port. Once the fleet arrived, treasure and other goods were sent up from Panama to be loaded aboard the ships. With this work completed, the merchants and government officials returned to Panama, where the climate was more agreeable.[59] All this had happened several weeks earlier.

When Drake and Raunse arrived at the Isle of Pines, they found two frigates from Nombre de Dios with crews of black slaves loading lumber. Taking the men prisoner, Drake and Raunse questioned them closely, learning that the town was undefended, though some soldiers were expected from Panama within a short time. It is not clear whether the prisoners told Drake and Raunse that the fleet had already departed, taking all the goods and treasure to Spain. It is clear that they told him the town might have a moderately heavy guard, including an artillery battery on a hill to the east.[60]

Raunse may have had misgivings about continuing with the attack. As it turned out, he stayed behind with the three ships at the Isle of Pines, sheltered in a bay that they named Port Plenty. Drake took his own three pinnaces, along with a shallop that belonged to Raunse, and headed up the coast for Nombre de Dios. He left behind twenty of his own men to guard the ships, while Raunse sent twenty of his men in the shallop.[61]

Five days later, on 28 July 1572, Drake landed his men at the Isla de Cativas, about twenty-five leagues east of Nombre de Dios. Issuing a weapon to each man, Drake spent one morning dividing them into two companies and drilling them on proper tactics. Shortly after noon they set sail again for the town, arriving before sunset at Rio Francisca, about two leagues away. From this point they kept very close to shore, rowing in darkness into the mouth of the bay. About three in the morning, just as the moon rose, they spied a Spanish merchantman from the Canaries sitting across the harbor. The Spanish lookout realized immediately what was afoot, and the Spanish captain tried to send his boat ashore to give the alarm. But Drake's pirates beat the Spanish boat to the sandy beach, where by chance they captured the entire armament of the town, six culverins and demiculverins. Knocking these guns from their carriages, Drake split his force into two companies of thirty men each, leaving a dozen to guard the pinnaces.[62]

Leaving one company as rear guard, Drake proceeded to march up the hill east of town to capture the supposed artillery emplacement. Finding none, he came back down and regrouped his men. This time he put his brother John in charge of a group that included John Oxnam and sixteen other men, plus a drummer, a trumpeter, and three fire pikes. Drake himself took the rest of the men and marched toward the central plaza from the north, while John and his company circled around to approach from the east side of the plaza.[63]

The exact configuration of the plaza at Nombre de Dios is not clear, though it seems to have been built in the grid plan specified for Spanish settlements in the New World. Two streets met at each corner of the plaza, and the corners were located at the cardinal points of the compass. The church was on the southwest side, government buildings on the southeast, the "king's treasure house" on the northeast side, and trading houses on the other.[64]

There was no longer any question of surprising the inhabitants, who eventually numbered thirty-five or forty men and women, black and white, arrayed along the southern side of the plaza. Another group of two or three men marched about with burning matches on the western side, as though another force of harquebusiers were lining up there. The ruse worked only until Drake's men fired at the burning matches. When there was no answering volley, the pirates charged across the plaza and drove the poor fellows away. Drake then had his pinnaces fire their guns toward the plaza, while his men concentrated their fire at the southern end. Meanwhile, the Spanish citizenry managed to rouse themselves for defense, firing low, killing Drake's trumpeter and wounding a number of men, including

Drake himself. Almost at that very moment John Drake's company joined the attack from the east side, and together the pirates drove the inhabitants back out through the gate and along the road to Panama.[65]

Throughout the brief battle someone inside the church kept ringing the bell, to give the alarm. Even when the Spanish forces were driven out of town, the bell continued to ring, and because the doors were locked, nothing could be done about it. Instead, Drake ordered his brother's men to break into the treasure house, which proved to be empty. Drake stayed in the plaza with the rest of the men to fend off the expected counterattack. Aided by a driving rain, a dozen or so citizens finally gathered themselves together and drove the pirates back to their pinnaces. To save their foray from total failure Drake and his men took the Spanish ship loaded with wine, then barely made it out of the harbor before the Spanish got one of their guns back on its carriage and into firing condition.[66]

The raid was a dreadful failure. The blacks taken at the Isle of Pines, obviously badly informed about Nombre de Dios, had told Drake that there was a Spanish garrison in town, with artillery planted on the hill overlooking the place. They also said that the town was rich and heavily populated. None of this was true. Another black taken prisoner in Nombre de Dios apparently told Drake that there was a trained force of 150 men poised for a counterattack. This was also untrue.[67] This was a discouraging way for Drake to learn that information from captives was often badly mistaken.

Even more serious was the failure in planning. The men were totally untrained. The guard left with the pinnaces was apparently convinced that the two or three men parading around in the dark with burning matches constituted a great force of armed soldiers. Drake himself was unprepared for the attack. If the Nichols narrative is correct, he divided his men into separate forces on the spot, then regrouped them several times with no apparent plan of action. Even so, Spanish losses were great, four or five killed, the same number mortally wounded, perhaps thirty in all killed and wounded. In comparison, Drake lost one man killed and several more wounded.[68]

The crowning irony is that there was almost nothing in Nombre de Dios worth stealing. The small amount of booty that the pirates managed to take was not of sufficient value for the citizens to make a claim. Even the wine ship was of little value. It was owned not by a Spaniard but by a Canary Islander, who offered only 2,000 pesos to help get it back.[69]

No doubt embarrassed by these facts, Philip Nichols reported a half century later that the pirates had indeed found a great treasure in the government house, but they refrained from taking it. As Nichols wrote the story, once the battle in the plaza was over, the men approached the government building and found the gate open, with a mule standing ready for someone to make an escape. In the dimness of a lantern, so Nichols reported, they spied a great pile of silver bars, seventy feet long, ten feet wide, and twelve feet high, each bar weighing thirty-five or forty pounds. Drake ordered his men not to touch a single piece of silver, or so Nichols said. His reason? The treasure house was filled with gold and jewels more than sufficient to load all four pinnaces. So, ordering some men to break into the treasure house, Drake took the rest of the men to stand guard in the Plaza, where he fainted from loss of blood. Panicked at the thought of losing their commander, the men abandoned the treasure house, carried the unconscious Drake back to the pinnaces, took command of the Canary wine ship, and sailed away.[70]

Withdrawing from the harbor, Drake's four ships sailed three leagues to Bastimentos Island, where the people of Nombre de Dios had large plantations of pineapples, bananas, and a soft-fleshed fruit called *guanábanas*.[71] Drake and his men spent the next two days regrouping, while the people of Nombre de Dios sent an emissary out to parley. Afterward, Drake retreated to the Isle of Pines. Displaying again the indecision that had come to typify this voyage, Francis Drake stopped in the middle of the return trip and sent his brother John and another seaman named John Hixon in one of the pinnaces to report on conditions in the Chagres River. When Captain Raunse learned that Francis Drake was such an undependable ally, he withdrew from the partnership, not even waiting for John Drake to return.[72]

A few days later, about 7 August 1572, Drake took his two ships and three pinnaces east toward the port of Cartagena. Arriving just about nightfall on the thirteenth, Drake left the two ships safely at anchor in the *boca chica* or narrow inlet near the Isla de Carex. He then took the three pinnaces and rowed silently into the harbor. Unfortunately, the alarm had already been given, and all he found was an empty fragata with an old man aboard to serve as watchman. Questioning the old man, he learned that a merchant vessel from Seville lay just around the next point, ready to depart in the morning. Drake attacked the ship with his pinnaces and finally caused it to run aground, where Spanish horsemen boarded the vessel and kept it from falling into the hands of the pirates. Just what sort of vessel it might have been remains unclear. The story related by Nichols describes the vessel as "a great ship" of "two hundred fortie Tunne." The Spanish report says it was only a fragata, though loaded with valuable goods.[73] In any event, the attack failed, and Drake's ships retired to the outer anchorage, where the next day they looted a vessel carrying dispatches from Spain, plus another with messages from Nombre de Dios. Setting the sailors ashore, Drake burned both dispatch boats.[74]

If the next event related by Nichols is true, then it is easy to understand just why Raunse decided to end his partnership with Drake. While anchored a few leagues off the entrance to the port, Drake decided that he could operate more efficiently with just one ship. He would get rid of the *Swan,* the ship his brother commanded—and loved. Calling the carpenter, Thomas Moone, into his cabin, Drake ordered Moone to go aboard the *Swan* and secretly bore holes in the bottom, being careful to place a baffle over the holes in order to muffle the noise of the water. By the time John and his men discovered the leak, it was too late to save the ship. To ease John's grief at losing his ship, Drake then gave him command of the *Pascoe* and assigned the extra men to serve in the pinnaces. This story of colossal arrogance and recklessness on the part of the expedition commander can scarcely be true. It is not the only possible explanation for the loss of the *Swan,* which was anchored in the boca chica and had taken fire from Spanish culverins.[75] Moreover, John Drake had money invested in the *Pascoe,* no doubt in partnership with his brothers, and it was therefore unexceptional for Francis to give him command of the ship.[76]

Sailing south into the Gulf of Uraba, Drake gave his men a two-week rest. With the help of Diego, the escaped black slave from Nombre de

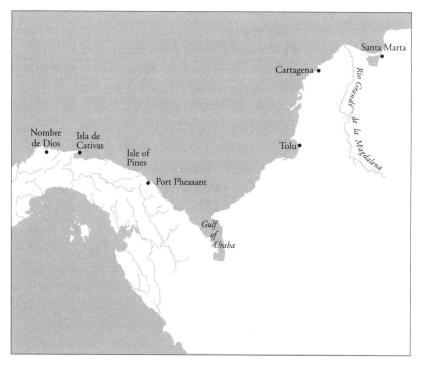

Drake in Panama, 1572–73

Dios, the men built huts ashore and spent alternate days hunting, refitting the vessels, and playing various games. On 5 September he sent John Drake with the *Pascoe* and the pinnace named *Lion* to make contact with the cimarrones who lived on the isthmus. Then, taking the other two pinnaces, *Minion* and *Bear,* Drake sailed eastward to the Rio Grande de la Magdalena, the dividing line between the districts of Cartagena and Santa Marta and the supply route for the interior of Nuevo Reyno de Granada.[77]

Fighting off the mosquitoes that infested the riverbanks, the pirates made their way upriver to a small trading post, manned by a lone merchant. The man fled at their arrival, and Drake's men filled the two pinnaces with fresh provisions from his stores. Apparently disappointed with what they had found, the pirates drifted downriver back to the Caribbean and chased about for several days between Cartagena and Tolu, stopping a few Spanish fragatas and keeping possession of two that had especially fine cargoes of provisions.[78]

Still frustrated at their failure to capture any valuable prize, Drake then took his men back to the Isle of Pines and the place his men called Port Plenty. With the supplies from the frigates that they had captured near Cartagena, Drake established depots at several places in the nearby islands, hoping that if one were lost the others might remain undiscovered. John Drake met him at Port Plenty with the news that he had used Diego's good offices to establish an alliance with some of the cimarrones on the coast. Taking the advice of his brother and his new friends the cimarrones, Drake moved his men to an island near Cabo Cativa, where he again built a fortification. The walls of the new fortification, made of logs and earthworks, were thirteen feet high. One or both of the ships taken at the Rio Grande drove onto some reefs at Cativas, and timber from the wreck was used for construction of what was called Fort Diego.[79]

In mid-October 1572 Drake was again in the boca chica at Cartagena. Capturing a 50-ton merchantman from Santo Domingo and another en route to that island, Drake spent several days trying to take them out of the harbor. Harassed by continuous Spanish sorties and unable to take the vessels away, Drake scuttled one and burned the other. For the next two weeks he continued sailing in and out of the inlets around Cartagena, looking for suitable victims and finding none.[80]

A second trip up the Rio Grande de la Magdalena was also fruitless. The trading post was deserted, and all the inhabitants had fled to the interior. Consequently, Drake decided to try his luck at Santa Marta. Again the inhabitants had been forewarned, and after a warning shot from the fort there, Drake and his pinnaces again made for the open sea. With both pinnaces running perilously short of food, some of the men threatened to go ashore and forage there. After some argument, Drake sailed away, and the crew of the *Minion* followed reluctantly. Within a short time, they fell upon another merchant ship, loaded with dried provisions, an obvious gift "of Gods great mercie."[81]

By mid-November, with many of the men sick and one dead, Drake sent the *Minion* back to Fort Diego, following at a slower pace in the *Bear*.

There, according to the Nichols account, at least, he heard tragic news: his brother John and another man had been killed about 9 October in an unsuccessful attack on a Spanish *fragata*. The public records say something different. A nuncupative will filed in 1574 by the agent of Francis Drake states clearly that John Drake died "about the ix^th or x^th daie of June last past in anno domini 1573," having been "sodenlie stroken with a gunne shott." The Nichols narrative has no dated events between 4 April and 9 August 1573, and there is nothing else to give a clue that would explain the eight-month discrepancy.[82]

Faced with a lengthy series of failures and losses, Drake resolved to wait ashore at Fort Diego until the return of the convoy in the spring. All went well for a month or more, but early in January men began dying from a sudden illness, apparently yellow fever. One was Drake's other brother Joseph. Resolved to find the cause of the illness, Drake instructed the surgeon to perform a postmortem. "The Surgeon . . . found his liver swolne, his heart as it were sodden, and his guts all faire. This was the first and last experiment that our Captaine made of Anatomy in this voyage."[83]

Naturally, the surgeon himself was infected during the surgery, and he died within a few days. The boy who assisted him became very ill and did not fully recover until the company returned to Plymouth. In all, twenty-eight men died of the disease. With the losses from other causes, Drake had no more than thirty-five or forty men left.[84] Only a stubborn tenacity kept him from giving up altogether.

These were the days when the name of Francis Drake first began to appear in Spanish records, an indication that colonial officials had begun to single him out from all the other pirates as someone to watch. Morgan Tillert (Miguel Morgan), a seaman who had sailed earlier with Hawkins, testified to his Spanish captors about some of the more important seamen who came with Hawkins. Harry Newman, Francis Drake, and Nicholas Anthony, he said, were men "widely and publicly known to be great Lutherans." Not quite the terror of the seas, Francis Drake was nonetheless coming to be seen as a threat to Spanish society.[85]

Drake's newest plan was to attack the warehouse at Venta de Cruces and perhaps try to intercept the treasure train on the road between Panama and Nombre de Dios. Despite the faulty intelligence that the cimarrones had given him previously, Drake had little choice but to accept the advice and assistance of the cimarrones, who became his friends because he was an enemy of the Spanish. Early in January 1573 they told him that the fleet had arrived at Nombre de Dios, and this was partly confirmed when the *Lion* returned from patrol with a provision ship and the news of ships moving again between the ports. Leaving Ellis Hixon in Fort Diego to guard the *Pascoe,* Drake took the healthiest of the survivors and set out overland for Venta de Cruces.[86]

There were eighteen Englishmen and thirty cimarrones in his party. Drake's sailors had all they could do to carry themselves and their weapons through the dense tropical forests, across rivers, over mountains. The cimarrones did most of the real work, scouting out the route, carrying all the supplies, building shelters, and hunting and gathering food that the forest supplied in abundance to those who knew what to look for. On the third day out of Fort Diego they stopped at a cimarrón village, a place of more than fifty houses built along a wide street, where the people were nicely dressed and moderately prosperous.[87]

At one point in the journey the cimarrón guides led Drake and his men to a tall tree from which they could see both oceans, Atlantic and Pacific. Drake vowed to sail one day on the Pacific, and John Oxnam promised to go as well. By the end of January, two weeks into their journey, Drake and his allies were within sight of Panama. Here they stopped in a clump of mangroves while one of the cimarrones went into town to find out when one of the treasure trains would head for Nombre de Dios. The man soon returned with the news that the treasurer of Lima would be on the road that very night with a train of fourteen mules loaded with gold and jewels.[88]

Starting immediately, Drake and his party set out for Venta de Cruces. While they were still about two leagues from the settlement, two of the cimarrón scouts returned with a Spanish prisoner whom they had found sleeping beside the road, the match for his harquebus still burning in case he had need to fire the weapon. They took him to Drake bound and gagged, nearly strangled and ready to talk. The man confirmed the story of

Drake's cimarrón spy, telling Drake that he was part of an advance guard, sent ahead to secure the road for the mule train. This was as good a place as any for an ambush, so Drake broke his men into two companies. John Oxnam and the cimarrón allies stayed on one side of the road, while Drake and his small unit lay on the other, far enough apart that they could catch the pack train between them.[89]

As the pack train approached, a Spanish horseman rode out in advance. One of Drake's men stood up, his white shirt gleaming in the moonlight. Realizing that it might be an ambush, the horseman rode back to give the alarm. The treasure train was sent back to Panama, but some trains of less valuable goods were allowed to go through. These Drake seized, but the pickings were poor. The most useful prizes were the mules, which some of the men decided to ride.[90]

With their presence again discovered, there was no choice but to retreat. There was a choice of routes, and Drake with his typical lack of concern for personal danger decided on the short and daring road through Venta de Chagres. Just at the outskirts of town they surprised a troop of Spanish soldiers escorting some Dominican friars to Panama. In the brief battle, several soldiers were killed and one friar mortally wounded.[91] Continuing their march to Venta de Cruces, they allowed the cimarrones to loot the warehouses, then burned the town.[92]

With the aid of their cimarrón guides Drake and his men then made their way back through the dense tropical forest and rejoined their company at Fort Diego. They could not have made it without the help of the cimarrones, who sometimes carried the men who were too sick to walk. With supplies in the fort again running low, Drake sent John Oxnam in the *Bear* to sail east toward Tolu, hoping that he would find a provision ship along the way. Lacking the crew to man three pinnaces, Drake sunk the *Lion,* then took the *Minion* and headed west for Veragua, the province just west of Nombre de Dios. The placer mines in that vicinity were said to be so rich that every black slave could pan a peso of gold each day.[93] Desperate to find something worth stealing, Drake hoped to meet a ship loaded with treasure from the mines. This did not happen. The governor of Honduras reported an encounter on 25 March with a well-armed English raider from the vicinity of Nombre de Dios.[94] Despite continual raids during the next two weeks, Drake returned empty-handed.[95]

The *Bear* had better luck. Near Tolu, Hixon and his men took a 20-ton *fragata*, loaded with food. When Drake saw the ship, he realized that it was better than either of his frigates, so he decided to arm it as a third ship of war. Having done this, he sailed with all three vessels toward Cabo de Cativas, where he fell in with a French captain whom Nichols called Tetu, probably Guillaume Le Testu. Quickly coming to an agreement, Drake and Le Testu decided to make one more attack on the mule trains traveling the road between Nombre de Dios and Panama.[96]

Sailing their combined fleet to the Rio Francisco, Drake and Le Testu landed their shore parties just east of Nombre de Dios. Drake took fifteen men and his cimarrón allies, while Le Testu took twenty of his own men. Telling the ships to return on the fourth day, they headed inland to a spot about two leagues south of Nombre de Dios. Drake, Le Testu, and the cimarrones reached the place of ambush on 29 April 1573. Almost immediately they heard bells signaling the arrival of the mules.[97]

This time the pirate attack was a complete surprise. The Spanish guards were quickly driven off, but not before several of the French pirates and one of the cimarrones were killed. Le Testu himself received a mortal wound and had to be left on the road. Once the remaining Spanish guards had fled, Drake and the other pirates looted the packs of much of the gold. There was so much silver, though, that they could not carry it away. Instead, they shoved many of the bars into animal burrows and buried the rest along the road before making their way back to shore.[98]

Considering all the problems that had arisen on the voyage, Drake was probably not surprised to find a fleet of Spanish frigates waiting offshore, rather than his own pinnaces. He was forced to construct a raft and sail out to an island about three leagues away, where the pinnaces eventually came for him. United once more with his crew, Drake sent a rescue party back to the isthmus in hope of rescuing Le Testu, as well as some of the buried treasure. The search was only partially successful. Le Testu was dead, one of his men captured and executed. Nearly all the buried treasure had been recovered by the Spaniards, who learned from the French captive where it had been hidden. Even so, the rescue party managed to find some that had been overlooked. This was later placed in the common hoard and divided equally between the French and English crews.[99]

With something to show at last for their months on the Spanish Main, Drake decided that it was time to go home. Perhaps it was early June when he headed again for the Rio Grande de la Magdalena. Here the pirates captured a 25-ton fragata loaded with food. Taking the fragatas and pinnaces back to port at the Cabo de Cativas, they careened them and scraped them and tallowed the bottoms to make them sound enough for the trip home. The two remaining pinnaces they burned, giving the ironwork to the cimarrones. Setting sail for home, they went by way of the Straits of Florida, which they cleared about the middle of July. They were in Plymouth harbor on Sunday, 9 August 1573. They had been gone so long that many had given up hope of their return. When the news came, everyone in Plymouth was listening to a Sunday sermon. As the word spread through the church, one after another got up to leave, until the parson was left nearly alone. That, at least, is the story.[100]

After his return Drake applied for appointment as executor of John's estate, saying that this was his brother's dying wish, stated before witnesses. On the strength of a nuncupative will, drawn up later and witnessed by John Prouse and John Crockit, Drake took control of John's share in the proceeds of the voyage. The undated will is very brief:

> In the name of God amen anno 1573 John Drake late of
> plymouth in the countie of Devon maryner being on a
> voyage to the Indese sodenlie stroken with a gunne shott
> and nere his death and being then at that instant which
> was about the ix[th] or x[th] daie of June last past in anno
> domini 1573 in good and perfect memorie was demaun-
> ded by two or three of other mariners in the same shipe
> at that present tyme whether he had made his testament
> left at eny place—whoe answered them that he had
> made none at all / wherefore saied he I doe nowe nomy-
> nate and apoint my brother Francis Drake to be my full

and whole executor of suche goods as I have / excepting
myne adventure of xxx[li] which I have in this shippe
called the paschoe of Plymouth the which xxx[li] with the
proffitt of the same adventure cominge I give unto Alice
Drake my wief, and I shall desier my brother Francis to
see it trulie paied and consented to my saied wief, and
because my wief is a yonge woman I have made my
saied brother executor to the extent that he maie be an
ayde and helper unto my saied wief (as I trust he will)
Theie witnesses John Crockit John Prouse.[101]

In accordance with the terms of the document, Francis Drake was appointed executor on 12 February 1574.[102]

Within a short time John's widow remarried, and she soon brought suit,
questioning the authenticity of the will. William Drury, speaking for the
Prerogative Court of Canterbury, gave his decision on 28 November 1575.
In his decision Drury said: "We ascertained and clearly discovered on the
part of the said Francis Drake his intent in his particular allegation and
purported will, . . . we hold and we are of the opinion that it is in no way
founded or proven but in every aspect of its proof it is deficient and it
fails."[103] Beyond this, Drury seems to have decided that Drake could not
recover the moneys he had already spent on Alice. "We condemn the aforenamed Francis Drake in the legitimate payments already made and being
made on the part of and by the part of the said Alice Cotton, alias Drake,
in this matter, through this our definitive sentence and this our final decree."[104] Legal circumlocutions aside, the commissioner clearly did not
think Francis Drake had behaved in an honorable way.

This is not the only problem presented by the will. There is the matter
of the eight-month discrepancy in the date of John Drake's death. According to the Nichols narrative, John Drake died about 9 October 1572,
"two dayes after our departing from them."[105] The narrative is very clear
on this point, and John is omitted from all the actions that take place
thereafter in the narrative. On the other hand, the will is just as clear in
saying that John Drake died "about the ix[th] or x[th] daie of June last past in

anno domini 1573."[106] Both Francis Drake and the witnesses, John Prouse and John Crockit, knew when John Drake died. If they could not remember the exact day, they could surely give an estimate that was less than eight months in error.

If the date given in the will is the correct one, then John Drake probably received his fatal wound during the battle for the Spanish *fragata* near the Rio Grande de la Magdalena. As we have seen, this took place in the early part of June 1573. It is simply impossible to know why the records of his death are so much at odds with one another.

It is less difficult to gauge the success of the voyage. Three pinnaces and the *Swan* were lost. More than half the crew were dead, including Drake's brothers Joseph and John. The booty taken on the April raid near Nombre de Dios had netted about 80,000 pesos in gold, of which half was distributed to the French pirates.[107] Drake and his men could have come home richer by nearly 50,000 pesos, or about £20,000. This was an enormous sum, and Drake's share must have been enough to make him rich. In addition Drake had the two *fragatas*, one belonging to James Raphael and the other to Sebastian Proença. Both were fine ships, and Drake still had them in 1575, though one was then on a voyage to the Indies.[108]

Beyond his acquisition of wealth, Drake had struggled against immense difficulties for nearly a year, gaining valuable experience as an independent commander. Poorly organized and indecisive at first, he finally realized that planning and discipline were of primary importance for a commander. In spite of a tendency to change intermediate objectives on the merest whim, he showed a surprising tenacity for his ultimate goals. Nothing was allowed to stand in the way of his determination to be a rich man and to earn the respect of his comrades. One thing he did not have to learn: bravery. He was absolutely fearless in the face of odds that would have made a lesser man choose some alternative.

Nevertheless, he had serious character flaws that he never overcame. He did not flinch at deserting a comrade under fire, as he had done earlier with Hawkins at San Juan de Ulúa and as he did this time with Le Testu on the road to Nombre de Dios. Beyond this, he had a taste for violence, and he lacked a strong sense of family attachment. When his two brothers died, Drake did not end his pirate raids. Instead, he used the deaths to show his men that nothing could change his determination to stay in the Indies until he had managed to seize some grand treasure. As though to emphasize his iron will, Drake had the surgeon dissect the body of his brother Joseph, saying that he wanted to learn the cause of his death. This seems like an act of extreme callousness, even for the sixteenth century. A final flaw, ever present, though not so serious, was the streak of covetousness that let Drake deprive friends and relatives of the money due them.

4

The Successful Merchant

WHEN FRANCIS DRAKE RETURNED HOME in the late summer of 1573, he was rich enough to do just as he pleased. Beyond riches, what pleased him most was the sea and, next to that, a good fight. Even so, he had a wife to accommodate and business associates who expected to share in the profits of his voyage.

Perhaps Drake used his own share to buy a house in Plymouth. An item in the Plymouth Record Office indicates that a building on Notte Street was held by "Francis Drake, merchant," in 1576, though he may not have lived there. In 1581 the Drakes were living in leasehold property belonging to "Thomas Edmonds, gentleman," and they may have been living on the property much earlier.[1]

Because he was rich enough to have servants, Drake took his young cousin to serve as a page. The boy was named John, a lad of ten, son of Robert and Anna Drake, Francis's uncle and aunt. Born about 1563, John had lived with his grandmother from the time he was six months old. When his grandmother died in 1571, John returned to his mother's house for a brief time before his cousin Francis came home from the Indies a rich man.[2]

For some months Francis Drake was involved in settling accounts for his voyage, managing the estate of his brother John, and perhaps taking care of matters for his deceased brother Joseph. One of the ships taken from the Spanish was sold to Sir Arthur Champernown. Another went to John Hawkins. Drake kept the third ship; he still had it in 1575.[3]

No doubt he spent some of his money on the ship. In 1575 he was listed as "Captaine of a Barque called the Falcon." There is no record to show the

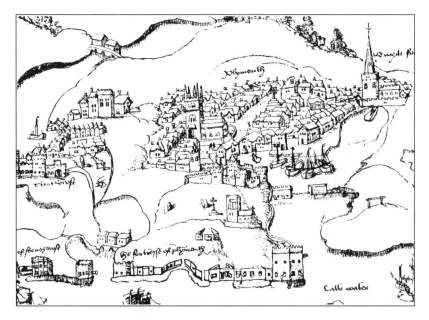

This view of Plymouth is from a map drawn about the time Francis Drake was born. Later maps indicate that the town may have had a more distinct street arrangement when Drake moved there. Reprinted from BL Cotton MS, Aug. 1, vol. 1, no. 38.

size of the *Falcon,* but the ship was large enough to be served by its own pinnace. Aside from Drake himself, the crew of the *Falcon* consisted of a master, a pilot, a boatswain, a carpenter, a steward, and a gunner, plus eighteen mariners. The pinnace carried eight mariners.[4] With a crew of that size the *Falcon* may have been 25 tons, the same size as the ship taken at the Rio Grande de la Magdalena in June 1573.[5] The pinnace was probably 8 or 10 tons. Drake also had a third vessel, the bark *Frigacie.*[6]

He undoubtedly used the ships for commerce, but by early 1575 Drake enlisted them in the Irish campaign of the earl of Essex. For some years the Irish had been up in arms, dating from the 1494 attempt by Henry VII to subordinate the Irish parliament. Irish resistance rose to a fury after 1541, when Henry VIII assumed the title of King of Ireland and attempted to enforce his ecclesiastical changes there. In the ensuing decades, vast quantities of money and great numbers of men went into the effort to subdue Ireland, but with little success, except in the Pale around Dublin. Military efforts languished during the reigns of Edward and Mary, but were renewed by Elizabeth, whose major objective was to extend English control in Ireland beyond the Pale.[7]

In general the English plan was to eliminate the Irish nobility and to reduce the "Irish churl" to a servitude somewhat like that of the Indians in the Spanish *encomienda* system. An assortment of men had tried their hand at suppressing the recalcitrant Irish, all to no avail. Then in 1573 Walter Devereaux, earl of Essex, sent an expedition to occupy Ulster. Mortgaging his English lands to the queen for £10,000, Essex agreed to use the money to contribute four hundred foot soldiers and two hundred horsemen for service in Ireland. In return the queen agreed to contribute the same numbers of men and to grant Essex a large estate in County Antrim along with sweeping governmental powers. Private individuals were encouraged to invest in the project and to receive smaller grants in exchange.[8]

When the local chief, Sir Brian MacPhelim O'Neill, heard the details of the scheme, he protested the arrangements and led others in resisting change. Still, Sir Brian remained loyal to the queen and for a time worked with Essex. For his part, Essex soon saw how difficult it would be to attack Sir Brian. Consequently, Essex lured the man's followers into a trap at a feast, treacherously slaughtered them, then had Sir Brian himself executed in Dublin. There was great popular indignation in Antrim but no public reproach for Essex from the queen. In fact, Essex seems to have been proud of the clever way in which he had managed to eliminate the opposition.[9]

This task completed, Essex turned his attention to Rathlin Island, where he wanted to establish a permanent fort. A tiny island off the north coast of Antrim, Rathlin had served for as long as anyone could remember as an outpost for Scots moving into Ulster. Indeed, Rathlin was already well fortified, so well that the local Scots chief, Sorley Boy, sent his women and children there for safety.[10] To take the island, Essex required a fleet. Enter Francis Drake.

By the end of 1574 Essex was talking about the ships that Francis Drake had brought back from the Indies.[11] Within a few months, Drake was in charge of a small naval force that Essex planned to use in the Rathlin operation. As he had the means to do so, Drake no doubt invested money in the Antrim venture, though it is unclear how much or what the return was to be. What is clear is the value of Drake's small ships. The same qualities that made Drake's vessels useful in the ports of the Caribbean were the ones needed for navigation in Irish ports. "They will brooke a sea well," said Essex, "and yet they drawe so little water, as they maie passe into eny river Island or Creek."12

Although Essex paid some of the expenses of the little fleet, the payments scarcely covered the cost of the operation. That was to be recovered from goods seized during the raid. As captain, Drake received a salary of forty-two shillings per month. The master received twenty-six shillings eight pence, and the pilot twenty shillings. The other officers received eleven shillings eight pence each month. In the pinnace the work of the seamen consisted mainly of rowing, so they were paid more than the seamen in the *Falcon,* eleven shillings eight pence in the pinnace, compared with six shillings thirteen pence for the seamen in the larger ship.13 As the earl of Essex put it, "Ordinarye saylers care not to pull at an ore."14

For Drake the Irish campaign was brief, lasting from the first of April to the end of September 1575.15 It was also costly, if we may believe the contemporary accounts. Edmond Howes wrote that Drake paid the entire cost of the fleet: "He furnished at his own propper charge, three friggots with men, munition, and served voluntary in Ireland under Walter Earle of Essex: where he did excellent service, both by Sea, and land, at the winning of divers strong Forts."16

A fellow sailor said much the same thing. When asked a few years later whether Francis Drake had formed an alliance to go to the Pacific with John Oxnam, John Butler replied: "Francis Drake is a poor man who has not the means for this, for he owns nothing more than what he took in the Indies, and all this he spent on some islands over there toward Ireland."17

If Drake indeed squandered his new wealth this way, it was totally in character, an attempt to buy approval from rich and powerful people. He did much the same thing after his voyage around the world, when people said that he spent the greater part of his fortune trying to buy the approval of the queen and her councillors.18 His collateral descendant Henry H. Drake put the matter somewhat differently: "When ruined he could still fit out an expedition, for his quasi-fathers, Francis Russell and Edmund Tremayne, were of Elizabeth's Privy Council; and the secret cause of his devoting the first wealth he acquired to fitting out three ships for the public service in Ireland is, that those two men were then employed to quell rebellion there."[19]

In fact, the Irish expedition was not quite a public service. It was a business venture from which Essex and his partners hoped to make a profit, and profit they did, in both land and money.

With preparations under way in various places and ships in various ports, it is a wonder that the Irish in Rathlin were not forewarned. Yet somehow everything was kept secret. Essex had his fleet ready in Carrickfergus, on the southeast coast of Antrim, by July 1575. Retiring to the Pale with most of his troops, Essex sent Captain John Norris to Carrickfergus with several hundred picked troops. Part of his force was intended as a garrison for Carrickfergus, the rest for a siege force in the attack on Rathlin. Arriving in Carrickfergus, Norris brought with him letters from Essex to Drake and the other ship captains, instructing them to transport Norris and his troops to Rathlin Island.[20]

Assembling all the local shipping that they could commandeer, Drake and the other commanders left for Rathlin Island early on the morning of 20 July 1575. While the distance is not great, stormy weather separated the ships and kept them at sea for more than two days. Still, they all managed to assemble at the appointed place, probably Church Bay, on 22 July.

Not entirely taken off guard, the islanders saw the fleet as it approached, and they were able to mount a defense on the beach. Even so, it was impossible to stop the overwhelming numbers of men and animals from landing. Contesting every foot of ground, the islanders fought bitterly, then retreated to a fortified castle, probably Bruce. Bringing in two cannons from one of the ships, Norris and his army bombarded the castle for several days, finally breaching the walls. When this happened, the constable in charge of the castle asked for terms of surrender. Norris gave almost nothing, but the commander surrendered anyway on 26 July.[21]

If the battle was bloody, the surrender was worse. The constable had

Drake's service in Ireland, 1575

bargained for his own life, plus that of his wife and child and a hostage he held, but "all the rest were to stand on the curtesy" of Essex and his army. That courtesy proved to be scant. As the Scots filed out of the castle, they were set upon by the English soldiers. Two hundred people were killed, men, women, and children. Then for several days, the soldiers searched through the tiny island, tracking down survivors in caves and crevices and killing them as well.[22] In all, perhaps five hundred people were put to the sword. Essex wrote to Walsingham that Sorley Boy had watched it all from the mainland, desperate with grief.[23] If he did, his eyesight was marvelous, for the distance is a good five miles.

Whether Francis Drake had a direct role in the attack and the massacre is unknown. In his previous voyages Drake had always joined the landing parties and participated in their assaults. Considering this previous experience, it is difficult to imagine that he would not have been given command of a troop of men at Rathlin Island. Whether Drake participated or not, the victory proved to be of no lasting value. The English garrison lived in wretched isolation and finally abandoned the place.[24]

The real reason for the attack was not malice, it seems, but greed. Rathlin was an extremely rich prize, no doubt made more so by the lack of survivors to claim the property. In his report Essex listed 3,000 sheep, 300 cattle, 100 brood mares, grain enough to supply two hundred men for a year, and much in the way of personal goods.[25] How this booty was divided is now unclear, but Francis Drake must have received some of it, as was the custom.

In spite of the ghastly victory, Essex was never able to defeat Sorley Boy or to take control of Antrim, and he was soon out of the picture. His supposedly faithful retainer Thomas Doughty began to conspire against him, perhaps with the knowledge if not the connivance of Drake. During his service in Ireland and perhaps even earlier, Drake became friendly with Doughty, a man of his own age and of equal ambition. Working with Christopher Hatton, captain of the queen's guard, and with her current favorite, the earl of Leicester, Doughty managed to open a place for himself at court, while discrediting Essex.[26] In due time Sir Henry Sidney was dispatched to Ireland as the new Lord Deputy, sailing in the *Frigacie*, one of Francis Drake's ships.[27] Finally, in September 1576, Essex suddenly took sick and died. Some said he was poisoned. One man said the poisoner was Francis Drake, though others said it was the earl of Leicester.[28] Regardless, the Irish interlude was over.

Within a short time, Drake and Hawkins were involved in business with a merchant named Acerbo Velutelli. In 1575 Velutelli received a grant from the queen, giving him a ten-year monopoly on the importation of "currants and sweet oyle" from Zante, an island in the Ionian Sea. During the first year, John Hawkins took two shiploads of goods there and brought cargoes back, though Velutelli says he lost money on the deal. In 1576 Francis Drake joined Hawkins in the venture, only to lose one of his ships in a wreck near Dover.[29]

No doubt there were other voyages and other commercial arrangements about which there is no evidence. What we do know is that by this time Francis Drake was in the midst of plans for another trip to the New World. During their months serving Essex in Ireland, Drake and Doughty began to discuss the possibility of a raid on Spain's Pacific ports. When they returned to England, both Drake and Doughty developed a close relationship with the queen's good friend Hatton. Doughty became Hatton's private secretary. One or another of the men, probably Doughty, suggested to Hatton that he secure official permission and financial backing for this new trip to the Spanish Indies. As close friends sometimes do, Drake and Doughty later fell out, and each claimed to have been responsible for working out the details with Hatton.

John Cooke, who did not like Francis Drake, gave this as Drake's account of the matter: "My lorde of Essex wrote in my commendations unto secretarye Walsingham more than I was worthy, but belike I had deserved somewhat at his hands, and he thought me in his letters to be a fite man to serve against the Spaniards, for my practice and experience that I had in that trade."[30] This can scarcely be a direct quotation, for Cooke heard it in 1578 but did not put it on paper for some years.[31] Still, it suggests the interpretation that Francis Drake put on events.

As Cooke recalled Drake's words, Sir Francis Walsingham came to Drake and said he had been asked by the queen to make quiet arrangements for a raid on possessions of the king of Spain, who had caused her "divers in-juries." Continuing with the words of Drake as he recalled them, Cooke wrote:

> And with all he shewed me a plott, . . . willinge me to
> set my hand, and to noate downe where I thought he
> myght be moaste annoyed, but I tolde him some parte
> of my minde, but refused to set my hand to any thinge,
> affirminge that hir maiestie was mortall and that if it
> should please God to take hir maiestie awaie it might so
> be that some prince might raigne that myght be in
> leauge with the Kinge of Spayne and then wyll myne
> owne hand be a witnes agaynst my selfe. Then was I
> very shortly aftar and in an eveninge sent for unto hir
> maiestie by secretary Wallsingham, but came not to hir
> maiesty that nyght, for it was late, but the next daye
> cominge to hir presens, thes or the lyke words . . . Drake
> so it is that I would gladly be revenged on the kinge of
> Spayne for dyvers Iniuries that I have receyved.

The queen then bound Drake to secrecy, saying that anyone who let the king of Spain hear about the plan would lose his head.[32]

Of course, Doughty had a different story. According to an account writ-ten later by his friend Francis Fletcher, the negotiations started with a con-versation between Doughty and Hatton. Like Cooke, Fletcher managed to reconstruct lengthy dialogues many years after he heard them. Like Cooke as well, Fletcher was no great friend of Drake's. Still, this sort of evidence is all we have, and the partisanship of his friends certainly did not help Doughty. This is the way Fletcher remembered the conversation:

> The said T. Doughtye sayd that he was the first that
> preffered our Captayne to the Earle of Essex, and . . .
> when the earle of Essex was dede, that then the sayd
> T. Doughty preffered our captayne to his master Master
> Hatton and that he the said T. D. & our captayne

confferred about this viage in Iarland. . . . And then
the said T. D. . . . went to Mr. Secretary Walsingham
and to Mr. Hatton, and like a true subiect brake the
matter to them, & they brake it to the queens maiestye,
who had greate goode lykinge of it & and cawsed our
Captayne to be sent for and commanded this viage to
goe forwarde.[33]

There is no way to know which story is right, though the most reasonable
choice seems to be the Fletcher-Doughty version. Doughty saw Hatton
daily and through him had access to Walsingham and the queen.[34]

If the plan finally agreed upon was written out in detail, that document
has not come down to us. There are, however, a few fragments copied
from a preliminary version drawn up about May or June of 1577. Usually
called a "draft plan," this document is evidently a brief prepared by a secretary for the information of the man who would discuss the matter with
the queen and some of the other investors. It is possible that the original
pages were written by Thomas Doughty for the use of Christopher Hatton
and Francis Walsingham, but there is no way to be certain about this. No
matter. The fragments are clear enough to show the general ideas of the
people who backed the voyage.[35]

Though badly burned at the top, and less so at the sides, the surviving
pages contain enough intelligible detail to show the general route that
Drake would follow. He was to sail across the Atlantic and along the coast
of South America, entering the Pacific through the Strait of Magellan, and
looking for places to trade:

cours
the powlle
the sowthe sea then
far to the northwards as
alonge the saied coaste as
as of the other to finde out pl
to have trafiek for the ben
of thies her majesty's realmes, wh

they ar not under the obediens of
prince, so is ther great hoepe of
spiecs, drugs, cochinillo, and
speciall comodities, suche as maye
her highnes dominions, and also
shippinge awoorke greatly / and
gotten up as afore saied in to xxx d
the sowthe sea (if it shalbe thought
by the afore named frauncs Draek to proc
far) then he is to retorne the same way
whome wards as he went out. Which viage
by gods favor is to be performed in xiiith month
all thoughe he shuld spend .v. monthes in
taryenge uppon the coaste to get knowle
of the princs and cowmptres ther[36]

In spite of the missing words, it is clear that Francis Drake was to lead an expedition around the tip of South America, carefully exploring the coast south of 30° but avoiding Spanish settlements in the interior.[37] This cautionary rule meant that Drake was to avoid the inland raids that had proven so costly on his previous trip.

The "princes and countries" mentioned in the last line are no doubt intended to imply societies of the same stature and wealth as the Aztecs of Mexico and the Incas of Peru. Even so, there can scarcely have been any hope of finding such places in South America, whose coast had been fairly well explored by earlier Spanish expeditions.[38] Indeed, the investors did not really expect to do much in the way of negotiation with other sovereigns, for only £50 was budgeted for "presents to be geven to the head of the cowmptres of divers sorts."

The introductory part of the manuscript contains a list of the supplies to be taken on the journey, including all the tools that shipwrights needed to build and repair seagoing vessels, a great deal of ordnance, and seven pinnaces to be carried aboard the other ships. From this list it can be seen that the new journey was intended to repeat the successful aspects of

Drake's previous voyage. The armaments and the pinnaces would be used for raids on Spanish shipping, as they were in 1572 and 1573.[39]

There were no orders for the commander, nothing more than a general outline of the route out and back. The description was intended to let the queen know what the investors were involved with, but the commander as usual would have to make up his own mind about operational details:

> Matters nessesare for your honnr [to] remember, viz.
> That it might pleas her majestie to graunt th
> her highnes ship the swallowe with her tools
> apparrell. and only iiii d colverins with ii falcons
> of brase might be left in her to pose in the way
> and that the same ships with the ordnaunce afore
> named might be vallewed by indifferent persons
> and of the chance which the same shall amount
> with her highnes to beare such partes as she
> shall lieke. and for the rest the same to be
> borne by the parties that shalbe thought myet
> uppon good assurans to be geven into the exchequer
> that the Q. majestie mayebe made prive to the trewthe
> of the viage. and that the coollar to be given out for
> Allexandria with no effect is all redy don by the
> licens procured from the Turkes.[40]

What were the trade goods? There were none. The list of supplies did not include trade goods, for trade was not the real object of the venture. The expenses of the voyage, and profits for the investors, would have to come from captured Spanish cargoes. The new voyage would offer English officials the opportunity to share in the wealth that the previous voyages of Hawkins and Drake had shown to be available in the undefended Spanish colonies. In a word, the purpose was piracy. That was the reason for secrecy, the explanation for the story that the ships were going to Alexandria.

Several variant interpretations of the plan have been proposed, all of them disposed of neatly by Kenneth R. Andrews.[41] The basic thrust of each of the variant views is that Francis Drake was selected to implement some new aspect of Elizabethan foreign policy. Each of these interpretations ignores the fact that Drake was clearly not equipped to play such a role, for he lacked the education, the experience, and the sophistication necessary in matters of state. As one government memorandum of 1581 put it, Francis Drake was "a private man of mean quality" when he set forth on his voyage.[42]

Julian Corbett was one of the first historians to assign Drake a significant role in the formation of Elizabethan foreign policy. In Corbett's version of events Drake was chosen by a "war party" of influential men who hoped to force Spain into war with England. For them Drake's plan to sail to the Spanish ports in the Pacific was a perfect provocation. Drake was a "statesman" in Corbett's view, and his voyage was "a calculated affair of state."[43]

Henry Wagner has dismissed Corbett's labored defense of this concept with little trouble, substituting one of his own. In Wagner's view the real aim of the voyage was to establish trade with the Moluccas or even China.[44] Everything else was secondary. Almost in passing, Corbett had suggested the possibility that Drake was supposed to establish English colonies in North America and the South Pacific.[45] Elaborating upon this theory some years later, Zelia Nuttall credited Drake with a plan to establish a colony on the California coast as a bar to further Spanish expansion. It was "Drake's dream," she wrote, to found a "New English Protestant colony" that would serve as a model for peaceful conversion of the native inhabitants.[46]

E. G. R. Taylor presented a different view in 1930 when she published the "draft plan" for the first time, interpreting it as evidence that Drake was supposed to explore the coast of Terra Australis, the supposed but as yet undiscovered southern continent. Taylor also submitted evidence to show that Drake had instructions to go to the Moluccas.[47] Another historian, Richard C. Temple, ignored these elaborate arguments and decided that Drake had intended all along to sail around the world, just as Magellan had done.[48] With similar lack of evidence, both Nuttall and Taylor thought that Drake had orders to look for the Strait of Anian, a supposed northern passage between the Atlantic and Pacific oceans.[49]

Based as these theories were on little more than inference and conjecture, it was only a matter of time before some scholar would expose the flimsy foundations on which they were built. Kenneth R. Andrews did so in his 1968 study of Drake's expedition. In his view Drake's primary purpose was to explore the southern coasts of South America, looking for future trading opportunities. A secondary aim was to pay the costs of the voyage from piracy.[50]

Although this order of affairs may have reflected the intentions of a few of the people who invested in the enterprise, it is doubtful that Francis Drake looked upon himself primarily as a merchant. For Francis Drake the plan all along was to raid lightly defended Spanish ports and to capture Spanish merchant ships. He said so himself, if we can believe the version of his statement handed down by John Cooke. As Cooke recalled the words, Drake claimed "to be a fite man to sarve against the Spaniards, for my practice and experience that I had in that trade." In other words, he was selected to command the expedition because of his experience as a pirate.[51] Any plans for future trading opportunities were plainly secondary in Drake's mind and no doubt in the minds of most of those who chose him for the voyage.

Because the plans so clearly involved piracy, the investors wanted to keep the details secret. That was not easily done in a society where court secrets became common knowledge almost immediately. Realizing this, the investors decided to turn court gossip to their own advantage. In June 1577 John Hawkins sent a letter to Secretary Walsingham, describing a fictitious plan for Drake to command a merchant fleet sailing to Alexandria, Tripoli, and Constantinople. The ships were those listed in the private memorandum, Drake's ship *Francis* or *Pelican* and the queen's ship *Swallow*.[52]

The ruse was partially successful—as successful as anyone could have hoped. By early fall 1577, the acting Spanish ambassador in England knew about the plan for a trading voyage to North Africa and also knew that it was a screen for another raid on Spanish colonial towns. The Spanish ambassador Antonio de Guaras was informed by one of his agents: "Francis Drake is going to the Antilles, although they are spreading the rumor that they are going to Tripoli. Even so, there is no doubt they are going where I say, and they will do much harm if your mercy does not take measures to keep them from going."[53] The agent did not know specifically where the ships were going. But as more information came from court informers, the piratical nature of the scheme became more obvious. Guaras called it "an enterprise of much importance to Spain." As he noted: "These are proceedings that promise to bring in a great deal of treasure. The queen is also involved, and others from the council, because they hope to gain much in this business. It is important for Spain to know the location in order to send them to the bottom of the sea."[54]

Ambassador Guaras may have known the names of the Privy Council members who were involved, but he did not list them. We know some of them from the list in the memorandum outlining the preliminary plans for the trip. Investors included the earl of Lincoln, who was lord admiral of England, and the earl of Leicester. The secretary of state, Sir Francis Walsingham, was also included, as was Sir Christopher Hatton, captain of the Queen's Bodyguard. The list was rounded off with Drake's relatives and friends: his cousin, John Hawkins, and the Wynter brothers. George Wynter was clerk of the Queen's Ships, and William Wynter was surveyor of the Queen's Ships.[55]

The amount contributed by Drake was £1,000. He later claimed that the queen contributed a like amount, though there is no contemporary record to prove that she did. Very likely her investment was the value of her ship, *Swallow*. Sir William Wynter was listed for £750, while George Wynter and John Hawkins were down for £500 apiece. The portion of the manuscript listing the contributions of the others has been burned away.[56]

Drake's own investment may have been the value of his new ship, called the *Francis* in the draft plan but actually christened the *Pelican*. The name probably originated from Queen Elizabeth's own fascination with the pelican as a religious symbol. Just as the bird was said to pluck at its own breast to feed its young, Elizabeth liked to think of herself as pouring out her life's blood for the good of the English people.[57] The name itself hinted at Elizabeth's involvement in the voyage, a fact that would scarcely have escaped the notice of Spanish informers at court.

The *Pelican* seems to have been built in the fall of 1574, just before Drake joined the expedition to Ireland, where he presumably spent much of his newly acquired wealth.[58] A couple of years later, on 9 July 1577, Drake claimed the royal bounty for construction of the ship: "The same Fraunces hath of late caused to be erectid made and builded at his owne expenses proper coste and chardge one ship or vessell callid the Pellican of Plymouthe of the burthen of one hundrethe and fiftye tonnes . . . the said Francis Drake hath so built and made the said shippe callid the Pellican newe from the stocke."[59]

As was the usual practice, the complement of fleet personnel was made up from friends and relatives of Drake and the other investors. From his own family Drake took his brother Thomas, "not the wisest man in Christendom," and his cousin John.[60] John Hawkins sent his nephew William Hawkins and no doubt other relatives as well.[61] George Wynter sent his son John.[62] Thomas Doughty brought his brother John and his good friend Leonard Vicary, a lawyer from the Inner Temple.[63] John Brewer the trumpeter and John Thomas came at the recommendation of Christopher Hatton.[64] The chaplain, Francis Fletcher, seems to have been sent by Francis Walsingham.[65] Francis Drake was commander of the fleet, but the exact details of command were not clearly defined. Drake, John Wynter, and Thomas Doughty were considered to be "eqwall companions and frindly gentlemen" in the enterprise.[66]

Not a man to concern himself with details, Drake left most of the work of preparation to others. John Wynter, captain of the *Elizabeth*, brought his 80-ton ship and the 15-ton *Benedict* from London to Plymouth in September 1577, fully armed, supplied, and ready to sail. Such was not the case in Plymouth, where little or nothing was ready. "The ships," he said, "weare moste untakled, most unbalested, and unvictualled."[67] James Stydye, with whom Drake had served in Ireland, was in charge of preparing and loading all the ships.[68] The supplies are not listed completely, but they no doubt included pickled and salted beef, beer and wine, codfish, cheese, oatmeal, and such condiments as vinegar, mustard, salt, and oil.[69]

The largest ship in the fleet was the *Pelican*, a vessel of no more than 150 tons. This is the size stated by Drake in July 1577.[70] A month earlier John Hawkins described the *Pelican* as a ship of 120 tons.[71] A year before that a government report listed the *Pelican* at 110 tons.[72] In the sixteenth century various methods were used to determine ship size, and it should come as no surprise to learn that the ship owners used the most generous method for computing their bounty claims.[73] This tonnage describes a ship with a beam of perhaps 19 feet, a keel between 47 and 59 feet and a length between perpendiculars in the range of 68 to 81 feet. The depth of the hold was about 9 feet. The vertical clearance was 5' feet between decks, 5 feet under the forecastle and halfdeck, and 6 feet in the great cabin.[74]

In spite of the small size, the *Pelican* was heavily armed, as were all the ships in the fleet, a lesson learned from the Hawkins voyages. The best description of the armament comes from Nuño de Silva, who was a sort of prisoner-pilot in the ship for more than a year. He described the *Pelican* as the largest in the fleet, 220 *toneles,* or about 150 tons.[75] By Silva's account the ship was well made, with double planking on the hull but no lead sheathing. There were seven gun ports on each side, plus another four guns in the bow. Thirteen of the guns were cast in bronze, the others iron.[76] The masts, sails, and rigging were new and in excellent condition. The ship was fast and answered the helm quickly.

Two other ships were smaller than the *Pelican* but equally well armed. The *Elizabeth* was a new vessel of 80 tons, called 150 toneles by Nuño de Silva.[77] Built by the Wynter brothers on the Thames, it was later said to have been constructed with timber from the queen's private naval stores.[78] It was armed with eleven cast-iron cannons. Twelve additional guns were parceled out among the other three ships.[79]

The small ship *Marigold* was 30 tons, rated at 50 toneles by Nuño de Silva.[80] Its armament was six guns.[81] The provision ship or flyboat, improbably called the *Swan,* was an ungainly and flimsy vessel of perhaps 50 tons that was stout enough to carry only five guns.[82] In addition there was the *Benedict,* a pinnace of 17 tons armed only with "a few versos."[83]

The crew consisted of about 170 men and boys, according to the best estimates. Francis Fletcher said the company consisted of "150 men and some boyes."[84] John Cooke said that there were "164 men[,] gentlemen and saylers."[85] John Drake, who should have known, said in 1582, "In the whole armada there were no more than a hundred and sixty soldiers."[86]

Putting it another way in 1587 he said, "Between men of war and mariners, the whole armada included a hundred and forty men."[87] Counting a dozen and a half lads who served as pages and cabin boys, there is surprising agreement between the sources. With one exception. The testimony of Nuño de Silva, who also should have known, is that there were 270 men.[88] But Miss Nuttall thinks this was a clerical error for 170, and perhaps it was.[89]

The problem with Silva's account provides a good excuse for discussing the various sources of information about the voyage. Kenneth R. Andrews called this journey "one of the most richly documented Elizabethan voyages," and this is certainly true.[90] It is equally true that there are almost no real firsthand accounts of the trip. The narratives that do exist have without exception been filtered through the hands and minds of clerks, copyists, editors, and interpreters. Even more important, the two accounts upon which the most reliance has been placed are the ones whose authenticity is the least certain: Richard Hakluyt's "Famous Voyage," and *The World Encompassed,* which is based mostly on a manuscript attributed to Francis Fletcher.

The Hakluyt account is a curious item. Published as a ten-page insert to be placed in his *Principall Navigations,* this addendum contains no indication of authorship or date of publication. The reasons for this are obscure, but they probably arise from a government desire to keep the voyage secret, even after Drake returned.

Late in 1584 Sir Edward Stafford, Elizabeth's ambassador in France, wrote to Secretary of State Walsingham, reporting what he had heard from his own secretary, Richard Hakluyt: "Drakes jorney . . . is varie secretlye kept in Ingland," but "here . . . it is in everie bodies mouthe." Stafford thought it ridiculous that he and others were kept in ignorance and that all were left to guess at what Drake had actually accomplished.[91] Secrecy about the Drake voyage was maintained through the rest of the decade. When a new edition of Holinshed's *Chronicles* was published in 1587, it was immediately recalled and censored, and long paragraphs about Francis Drake were removed.[92] Censorship was still the policy two years later, when Richard Hakluyt began publishing his compilation of journals and documents on the great English voyages. Though he wanted to include Drake, Hakluyt was prevented from publishing an account of Drake's circumnavigation.[93] One reason was doubtless the continuing controversy in England and abroad over Queen Elizabeth's retroactive approval for Drake's acts of piracy.[94]

The secrecy policy was not greatly changed in the 1590s, when Hakluyt finally published his brief account of Drake's journey. The story Hakluyt told was filled with embellishments, partly intended to support a questionable English claim to discovery on the northwest coast of America. No one knows exactly how the Hakluyt report was written. Henry Wagner, who published the first twentieth-century critique of the Drake sources, thought it appeared about 1595, which is perhaps a little early. Wagner and others have shown that Hakluyt's story of Drake's "Famous Voyage" is related in one way or another to now-missing original accounts drawn up by John Cooke and several other members of the expedition after their return. The most important of the surviving accounts is a heavily edited version of the journal of Francis Fletcher.[95]

The Hakluyt version certainly had not appeared in print by January 1593, when Drake addressed a letter to the queen, complaining that reports of his journey "hitherto have been silenced." John Stow, the famous chronicler of Elizabethan England, obviously had not seen the Hakluyt story before he issued the revised edition of his *Annales of England.* Stow's Drake narrative was written between 1585 (the publication date for a quotation he used to describe the "valorous," "prudent," and "fortunate" Drake) and 1592. Stow used Hakluyt's description of the Cavendish voyage but had to rely on John Cooke for his brief account of the Drake voyage. The surviving manuscript of Cooke's narrative is in the handwriting of Stow, which probably means that Hakluyt was able to consult and copy it only after Stow's 1592 *Annales* were published.[96]

At about this same time, in the early 1590s, other bits of the story began to appear. Emanuel van Meteren, a Dutch historian and the dean of the Dutch merchant group in London, had lived in England since the middle of the century. He was a good friend of Richard Hakluyt and, like Hakluyt, made a strenuous effort to collect reliable information on the English voyages and other important events of the time. In his first manuscript history, written before 1593, van Meteren was forced to rely on his own research into Drake's circumnavigation, apparently because the Hakluyt insert sheets were not yet in print. There is similar evidence in the work of Jan Huygen van Linschoten, the Dutch merchant and historian, who had lived in Spain and Portuguese India. When Linschoten's *Itinerario* was approved for publication on 8 October 1594, the author had to use an incomplete account of the Drake voyage written by Nuño de Silva. Once Linschoten's work was published, Richard Hakluyt obtained an English translation and used it in the revised edition of his own work (1600).

That Hakluyt and Meteren worked closely together is apparent from several sources. In 1595, for example, Emanuel van Meteren was able to secure from Hakluyt a copy of Francis Pretty's journal of the 1588 Thomas Cavendish voyage around the world, and he used that journal in revising his own notes about the Drake voyage, which Cavendish had imitated. All of this doubtless means that the story Hakluyt finally published about Drake's circumnavigation was drawn up after 1595 in response to pressure from home and abroad to give an official account of Drake's voyage.[97]

The early-twentieth-century historian Henry Wagner thought the author of Hakluyt's Drake story was Richard Hakluyt himself.[98] David Quinn, dean of the modern historians of English exploration, thinks the Drake story was drawn up by Hakluyt with "conflation and contraction" by his assistant, the Reverend Philip Jones.[99] A contemporary Dutch broadside account of the voyage credits "her English majesty's deputy printer," doubtless meaning either George Bishop or Ralph Newberie, publishers of the original Hakluyt volume, where they are listed as "Deputies to Christopher Barker, Printer to the Queenes most excellent Maiestie."[100]

This Dutch version appears to be a translation of the story of the Drake voyage that Hakluyt originally intended to publish. Hakluyt did not do so, as he said in his introduction, because he did not want to preempt someone else's plan to publish the story of Drake's voyage around the world.[101] Fortunately for historians, the original version was published in Dutch, so we have the story as Hakluyt originally intended it, as well as the English version that he finally issued. The publication of the Dutch edition in about 1595 may have provided the motivation for Hakluyt to print the story as an addendum to the second volume of his 1589 work, the *Principall Navigations.*[102]

One of the main sources of information about the Drake voyage around the world has been the account by Nuño de Silva that was published by Richard Hakluyt in 1600. Though widely accepted as a direct translation, this also is a derivative account.[103] When Hakluyt published his copy of Silva's story, he used not a Spanish manuscript but a translation from the Dutch version published earlier by Linschoten. Linschoten had his copy from the Portuguese viceroy in India.[104] The Dutch edition appeared in 1596, and an English edition of Linschoten was on the market in 1598, well before the Hakluyt version came off the press in 1600.[105] The point is that many of the printed accounts of this voyage that are usually considered original are clearly nothing of the sort. In addition, several of the manuscripts attributed to people who were on the voyage are not firsthand accounts.

An example already mentioned is the John Cooke manuscript, which is in the handwriting of John Stow.[106] There are others. The testimony about the voyage given by John Drake is not in his own hand, nor even in his own exact words. Instead, John Drake's testimony is in the standard format of sixteenth-century Spanish legal testimony.[107] Witnesses were questioned before a notary, who was obligated to convert the often rambling testimony into a readable narrative. For the most part such narratives were written in the third person, with occasional first-person pronouns and other bits that seem to record the actual words of the witness. In the Spanish system, once a notary finished his account, the witness was required to read it and say whether the narrative was correct or not. If the witness wished to change anything, the notary was obliged to add the changes at the end of the document. This is not so different from the present American system, except perhaps that a modern American reporter would put the account in the first person, as though the witness had said the exact words.

Even the narrative attributed to Francis Fletcher is obviously not the original manuscript. That document was apparently removed from Fletcher's hands as soon as the voyage was over, and from that time numerous additions were made.[108] The more obvious additions are a reference to the later voyage of Thomas Cavendish; a lengthy section apparently added after 1616, refuting the Dutch claim to have been first around the cape at the tip of South America; numerous long and erroneous descriptions of native peoples; and even a section referring to the renaming of Drake's ship.[109]

So, the voyage around the world is reasonably well documented. Indeed, it is "one of the most richly documented Elizabethan voyages," as Andrews noted. But the story that emerges is not entirely clear, for several reasons. Lamentably, there is no holograph narrative of the journey. And there is little firsthand information about the voyage, none for the route from the Mexican coast to California. Despite all this, it is possible to describe the trip in considerable detail, recounting the first circumnavigation of the world by an English commander and a largely English crew, sailing a half century after Magellan and El Cano did it for the first time with a largely Spanish crew.

II

AROUND THE WORLD

5

Plymouth to Cape Horn

WITH ASTONISHINGLY LITTLE ATTENTION from Francis Drake himself, the fleet finally made sail on 15 November 1577. The trip was shorter than anyone expected. A sudden squall drove the ships into Falmouth harbor in Cornwall, where they were badly beaten by wind and waves. To avoid running aground, the *Pelican* and the *Marigold* had their mainmasts cut away. Even so, the *Marigold* was driven against the rocks. So severe was the damage that the fleet was forced to return to Plymouth for repairs. Arriving on 28 November, the ships were repaired while Drake berated James Stydye about the way the ships had been loaded. By 13 December, when the fleet left once more, Stydye had been dismissed.[1]

There were other storms, one of which washed a cabin boy into the sea, but the voyage was otherwise unremarkable for the next few days. By Christmas Day the sailors had sight of land, Cape Cantine on the Barbary Coast of Africa.[2] Two days later they made anchor at a tiny island called Mogador, just off the Moroccan coast. Experience on earlier voyages had shown these waters to be fine places for capturing unarmed Spanish and Portuguese ships, so Drake ordered the carpenters to assemble one of the pinnaces that had been brought along for raiding purposes.[3]

While this work was going on, a crowd gathered on the mainland, looking at the strange vessels. Drake sent a party ashore to talk with the people and see what could be learned about the local ship traffic. One man in the fleet who had been held prisoner in Morocco was able to act as interpreter. Preliminary conversations were promising, so the shore party left a hostage and took two Moors aboard ship for a conference. Drake was pleased enough with the information that he gave the two Moors some pieces of cloth, shoes, and other rewards.[4] After they returned ashore, the hostage

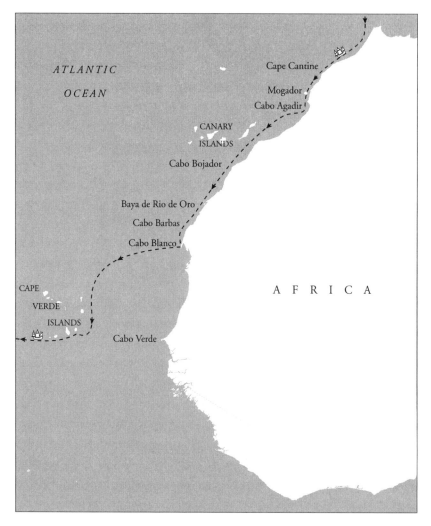

Drake's route along the coast of Africa, 1577

reboarded the ship. For some reason, though, the atmosphere was very different the next day. A similar party went ashore, and an Englishman named John Fry was taken captive.[5] If Drake made any attempt to rescue the man, the effort was unsuccessful. The fleet stayed a few more days in port, where many of the men fished and rested. When the pinnace was finished at the end of December, the fleet set sail once more.[6]

On 7 January 1580 the raiding pinnace found its first victims, three Spanish fishing smacks, near Cabo Agadir.[7] The Spanish vessels and crews were promptly impressed into the fleet. A little later three Portuguese caravels were added to the growing armada. The first of the caravels was taken on 10 January southwest of Cabo Bojador at the Baya de Rio de Oro, the second on 15 January at Cabo Barbas. On 17 January at Cabo Blanco the English raiders found a third caravel at anchor and took it as well. For a few days the fleet remained at Cabo Blanco, taking on supplies and water, while the military commander, Thomas Doughty, took his soldiers ashore for field training.[8]

The six additional ships were an embarrassment of riches, more captives than Drake and his party could easily handle. After taking what he wanted from the cargoes, Drake set most of the men and ships free. One caravel was heading to Maio in the Cape Verde Islands for a load of salt. Because the pilot of this vessel knew the coast, Drake kept the ship in his fleet for a time. In addition, he forced the captain of a Spanish fishing smack to trade his 40-ton vessel for the 15-ton *Benedict*. Renamed *Christopher,* the fishing smack became a permanent part of the English fleet.[9]

The evidence is not absolutely conclusive, but it seems clear that most of Drake's men had expected from the beginning to be involved in raids on foreign ports and shipping—in a word, piracy. This is what Drake had done on earlier voyages, and there was no reason for any of the men to think that he might have changed. Writing later about the capture of the first three fishing boats, John Cooke noted that it was "not contrary to our expectacion."[10] Even so, John Wynter later insisted that "I did never give my consente or allowance any way to the taking of any shippe or goods unlawfully."[11] Some years after this, John Drake said that "when they left England, not two men in the fleet knew where they were going, nor did this witness know."[12] The testimony of John Cooke seems more dependable in this case, because both John Wynter and John Drake were defending themselves in court, and both were eager to absolve themselves of any blame. With such meager evidence, it is remotely possible that neither man knew what was planned when the ships left Plymouth, yet their statements are oddly phrased, and they sound very much like careful attempts

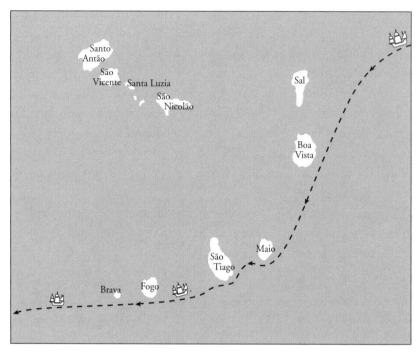

Drake's route through the Cape Verde Islands

at evasion. John Wynter's friend Thomas Doughty certainly knew of the prospective piracy, if the statements later attributed to him can be believed. Before the fleet left Plymouth, Doughty told one of the crew that "if we brought home gold we shuld be the bettar welcom."[13] Whatever the case might have been early in the voyage, by the end of January 1580 every man in the fleet knew exactly what sort of expedition they were on, even though neither Drake nor any of the other leaders had announced their plans publicly.

Drake did not stop at Tenerife, as Hawkins usually did, but sailed on to Cape Verde, where he knew from experience that Spanish and Portuguese merchant ships tended to gather. Arriving at the island of Maio on 27 January, Drake sent John Wynter and Thomas Doughty ashore with a force of seventy men to look for plunder. Somewhat to their surprise, the raiders discovered that other pirates had raided the place earlier. All the inhabitants were in hiding, and there was nothing to take but water and a little goat meat.[14]

Leaving Maio the next day, the fleet sailed to the nearby island of São Tiago, where they arrived on 30 January. Here the English ships were even less welcome. While sailing along the coast, they were fired on from the island forts, which apparently had advance word of their arrival. Unable to land, they nonetheless managed to capture another ship, this one a big Portuguese merchant vessel, the *Santa Maria,* laden with wine and other goods.[15] The commander was Nuño de Silva, an experienced pilot who knew the coast of South America. Adding Silva and his ship to the fleet, Drake sailed to the islands of Fogo and Brava, hoping to load a supply of firewood and fresh water for the long voyage across the Atlantic. In both places they found themselves unable to anchor. At Fogo the volcano was too active; at Brava the coast was rocky and the water too deep for an anchorage. Rather than risk a longer stay in these inhospitable islands, Drake decided to sail on across the Atlantic with only the provisions that were already aboard. Putting the Portuguese captives in the new pinnace, Drake gave them a little wine, bread, and fish, and set them adrift. If this seems like inhumane treatment, it was better than most of Drake's crew expected of him. Nuño de Silva fared somewhat worse, as it turned out. He was taken along to serve as pilot of Drake's fleet.[16]

Before leaving the islands Drake named Thomas Doughty as captain of the Portuguese ship and told him to be particularly careful of the valuable cargo. What happened next is not entirely clear. The earliest account, by John Wynter, reported "a very plentiful prize of wine and bread" and referred to "the discommodities that it bred through disorder." While not completely clear, Wynter seems to be writing about sailors who drank too freely from the newly acquired cargo of wine.[17]

A later narrative by John Cooke reports that Doughty found Thomas Drake stealing from the cargo of the captured Portuguese ship. According to Cooke, Thomas Drake begged Doughty to say nothing to his brother, but Doughty reported the matter anyway. Enraged, Francis Drake turned on Doughty with a string of oaths. Drake viewed the charge against his brother as an accusation against Drake himself. Furious, but seemingly uncertain about taking action against his "eqwall companyon," Drake and his brother Thomas argued the matter vehemently with Doughty and his friends, among whom was the lawyer Leonard Vicary. In the end Drake himself went on board the captured ship, now commanded by his brother Thomas and called simply the *Mary*. Doughty took charge of the *Pelican*. On 2 February the fleet set out across the Atlantic Ocean.[18]

The ocean crossing was long and tedious. For three weeks the fleet lay becalmed in the equatorial heat, while water, provisions, and tempers grew short. Men who had seemed to get along when in sight of land found that they could not agree at all when out at sea. In particular Doughty and Wynter found themselves increasingly at odds with Francis Drake, who seemed unable to endure the least criticism. The root of the problem was the matter of authority; the three men could not really be "eqwall companyons." Thomas Doughty said as much to the crew when he took command of the *Pelican*. "There hathe benne great trales, fawlings oute, and quarills among you," he said. "Everie [one] of you have benne uncertaine whome to obeye because there wear manye which toke upon them to be masters." Doughty then went on to say that he derived his own authority from Drake, who had his from the queen.[19] This should have mollified Francis Drake, but it did not.

On board the *Mary,* Thomas Drake and his friends took every opportunity to vilify Doughty. Not only had Thomas Drake been falsely accused of theft, they said to Francis Drake, but Doughty himself was a thief.[20] Drake took it all in, magnifying every bit of gossip into a personal attack by Doughty on Drake himself. In the end Drake determined to provoke some sort of reaction from Doughty that would allow for his complete removal.[21]

Only vaguely aware of what was going on, Doughty underrated the threat from his traducers. While he no longer thought himself to be one of the "eqwall companyons," he did believe that Drake considered him to be "his friend whom he trusteth." This soon changed. One day, while the ships were becalmed, Drake sent his trumpeter, James Brewer, aboard the *Pelican* on some unspecified errand. As might have been expected, the crew gave him the sort of ribald welcome that sailors reserve for mates not seen for a while. They "offered hym a Cobbey," which is to say that some of the men held him while others beat him on the buttocks with a paddle. Brewer seemed to take it in good spirit until Doughty himself joined in, striking Brewer lightly with his hand. Thereupon Brewer turned to Doughty and said: "Gods wounds doughty what doste thou meane to use this familiaritie with me consyderinge thou art not the generals frinde?" Doughty protested his great friendship for Drake, and half jokingly said to Brewer: "I pray the lett me lyve until I come into england." Unappeased, Brewer returned in a huff to the *Mary*, where he went immediately into Drake's cabin. Somewhat ominously, the ship's boat was not taken aboard but waited while Drake and his friends discussed the next move.[22]

There is no report of their conversation, but in a short time the boat went back to the *Pelican* with a request that Doughty come aboard the *Mary* to explain himself. Doughty immediately complied, but when the boat drew alongside the *Mary*, Drake refused to allow him aboard or to listen to any explanations. Instead, he ordered his sailors to take Doughty to the *Swan,* the supply ship.[23]

Perhaps by accident, perhaps by design, Drake had found a perfect way to separate Doughty from his friends and to humiliate him. Publicly rebuked by his commander, Doughty felt like a prisoner and said so to the men on the *Swan.*[24] Even so, he outranked John Chester, who had been captain of the little ship, so Chester had to step aside while Doughty became captain. In such a small vessel, the rank did not mean much, as the real command was taken by the ship's master, who handled navigation and took charge of the seamen. During the ensuing weeks Francis Drake became obsessed with Doughty, talking to the sailors and asking for the least bit of gossip that might be used to cast the man in an unfavorable light. At the same time Drake began to emphasize the separation of the officers and gentlemen on the one hand, many of whom sided with Wynter and Doughty, from the ordinary mariners on the other, who were flattered to be taken into the commander's confidence.[25]

Reduced to titular command of the little supply ship, Doughty became morose and began speaking bitterly about Drake to various men on the *Swan*. To Chester, who had been captain of the little ship before his own arrival, Doughty said: "I marvayle, Mastar Chestar, that you will take it at his hands to be thus used." On another occasion the master of the ship spoke impudently to Doughty, who turned to Chester and said: "Let us not be thus used at thes[e] knaves hands. Lose nothing of that aucthoritie that the Generall hathe commytted unto you. If you will, we will put the sworde again into your hands, and you shall have the governement [of the ship]." This was not the most judicious statement he could have made, and it later became the basis for a charge of inciting the men to mutiny.[26]

Sailing south and southwest, the fleet crossed the equator on 20 February. By the end of the month they passed near, perhaps within sight of, Isla Fernando de Naronha, 250 miles off the coast of Brazil. On 10 March the fleet was in the outer reaches of the Bahía de Todos Santos, where Nuño de Silva had been led to believe he would be released with his ship. But Drake had begun to see how valuable this experienced pilot could be on his voyage and decided to keep Silva in the fleet a while longer. Consequently, the fleet did not stop but sailed on down the coast for three more weeks, perhaps deliberately avoiding land for fear of meeting Portuguese men of war.[27]

On 5 April sailors from the *Elizabeth* and the *Mary* had their first certain view of the coast of Brazil, and the next day the other ships did as well.[28] They failed to find a good anchorage, and on the seventh some of the ships were lost in a storm, including Doughty's vessel, the *Swan*. Several more days passed before all were gathered together again at Cabo Santa María, the entrance to the Rio de la Plata. Drake called the place Cape Joy and remained there for several days while the ships drew in fresh water from the river. The men also killed a few seals for fresh meat, and the ships spent a few days sailing along the north and south banks of the river. Still finding no place where he wanted to stay, Drake ordered the fleet to sea once more, where Doughty's little *Swan* again became separated from the rest of the fleet in a storm.[29]

During the long passage Drake allowed his anger at Doughty to simmer, uttering one invective after another against his absent partner. The man was a witch, he said, a conjurer who brought these storms on the fleet by his own machinations.[30] Taking their cue from the commander of the

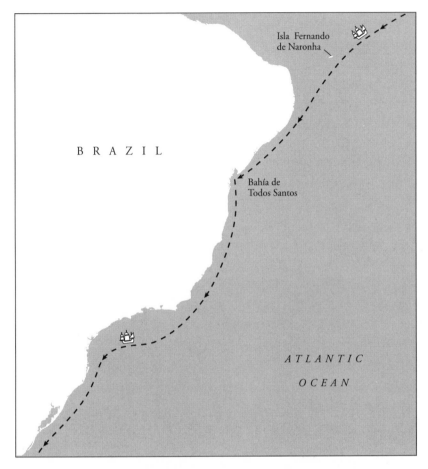

Drake's first landfalls on the coast of Brazil

fleet, Drake's friends also began to treat Doughty with contempt. The master of the *Swan,* for example, no doubt acting with approval from Drake, began to eat his meals with the seamen, to whom he issued a generous allotment of food, while Doughty and his gentleman companions were kept on short rations. Doughty complained about this, the two men came to blows, and the master finally offered to give Doughty something to "eate that falls from my tayle."31

Meanwhile, all the ships were making their way down the coast, the *Swan* still separated from the rest of the fleet, and other ships disappearing

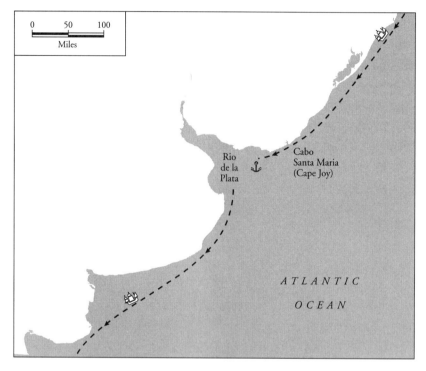

Anchorage at the Rio de la Plata, April 1578

for a day or so in the stormy weather. On 13 May most of the fleet was anchored in the road off Cape Tres Puntas, which Drake called Cape Hope. In order to look for a sheltered cove with better protection from the weather, Drake called for the boat from the *Elizabeth* to come over to the *Mary* and take him up into the little bay. While the sailors were rowing him ashore, another storm blew up, and the *Mary* was forced to run for the open sea. The *Pelican* soon followed, and the *Elizabeth* as well. Had John Thomas, captain of the *Marigold,* not decided to run through the uncharted entrance to the bay, Drake might have been left to face the storm in an open boat. But Thomas saved the commander, and the next day Drake took a party ashore to make a signal fire and draw the rest of his ships into the little harbor.[32]

When the wind died down and all the ships but the *Swan* and the *Mary* were assembled, Drake took his fleet to sea once more. A short distance to

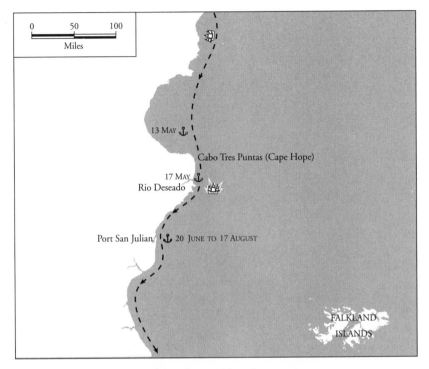

Drake's anchorages, May–August 1578

the south, in the mouth of the river now called the Deseado, he found the safe harbor that he had been looking for. Leaving the *Marigold* and the *Christopher* in the harbor to find a suitable anchorage, Drake went aboard the *Pelican* and made preparations to bring in the lost ships. Sailing northward, Drake located the *Swan* and brought it into port. The *Elizabeth* sailed south, searching in vain for the *Mary*.[33]

The *Swan* and the *Pelican* reached port together on 17 May 1578, Whitsunday. The *Marigold* and the *Christopher* had found a suitable anchorage, and the ships all stopped there. Then, drawing the *Swan* alongside the *Pelican,* Drake ordered all the remaining supplies and provisions to be transferred to the flagship and had his men begin to strip away the fittings and prepare to abandon the vessel. Doughty, of course, was enraged at the prospect of losing his last vestige of command. Confronting Drake on the deck of the ship, Doughty reminded his former comrade in arms of their partnership agreement. He then declared that he had lost all confidence in Drake and now thought that Drake's word was worthless. Losing his temper, Drake struck Doughty and ordered him bound to the mast, an order that the *Swan's* master carried out with great delight. When the ship had been completely stripped, Drake had Thomas Doughty and his brother John put aboard the *Christopher*. The *Swan* was then driven ashore and burned so that the iron work could be salvaged.[34]

The expedition remained there for two weeks, taking on a supply of seal meat and visiting with the natives. The local people lived a very simple existence, using long bows and arrows, eating seal meat, and wearing short sealskin tunics. The Englishmen and the scantily dressed local people seem to have enjoyed themselves immensely, dancing together to the music of the trumpeters and fiddlers among Drake's crew. John Winter was a particularly avid dancer, among others. Drake, too, seems to have joined the fun, and one of the locals became so close a companion that he was able to seize the red velvet cap off Drake's head and keep it.[35] What other diversions the crew engaged in can only be imagined, though they seem to have included those that traditionally take place when the "sonnes of God" meet with the "Daughters of men."[36]

Leaving port about the first of June, the ships headed once more out to sea, but almost immediately the *Christopher* became separated from the rest of the ships. Within a day or two it turned up again, Drake in the meantime taking the opportunity to condemn Doughty publicly for causing more trouble. On 3 June, Drake ordered the ships back to port, where the *Christopher* was stripped and abandoned.[37]

Drake then put Thomas and John Doughty aboard the *Elizabeth*, forbidding them to read or write anything except in English, and warning the crew not to have any contact with the two brothers.[38] Thomas Doughty was a conjurer and a seditious person, said Drake, while his brother was a witch and a poisoner. Any man who consorted with them would be Drake's enemy and have no share in the profits from the voyage. On the other hand, anyone who sided with Drake in the dispute would be so well rewarded that even the poorest seaman would be able to live like a gentleman for the rest of his life. In spite of this promise of reward and punishment, a good many men in the *Elizabeth* sided with Doughty, Captain John Wynter being one of them. He allowed Doughty to have a cabin of his own, even though Drake had intended that Doughty sleep and eat with the seamen.[39]

All this seems strange, but superstition of this sort was common in sixteenth-century England. The conjuring accusation and the prohibition on reading and writing in languages other than English may have been based on a fear that Doughty was an astrologer, who needed the Ephemerides and other Latin reference books for his work. Beyond this, Doughty may have been keeping a diary or other notes in Latin, as Richard Madox did a few years later, much to the chagrin of his own commander.[40]

Setting off once more, the fleet sailed south for another two weeks, finally coming upon the *Mary*, sailing southward toward Port San Julian. This may seem like phenomenally good luck, but apparently the fleet had agreed to meet there at Magellan's old winter headquarters.[41] On 20 June Drake took the reunited fleet into port. There, according to Francis Fletcher, the *Mary* was found to be in extremely poor condition, and for that reason it was put ashore, stripped, and abandoned.[42] This was an odd development: all of the ships connected with Doughty and at one time or another separated from the fleet were abandoned as soon as the fleet was reunited. Did Drake really believe that Doughty had put a witch's curse on the vessels? John Cooke did not think so, though he did think that Drake wanted the seamen to believe that sorcery was involved.[43]

On 22 June, Drake went ashore with a small party of armed men in order to locate a suitable camping spot. Almost as soon as the group landed they were stopped by a band of Indians, armed with bows and arrows. One of Drake's men, Robert Winterhey, started to fire a warning arrow at the Indians, but his bowstring broke. Regardless of Winterhey's intention, the Indians interpreted his action as a hostile move. They fired off a volley of arrows, one of which wounded Winterhey. Oliver, the master gunner, then tried to fire his fowling piece, but the powder was wet and would not ignite. One of the Indians then shot Oliver, and the whole party had a very difficult time fending off the attack. Finally, while the men with shields set up a defense line, Drake managed to recharge Oliver's fowling piece, shot one of the attackers in the stomach, and "sent his gutts abroad." This took the spirit out of the rest of the Indians, and the Englishmen were then able to retreat to their ships, taking the wounded Winterhey with them but leaving Oliver's body on shore. Winterhey died within a few hours, having been shot through the lungs. The next morning a rescue party managed to recover Oliver's body, and both men were buried ashore with full honors.[44]

Having been so long at sea and faced with a stormy passage in the strait, Drake needed a winter anchorage to refit his fleet and allow his seamen to rest. In addition, he was eager to deal with Doughty and thus to consolidate his own leadership. So he decided to ignore the loss of the two men in battle and stay in Port San Julian for the rest of the winter. He also determined to put Thomas Doughty on trial for mutiny.[45]

On 30 June 1578 Drake brought the entire company ashore and had everyone assemble for the trial. John Thomas, captain of the *Marigold* and a good friend of Drake's, presented the commander with a bundle of papers that contained reports from various crew members about the supposed delinquencies of Doughty. With the papers untied before him, Drake began the proceedings, reading his main charge: "Thomas Doughty, you have heare sought by divers meanes in as mych as you maye to discredite me to the great hinderaunce and ovarthrowe of this voyage." If proven guilty of these and other charges, said Drake, Doughty would deserve death.[46]

In reply Doughty said first that he had never done any such thing and told Drake that he would be glad to defend himself in an English court. "Nay, Thomas Doughtye," said Drake, "I will here impanell a jurye on you." Doughty answered that he hoped Drake had authority for holding such a trial and asked to see Drake's commission. Ignoring the request, Drake had Doughty's arms bound behind his back and told John Thomas to read the various charges.[47]

The charges were apparently those contained in a series of manuscript notes now in the British Library. These seem to be reports of private conversations had at various times with Thomas Doughty. Names of witnesses are appended to most of the notes, though not all of the witnesses appear to have been involved in the conversations. Francis Fletcher, for example, was certainly not a passenger on the *Swan,* where most of the conversations were said to have taken place.[48] If Fletcher was indeed a witness, he probably did nothing more than to serve as a notary at the trial, verifying that the conversations were written down just as they were reported. In fact, John Cooke says the charges were recorded on oath at the trial. The oaths were administered by John Thomas, and the written allegations were then delivered to John Wynter, who had been made foreman of the jury.[49] All this gave the trial the appearance of fairness, with three of Doughty's closest friends serving as court officials.

The two most serious charges were incitement to mutiny and a statement to Edward Bright that the queen and council might be corrupt. The others were scarcely more than squabbles between the partners: that Doughty had given a copy of the plan to the lord treasurer; that Doughty was the man who really conceived the plan for the voyage; and similar bits of gossip.[50] Few of the gentlemen seemed to agree with the proceedings. Leonard Vicary, the lawyer, said to Drake, "This is not lawe nor agriable to justice." Drake was not concerned about legal niceties. "I have not[,] quoth he[,] to do with you crafty lawyars, neythar care I for the lawe, but I know what I wyll do." Vicary still objected, finally saying, "There is I trust no matter of death." To this Drake replied, "No, no, Mastar Vickarye."[51]

The problem for Vicary and others was that, although most of the allegations were petty, some of them were true. In particular, there were good witnesses who could verify Doughty's furious remarks to Chester when he was provoked to anger by the impudent seaman who was master of the *Swan.* This outburst could have been seen as a serious attempt to incite mutiny had it not been made in the heat of anger. The jury members were inclined to think that the whole matter should be forgotten, but they were afraid to act counter to Drake's obvious will. So with Drake's seeming assurance that Doughty would not be executed, the jury members had a convenient way out of their dilemma. They decided that the charge of inciting to mutiny was indeed true, as were some of the less serious allegations. But the jury rejected the charge of lese majesty, saying that it was impossible to take the unsupported word of such a man as Edward Bright.[52]

Drake was elated. With the guilty verdict in hand, he took the seamen off to one side, away from the Doughty brothers. There he pulled out a bundle of documents that he had brought from his cabin on the ship and began to read them aloud. There was a letter from Hawkins to Essex; a letter from Essex to Walsingham; a letter from the queen's favorite, Christopher Hatton, offering to Drake the services of his men John Thomas and John Brewer. But something was missing. "Gods will," said Drake, "I have left in my cabyne that [which] I shuld especially have had." And then, as Cooke recalled later, Drake pretended that he had forgotten to bring the copy of the supposed royal commission that gave Drake himself full authority on the voyage. In fact, the only paper he had with any sort of royal connection was a document showing that the queen had invested money in the voyage. Even so, the seamen were greatly impressed at the collection of papers, which included the signatures of so many important people.[53]

Drake did not send for the missing paper. Instead, he recalled his original accusations against Thomas Doughty, and he asked the men whether they now agreed that Doughty had tried to discredit him. As Drake explained it, "discredit" meant "takynge away of my good name and altogether discreditinge me, and then my life." If this happened, he said, it would mean the end of the voyage, for the crew would be leaderless and so divided against one another that they would not be able to find their own way home. On the other hand, by simply getting rid of Doughty the troublemaker, Drake promised again, they could be assured of success beyond their wildest dreams. The lowest sailor would be a rich man, he said. "The worst in this flete shall become a gentleman." Then, claiming that all this would be impossible if Doughty should continue to live, Drake said, "They that think this man worthy to dye let them with me hold upp theyr hands and they that think him not worthye to dye hold downe theyr hands."[54]

Few, perhaps none, dared to leave their hands down and show their friendship for Doughty. As Cooke recalled, some men raised their hands because they resented Doughty's gentlemanly demeanor. Others raised their hands in support of Drake, because they were afraid to oppose him. A final group lifted up their hands, but also lifted their "very hartes unto the Lorde," silently praying for deliverance from the hands of Francis Drake.[55]

Noting this reluctance in a few of the men, Drake explained that there was no alternative to Doughty's execution. He offered to cancel it entirely if anyone could offer a reasonable alternative. Doughty himself spoke up, saying to Drake, "I pray you, cary me with you to the Perwe [Peru] and there set me a shore." To this seemingly reasonable offer Drake replied, "No, truly, mastar doughty, I can not answere it to hir maiestie if I shuld so do." No doubt it was better to put a man to death than to set him free in Spanish territory.[56]

Continuing to tease his victim, Drake then said he would put Doughty in the hands of anyone who would offer to keep him in custody for the rest of the voyage. Hearing this, Doughty asked John Wynter to be his jailer, and Wynter agreed. Thereupon Drake replied that he would permit it only if they put Doughty in the hold, nailed the hatches securely over Doughty's head, canceled the voyage, and sailed straight home. Hearing this unpleasant alternative, a noisy group of sailors shouted, "God forbyd, good generall." And Doughty's fate was sealed, 30 June 1578.[57]

For a day and a half Doughty prepared himself for death, praying, setting his affairs in order, and talking with the few friends who dared to visit him. On the second of July, Doughty asked Drake for permission to receive the sacrament. Drake not only granted the request but received the sacrament with him. Then after a meal, Doughty said that he was ready for execution. Commending himself to all present, Doughty thanked his friends who had remained faithful and expressed regret that they were now in jeopardy themselves. Immediately one of them, Hugh Smith, asked Doughty to please explain to everyone that they had never conspired against Drake. Doughty did so and begged Drake not to punish the poor man. "Well, Smith," said Drake, "I forgive the, but by the life of God . . . I was determined to have neiled thy ears to the pillary." With that, Doughty thanked Drake, embraced him, and called him his good captain. He then lay his head on the block, and the executioner chopped it off. Afterward, Drake had the head held up before the assembled sailors, telling them, "This is the end of traitors."[58]

To this day no one has been able to explain just why Francis Drake thought that he needed to take the life of his onetime friend. He obviously wanted Doughty out of the way permanently, and just as obviously he had no legal right to try or to execute the man. Several times during the expedition he claimed to have a document from the queen giving him such authority, but he never showed it to anyone, then or later.[59] After the voyage, John Doughty took legal action against Drake for murdering his brother. A commission from the queen such as he claimed to have had would have been a perfect defense, but again Drake did not produce such a document. Instead, he employed a series of legal maneuvers to avoid trial. We can only suppose that the commission did not exist.[60]

At a loss to explain Drake's abominable behavior, some members of his family later claimed that Doughty had committed a great outrage that sullied Drake's honor and forced him to seek revenge. In 1582 Richard Madox wrote one version of such a story in his diary: "We dined on the Edward. Walker disclosed to me that he was told by Whitaker that Thomas Doughty lived intimately with the wife of Francis Drake, and being drunk he blabbed out the matter to the husband himself. When later he realized his error and feared vengeance, he contrived in every way the ruin of the other, but he himself fell into the pit."[61] The Walker in this story was the Rev. John Walker, chaplain of the *Edward*. Whitaker was Henry Whitaker, receiver of the port of Plymouth, whose wife Judith was sister of William Hawkins. The conversation between Walker and Whitaker took place when they all dined at the Hawkins home in Plymouth on 1 June 1582, just a few months after the death of Mary Drake.[62]

The story may be nothing more than family gossip. Drake obviously wanted to be rid of Doughty permanently, though he lacked the legal authority to do it, and bullied officers and crew into sharing the blame. John Wynter, the third "eqwall companyon" and Doughty's close friend, later said that from the first capture of the Portuguese ship he had opposed Drake's plan to change the voyage into a pirate raid, and Doughty seems to have held the same opinion. But Drake manipulated the crew so successfully that Wynter was terrified and would not oppose him publicly. "Yf I shoulde have contraryed him," said Wynter, "or gone aboute to practise to withstand him in anie parte of this his doinges, he would have punished me by death."[63]

In fact, Drake threatened to execute any other member of the crew who might commit a similar offense. No doubt this is why he ordered them all to receive Communion the following Sunday, confessing their sins beforehand to the priest Francis Fletcher.[64] The idea presumably was that no Christian could receive the sacrament while contemplating mutiny. Moreover, any who had harbored such thoughts in the past would have to confess them to the priest, who could then be bullied into telling Drake.

The use of confession and Communion provides an interesting insight into Drake's religious practice. The English church had not abandoned private confession. There were formulas for general confession and absolution, but provisions were also made for private confession and absolution for those souls who wanted them.[65] One of Drake's friends, Morgan Tillert, had sailed with Drake on an earlier voyage. Taken captive, Tillert later told the Inquisition that Drake did not believe that a man had to confess his sins to a priest. "It was sufficient to confess to God in his heart."[66] This seemingly contradictory attitude is typical of Drake's expedient approach to religion. He had the same flexible theology that he had seen at work in the Hawkins family. Just as John Hawkins could pretend to be Catholic when it was convenient, Drake could do the same—particularly if a little Romish dogma might be useful in rooting out mutineers.

None of the men appears to have been taken in by the plan. The men told Fletcher only what it seemed safe to say. John Cooke, for example, held back the whole truth of his confession "for feare of ther tiranyes in that place."[67] Fletcher was equally circumspect in giving advice to the penitents. "As the Lord enabled me I performed," said Fletcher, "with exhortation to repentance every man as he felt the guilt of his owne conscience."[68]

Unsatisfied with the outcome of the enforced sacraments, Drake called the men ashore a few days later for a special meeting. Speaking at some length, Drake said he wanted no more grumbling, as this would inevitably lead to mutiny. According to Cooke's report of the speech, Drake thought that the main cause of dissatisfaction was the division between sailors and gentlemen. This would change. Henceforth both groups would labor side by side, though sailors would still have to obey orders as before.[69]

A further source of worry, as Cooke recalled, was the continuing uncertainty about the source and extent of Drake's authority. Some of the men had been saying Drake was sent out by Sir William Wynter or by Christopher Hatton or by John Hawkins, but Drake said his authority came from none of those men. Rather, Sir Francis Walsingham had called Drake to his quarters and told him that he was being commissioned to take vengeance upon the possessions of the king of Spain for damages suffered by the queen of England. A day after this meeting, said Drake, the queen herself ratified his appointment in a personal interview. She then asked his advice about the proposed voyage, Drake said, and he told her that it would be better to attack the king's possessions in the Indies than to attempt any attack on the Spanish ports in Europe.[70]

Again, as Cooke remembered, Drake brought out his bundle of papers, showing the men a document recording the queen's investment of a thousand crowns, along with other financial records. And again he failed to produce a copy of the alleged commission signed by the queen. Instead he said that he had sworn to keep the entire plan secret from everyone in the realm.[71]

In the midst of his long and rambling speech, Drake paused to ask what the seamen expected from the expedition. Wages? Or were they were willing to give up their wages and rely on his generosity? They all said they were, in effect committing themselves to his newly revealed plan for pirate raids on Spanish ports and shipping. Then he turned to the officers, most of whom held their commands by appointment from the ship owners. In front of the seamen Drake called the officers forward and formally relieved them of their commands. Once this was accomplished, he reinstated them, or most of them, as his own appointees. The exception was office of master on the ship *Marigold.* Edward Bright, the ship's carpenter who had testified so eagerly against Doughty, was made master under John Thomas, who retained the job of captain.[72]

It was a strange appointment. Clearly Drake wanted to reward Bright for his leading role in the Doughty trial and execution, but there may have been another reason. Captain John Thomas was one of Doughty's friends, and Bright may have been appointed to keep an eye on him, just as he had on Doughty. Beyond this, it seems clear that many of the disaffected men were on board Wynter's ship, the *Elizabeth.* A few days after the recommissioning Drake came aboard the *Elizabeth* and threatened to hang half the crew, telling Worrall that "his case was worse than Doughties."[73]

It was a marvelous performance. With oaths that shriveled the hearts of the men on the *Elizabeth,* Drake turned on Wynter and demanded, "Where is your man ulisses." When Wynter said nothing, Drake continued, "By gods lyfe yf he were my man I would cut of his ears yea by gods wounds I would hang him." John Cooke, who wrote it down later, added in puzzlement that he did not understand what the men had done: "Truly I do not knowe."[74]

There can be no doubt about Drake's purpose in this incident. He wanted to make certain that the men were afraid of him. But fear works both ways, and it was the great leveler on this expedition. The officers were afraid of the men and the men of the officers. Nearly everyone was afraid of Drake, but Drake was afraid of the men as well and kept an armed guard nearby.[75] No doubt some of the men were planning to desert, but it was obvious to everyone that any such move would have to be done carefully. Doughty's freshly dug grave was a reminder of what could happen to the incautious. If this were not enough, there were age-blackened timbers on the shore, surrounded by human bones, thought to be relics of the executioner's work in the Magellan expedition. With the headless body of Doughty fresh in the grave and the rest of the crew beginning to feel the pangs of starvation, everyone was eager to be away from that awful place.[76]

Only three ships were left in the expedition: the *Pelican,* commanded by Francis Drake, on which Nuño de Silva served as pilot; the *Marigold,* commanded by Captain John Thomas; and the *Elizabeth,* with John Wynter as captain. The fleet left Port Saint Julian on 17 August, and by August 21 they were in the Strait of Magellan.[77] At about this time Drake is said to have held a ceremony, renaming his ship. The *Pelican* became the *Golden Hind,* or so the story goes. It is a curious tale, not clearly supported by contemporary evidence. In fact, there is no firsthand record of the ceremony, and if we may judge by their silence in the matter, none of the members of Drake's crew was aware that the name of the ship had been changed. John Wynter certainly did not know, for he continued to call Drake's ship the *Pelican.*[78]

Drake's route to the Strait of Magellan

The only manuscript that mentions the rechristening is the one attributed to Francis Fletcher. The brief remark appears in the section of the
story after the ships had passed through the Strait of Magellan and endured the storms that blew them far to the south. "The storme not onely
continewing but increasing upon us more & more our shipp I meane the
Admirall if shee had retained her old name shee had when shee came out

of England being called the Pellicane which was changed into the Golden Hinde by the generall for the Honour of the Honourable Sr Christopher Hatton his master she might have been said to bee a Pellicane in the wildernes."[79]

As will be seen, that manuscript was extensively revised after it left Fletcher's hands. One obvious revision was the religious service held on Sunday, 17 August, at Port Saint Julian. When preparing the Fletcher manuscript for publication, the editor changed the date of this observance to the twentieth, when the fleet was about to enter the Strait of Magellan.[80] Here Fletcher said Francis Drake ordered his three ships to lower their topsails, allowing them to drape over the lower sails, as a salute to the queen: "At this cape our generall caused his fleet, in homage to our soveraigne lady the Queenes majesty, to strike their top-sailes upon the bunt, as a token of his willing and glad minde, to shewe his dutifull obedience to her highnes, whom he acknowledged to hafe full interest and right, in that new discovery; and withall, in remembrance of his honorable friend and favorer, Sir Christopher Hatton, he changed the name of the shippe, which himselfe went in, from the *Pellican* to be called *the golden Hinde*."[81]

The name *Golden Hind* first appeared in the historical record on 20 May 1579, when Nuño de Silva read into his testimony a copy of a letter written by Francis Drake. In this letter Drake's ship was called the *Gama Dorado*.[82] Four years later, perhaps imperfectly recalling this letter, Pedro Sarmiento de Gamboa said that he thought Drake's ship was named *Aguila Dorada*,[83] or the *Golden Eagle*. For a number of years the Spanish seemed to be alone in their belief that the ship was called something golden. A Dutch merchant living in London finished a comprehensive history of Europe in 1586 and sent it to a printer in Germany. Although the book was not published for another dozen years, the name as recorded there was *Publicanus*, which seems closer to *Pelican* than to *Golden Hind*.[84]

The earliest printed reference to the name of the ship appeared in the 1592 edition of Stow's *Annales*. Stow referred to the vessel as "the golden Hind (or Pelicane I think)."[85] Four years later the Dutch historian Jan Huygen van Linschoten published the first edition of Silva's record of the voyage, calling the ship "het vergulde Hert."[86] Following his lead, the English translator of this work called the ship "the golden Hart."[87] When Richard Hakluyt copied this material for the second edition of his own work on exploration, he amplified that translation a bit and referred to the ship as "the Pellican or the golden Hinde," apparently because he thought no one would recognize the ship if he called it simply *Golden Hind*.[88]

All of this indicates fairly clearly that the name *Golden Hind* was not in common use among the members of Drake's crew during the voyage—or, for that matter, anywhere in England during the years immediately after the ship returned. One likely reason is that Elizabeth had adopted the pelican, as she did so many other Christian symbols, to signify her own un-stinting love for the English people and her position as head of the English church.[89] Seen in this light, the renaming of the ship, if it actually took place, was something of a blunder on Drake's part. But by 1628 Elizabeth, Drake, Fletcher, and most of the others were dead, and it was possible to resurrect this name and to use it as part of the continuing effort to change Drake from "a real man into a national legend."[90]

On 24 August the fleet stopped at an island covered with flocks of penguins. Wading in with clubs, the men managed to kill enough of the flightless birds to replenish their depleted stores. The Fletcher manuscript put it this way: "Within small tyme continueing our way we chanced with 3 Ilands a little distant one from another at 2 whereof wee arived & gave the names to all of them. The first wee named Elizabeth, the 2 Bartholomew the day being called by this name, & the last George his Iland according to custom of our country."[91]

As the story was adapted for the *World Encompassed* it was also made more dramatic. One was indeed named Bartholomew, for the saint on whose feast day it was discovered, and another Saint Georges, in honor of the patron of England. These two islands were "exceeding usefull," for the men were able to land on both of them and take in a supply of penguin meat. The third island was "very faire and large and of a fruitfull soile." Drake landed here with a party of gentlemen and seamen, took formal possession in the name of the queen, and called it "Elizabeth Iland."[92]

Interestingly, the sole source for the act of possession is the *World Encompassed*, published in 1625. None of the men on the expedition recorded this

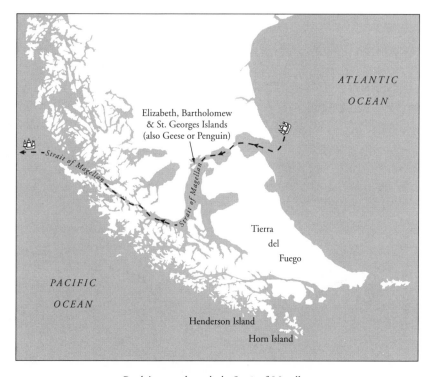

Drake's route through the Strait of Magellan

event; they noted simply that the fleet stopped at an island and killed a supply of penguins.[93] This is almost exactly what Richard Hakluyt wrote in a description of the Drake voyage published about 1596 in a twelve-page insert for his *Principall Navigations:* "The 24. of August we arrived at an Island in the streightes, where we found great store of foule which could not flie, of the bignesse of geese, whereof we killed in lesse then one day 3000."[94]

In 1584 John Drake testified about the journey and recalled only that there were many islands in the strait and that "the said islands contain many birds."[95] Three years later he recalled that "Captain Francis went sailing toward the strait, which was in fifty-two degrees. At the entrance he found three small islands. He landed on one and called it Elizabeth. Here there were many featherless birds which could not fly."[96]

When Thomas Cavendish went through this passage in 1587, apparently

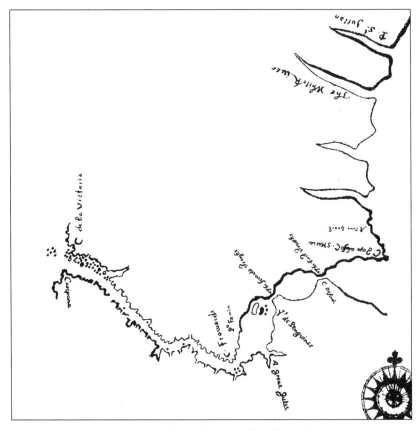

Route through the Strait of Magellan Mapped by Thomas Cavendish 1588
Adapted from Algemeen Rijksarchief, The Hague, VEL, 733.

using maps obtained from Drake, he failed to mention any island named
Elizabeth. Instead, he noted: "We came unto two islands named by Sir
Francis Drake the one Bartholomewe Island, because he came thither on
that Saints day, and the other Penguin Island."[97] If Drake had found three
islands and named one for Queen Elizabeth and the other for Saint George,
Thomas Cavendish seems to have been totally unaware of it. Cavendish,
in fact, made his own map of the strait, showing a group of five islands,
two of them relatively large and three very small.[98] His map shows the
name of only one of these islands, Penguin Island.[99]

John Wynter was seemingly unaware of any ceremony or the christening of an island for the queen. His account of the visit includes only this brief remark: "The 20th daie of this month at night we entered the straite in the middest almost whereof we found an island where we found certain sea fowls with which this Island was most abundantly stored. Here we killed so many as served 140 men seven weeks."[100] If Francis Drake took part in any ceremony of possession, John Wynter did not know about it. Edward Cliffe, one of the seamen who sailed with Wynter, is credited with saying that the three islands were named after Elizabeth, Saint George, and Saint Bartholomew. But the original copy of his account is not extant, only the version printed by Hakluyt in 1599.[101] Wynter himself returned to the island, which he called the Island of Geese, on 3 November.[102] In 1618 Wynter told Samuel Purchas that he had himself landed on an island in the strait and taken possession in the name of the queen.[103] It seems possible, even likely, that the story in Cliffe and in the *World Encompassed* is Wynter's account, transferred and embellished.[104] As will be seen, another story involving Wynter was added to the Drake account in much the same way.

The fleet came out of the strait on 6 September, directly into the face of a great storm. Hoping to find a place of refuge, they headed northwest, where their maps showed the coast. But running northwest, the sailors found only open sea. The actual coastline ran north and even a bit to the northeast. In the manuscript of Francis Fletcher it was said that the faulty maps had been circulated by the Spaniards "of a Malitious Purpose" to lead any ship astray that might try to reach Spanish possessions in the Pacific.[105] The real explanation is much simpler. Spanish cartographers generally stated that the coast ran roughly north and south. This is the way it was reported by the Magellan expedition.[106] Francisco Ladrillero reported the same thing after his journey through the strait in 1558.[107] This information became available elsewhere in Europe during the next decade, but few cartographers made use of it.[108] The longitude problem persisted for decades.

Before the voyage of Ladrillero it was common to show a gap in the lower west coast of South America or to use some other device to indicate that the area had not been fully explored. Once the full coast had been explored, it became obvious that something was amiss. Using Ladrillero's detailed description of the Strait, Juan López de Velasco was able to report in 1570 that the problem with the maps arose from a difference in opinion among navigators about the longitude of each coast of South America. With the instruments available, it was difficult to determine the actual longitude. As Velasco put it, "If the longitudes and latitudes are preserved, you must change the directions and locations; and if these are based on observations, you must discard one or the other, perhaps both; so cosmographers disagree about the longitude of the strait."[109]

Once the coastline became known, geographers had to decide just where the corrections should be made. Early solutions to the problem were less than perfect. In the case of the Sancho Gutiérrez planisphere of 1550, the cartographer produced his famous double coastline. One line ran roughly north-south, with a gap between the end of the line and the mouth of the strait. The other, newer line connected the mouth of the strait with another point above the port of Valdivia. Viewers could decide for themselves where they would like to have the coastline located.[110]

Some cartographers thought that it was easier simply to join the ends of the previously plotted coastlines, adding the names of the bays and ports reported by Ladrillero. This is what Bartolomé Olives did with the new map of the strait that he produced about 1562 or shortly thereafter. To do him justice, Olives also added an important caveat in large letters: "One should note . . . the new description of the entire coast of Chile up to the Strait [of Magellan] that S[eñor] D[on] Garcia [Hurtado de Mendoza] produced this year of 1562. It appears to conform with the derrotero of the same [Strait of] Magellan that by good fortune came into our hands. In it the coast runs partly west-southwest and partly a quarter to the west a quarter to the southwest. So we describe it here [only] until we can obtain a more complete report, not changing the locations of the ports nor their altitudes, from the way they have been previously shown."[111] Olives thus drew the coastline on his map erroneously but explained why he was doing so. Others apparently followed his lead, drawing the coastline the same way but omitting the disclaimer. Two prime examples are the printed world maps of Abraham Ortelius issued in 1564 and 1570.[112] At least one of these

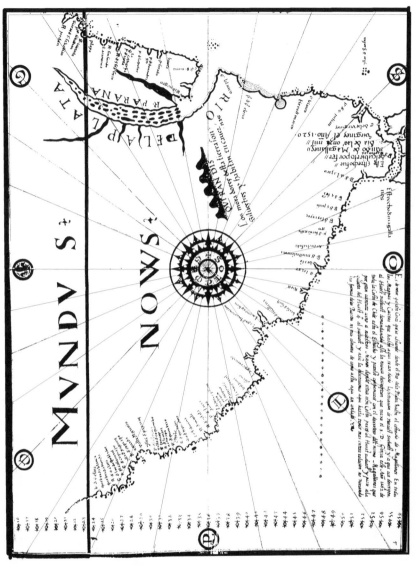

West Coast of South America, from the 1562 atlas of Bartolomé Olives. From Biblioteca Apostolica Vaticana, Urbinates Latini 283, atlante nautico, tav. X.

maps was probably in Drake's map case during the voyage, perhaps accounting for his confusion about the location of the coast.[113]

Sailing northwest toward the putative coast, the three ships found no harbor and were instead storm driven for several days to the west-southwest.[114] For a time the storm abated, and on 15 September there was a clear sunset, after which they observed an eclipse of the moon. New winds then drove the ships back toward the strait. The storm increased in fury, so much so that it was impossible to keep the little fleet together. On the last day of September the *Marigold* disappeared, effectively solving Drake's problems with Doughty's close friend Captain John Thomas.[115]

What happened to the ship is unknown. The Fletcher manuscript tells a story of cries in the night and the sound of a ship breaking up on the rocks, but this is clearly one of the many embellishments later added to the original account. The ships were still a week away from finding land, and the other crews simply did not know what had happened to Thomas's little ship.[116] In fact, though the *Marigold* was not seen again by Drake and his people, some of its crew may have survived and later reached England.[117]

On 7 October, still struggling against the stormy seas, the two remaining ships found their way into a rock-strewn harbor near the mouth of the strait. Tossed by the high seas, Drake's ship lost both anchor and cable and was unable to remain in the bay. He signaled Wynter to leave the harbor with him and sail as close to the wind as possible. Still buffeted by the storm, the two ships lay outside the harbor for a time, hauling into the wind. By evening the *Elizabeth* was still headed toward the north, while Drake's *Pelican* rode two or three miles astern, but still in view now and then. Somehow during the night the ships separated, the *Elizabeth* driving toward the north shore and the *Pelican* sailing out to sea again, west-southwest.[118]

Finding himself alone and near a rocky shore, Wynter says he took refuge in a harbor in the mouth of the strait. There he remained for more than three weeks, lighting signal fires and waiting for the return of Drake and the *Pelican*. While he awaited Drake's return, Wynter went ashore to inspect the country.[119] "The 20th daie of october I went ashore and landed on a highe mountaine beinge the highest in all the straite in the tope whereof I ingraved her majesties name and we praised god together for the danger we escaped." If Wynter took possession of the island, he did not say so. The accounts in the Fletcher manuscript and the *World Encompassed* simply do not find any corroboration in the stories told when the men first returned to England.

When it became obvious that Drake was not coming back, Wynter announced to his crew that he intended to sail on to the Moluccas.[120] This seems to have been part of the plan; if the ships became hopelessly lost, they would head for the Moluccas and meet there.[121] When Wynter said he hoped to rendezvous with Drake in the Moluccas, his crew announced that they felt differently about the matter. Only a few weeks earlier Drake had threatened to execute thirty of them.[122] Led by the master of the ship, they refused to go on. Wynter reluctantly ordered a return to England.[123] At least, this is the story Wynter told when he returned home, and the moderately favorable reception he got at court is evidence that it was considered to be a factual account of what took place.[124]

Still, there was an undercurrent of doubt. A Spanish mariner dispatched in 1579 to gather information about English shipping reported that Wynter was considered to have deserted the fleet out of cowardice.[125] This became the predominant view in England when Drake came home. Wynter was charged with desertion and put into prison for a time.[126] Drake himself seems to have had a hand in this, though he earlier had told a Spanish prisoner that he expected to meet Wynter and Thomas in the Moluccas.[127] In any case, the members of Wynter's crew soon took their lead from Drake and began to say that they had wanted to continue the voyage, while Wynter had insisted on returning home.[128]

There were others who did not continue the voyage with Drake. Years after the expedition was over Peter Carder turned up in England, claiming to be the survivor of a group of eight men from the expedition who had been in a pinnace in the strait when a storm came up that separated them from the ship and drove them ashore.[129] Very likely Carder and his companions were in one of the three pinnaces lost by Drake in the course of his voyage around South America, though one writer has suggested that

Carder was really in one of Wynter's pinnaces and was lost off the coast of Brazil during Wynter's return to England.[130]

None of this is very certain. The *Marigold,* the *Elizabeth,* and the several pinnaces could have been lost in a storm, but it is also possible that they simply took advantage of the storm to get away from a tyrannical commander. And although some have persisted in calling John Wynter a deserter, there is good reason to think it was the other way around.[131] Drake may have abandoned the other ships because he wanted to rid himself of potential troublemakers.[132] Certainly, he appears to have made no effort to locate the missing ships, even though he passed within easy sailing distance of the mouth of the strait, where Wynter waited for him.[133]

Whatever happened to the others, it is clear that the storm blew Drake's ship far to the south, though it is difficult to know exactly how far. Nuño de Silva said the *Pelican* reached 57° and anchored in the cove of a small island.[134] John Drake said that they sailed as far as 56° south latitude, taking refuge "at a very good island where they took on water and wood and some herbs that they knew about."[135] Neither Silva nor John Drake seems to have thought they had reached any point of unusual geographical interest. It was very different in England after John Wynter arrived home.

Working with data supplied by Wynter, and no doubt reviewing information from the earlier Spanish expeditions to the Strait of Magellan, the English government began to circulate the story that Wynter had returned home without passing through the strait again.[136] Using a double agent as an intermediary, this information, or misinformation, was passed to the Spanish ambassador in London, Bernardino de Mendoza. Two years later, when Drake arrived home, the official story was changed. This time, Drake was the man who had sailed south of the continent into the open sea, bypassing the strait altogether.[137]

As time passed the story took on a certain permanence. During the 1590s, when Richard Hawkins was a captive in Spain, he was interviewed by the chronicler Antonio de Herrera, particularly about his voyage of 1593. According to the story that Herrera later published, Hawkins sailed into the Strait of Magellan and saw that there were only islands to the south. He then turned south through these islands, navigating clear to 56°

south latitude, where he determined that there were no more islands, only open sea. Hawkins then retraced his route through the islands and resumed his passage through the strait. In recounting the brief Hawkins journey, Herrera noted that Francis Drake had done much the same thing in 1579, sailing first through the strait, then "rounding the archipelago" from the Pacific to the Atlantic and back again.[138]

Herrera's statement that Drake had sailed around the tip of South America from the Pacific to the Atlantic is probably based on the story that the English government circulated in 1579, after John Wynter returned home.[139] Reconstructing this earlier version of the story, it appears that all three of Drake's ships had first passed through the Strait of Magellan and then sailed south to the tip of Tierra del Fuego. Wynter then sailed back north without ever entering the strait again. The queen was said to have a map of the route, but Mendoza was not shown one or allowed to know the latitudes involved. His information came from an agent who claimed to have seen the map and to have heard the story from officials who had it first from Wynter and later from Drake himself.[140]

Obviously, this was a story for foreign consumption and not for good English seamen who wanted to find their way into the Pacific Ocean. Just as obviously, the whole story was fiction. The seamen who were with Drake on the *Pelican* were totally unaware of any such discovery, at least in the years immediately following their return. John Drake, William Hawkins, and two pilots named Thomas Blacollar and Thomas Hood all sailed on the *Pelican* during this voyage. In 1582 all four went with Edward Fenton on another voyage to the straits. When Fenton asked their opinions about avoiding the new Spanish fortifications in the strait, they told him there was only one alternative route, the Cape of Good Hope.[141] They had seen no cape south of the Strait of Magellan, and in fact they did not have a clear idea about the location of the various islands they had seen in the archipelago. All they knew was that there were "certain gaps in the land and long recesses in the sea."[142]

The misinformation came, as Madox had guessed, from Drake himself, who was willing to spread confusion regarding the exact route of his voyage, even though it meant misleading other English sailors. In 1582 Drake furnished the Fenton Expedition with an extremely detailed map of the strait. The actual map is not now available, but the information it contained was so precise that the men on the expedition refused to believe that Drake could have seen the places shown on his map. His voyage through the strait, they knew, had taken only about two weeks, and most of that time had been spent battling contrary winds and stormy seas. The Reverend Richard Madox, who was with Fenton, concluded that Drake had simply lied about the whole thing. "I am convinced that that Drake of ours either found some kind of draft among the Portuguese or Spaniards and thus put forth their little commentaries as his own or I believe him to be a man who has cast off all shame and dared boldly to determine things unknown and to present them to her majesty as explored and already claimed. Either of these things should be reproved."[143] In order to understand how the story developed, it is necessary to look at the Drake maps and manuscripts produced in England at this time and to compare them with similar materials from Spanish sources.

During the sixteenth century Spanish navigators and cosmographers amassed a surprising body of information about the straits region, and, following their usual practice, transferred this information into the derroteros carried by pilots of Spanish ships. Antonio de Pigafetta, reporting the results of the Magellan expedition, said that it was possible to see a body of water between some of the islands south of the strait. Even so, he did not explore the area, and it was unclear to him whether there was a land mass or open sea beyond this group of islands.[144]

This uncertainty was soon dispelled. Andrés de Urdaneta, reporting on the discoveries of the Loaysa expedition of 1525, said that one of the ships had gone down the Atlantic coast beyond the mouth of the strait, following the coastline clear to the open sea: "The other caravel of Francisco Doçes sailed beyond the strait, following the coast south to fifty-five degrees, and they said later that they turned back at what appeared to them to be the end of the land."[145]

A few years later Francisco de Camargo, brother of the bishop of Plasencia, led another expedition to the strait. With one of his ships Camargo reached the Pacific Ocean, then sailed south to 56°. Reports from these expeditions enabled the royal chartmaker Alonzo de Santa Cruz to state confidently that Tierra del Fuego "is certainly an island." More than this, he managed to describe the region on the Pacific side with considerable accuracy as "two very large islands alongside an archipelago of very small islands." Santa Cruz also said there was no evidence for the imaginary southern continent shown on the maps of Oronce Finé and other European cosmographers.[146]

Challenged, no doubt, by the stunning achievements of their early explorers and mapmakers, the Spanish government continued to investigate the Strait of Magellan. Two new expeditions went to the strait in the 1550s, making their approach from the west. The report from the first expedition seems to have been lost during the Chilean Indian revolt of 1554, but the reports from the second expedition were sent to Seville in 1559, adding considerably to Spanish knowledge of the numerous islands in the archipelago.[147] Thus by 1560 the Spanish cosmographers had a fair grasp of the geography of the Strait of Magellan and Tierra del Fuego, even though no one had yet reported rounding the cape. Because of this, official Spanish charts (the *padrón real*) depicted Tierra del Fuego as an archipelago, with a large island and an open coastline on the south and east and smaller islands on the west. The imaginary southern continent favored by other European mapmakers did not appear on official Spanish maps.[148]

Richard Madox no doubt had it right. Working with information from the Spanish maps and derroteros that circulated through Europe, Drake was able to infer the existence of a free passage between the Atlantic and Pacific Oceans, even though he had not made the passage and did not understand the true geography of Tierra del Fuego.[149] Drake's imaginary geography was depicted on a map that he gave to the queen upon his return to England. Kept secret for some years, by 1625 the map was hanging "in His Majesties Gallerie at White Hall, neere the Privie Chamber."[150] As with every other original account of the voyage in English, this map is now unknown, but a number of cartographers were allowed to make copies, and from these it is possible to see what Drake had in mind. Moreover, it is possible to compare Drake's geographical inferences with others made from Spanish data.

All of the copies of Drake's map depict a scattering of tiny islands at the southern tip of South America, including an island named Elizabeth, in one language or another. This island is not named in any of the accounts known to date from the time of the voyage, and it must be considered as an afterthought, something that Drake later wished he had done. The only early reference is in the Fletcher manuscript, which now exists only in a heavily edited version.[151]

One of the earliest maps based on the Drake map is the small manuscript sheet now called the Drake-Mellon map. Although this map is undated, it shows the Drake voyage around the world, plus a voyage in 1585–86 to the West Indies. Thus the Drake-Mellon map is from the period 1586–87 or later.[152]

Other contemporary copies of the Drake map were printed. These include a map done by Nicola van Sype that shows much of the same geographical detail as the Drake-Mellon manuscript map. Because the van Sype map includes a small portrait of Drake at age forty-two, the map was prepared about 1582 or later.[153] The van Sype map was also published in a French edition, probably done about the same time.[154]

Two additional printed maps with somewhat similar depictions of the Strait of Magellan and Tierra del Fuego were published in 1587 and 1589. The first was engraved by Philipp Gaulle and appeared in an edition of Peter Martyr's *De Orbe Novo,* published by Richard Hakluyt while he was in Paris.[155] The second is a small world map engraved by Jodocus Hondius in 1589.[156]

Perhaps the most famous of the various copies of the "secret" Drake map is the one printed by Hondius in Amsterdam in 1595 or 1596. Various libraries have copies of the map, but the one most frequently reproduced is in the British Library. Because this copy has a Dutch broadside text pasted around three edges, the map is often called the Drake Broadside map. The map contains no publication information, but a study of the typefaces used on the map and in the broadside makes it possible to date both with a fair degree of certainty.[157]

All these maps employ an entirely imaginary depiction of the islands at the Strait of Magellan. One map that does not is the manuscript atlas drawn by Joan Martines in 1591. Apparently in response to the numerous stories circulated by the English government, Martines did his own research and produced a map that shows Tierra del Fuego with a fair degree of accuracy but in a manner completely different from the English maps. The most significant difference is the legend written in the open sea below this large island: "Canal descubierto por nugno de Silva piloto portugues de fran[cis]co drache."[158] Evidently Martines used information from reports of Nuño de Silva, as well as information from the earlier Spanish voyages to the strait.[159]

The tale of Drake's having doubled the southern tip of the continent was just one of many stories about the voyage circulated by English officials to annoy and confuse their adversaries in Spain. The efforts met with a good deal of success. In August 1579, shortly after being informed of John Wynter's supposed route home, the Spanish government began an official inquiry to determine whether such a voyage could really have taken place or not. The immediate answer was maybe.[160] Investigations continued into the next few decades.

Spanish mapmakers were not alone in doubting the truth of the English claim. Other European cartographers held the same opinion, and most of them refused to believe that Drake had seen the cape or the other places that he claimed to have discovered. The German cartographer Gerard Mercator complained to his Dutch counterpart that the English were deliberately "concealing the course followed" by Drake and "putting out differing accounts of the route taken and the areas visited."[161] A French observer noted that it was impossible to give credence to Drake's claims because the English government would not produce records of the voyage.[162]

To be sure, the early accounts of the voyage published in England mentioned no such discovery. The first such publication appeared in 1625, when Drake's nephew, also named Francis, published his book entitled *The World Encompassed by Sir Francis Drake*. As the title page asserts, the small volume was "carefully collected out of the notes of Master Francis Fletcher Preacher in this imployment and divers others in the same." For more than a century this remained the major English source for the voyage, but after the middle eighteenth century a number of manuscripts became available, including one that bore the name of Fletcher himself. Since its discovery, the manuscript has been considered to be the set of "notes" made by Fletcher that served as the basis for the *World Encompassed*. Cataloged as Sloane No. 61, the manuscript is not an original document but a copy made in 1677 by London apothecary, John Conyers.

The Fletcher manuscript is a strange document of forty-three pages. It is not a set of notes but a rambling narrative. There are illustrations to accompany the text, including a crude map of the straits alongside a story about reaching the southernmost part of the world. Including about four pages of text, this is the longest account of the supposed discovery that is now available. Some historians, following the lead of Corbett, treat the manuscript as though it were in the original form.[163] Others, following Wagner, assume that the original Fletcher manuscript has been heavily edited.[164] In fact, Wagner was of the opinion that the manuscript was not completed very long before the publication of the *World Encompassed* in 1628.[165] Since the Fletcher manuscript is apparently the only firsthand account of the discovery, it is necessary to look at the document more closely.

Several pieces of internal evidence contain clues about the date of composition. A reference to the voyage of Thomas Cavendish has been assumed to date from about 1588 or shortly thereafter, when Cavendish returned from his own voyage around the world. A close reading of the text, though, shows that the reference in the Fletcher manuscript is much later. The manuscript refers to a Latin legend on the 1595 Hondius broadside map. Translated into English, the legend reads: "Francis Drake mapped these islands at Magellan Strait, but Thomas Cavendish and all Spaniards deny it, affirming that there is nothing but a strait, and it is possible that Drake, driven by tempests from his course did not make regular observations, as he lost two ships here."[166]

The Fletcher manuscript contains a direct response to this assertion: "Toucheing Mr Candish a Gentileman worthy of immortall fame for his Rare Enterprisre in Travailes, I say littel: onely this I observe that he was able to say no more either to proove that that terra australis is a continent or that the passag a streite: then Magilanus himselfe as by the line of his course in the mapp may appeare leadeing imediatly from the Passage by

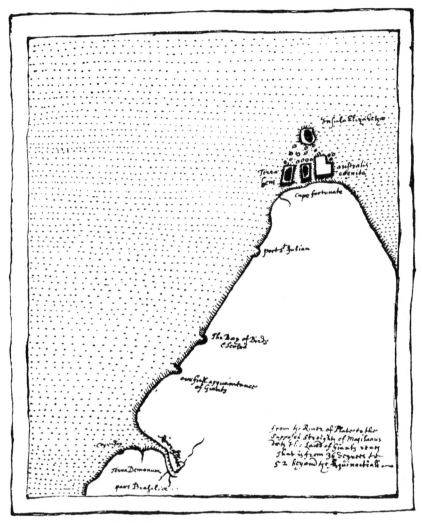

Map of the Strait of Magellan, said to have been copied in 1677 by John Conyers from an original drawing made by Francis Fletcher. In this map south is at the top. Reprinted from BL Sloane MS 61, fol. 35v.

the South cape of america towards the line without anny touch of anny point further to the Southward to make anny proofe or tryall."[167] In other words, one need only look at the Hondius broadside map to see that Mr. Cavendish did not sail south of the strait and therefore could not make a definite judgment about the accuracy of Drake's claim.

It is not necessary to think that the Reverend Francis Fletcher was attempting to deceive us. As David Beers Quinn says, "it is highly probable, indeed almost certain," that Drake seized the journals or notes of Fletcher and others, either just before or just after the ship returned to England. Sections of the journal such as this one are no doubt later additions to Fletcher's original brief notations.[168] Some of the amendments are obvious. For instance, the Fletcher manuscript now contains several pages describing the native people of the Strait of Magellan. All of this was plagiarized from Pigafetta's story of the Magellan expedition.[169] In fact, the Pigafetta account was very likely well known by members of the expedition. Nuño de Silva referred to three books of navigation that Drake had brought with him, "one in French, one in English, and the other was the discovery of Magellan."[170] Even if we did not know the source, it is clear that Fletcher himself would not have described seeing giants there, for the other members of the expedition were familiar with Pigafetta's story and thought it was ludicrous.[171] Perhaps the most curious connection between the Fletcher manuscript and the Pigafetta story is the way in which the account of the trial of Thomas Doughty parallels the trial and execution of Magellan's mutineers.

Of more importance for the present discussion is the Fletcher manuscript's first-person account of the author's experiences on this southernmost island in the hemisphere: "My selfe being landed did with my Boy travill to the Southermost point of the Iland to the Sea one that Syde. Where I found that Iland to be more Southerly three partes of a degree then anny of the Rest of the Ilands. Where having Sett up an end of Stone of som biggnes & with such tooles as I hadd of purpose ever about mee when I went one shoare, had engraven her majestyes name, her Kingdom, the yeare of Christ & and the day of the moneth."[172] In another place the Fletcher manuscript called this place Elizabeth Island. Obviously, there was a conflict with the island of the same name in the strait. The conflict was resolved in the *World Encompassed* by saying that Drake decided to refer to all the islands south of the strait as Elizabethides.[173]

The account in the Fletcher manuscript is so similar to the one related by Richard Hawkins in his 1622 memoir, and indeed to the story told by

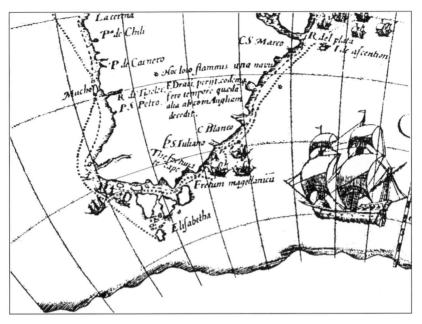

*Map of the routes of Drake and Cavendish through the Strait of Magellan
(detail; some features removed). Reprinted from* Vera Totius Expeditionis Nauticae,
(Amsterdam: Cornelis Claesz, c. 1596).

John Wynter, that one version evidently depended upon the other. Here is
what Hawkins said:

> Francis Drake told mee, that having shot the Straits, a
> storme took him first at North-west, and after vered
> about to the South-west, which continued with him
> many dayes with that extremitie, that he could not open
> any sayle, and that at the end of the storme, he found
> himselfe in fiftie degrees, which was sufficient testimony
> and proofe, that he was beaten round about the Straits,
> for the least height of the Straits is fiftie two degrees and
> fiftie minutes; in which stand the two entrances or
> mouthes. And moreover, hee said, that standing about,
> when the winde changed, hee was not well able to dou-
> ble the Southernmost Iland, and so anchored under the

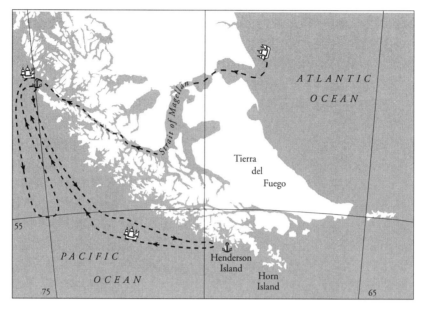

Drake's route south of the Strait of Magellan (conjecture)

lee of it; and going ashoare, carried a Compasse with
him, and seeking out the Southernmost part of the
Iland, cast himselfe downe upon the uttermost point
groveling, and so reached out his bodie over it. Presently
he imbarked, and then recounted unto his people, that
he had beene upon the Southernmost knowne Land in
the World, and more further to the Southwards upon it,
then any of them, yea, or any man as yet knowne.[174]

The only way to make much sense of this section of the Fletcher manuscript is to take it as a draft copy of the *World Encompassed* rather than a
heavily edited version of Francis Fletcher's original journal. With this understanding, it is possible to conclude that Francis Drake and not Francis
Fletcher is intended to be the narrator. In this way the Fletcher story about
reaching the point farthest south on this island can be seen as an early draft
of the story, one that was discarded along with many other fanciful sections
of the manuscript before the *World Encompassed* went to press in 1628.

The same portion of the Fletcher manuscript contains evidence that dates it at about 1619 or later. In 1616 Jacob Le Maire and Willem Schouten van Hoorn successfully navigated the cape at the tip of South America and named it Von Horn. The results of the voyage were first published in Dutch in 1618, quickly followed by editions in other languages, including an English version that appeared the following year.[175] No doubt this first successful voyage around Cape Horn was the reason for the insertion of a long and rambling section in Fletcher's text, insisting that Francis Drake had been the first to sail around the southern end of the continent.[176]

There is no reason to doubt that Drake reached an island at 55° south latitude, just as other navigators had done before him.[177] There is no reason to doubt that he thought there might be open sea beyond this point. Spanish navigators had reported this possibility. But John Drake, William Hawkins, Thomas Blacollar, and Thomas Hood, who were with Drake on the *Pelican,* all said that they had not seen such an open sea.[178] And if they had not seen it, Francis Drake did not see it.

Wagner went to some pains to determine exactly which island Drake might have reached. His conclusion was that Drake reached Henderson Island, north and considerably west of the Cape Horn Islands. Cape Horn, as Wagner indicates, is a mountain fourteen hundred feet high and not at all like the island described by Hawkins or by the editor of the Fletcher manuscript. If, as seems likely, Drake failed to discover the cape at the tip of South America, he did make an important contribution. He started a widespread discussion of information that had been gathered by earlier Spanish expeditions, and he popularized the idea that there might be an open channel south of Tierra del Fuego. Wagner put it in proper perspective when he said that by sailing around Cape Horn from the Atlantic to the Pacific, Schouten and Le Maire had shown that "Drake's theory that the seas were one" was correct.[179]

This claim of important geographical discovery is one of the earliest examples of a remarkable phenomenon noted by E. G. R. Taylor: the way in which "the story of the Drake voyage has been edited and worked up for publication."[180] These inflated claims, by the English government in the sixteenth century and by some Drake fans today, obscure Drake's real character and his place in history. He was a pirate, and a good one, largely because he was untroubled by a conscience that in most men would murmur against theft or murder.

Drake also began to display an unusual quality of leadership. He found that he could manipulate the men who served with him, even when they neither liked nor trusted him. He learned how to make piracy an act of patriotism, subverting the consciences of officers and men alike. Ignoring the command structure, Drake discovered that it could be useful to tell the men in the lower ranks that their services were as valuable as the services of the officers. The officers might grumble, but they would follow him anyway. Drake's feud with Doughty and the quasi-judicial murder of this former friend provided his most stunning revelation. Entirely by accident, Drake began to understand that a skillful commander could use foul language, ridicule, humiliation, and even death to isolate the men who opposed him, and no one would dare to defend his victims.

6

Cape Horn to Guatulco

SAILING NORTH ONCE MORE ON 28 October, Francis Drake and the crew of his ship left the Strait of Magellan and the southern islands behind. There were no more than eighty men left in Drake's crew when he started the voyage northward in the Pacific.[1] Presumably these were the most loyal and dependable of the 170 or so who started the trip. Most of the enormous loss of crew came at the Strait of Magellan, though some had perished earlier. As we have seen, a cabin boy washed overboard during the first few days out of Plymouth. John Fry was captured at the island of Mogador and presumably was never ransomed. Robert Winterhey and a seaman named Oliver were killed in a battle with Indians at Port Saint Julian. John Doughty was executed in the same place. This accounts for a half-dozen men, and probably a dozen others died, deserted, or were otherwise lost, if we can credit John Wynter's account. Wynter said that there were 140 men in the fleet on 20 August.[2] Although this total reflects a significant loss, it appears that the real casualties came in the Strait of Magellan.

According to Nuño de Silva, "Many men died from the cold during the passage through the strait."[3] This seems to be a blanket statement intended to cover losses from hunger and disease. With little to eat for the next few weeks except penguin meat, the men all began to show symptoms of scurvy.[4] John Drake said that when they were in port for wood and water at an island in 54° south latitude, they began to gather plants to cook and eat. One of the plants, he said, "was an herb that Captain Francis had heard described as medicinal." They squeezed the juice from the leaves of this plant, mixed it with wine, and gave it to the sick men to drink.

"Nearly everyone was sick with swollen legs and gums, but all recovered, except two men who died later."[5]

The biggest losses came with the disappearance of entire ships with their crews. On 30 September the *Marigold* seems to have run aground. It carried a crew of perhaps twenty men, and though some may eventually have reached England, they were all lost so far as the expedition was concerned. Scarcely a week later, on 8 October, the *Elizabeth* and the *Pelican* were separated in a storm. Captain John Wynter eventually managed to bring the *Elizabeth* back to England with its crew of fifty, but this group was also lost to Drake. A pinnace carrying eight men disappeared somewhere in the strait. Peter Carder and possibly one or more other survivors from this little vessel reached England several years later after numerous harrowing adventures. Two other pinnaces may also have been lost, accounting for perhaps an additional sixteen men. Thus the passage through the Strait of Magellan cost Drake at least eighty souls, perhaps more.

On 30 October the *Pelican* stopped at an island near the mouth of the strait, lowered the sails, and sent a boatload of men ashore. Again they harvested a supply of penguin and seal meat. On 1 November 1578 the ship left the harbor. For a few days they sailed to the northwest, then for another day or two to the northeast. For another week they sailed northwest again, and then northeast, still trying to locate the coast. Finally, they changed to a northward course and on 25 November, after another week, they reached the island of Mocha.[6]

This was the first landfall in nearly a month, and the first opportunity to search for firewood, water, and fresh food. It was also the gateway to La Imperial, the major gold-mining city of Chile. It was said that each Indian laborer could take an ounce or two of gold every month from the gold-bearing sands of the Madre de Dios and other rich mines. The Spanish landlords or *encomenderos* had three hundred thousand such laborers, who spent most of their lives resisting forced labor. For this reason, the place was known as a *tierra de guerra* — land of war.[7]

Had Drake known the reputation of the place, he might have sailed on. Instead, he anchored in the harbor, noting that the island was heavily populated with Indians.[8] Lowering the ship's boat, Drake took a party of

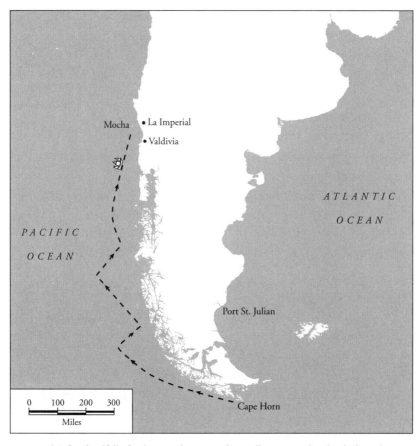

Drake's first landfall after leaving the Strait of Magellan was at the island of Mocha.

eleven bowmen and harquebusiers ashore, where he traded with a few of the Indians, obtaining shellfish and two Spanish sheep. The next day, Drake took the same party ashore again, hoping to get wood and fresh water. He must have expected trouble, for only two men went ashore, while the other ten waited in the boat. Rolling their barrels up to the watering place, the two seamen walked directly into an ambush. The battle was brief but furious. The Indians seized the two seamen, and when Drake and the soldiers came to the rescue, they, too, were attacked with stones and arrows. Drake received two arrow wounds, one just under the right eye and another in the head.[9] All of the other men were wounded as well. For a time it seemed that no one would escape, but the remaining men finally pushed their boat away from the shore. Even while Drake's men tried to row away, the Indians pressed their attack, grabbing the oars out of the hands of two of the oarsmen.[10] One or two of the wounded crewmen later died.[11] Drake never discovered what happened to the two who were taken captive, though it was presumed they were also killed.[12]

Silva located this island in 39° south, exactly the latitude given in the Spanish derroteros. Silva's own astrolabe had been taken aboard Drake's ship when he was captured. As Drake's chief pilot, Silva certainly knew how to use the astrolabe, and he was surely allowed to use it from time to time.[13] Other seamen may have been allowed to use it to make their own observations, but it seems likely that the latitudes given in most of the accounts were written after Drake acquired Spanish derroteros of the Pacific ports. In fact, the same caveat applies to many of Silva's latitudes, including the one for Mocha. For these reasons it seems pointless to list or compare the various latitude estimates in the accounts of the voyage along the Pacific coast.[14] The best that can be said of all sixteenth-century latitude estimates is that they were often extremely accurate for places close to the equator and became progressively less accurate nearer the poles. Errors of a degree or so could be expected in the latitude of Mocha, as much as two degrees at Cape Horn.

Having been mauled so badly by the Indians, Drake and his men were unable to entertain any thought of a raid on La Imperial or the nearby port city of Valdivia. Instead, they sailed north for several days, nursing their wounds, and finally anchoring in an unnamed bay well to the north of Valparaiso, possibly Quintero. The latter place was the seaport for the Chilean capital, Santiago. It was a wonderful choice for a pirate raid, as the gold mines at Santiago were even richer than those at Valdivia.[15] But the harbor was empty, except for some Indians fishing in a canoe. One of the Indians, a man named Felipe, could speak Spanish. Asked whether there might be some other ship nearby, Felipe said there was indeed, in the port of Valparaiso.

As it turned out, Valparaiso was quite a small harbor, fit to shelter only a few ships at one time.[16] The English offered to pay Felipe if he would guide them there, and Felipe agreed.[17] It is not clear who carried on this

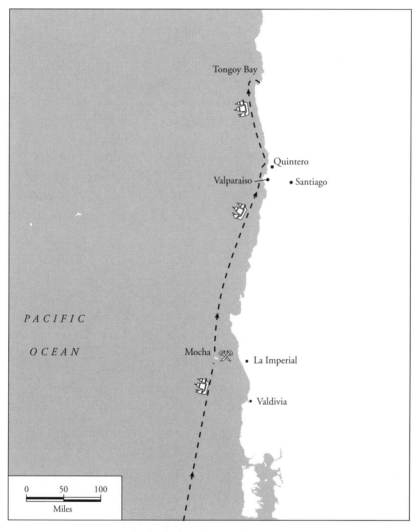

Drake's raids along the central coast of Chile

conversation. Some of Drake's men could speak Spanish, including Silva and one of Drake's black servants, both of whom spoke English as well. There is less certainty about Drake's own ability with the language. He certainly knew some words and phrases, and he liked to use them with Spanish prisoners. But he also employed an interpreter for important matters and for conversations of any length.[18]

It was completely dark by the time the ship reached the harbor at Valparaiso, on 5 December 1578. Drake took his ship in close enough to exchange greetings and convinced the Spanish crew that they were countrymen.[19] The Spanish ship, called *La Capitana,* had served as the flagship in the expedition of Pedro Sarmiento de Gamboa to the Solomon Islands a decade earlier.[20] By this time it was old and probably in poor condition, for the owner used it only to take cargo up and down the coast. The crew consisted of five or ten Spanish sailors and two or three black slaves.[21] Drake dispatched a party of eighteen men, armed, but probably concealing their weapons. The sailors on *La Capitana* greeted them as friends, with a drumroll and an open cask of wine.[22] They were soon disabused of their error.

Tom Moone, the seaman who had sailed with Drake on the earlier voyage to Nombre de Dios, leaped aboard *La Capitana* and struck the pilot in the face. "Abajo, Perro!" he said—"Get below, you dog." All of the Spanish crew was locked away below deck, except for one man who jumped overboard and swam ashore.[23] Drake then boarded the ship and inspected the cargo. There was gold, of course, 24,000 pesos, but there was other cargo, as well, including wine and a quantity of sawed lumber. Leaving a guard on the ship, Drake went ashore with two boatloads of men. All the inhabitants of the town had fled, so the men broke open some warehouses and helped themselves to the wine and food stored there.[24] Other men found a little chapel, from which they stole a chalice, some cruets, vestments of damask, a missal, and the sanctuary bell. All these items Drake presented to the chaplain, Fletcher.[25] It was a joke, of course. Fletcher would not use such Popish paraphernalia, and it was all promptly destroyed.[26]

Of all the booty Drake and his crew managed to seize at Valparaiso, the most valuable was the derrotero of the pilot and master Juan Griego. This document was a set of charts and sailing instructions for all the ports on the coast, and Drake was able to use it for the rest of the journey, perhaps having it translated as he did the derrotero of Nuño de Silva.[27] According to Silva, this document was so valuable that Drake intended to present it as a gift to the queen.[28] He also pressed Griego into service as his own pilot, for Silva was not familiar with the Pacific ports. Loading his loot onto *La Capitana,* Drake sent all but two of the Spanish seamen ashore and placed a crew of his own sailors aboard.[29] With two ships, Drake had a fleet once more. He sailed out of Valparaiso and back to Quintero Bay, where he deposited the Indian guide, Felipe.[30]

Once again Drake was in his element. He was an expert at capturing merchant vessels and looting defenseless towns. His first raid was a total success. The 24,000 pesos of gold was apparently only the amount listed on the official register, from which the king's fifth would be calculated. Unregistered gold may have brought the total to 200,000 pesos, the amount of the Spanish damage claim registered in London in 1580.[31] One man who was on the voyage said that the gold was packed in three large chests, covered with leather and bound with iron. The fourth and largest chest, no doubt contraband, was found hidden under the helmsman's cabin.[32] Of more immediate interest to the sailors was the huge store of looted wine, such a great quantity that everyone was gratified a few weeks later when several barrels of tar were used to waterproof the decks and hull, freeing deck room for wine storage. Most notably, if the tone of the narratives is any guide, Drake became his usual boisterous self. If he had really deserted the luckless *Elizabeth* and *Marigold* at the straits, he now began to think of looking for them along the Pacific shore.[33]

Taking his little fleet a short distance north, Drake hugged the coastline for a few days. The first stop came on 11 December at Tongoy Bay, in about 31°. It was here that Nuño de Silva said that they had arranged to meet the *Elizabeth* and *Marigold* if they became separated.[34] Firewood and fresh water were always in short supply on sailing vessels. Drake sent a party ashore on 12 December to look for water and wood. The seamen found salt pans, where the local people made salt from seawater, but there was no drinking water. Moving on to the north, the ships stopped again in the bay at La Herradura, where another party went ashore. Working quickly, they managed to capture some of the pigs that ranged loose along the bay, and they also took on a few jugs of water. Suddenly, someone heard a gunshot. A lookout sent by Drake to the crow's nest soon spotted a party of fifty or so horsemen on the land, apparently citizens of the nearby town of La Serena coming in search of Drake's raiders. Drake quickly gave the signal for

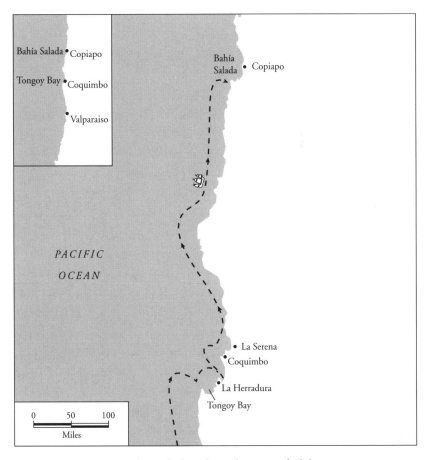

Drake's raids along the northern coast of Chile

the shore party to return, but one man failed to make it. The Spanish harquebusiers shot him as he tried to defend his comrades, who were clambering over the rocks and into the boat.[35] Seeing that the man was dead,
the Spanish soldiers waded into the surf and retrieved the body. They cut
off the head and carried it away on a pike. Once the Spanish were gone,
Drake sent another party ashore to bury the headless corpse. Thereupon
some of the Spaniards returned to the beach, and Drake decided once again
to look for a more agreeable port.[36]

Leaving the bay at night on the twentieth, Drake took his ships north
again, intending to stop at the town of Coquimbo on the other side of the

peninsula for another try at raiding. In the darkness his flagship nearly ran aground on a reef north of the bay. While maneuvering the ship out of this spot, his fleet passed beyond the entrance to Coquimbo, and Drake missed another chance at a raid on a rich Spanish port.[37] He tried next day to moor his ships in one of the Islas de Pajaros, north of the bay of Coquimbo. Here a shore party managed to gather a good supply of birds, but the anchors dragged, and Drake had to let the wind carry the ships farther north.[38] On 22 December they finally found the good harbor that they had been seeking, Bahía Salada on the desert coast of Chile. The whole countryside was dry and uninhabited, an ideal place to hide from the angry Spanish citizenry and to careen the flagship. On the other hand, there was little drinking water, and no one dared to go inland in search of it.[39]

Intending to stay for a refit in Bahía Salada, Drake first ordered the crew to take out of the hold a pinnace that had been cut to size in England and stored disassembled aboard the *Pelican-Golden Hind*.[40] Within two weeks, the carpenters had the pinnace ready for caulking. By 9 January the sails had been cut and sewn; a small bronze gun was placed in the bow, and the pinnace was launched.[41] While this was going on, Drake selected a crew of fifteen men for the launch, with Juan Griego as pilot. Sailing south, he took the new vessel on a trial run, intending to fill the water barrels and to look for some sign of the *Elizabeth* and the *Marigold*.[42] He was gone for two days but found no trace of the other ships. Worse, he was unable to go ashore anywhere because of hostile Indians all along the coast.[43]

While Drake was gone, the seamen emptied the flagship so that they could get at the guns stored beneath the ballast stones. Drake arrived just as this work was completed and decided that this would be a fine opportunity to careen the ship on the beach and repair the hull, which leaked badly.[44] An unballasted ship is very hard to handle, and at one point the men lost control and nearly capsized the ship. Somehow they managed to secure the tackle to the mainmast and heel the ship over on its side. It took another week to clean the hull and to cover the decks and the sides with the usual mixture of grease, sulfur, and tar.[45]

While the work continued, Drake's men were nearly defenseless, and during the first days most of the men stayed on board. One day two

Spanish horsemen fired on the camp where the pinnace was under construction, and a short time later a group of Indian "spies" appeared.[46] But there was no attack, and Drake was able to complete work on his ship. The flagship became a floating artillery battery. The crew of the *Pelican* served eighteen guns, three of bronze, and the rest of cast iron.[47] Fourteen guns were placed at gun ports below deck, seven on each side. The rest were mounted above deck, two large cast iron guns in the poop, and two smaller guns in the bow.[48] There was nothing else like it on the Pacific coast.

Leaving Bahía Salada on Monday, 19 January 1579, Drake sailed north once more, a pirate captain who had armed himself, while his prey sat by and watched. Perhaps they could do nothing. In the entire province there were only eleven Spanish towns, with an average of a hundred and fifty Spanish settlers in each place. The nearby town of Copiapo was nearly deserted, and there were fewer than a hundred Indians living in the vicinity. The larger towns and the majority of the people were located in the salubrious southern part of Chile and had almost no overland contact with the northern region. Even there most of the Indians were hostile, and an armed group of settlers heading north to attack Drake's camp might well have found itself fighting Indians rather than Englishmen.[49] Beyond this, the ship of Juan Griego seems to have been the only Spanish vessel in the region. It was certainly the only one that Drake's fleet encountered. Even so, the Spanish ought to have been able to manage more than two harquebus shots from horseback at the pirates in a month.

So inconsequential was the Puerto de Copiapo that Drake's ships passed the town without seeing it, sailing on to a small island, where they found a few Indian fishermen.[50] After distributing some gifts, Drake and his men learned that there was a watering place ashore. Looking the next day, they discerned that the spring was a mile or more from the beach, so they decided to sail on.[51] The new pinnace had begun to leak, and a few days later, when they finally found a good watering place, they stayed for two days, putting more pitch on both the pinnace and the ship's boat.[52] The place where they stopped was called Morro de Jorje. In a nearby Indian village, called Morro Moreno, Drake's seamen found a supply of dried fish, already packed into bundles. When they departed the next day, the En-

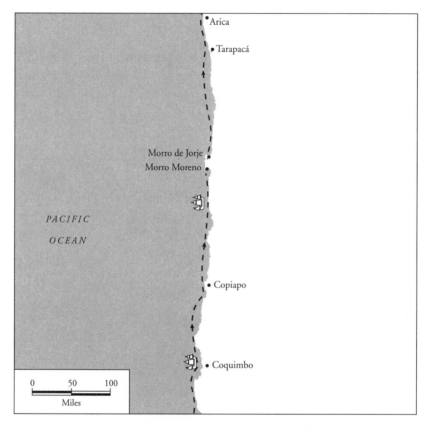

Drake's raids on the desert ports of northern Chile

glish pirates took half the village's fish, along with three of the fishermen. Whether they paid for the fish is unclear. The pilot Juan Griego seemed to think they did. Nuño de Silva and John Drake thought they did not.[53] In any case, one or all of the Indian captives were released about fifty miles up the coast, near a place called Compisa or Paquiza.[54]

On Monday, 2 February 1579, Drake and his seamen met the first seagoing vessel they had seen in nearly two months. It was a fishing boat, crewed by four Indians, who were returning to port with a full load of fish. Taking the Indian fishermen captive and tying their boat to the bow of *La Capitana,* Drake sailed onward. During the night, however, the Indians who remained in the boat quietly untied their vessel and drifted silently away.[55]

Perhaps Drake had second thoughts about the fishermen and allowed them to escape.

In any case, he kept one of the Indian fishermen on the flagship to guide his ships to the next watering place. This was a little bay about a hundred miles farther north, called Puerto de Tarapacá. The bay was formed by an island about four miles from shore that sheltered the port. Stopping some distance out in the bay, Drake took a party ashore in the pinnace. Somehow, perhaps with Spanish banners or Spanish conversation, he managed to make the local people think that his ships were Spanish. The two Spaniards in Tarapacá were taken by surprise, and Drake quickly made them his prisoners. One of the men was a courier who had just arrived from Potosí. His seven pack llamas carried silver bars worth three thousand pesos. In Tarapacá, Drake also seized a large quantity of dried beef *charqui* and some chickens, adding considerable variety to the fish diet that his men had endured for several weeks.[56]

Taking one of the Spanish prisoners as a guide, Drake sailed on to the next port, Arica, where he expected to find more booty. He was not disappointed. Arriving there on 5 February, Drake found two ships and three fishing boats in the harbor. One of the ships belonged to a merchant named Felipe Corso and carried thirty or forty bars of silver.[57] The second ship, belonging to Jorje Díaz, carried only clothing from Castile and wine. Drake took the silver and the wine. The second ship was then burned, with the clothing in it. The burning, according to John Drake, was done without Drake's knowledge, perhaps by a drunken seaman taking a lamp into the hold to look for more wine.[58]

During the night the gunners on Drake's flagship fired now and then at the town, while other seamen played music and enjoyed the wine that they had found.[59] The next day Drake ordered men into two of the boats he had seized, intending to go ashore and look for more booty. However, the sailors had scarcely seated themselves in the boats when they saw a group of men—perhaps sixty horsemen, harquebusiers, and archers—lined up on shore and ready for a fight. Faced with this determined opposition, Drake deceed to leave Arica for other, richer places.[60] One of the Spanish sailors whom Drake had taken captive in Santiago was loaded into one of the fishing boats, along with the man taken prisoner at Tarapacá. These men Drake released in the outer harbor, but he kept Nicolas Jorje and a black slave, both of whom had been aboard the ship of Felipe Corso.[61] Then he sailed away with a fleet newly enlarged to three ships.[62]

Under cover of darkness, the men in the fishing boat sailed out to give warning to the ports in the north.[63] Drake had heard that there was a ship loaded with silver in Puerto de Chule, the port for the city of Arequipa.[64] For some reason he could not get much speed from his ships, and the Spanish fishing boat reached Chule before he did.[65] Unaware of this and exasperated with the slow sailing of his fleet, Drake put a party of armed men aboard the pinnace and sent it ahead to Puerto de Chule. When this vessel arrived in the harbor at Chule on 9 February, the men found the treasure ship, empty.[66] It was wet above the waterline, indicating that a cargo had just been unloaded. People on shore spotted the pinnace and shouted that they had fooled the thieving Englishmen. Unwilling to leave empty-handed, Drake's men took possession of the empty ship and headed out of the harbor.[67] When Drake came near the port a short time later, he saw a line of pack llamas on the trail above Chule, guarded by horsemen. They were taking the silver out of harm's way.[68] Drake might have gone ashore to capture the pack train, but a group of Indian archers was lined up along the shore to resist any such attempt. Disappointed at Chule, Drake determined not to provide any other opportunity for messengers to precede him along the coast. He kept his men aboard the empty ship, the property of a man named Bernal Bueno, and took it to sea with the rest of his fleet.

With a fleet now numbering four ships and a pinnace, Drake had too many vessels for the swift, silent work of piracy. His experience in the Caribbean had shown convincingly that a well-armed ship and a pinnace were all that were needed. Consequently, he ordered his men to take everything of use or value out of the three captured ships. Then with all his crew and prisoners aboard the *Pelican*, the sails were set on the three empty vessels, and Drake watched them move out to sea.[69] With the losses incurred at the island of Mocha and the bay of La Herradura, Drake's crew

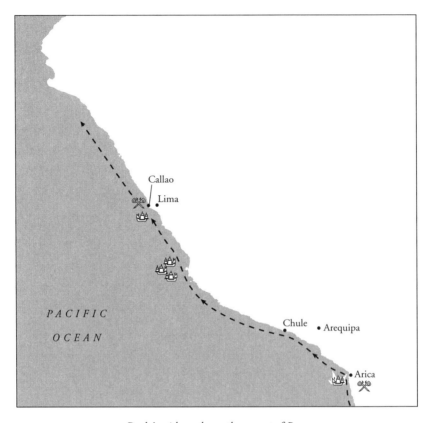

Drake's raids on the southern coast of Peru

was reduced to a bit more than seventy men, only about thirty of whom were fit to fight. This total is from Nicolas Jorje, the prisoner taken at Arica, who said that he had counted the crew members while no one was looking.[70] In addition to his own men, Drake still had three prisoners, Juan Griego, Nicolas Jorje, and the unidentified black slave.

Sailing on for about fifty miles, Drake sighted three ships and gave chase, capturing one of them. There was nothing aboard worth taking, but Drake talked to the officers and took three of them prisoners. How Drake encouraged them to talk is not clear, but talk they did. Gaspar Martín, the captain, told Drake that two ships were expected to arrive in Callao, the port for the city of Lima, bringing merchandise from Panama, plus a great quantity of silver. One of these vessels was the ship of Miguel Angel, and the other the ship of Andrés Muriel. In addition, Sant Juan de Anton had just left Callao de Lima with a big load of silver. He was bound for Panama, with stops at several other ports along the way.[71]

One of the prisoners was a Portuguese pilot, and Drake immediately ordered the man to guide them into Callao. They arrived about midnight on 13 February and immediately began making their way into the harbor. At one point Drake's ship scraped over a sand bar. Drake immediately accused the pilot of having "maliciously" led them astray and threatened to cut off the poor man's head. There were no more problems with the pilot.[72]

Callao was at that time the official port of entry for all merchandise going between Spain and Peru or Chile. The bay is partially enclosed on the west by an island, called in those days the Isla del Puerto. The wide entrance on the north side of the island was used by ships from Panama, while the ships from Chile used a narrow channel on the south.[73] Certain that there were no other ships approaching from the south, Drake approached the harbor with perfect confidence. In fact there was nothing to fear from other ships, for all the vessels in the Pacific ports were unarmed merchant ships, but Drake also knew that surprise was an essential element in a successful pirate raid.

As his ship was anchoring in the bay, another vessel came alongside, and the lookout asked Drake's crew where they were from. Drake had one of the Spanish prisoners reply that the ship came from Chile.[74] He learned in reply that the other ship was from Panama and belonged to Alonso Bautista.[75] Perhaps things would have gone better for the English had not a boat put out from the custom house to learn the identity of the new visitors. The port inspectors were satisfied with what they heard from the lookout on the ship from Panama, and they decided to wait until morning to go aboard for further inspection. But one of the Spanish prisoners on Drake's ship told the inspectors that the ship belonged to Miguel Angel and came from Chile. The inspectors knew that Angel had just arrived from Panama, and one of them climbed aboard to take a better look. As soon as he saw the guns on deck, he knew that something was wrong. Clambering back down to the boat, he and his comrades rowed furiously for shore, peppered by a hail of arrows from the men on Drake's ship and crying out "Franceses,"—Frenchmen.[76]

Not daring to delay any longer, Drake sent a boarding party to the ship from Panama. As a merchant vessel, it carried no soldiers or cannons, yet somehow the Spanish crew managed to fire a harquebus at Drake's pinnace and kill one of the pirates. Seeing that the Spanish sailors were determined to resist, Drake ordered one of his cannons to fire on the ship. The iron ball went clear through the hull, in one side and out the other. This was too much for the merchant sailors. They dropped their own ship's boat into the water and rowed hurriedly for land, while Drake's men took possession of the abandoned ship.[77] Three Spanish seamen and a black slave remained on board and were added to the group of prisoners.[78]

Having lost the opportunity for surprise, Drake put twenty or thirty men into his pinnace, plus another six or seven in the ship's boat, and sent them around the harbor to look for the vessels that belonged to Miguel Angel and Andrés Muriel.[79] Failing to find any trace of the alleged cargo of silver, the men cut the cables on the eight or nine ships remaining in the harbor, allowing them to drift. During this maneuver Drake and his men were very likely able to question a few Spanish seamen and to learn from them that some of Drake's old comrades were prisoners in Lima. One of the captives was John Oxnam, who had been with Drake on the raid at Nombre de Dios in 1573. As John Drake recalled events, Drake hoped that the ships would drift toward the mouth of the harbor so that he could gather them up and hold them as ransom for the release of Oxnam and his fellow pirates.[80] This did not happen, for the ships simply drifted ashore. Drake left Callao disappointed at the results of the raid. Outside the port his men sorted through the merchandise from the Panama ship, taking what they wanted, then setting it adrift, with the four men who had been taken captive in Callao.[81]

By daylight it appeared that two or three ships had come out of Callao in pursuit.[82] Seeing them, Drake assumed that they had come for a fight, and he immediately began to prepare his crew for battle. He ordered his seamen to leave the ship he had captured in Callao, and when he thought that they were not moving quickly enough, he went aboard himself and shouted at them to get moving. Once the crew was safely aboard the *Pelican,* Drake ordered Juan Griego and the men he had taken as captives a few hours earlier to go on board in their place. Setting the ship adrift, he waited for the vessels from Callao to arrive and give battle. Nothing happened. The Callao ships came within a mile or two, then turned and headed back to port.[83]

Although Drake did not know it, the Spanish vessels had come ill prepared for a fight. They were unballasted and difficult to handle. Most of the men in the ships were citizens of Callao, unused to the sea. When the ships hit open water, these nautical novices became deathly sick and were in no condition for battle. Perhaps worst of all, the flagship belonged to Miguel Angel, who later proved himself to be less than eager to fight pirates. His vessel lost the wind just outside the harbor and did not move for hours. No one could say whether this becalming was deliberate or not, but many had their suspicions. While Drake sailed northward with his own flagship, the Spanish merchantmen returned to port to face the blistering criticism of the viceroy.[84]

As he sailed up the coast, Drake kept the ship out three or four miles from shore, sending the pinnace close in to scout the bays and inlets. After a few days, when the pinnace was just outside the port of Trujillo, it captured an unarmed ship belonging to a man named Cataro.[85] The prey was a small vessel loaded with local trade goods. Except for a silver jug and a platter, none of the merchandise was of much interest to the pirates. When he had taken what he wanted, Drake lined the crew up and asked whether anyone had seen a ship from Lima sailing along the coast. The pilot said "No," and everyone else said "Yes," so they knew that they had hit upon a sensitive subject. They also knew that no one had sent word onward, warning of their approach. Their luck could scarcely have been better, and to keep their arrival secret, they put a crew on the Spanish vessel and kept it with the flagship for a few more days before setting it adrift.[86]

About 24 February they arrived at Paita, a small settlement but a fine port, where all the ships called on their journeys between Panama and Lima.[87] Again the pinnace entered the port and the armed pirates prepared

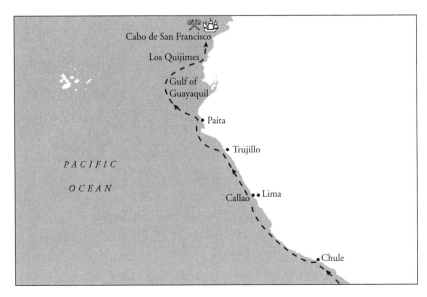

Drake's raids along the coasts of Peru and Ecuador

to board a vessel anchored there. Once the Spanish seamen saw what was happening, they quickly lowered their own boat and rowed for shore, leaving behind the master, the pilot, and some black slaves. The merchandise was of no interest, but there was a good supply of food aboard. The English sailors loaded their pinnace with bread, chickens, and even a pig, then sailed out of the port, taking the ship along. Once outside the port, Drake came aboard and questioned the officers. Yes, they had seen the ship of San Juan de Anton; it had passed through Paita only two days earlier.[88] Drake took the pilot, Custodio Rodríguez, but set the ship adrift, relatively certain now that no one was going ahead to give the alarm.[89]

About twenty miles north of Paita, the armed pinnace met and captured still another Spanish merchant ship, this one belonging to Gonzalo Alvarez. One of the passengers said that once they saw the armament in the pinnace and looked at the more heavily armed flagship some distance away, they knew that resistance was useless. Drake kept them prisoners for a few hours, questioning everyone closely but taking nothing from the cargo.[90] Even so, he did not leave empty-handed. He knew the value and utility of black slaves, and he took the black man that he found aboard the Spanish ship.[91]

Perhaps because he had information about a ship that had recently left the port, Drake avoided the Gulf of Guayaquil and sailed on north.[92] Approaching the Cabo de San Francisco, they came to another favorite stopping place for ships coming from Panama. This was Los Quijimes, a place along the coast where four rivers empty into the bay and where there is plenty of firewood and fresh water.[93] Here on 28 February they found the richest prize to date, a ship coming from Guayaquil and belonging to Benito Díaz Bravo. The ship was riding at anchor, its crew completely unaware of the approaching danger. Drake's men boarded the ship without opposition and discovered a huge quantity of gold and silver, plus tackle, maize, salt pork, hams, and other merchandise. He loaded everything possible onto his own ship, then took Díaz Bravo's ship out to gauge its speed. Discovering that it was faster than the *Pelican,* he put two of his own guns on the Spanish vessel, saying that he intended to use it as an auxiliary to his own. This accomplished, he sent the passengers and crew ashore in the ship's boat, retaining Díaz Bravo and his nephew Francisco Jácome, who was the clerk of the ship and presumably knew where all the most valuable items were stowed. As usual, Drake also retained several black slaves, this time because he thought that they might be able to provide him with useful information.[94] Two of the passengers were Dominican friars, and as a result the members of Drake's crew referred to it as the friars' ship.[95] By the time they were back in England, some were saying that the ship was owned by one of the friars.[96]

The treasure in Díaz Bravo's ship amounted to "80 li[bras] weight of gould." There was also a great golden crucifix and "certaine emeralds neere as longe as a mans finger."[97] Díaz Bravo said the treasure amounted to 18,000 pesos of gold and silver, either "registered or to be registered." The other goods were valued at an additional 4,000 pesos.[98]

During the night Drake had the slaves questioned concerning the amount of treasure carried on the Spanish ship. Convinced that some gold was still being hidden, Drake boarded the Spanish ship and had several captives strung up with ropes around their necks, threatening to hang them if they did not tell him where the gold was.[99] They insisted that there was nothing more, but Drake was still not satisfied. Taking the clerk back to his own ship, Drake strung the poor man up again and demanded again to know whether any more treasure was hidden in the hold. The clerk, Francisco Jácome, said "No," but the slaves said "Yes." When Jácome insisted that the slaves were lying, Drake had him strung up by the neck on a pole and dropped into the sea. The pinnace fished him out and took him back aboard, where Drake was finally convinced that he had told the truth.[100] Another member of the Spanish crew actually took two gold ingots *(dos texos de oro)*, and for that he was hanged until he was dead.[101]

Drake experimented again with the second ship that night and began to consider how he might divide his crew among the three vessels. Finally he decided that he simply did not have enough men and that an additional ship would be too much trouble. The next day, Sunday, 1 March, he ordered the guns taken out of the Spanish ship, cut away her sails and anchor, and let Díaz Bravo and his nephew go free. But he kept the black slaves.[102]

It was not charity that had prompted their release. Rather, the lookout had spied the ship of San Juan de Anton on the horizon.[103] In order to keep his own ship from moving too swiftly and thus frightening off his prey, Drake had the pinnace hauled up on deck. Then, with ropes and cables trailing from the poop and all the sails shortened, the flagship began to run along so slowly that it was nightfall before they met the ship of San Juan de Anton. Again lowering the pinnace into the water, Drake brought his own vessel close alongside the other ship. The men from the Spanish ship hailed the strange vessel and asked who they were. As usual, Drake had someone answer in Spanish that it was the ship of Miguel Angel.[104]

Somewhat more suspicious than his fellow pilots, Anton replied that this could not be, for he had seen the ship empty in Callao. He then told the pirates that they should lower their sails in the name of the king. Drake himself then replied, "You must strike your sails in the name of the queen of England." This, at any rate, is the way John Drake recalled the first moments of their encounter, when he was asked to describe it in 1587.[105] But San Juan de Anton had a different recollection, and his testimony was given within days of the event. According to Anton, someone called out from the other ship, "English! I order you to strike your sails!"

Anton replied, "What England demands that I strike sail? Come and do it yourself."[106] With that the English ship opened fire, and the first shot carried away the mizzen mast of Anton's ship. Other guns joined in, and in the flurry of shot and arrows Anton himself was wounded.[107] Meantime, Drake's ship came in close enough for men to board the Spanish ship. Other armed men from the pinnace swarmed up rigging on the other side. They found Anton alone on the deck and took him back to Drake's ship as a prisoner.[108] The rest of the passengers and crew they herded into the cabin at the poop and locked them up.[109]

The treasure in the Spanish ship was more than any of the pirates had seen before. There were the usual stores of merchandise—flour, sugar, preserves, and salt pork—as well as ship fittings, including tackle, sails, canvas, and a cable.[110] The treasure, according to Anton, amounted to 362,000 pesos, variously denominated in silver bars, *reales* (silver coins), and gold. Of this amount, some 160,000 pesos belonged to the royal treasury, and the rest was privately held. In addition, there were about 40,000 pesos of unregistered gold or silver.[111] The anonymous English witness described it in different words but with much the same meaning. The weight of the gold was eighty pounds. There were thirteen chests of reales, and there was so much uncoined silver that it was used as ballast in place of the usual ballast stones.[112] Nuño de Silva said about the same thing: there were 1,300 silver bars, plus fourteen chests filled with reales and gold. He had been told this by the passengers, and he suspected that there might even have been more.[113]

There are several interesting stories—legends perhaps—that have attached themselves to the ship of San Juan de Anton. One, having to do with the name of the owner and pilot, was contributed by Zelia Nuttall, who translated and published the testimony of Anton and his Spanish colleagues for the Hakluyt Society. Because the man's name does not conform to standard Spanish usage, Miss Nuttall surmised that it must really be Saint John de [South]ampton. Her evidence is that Nuño de Silva once said that "Anton had been brought up in England and spoke English."[114]

With the Nuttall surmise to guide her, Eva G. R. Taylor took the speculation on San Juan de Anton a step further. After he was released by

Drake, Anton gave an account of his captivity to the Spanish authorities. Professor Taylor located a manuscript in the British Library that she believed to be an English version of Anton's Spanish account, perhaps written and corrected by Anton himself.[115] In this document, the man's name is written out as St. John de Ampton (for Southampton, Taylor assumed).[116] The Spanish ship captain's English origins are said to explain Drake's considerate treatment of the man—if theft of a king's ransom in treasure can be termed considerate.

The second interesting story has to do with the name of Anton's ship, or to be more precise, the nickname. The official name of the ship was *Nuestra Señora de la Concepción,* but the unknown English witness insisted that the Spanish called her by the unlikely name of *Cacafuego.*[117] This translates directly, though not very elegantly, as Shitfire. Nuttall presented the interesting theory that the nickname was really *Çacafuego* (phonetically Sacafuego), or Spitfire.[118] If this is so, it ruins an otherwise amusing seaman's yarn. The pilot of the ship, on being released, supposedly said to Drake, "Our ship shalbe called no more the Cacafogo but the Cacaplata, and your ship shalbe called the Cacafo[go]."[119] This is the version of the story told by the unknown English witness. But he had the pilot's name wrong, calling him Don Francisco, and he seems to have been mistaken about the things taken from the ship. Perhaps to make the anecdote more believable, Hakluyt edited it a bit before publishing his c. 1596 version, attributing the remark to "the Pilots boy."[120] To add to the confusion surrounding the nickname, Nuño de Silva on one occasion called the ship *La Plata* and on others *La Nao Rica.*[121] In his log he referred to the ship in Portuguese as the *cagua fogo,* which may be an indication that the uncomplimentary name was used by Drake's sailors and not by the Spanish seamen.[122]

On the subject of Silva, it ought to be noted that several of Drake's Spanish captives thought that they recognized Nuño de Silva as Hernán Pérez, a man who had been involved some twenty years earlier in the theft of a great deal of gold at a place near the Punta de Santa Elena.[123] The witness who made the most vehement denunciation of Silva was none other than San Juan de Anton.[124] Possibly Silva claimed Anton was English simply to retaliate for Anton's own charges against Silva. In any case,

*This seventeenth-century view shows the men on Drake's "Caca Fogo"
firing at the ship of San Juan de Anton, called the "Caca Plata" and
depicted with cannon, though it was actually unarmed. Reprinted from*
Hulsius, *Sechste Theil.*

Silva seems to have established his true identity to the satisfaction of the
authorities both in Mexico and in Spain.

It took six days for Drake and his pirates to rifle the ship of San Juan de
Anton and to transfer the booty to their own ship. Custodio Rodríguez
said that he saw the pinnace go back and forth five times, carrying a full
load to the pirate ship each time.[125] Once they were finished, Drake distributed "gifts" to some of the captives. Because these were items that
Drake had stolen from other people, the Spanish authorities were not inclined to allow the recipients to keep the gifts. San Juan de Anton, for example, received a German musket, a gilded corselet, and a silver bowl, in
the bottom of which the words *Francisqus Draques* had been inscribed. Be-

yond this, Drake gave Anton a supply of iron, tar, and other stores. To
other men he gave thirty or forty pesos, plus such gifts as a set of pistols, a
sword and shield, some fans for ladies, linen cloth, and various implements. The most interesting gift was a letter of safe-conduct, written in
English and addressed to John Wynter.[126]

The original letter has not survived. A copy published by Hakluyt
in 1600 is often said to be taken from the English original, but it is really
an English retranslation of a Dutch version published earlier by Linschoten.[127] Nuño de Silva was given a copy of the letter and it was later attached to testimony he gave to Spanish authorities concerning his voyage
with Drake. From this copy it is possible to determine more or less what
Drake said. Beyond that, Silva tells us that Drake referred to his own ship
as the *Gama Dorado,* the *Golden Hind.*

> Letter that the English Captain Francis Díaz [Drake]
> (who entered into the Mar del Sur by the Strait of Mag-
> ellan) wrote from his ship named the Golden Hind with
> the ship named San Joan de [ ] (that his companions
> robbed and that he left behind).

> Señor
>   Mister Winter, if God wills that you should meet
> with Mr. St. Joan then I ask that you treat him well, in
> accordance with the promise I have given him. And if
> you should lack any of the things that Sant Joan carries
> with him, then you should pay him double from our
> own stores, that you are carrying. And you should order
> that none of your soldiers do him harm nor injury. I
> will fulfill the decision that we made together to return
> to our own country, God willing. Even so, I greatly
> doubt that this letter will get to you because of the
> Spaniards.
>   I continue praying always to Our Lord who can turn
> both us and everyone else to salvation or condemnation.
> To him I give thanks always. Amen.

This letter that I write is not just for Mr. Winter but
also for Mr. Thomas and Mr. Arle [Charles? Chester?]
and Combe [Cook?] and Mr. Anthony, along with all
the rest of your friends. I trust you all might keep us in
mind. Even so, I maintain a hope in God, that he will
not load us with great burdens but will help us in our
tribulations. I pray you, by the Heart of Jesus Christ,
that should God allow you to have some tribulations,
you will not dispair of the great mercy of God. He will
hold you and He will guard you until He turns again to
grant life from among His great gifts. And He will man-
ifest his mercy and honor and power and empire forever.
Amen.

> With sorrow. I have a very heavy heart.
> Francis Díaz [Drake][128]

It seems that the Spanish authorities received another copy from San
Juan de Anton. Within a few days this copy was dispatched to Lima, where
John Butler, an English prisoner captured with Oxnam, translated it.[129]
This was done not because Butler was the only person who could translate
English but rather because Butler was also a pirate, and he knew Drake.
The authorities hoped that he could help identify the people mentioned in
the letter and determine whether there was any reason to expect other raids
on the Pacific ports. No doubt this is exactly what Drake wanted the Spanish to do, for if they were busy chasing other, perhaps imaginary vessels,
there would be just that much less opportunity to chase him.[130]

Drake was elated with the results of his raids. The treasure surpassed anything that he had ever considered, and he used some of it to impress his
prisoners. This generosity is uncharacteristic of Drake, but not difficult to
understand. Other robbers had done the same, and others would do so
again, in the Robin Hood tradition. It is easy to be generous with some-
body else's money.

Success made Drake expansive. He boasted about his exploits, real and
imaginary, and his captives hung onto every word. Drake told Anton that

he had a license from the queen to rob Spanish subjects and recover the 7,000 ducats that Hawkins had lost in his dealings with the viceroy of New Spain. Once this was accounted for, everything else would go to the queen.[131] He told Domingo de Liçarça that he knew about the executions of English pirates in Panama and also about the men held prisoner in Lima. If any of the Lima prisoners should be harmed in the future, Drake would cut off the heads of 3,000 men in Peru and cast them into the bay at Callao. This man, who must have been more credulous than the others, was also told that Drake had seen giants at the Puerto de San Julian and that "next to the giants they looked like little boys."[132]

In most of his conversation with Anton and his men, Drake gave little away. The question in everyone's mind was how he would return home (and whether it would be possible to intercept him when he did). In answer to these questions, Drake pulled out a beautiful world map, some six feet long, that he said he had purchased in Lisbon. Pointing to the map, he said there were only two ways to go, east or west, back through the Strait of Magellan or ahead through the Moluccas. Both of these routes involved voyages in the South Pacific. Two other extremely doubtful routes had often been discussed in the North Pacific. One way was the route that some geographers said cut through the northern part of North America. Variously called the Strait of the Bacallaos or the Strait of Anian, this route had never been navigated. Some geographers placed it on their world maps, but mostly for decoration. The other way, north of China, was considered possible, but so difficult as to be unthinkable. Drake discussed them all, telling his avid listeners that he might take any one of the routes.[133] The impression was that he had not yet made up his mind.

On 6 March he ordered San Juan de Anton and the three recently captured pilots to be put into Anton's ship, then he let them sail away. While Anton and his lightly laden ship headed for Panama, Drake sailed for the Isla de Caño to take on fresh water. He was cocky and confident. Anton knew that this was where Drake would go, and he informed the authorities.[134]

It was more than a week before the English ship arrived at Caño, about 18 March.[135] For two days Drake searched for a beach suitable for careening his ship, which was leaking and covered with barnacles. In the mean-

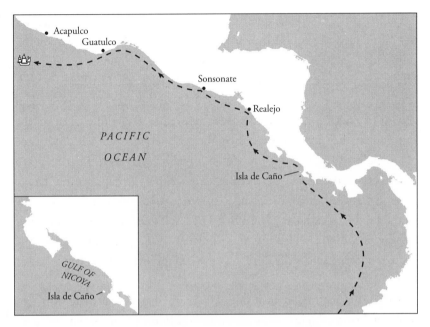

Drake's raids from the coast of Ecuador to Guatulco

time he dispatched the pinnace to keep a watch for other vessels, those coming in pursuit and those simply passing by. On the afternoon of the eighteenth, about five miles from the island, the pinnace came upon a merchant ship, sailing south from the Gulf of Nicoya. The vessel belonged to a Panama merchant named Rodrigo Tello. Drawing near to the ship, the men in the pinnace fired a few shots from their harquebuses and managed to wound one of the passengers. Resistance was useless, so Tello surrendered his ship.[136]

Once the pinnace arrived at the island, bringing the new captive, Drake had the treasure transferred from his vessel to that of Tello, except for the silver bars, which were thrown onto the river bank. As the ship rose out of the water, the seamen tipped it first on one side, and then the other, in an attempt to clean the bottom and caulk the leaks. The whole process took about a week. At the end of the time, the ship looked new again, but the leaks persisted, and it was obvious that she would have to be careened again before returning to England.[137]

During this time Drake questioned his prisoners closely, though he was not as friendly, not as talkative, as he had been with the gentlemen on the ship with San Juan de Anton. These were men of humble origins, and Drake saw no need to waste gifts on their ilk. Most of the time they were confined to the pinnace under guard.[138] During prayers they were taken aboard Drake's ship, though they were allowed to gather fore or aft on the ship and say their rosaries. Even then, the prisoners were not left alone. One of the sailors stomped on a crucifix, crushed it, and threw the pieces into the sea before the eyes of the horrified crewmen.[139] Perhaps because Drake generally ignored them, the Spanish prisoners were able to talk with some of the English seamen and learn that Drake planned to return to England by way of China.[140] This was the common Spanish terminology for the route that went across the Pacific to the Philippines and the Moluccas or Spice Islands.

After searching the Spanish ship, Drake discovered that there were two pilots on board who knew the route to the Moluccas and who had proper sea charts and navigating instruments. The older of the two was Alonso Sánchez Colchero, a gray-haired man of fifty, who was said to be an expert pilot in the China trade. Taking Sánchez Colchero aside, Drake told the man that he wanted to hire him as pilot for the trip across the Pacific. The seaman refused, saying at first that he was only a simple sailor and knew nothing of navigation. When Drake showed the man that he was listed as a pilot in the ship's register, Sánchez Colchero begged to be left behind for the sake of his wife and family. Drake thereupon promised to pay the pilot a thousand pesos when they reached England, gave him fifty pesos to send to his wife, and pronounced the matter settled.[141]

By 26 March the work on the ship was completed.[142] It still leaked badly, so Drake determined to take Tello's small vessel along to ensure having a ship with a sound hull. Ordering the prisoners into his pinnace, Drake gave them some supplies, a keg or so of water, a bag of flour, and a little maize. This time there were no gifts. Drake told the men that they would find all they needed on shore at the Rio de Barranca, a few miles away. They did so as they watched the two ships sail northwest toward Realejo.[143]

With an English crew sailing the Spanish ship, Drake took his pirate fleet to sea once more.[144] From the sailing charts of Sánchez Colchero, Drake knew that the sea route to the Moluccas began at Acapulco. This was the route pioneered in 1564–65 by the Augustinian Friar Andrés de Urdaneta, and his course computations were on the charts of every Spanish pilot who sailed the route thereafter.[145] Drake intended to go the same way. He took his ships up the coast, hoping to be able to careen the flagship once more in a shipyard along the way, perhaps at Sonsonate or farther north in Acapulco or Colima.[146] The unhappy pilot Alonso Sánchez Colchero went with him.

As they approached the entrance to the port of Realejo, Drake told his new pilot that he wanted to enter the port and burn the place, along with a ship that was being built there for the China trade. At first Drake asked the man simply to "become a Lutheran" and join with them. Met with a refusal, he ordered the prisoner to pilot Drake's ships into the port, which was blocked by a treacherous sand bar. Finally Drake had a rope put around the prisoner's neck and strung him up. Twice he did this, stopping only when the man began to lose consciousness. Drake spared the poor man's life but put him in an iron cage in the ballast.[147] Apparently he was beginning to see that Sánchez Colchero would be of little use as a pilot on the voyage across the Pacific.

Still sailing northward, they passed the port of Sonsonate, where they began to see the volcanoes of Honduras and Guatemala. On 4 April 1579, shortly before dawn, they encountered another Spanish ship that was sailing south from Acapulco. The helmsman of the Spanish vessel called to Drake's ship that it must keep away, but the English pretended not to hear. Keeping silent, Drake brought Sánchez Colchero up on deck. When the Spanish helmsman called out again, asking what ship it was, Sánchez Colchero spoke up, saying it was the ship of Miguel Angel from Peru. As the ship came closer, the Spanish sailors could see the smaller ship at the prow, as though she were towing the larger one. Suddenly there was a flurry of activity. Drake's larger ship came around behind the Spanish vessel, and several men fired down on the deck. Scarcely a half-dozen men were awake on the Spanish ship, and in any case there was no way for them to resist.[148]

There was a hidalgo aboard the Spanish ship, Don Francisco de Zárate. This knight of the Order of Santiago was no doubt the most fawning, cowardly creature the pirates had yet encountered on their voyage. Drake loved him. As Zárate boarded the pirate ship and saw Drake pacing the deck, he bowed to the pirate and kissed his hands.[149] Never before having been the object of such deference, Drake took the trembling hidalgo to his cabin, sat him down, and began to interrogate him.

"I am a friend of those who tell the truth," said Drake, "but I am annoyed with anything else."[150] The truth was the only thing Drake wanted to hear, he said.

"How much silver and gold do you carry?" "None," said Zárate. The question was repeated, and Zárate replied, "None, except for some plates and cups I use at table."[151]

Well, said Drake, was there any relative of the viceroy aboard? "No, señor," said Zárate. Well, if there were, said Drake, "I would show you how a gentleman should keep his word."[152]

Drake then took Zárate down to the ballast, where Alonzo Sánchez Colchero was imprisoned. "Sit down," he said. "You must stay here." As the man began to sit, Drake stopped him. "Not just yet," he said. "Just tell me the identity of that man." Zárate said he really didn't know. "Well," Drake said. "That's the pilot the viceroy was sending to Panama to take Don Gonzalo to China." Having shown his contempt for the viceroy, Drake then took the hidalgo back on deck, where they had a pleasant conversation until lunch time.[153]

At lunch Drake served Zárate from his own platter and told him to quit worrying. He and all his property were safe. Once more the poor man kissed Drake's hands. Zárate noted that the English officers and gentlemen who ate with him at Drake's table were afraid of their commander. None of them would take a seat or put on his hat until Drake told him repeatedly to do so. One of the gentlemen who took Zárate's particular attention was John Doughty, the brother of the man who had been executed. Young Doughty ate at the table with the other gentlemen, but he was never left unguarded and never allowed to leave the ship. Asking about Drake's silver and gilt table service, Zárate was told that Drake had it decorated with his own coat of arms and that much of it was a personal gift from the queen. Zárate believed every word.[154]

The next morning Drake asked to see what Zárate had in his bales and storage chests. With all the Spanish seamen removed to the other ship, Drake remained aboard Zárate's vessel all day, taking what he wanted.[155] There were bales of silk and linen and crates of fine china.[156] Zárate noted that none of Drake's men dared to touch a single item until told to do so. Although he gave his men favors, Zárate noted, "He punishes the least fault." Still, Zárate had little to complain of on his own account. "He took very little from me," the hidalgo said. "In fact he was very polite." Intrigued by the curious trinkets in Zárate's possession, Drake took some of them "for his wife." In return, Drake gave Zárate a cutlass and a little silver brazier. Drake's gifts were of little value, it seems: Zárate said that his captor "lost nothing at the fair." Drake then told Zárate he would be released the next day, and Zárate thanked him.[157]

The next morning bright and early, Drake took Zárate back to his own vessel. Lining up the Spanish sailors, Drake gave each man a few silver reales. A few of the passengers looked a bit the worse for wear, and Drake gave them some reales as well. Then turning to Zárate, Drake instructed him to "tell the Englishmen in Lima that I met him on 6 April and that he is well."[158] Drake was tired of Alonso Sánchez Colchero and ordered him to be put in Zárate's ship. In his place Drake took Juan Pascual, a Portuguese seaman recommended by both Sánchez Colchero and the captain of Zárate's ship. Despite Pascual's protests to the contrary, Drake was convinced that the man would be able to guide him to Guatulco, which he apparently told Sánchez Colchero was to be his next stop.[159] In addition to Pascual, Drake also took a young black man and woman he had seen on Zárate's ship. The young woman's name was María, and the unidentified English informant called her "a proper negro wench," leaving little doubt about the reason for taking her along.[160] The trip across the Pacific was going to take seventy or eighty days, and there was no sense in getting lonely.[161]

From 7 April to 13 April 1579, Drake sailed along the coast, no doubt stopping once or twice for wood and water. He came upon the port of

Guatulco in broad daylight and saw a single small ship in the harbor. It was a small place, just as he had been told, seldom used since the middle of the century, when it was superseded by the ports of Navidad and Acapulco. There were only three hundred Indians in the district and fewer than a half-dozen Spanish residents.[162] Approaching the port about noon, Drake sent a boat ashore with twenty or twenty-five armed men.[163] The surprise was complete. Gaspar de Vargas, the alcalde, tried to muster a force in the village plaza, but everyone scattered when the English fired their first few shots.[164] The priest, Simón de Miranda, was taken prisoner, along with a guest who had come for Holy Week. Also taken to the ship was Francisco Gómez Rengifo, the local *encomendero*—a landowner with a royal grant entitling him to service and tribute from the Indians. There were nearly as many Spanish visitors in Guatulco as citizens. One such man was Bernardino López, lieutenant governor of the province. López was there because he owned the cargo that had just been loaded on the ship.[165]

Gómez Rengifo was definitely the rich man of the town. Tom Moone, who must have been a favorite of Drake's, was the first to enter the man's house. He found the encomendero getting ready to flee and took a large gold chain from him, along with some 7,000 pesos in money and goods. He also took a crucifix from the wall and smashed it against a table, telling the poor man that it was nothing but a pagan idol.[166]

Finding that the ship was mostly loaded with local produce, Drake and his men began to ransack the town. Once they finished with the house of Gómez Rengifo, the only other place to sack was the church. Here they stole the chalices and the monstrance, as well as the damask vestments, a satin cope and matching canopy, surplices, and altar cloths. The expensive fabrics were taken to the ship; the others used for towels. The seamen scattered and trampled the unconsecrated altar bread, then turned to smash and slash the images and the crucifix.[167] When they got back to the ship, where the captives were, Tom Moone noticed the friar saying his rosary. He grabbed the rosary out of the priest's hands and pulled off a gold medal bearing an image of the Virgin Mary. Moone then bit down on the medal, making a great face, and finally pretended to throw it into the water.

With the pillaging completed, Drake had a meal set on board the ship and invited his prisoners to eat, knowing that they were supposed to fast during Holy Week. All but the priest dined, and all watched later when Drake made a great show of leading religious services.[168] Drake was angered when he saw Gómez Rengifo looking at the cover of his copy of Fox's *Book of Martyrs*. His attitude quickly changed, though, and he told the man this was "a very good book." Drake pointed to pictures in the book of Englishmen who had been "martyred and burned in Castille." Another picture showed European kings kissing the foot of the pope, which Drake said showed the pope's great arrogance.[169]

The next morning Drake sent a party ashore for water, putting Juan Pascual in chains and ordering him to show them the way. This accomplished, he returned to the ship and set the prisoners free. Just as he was about to sail out of the harbor, Drake summoned Nuño de Silva and had some of his sailors put Silva on the deserted ship. No one could have been more surprised, except perhaps the citizens of the town, when they later heard Silva calling them to come with a boat and take him to shore.[170]

Drake could have had only one motive for this cynical move. Silva, by all accounts, had joined Drake's pirates and had begun to practice Drake's religion. Obviously he was in for serious legal proceedings when the Spanish authorities got their hands on him. But Drake had suddenly realized that everyone knew of his plan to return home by way of the Moluccas. Thus he carefully primed Silva with the misinformation that he had changed his mind and was going home another way, perhaps by the northern passage. Silva dutifully repeated this account to the authorities, who generally refused to believe it.[171]

During his voyage northward along the Pacific coast of South America Drake began to experiment with new techniques to control his visitors and his own crew. With most of the visitors, especially those of good social position, he talked—almost incessantly. He boasted that he controlled the entire coast and could sail wherever he wished.[172] To show that he was not afraid of pursuit, he told everyone that he intended to return home by crossing the Pacific and following the route through the Moluccas and Spice Islands, around Africa, and on to Europe. At one point Drake began to think he had talked too much, but the Spanish officials were convinced that it was a trick. If Drake said he would cross the Pacific, he would do just the opposite, returning by way of the Strait of Magellan.[173]

Drake also took pains to demonstrate his complete control over the lives of his captives and his own crew. When Spanish authorities later asked the captives why they always showed Drake where to find firewood and fresh water, they replied that he threatened to cut their heads off if they refused.[174] To emphasize his willingness to do so, Drake bragged to some of the captives that he had decapitated one of his own officers for a minor act of insubordination.[175] One captive said that Drake's men were so afraid of him that they trembled at the sight of him. When he passed by they doffed their hats and bowed to the floor.[176]

This open display of arrogance may very well explain one of the most intriguing changes in Drake's behavior during this part of his voyage, officiating at public prayer. Even though he had a chaplain, the university graduate Francis Fletcher, Drake himself began to lead the prayers, to read from the Scriptures, and now and then to give the sermons.[177] This was not his practice during the early months of the voyage, when Fletcher was the undisputed leader of religious activities. In fact, Drake officiated for the first time on the Sunday after the execution of Thomas Doughty. By the time his pirate ship reached the coast of Peru this was a standard part of Drake's repertoire, at least while visitors were present.

No doubt there were several reasons for the change. First, Drake's Spanish captives had, perhaps unconsciously, shown their general belief that Drake was nothing but a common thief. "You will be saying," Drake told one man, "this man is a devil who robs by day and prays at night." Insisting once more that he took their goods in the name of the queen, he also said that he realized this might seem to be an insufficient explanation.[178] For this reason he seems to have gone to some pains to imply that God himself approved of what his pirates were doing.

Beyond all this, Drake's new emphasis on his position as a religious leader demonstrated his total control—not only over the lives of his captives and his crew but over their souls as well. This was a huge step in the development of his character. The man who had started the voyage as a part-time pirate and prosperous English merchant sailor had become something very different. In the first stage this self-proclaimed emissary of the queen had made piracy an act of patriotism. During the voyage along the Pacific coast Drake's role changed once more. He was very nearly an agent of God. Drake the pirate was no longer a simple patriot, working to serve his queen. Now he seemed to be almost a missionary, working for God.

7

Guatulco to the Pacific and Home

WHEN HE LEFT THE PORT of Guatulco, Drake also left the distinct impression with everyone that he intended to sail for Acapulco, where there were shipyards with good beaches on which to careen his leaky flagship. So convinced were his Spanish captives that this was his next destination that local authorities made a special effort the following spring to determine just why Drake had failed to appear. One man said that it was because they had managed to deceive Drake about the port. Juan Pascual testified that he and other prisoners had agreed to give Drake misleading information about the place in order to discourage him from going there. Specifically, when "the said Englishman asked him and others whether there were ships and men in the port of Acapulco," he answered that there were. The inference is that Drake did not want to go where there was a chance of meeting men ready for a fight.[1]

Nuño de Silva had a slightly different story. According to his account Drake had intended to go to Acapulco only for water. Because he was able to get water in Guatulco, it seemed likely that he would bypass Acapulco. Instead, he would probably sail north to look for the Strait of the Bacallaos (Anian). When he failed to find that he would probably go by way of the Moluccas.[2] This bit of misinformation caused enough uncertainty among Spanish officials that they spent the next few weeks looking for Drake near the ports around Acapulco. Seeing no trace of him there, the viceroy concluded that Drake had gone home another way.[3]

The idea that Drake might return home by a northern route seems to have originated in a conference Drake had with Silva and his other pilots while they sat in the port of Guatulco. Drake showed this group a map on

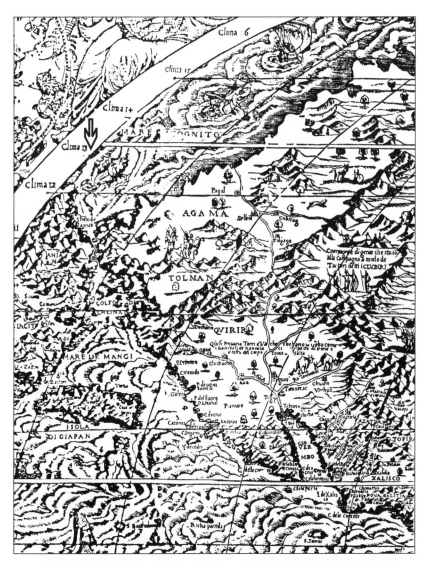

The 1561 world map of Giacomo Gastaldi was the first to show the imaginary Streto di Ania[n]o (arrow). The map has been edited for clarity. From British Library Map Room, C.18.n.1.

which there was a strait in about 66° north latitude and said this was the way he would go home.[4] The mythical Strait of Anian was first described by Giacomo Gastaldi in 1561, and it very quickly became a feature of the printed maps of the world prepared by other geographers.[5] This putative strait was widely discussed among pilots and geographers. In 1574 the famous pilot Juan Fernández de Ladrillero testified before officials in New Spain in 1574 that he believed there was such a strait, and some took him seriously.[6]

It is almost inconceivable that Drake had any real intention to go this way. No doubt he wanted Silva to tell the Spanish authorities that this was his destination; otherwise he would not have released the man immediately after the meeting was over.[7] But all the evidence indicates that Drake's real intention was to do what he had been saying he would do, take the Moluccas route across the Pacific. There was really no other alternative. It would be extremely difficult to go back through the Strait of Magellan, for the prevailing winds along the South American coast are from the south. These winds had helped Drake during his voyage north, but they would be against him on the return trip and make him easy prey to the Spanish ships that might lie in wait there.[8]

Still, there was a problem with the Moluccas route—the season. Winter was the best time to catch the winds for the trip across the Pacific. All the details had been carefully recorded by Andrés de Urdaneta, who advised that October or November were the best months to start.[9] Drake would have to find some haven along the coast in which he could careen his ship and take shelter for several months. Fortunately, this was the season for sailing north, as the local sailors knew well.[10]

The stories published after Drake returned home indicate that he stayed in a harbor somewhere along the coast of Upper California. A number of Spanish expeditions had sailed along the coasts of Lower and Upper California during the previous half-century, and it was apparently well mapped during these years.[11] Urdaneta later made special efforts to assemble information about those voyages, and the maps no doubt served as the basis for the California portions of his derrotero.[12] This is the document that Drake had taken from Colchero.[13]

Using these navigational aids, Drake is supposed to have sailed from Guatulco, taking his fleet of two ships, the *Pelican* and the nameless ship of Rodrigo Tello. From that point he disappeared into the west, making land again in latitude 44° north. The firsthand sources for this part of his trip are minimal, nearly nonexistent. John Drake has two remarks about the voyage north, the first in 1584:

> They left Aguatulco . . . in April and they went to sea. They sailed continually to the northwest and the north-northeast. They traveled for the entire months of April and May, until the middle of June. From the said Aguatulco, which is in 15 degrees, they went to 48 degrees. They encountered great storms along the way. The whole sky was dark and filled with clouds. Along the route they saw five or six islands. Captain Francis gave one of them the name Saint Bartholomew and the other one Saint James. These islands were in 46 and 48 degrees. To the land in 48 degrees Captain Francis gave the name New England. They remained there a month and a half, taking on wood and water and careening the ship.[14]

Three years later John Drake gave a somewhat different description:

> They departed from here and took a course for the northwest and the north-northwest. They sailed a thousand leagues up to the latitude of forty-four degrees, always sailing close to the wind. Afterward the wind changed and they went to the Californias. They discovered land in forty-eight degrees. They landed there and built huts. They remained for a month and a half, careening the ship. Their food was shellfish and seal. During their stay the Indians came many times. When they saw the Englishmen, they wept and bloodied their faces with their fingernails. Since they did this as a sign

of adoration, Captain Francis told them in signs that
they should not do that, because they were not gods.
They were always peaceful, doing no harm, even though
they gave [the Indians] no food. The people are the
same color as these Indians. [They are] well disposed.
They carry bows and arrows, and they run around
naked. It's a temperate climate, more cold than hot,
with a fine appearance. Here they careened the large
ship, and they left the one they had taken from Nicaragua. When they departed, the Indians seemed to be
sad.[15]

The unknown English writer also has a very brief description of the place:

Here Drake watered his ship and departed, sayling
northwards till he came to .48. gr. of the septentrionall
Latitud, still finding a very lardge sea trending toward
the north, but being afraid to spend long time in seeking for the straite, hee turned back againe, still keping
along the cost as nere land as hee might, untill hee came
to .44. gr. and there hee found a harborow for his ship
where he grounded his ship to trim her, & heere came
downe unto them many of the contrey people while
they wer graving of their ship & had conference with
them by synes, in this place drake set up a greate post
and nayled thereon a vi[d] [sixpence coin], which the
countreye people woorshipped as if it had bin god
also hee nayled uppon this post a plate of lead, and
scratched therein the Queenes name, and when they
had graved and watred theire ship in the latter ende of
August they set sayle.[16]

No doubt these three brief accounts contain elements of truth. They
may indeed be very largely true. But they are also partly imaginary. The latitudes, for example, do not agree with any latitudes shown on maps of the

voyage published in the years following Drake's return. Beyond this, they do not agree with the latitudes published by Hakluyt about 1595 and later, or with the latitudes published by Drake's nephew in 1628. The reason for this seems to be that English authorities had determined to keep details of the voyage secret after Drake returned. Obviously, the Spanish were able to trace Drake's route through their ports in Central and South America. Only the later portion of the voyage could really be kept secret, including his trip from Guatulco to the Moluccas. To accomplish their goal, English authorities gave out a series of changing and conflicting accounts. A few weeks after Drake's return the German geographer Gerard Mercator wrote to his Dutch friend Abraham Ortelius, complaining that English officials were "concealing the course followed" by Drake and "putting out differing accounts of the route taken and the areas visited."[17] The Drake story was still in a state of flux in 1582, when John Drake left England on a voyage that ended in his capture. The two stories he later gave to Spanish authorities probably reflect the version being circulated when he left.

Although it might have served the foreign policy interests of the crown, the secrecy was an annoyance at home and abroad. Late in 1584, Sir Edward Stafford, Elizabeth's ambassador in France, wrote to Secretary of State Walsingham, reporting what he had heard from his own secretary, Richard Hakluyt. "Drake's journey is kept very secret in England, but here it is in every one's mouth," he wrote.[18] The secrecy policy became something of an embarrassment in 1589, when Hakluyt began to publish authoritative accounts of English navigators—all except Drake.

Hakluyt was finally able to add a report on the Drake voyage to his original volumes. No one knows exactly how the Hakluyt report was written or when it was published. Because Hakluyt's account is the earliest extensive story of the voyage, it might be worthwhile here to consider how and when it was written. Henry Wagner thought it appeared about 1595, which is perhaps a little early. Wagner and others have shown that Hakluyt's story of Drake's "Famous Voyage" is related in one way or another to now-missing original copies of John Cooke's story and several manuscript accounts drawn up by members of the expedition after their return, especially the heavily edited version of the journal of Francis Fletcher.[19]

The Hakluyt version certainly had not appeared in print by 1 January 1592, when Drake wrote to the queen that reports of his journey "hitherto have been silenced."[20] John Stow obviously had not seen the Hakluyt story before he issued the revised edition of his *Annales of England*. Stow's Drake narrative was written between 1585 (the publication date for a quotation he used to describe the "valorous," "prudent," and "fortunate" Drake) and 1592.[21] When Stow wrote about Thomas Cavendish, he was able to use Hakluyt's description of the Cavendish voyage. Because he had to rely on John Cooke for his brief account of the Drake voyage, it seems clear that the Hakluyt story about Drake was not yet in print. The surviving manuscript of Cooke's narrative is a copy made by John Stow, so it seems reasonable to assume that Hakluyt himself was not able to consult it until Stow's 1592 *Annales* were published.[22]

By the early 1590s other bits of the story began to appear. Emanuel van Meteren, a Dutch historian and the dean of the Dutch merchant group in London, had lived in England since the middle of the century. He was a good friend of Richard Hakluyt's and, like Hakluyt, made an effort to collect reliable information on the English voyages and on other important events of the time. In his first manuscript history, written before 1593, Meteren was forced to rely on his own research into Drake's circumnavigation, seemingly because the Hakluyt insert sheets were not yet in print.[23]

Similarly, the Dutch merchant Jan Huygen van Linschoten, whose *Itinerario* was approved for publication on 8 October 1594, wanted to publish the story of Drake's voyage. However, Linschoten had to use Nuño de Silva's incomplete account of the Drake circumnavigation. When Linschoten's work was published, Hakluyt had it translated into English, then copied portions for the revised edition of his own work.[24]

In 1595 Meteren was able to secure from Hakluyt a copy of Francis Pretty's journal of the Thomas Cavendish voyage around the world. Meteren used that journal in revising his own notes about the Drake voyage. This no doubt means that Hakluyt's story of the Drake voyage was not available in the early part of 1595. It also means that the story Hakluyt finally published was drawn up after this time in response to pressure from home and abroad to give an official account of Drake's circumnavigation of the globe.[25]

Wagner attributed Hakluyt's Drake story to Richard Hakluyt himself.[26] David Quinn thinks that the story was drawn up by Hakluyt with "conflation and contraction" added by his assistant, the Reverend Philip Jones.[27] An early Dutch account of the voyage credits "her English majesty's deputy printer," doubtless meaning either George Bishop or Ralph Newberie, publishers of the original Hakluyt volume, where they are listed as "Deputies to Christopher Barker, Printer to the Queenes most excellent Maiestie."[28] It is not yet possible to determine exactly who wrote Hakluyt's Drake story. Even so, it was considered important enough to appear as part of one of the first printed maps of the voyage, the map engraved and printed by Jodocus Hondius about 1596.[29]

The Hondius depiction of the voyage was not the first to appear in print. The earliest one appeared in the Low Countries in the early 1580s, engraved by Nicola van Sype. On this map Drake is shown as having stopped at an island just off the northwest coast of America, part of a chain lying in about 42° north latitude.[30] The van Sype map was then reproduced in a Dutch-language edition.[31]

The important thing about these maps is that they were likely copied from the large world map of the voyage that Drake presented to the queen upon his return.[32] It was a very large map, almost certainly the same one Drake showed to his Spanish prisoners, the map that he told them he had purchased in Lisbon.[33] Judging from the vignettes that appear on the copies, it seems probable that the map Drake gave to the queen had been similarly enhanced around the edges. This ornamentation was probably added by John Drake, who was said to have spent his full time in Drake's cabin, making drawings of the coastlines as well as the flora and fauna.[34] Kept secret for years, the map was later placed on display in Whitehall, but it has since disappeared.[35] Even so, it is clear that the map contained information that fit the story that English officials wanted the Spanish to know. As has been seen, some of the contents of the map were carefully revealed to the Spanish ambassador in London. He was not allowed to see the map itself, no doubt because he would then have realized it did not contain sufficient information to verify the new discoveries that were being claimed.[36]

Drake's route shown on the map printed by Jodocus Hondius about 1596 was probably copied from the large world map that Drake presented to the queen after his return. (A dashed line showing the later voyage of Thomas Cavendish has been deleted.) Vera totius expeditionis nauticae.

This map, attributed to Nicola van Sype, was apparently copied from the map Drake gave to the queen. The dotted lines show Drake landing on an island off the coast of California. Reprinted from La Herdike Interprinse, *fold-out bound with [Bigges,]* Expeditio Francisci Draki. *Huntington Library 9074 (only copy).*

When John Drake testified about the voyage in 1584, he said that Drake found "five or six islands" on the voyage north. He named one of them Saint Bartholomew and the other one Saint James. "These islands were in 46 and 48 degrees," continued John Drake. "To the land [*terra*] in 48 degrees Captain Francis gave the name New England." This is a pretty good description of the Upper California portion of Drake's voyage that appears on the van Sype copy of Drake's world map, although the latitude of the islands appears to be more in the neighborhood of 41 and 45 degrees. The map shows Drake landing on one of the islands, rather than the mainland. The word *terra,* as used by John Drake, could refer to an island or to the mainland.[37] But several writers of that day interpreted the evidence to mean that Nova Albion or New England was an island.

Antonio de Herrera, who saw and used John Drake's testimony to give an official account of Drake's circumnavigation of the globe, wrote: "Francis Drake saw along this route five or six islands of good land [*terra*]. He named one S. Bartolome, another S. Jayme, and another that seemed larger and better, *Nueba Albion.*"[38]

Another person who thought that Drake had landed on an island off the coast of Upper California was Pedro Sarmiento de Gamboa. After leading the expedition in pursuit of Drake, Sarmiento was captured by the English and taken in 1586 to London, where he talked at length with Drake and the queen. Upon his return to Spain some years later he repeated the conversations to Bartolomé Leonardo de Argensola, who published the information in 1609. According to Argensola, Drake sailed north by a variety of routes until he arrived at a group of six islands. One of these he named San Bartolomé, another San Iayme, "and the one that seemed to be the largest and most fertile, New Albion."[39]

A similar story, attributed to "her English majesty's deputy printer," appears in the Dutch text attached to the edges of the "Drake Broadside" map. It contains information not included in the Hakluyt version but is otherwise so close to the Hakluyt narrative that it may well be the story that Hakluyt originally intended to publish. In any case, the Dutch story locates Drake's harbor in an island that he named Nova Albion.[40]

In 1599 Theodore de Bry published a Latin version of the Drake circumnavigation. Translating from the Dutch text, de Bry called Drake's place an island. "*Insulam hunc* [*sic*] Draco Novum Albionum vocabit," says the Latin edition. The German edition is similar: "*Von Dracken murde diese Insel* Nova Albion *genannt.*"[41]

As John Drake said when he testified as a Spanish captive, Drake took two ships when he left Guatulco, the *Pelican* and the bark captured off the coast of Nicaragua.[42] During a visit to the Channel Islands in 1602, Sebastián Vizcaino heard that the remains of a bark were washed up on the shore of Catalina Island. Vizcaino noticed that many of the children on the island were "white and blonde." According to an Indian woman who still had two pieces of "Chinese damask" given to her by one of the men, the wrecked ship had run aground and broken up on shore somewhere north of the main village. The Indians still recalled the visitors, including the curious black slaves who were aboard the ship. In a Dutch account of the Drake voyage, Emanuel van Meteren wrote that the journey north from Guatulco took Drake to 33° north latitude. This is just where the Channel Islands were located on the Spanish maps of the period, maps that formed the basis for those that Drake seized from Alonso Sánchez Colchero.[43]

Another story, also from Spanish sources, seems to place Drake's landing place in the peninsula of Lower California. During the later part of the 1620s Father Jerónimo de Zárate Salmerón wrote about the region, giving as his source Father Antonio de la Ascención, who had been to California with Vizcaino. According to this story, a Portuguese pilot named Morera had appeared on the Mexican frontier at Santa Barbara, from which point he made his way to Sombrerete, Nueva Galicia, about 1585 and told the governor that he was a survivor of the Drake expedition. He had been put ashore by Drake in or near the Strait of Anian and had crossed an arm of the sea in order to reach Mexico.[44]

In spite of all this evidence for a landing on one of the Channel Islands, Drake's route between Guatulco and the Moluccas is still largely a mystery. One thing is certain, though: the "Portus Novae Albionis" inset on the "Drake Broadside" map of Jodocus Hondius is of absolutely no value for locating any place where Drake might have stopped on the California coast. The inset does not depict a harbor in Upper California. It is simply a mislabeled sketch of the harbor at Acapulco, a deep bay, sheltered by a peninsula alongside an island of nearly equal length.[45] A view of Acapulco drawn by Adriaen Boot in 1628 shows the harbor in great detail, with a town on the far shore. Prominently featured are the curious rock formations that appear on the Hondius inset.[46] The original view copied by Hondius doubtless came from the derrotero that Drake took from Alonso Sánchez Colchero. The same view, perhaps mislabeled, probably appeared on the margins of the map given by Drake to Queen Elizabeth. This is important only because so many modern fans of Drake have tried to use the inset to prove that Drake landed in one or another of the bays in and around San Francisco.[47]

A second supposition is almost equally certain. The various latitudes given in the several accounts of the Drake voyage are of little or no value in determining Drake's landing place. After talking with William Hawkins or John Drake in October 1582, Richard Madox wrote that Francis Drake had "graved and bremd his ship the[r] at 48 degrees to the north."[48] In 1584

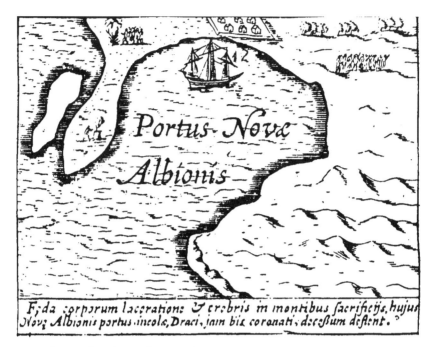

This inset from the Hondius map of Drake's expedition is really a mislabeled map of the port of Acapulco rather than a place on the coast of California. Source: Vera totius expeditionis nauticae.

John Drake told his Spanish interrogators that his relative's ships went as far north as 44° or 46° and that they found a harbor for careening the ships at 48° of north latitude—about the site of today's Seattle.[49] These figures are such clear exaggerations that no competent historian accepts them. In all likelihood they simply reflect the state of the story being circulated in May 1582, when John Drake left England on the journey that landed him in a Spanish prison. Emanuel van Meteren, who wrote one of the earliest foreign language reports, said that Drake went only to 33° north latitude (the current San Diego).[50] Hakluyt at various times gave the northward limits of the journey as 42° and 43° and said that the harbor where Drake stopped was in 38° (today's San Francisco).[51] The composite account published in 1628 by Drake's nephew, *The World Encompassed by Sir Francis Drake,* locates Drake's California harbor at 38°30' north latitude.[52]

These last two figures are the basis for the claims that Drake stopped at

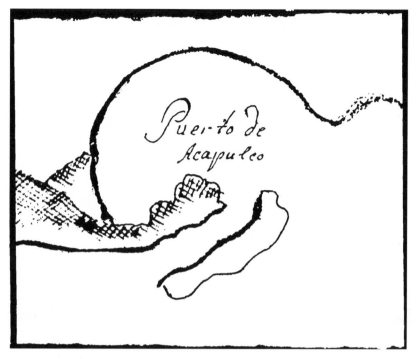

Sketch of the port of Acapulco, detail from the "Ringrose Atlas," one of a series of copies of a derrotero similar to the one that Drake took from Alonso Sanchez Colchero. Reprinted from Ringrose, "South Sea Waggoner." National Maritime Museum, London, MS P.32.39.MS9944.

Bodega Bay, Tomales Bay, Drake's Estero, Drake's Bay, Bolinas Lagoon, or San Francisco Bay, all of which are located in that general area. The weakness of the argument for any one of these locations is that Drake used maps captured from Spanish pilots, maps that very likely overestimated the latitude by a degree or two.

Consider a few examples. When Juan Rodríguez Cabrillo was at Catalina Island, he said that the latitude was just a bit more than 34°, about a degree too high. When Cabrillo was near Drake's Bay, he called the latitude 40°. By his estimates 38° would have put him in Monterey Bay.[53] When Alvaro de Mendaña reached the San Benito Islands in 1567, he thought that he was at 30° north latitude, an exaggeration of a degree and a half.[54] If Drake, using Spanish maps, actually sailed to what he thought was 38° north latitude, he may very well have been in Monterey Bay, the same

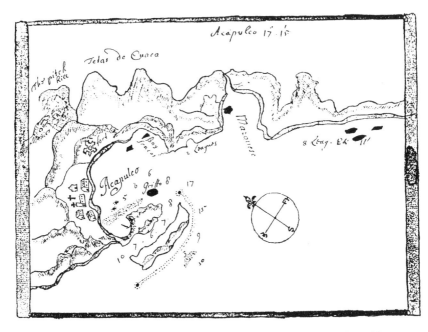

This seventeenth-century view of the harbor at Acapulco shows the narrow channel between the island and the peninsula, the only safe entrance to the port. Reprinted from Ringrose, "South Sea Waggoner."

place where Cabrillo's little fleet sheltered after a storm. There is some sense in this conclusion, because maps of the early seventeenth century described Monterey Bay as "a grand haven" for ships engaged in the China trade—"muy buen puerto para socorro de las naos de China."[55]

On the other hand, there is equally convincing evidence that Drake did not go this far north. When Richard Madox referred to the voyage in 1582, he wrote that the ships had stopped in "Calphurnia."[56] When John Drake testified about the journey a second time, in 1587, he told his Spanish interrogators that the ships "went to the Californias."[57] The word in those days was used to describe locations in the Baja California peninsula.[58] It was here in 1587 that Thomas Cavendish stopped in "a great bay called Aguada Segura; into which bay falleth a faire fresh river."[59] If Francis Drake careened his ship in "Calphurnia," he may well have done so in the same harbor near the tip of the California peninsula.

When the Hakluyt account was published in late 1595 or early 1596, it was made as a twelve-page insert to be placed after page 643 of the 1589 edition. This version of the story is important largely for the fanciful details of the lives and customs of the native inhabitants. Among the details is a word supposedly in the language of the people who lived on the shore where Drake careened his ship. In Hakluyt's English edition it was *Hioh;* the Dutch and German versions of the Drake voyage had *Hioch,* which seems to indicate that the final consonant has a hard sound.[60] When the *World Encompassed* appeared in the seventeenth century, several other supposedly Indian words appeared. One was *Tobáh* or *Tabáh* in place of "tobacco," which had appeared in Hakluyt's English account. Another was *Petáh,* which was explained as "a roote . . . whereof they make a kind of meale, and either bake it into bread, or eat it raw." *Hioh* was the same: *Hióh* or *Hyóh.* A third new term was *Gnaáh,* "by which they intreated that we would sing." The word *Oh* was spoken as an expression of approval.[61]

To this list can be added a few words and phrases copied by Richard Madox in 1582, when he was on a voyage with John Drake and William Hawkins, two of the men who were with Francis Drake. As Madox understood it, the California Indians used the word *cheepe* to mean bread, *Hioghe* to mean king, the expression *Nocharo mu* for "tuch me not," and *Huchee kecharoh* to mean "sit downe." *Hodeli oh heigh oh heigh ho hodali oh* was "ther song when they worship God."[62]

In 1942 anthropologist Robert F. Heizer published a study in which he identified several of these words and phrases as being from the Coast Miwok language, though he had to change some definitions in order to make them fit. According to Heizer *Hioh* or *Hioghe* is the same as *hoipu,* the Coast Miwok word for chief. *Cheepe* was Coast Miwok *tcipa,* the word for acorn bread. And *Nocharo mu* was *notcáto mu,* "keep away." Those were the easy ones.[63]

Gnaah, according to Heizer's study, "can possibly be likened to the Coast Miwok *koyá,* 'sing.'" The best he could do for *Huchee kecharoh* was *atci kotcáto* "step into the house," or *hoki kotcádo,* "go into the house." *Oh* was indeed an expression of approval, similar to that used by the Pomo. *Tabáh* or *Tobáh* and *Petáh* or *Patáh* were simply impossible for Heizer to identify with any certainty, nor could he do much with the chanted phrase, *Hodeli oh heigh oh heigh ho hodali oh.*[64]

In 1974 Heizer reprinted his earlier study, adding a few corrections. He thought *petáh* and *tobáh* might be "renderings for potato and tobacco." On this occasion Heizer decided that the word *Oh,* undefined in Miwok dictionaries, could be *Oiay* (God) or *Oiya* (friend). In addition, he changed his mind about *koyáh* as a cognate for *Gnaah.* This identification, he said, "cannot be argued strongly."[65]

But is it really necessary to believe these are true Indian words? Some of them can be identified as Spanish. *Cheepe,* for example, is surely the Spanish *Chipa,* or manioc bread. The Spanish word fits the description given by Hakluyt: a root ground into meal and baked into bread. *Tabáh* and *Patáh* are just as easily identified with the Spanish words for tobacco *(tabaco)* and potato *(patata).*[66] Similarly, *Nocharo mu* could be *no tocarme,* do not touch me. And *Hioh* or *Hioghe* could easily be the first word of *Hijo de Dios,* the Son of God. The phrase *Huchee kecharoh* could be *aquí quedará* (you will stay here). Indians at Aguada Segura and other Spanish outposts in Baja California would almost certainly have known these and other Spanish words and phrases and would very likely have used them to impress visitors.

The enthusiasts who identify Drake's Bay as the stopping place of the Drake expedition often point to the many fragments of Chinese porcelain found along and near the bay as evidence that Francis Drake really stopped there. In this version of the Drake story, the expedition is said to have abandoned several cases of porcelains at the bay. As luck would have it, Drake's porcelains were left in exactly the same place where Cermeño is also said to have left broken porcelain when his ship was wrecked there in 1595. According to this argument it is possible to distinguish between the "crude," "surf-worn" fragments from the Cermeño expedition and the "sharp-edged, high-quality porcelain sherds" that could have been left by no one but Francis Drake.[67] In any case, Chinese porcelain fragments of a similar age have been found elsewhere along the Pacific coast.[68]

One of the most persistent stories about the place where Francis Drake stopped on the California coast is that Drake claimed the land for England, marked his claim with an engraved brass plate, and that the very same brass

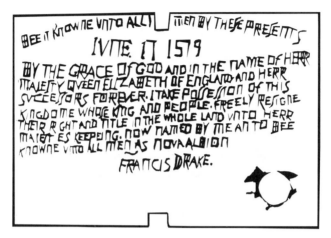

*Author's sketch of the controversial "plate of brass" now in the collection
of the Bancroft Library.*

plate was found near San Francisco and placed in the Bancroft Library of the
University of California. First branded genuine, then a hoax, then genuine
again, and then a hoax again, the "plate of brass" still has its enthusiastic
supporters.[69] The documentary evidence for the existence of such a plate is
contradictory to say the least. Richard Hakluyt called it "a plate, nailed
upon a faire great post" with a sixpence "under the plate."[70] The anonymous
manuscript in the British Library says that Drake "set up a great post and
nayled thereon a vi[d] [sixpence]" and a "plate of lead."[71] The Dutch version
of the story says the plate was silver.[72] The latest of all the versions, *The
World Encompassed by Sir Francis Drake,* says the plate was brass.[73]

Records of the inscriptions also vary. The anonymous manuscript says
that the queen's name was on the lead plate.[74] Hakluyt's story says the text
included "her maiesties name, the day and yeere of our arrival there, with
the free giving up of the province and people into her maiesties hands" plus
"the name of our Generall."[75] The *World Encompassed* adds that the surrender of sovereignty was made "both by the king and people."[76] The Bancroft
Library plate of brass moots the issue by including all these elements.

Of the several animals said to have been seen by Drake and his men at
Nova Albion (and by Cavendish at Aguada Segura), none are more puzzling than the "Connies." Here is the way Hakluyt described them in the

sixteenth century: "We found the whole Countrey to be a warren of a strange kinde of Connies, their bodies in bignes as be the Barbarie Connies, their heads as the heads of ours, the feete of a Want and the taile of a Rat being of great length: under her chinne on either side a bagge, into which she gathereth her meate, when she hath filled her bellie abroad. The people eate their bodies, and make a great accompt of their skinnes, for their Kings coate was made of them."[77]

Now a "cony" is a rabbit. And California rabbits simply do not look like this. Nor does any other animal. Seth Benson, emeritus curator of mammals at the Museum of Vertebrate Zoology at the University of California, Berkeley, put it best: "The cony described in Hakluyt's 'Famous Voyages' and in Drake's 'The World Encompassed' cannot be identified with any known mammal living anywhere in the world, let alone California."[78]

Probably the most interesting part of the early stories about Drake's sojourn in Upper California is the account of his relations with the Indians. The usual exchange of gifts took place, including "bags of *Tobacco*" from the Indians. Then ambassadors appeared, to announce the imminent arrival of their king. The king came with a group of courtiers, preceded by a man bearing his scepter, from which were hung the two royal crowns, along with three long chains "made of a bonie substance." After much pomp and ceremony, the king asked Drake to "take their province & kingdome into his hand, and becomme their king." The people made "signes that they would resigne unto him their right and title of the whole land, and become his subjects." Renouncing his own sovereignty, the king then put the crown on Drake's head, placed the chains around Drake's neck, and proclaimed him to be the new ruler of the country. Drake, for his part, accepted in the name of the queen.[79]

This story is entirely fictitious. The local people were unsophisticated food gatherers, who occupied a very restricted area. They had no idea of sovereignty, and their cultural accouterments were not like those described in the story. They did not wear the clothes, nor travel in canoes, nor live in the houses described by Hakluyt. In fact, the descriptions are so fanciful that Henry Wagner concluded that the author of the Hakluyt narrative simply included cultural features of all the native societies that Drake had seen.[80]

When the *World Encompassed* was published in 1628, the Hakluyt story of Drake's landing place was included, with additional embellishments. One scientific critic has described the various stories in a way that allows us to dispose of them: "The accounts concerning the cony are fabrications. Also, other statements concerning the biology and ecology of the region, including the weather, have no certain identifying values, or are contradictory, or false. If the various statements in these accounts are weighted equally, the conclusion must be drawn that they cannot be used to identify a specific landing site in California. Indeed, so much of the accounts are fabrications that they might be used to support the argument that Drake did not visit California."[81]

The early assertions by John Drake and Richard Madox that Drake sailed to 48° north latitude were repudiated by inference in the mid-1590s, when Richard Hakluyt said Drake sailed as far north as 42°, and by Emanuel van Meteren, who said in his corrected work that Drake sailed only to 33° north latitude.[82] Nonetheless, the earlier assertions of John Drake and Richard Madox were renewed in 1628 when the *World Encompassed* appeared.[83]

Professor George Davidson, who made the initial U.S. surveys of the West Coast, described in 1908 the route Drake would have taken to reach 42° north latitude. Based on his own experience in sailing ships and his own study of the Pacific Coast pilot charts, Davidson concluded that the route would have involved a long sail to the west-southwest, followed by careful sailing to the west-northwest, northwest by west, and north-northeast. The total distance would have been nearly 3,000 miles beyond Guatalco.[84] Such a journey in a leaky and overloaded ship seems very unlikely for a commander who had never before sailed anywhere without good charts and good pilots.

The most reasonable conclusion is that Drake did not head out to sea for a month or more, then sail to Upper California, as stated in the early accounts. Instead, he probably followed the coastal route taken by early Spanish explorers. In the Colchero derrotero Drake had full information about this route, including descriptions of all the good harbors in Lower California. The best of these for his purposes would have been the sandy beaches in Magdalena Bay or one of the small harbors in Cedros Island and the San Benito Islands. There is interesting circumstantial evidence that Drake might have sailed as far north as the Channel Islands, stopping at Catalina Island. This is supported by Meteren's statement that Drake reached 33° north latitude. Even so, Catalina seems too far north for a commander looking for a convenient place to careen his ship.

Of all the unlikely voyages, the least likely is that Drake took his leaky ships in search of the Strait of Anian. The most positive thing that can be said about such a voyage is that English mariners had long hoped to find a northern route to the Pacific but thought it unlikely that such a route existed. A voyage by Drake's treasure-laden ship in search of such a strait is equally unlikely.

The best explanation for the English stories that Drake had sailed to 48° north latitude was their perennial desire to annoy the Spanish. When the ships of Juan Rodríguez Cabrillo returned from the voyage to the northwest in 1543, his men reported that they had gone as far north as 43° or 44° or perhaps a bit more. His accomplishments, along with those of the other Pacific navigators, were carefully studied by Andrés de Urdaneta in the 1560s, when he was making his plans for the successful passage to Manila and back. Urdaneta's work made these explorations the subject of common conversation in the ports of Mexico and Guatemala.[85] When Drake visited, he no doubt heard the stories. Drake's claim to have sailed farther north then Cabrillo and to have camped at a place farther north than Cabrillo's winter camp was a way to tell Spanish authorities that an English navigator had done better than his Spanish predecessors.[86]

Once Drake had completed the repair of his ship, he was ready to leave on the long voyage to the Moluccas and then home to England. He decided not to take the captured ship with him, abandoning it and perhaps leaving some of the crew.[87] There were several reasons for this. First, the captured ship was a small vessel, not strong enough for a long sea voyage. At one point Drake had thought of strengthening the hull of this ship and fitting it with additional sails and oars.[88] No doubt this proved to be more work than he could undertake, and Drake finally decided to abandon the vessel. Some authors have speculated that Drake also abandoned a dozen

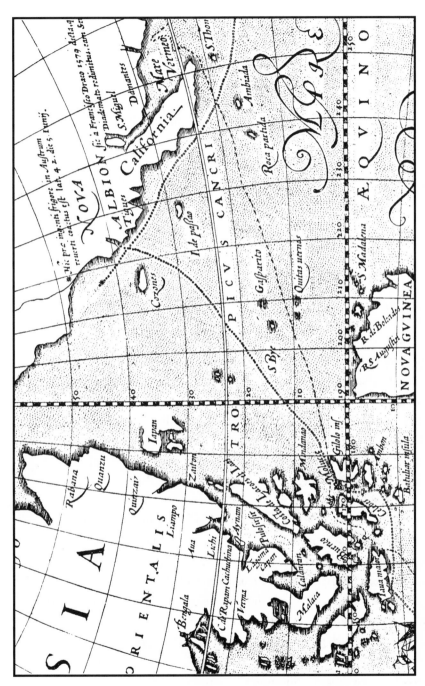

Jodocus Hondius showed Drake sailing southwest across the Pacific, a most unlikely route, because of the prevailing winds and currents. From Vera Totius Expeditionis Nauticae.

or so men.[89] Perhaps he did, for only sixty men were left in his crew when he reached the Moluccas.[90] It is even possible that the Portuguese pilot Morera was one of them.

The anonymous English account says that Drake left his anchorage "in the latter ende of August" and did not see land again until the end of November.[91] According to two other accounts they left in July, stopped for a day at islands offshore to hunt for seals and birds, then set off again the following day. The first of these, the Hakluyt story, says that they left on 25 July and made their first landfall on 13 October.[92] The *World Encompassed* says that they left on 25 July and had their first landfall on 30 September, after sixty-eight days at sea.[93] The anonymous account is presumably by an eyewitness. The others were written after many opportunities for correcting and embellishing the narrative. It is not possible now to know which account, if any, is correct.

The route they took must have been the same as the route taken by the Manila galleons, for that was the route on their derrotero. This meant sailing southwest to about 13° of north latitude, perhaps still looking for the Bajos de Abreojo or the Bajos de San Bartolomé, where some mariners had thought that they might find the islands and treasure mines visited by King Solomon's ships. From here they would sail west at about 10° north latitude, looking for the island Ruy López de Villalobos called Los Corales. This was in the Radak chain of the Marshall Islands, and Drake missed it, just as others had done. He also missed the island of Kwajalein, where natives in boats had greeted Villalobos, calling out, "Buenos días, Matalotes" —"Good day, mates."[94]

The problem was a treacherous wind, which drove them south to 1°30' north latitude.[95] Continuing on this route, Drake passed the Marshalls and most of the Carolines before correcting his course. His first landfall was made at one of the Palau Islands, probably Babelthuap. A fleet of dugout canoes came to meet his ship. These boats sported a brilliant coating of shiny red paint, with festoons of cowrie shells draped here and there. Both ends of each canoe pointed upward in symmetrical fashion, and there were outrigger booms and floats on most of the boats. Depending on the size, the crews varied from four or six to fourteen or fifteen men in each

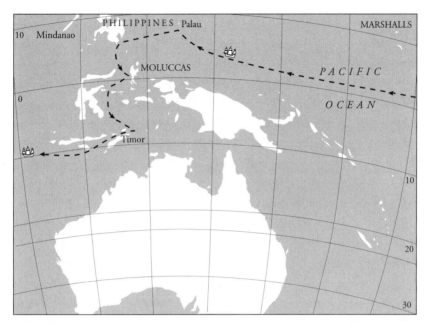

Drake's route through the South Pacific

vessel.[96] These are described in the Hakluyt account as follows: "Their Canoas were hollowe within, and cut with great arte, and cunning, being very smooth within and without, and bearing a glasse as if it were a horne daintily burnished, having a prowe, and a sterne of one force, yeelding inward circle wise, being of great heigth, and full of certain white shels for a braverie, and on each side of them lie out two peeces of timber about a yard and a halfe long, more or lesse, according to the smalnes, or bignes of the boate."[97]

At first the canoemen traded with Drake's sailors, fish for beads. But they soon tired of this, became noisy and indignant, and demanded beads for nothing.[98] One man grabbed a knife and refused to return it. A scuffle ensued. The canoemen hurled stones at the sailors. Drake ordered a cannon to be fired at the boats. Twenty islanders were killed and more were injured.[99] The Englishmen decided to name this place the Island of Thieves, *Los Ladrones.*[100]

Drake and his men remained in Palau for another day or two, no doubt taking on wood and water. The Palau islanders were tough and warlike, not discouraged by the first encounter with the English sailors. Trading continued while they were in the islands, and Drake's pilot was able to make a reasonably accurate determination of their general location, 9° according to John Drake, 8° according to Hakluyt.[101]

Again sailing west for a week or more, they came to the Island of Mindanao and searched the rugged coast for several days before finding a place to stop for wood and water. From there they headed south, passing several islands on their way to Ternate in the Moluccas. John Drake said that one of the islands was named Borney.[102] According to Hakluyt they saw three Portuguese islands: Tagulada, Zelon, and Zewarra.[103] The *World Encompassed* records that they passed five islands. The first was Talao, located on maps of the day in 3°40' north latitude. The other three were Teda, Selan, and Saran, "Islands so named to us by an Indian." Selan was then thought to be at exactly 3° north. A fifth island was Suaro in 1°30' north latitude, the last island seen before reaching the Moluccas.[104] There is an obvious similarity in some of the names, so the lists are probably not exclusive. In what is certainly the most exhaustive study of the problem, William A. Lessa identified four of the islands as two peninsulas and two islands in the Davao Gulf.[105] On the other hand, it is reasonable to think that Talao is the island now called Pulau, while Tagulada and perhaps one or two others are islands nearby.[106]

While sailing on this course, they met another ship and asked for supplies, pleading great need. When the commander of the other vessel discovered the ship was English, he refused to help, saying he would not give aid to Lutherans. Drake then declared that he would take what he wanted. He followed the other ship the rest of the day and all night, unlimbering the guns that had been stored away for the trip across the Pacific. The next morning he drew close to the other vessel and ordered its captain to surrender. When the other captain refused, Drake ordered his guns to fire, several times, but they apparently missed each time. Finally, the ship took refuge in a shallow bay, and Drake thought it wiser to sail on. Perhaps because of the distance involved during their shouted exchanges, no one on Drake's ship was certain of the identity of the other ship.[107]

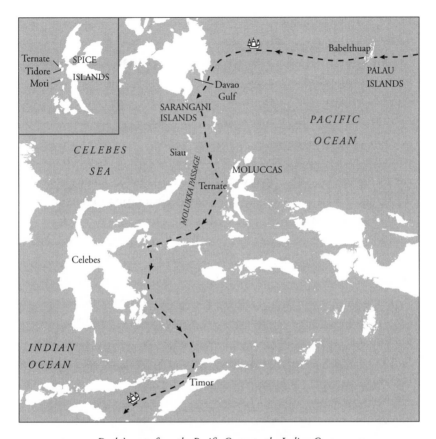

Drake's route from the Pacific Ocean to the Indian Ocean

Drake's objective on this leg of the journey was the island of Tidore in
the Spice Islands. Most of the islands in this region grow spices of various
sorts, but the traditional trade in cloves was limited to several tiny islands
on the east side of the Molukka Passage. Just how Drake decided on one
island rather than another is not clear, though the earliest account published by Hakluyt insists that he originally intended to land at Tidore.[108]

Sailing through the Sarangani Islands, Drake stopped at the island of
Siau, where he convinced two fishermen to show him the way to Tidore.
Following their directions, Drake sailed southeast across the Molukka Passage, stopping first at another small island, perhaps Moti, where a "Portuguese mestizo" promised to take them to a place where people would give

them provisions. Fortunately for them, a well-dressed "Moro gentleman" with a gold chain around his neck and a silver chain full of important-looking keys at his waist approached just then. He warned the Englishmen not to go with the Portuguese, as they were not to be trusted. Instead, he suggested that Drake come to meet with his own king, who would treat him royally. With this last man as guide, the English pirates then sailed the short distance to Ternate.[109]

Drake and his crew were well received in Ternate. They had an interview with the king and then were directed to a better anchorage, where they could load the provisions they wanted. In addition to the provisions, Drake took on ten tons of spices, including about six tons of cloves, plus additional supplies of ginger and pimiento. Everything was paid for with linens—surprisingly, not with gold or silver.[110] The provisions included cassava, plantains, and chickens.[111] Apparently thinking it best not to mention that he was ruled by a queen, Drake told the king of Ternate that the English king was a brother to the king of Spain. Impressed by this, the king of Ternate offered Drake the freedom of the island and invited him to visit him ashore, but Drake declined, sending some of his officers instead.[112]

This is the simple story that was recorded by John Drake. Years later, the tale became much more elaborate. The "Moro gentleman" did not accompany Drake to the island but instead went ahead to warn the king that important visitors were coming and to prepare a reception. As soon as he arrived, Drake sent a gift to the king, a velvet cloak. In exchange, the ruler of Ternate sent Drake a signet ring and went out in his own boat to meet him and direct him to a proper anchorage. Whether true or not, the account of this first meeting is a colorful tale:

> The King purposing to come to our shippe, sent before
> 4. great and large Canoas, in every one whereof were
> certaine of his greatest states that were about him,
> attired in white lawne of cloth of Callicut, having over
> their heads from the one ende of the Canoa to the
> other, a covering of thinne perfumed mats, borne up

*Drake's ship being towed by the canoes of the ruler of Ternate.
Reprinted from Hondius,* Vera Totius Expeditionis Nauticae.

with a frame made of reedes for the same use, under
which every one did sit in his order according to his dig-
nitie, to keepe him from the heate of the Sunne, divers
of whome being of good age, and gravitie, did make an
ancient and fatherly shewe. There were also divers yong
and comely men attired in white, as were the others: the
rest were souldiers, which stoode in comely order round
about on both sides, without whome sate the rowers in
certaine galleries, which being three on a side all along
the canoas, did lie off from the side thereof 3. or 4.
yardes, one being orderly builded lower then another,
in every one of which galleries, were the number of 4.
score rowers.[113]

There were further visits and further conversations. The king promised
to send provisions to the ships, and he was as good as his word. There were
rice, chickens, raw sugar, syrup, sugar cane, and a meal called Sago, "made
of the tops of certaine trees, tasting in the mouth like sowre curds, but melt-
eth like sugar." Beyond this, the king offered to "yeeld himselfe and the

right of his island" to the queen of England.[114] After another twenty years, when the *World Encompassed* was published, the story became even more elaborate and less plausible.

The stories soon became current in Spain as well as in England. Bartolomé Leonardo de Argensola included some additional details in his 1609 history of the Moluccas. In one part of his account, Argensola said that Drake tried to purchase cloves without the permission of the king of Ternate, called Babú. As a result, Babú threatened to have Drake put to death. Only by sending additional gifts to the king was Drake able to extricate himself. Once this was done, though, the king and Drake became fast friends. Drake, presenting himself as a representative of the queen, promised to establish trading facilities in Ternate.[115] Argensola had already seen the Hakluyt story, but he had independent confirmation for the negotiations. These came from Francisco de Dueñas, a representative of the Spanish governor in Manila, who visited the region within three years of Drake's visit. It should be noted that in the Spanish accounts, the king of Ternate did not go out to greet Drake or offer to become a vassal of the English ruler, or any of the other imaginary things mentioned in Hakluyt and the *World Encompassed*.[116]

After staying for five or six days in Ternate, Drake sailed on, looking for a place to careen his ship once more. He soon found a tiny island, deserted and without water but with a supply of wood and full of crabs and lobsters. Drake called the place Crab Island, and located it in about 4° north latitude. He stayed here for a month or more, bringing drinking water from a nearby island and thoroughly refurbishing the ship for the remainder of the voyage home.[117]

While they were on this island Drake had an argument with a man named Will Legge, the ship's steward. After the capture of the *Capitana* off the coast of Peru, Legge had been rifling through a chest and discovered six and a half pounds of gold, which he gave to Drake. In gratitude, Drake gave Legge a wedge of gold weighing about twenty-nine ounces. After their argument, Drake took the gold away from Legge. Later, realizing how this looked to the men, Drake marked the bar with a chisel and assured Legge that he would return that very bar to the steward when they reached

England. According to Legge, this was never done. In fact, Legge later claimed that he was arrested on a charge of owing Drake fifty pounds.[118]

Another incident on Crab Island deserves mention, though many Drake biographies gloss over it or skip it entirely. The two eyewitness accounts give the details. John Drake told his Spanish captives that when the mariners left the island "they left there the two black men and the black woman Maria."[119] The anonymous account gives more details. The black woman, taken aboard seven months earlier, was pregnant, "being gotten with childe and now being very great."[120] No doubt there was good reason for abandoning her. There was uncertainty about the father, but suspicion fell on Drake and others. She was "gotten with child between the captaine and his men pirats."[121] The embarrassment when they reached England would be more than Drake could have wanted to face. Beyond this, another long voyage across the Indian and Atlantic oceans might be too hazardous for her and the child as well. John Drake put it succinctly. They left the three "with rice and seeds and fire to populate the place."[122] As luck would have it, the story did get out after they returned home, and Drake was criticized roundly. William Camden wrote later that Drake had "most inhumanely" left the "Black-more-Maide who had been gotten with Child in his Ship" to fend for herself on an island.[123]

The version of the anonymous English manuscript account published by W. S. W. Vaux has left the impression that the island was called Francisca in honor of one of the two men. However, this seems to be an error. The manuscript originally had the woman's name listed as Francisca and said the island was named after her. The name was then corrected to Maria, and the manuscript was changed in such a way as to say that the island was named after "one of the ii negrose." Francisca is an unlikely name for a man, and, given the circumstances, it is equally unlikely that the island would have been named after one of her companions, rather than the woman herself. If the island had another name, it was probably Maria.[124]

Having abandoned the three black slaves, Drake and his men headed south, looking for a way out of the Moluccas and into the Indian Ocean. For a month they tacked, first in one direction and then another, but could not find the route. Somewhere off the Celebes on 8 January at about 8 P.M.

they struck fast on a reef and could not get the ship free. First they threw overboard most of the cargo of food and spices, plus several cannons and other materials. It was a terrible spot. Intending to haul the anchor aft and winch themselves off the reef, they sounded the depth but found no bottom at 300 fathoms. Nothing they did seemed to help.[125]

Drake then told Fletcher to hold a communion service. The sermon seems to have been on the subject of Thomas Doughty. The stranding was a punishment for the death of Doughty and all the other evil that they had committed on the voyage. There was not much hope of getting away safely. "Every theefe reconciled him selfe to his fello theefe," said the anonymous chronicler, "and so yelded themselves to death." Then late in the afternoon a gale came up and blew them off the rocks.[126]

Not a man to forget an insult, Drake immediately called Fletcher on deck and berated him mercilessly. More than this, he had the poor cleric chained to a hatch cover. Drake then seated himself on a sea chest and, with his slippers in his hands, said: "Francis Fletcher, I doo heere excomunicate the out of the Church of God and from all the benefites and graces therof, and I denounce the to the divell and all his angells."[127] Continuing, Drake told Fletcher to stay aft where he belonged, saying that if he came before the mast again and talked to the men, he would be hanged. He then had a little verse written and told Fletcher to wear it permanently on his arm "or be hanged." The verse was: "Francis Fletcher, the falseth knave that liveth." The author of this story, perhaps using information from Will Legge, added his own editorial remark: "Save Francis Drake, quoth the writer hereof."[128]

Once free of the reef, the ship sailed onward. Because so much had been thrown overboard while they were lightening the ship, it was necessary to stop again to purchase food and to get additional water and firewood. The first stop was made on 8 February 1580 at an island called Baratina, where they took on various "fruits of the land."[129] The account in Hakluyt says, "To confesse a trueth, since the time that we first sett out of our owne Countrey of England, we happened upon no place, (Terenate onely excepted) wherin we found more comfortes and more meanes of refreshing."[130]

From this point they sailed to the southern coast of Java and stopped

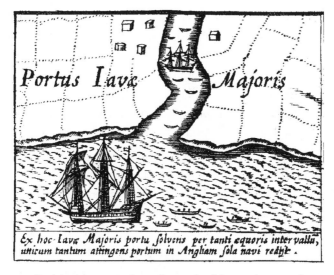

Drake's anchorage on the southern coast of Java as shown on the
Hondius map.

there for two weeks or more.[131] Here they were able to buy six or seven tons of rice, plus plantains, coconuts, and sugar cane.[132] Because of the map inset printed in the Hondius "Drake Broadside" it is usually assumed that the ship stopped at the major port on the southern coast, Tjilatjap.[133] Perhaps this was the port, though we have seen that the inset maps do not necessarily show the places visited by Drake. In any case, they were treated well. John Drake says they met nine kings, though the Hakluyt story mentions five and names only three. They were Rajah Donaw, Rajah Mang Bange, and Rajah Cabuccapollo. The people were more than cordial. Whereas the men at Ternate guarded their women carefully, the men of Java offered to share them. Even the kings did this. An unfortunate result was the French pox, common to all, but curable by sitting naked in the sun and letting the evil humors boil out.[134] This was a place to store up for the voyage home. They managed to buy beef for the first time since leaving England. There were also rice and chicken and cassava.[135] Again they paid in trade goods, though the prices were high. According to Thomas Hood, the people wanted nothing but the finest silks and linens, and it cost Drake £4,000 worth of goods to buy enough food for the voyage home.[136]

From Java to the Cape of Good Hope the voyage was an uninterrupted passage of two and a half months on the open sea.[137] John Drake said that they did not stop at the cape because there were no good harbors.[138] The anonymous writer says they stopped at a harbor on the west side of the cape but were unable to land. Then some heavy rains renewed their water supplies, and they sailed on for another month or more. Finally, they stopped for water and provisions at Sierra Leone on the Guinea coast. It was the twenty-second day of July 1580.[139]

After two days taking on wood and water they left the Guinea coast and sailed northwest to the latitude of the Azores. From here they caught a westerly wind and sailed on to Plymouth, or so the anonymous informant says.[140] Another informant, a certain Pedro de Rada, heard that Drake had stopped at Belle Isle, where he unloaded some of his treasure, and then had gone on to New Rochelle, where he hired additional crewmen and repaired his ship a bit.[141] No other information has ever come to light about this incident, which may or may not be true. With his crew weakened by disease and hunger, Drake might have welcomed replacements. No doubt he also wanted to know what sort of reception might await him in England.

Perhaps he obtained all this in New Rochelle and Belle Isle. Perhaps not. The only thing known with certainty is that Drake's ship arrived in the harbor at Plymouth late in September 1580, after a voyage of nearly three years. With such a dearth of precise information about other aspects of the voyage, there is no reason to be surprised that the exact date of return is not clear. John Drake said a few years later that he thought it was "in the month of October."[142] A Dutch version of the journey said it was "the third of November in the year 1580."[143] Drake's nephew Francis, writing in 1626, said that they reached Plymouth "the 26. of Sept.," and most historians accept this date.[144]

III

A Pirate and a Gentleman

8

Honors and Riches

WHILE DRAKE WAS ON HIS three-year voyage around the world, he had no communication with anyone in England. Still, news of his exploits arrived there, even before he began his raids along the Pacific coast. Most of the information came in the form of complaints lodged by the Spanish ambassador, Bernardino de Mendoza, though other news reached England from travelers on the Continent. John Wynter's report was already in the hands of government officials. Wynter himself was charged with piracy for his supposed role in seizing the ship and cargo of Nuño de Silva, but the remaining goods were eventually returned to their owners, and the charge of piracy was dropped.[1] With this precedent, an official attitude developed toward Drake and his voyage—a very favorable one, as it turned out.

During these years the Spanish representatives in England managed to organize remarkable sources of information about Drake's voyage, undependable at first, but much improved as time passed. A few weeks before Drake left the country in 1577, the unofficial Spanish representative in England, Antonio de Guaras, had written to authorities in Spain, telling them that "Drake the pirate" was thought to be going to Scotland to capture the prince.[2] Before he could get his information straight, Guaras was accused of some crime, perhaps complicity in a plot to free Mary, and thrown into prison.[3] Guaras was soon replaced by an ambassador, Mendoza. By the end of March 1578, Mendoza was able to supply a slightly more factual account of Drake's intentions. Drake had left a month and a half before Christmas with a pretended objective of Alexandria, where he would purchase a cargo of currants. From his sources Mendoza learned that the trading voyage to Alexandria was a cover for another raid on Spanish ports. At first he was convinced that the real objective was Nombre de Dios once again, repeating the raid that Drake had made earlier with John Hawkins.[4] In this he was wrong, but he understood Drake's general inclination.

As a new man in London, Mendoza had to organize a dependable group of informants. Within a few months this was accomplished. John Wynter returned to England on 2 June 1579 and immediately submitted a written report to the Privy Council.[5] Scarcely a week later Mendoza wrote to Spain with a description of Drake's voyage to the Strait of Magellan, including the trial and execution of "a gentleman" (Doughty).[6] Either Mendoza had obtained a copy of Wynter's report or he had a summary of the report, plus other important details. Among his details was information that Wynter had been granted a private audience with the queen. Obviously pleased with what she heard from Wynter, the queen ordered that the captain and his crew should be treated honorably. She also decided to defer an investigation into the death of Doughty until after Drake's return.[7]

A few weeks later Drake's real objective became abundantly clear, both in Spain and in England. The viceroys in Peru and New Spain had sent dispatches to the Spanish king, informing him of Drake's raids. Philip was annoyed, but less so than we now tend to think. The attacks that Drake made on Spanish Pacific ports were really minor matters when viewed in the context of Spain's other interests in Europe and around the world. Philip's real priority was to learn whether Drake's raid was a signal of English intentions to open a general war against Spain. Would there be similar raids on the Spanish coast as well?[8] It was a serious possibility. With the Spanish army busy fighting rebellious subjects in the Low Countries, the English government had very little to fear from an expanded policy of tormenting the king of Spain.

The first reports were followed within a few weeks by messages arriving in London from English merchants in Seville. Drake's booty was thought to be 600,000 ducats, a third of it the property of the Spanish crown. Drake's English investors, presumably including the queen, were overjoyed. And, yes, Mendoza could report, other private citizens were thought to be planning similar raids.[9]

As always, there were two sides to the Drake question. Those who had invested in Drake's voyage rejoiced, but the merchants who traded with Spain were more than a little apprehensive. Some feared that their own goods in Spain might be subject to seizure and forfeiture. Many of them purchased insurance against such an eventuality, paying a premium of as much as 4 or 5 percent of the value of their cargoes. When these merchants went to the Council to ask for some official assurances, Mendoza reported to his government, they were told that Drake was simply on a private voyage of discovery.[10] There is no evidence that Mendoza had a sense of humor. Perhaps members of the Council did.

In preparation for Drake's return, the members of the Council who had money invested in his voyage sent word to officials in Plymouth, ordering them to give Drake every possible assistance in landing and guarding his spoils. So self-assured were they that Mendoza was reluctant to discuss the Drake matter at all with the queen. Any complaint would amount to an admission that Spain simply lacked the extra men and ships to pursue Drake.[11] As Spanish impotence became more obvious, the investors began openly to appoint men in each of the ports to be ready to assist Drake whenever he might return.[12]

Meanwhile, Mendoza had begun general negotiations for the recovery of all goods stolen by pirates. An agreement for reciprocal return of stolen property was formalized at Bristol in 1579, but it was never taken seriously by English authorities. English commissioners at first refused to convene. Later they said it would be necessary to interview the alleged pirates before any other action could be taken. Finally, they refused to deal with anyone other than the owners of the property alleged to have been stolen. Ambassadors could negotiate only for the return of government property.[13]

Some of the owners did appear and ask for their property, but they were able to recover little or nothing. In one case the owners of a cargo of fish tried to recover the value of the goods from the men who had signed as sureties. They quickly discovered that all the names given as surety were fictitious.[14]

In the midst of this minor squabble about piracy, Spain's foreign problems began to grow. The civil war in the Netherlands, far to the north, coincided with other troubles in Fez-Morocco, to the south. Philip scarcely wanted another war, but he soon had one. When the Portuguese throne became vacant in 1580, Philip considered himself the legitimate heir. He found that armed intervention was necessary to sustain his claim to the crown of Portugal. Anti-Castilian groups promptly threw their support behind an illegitimate claimant, Dom Antonio, who also attracted the interest of France and England.

There were problems closer to England as well. Catholics there and in Ireland lived in daily expectation of aid from abroad to relieve their persecution. Pope Gregory XIII had dispatched a force of volunteers to Ireland to help organize a rebellion against English rule and had implored Philip to provide assistance in this venture. The king was also under considerable pressure to do something about seminary priests, who were tried and hanged almost as soon as they landed in England.

Trade was another problem. Along with the French and the Dutch, English merchants were showing an interest in direct trade with the Levant, as well as in the Far East and the Indies. But grain farmers in Andalusia were horrified by the thought of war, for they depended on foreign markets, especially those in England.[15] To cap all these troubles, the new Spanish ambassador to England was not allowed to present his credentials to the queen, who initially received him only as a private citizen.[16]

Faced with these difficulties, the merchants of Seville sent their own representative, Pedro Zubiaur, to London to try to deal privately for the recovery of their goods or their money.[17] The Spanish merchants seemingly felt that they could enlist the aid of the English merchants who traded in Spain and, through private negotiations, recover some part of their losses. These English merchants were said to be indignant that their property must be placed at risk for the benefit of a few of Her Majesty's favorites who had invested in Drake's voyage.[18]

In the midst of these developments, Drake's backers in England began to suspect that he might not be coming home after all. At first they expected him to be in England by January 1580.[19] When he failed to appear, there was some thought of sending a ship to search for him, but no one knew exactly where to go.[20] So it was a distinct and pleasant surprise when the ship appeared in Plymouth harbor late in September 1580. The exact date is unknown, but Ambassador Mendoza was aware of Drake's return on 28 September.[21] Thus most historians accept 26 September as the date of his arrival. This was the date given by Drake's nephew.[22]

When Drake's ship first entered Plymouth harbor, some of the crew hailed two men fishing in a small boat and asked whether the queen were still alive. Hearing that she was alive and well, Drake took the ship into the bay. Anchoring in the bay, the sailors were advised not to land because of a pestilence in the city. Even so, Drake's wife, Mary, came to the ship, as did the mayor of Plymouth. No doubt acting on their advice, Drake sent John Brewer to London with information about their voyage.[23] Brewer was Hatton's man and could be trusted with confidential business. He carried messages to the queen and to several private individuals, presumably the people who had invested in the voyage. Drake likely took on additional supplies before leaving the harbor and anchoring again off a nearby island to await a reply from London.[24]

The initial reply was distressing. Drake was advised that the queen had been greatly embarrassed by his actions and that the Spanish ambassador was asking for restitution.[25] No doubt this was all said for the benefit of Mendoza, who could be expected to learn the substance of the dispatch immediately. A short time later Drake received private messages from the queen, telling him that he had nothing to worry about. With this assurance Drake landed his treasure in Plymouth and left it in the care of his friend John Blitheman, the new lord mayor.[26] According to the information Mendoza received, the treasure was locked in a tower near Saltash and guarded by a detachment of forty men.[27]

As soon as the treasure was secured, probably about 12 or 13 October, Drake departed for London. In her message the queen had asked him to bring a few samples of his cargo. So he brought a small party of men with several pack horses loaded with gold and silver.[28] Once in London, he was led into the queen's presence for a private audience that lasted for perhaps six hours, interrupted from time to time by brief conferences with members of the Privy Council.[29] There is no record of the conference, but it seems certain that Drake gave the queen a complete description of the

This map, attributed to Nicola van Sype, is thought, like the map drawn by Jodocus Hondius, to be a copy of the map that Drake gave to the queen. Both maps, as well as a third by van Sype, contain similar vignettes, supposedly copied from views drawn by Francis Drake and his nephew John Drake. The other van Sype map contains a statement that it was "viuee et corige par le dict signeur drack" (seen and corrected by the said Sir Drake).

RAECK DAVOIR CIRQVIT TOVTE LA TERRE

plunder, plus a few samples as gifts. He appears to have emphasized the point that most of the treasure had not been registered by the owners, who were trying to evade the Spanish levy on shipments of gold and silver. Because the goods were contraband, the owners could scarcely ask their government to negotiate for their return. And because the registration was incomplete, the Spanish government could not know how much Drake had taken.

At first the council prepared an order that all the treasure was to be inventoried and placed in the queen's possession in the Tower of London. When the absent councillors, Leicester, Hatton, and Walsingham, learned of this plan, they prevailed upon the queen to rescind the order. They reasoned that the Spanish government did not know how much booty was involved and that there was no reason to give the Spaniards the benefit of an inventory. The less treasure registered in the Tower, the less the English might later have to return to Spanish owners. The queen quickly endorsed that logic, ordering instead that a report should be circulated that Drake had brought home little or nothing.[30]

With the preliminaries out of the way, Drake returned to Plymouth on 23 October, accompanied by the queen's representative, Edmund Tremayne, who was to take charge of some of the treasure.[31] But as Tremayne knew, Drake hid a large portion of the treasure elsewhere. Tremayne took the rest to the tower near Saltash, where the mayor had been keeping the treasure under guard.[32] It appears from a later letter of Tremayne's that he was simply to guard the treasure, while Drake himself was to exercise control over the items. Only Drake and the queen knew the total amount of the treasure. Writing to Walsingham later to report what he had done, Tremayne mentioned the "portion that was landed secretly," as though this was part of some prior agreement. Referring to Drake's authority in the matter, he continued, "I have only taken notice of so much as he has revealed."[33]

Before leaving London, Drake gave the queen a diary covering the entire three-year voyage, plus a large map showing the route he had taken. No one knows what information was recorded in the diary or what places were shown on the map because the queen ordered everything kept secret under pain of death.[34] The whole point was to tantalize the Spanish government by giving away none of the details of the voyage, pretending instead that nothing significant had happened.

Pursuing this policy, Elizabeth dispatched two of the secretaries of the Council to tell Mendoza that she had heard of his complaints about Drake and the warm reception that he had received at court. The emissaries told Mendoza that Elizabeth had made inquiry about the voyage and learned that Drake had done no damage either to Spanish subjects or to Spanish territories. This being the case, she did not wish to talk about Drake until she was reimbursed and otherwise satisfied for the Spanish king's interference in Ireland.[35]

When Drake returned to Devon with Tremayne, he had the queen's authority to appropriate an extra £10,000 of gold for himself.[36] Either then or later there were additional sums for the investors and the crew. John Drake said that the crew shared £40,000, and Mendoza reported that the private investors were to have double their money back.[37] On 30 October the queen ordered Drake and Tremayne to return to Devon and move the registered treasure once more. They did so, loading it on pack horses and taking it to Sion House in Richmond. After the first of the year it was moved to the Tower, out of the somewhat reluctant supervision of Edmund Tremayne. Mendoza's informants told him about the plunder that went to the Tower: "They say he is bringing twenty of this country's tons of silver, each one 2,000 pounds; five boxes of gold, a foot and a half in length; and a huge quantity of pearls, some of great value."[38] The official records show that Mendoza's sources of information were accurate.

Tremayne's inventory listed forty-six parcels whose undisclosed contents weighed a bit more than 200 pounds apiece, a total of nearly five tons.[39] This was only part of the treasure. Another inventory showed 650 ingots of silver weighing nearly 23,000 pounds, plus 36 parcels of gold, weighing a bit more than a hundred pounds.[40] A list compiled five years later showed that more than eleven tons of silver remained of this original total. Of the 650 silver ingots, some £40,000 had been coined, and 243 ingots were left. Beyond this, there were some £205 in gold coins made from ingots and cakes of gold. In addition numerous small pieces of silver were valued at £512.[41] Most or all of the unregistered booty apparently remained in

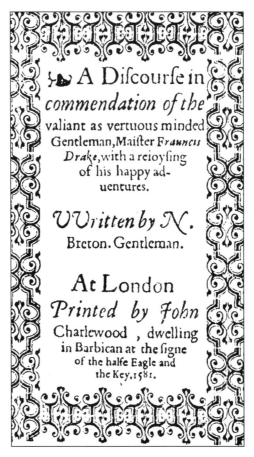

Shortly after Drake's return to England, Nicholas Breton,
a literary gentleman, published this eight-page pamphlet,
congratulating Drake on his stunning accomplishments
of sailing around the world and bringing home a
shipload of treasure.

Drake's hands, making him one of the richest men in the country.[42] The total value of the treasure was unknown, but Mendoza thought a million and a half (pesos?) might not be far wrong, and another source suggested a worth of two million.[43]

Drake, for his part, had taken up residence in London, where he soon purchased a house in Elbow Lane.[44] He appeared at court as often as possible, visiting with the queen and showering her with presents.[45] As a New

Year's gift Drake gave her an emerald-studded crown and a diamond cross, together worth more than 50,000 ducats. He also made gifts to influential people at court, including the chancellor, the secretaries, and others. On the other hand, he was said to be tightfisted with his crew, giving them something now and then to live on but not sharing the loot, as he had frequently promised to do.[46] This generosity to influential strangers was not new. Drake had done the same with the dignitaries he took prisoner during his raids on the Pacific ports. Drake's open attempt to buy the respect of men of power and influence sometimes worked with his enemies but often not with associates in England.[47]

This was to be a continuing problem for Drake. He was a pirate, and the queen did not care. In fact, she was at great pains to show how much she liked him.[48] But many of the people whose respect was important to Drake refused to have anything to do with him. Burghley rejected a gift of ten bars of gold, saying that he could not in good conscience receive stolen goods.[49] At a dinner party one evening, when Drake was boasting about his exploits, Lord Sussex declared that it was not a great accomplishment to capture an unarmed vessel with a well-armed ship. When Drake persisted, the earl of Arundel told Drake that he was impudent and had no shame.[50]

When the Spanish ambassador began to realize that Drake would be allowed to keep what he had taken, Mendoza submitted a memorandum that described Drake's stolen treasure and enumerated some of the injuries he had caused in the process of accumulating it.[51] Ever sensitive to criticism, Drake decided to reply to this list of accusations. First, he flatly denied having taken any "unregistered" gold or silver. He then assembled the members of his crew and instructed them to testify in his behalf. In fact, one man testified briefly and forty-eight others signed a paper specifying that they agreed with everything the first man had said. The testimony is instructive. The sailors knew that gold and silver had been taken but did not know how much. They knew that some ships had been taken, but it was not true that any had been sunk with their men on board. Drake's men knew of no Spanish sailor who had been killed and only one who had been injured.[52]

One signature did not appear on the document, perhaps because the man refused to sign. The holdout was John Doughty, who was determined to see Drake answer in court for the death of his brother Thomas. Because the incident had occurred outside England, the only court that could hear the case was the Earl Marshal's court, the High Court of Chivalry and Honour. When Doughty attempted to bring Drake before the court, Drake apparently raised the question of jurisdiction. Doughty thereupon appealed to Chief Justice Wray, who, along with the other justices, gave Doughty permission to proceed with his case. As he might have expected, the queen had the last word. Cases involving offenses committed outside the realm had to be heard before the Earl Marshal and the Chief Constable. The post of Lord High Constable was vacant in 1581, and Queen Elizabeth refused to appoint a new one to hear the case. As a result the appeal became dormant.[53]

Not the least concerned about the constant undercurrent of gossip about Drake, the queen ordered that his ship be taken ashore at Deptford and placed in a dock as a permanent memorial of his voyage.[54] More than this, the queen said she would be glad to be Drake's guest at a banquet there, and one was immediately arranged. It was a grand affair, finer than anything seen in England since the reign of Henry VIII. The ship was scrubbed and adorned. There were banners flying, and crowds pressing in closely to catch a view of the distinguished guests. When the queen arrived, accompanied by the Marquis de Marchaumont, agent of the Duke of Alençon, she showed Drake a gilded sword and said that she had come to cut off his head. Then the queen told Drake to kneel. She handed the sword to Marchaumont and told him to be her representative, knighting Drake. This done, Drake presented several gifts to the queen, including a large silver coffer and a diamond-studded jewel.[55] Usually described as a "frog," *rana,* the jewel may in fact have been a sort of frivolous "vanity," *vana.*[56]

In the wake of this happy ceremony, the banquet on board Drake's ship was a somewhat raucous affair. As the queen came aboard the ship, Marchaumont noticed that her garter had slipped down and was trailing. He bent to pick it up unobtrusively, but the queen told him to hand it to her and proceeded to put it on in front of him.[57] Later, as the crowd surged onto the flimsy bridge that had been built from ship to shore, it collapsed, throwing a hundred or so people into the muddy water.[58]

The knighthood ceremony was not something done on the spur of the moment. Apparently encouraged by the queen, Drake had been expecting it for some time.[59] But it was necessary first to be a gentleman of property. As early as November 1580 he began negotiating to purchase Buckland Abbey from Sir Richard Grenville. John Hele of Plymouth and Christopher Harris of Plymstock acted as his agents, handling much of the detail, though Grenville always knew that Drake was the real purchaser.[60] Because Grenville held the property under a grant from Henry VIII that required knight service, royal approval was necessary before the sale could proceed. On 1 December 1580 letters patent were issued under the great seal of Queen Elizabeth, allowing Sir Richard Grenville and his wife to sell Buckland Abbey to Hele and Harris.[61] Such royal approval was very close to an announcement that the new purchaser would also be a knight. In fact, Mendoza more or less confirmed this when he told his king that Drake's knighthood was made on the basis of his recent purchase of property.[62]

With royal approval, Drake's agents could proceed with the actual purchase. On 19 December they gave Grenville the sum of £3,400 as full payment for the lands, buildings, contents, implements, and household furnishings of Buckland. In his agreement Grenville promised to deliver the property to Hele and Harris or their assignees on or before 25 March 1581, the feast of the Annunciation. An interesting provision in the agreement allowed Drake to keep the property for three years, then sell it back to Grenville if he wished, for the same £3,400, less wear and tear. While Drake's name is not mentioned in the body of the indenture, it does appear in an endorsement "sealed and delivered the day and year within written by the within named Sir Richard Grenefylde knight to the within mencioned Frauncis Drake esquire."[63]

The exact date on which Drake took possession of Buckland is not clear. The knighthood ceremony of April 4 and Mendoza's letter of April 6 are strong evidence that Drake was considered to be the owner of the property at that time. But the final indenture is dated in Trinity Term 1581, which could mean that Drake did not take possession of Buckland until some time after Trinity Sunday, 21 May 1581.[64] Less than three months later, 10 August 1581, Drake transferred to Hele, Harris, and Edmund Tremayne the remainder of his leases on two houses in Plymouth.[65] This is pretty clear evidence that he was living at Buckland before that date, though a clause in the transfer document provided that Drake might nullify the transfer by simply paying one shilling to Tremayne, Hele, and Harris.[66]

Other legal maneuvers followed. On 3 October 1582, Hele and Harris signed an indenture formally transferring the property to Drake and noting that the purchase had been made for "the onely use of him the said Sir Francis."[67] Finally, on 7 June 1583, Royal Letters Patent were issued to Drake, confirming his possession of the Buckland estate.[68]

A former Cistercian foundation, Buckland was a marvelous property, with extensive buildings, orchards, and a great tithe barn that still stands. The elder Sir Richard Grenville had bought the abbey from the crown in 1541 for £400. Forty years later it was very likely deteriorating and perhaps not worth the £3,400 that Drake paid to the Grenvilles.[69] Obviously Drake wanted it badly enough to hire two agents to handle the protracted purchase arrangements. While the abbey buildings had languished in the first years after the Grenville family purchased the place, Richard Grenville had tried to transform Buckland into a private estate. He converted the great church into a house and sold it fully furnished. All Drake had to do was move in. Drake, now enormously wealthy, apparently did not worry about obtaining the lowest possible price.

Although some English monasteries were places of great architectural merit, Buckland was not. Cistercian buildings were typically simple, austere structures, the most lavish being the church. Constructed as they were for the use of monks, these simple buildings were not easily converted into ornate homes. The conversion of Buckland took place over several decades. For a brief time after the dissolution, George Pollard of London leased Buckland from the crown, though it is not clear that his family lived there.[70] Two years later the elder Sir Richard Grenville purchased the place as an estate for his son Roger. He was the first member of the Grenville family to live at Buckland, and he seems to have made a family dwelling of the dorter and kitchen, where the monks had once lived. These structures proved to be too rough and spartan for Roger's son Richard, who had them pulled down. The abbey church then became the main dwelling.[71]

*Francis Drake bought Buckland Abbey in 1580, after the old church
had been converted into a three-story residence. The roofline of the
missing south transept can still be seen in the stones of the central tower.
Author's drawing, based on a sketch from the National Trust leaflet
"Buckland Abbey," 1988.*

The Grenvilles reversed the usual treatment of the confiscated religious
properties. As a general rule the churches were used as quarries of building
stone required to refurbish other parts of the monastic enclosure. At Buckland the domestic abbey buildings were quarried for material to convert
the church into a private house. The remodeling work must have begun
about ten or twelve years before Drake purchased the estate.[72] The principal change was the installation of two wooden floors inside the nave, which
changed the abbey church into a three-story dwelling. The arcades to the
side chapels were blocked with stone, and a great hall was constructed in
the space under the crossing tower. The great hall occupies only a single
story, but Grenville had it embellished with oak paneling and intricate
plaster work, making it the finest part of an otherwise economical construction project. The date 1576 worked into the plaster above the fireplace
is usually taken to be the year that Grenville completed the renovation of
the building.[73] As part of this work the south transept was removed, allowing installation of the windows that bring light into the great hall.

With the building so recently renovated it was not necessary for Sir

Francis Drake to undertake additional work himself. This is no doubt the reason that so little of the present dwelling at Buckland can with certainty be identified as Drake's contribution. It was said at one time that an oak paneled drawing room was "Sir Francis Drake's major structural contribution to Buckland Abbey."[74] An 1830 watercolor has since been found, however, showing this room with plain plaster walls. The plaster in the great hall is now painted entirely white, but paint analysis shows that some of it may originally have been colored. In particular, some decorative shields bore the arms of Grenville. These were almost certainly painted out by Drake, though not covered over with his own arms, it seems.[75]

Exactly what those arms may have been was a matter of some dispute. Drake insisted from the start that his family was entitled to use the arms of the Drake family of Ashe: a dragonlike wyvern gules crested with an eagle displayed.[76] There is some evidence that Francis Drake began to use these arms as soon as he was knighted. According to this story Sir Bernard Drake of Ashe objected, saying that Francis Drake was not related to his branch of the family. When Francis Drake persisted, Sir Bernard became so enraged that he accosted him in public and boxed his ears. Hearing this, Queen Elizabeth promised to give her favorite sailor "a new coat of everlasting honour," devising a coat of arms and crest for him.[77]

This may have been so, but the relationship between Sir Bernard and Sir Francis seems to have been pleasant enough, and Bernardino de Mendoza thought that Bernard Drake might indeed be Francis's uncle.[78] But Drake family genealogists have been unable to prove that there was a connection between the two families.[79] In any case, it is abundantly clear that Sir Francis Drake did use the old Drake family arms; he may have used others at an earlier date.

There are a few indications that Drake claimed and used a coat of arms during his voyage around the world. Francisco de Zárate reported seeing Drake eat from silver dishes on which his arms were engraved.[80] Nuño de Silva said that Drake showed him the coat of arms embossed on the breech of a cannon and claimed that it had been granted to him by the queen.[81] Of course, Drake had no arms then, but Silva's description of the figure embossed on the cannon fits in a general way the arms that Drake was later

The Drake coat of arms displayed at Buckland Abbey.

granted by the queen and indicates that he was already thinking about the royal favors he might receive. The device that Silva was shown included a globe and a north star, both of which are features of the arms and crest the queen granted to Drake on 20 June 1581: "Of sable a fece wavy argent be-tweene tow starres argent: the heaulme adourned with a globe terrestriall, upon the height wherof, is a shippe under sayle, trained aboute the same with golden haulsers by the direction of a hand appeering owte of the clouds all in proper colour a red dragon volant shewith it self regarding the said direction, with these wordes Auxilio divino."[82] If the whole thing is not simply a coincidence, then Drake must have decided very early exactly how he wanted his arms to appear.

This supposition is borne out to some extent by the documents. The of-ficial papers granting the arms were rewritten twice, but still not to Drake's entire satisfaction. He insisted that the final document must state that he was entitled to use the Drake family arms. As a result this addendum was composed on a separate piece of paper: "Notwithstandinge that the said Sr Francys Drake, beinge well borne and descended of worthie ancestors such as have of longe tyme born Armes as tokens and demonstrations of their race and progenie which lykewyse to him by iust descent and perog-ative of birth are duly deryved, may for the Armes of his surname and family beare Argent a Wever dragon volant gules with the difference of a third brother, as I am credibly enfourmed by the testimony of Bernard Drake of [blank] in the countie of Devon Esquire chief of that Coatearmure, and sondrey other of that family of worshippe and good credit."[83] There are a number of problems with this addendum, including the fact that it was not part of the official document and that it was not signed by Sir Bernard Drake.[84] Even if the addendum had been written into the official document, this would have been a curious way to handle the matter. The usual method would have been to cite the hereditary arms and state that they were augmented by the new royal favor.[85]

The crest was another problem. Sir Francis Drake was not pleased with the new crest granted to him by the queen, and he did not use it. Instead, the crest he used was an eagle displayed. A family biographer wrote: "There is not a single instance known of Sir Francis sealing with the new ship crest, although from the time he was knighted he used the arms the Queen gave him quarterly with his own waver dragon."[86]

The newly minted knight was not content with royal recognition for his stunning accomplishments. He resented any reference to his humble origins and always tried to claim kinship with a family of recognized gentility. In attempting to force this recognition from the heralds, Drake initiated a process that continued for the rest of his life and beyond, editing and embellishing the records and prevailing upon others to assist in reworking his place in history.

Elements of Drake's coat of arms appear on a number of items now kept at Buckland. They are displayed in a long room on the second floor called the Drake Gallery. Clearly the best known if not the most important item in the room is the Drake Drum. It is a colorful piece with a walnut barrel painted gold and decorated with Drake's arms. The authenticity of this and other pieces is not entirely clear. The barrel is arguably of the late sixteenth century, and the drum heads may be as well. The rim bands are replacements made in 1889. Legend dating perhaps a half-century earlier and immortalized in Henry Newbolt's 1895 poem held that the drum would roll whenever the fate of England was in jeopardy.[87] Among the other items in the gallery are eight banners said to have been used to decorate Drake's ship at Deptford when he was knighted by the queen and her guest from France.[88]

Additional pieces perhaps ought to be at Buckland but are not. These include a chair made from timbers of the ship and presented to the Bodleian in 1662. At least two other such chairs existed at one time, and they may once have been in the house.[89] A carved panel also made from the ship's timbers was removed to Nutwell Court in the late eighteenth century.[90]

With his newly acquired status as a gentleman, Drake began to think about other ways to assure his place in society. First, he arranged to sit for portraits. One of the most popular portrait artists and miniaturists of the time was another Devon man, Nicholas Hilliard. His miniature painting of Drake is marked "Aetatis Suae. 42. Ano D[omi]ni: 1581."[91] Now in the National Portrait Gallery, this miniature is probably the most charming of all the Drake portraits, and it is very likely the earliest as well. It shows a round-faced Francis Drake with dark, receding, curly hair and a light reddish beard. Hilliard did a similar but somewhat larger miniature of Drake at the same time. Not the most popular of the Drake portraits, these are nonetheless the best, and there is a reason. Hilliard and Drake were close, perhaps relatives. According to Hilliard's most recent biographer, the artist's son Francis was baptized on Christmas Eve 1580. It is "more than probable that the godfather was Francis Drake."[92]

Another miniature from an even earlier time that is said to be the work of Isaac Oliver shows a round-faced young man of about thirty, with a mustache but no beard. Lady Elizabeth Eliott-Drake believed that it is the earliest portrait of her illustrious kinsman, but modern authorities doubt that it is Francis Drake.[93]

An engraved picture, only slightly larger than the Hilliard miniatures, appears on the map made by Nicola van Sype. The picture includes the legend, "A[e]tat Su[a]e 42," but it is not certain this was drawn from life. The man in the picture is thinner than Hilliard's Drake. He has a full head of light-colored hair but a dark beard.[94]

An engraved portrait usually attributed to Jodocus Hondius and done about the same time as the Hilliard miniatures shows the head and torso of Sir Francis Drake. The inscription reads in part: "Ano. Aet. Sue. 43." As be-

The Nicola van Sype portrait, probably not drawn from life, is one of the earliest printed likenesses of Sir Francis Drake.

fore, this is Drake at the age of forty-two or in "the forty-third year of his age." This is a round-faced Drake with a full head of curly hair and a very stout body.

One engraving published a decade later by Cornelis Claesz shows Drake at the age of forty-three. The receding hairline is very definite here, but the view shows only his head.[95] A similar engraving evidently derived from the same original is said to be the work of Thomas de Leu, based on a still-unknown painting by the French artist Jean Rabel. There is some speculation that Rabel copied from an English original sent to Paris by the French ambassador in 1586.[96]

A final Drake portrait is worth noting here. Attributed to Marcus Gheeraerts the Younger, the painting is dated 1591 and shows a decidedly aging Sir Francis Drake. Thick of body, thin of hair, with a beard decidedly gray and a chin just the least bit sunken, this Drake is gazing at a globe and wearing the jewel presented to him by Queen Elizabeth in 1588.[97] He has the look of a man both self-satisfied and self-assured. A notable feature of this portrait is the coat of arms. When the portrait was purchased for the Royal Naval Museum in 1932, the head of the management committee, in an interview with a newspaper reporter, cited the curiously truncated coat of arms as evidence that the picture was genuine: "I was able to establish the authenticity of the picture through two features. One is that the space for Drake's coat of arms is blank. It is a fact that because he did not like the coat of arms drawn up for him by the College of Heralds he would never use it."[98] Where the reporter quoted him as saying "coat of arms," he probably said "crest." There was some speculation that the crest might originally have been in the picture and then have been removed at Drake's insistence.[99] This conjecture has not been demonstrated conclusively, and its likelihood remains one of several disputes regarding this picture. Another copy that includes the crest is dated 1594. Some authorities feel the latter one is the original.[100] Others say it is a later copy, perhaps done by Abraham Janssen.[101]

Even without these pictures, we might recognize Drake from the descriptions left by those who knew him. Nuño de Silva noted that he was short, stout, and extremely strong. His reddish-blonde beard did not quite cover the slight scar from an arrow wound on his right cheek. A bullet wound in his right leg apparently caused no limp.[102] Drake's tendency to heaviness became more pronounced as time passed. García Fernández de Torrequemada saw Drake a few years after this and said that he was "more fat than thin."[103] Five years later Marcus Gheeraerts the Younger painted a Drake who was distinctly fat and who no longer looked very strong.

When Drake purchased the estate of Buckland, the citizens of Plymouth seem to have become alarmed at the possibility of losing their most famous merchant-seaman. Purchase negotiations had scarcely been concluded when the aldermen and burgesses named Sir Francis Drake to be the new lord mayor for the term beginning at the end of September 1581. Almost nothing is known about his term of office, but the position of mayor may have been largely ceremonial in any case. The election likely took place on Saint Lambert's Day, 17 September, which was the traditional election day. Just as likely one of Drake's first duties was to walk around the boundaries of the

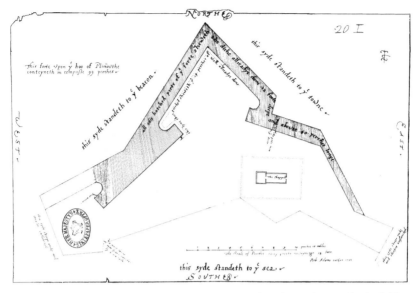

In this 1593 map of the proposed fortifications at Plymouth, Robert Adams used a shaded line to show the ditch or moat. A dotted line inside that area indicates a section of wall "allreadye done," perhaps the wall built during the mayoralty of Francis Drake. From PRO, SP 12/245, fol. 31.

borough with the outgoing mayor, his friend John Blitheman. On Michael-mas Day, 29 September, the new mayor customarily took his oath of office in the guildhall, then walked to Saint Andrew's to receive the blessing of the church.[104] Following this, he no doubt went home. Perhaps Lord Mayor Sir Francis Drake went to the house he held on lease from Thomas Ed-monds—that is, assuming he had nullified his earlier assignment of the lease to Hele, Harris, and Tremayne.[105]

The "Black Book," the seemingly official annals of Plymouth, contains one lone entry for Drake's term of office: "The newe compasse made upon the Hawe." What this means is unclear; perhaps a new wall was built ad-joining the castle on the Hoe that had been repaired the year before.[106] If so, it is not quite the record of inaction attributed to Drake by one local historian. After reviewing recently discovered Plymouth municipal records, R. N. Worth said: "It is a remarkable fact that a man of so much energy as Drake should have had one of the most unimportant mayoralties of that generation."[107] What disturbed Worth the most was his discovery that a local legend was not true. Drake had not built and donated a new water system to the borough.

According to the legend, Lord Mayor Francis Drake noted a periodic shortage of drinking water in Plymouth and, recalling canals he had seen in Peru, took it upon himself to build a leat or ditch to bring the first outside supply of water into Plymouth.[108] In reality there had been other attempts to bring water to the town. As early as 1559-60 borough officials had taken steps to solve the water problem, though with indifferent success. Efforts continued in succeeding years, and no doubt the problem was discussed during Drake's term as lord mayor. Finally, in 1585 the Corporation of Plymouth prevailed upon Parliament to pass a Water Act, empowering the city to excavate a ditch and bring water from the river Meavy.[109]

Nothing much happened for the next few years, while municipal officials were kept busy preparing to defend the town against the threat of Spanish invasion. Then in 1589 Robert Lampen was hired to survey the line for a canal and to prepare drawings. Municipal officials then signed a contract with Francis Drake, agreeing to pay him £300 to undertake the construction. Of this amount £200 was for Drake himself, while the other £100 was to be used to compensate the owners of the land over which the leat was dug.[110]

Drake had good business reasons for becoming involved in this project. For some years Drake had been renting and operating the old gristmills at Millbay. In the leat project Drake was allowed to build six new gristmills on the leat and to use them for the next sixty-seven years, after which title would revert to the Plymouth Corporation. It was an extremely profitable arrangement for Drake. Worth estimated that the leat construction cost him £110, leaving £90 to pay for the construction of the new mills. From these new mills Drake and his successors for the next sixty-seven years probably enjoyed an annual income of about £200.[111]

Drake's construction work began in December 1590, and he lost no time in bringing it to a successful conclusion. For the first few miles of canal an old leat was deepened and widened. An additional eight miles or so of trench was completely new, six or seven feet wide and a couple of feet deep. Within about four months, four of the six gristmills were finished, and the leat was carrying water. There was a grand opening on 24 April 1591, and Drake celebrated the occasion with a demonstration of corn grinding at one of the new mills.[112] After Drake's portion of the work was completed, the Plymouth Corporation proceeded to install conduit in the town and to make other improvements that turned the Plymouth leat into a functioning municipal water system. The total cost of the whole system was about £800.[113]

As a contractor Drake did the initial construction work quickly and well. No doubt the Plymouth municipal officials recognized this ability to get things done and retained his services as contractor for just that reason. On the other hand, he did not pay all the landowners for the right to cross their land. This was something he had agreed to do, and another important reason for retaining his services. As a result of his oversight, if that is what it was, at least two landowners later brought suit against the Plymouth Corporation, and the court decreed that Plymouth would have to compensate them for their property.[114]

The position of lord mayor gave Drake the opportunity to look over property in Plymouth with an eye to expanding his investments there. On 20 October 1582, shortly after his term as mayor ended, Drake paid his uncle William Hawkins £1,500 for forty separate pieces of property in Plymouth, along with an interest in the Plymouth town mills and other properties. This was an enormous investment, making Francis Drake one of the largest landholders in Plymouth. Only two others had more: members of the Hawkins family still had sixty freeholds, while the Plymouth Corporation had fifty. Drake had paid an inflated price for Buckland, and to judge from the records he did the same in Plymouth. The properties he purchased in 1582 for £1,500 had sold for £720 in January 1579.[115]

The new holdings were scattered all over Plymouth. Five were in Batter Street, three in Bretonside, one in Finewell Street, two in High Street, one in How Street, one in Kinterbury Street, seven in Looe Street, one in Lynam Street, one in Old Town Street, one in Patrick Street, one in Saint Andrews Street, seven in Southside Street, one in Stillman Street, three in Treville Street, one in Vauxhall Street, one in Whimple Street, and three others in a street whose name is not given in the documents. Most of the properties, twenty-nine in all, were residences, though they may also have included portions that were commercial. Others were used exclusively for business, including a bakehouse, warehouses, and a vault. There were two stables and four gardens. One tenant was Robert Spry, who seems to have been the man who drafted the plan of the Plymouth Leat.[116]

Drake's other investments in real estate were substantial. The Drake Papers in the Devon Record Office contain numerous copies of deeds and leases that record his investment activity. The most important of the manors were Yarcomb, which he purchased from Richard Drake in 1582; Sampford Spinney, which he purchased from Jerome Mayhew; and Sherford, which came as a grant from the queen in recognition of his "viadge, compassinge and goinge aboute the whole worlde."[117]

With money to invest, Drake continued to expand his maritime interests. The records are slim on this point, but the evidence indicates great activity. In June 1581 Mendoza reported that Drake was arming seven small vessels to go to Terceira.[118] In September of the same year he had three more ready to sail from Plymouth.[119] In November Mendoza reported that one of Drake's ships had returned from Terceira, while others were ready to leave.[120] Much of this activity was performed in behalf of Dom Antonio, but trade was no doubt involved as well. In November 1582 two of Drake's ships were reportedly ready to go on another voyage.[121] No doubt some of this is unfounded gossip, but the stories are based on public knowledge of Drake's investments in ships.

In spite of Drake's newfound wealth and honor, one man was determined to be his enemy. John Doughty still burned with anger about the execution of his brother. Frustrated in his attempt to have Drake tried for murder, Doughty carried his complaints to every person who would listen. In one letter John Doughty wrote: "When the Queen did knight Drake she did then knight the arrantest knave, the vilest villain, the falsest thief and the cruelest murderer that ever was born."[122] It was to be expected, then, that Doughty would soon be implicated in a plot against Drake.

When the Spanish agent Pedro de Zubiaur began his efforts for the recovery of Drake's booty, the influential people who shared the profits of the voyage took offense. Finally, Zubiaur managed to annoy them to such an extent that late in March 1582 he was thrown into jail.[123] Debt was the stated reason, but he was also said to have dealt with an English merchant named Patrick Mason. Arrested as a spy, Mason was questioned on 15 May 1582 about his knowledge of Spanish plots against the realm in general and against Drake in particular. At first he denied any such involvement.[124] The interrogators were not satisfied with the first confession, so they questioned Mason once more, the second time under torture. This time Mason admitted that he had conspired with Zubiaur. In his new testimony Mason said that the Spanish agent had shown him letters from Spain, saying that the king would give 70,000 ducats to anyone who would recover the treasure or bring him Drake's head—either would do. Either Zubiaur or Mason, according to the confession, which is not clear, encouraged John Doughty to take up the offer: "[He] dyd procure and geve John Doughtie to understande therof that yf soe be yt, he woulde take upon him to doe that exployte, he shoulde benyfytt him self of soe muche & that he woulde be bounde to see the that [*sic*] game performed; and besyde yf that John Dowghtie shoulde be apprehended in doinge of this, & comyted unto pryson, he should not wante monye to mayntayne him."[125] It is not clear whether Doughty agreed to this or not, but he was soon in prison, and there he remained. Doughty was still interned at Marshalsea in late 1583, seemingly with no hope of pardon.[126] He had been sixteen months in prison, and there is no record that he was ever released.

During this time Drake was involved in numerous projects to reprise and expand upon his recent voyage. Sir Francis Walsingham suggested the formation of a corporation to exploit the discoveries Drake had made beyond "the Equynoctyall lyne." The purpose of the new venture was to establish an English equivalent of the Spanish Casa de Contratación. Drake himself was to be governor and was to have a tenth of the profit. As in Spain, the queen would receive part of the profit from any mines of gold and silver that might be established in countries "not lawfully possessed by any other Christyan Prynce."[127]

A little later, in early 1581, there was a proposal to send Drake with a fleet of ten ships to the Moluccas by way of the Cape of Good Hope. There he would meet a similar fleet headed by Henry Knollys, who would travel by way of the Strait of Magellan, pausing to raid the Spanish ports along the Pacific coast, just as Drake had done.[128] There were more consultations in April between Walsingham, Leicester, Drake, Hawkins, Frobisher, Wynter, and Bingham, but the new plans conflicted with the queen's own interest in the matter of Portugal. She was becoming more closely involved with Dom Antonio and was reluctant to approve any ventures that might conflict.[129] Drake was sent to Plymouth to prepare a fleet for the Indies, but early in May the queen decided to send him to the Azores instead. The plan was to establish Dom Antonio in possession of Terceira. From that point it was thought that English ships could prey at will on Spanish vessels going to and from the Indies.[130]

Drake and Hawkins were delighted with this plan, which would allow them to renew their old trading connections in the islands. In June, Dom Antonio arrived in England, seemingly penniless and asking for a loan from the queen to continue the Azores project. By early July he was meeting with Francis Drake, John Hawkins, and John Wynter at his temporary lodgings near Greenwich.[131] The immediate result of these negotiations was a plan called the First Enterprise. Operating under the Portuguese flag, Drake would take a fleet of eight ships, plus pinnaces, to establish a base in Terceira. He would wait there for the treasure fleet from the West Indies, and if he missed that, he would cross the Atlantic and raid the West Indies ports. Dom Antonio would pay one-fourth of the cost of equipping the fleet, and the investors would pay the rest. The English parties to the venture included Edward Fenton, Gilbert Yorke, and Luke Ward, in addition to the men who had been involved all along. Piracy was the aim, but this time with official approval, a third of the profits going to the crew and two-thirds to the investors.[132]

For some reason the queen suddenly lost interest in the project, partly because of the expense but also because of other difficulties. By early August the ship captains were beginning to grumble. When they learned that Drake was to be the admiral of the fleet, they refused to go unless someone else would guarantee their pay. With finances suddenly in jeopardy, Dom Antonio brought out bundles of jewels, including an eighty-carat diamond which he offered as surety.[133] In the middle of August, with ships ready to sail, Dom Antonio demanded an additional loan.[134] The queen suddenly became "very cold" to the plan. By the end of the month it was all over. Drake, Hawkins, and Walsingham decided to discharge the crews and sell the supplies.[135] Dom Antonio determined to try his luck in France, but he was not allowed to leave until he covered his debts. To manage this he was forced to pawn his diamond and other jewels to the queen, who thereupon guaranteed his debts to the merchants and investors.[136]

With the first plan a total failure, the English investors came up with the Second Enterprise. This was a scheme to send ships to Calicut on the Malabar coast and establish an English outpost for trade with the Moluccas. As the plan involved areas that were nominally Portuguese, the English sought and received the blessing of Dom Antonio, whom they insisted on calling the king of Portugal. The principal investors were the earl of Leicester, Sir Francis Drake, and Henry Owtread. Owtread was a prosperous shipowner from Southampton who had previously been engaged in piracy. John Hawkins refused to become involved this time, not wanting to lose any more money in what he saw as a very hazardous enterprise. There were numerous other investors, including some from the earlier projects of the Muscovy Company and the Levant Company.[137]

The new fleet consisted of four ships. The galleon *Leicester,* with Edward Fenton as captain and admiral, was owned by Leicester and Owtread. The *Edward Bonaventure,* with Luke Ward as captain and vice admiral, was probably a ship supplied by the Muscovy Company. The bark *Francis* belonged to Francis Drake, who appointed his young cousin John Drake to be captain. The bark *Elizabeth* was added later to carry provisions, with Thomas Skevington as captain. While Leicester had responsibility for the appointments, he probably relied heavily on Francis Drake's advice. Two of the pilots, Thomas Hood and Thomas Blacollar, had sailed with Drake, as had many of the seamen.[138]

The fleet left the shores of England on 1 May 1582, and most of the men did not see those shores again. From the start there was disagreement. The captains could not get along with the admiral, the seamen wanted to plunder Spanish ships and ports, and Fenton himself was not at all certain that he wanted to go to the Moluccas. There was a long delay in Sierra Leone, where the *Elizabeth* was sold. Continuing to the coast of Brazil, the fleet captured a Portuguese vessel and from its crew learned that Pedro de Sarmiento had sailed recently to fortify the Strait of Magellan. This news convinced Fenton that he should not attempt passage of the strait. Disgusted with Fenton's cowardice and indecision, John Drake and his crew in the *Francis* slipped away one night, determined to continue the voyage on their own.[139]

Thinking that they could find water, firewood, and provisions in the Rio de la Plata, John Drake made that river his first objective. With abominably bad luck, the ship ran aground in the river and had to be abandoned. The crew all made it safely ashore in the ship's boat, but their troubles were only starting. Almost immediately they were captured by Indians, who held them as slaves for more than a year. John Drake and two companions finally made their way to Buenos Aires, where Drake was recognized as the protégé of Sir Francis Drake. They were interrogated by local officials, and after some months of delay John Drake and another Englishman were sent to Lima. There Drake was questioned by the Inquisition and imprisoned for a short time. Because he repented having been a "Lutheran," he was allowed to wear the yellow *sanbenito* and red cross and to walk in the *auto-da-fé*. Afterward he was sentenced to remain in Spanish territory for the rest of his life.[140]

Fenton with the *Edward* and the *Galleon* went to the nearby port of São Vicente, ostensibly for trade. After some conversations with the officials of the town, the English were advised that the local officials were afraid to allow them ashore. Finally three Spanish ships appeared in the harbor, and a fight ensued, during which several English sailors were killed. This was the final blow for the expedition. The officers of the *Edward,* exasperated by the lack of support from Fenton, determined to returned to England, where they arrived 29 May 1583. Fenton continued to lurk about the coast of Brazil for some time, until he and young Hawkins came to blows. Then he headed for home, arriving there on 29 June, with Hawkins in irons. There was an investigation into the failure of the voyage, but the result is not clear.[141]

Even while Drake was feted in Plymouth and London, honored by the queen, and toasted by crowds of admirers, tragedies seemed to dog him. Mary Newman Drake, the long-suffering wife who had been separated from him for such long periods since their marriage in 1569, died about 24 January 1583. She was buried in Plymouth, which may mean that she spent her last days in that town, rather than at Buckland. The burial probably took place at Saint Andrew's, where the parish register lists the burial on January 25 of "The Lady Marie the wiffe of Sir Frauncis Drake knight."[142] A second registration was placed in the records of Saint Budeaux, simply to complete the record at the parish where the two had been married.[143] We can only guess that Drake was devastated by the loss of his wife, for there is no record of his thoughts. There were no children in the marriage, and we know of no other family relationships. Lady Elizabeth Eliott-Drake, who compiled the official family biography in 1911, suggests that Mary had a sister whose son Jonas was left fatherless. The boy was then taken in by Francis Drake and raised in his home.[144] A modern biographer suggests that Mary may have had a brother and four sisters and that one of her sisters was the mother of Jonas Bodenham, who became Sir Francis Drake's page at about this time.[145] Either or both of these may be true, for one Jonas Bodenham did become Drake's retainer and agent and was later remembered in his will.

It was almost inevitable that a man as popular as Sir Francis Drake would be named to sit in Parliament. The two most likely places for him were "the docile boroughs of Bossiney and Camelford" in Cornwall.[146] When the Fourth Parliament convened for the Third Session, beginning 16 January 1581, Francis Drake was a member. What seat he held and what he did are unknown. An entry in the journal for 17 February 1581 confirms his membership: "Francis Drake Esquire was Licensed this day by Mr Speaker to depart for certain his necessary business in the service of her Majesty."[147] No other evidence of his service during this session has been found. As a new member he may have thought it best to watch proceedings rather than attempt to participate.[148]

His second term in Parliament was somewhat different. In 1584 Drake was named at the October election as one of two members from Bossiney.[149] On 27 November he was named to serve on a committee that included Richard Grenville to consider the "Bill for the better and more reverent observing of the Sabbath day." A version of the controversial bill was passed on 7 December and sent to the House of Lords.[150]

On 5 December, Francis Drake was named to a committee considering a "Bill for bringing in of staple Fish and Ling [cod]."[151] Somewhat more important, he was on the committee that debated the bill "for the Confirmation of Letters Patents made unto Mr Walter Rawleigh."[152] This bill resulted in the planting of an ill-fated colony on Roanoke Island, whose survivors were later rescued by Drake. Service on this and other Parliamentary committees gave Drake the opportunity to work with such men as Philip Sidney, Hatton, and Grenville, men whose friendship and influence he was happy to have. It was also an opportunity for Drake to acquire the sophistication and polish that were lacking in his training at sea.

On 21 December, Drake was named to a committee for a bill close to heart and home, the "Bill for the preservation of the Haven of Plymouth." The committee brought in a version of the bill on 18 February, but it was sent back for amendments. Returned with a proviso on 20 February, the bill was finally accepted for general debate on 23 February. It passed Commons on 27 February and was sent to the House of Lords, along with a request for information about the fate of the Sabbath bill.[153]

This inquiry brought some results. The Sabbath bill came back with so many amendments and additions that it was scarcely recognizable. The new bill prohibited bear baiting, hawking, hunting, wakes, and similar activities. Passed on 17 March, the Sabbath bill was sent to the queen, who refused to sign it.[154] Bernardino de Mendoza might have predicted her veto, for he had been mildly shocked at the queen's interest in bear baiting when she invited him to attend an exhibition of the sport a few years earlier.[155]

Drake had one other committee assignment on a subject of concern to his constituents, the manufacture of Devonshire woolens, more precisely a "Bill against abuses in making Devonshire Kersies."[156] One important committee did not include Drake: a committee for the "Bill for the suppression of Pirates and Piracy," a subject that greatly annoyed Drake, who considered himself more a patriot than a pirate.[157]

Before the parliamentary session ended Francis Drake was married once more. It was something of a coup. His new wife was Elizabeth Sydenham. She was much younger than her new husband, and the only child of Sir George Sydenham and his wife Elizabeth. The family was rich and well connected, with an impressive house at Combe Sydenham in Somerset.[158] The girl was beautiful, intelligent, and well mannered. There was no apparent reason for her to choose Francis Drake as a husband or for her father to accept such a match. And yet it happened. The date of the marriage is not known, but it probably happened shortly before 9 February 1585. On that date Francis Drake signed a marriage settlement, pledging his estates at Yarcomb, Sherford, Sampford Spinney, and Buckland for the enjoyment of his new wife and their heirs. As it turned out, Drake gave up nothing in this carefully worded document. He simply committed his estates "to the use and profit of the aforesaid Francis Drake and the Lady Elizabeth his wife and the heirs and assigns of the aforesaid Francis for ever."[159] In effect Sir Francis Drake promised to support his wife in the manner to which she was accustomed, but he still retained full power to dispose of his property as he might see fit.

Recognizing that his most stunning success had come on the sea, Drake continued to maneuver for royal permission to sail once more. At the end of 1582, Mendoza reported that Drake had contributed two more ships, with pinnaces stowed on board, for a fleet that William Hawkins was assembling. The objective again was to go to the Moluccas.[160] Later the Cape Verde Islands became the destination. When resistance was met there, the fleet went to the West Indies and returned home the following year with a rich cargo of treasure, pearls, hides, and sugar.[161]

Relations between England and Spain deteriorated rapidly. Elizabeth had encouraged the rebels in the Netherlands, and when the Prince of Orange was murdered, she took the matter as a setback to English interests.[162] Catholic forces in Europe still continued to encourage invasions or rebellion, first in Ireland, then Scotland. Finally, some people began to talk about an invasion using Spanish troops from the Netherlands. Known as the Throckmorton Plot, the whole thing quickly fizzled. Though there was probably never much support for the plan in England, Ambassador Mendoza was expelled in January 1584.[163] John Hawkins, who was treasurer of the navy at the time, began urging a program to send privateers against Spain under the flag of Dom Antonio. Somehow he managed to rebuild the twenty or so old ships in the fleet so that when Drake and others were appointed to inspect the state of the navy, they found it in good condition for service.[164]

The prospect of additional service at sea appealed to Drake. A document dated 20 November 1584 shows the Queen, Drake, John and William Hawkins, Leicester, Raleigh, and Hatton involved in planning a fleet of eleven ships, four barks, twenty pinnaces, and 1,600 men for a voyage to the Moluccas. Drake was to be the commander.[165] His commission was signed on Christmas Eve 1584, but things changed before he was ready to sail. The new destination was the West Indies.[166]

This son of a poor family from Tavistock had gone to sea as a boy, dabbled in piracy, and gained modest success as a merchant. Then with astonishing astuteness, he discovered a way to take advantage of the religious hostility that was beginning to intensify the national differences between Spain and England. Drake calculated that thefts from Spaniards, if grand enough, might not be punished by his queen. Thereupon he embarked on a series of pirate raids on undefended Spanish ships and ports, and in the process gained an enormous pile of booty, probably more than had ever been seen in England. Lavishly sharing this wealth with the queen and her closest councillors, he quickly preempted Spanish demands for punishment and retribution. Knighted and thus made a gentleman by royal command, he entered politics and business, aligning himself with the most influential men in the country. Within a few years he had married into a good family and had received a royal commission to carry out one more raid on Spanish ports and shipping.

9

Raid on the West Indies

EVER SINCE DRAKE'S RETURN FROM his voyage around the world, plans had been made and remade for another voyage. At one time or another there were plans to go to the Azores or the West Indies, to sail once again to the Pacific, or even to establish a trading post in Brazil. Drake actually sent a few ships on one or another of these voyages, but the queen seemed reluctant to allow her favorite pirate to sail himself. Finally, in the summer of 1584, Francis Drake was placed in charge of organizing a fleet that would go to the Moluccas.[1]

At first, little or nothing came of this authorization. The other investors were reluctant to advance any money until they were certain that Drake's fleet would actually receive final permission to sail.[2] By November, Drake had pledges from other investors, but still no money. The queen herself was a principal investor, with £10,000 in cash, plus credit for several thousand more from two ships that she would make available for the voyage. These vessels really had little value, but the credit gave her an added share in the projected profits of the voyage.[3] Other investors pledged varying sums, sometimes in cash, though frequently in the form of ships and supplies. The partners included Sir Francis Drake, with an investment of £7,000; the earl of Leicester, £3,000; John Hawkins, £2,500; William Hawkins, £1,000; and Sir Walter Raleigh, £400.[4]

Dormant for a while, interest in the project began to revive in February 1585. On the twenty-second of the month Ambassador Mendoza, safely transferred to Paris, reported to his king that Drake was preparing a fleet of twenty-four ships and twenty pinnaces for a raid on the West Indies. The queen was investing £20,000 and others were contributing lesser sums. Drake was to command a force of two thousand men, and he hoped to capture the treasure fleet.[5] As usual, Mendoza's information was good. This is very nearly the description of the fleet Drake commanded. Still, there were delays. By early April it seemed that the queen had changed her mind again and that Drake might not go after all.[6]

All this was cleared up when the Spanish king placed an arrest order on all English ships that happened to be in his ports.[7] Faced with this new crisis, Elizabeth spent a few weeks in indecision. Finally, she decided to respond by ordering Drake to proceed with his fleet to Vigo, where most of the ships were confined, and to negotiate for their release. Her decision was implemented on 1 July 1585 with an order renewing Drake's commission.[8] A few days later the Privy Council issued general letters of marque, with provisions for English merchants whose goods were under embargo in Spain to seize Spanish goods in reprisal.[9] Following this, the queen received a new delegation from the Netherlands and promised to give them open and substantial assistance in their war for independence from Spain.[10]

Drake's orders for freeing the ships were clear, but those seem to be the only orders he had. Exactly what Drake was supposed to do once the merchant ships were free is not clear. Perhaps his orders were never put into writing. From reports submitted after his return home it is possible to conclude that Drake was expected to intercept the Spanish treasure fleet coming from the Indies. If successful, he would return to England. Failing that, he would go to the Indies and carry out raids on Santo Domingo, Cartagena, and Panama. He may have been told to occupy Havana, but this is not clear.[11] In keeping with the queen's wishes, there was no declaration of war. In fact, Elizabeth retained the right to disavow Drake's actions if necessary.[12]

Even after a year of planning, the fleet was not ready to sail. From all appearances, very little had been accomplished in preparation for the voyage. Although Drake received his orders in early July, the ships did not leave Plymouth for another two and a half months. Even then they were not fully equipped, for reasons that are not entirely clear. Money was surely not the problem. Elizabeth's cash contribution of £10,000 had been disbursed in the summer and fall of 1584, nearly £7,000 going to Drake himself.[13] Very likely the privately owned vessels were not yet ready to go to sea. The John Hawkins ship *Primrose* is one example.

Early in May, Mendoza had reported to his king that the ship was slated for service with Drake.[14] Nonetheless, Hawkins appears to have sent the *Primrose* later in the month to Bilbao, where the Spanish authorities attempted to seize it by force. Expecting trouble, the English sailors resisted bravely, tossed most of the Spanish soldiers into the bay, and promptly sailed for home.[15] There were problems with other ships as well. Some, including the privately owned *Sea Dragon,* were still in the royal naval yard at the end of July 1585.[16]

There were also the command problems. No one was named to be military commander until Christopher Carleill was recalled from Ireland.[17] The overall command was also in question for a time. Sir Philip Sidney appeared in Plymouth at the end of August or the first of September and announced that he was going with Drake. Because Sidney held an important place in the queen's retinue, his presence on the voyage would make him effectively joint commander. Annoyed with this development and certain that the queen did not know what Sidney was doing, Drake took pains to see that she was fully informed. Elizabeth immediately sent orders that Sidney was to return to London and that Drake was not to depart until Sidney was well on his way.[18]

One more problem arose just before the fleet was ready to sail. On 7 September the pretender to the Portuguese throne, Dom Antonio, arrived in Plymouth.[19] Drake found room for him at his Buckland estate, along with Sidney. Dom Antonio also wanted to go on the voyage, but some correspondence with the queen soon convinced him that this was impractical, and he left for London with Sidney.[20] Drake's meeting with the would-be king of Portugal developed into a long friendship, in which each man tried to take advantage of benefits the other might confer. Drake could provide the pretender with military and naval assistance, while Drake could look for trade concessions if Dom Antonio should be successful in taking the throne of Portugal.

On 14 September 1585 Drake took his fleet to sea, though the ships were not yet fully provisioned. As Christopher Carleill explained in a report: "Because the winde being faire upon our coming from Plymouth wee weare loath to lose the same for any smale matters coming so rarelie as it doth there, and withall wee not the most assured of her Majesties perseverance to let us go forwarde."[21] In short, the fleet left port somewhat prematurely to take advantage of a favorable wind and to deprive the queen of any opportunity to change her mind. As it turned out, the queen indeed wondered whether she had made the right decision, and the fleet was not beyond recall. Buffeted by contrary winds, Drake's ships took a week or more to clear the coast of England. Fearful of a change in the royal order, Drake told one of his commanders that he would put into France or Ireland, if necessary, rather than risk returning to an English port.[22]

At one point Spanish spies reported that Drake's ships were riding off the Isle of Wight while the queen decided whether they could proceed. The reported reason was her reluctance to leave the realm without naval defenses.[23] The spies had part of it right. The royal reluctance was real, but the location of the fleet was probably imaginary. Drake's course, from Plymouth to Falmouth, then mostly south toward Cape Finisterre, took him nowhere near Wight.[24]

The fleet under Drake's command included about two dozen ships and eight pinnaces. The largest ship was the 600-ton royal naval vessel *Elizabeth Bonaventure,* a twenty-five-year-old ship that had been recently rebuilt as a galleon.[25] This was Drake's flagship or "admiral." Hawkins's 300-ton *Primrose* was commanded by the distinguished seaman Martin Frobisher and served as "vice admiral." Drake himself owned three or four of the ships in the fleet. The largest was the *Thomas,* captained by his brother Thomas Drake. At one time this ship was apparently called the *Hastings* and was rated at 100 tons. No doubt it was rebuilt on a larger scale, for there is evidence that the ship was rated at 200 tons. The *Francis,* a ship of 60 or 70 tons, was commanded by Thomas Moone, who had sailed with Drake in 1573 and again in the voyage around the world.

Not all of Drake's commanders are known. The 70-ton *Elizabeth,* or *Elizabeth Drake,* was probably owned by Drake and may have been captained by John Varney. The 40-ton *Mathew* also belonged to Drake, though the captain is unknown.[26] Other commanders were prominent. The veteran Thomas Fenner was captain of the *Bonaventure,* Drake's flagship. Sir William Wynter's son Edward was captain of the royal naval ship *Aid.* Christopher Carleill was captain of the *Tiger,* as well as commander of the military forces.

A journal of the voyage was kept by one of Carleill's lieutenants, who made entries largely at Carleill's direction. Another one of Drake's subordinate commanders, Captain Walter Bigges, was apparently responsible for the preparation of another account that was later edited and enlarged for publication.[27] Drake himself intended to keep a "whole and perfect booke" of the voyage but apparently did not do so.[28] He may have intended the work to be done by his chaplain and confidant on this expedition. This was Philip Nichols, who later wrote an account of Drake's voyage of 1572–73 and may have had a hand in the preparation of *The World Encompassed.*[29] If Nichols did prepare a manuscript of this voyage, it has not survived.

For some reason, perhaps because Carleill did not arrive until the last minute, no thought was given to the preparation of sailing orders until the vessels were well out to sea. On the afternoon of 14 September, Carleill and others went aboard the *Bonaventure* and worked for several hours in preparing sailing orders. These were ready the next morning, and copies were handed to the assembled captains. The expedition was Drake's first experience with a large command, and he very quickly found that he did not like the responsibility, particularly the need for continual consultation with his captains. By 17 September he had decided on an informal advisory group consisting of Frobisher and Carleill. Flattered by this attention, Carleill noted in his journal, "I can not say that evar I had to deale with a man of greatar reason or more careful circomspection."[30] Two other trusted advisers were perhaps closer to Drake because they sailed on the *Bonaventure.* These were Chaplain Philip Nichols and Captain Thomas Fenner.[31]

Just off the northwest coast of Spain the *Tiger* and the *Bonaventure* captured a ship whose master claimed to be heading from Newfoundland to St. Jean-de-Luz with a cargo of dried fish. A companion to the captured vessel was sunk during a brief fight.[32] Overnight questioning of the captive captain and crew convinced Drake that they were headed not for St. Jean-de-Luz, in France, but for San Sebastián, which lies across the border in Spain. Further searches uncovered certain "bulls from the pope," so Drake knew that these sailors were Catholics and seized both ship and cargo as a "lawfull prize."[33] The crew was set adrift in an open boat. In the process Drake considerably augmented his carelessly loaded stores.[34]

During the next two days the fleet rounded Cape Finisterre and came in toward land near Muros. Here they spotted seven more French ships, heading home with loads of salt.[35] One of the ships was brand new, and Drake immediately pressed her into the fleet, telling everyone that he would pay for her when the trip was over, "yf so it be adiudged."[36] It must have been so adjudged. According to the official account of the journey, *The Summarie and True Discourse,* the ship was renamed the *Drake* and was paid for at the end of the voyage.[37] This may be the incident recalled by Thomas Drake, who said some years later that "Sir Frauncis Drake was sued and prosecuted in the Admiraltie Courte by certen Frenchmen and others for provisions that were taken up on the seas in that voyage and ym-ployed in the same, so far fourth, as that by the sentence of that Courte he was adiudged to paie for the aforesaid provisions . . . the somme of twoo thousande poundes."[38]

On 27 September the fleet anchored near the Isles of Cies or Bayona in the mouth of the Vigo River. Loading some seven hundred soldiers into the pinnaces and long boats, Drake sent Carleill to land at the town of Bay-ona. On the way to shore the English landing party met emissaries sent by the governor of the town. Stopping to confer with them in the boats, Car-leill sent them back to the governor with Drake's reply. First, he said, the English intended to have their ships and sailors released from the embargo, or they would attack the place and release them by force. Second, he de-manded the right to purchase supplies to augment the meager store that had been loaded in Plymouth. Once this was done, Carleill proceeded to the beach outside Bayona. Here he landed the men, who immediately be-gan to amuse themselves by despoiling a chapel, while messengers went back and forth between Drake and the governor of the place.[39]

After the governor agreed that the English ships would be free to leave,

Drake's raid on Vigo

Drake himself landed. He wanted to speak to several of the English captains and satisfy himself that they were free to go. The captains seemingly affirmed what the governor had said and told Drake that the governor would meet with him the next day regarding his request to purchase
supplies. Negotiations were still inconclusive at midnight, when an approaching storm forced Drake to take his men back to the ships. Nonetheless, he determined to remain at Bayona until he had the supplies he
needed.[40]

As it turned out, the decision to remain at Bayona was a mistake, which
needed to be explained once the fleet returned to England. Carleill gave the
most convincing defense. First, there was still much to be done to make the
fleet ready for the voyage. The stores loaded so carelessly in Plymouth had

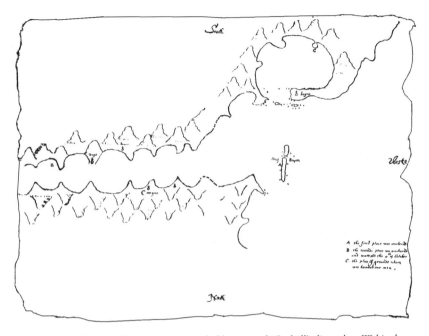

The harbor at Vigo and Bayona, a map probably sent with Carleill's dispatch to Walsingham in October 1585. The first anchorage at the Iles of Cies or Bayona is marked A; *the second beyond Vigo is marked* B; *the third inside the harbor at Bayona is marked* C. *In this map south is at the top. (Missing portions not shown; some detail added in dotted lines.) From PRO SP12/183/10, fol. 23.*

to be distributed to all of the vessels in the fleet. Then, too, it was apparent that some definite rules had to be formulated for maintaining discipline "both by sea and land." Finally, Drake wanted the king of Spain to know that Englishmen were on Spanish soil and that they were ready to take on whatever troops the king might send.[41]

Without intending to do so, Carleill embodied in his summary a description of his commander's dominant character traits. Francis Drake usually had a general idea of what he wanted to accomplish, but he did not become deeply involved in the work of advance planning. Records and administration interested him not in the least. Drake had little patience with other requirements of command, particularly the need to consult with his subordinates. He preferred to work through a small coterie of friends and to let these close associates relay his orders to the others. This was a command procedure designed to produce envy and resentment among the officers of the fleet.

But Drake had other qualities that made him a marvelous leader in combat. He was bold and absolutely fearless. When Drake told Sussex and Arundel, at a dinner in London, that he was quite willing to make war upon the king of Spain, it sounded like boasting but it was absolutely true.[42] He meant every word. Drake's personal bravery was accompanied by a complete lack of moral scruples. It did not bother him in the least to deprive someone, friend or foe, of life or property.

While Carleill worried about problems of organization, the storm raged through the fleet. Three ships, the *Talbot, Hawkins,* and *Speedwell,* lost their anchors and for a time were driven out to sea. They had scarcely made their way back into the bay on the last day of the month when Drake's scouts noticed boats leaving Vigo and carrying goods upriver. Taking this as a sign that the Spanish were prepared to deny his request for supplies, Drake quickly organized a raiding party to go in pursuit. As might have been expected, officers in the group were Drake's personal friends and family members. Carleill took the *Tiger,* Thomas Drake the *Thomas,* Tom Moone the *Francis,* and Richard Hawkins the *Duck,* which was an oared pinnace or galley, good for close fighting. Anchoring above Vigo to cut off the escape route, Carleill put his men into the ship's boats and the pinnace and set about capturing the Spanish boats as they tried to flee upriver. Carleill's raiders captured some booty, but not a great deal. One of the boats carried the silver cross and vestments from the cathedral of Vigo. Others were loaded with wine, sugar, and household goods. Carleill called it the "usuall pillage." It is not clear whether he meant to include in this description the "gentlewomen" captured in one of the boats, whose fate was not otherwise recorded.[43]

Their initial purpose accomplished, the English raiding party then went ashore and began a general pillage of the houses, convents, and churches in and around Vigo.[44] Most of the people had fled, and there was not much opposition, though there was one casualty. An English sailor from a merchant vessel that happened into port was caught alone, rummaging through a private house. Some local citizens strangled the unfortunate vandal and chopped off his head.[45] Total booty taken at Vigo was valued at about 6,000 ducats, though the Spanish loss was probably greater because of property destroyed.[46]

On the day following the raid, the governor sent a delegation to Drake, asking for a conference. This was arranged, and terms were agreed upon. The English were to be allowed to trade and take on water, and some English prisoners would be released from the local jail. In return the English raiders agreed to restore or pay for the plundered goods. The first two provisions were carried out, but there is no evidence of restitution or of payment for the stolen goods.[47]

Bold as ever, Drake kept his fleet in the harbor at Vigo for another week, taking on food and water. The shipload of fish captured before their arrival was parceled out to the ships in the fleet, while the vessel itself was broken up for firewood. A second shipload of fish was captured in port and commandeered in the same way as the first. Finally, on 9 October 1585, the fleet was ready. Hostages, given on each side at the beginning of the negotiations, were returned, and the fleet sailed down to the mouth of the bay. On the morning of 11 October a good northerly wind came up, and they went to sea once more.[48]

Why Drake tarried so long at Vigo is not clear, but it was just long enough to miss the Spanish treasure fleet. With a little more speed he might have taken the Spanish ships, some of which were sailing without an armed escort. There were two divisions. The New Spain fleet of thirty vessels reached the Spanish port of San Lucar on 22 September, by the new Gregorian calendar, which meant that Drake was still in Plymouth when the fleet arrived in Spain.

The Panama fleet was still to come. Arriving in Terceira on 7 October 1585, the fleet looked in vain for the naval escort supposed to have been sent from Spain. Authorities in Madrid knew at this time that an English fleet was hovering off Finisterre, and perhaps this is why Drake was allowed to remain so long unmolested in Vigo.[49] Whatever the reason, Drake missed his chance, and the second fleet also made port safely, while Drake and his men loitered in the harbor at Vigo.[50] Drake later told Burghley that he missed the second fleet by a mere twelve hours, but he was in fact late by several days.[51] Perhaps he was confused by the ten-day difference between the Gregorian and the Julian calendar dates.[52] The treasure he missed was the biggest such cargo Spain had seen in recent years.[53]

Leaving the shore of Galicia, Drake steered his fleet for the Canary Islands, intending to water there and sail on to the Cape Verde Islands. Once the fleet arrived at the island of Lanzarote, on 24 October, Drake convened a council to discuss the landing. Whether he announced the destination, as was his usual practice, or took advice, the decision was made to go to Palma. Passing Tenerife on the twenty-seventh, Drake's ships met a French raider who had also been hunting for the treasure fleet. The Frenchman told Drake that he had sighted the fleet off Cape Saint Vincent, just as it was about to enter Spanish waters.[54] The encounter came on 6 or 8 October, he said, giving Drake his first indication that he had completely missed the Spanish treasure fleet.[55]

Drake's ships reached Palma on 2 November. Heading into the bay, they were met with a barrage of cannon fire from the fortress. The cannoneers at Palma were great marksmen. Two shots struck the *Bonaventure,* one of them hitting the gallery where Drake was standing. The unknown narrator of the *Leicester* journal penned an interesting description of events: "The first shott was made at our Admirall, which went fayre over. The second being likewise shott at her strake atwixte our Generalls legges, standing in his gallery with Captain Frobusher and C. Carlell of the one side and Captain George [Barton] on the other, the splinters of the planke where on they stod hurte George a litell, but there was no more hurt done by it being a mynione shott."[56] A cannonball struck the *Leicester,* and other shots came close but did no damage. Faced with such firm resistance, Drake ordered the fleet out of the harbor and sailed on. The fleet went past the island of Gomera, where the desolate appearance of the land convinced everyone that the island had little wood or water available.[57]

During this part of the voyage orders were distributed to the land forces, no doubt the work of Carleill, but clearly also approved by Drake. The contents of the orders show their concern about the behavior of the troops at Vigo:

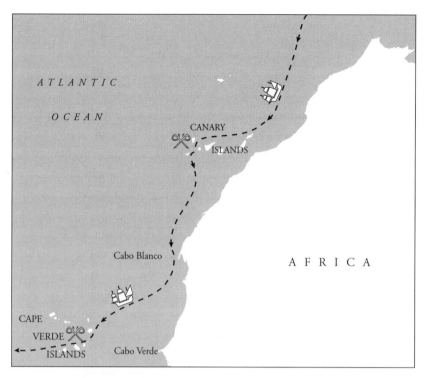

Drake's route along the coast of Africa, 1585

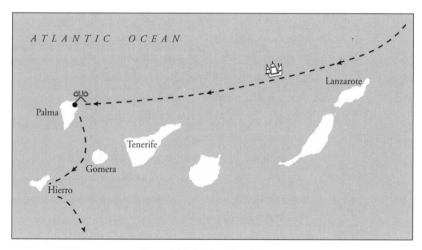

Canary Islands visited by Drake, 1585

1 In primis, that what person soever shall wander or stragle from his ensigne without commandment shall receue punishment according to the law of armes, to wit death

2 That no man offer to take any pilladge or make any spoyle before proclamation made vppon payne of death

3 That no souldier presume to breake or burne any church chest, locke, or doore, or any other thing locked or fastened, without order from his captain of whome chardge of any such thinge shalbe required

4 That no Captain gyve any such order for any breakinge of howses or chestes without direction from the generall or his deputy for the tyme being

5 That in every pinnasse or boate that shall lande any men the Captain & master do appoynt sum one especiall man of trust to kepe the same & that the saide person suffer not any man to [bring] abourd any pilladge whatsoever without order from the generall or his deputy and that no pinasse goe from the shore vpon payne of death

6 That no man of what condition soever retayne or kepe to himselfe any gould, siluer, Iewellry, or any thinge of speciall price, for that there shalbe order taken where the same shalbe deliverede. yf any souch thinge be founde with them or hereafter vnderstood & iustly approved that then he shall not only lose the benefitt that might growe vnto him by the voiadge, but shalbe reputed as a person non worthy of credit.

7 Item, for as much as we are bounde in conscience and required also in duty to yielde an honest account of our doinges & procedings in this action & that her Maiesty [ ] shalbe appoynted & persons of cerditt shalbe assigned, unto whom such porcions of goods of speciall price as golde, silver, jewells, or any other thinge of moment or valew shalbe brought and delyvered, the which shall remayne in chestes vnder the chardge of 4

or 5 severall kayes, and they shalbe committed vnto the custody of souch Captens as are of best account in the Fleet.

Youre loving Frende,

F. Drake[58]

Drake and Carleill appear to have decided that the disorderly conduct of the troops on land had contributed to the delay at Vigo. There must have been bickering about the uneven distribution of the plunder. The new orders were designed to prevent such misunderstandings in the future.

Pressing on, the fleet reached the island of Hierro on 5 November. Determined to keep discipline, Drake himself led the landing party, about seven hundred men. Among the first people he encountered was an English lad who had been born in Devon but had lived for some years in the island. The boy told Drake that there was not much likelihood of getting either provisions or plunder at Hierro, and so it proved to be. After waiting all day in the harbor for the rest of the fleet to join his ships, Drake set sail once more, making this time for the coast of Africa.

The fleet met the coast at Cabo Blanco, where the men spent some time fishing with lines and poles. They managed to catch a supply of sea bream or porgies, and dogfish—not much, but enough for a couple of meals for the fleet.[59] A day or so later they chased four French ships, managing to pick up a straggling pinnace, which was drafted into the fleet.[60]

From Cabo Blanco Drake headed to sea once more, directing his course toward the Cape Verde Islands. On 17 November the men on deck saw Boa Vista, then Maio, and finally São Tiago. This last island was Drake's next objective. During the night he landed a party of six hundred men, hoping to take the town by surprise. It was probably impossible to keep such a matter secret. The inhabitants saw the ships approaching and quickly fled, taking most of their valuables with them.[61]

The landing and march were militarily rather sophisticated. Carleill had divided his troops into three detachments to attack the town from three directions. On the right wing there were 250 men from the *Leicester,* the *Tiger,* and the *White Lion.* These were divided into several companies com-

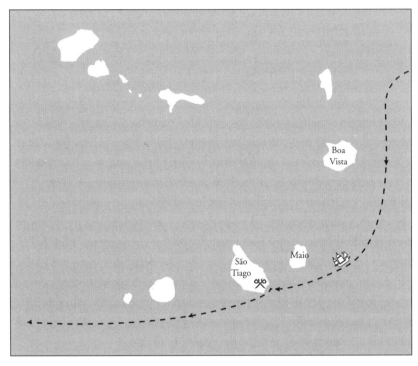

Drake's raid on the Cape Verde Islands, 1585

manded by Captain Francis Knollys and Captain Anthony Platt. Leading this wing were two forward detachments of 30 men each, with four ranks of harquebusiers and two of long bowmen, commanded by Captain John Sampson and Captain Richard Stanton. A similar advance force on the left wing was commanded by Captain John Goring and Captain George Barton, with Captain Anthony Powell apparently commanding the rear detachment of this wing. Carleill was in the center, commanding the main force. In the end there were about a thousand men. This careful preparation turned out to be quite unnecessary, as there was no resistance. When the sun appeared on the horizon, it was apparent that the entrance into town was by a narrow passage, and only one group could advance at a time.[62] Carleill thereupon sent the two detachments of Sampson and Barton into the town and finally occupied the place with the rest of his army.

In the fortifications along the seaward approach the soldiers found more than fifty pieces of ordnance, which they discharged as a salute for the queen's birthday.[63]

São Tiago was a large settlement of some six or seven hundred dwellings, with a cathedral, two other churches, a government house, and an episcopal residence. In addition to the cannons, all of which were brass, the troops found a dozen barrels of powder. There was also a huge supply of victuals, including wine, oil, bread, meal, and dried goat meat. There were oranges, sugar cane, and cocoa nuts, plus lemons, figs, dates, quinces, and potatoes. In the local shipyard Drake's sailors found a new caravel, which they added to the fleet. Seven other vessels in the harbor were stripped of cargo and fittings and set adrift.[64] What happened to the contents of these ships was something of a mystery. The author of the *Leicester* journal said that Drake kept it secret. "I have knowne not any made privie to it," he said, "but whome himselfe imployed in takinge out of all thinges within the said Carvells."[65]

While stopped at São Tiago, Drake repeated the blunder that he had made in dealing with the officers and men at San Julian. For some reason he thought it was necessary to put all the officers under oath, renewing their commissions in much the same way as he had on the voyage around the world. The loneliness of command seemed to create mistrust and suspicions that Drake could overcome only by making the officers absolutely subservient to his will. And it was not just the officers who were to be sworn. Everyone in the fleet was to take the oath of fealty. After this, Lieutenant General Carleill was to take an oath to the general, the captains to the lieutenant general, and the men to the captains.[66]

The whole plan was announced at a special meeting called on 19 November, where Chaplain Nichols read the oaths, which he seems to have written at Drake's direction, in consultation with Carleill and Frobisher. Knollys, who held the rank of rear admiral, was enraged that he had not been consulted about this. He was annoyed at being ignored by Drake, and he objected to the wording of the oaths. He was willing to take the oath of allegiance, but both he and his officers thought all the oaths were totally unnecessary.[67]

Knollys asked for time to consider the matter, made a copy of the oaths, and left. Outside the meeting room he met with Chaplain Nichols. As Knollys later reported, the chaplain berated him "with heathen and prophane examples." Then some of Knollys's men joined them, whereupon Nichols apologized and left. The next day was Sunday, and in his sermon Nichols announced that the oaths would be administered after dinner and declared that anyone who refused to take them was not fit to be in the fleet.[68]

When the council of captains was convened that evening, Knollys complained to Drake about Nichols's repeated insults, as he considered them. This was a mistake. Drake always became angry at criticism, either of himself or of his friends. Flying into a rage, Drake told Knollys that he and his men were seditious. When this happened, Knollys's friends and retainers— Masters Thorowgood, Willys, Longe, Stanton, and Chamberlain—came to his defense. There was no going back. Though Knollys offered to serve without taking the oath, Drake would not have it. During the next week there were several meetings, and Drake's anger grew at each one. Finally, Drake removed Thorowgood and the others from Knollys's command.[69]

Discipline was still lax, or so Drake thought. Before leaving São Tiago, he convened a court that among other things sentenced two men to death. One man had murdered an officer and was hanged for mutiny. Another had committed sodomy with two of the ship's boys, and he was hanged as well. With this accomplished, Drake then proceeded to impose discipline on the citizens of the island. With a force of several hundred men, he marched inland a dozen miles and burned the town of Santo Domingo. Drake then returned to São Tiago, set fire to that town, and on 28 November sailed out with his fleet. The next day, further along the coast, the fleet stopped at a place called Praya and set fire to that town as well.[70]

One place of curiosity for all visitors to São Tiago was the hospital. Situated next to the church, the institution had "as brave roomes in hit and in as goodlie order as any man can Device." The hospital rooms were filled with patients, twenty people sick of "fowle and fylthie Diseases." Drake's fleet was only a few days away from the islands when the same foul and filthy diseases swept through his ships, decimating passengers and crew.[71]

The chills and fever were like common ague, but some people had livid spots similar to those associated with plague.[72] Possibly it was bubonic plague, but the lingering lassitude of the survivors may be more typical of pneumonic plague.[73] In Drake's ship there were a hundred men sick; in the *Primrose,* sixty. For a week or more two or three people in each ship died every day.[74] As the epidemic spread, Drake called the ships together for a conference. Each ship came up to the flagship and reported its losses, whereupon Drake gave his own medical advice: bleeding.[75] According to the story later published in England, the losses were "above two or three hundred men."[76] Spanish informants who talked to men in the fleet said that losses were five hundred or more, with many others permanently disabled by the disease.[77]

The first landfall in the West Indies was the island of Dominica, reached on 18 December.[78] Here some of the men went ashore, where they took on water and traded for cassava bread, giving beads in exchange.[79] The native inhabitants were friendly, but the Englishmen, weakened by disease, were uneasy throughout their one-day stay. On 19 December the fleet began sailing northwest, along the line of the islands, toward La Española. Stopping on Christmas at the island of Saint Christopher, Drake sent the sick men ashore, hoping that the salubrious climate would help bring about their recovery. Twenty more men died on the island. Putting to sea once more after four days at the island, Drake captured a small vessel whose pilot guided him into the next port. On 1 January 1586 the fleet arrived at the bay of Santo Domingo, where Drake landed a thousand men and occupied the town.[80]

It was another night maneuver, the sort that Carleill and Drake seemed to prefer. Setting off in the pinnaces on the night of 31 December, while still out at sea, the troops landed early in the morning, unopposed, seven or eight miles west of the town.[81] The night before their arrival, the Spanish authorities received notice that the fleet was nearby. They were not worried. Everyone told them that no landing was possible except under the guns of the castle. Well, perhaps a landing could be made on the beach at Guibia, but a small guard was posted there to give the alarm in case of an attempted landing. There were natural defenses at Santo Domingo,

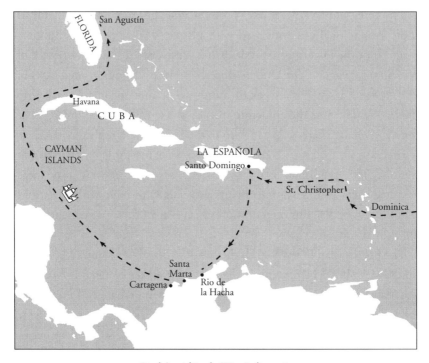

Drake's raid in the West Indies, 1585

though not sufficient, as it turned out. The entrance channel in the harbor was protected by a sandbar, and two or three ships were scuttled on the bar to make entry even more difficult. An armed galley under a professional navy officer, Diego de Osorio, took position inside this barrier to augment the cannons from the forts.[82] Once these preparations were made, everyone seems to have relaxed.[83]

The real weaknesses of the place became apparent only later. There was no garrison in Santo Domingo and very little in the way of fortifications. The walls shown on the detailed views of the town that Baptista Boazio drew after the town was occupied were mostly imaginary, often no more than a line of shrubbery.[84] A poorly armed and untrained citizen militia was called upon to defend the place against a trained English army.[85] No doubt this is what Drake expected to find, having seen Spanish defenses on his earlier visits in the Caribbean and his more recent visits in the Pacific ports.

Just how Drake and Carleill decided to land where they did is unknown. The official account said that the captured pilot told them about the beach at Hayna, but Drake probably had information about Santo Domingo from some of his own seamen who had visited there on trading vessels.[86] Regardless of the source of his information, Drake decided to land the army at Hayna and march his men toward the city. Meanwhile, his galleons would post themselves off the port, ready to give artillery support when necessary. Leading the way in the *Francis,* Drake took the pinnaces past the town to Hayna. Here he watched the men land in the surf and then set off marching through the jungle to Santo Domingo.[87] Their surprise was almost complete. The Spanish had seen the pinnaces sail past, but they believed that a landing was impossible. A small mounted force went out to reconnoiter, but there were too few to make any effective resistance. A few shots were exchanged, a Spanish horseman was killed, and the rest rode back to give the alarm.[88]

As the English army approached the city, the citizens began to flee. There were only 150 men in the Spanish force defending the city. They fell back to the Lenba Gate, which had stone portals but no actual gates. Here the city wall extended about fifty feet beyond the gate, a reasonably good place to establish a defensive line.[89] A few Spanish cannons were marshaled here, and one salvo was fired, killing an English soldier who stood next to Carleill. This was the last shot fired by the Spanish cannons. Supported by cannon fire from Drake's ships, Carleill's men charged the Spanish guns before the gunners could reload, scattering the Spanish defenders. The English then entered the city.[90]

On the Spanish side the disorder was complete. During the melee, someone gave the order to set the galley slaves free. Rather than giving the expected assistance to the defenders, the freed slaves immediately joined the English soldiers, roaming through the streets and looting the place.[91] A few soldiers remained in the fortress until noon the following day, when they also made their escape. It was a debacle beyond anyone's imagination, humiliating to the Spanish army and to the crown.[92]

Safely inside the city and victorious once again, Carleill set up his defensive perimeter, and Drake drew the fleet into the inner harbor. For sev-

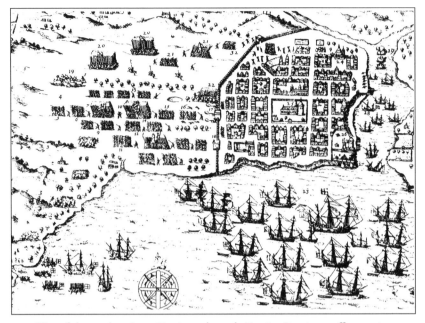

View of the attack on Santo Domingo, drawn by Baptista Boazio, an officer serving under Carleill. The town was not as large, nor the defenses as elaborate, as depicted. Reprinted from Bigges, Summarie and True Discourse *(1589). John Carter Brown Library at Brown University.*

eral days his men sacked the town, looting, burning buildings, and generally sowing disruption. Finally a Spanish emissary came to enquire what it would take to make the English leave. A million ducats, he was told.[93] It was impossible. Once the seat of Spanish power in the New World, Santo Domingo was in 1586 an isolated outpost, poor, sparsely populated, and living on memories of faded glory.[94] There was not enough silver and gold in the whole region to supply Drake's demand. So short was the supply of specie that the mint was making copper coins for use as local currency.[95]

For three more weeks English and Spanish negotiators met and talked. After each unsatisfactory session, Drake gave orders to burn another section of town, another church, another convent. Finally, when he realized that the citizens could not pay a large ransom, a compromise was made. With the bishop of Santo Domingo contributing the plate that had been saved from the cathedral, women giving up rings and earrings, and various merchants supplying the rest, a total of 25,000 ducats was finally assembled.[96]

Drake and his troops also looted what they could find in the houses. Everything movable was moved. Everything flammable was burned, including the Spanish galley, which had been under repair at the time of the attack. But the houses and public buildings were so solidly built of stone that they refused to fall. Even so, there was little booty except for a supply of food, several hundred hides, and some simple clothes.[97]

No doubt the capture of the town was a clear victory for the English troops, but it was not the great battle that has so often been described. The classic account was written a century ago by Julian Corbett. In his narrative English soldiers defeated a large force of Spanish regulars in a well-fortified town. This is simply not the case. His assertion that escaped slaves —"Maroons"—helped the English forces land is also without foundation.[98] A number of Spanish renegades and galley slaves joined the English after the city was taken.[99] But there is no evidence that the Spanish authorities thought that any of them had aided in the attack. In any case, Drake and his troops did not need assistance from anyone. The local citizen militia offered them scarcely any resistance.

When the story of Drake's West Indies voyage was prepared for publication a couple of years later, some curious stories were added to enhance their appeal and to modify the popular view of Drake. One such incident appeared later in two of the English accounts that deal with the occupation of Santo Domingo, but it was not mentioned at all in the Spanish records. According to the sailor who wrote the *Primrose* journal, a Spanish soldier on horseback appeared one day with a flag of truce.[100] For some reason not made clear in the account, Drake sent "a Nigro boie" to find out what the man wanted. The horseman talked to the boy briefly, then suddenly ran him through with his pike staff. When the Spanish negotiators appeared the next day to talk to Drake, he was furious and demanded that they hang the man who had killed the black boy. When that was not done, Drake took two friars who were his prisoners and hanged them in retribution. "The same Daie the Spaniardes came & carried awaie the fryers & 3 daies after, they hanged the same man that killed the Nigro boie where they friers weare hanged."[101] This story is repeated with some elaboration in printed editions of *The Summarie and True Discourse,* though not in the manuscript.[102]

Like all myths, this one may contain a bit of truth. A Spanish ballad composed some time later by Juan de Castellanos tells of two aged Dominican friars who were tortured and killed in their monastery by Drake's men.[103] There is no essential similarity between the two incidents, and both may be imaginary. But an English account of the voyage seems to support the Castellanos version. The journalist on board the *Leicester* told of being with a detachment sent to burn part of the town of Santo Domingo: "At our comming to the townes end we burnt an Abbey in which ley an old fryer dead, who was kilde by sum of the souldiors which weare dysorderly. We did burne divers other howses."[104] Drake's men did wreck every convent, monastery, and church they found, destroying images, altars, screens, and choirs, and attempting to burn what they could not otherwise ruin. All this was covered in reports that came from Santo Domingo.[105] There was nothing about the murder of two innocent friars, however, who would surely have been mentioned in official records if the authorities had known what happened. If the Spanish accounts failed to record the death mentioned by the *Leicester* journalist, it may be that the body was consumed in the flames. Spanish officials perhaps thought that the old man, known to be ill, had died of his illness.

Another story, not imaginary, involved Drake's capture of an escutcheon he found hanging in the *audiencia* building. The banner bore King Philip's motto: *Non Sufficit Orbis,* "The world is not enough." When the Spanish negotiators arrived to discuss a ransom, Drake asked them to translate the motto for him. Greatly embarrassed, they refused to say anything. Some of Drake's men then observed that perhaps Queen Elizabeth would force the Spanish king "to lay aside that proude and unreasonable reaching vaine of his."[106] Later, when they paid the ransom, the Spanish negotiators asked for the return of the escutcheon and got a blunt refusal from Drake.[107]

During the long stay at Santo Domingo, discipline again became a major problem. Several officers were involved in duels. The men quarreled as well, and some thirty or forty were placed in two of the cathedral chapels, which Drake converted to use as a jail.[108] One "Irisshe man" was hanged for murder.[109]

The trouble continued with Captain Knollys, who still refused to take the oath of allegiance demanded by Drake. After several additional meetings and a long letter from Knollys to Drake, demanding justice, Drake relieved Knollys of his command and placed him in the *Hawkins,* promising to send him home to England shortly.[110]

After thirty-one days in occupation at Santo Domingo, Drake took his fleet to sea once more. The fleet was larger when he left than it had been when he arrived. In the harbor was a merchant ship belonging to Juan Antonio Corço, which an admiring Drake took in exchange for one of his own that was leaking.[111] This was a large ship of 400 tons. In addition, there was a 200-ton vessel, and Drake took this ship as well, naming the two additions the *New Year's Gift* and the *New Hope.* The abandoned vessels were the *Benjamin* and the *Scout.* Three other Spanish ships taken from the port were very small, though one was a new fragata, just launched a few days before Drake's arrival.[112] The galley that Drake found in the port was in bad shape, partly dismantled for careening.[113] It was towed to sea and burned, along with Drake's leaky ships and several other vessels in the port that he did not want to take along.[114]

Along with his ships Drake took all the artillery he could find, some seventy guns of all sizes, loaded into Corço's ship.[115] Some of the galley slaves went along to help fill out the depleted crews. Others went into the hills. The same was true of many black slaves. Some went along with Drake, while others joined the free blacks in the hills.[116]

From Santo Domingo, Drake took the fleet directly south to the mainland. Intending at first to land at Rio de la Hacha, he was warned off by Spanish informants and went to Cartagena instead.[117] There is some indication that Drake had several such informants on board. Pedro, an Indian left by Drake at Cartagena, later told Spanish authorities that he had been Drake's servant since 1573, when Drake got him from a French pirate. Pedro told of others on Drake's ship who knew Margarita and Rio de la Hacha and Cartagena.[118]

According to Pedro some of these men were left behind at various ports to act as secret agents and help Drake on his next voyage. Pedro's testimony was given under torture, and much or all of it may be untrue, particularly the account of the agents, who he said invariably were short, bearded, and dressed in black. The Spanish authorities tried to trace the one man who was identified by name but found no such person. Still, Drake used local informants well during the Pacific voyage, and he is likely to have used them here.[119]

Cartagena was one of the principal towns of the Indies, though like Santo Domingo it was largely unfortified. The population in the early 1570s included only 250 vecinos, making it about half the size of Santo Domingo.[120] Except for the crews of two galleys and a galleass, there were no military people in the town. Still, the authorities in Cartagena had received advance warning and had taken some steps to fortify and defend the place.

Cartagena lay on the coast, but the bay was sheltered, reachable only through two small channels, Boca Chica and Boca Grande. The inner harbor was guarded by a fort at Boquerón, some distance from the town, where a chain had been placed across the channel to prevent entry. Between the town and the outer bay was a large island, connected to the mainland by a sand spit, La Caleta. A masonry wall four or five feet high, with a ditch in front, had been hurriedly placed across the spit, reaching most of the way and supplemented on the seaward side by some wine barrels filled with sand. Four guns were mounted behind the masonry wall, but the beach was open beyond the barricade of wine barrels with nothing else between the guns and the water some sixty or seventy feet away.[121]

For no very clear reason the Cartagena authorities decided to make their stand close to the city. The fortress at Boquerón was strong enough, they thought. The two armed galleys and the galleass were placed in the inner harbor, with the galleys drawn up bows to the shore at La Caleta to add their ten guns to the four behind the wall. A company of men was sent to guard the bridge connecting the town with the road to the fort at Boquerón, and another company was stationed at Boquerón. The remaining militia was placed at La Caleta, 300 harquebuses, 100 pikes, and 200 Indian bowmen.[122] Nothing was done to block Boca Chica or Boca Grande. It was an inadequate plan. If the galleys and the galleass had been placed in the channels, with the artillery pieces on the shore, Drake's ships could have been denied entry into the bay and he might not have been able to land.[123]

At about noon on Ash Wednesday, 9 February by the English calendar, ten days later by the Spanish, Drake sailed his fleet past the town. Peppered with cannon fire from the galleys and land batteries, his fleet sailed serenely onward and entered the bay unopposed through the Boca Grande.[124] Anchoring at about three or four in the afternoon, Drake summoned his captains into council and ordered them to prepare for a landing. Carleill would land with most of the troops at Hicacos Point. Frobisher would try to force an entry into the harbor under the fort at Boquerón.[125]

The landing was made at 2 A.M. the next day—under cover of darkness, as Drake and Carleill always preferred. The figures given in English sources seem to say that there were 1,700 men in Carleill's force, but this total probably included those who were scheduled to go with Frobisher.[126] Spanish sources estimate the numbers at a thousand in the attack on La Caleta plus another 600 in the pinnaces sent to Boquerón.[127]

Once Drake had his men ashore, he lined them up for a pep talk. It was short and to the point. They must attack and they must win. If they did not capture the town, none of them would be allowed back on board. Any man who retreated would be hanged.[128]

The force under Carleill made its way down the beach toward Cartagena, some four miles away. The Spanish had expected an invasion along this route and had planted sharpened, perhaps poisoned, stakes there.[129] English sources say that most or all of the men were able to avoid the stakes, though the Spanish report that "many" English soldiers were killed in this way.[130] This was only part of the Spanish defensive plan. A force of citizens and Indian auxiliaries lay in ambush out on the island. They were supposed to let Carleill's troops pass, then attack from the rear and cut them off. This may have been too sophisticated a maneuver for the citizen soldiers to understand. Rather than allowing Carleill to march beyond their position, when they would be cut off from Cartagena, the Spanish militia fell back in the face of Carleill's advance without offering any substantial resistance.[131]

It was still dark when Carleill's troops arrived at the masonry wall. As he drew his men together to charge, the Spanish defenders fired their can-

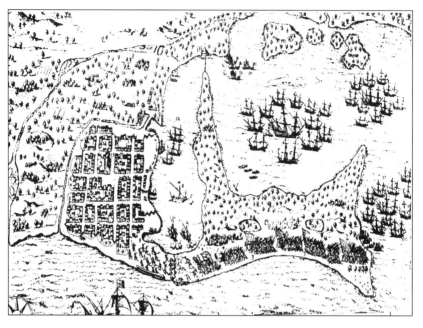

Boazio's sketch of Cartagena shows the inner and outer harbors. Carleill's troops are seen advancing across La Caleta. Reprinted from Bigges, Summarie and True Discourse *(1589). John Carter Brown Library at Brown University.*

nons, harquebuses, and arrows. The harquebuses in the galleys were fired as well, but they were of little use because of the distance. The cannons in the galleys were more effective weapons, though Carleill's men found a low part of the beach that was sheltered from the cannon fire.[132] At the insistence of the local people, the galley commander was stationed in the land battery to supervise defense from that point. But his untrained Spanish gunners were slow to reload.[133] Taking advantage of the delay, Carleill sent a force around the open flank and captured the battery.[134] There was a period of fierce hand-to-hand fighting in which the ensign bearer of Captain Alonso Bravo de Montemayor was killed and Bravo himself was wounded and taken prisoner. Following this someone cried out in Spanish, "Retire, gentlemen, we are lost." Local critics said that it was the galley commander Don Pedro Vique. Vique claimed that it was an Englishman trying to deceive his troops.[135]

It made no difference to the local militia. Hearing this, and faced with English pikes that were considerably longer than their own, they turned tail and went scurrying into the city.[136] As Carleill and his men entered Cartagena, they encountered a few barricades from which Indian archers fired at them with poisoned arrows. Some men were killed and others wounded, but most escaped without injury because Carleill's men were well armored. The Spanish militia and the Indians had none. The English quickly chased these defenders out of town.[137]

Surprisingly enough in the confusion, Don Pedro Vique managed to send an order to the galley commanders to push off from La Caleta and make their way out of the harbor. As the galleys approached the Boquerón channel, the commander of the fort signaled them to stop and give assistance against the English gunboats that had renewed their attack, still trying to pass the chain blockade. Coming closer, the galleys, too, came under fire from the English pinnaces that had been fighting in this area off and on since the battle started at La Caleta. On board one of the galleys a barrel of powder suddenly exploded, raining fire all over the ship. The galley slaves were unchained, and they immediately ran off into the countryside. Both galleys then ran ashore between the town and the fort, and that was the end of their escape attempt. Don Pedro Vique gave orders that night to burn the galleys.[138]

What the galley sailors did not know is that Frobisher's first attack on the fort had been driven off, after which the pinnaces returned to the fleet with the dead and wounded. Annoyed to see them back so soon, Drake himself took the pinnaces out, arriving at the fort at just about the time that the Spanish galleys were approaching. Angry with Frobisher for not having captured the blockhouse, Drake was determined to show his vice admiral just how it should be done. Arriving in range of the fort, Drake encountered the same withering fire that Frobisher had endured, losing a mast from his pinnace and seeing four or five of his men cut in two with chain shot. Still unable to capture the fort, Drake and Frobisher returned to the ships once more. Drake then took about two hundred men to La Caleta in the pinnaces. Under his direction the men removed the captured cannon from the wall on the sand spit and set it up on the wharf. From this point Drake bombarded the fort for the rest of the day, after which the Spanish soldiers slipped away in the darkness.[139]

Julian Corbett, who did not have access to the Spanish documents from Cartagena, thought that the attack at Boquerón was a feint to draw troops away from the real action at La Caleta.[140] In the Bigges account the naval attack is seen as a serious attempt to land a second invading force, and this conclusion is supported by evidence from Spanish sources.[141] As it turned out, Drake, Frobisher, and the pinnaces were unable to force an entrance, but the attack on Boquerón kept the Spanish defenders busy and prevented their giving assistance to the militia in Cartagena.

By midmorning it was all over. The battle of Cartagena did not last much longer than the battle of Santo Domingo. One local citizen said that the fighting was over within an hour.[142] Local wags said later that Drake was threatening to write to King Philip and complain about the lack of preparedness at Cartagena.[143] After the defenders at Boquerón slipped away under cover of darkness, Drake was able to enter the inner harbor.[144] Casualties on both sides are uncertain. The Spanish reported only a few lost but did not bother to count slaves and Indians. They thought that English losses were heavy, though the English would admit losing no more than thirty men.[145] The Spanish may have been counting graves. At least a hundred English soldiers and sailors died of wounds and disease while Drake waited in Cartagena, negotiating ransom payments.[146] Three of them were captains, including Tom Moone, who had served with Drake for the past dozen years.[147] Spanish observers thought that the loss to disease was huge, more than three times the number that Drake admitted.[148] The Spanish believed that the English were burying bodies secretly, and their reports mentioned "boatloads" of English dead.[149]

With an important prisoner, Alonso Bravo, plus three or four others, Drake felt that his ransom negotiations for Cartagena would proceed more smoothly than they had at Santo Domingo. In this he was disappointed. His first demand for 500,000 gold ducats elicited a counteroffer of 25,000.[150] One major problem was Drake's insistence on personal negotiations with the governor and the bishop. Bruised egos on both sides quickly made agreement impossible. When Drake first entered the governor's office to confer with these two, he found papers on the governor's desk that referred to him as a pirate. He flew into a rage and began shouting at the Spanish officials. During his tirade Drake made remarks about the Spanish king and grandees that offended the bishop, who thereupon insisted that no ransom could be paid.[151]

Largely as a result of this encounter Drake was compelled to remain at Cartagena for several more weeks, burning another part of the city after each unsuccessful negotiating session. The citizens seemingly thought that they could stall until the next fleet arrived from Spain. Drake assured them that he was not at all afraid of the fleet and that he might seek it out if it did not arrive before he left.[152]

While negotiations were at a standstill, Drake passed his time talking with Alonso Bravo, in whose house he lived. The two became close friends, or so Bravo thought. After being held prisoner for several days, he received news that his wife was dying at his country estate. Released to be at her side, the old man was later allowed to bring her body back to Cartagena for burial in the cathedral. Drake himself was present for the funeral, which was carried out with great pomp, "flags reversed and drums muffled."[153]

With this sort of relationship, Bravo might have expected special consideration when it came time to pay his ransom. In fact, Drake demanded 5,000 ducats from Bravo, saying that he really wanted 6,000 but was remitting 1,000 in recognition of his host's hospitality and gifts.[154]

An agreement on ransom of the rest of the city was finally reached after Drake's cannon destroyed the newly constructed cathedral. English sources say it was all an accident. Spanish say it was deliberate. Both agree that several arches in the unfinished nave collapsed after the cannon was fired, though the English say the collapse came from concussion and not from a direct hit.[155] In any case, the agreement was for a payment of 107,000 ducats. Some private houses and a monastery outside the town were ransomed separately. Drake also took what goods he could find and confiscated slaves as well, though he honored the request of those who specifically asked to be returned to their Spanish masters.[156]

Slightly more than a hundred thousand ducats was not much of a payment for such a great loss in English lives. Moreover, the payment was made not in coin but in bars and wedges of silver and gold. Some men felt that Drake was not absolutely honest in recording the ransom. Twenty mule loads of silver at eight wedges per load were brought to the house where Drake stayed and left there over night. The next day 116 wedges were counted.[157]

Most of the officers were discouraged. About the middle of the month Drake had a series of meetings, asking the land captains for their opinions about the course to be taken henceforth. Their answers were given in writing and later printed by Hakluyt when he published his own version of the *Summarie and True Discourse*.[158] They are illuminating, but Drake's questions are missing and must be inferred from the answers. The first question has to do with the ability to defend Cartagena. Some historians, taking their lead from Sir William Monson, have assumed that Drake had some intention of staying permanently in Cartagena or elsewhere in the Caribbean.[159] Nothing could have been further from his mind. The citizens of Cartagena had been delaying the ransom negotiations because they expected a fleet to arrive from Spain at any time and chase Drake away from town. Drake's question to the captains was whether they could defend Cartagena against a Spanish attack.[160]

First, they said, there were only 700 men fit for duty, with perhaps another 150 still sick. The troops were sufficient to defend the town from any Spanish attack but not to continue to Nombre de Dios or Panama, as Drake wanted to do.[161] The captains were disappointed with the booty so far obtained. Their experience so far showed that the towns of the Indies were not as rich as they had thought. Perhaps it would be better to return to England "with the honour already gotten."[162]

These remarks to Drake were couched in the most respectful language, but they masked an underlying resentment. From the very first there was a great disparity in the treatment of officers of the fleet. When quartering the troops at São Tiago, Carleill had given the best houses to his friends, and Drake had done nothing to correct the matter. Rather, he allowed it to continue, and the same sort of favoritism appeared in the distribution of captured guns and victuals.[163]

There is some evidence that women were a major problem throughout the voyage. Some black women were taken on board when the ships visited Cape Verde, and others were added at Santo Domingo.[164] Officers and men quarreled, fought, and dueled over matters that are not easy to understand from the records. The town of Cartagena had advance warning, so there was not much left there in the way of plunder. Perhaps because of this, slaves and servants were a source of discontent. Drake finally issued an order decreeing that no one under the rank of ensign could keep a slave, black or white, and establishing general rules for treatment of slaves.[165] There had been a prostitution problem in Cartagena before the English arrived, largely involving sailors with Indian and slave women, but with some Spanish women as well.[166] When Drake's fleet departed from the place, the great majority of the slaves carried on board were said to be female.[167] All of this evidence is circumstantial, but there is more than an indication that the "unrighteous intercourse," as one critic called it, continued after the English occupied Cartagena.[168]

Morale suffered another blow when Drake issued an order that every man who had Spanish coins must explain how he got them and offer them for exchange at official rates. Drake also wanted all gold and silver to be delivered to a central depository, but the captains so distrusted Drake and Carleill when it came to distribution of booty that this was apparently not done.[169] Alonso Bravo, who talked with Drake every day and developed a very close relationship with him, was able to meet and talk with many of Drake's captains. They told Bravo that they and their men were "aggrieved because [Drake] had promised them so much and they saw that their part would be small." Beyond this, "all the gentlemen said he would not again find any to go out with him from England."[170]

By the time Drake left Cartagena, discipline was a major problem. There was little for the soldiers and sailors to do there, and Drake had to rule his men with an iron hand just to stay in control. The dean of the cathedral thought that Drake was too firm: "This Francis treats his people harshly and hangs many."[171] Another said of Drake: "With the seamen he is harsh."[172] A third observer said, "He is feared and obeyed by his men," adding sarcastically that Drake was "not very cruel."[173]

Faced with all these problems, Drake was discouraged himself. He once said to Bravo that he had promised the queen a million ducats as her share of the profits, and he had nothing like that in his coffers.[174] Frobisher was disaffected as well, no doubt because Drake had questioned his bravery in the attack on the fort at Boquerón. One Spanish report had Frobisher complaining about the ransom money and about Drake as well. Why, he wanted to know, did the Spanish call "such a shameless rascal 'your excellency' when he was a low fellow who had been given command of the fleet because he knew this coast."[175]

After the final ransom payment was received, Drake took his ships away from the town and into the bay, where they took on water and underwent other housekeeping routines.[176] Several ships were careened while he was at Cartagena, and other repairs were also made.[177] Very likely Drake had already made up his mind to go directly to Cuba, which was his destination when he took his fleet out of the bay on 31 March.

Imagine the feelings of the Spaniards when two days later the English fleet was back in the harbor. All the captured ordnance was still carried in the *New Year's Gift,* seized by Thomas Drake from Antonio Corço at Santo Domingo.[178] Apparently new, this ship leaked so badly that it was feared she would sink. It was therefore necessary to unload the captured cannons she carried and distribute them throughout the fleet. Still as bold as ever, Drake spent an additional two weeks in Cartagena. On arriving the second time, he had found a supply of grain and decided to turn it into biscuit to take along on the next leg of the voyage.[179]

The disputes that had racked the fleet during the previous stay in Cartagena continued. Pedro Fernández de Busto said that this general discontent would prevent Drake from sailing against Havana as planned: "I am certain he will not attack Havana because they had many disputes with one another and they agreed on nothing. Three days before they left they had great arguments with one another. And so, I am sure that he went to Matanzas, and he was going to take on water and meat, and they were continuing their voyage to England."[180] Another man said that the dispute was between Drake and "the gentlemen and officers." He was not sure of the subject, but he did know that "both sides were drawing up documents."[181]

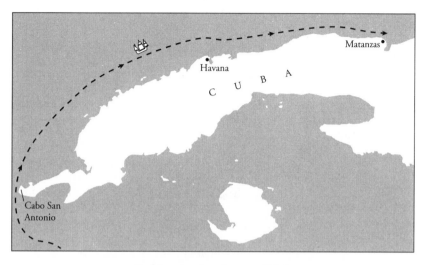

Drake's cruise along the coast of Cuba

Diego Hidalgo de Montemayor reported that the dispute was so serious that Drake had removed some officers from their commands and perhaps had even executed some of them.[182] These comments from Spanish observers would be of little interest if they were not supported by English sources. There were disputes among the officers almost from the first. The Knollys business had needlessly separated one group from Drake. He should never have let it happen. Other officers quarreled at São Tiago and even more at Santo Domingo.[183]

Sailing away from Cartagena once more on 14 April, Drake stopped briefly at the Cayman Islands, where his men shot a few alligators for meat.[184] From here they sailed to the westernmost point of Cuba, Cabo de San Antonio. Going ashore on 25 April, they found a frigate or two, which they set afire.[185] There was little or no water to be found, so the fleet continued to the east, passing Havana and chasing a small ship into the harbor. They attempted to land at Matanzas for water, but contrary winds kept them out of the bay.[186]

Returning again to Cabo de San Antonio, they arrived on 14 May. Desperately in need of water by this time, they landed and started gathering rain water. Losses from disease had continued, and it was necessary to send slaves and prisoners to help with the work. There was no running water, but recent rains had soaked the ground, and the men were able to dig pits, from which they bailed water. Drake himself labored alongside the men. Still strong as a bull, Drake waded into the sea up to his armpits, carrying barrels of water on his shoulder out to the waiting boats.[187]

While the fleet paused for the second time at Cabo de San Antonio, Drake called the captains into conference once more. With his numbers greatly reduced by disease and wounds, he told them that he would not attack Havana unless it could be done without risk.[188] Apparently thinking a successful attack impossible, he ordered most of the artillery to be put below decks, leaving only a few guns ready for service. Gun ports were closed and lashed down.[189] Perhaps to quell some unrest among some captured Moorish and Turkish galley slaves, Drake told them that they would be sent back to their own country as soon as he got them to England.[190]

Once the water casks were loaded, Drake ordered the fleet to sail back in the direction of Havana. Approaching the harbor, his lookouts spied a ship in the distance, and Drake sent a few pinnaces in pursuit. As the ships drew near to the port, they came under fire from the forts and were forced to turn back.[191]

Unable to enter the harbor, Drake took his ships to the nearby Guacuranao River, where the fleet remained at anchor for three or four days.[192] Most of what transpired here is unknown. The pinnaces still went out after the occasional ship, finally taking one small vessel laden with salt, from which the crew escaped in a canoe. Drake may have considered bringing the guns up again and waiting here for the fleet from Spain.[193] One of the Spanish prisoners who escaped at Cabo de San Antonio reported that Drake's soldiers wanted to wait for the fleet, but the officers opposed that strategy.[194] In the event, the English fleet departed without any further hostile move, passing the entrance channel to Havana Bay once more, then sailing off for the Florida coast.[195]

On 27 May, Drake's fleet reached San Agustín, which he determined to attack on the following day. The Spanish governor, Pedro Menéndez Mar-

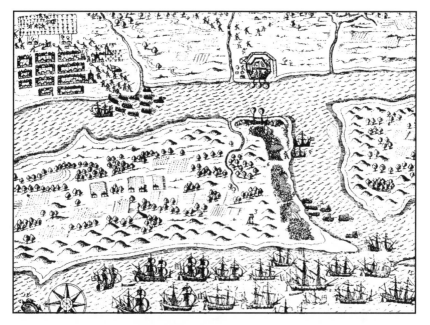

Boazio's view of the attack on San Agustín. Reprinted from Bigges, Summarie and True Discourse *(1589). John Carter Brown Library at Brown University.*

qués, had evacuated the town some days earlier after receiving warning messages from Santo Domingo. But with seventy or eighty men, he held the fort a mile or two up the bay. On 28 May, Drake began his attack on this post, bringing up artillery, which he placed across the river to begin an assault the next day.[196] Concerned about his ability to defend the unfinished log fort, and worried about leaving the townspeople undefended, Menéndez withdrew under cover of darkness, and Drake marched into the town unopposed.[197]

Drake remained at San Agustín for several days. As soon as the Spanish had left the town, the Indians entered and looted the place. Drake's men finished the job, burning the town, the fort, and the surrounding fields. Drake's men stripped the place of guns, tools, hardware, and everything else of value, including a chest with 6,000 ducats of the king's money. A small ship tied to the river bank was added to the fleet, replacing the vessel captured off Havana, which was burned.[198]

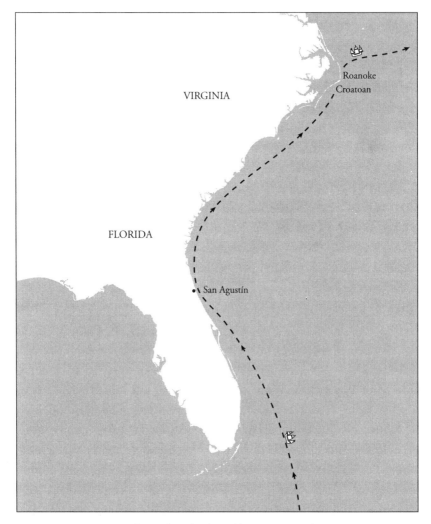

Drake's raid on Florida and his stop at Roanoke

Three Spanish deserters joined Drake at San Agustín, and three black
slaves deserted. They testified to Spanish authorities that Drake had told
them he had no intention of freeing them. Instead, they were going to the
English colony at Roanoke to labor there: "They said that he intended to
leave all the negroes he had in a fort and settlement established at Jacan by
the English who went there a year ago. He intended to leave the 250 blacks

and all the small ships that he had, and cross to England with only the large ones."[199]

Drake's determined destruction of every trace of the settlement at San Agustín may have been prompted by the loss of his sergeant major, Captain Anthony Powell, during a chase after the retreating Spanish troops. Whatever the reason, the pillage at San Agustín was not enough. Departing the first week of June, Drake directed his fleet to the nearby settlement at Santa Elena. He intended to sack and burn this settlement as well, but the shoals kept him out to sea, and he sailed past the bay.[200]

Continuing north, Drake's fleet passed along the Outer Banks and saw a signal fire at Croatoan Island. It was a party from the English settlement at Roanoke. This was a brand new colony, founded just a year earlier by a group of settlers brought to the island by Sir Richard Grenville, the partner of Sir Walter Raleigh. The local people guided Drake to their anchorage, but it was too shallow for most of his ships. Consequently, he anchored on the seaward side of the island. In response to Drake's messages, the governor, Ralph Lane, arrived the next day and asked for assistance. Drake offered food and supplies, including most of the materials taken at San Agustín. Seeing that Lane needed a ship, Drake offered him the use of the *Francis,* in which Lane proposed to return to England in August.[201]

These plans changed in the next few days. A hurricane blew the fleet from the anchorage, and the *Francis,* among others, did not return. With their settlement badly pounded by the storm, the Roanoke settlers were completely demoralized. Lane determined to return to England with Drake.[202] Abandoning their colony, the settlers left only a few ramshackle buildings as a reminder of their brief tenure. In addition, two men were left swinging from a gibbet, an Indian and an Englishman.[203] Whether these were the results of Lane's justice or Drake's is not known.[204] The fleet reached Plymouth on 28 July 1586.[205]

His new venture in command of a large fleet had brought out qualities in Drake that had only been suspected before. Always fearless and supremely confident, he proved to be unrelenting in battle. He was best at fighting in a ship, but he was effective in land assaults as well.

Yet the tenacity that made Drake a success in plundering unarmed merchant vessels proved to be a severe handicap in land warfare. His attempts to attack Spanish colonial settlements and hold them for ransom were uniformly disastrous. Ransom payments were always small, probably because he insisted on personal negotiations, at which he liked to show his charm and magnanimity. During the long stays in port, while negotiations dragged along, Drake's men were decimated by disease, and their ranks were torn by dissension.

Drake lacked some of the other attributes of a good commander. He hated the tedium of planning, preferring to let the future take care of itself. In any campaign he might have a general objective in mind, but he preferred to retain the right to change his mind at the last minute. Rather than take the trouble to purchase his supplies in advance, he would set off with enough for a few weeks. When he ran low, Drake would replenish his store from the next ship or settlement he happened to pass.

He hated the idea of a council of senior officers, which was the usual method of command at this period. Instead, he preferred to try his ideas on a few friends, then to make up his own mind without further interference. Naturally suspicious of others, Drake could not deal evenhandedly with his subordinate commanders. He was invariably partial to his closest friends, and he probably thought that any other concessions were unnecessary, even a sign of weakness.

Drake was warm and friendly with defeated enemies, especially those who were rich and influential, and he was usually pleasant with his officers. But he seemed to have a need to select one man as a nemesis and to make him the object of general vituperation. Moreover, he treated the ordinary sailors with contempt and punished them severely for the slightest infraction.[206]

The West Indies voyage was a failure so far as the investors were concerned, for they lost money. But England was quick to turn the voyage into a great triumph over Spain by the publication of *The Summarie and True Discourse of Sir Francis Drakes West Indian Voyage.* Suitably edited and augmented for publication, this little book quickly went through several editions in English and other languages.[207] In its pages Drake became a

Protestant leader of heroic proportions, fighting against the tyranny and bigotry of Catholic Spain. Privately, the authorities in England admitted that it was not "so good success as was hoped for."[208]

The results for Spain were worse. Several colonial towns had been destroyed and many citizens reduced to penury. Moreover, public buildings, fortifications, and military supplies had been plundered and destroyed. Funds that King Philip badly needed to carry on his war in the Low Countries had now to be diverted to America.[209] Drake was becoming more than an annoyance to Philip II. He was a major embarrassment.[210]

10

Raid on Cádiz

DRAKE'S FLEET SEEMS TO HAVE arrived in the bay of Plymouth on the night of 26 July 1586. Landing the next day, Drake immediately sent messengers to Lord Burghley, asking for funds to pay the seamen, who knew that the plunder was not enough to cover their wages.[1] The departure of the fleet had left a large dent in the male population of Plymouth, and their return meant that family life could return to normal.[2] Within a few days of the fleet's arrival, Ambassador Mendoza's informants in Plymouth had sent information about the treasure and the cargo of hides they had seen being unloaded.[3]

Mendoza's informants were so certain about seeing the fleet in Plymouth that it is scarcely possible to doubt their accuracy. Unfortunately, no contemporary record mentions the date. The earliest firsthand story of the voyage was published in 1588. This little book lists the place of arrival as Portsmouth and the date as 27 July.[4] This account was based on the unfinished journal kept by Walter Bigges, who died of fever shortly after the fleet left Cartagena. Early in 1588 the Bigges journal was used as the basis for a propaganda piece about the voyage, with numerous additions and changes being made by the editor Thomas Cates. Cates said that he was not certain who wrote the last part of the journal, adding that his own unspecified contributions were written from memory. In the English editions, published in 1589 and later, Cates or someone else changed the date of return to 28 July.[5] All editions of the *Summarie and True Discourse* say that the fleet went to Portsmouth.[6] But it is unlikely, even aside from the unequivocal testimony of Mendoza's agents, that Drake would land in Portsmouth rather than his home port of Plymouth, which was closer to hand as well.

With the West Indies voyage ended and the ships back in port, it was time to add up the profit and loss. On the loss side were 750 men out of

EXPEDITIO

FRANCISCI DRAKI

EQVITIS ANGLI

IN

INDIAS OCCIDENTALES

A. M. D. LXXXV.

Quà vrbes, Fanum D. Iacobi, D. Dominici, D.
Auguſtini & Carthagena, captæ fuére.

*Additis paſsim regionum locorúmque omnium
tabulis Geographicis quàm accuratiſsimis.*

L E Y D Æ,
Apud Fr. Raphelengium.
M. D. LXXXVIII.

*The best firsthand account of the West Indies voyage is the journal of
Walter Bigges, first published in a Latin edition in 1588.*

the 1,925 who began the voyage—almost 40 percent.[7] It was terrible news
for the families.

There was bad news for the investors as well. There was plunder, but not
much coin. Before the men could be paid, the investors would have to advance additional money, as Drake explained in his letter to Burghley.[8] At
first nothing was done. Early in September the Privy Council sent commissioners to pay the "Captaines, Souldiers, and Mariners."[9] As a con-

sequence, the men were given half pay, two or two and a half pounds.[10] Dissatisfied, they demanded full payment. Finally, the Privy Council sent a committee to investigate. The men were to be paid in full, and "if anie of the said mariners or souldiers shall shewe them selves obstinate," they were to be put in prison.[11]

True to form, Drake kept few or no records of the voyage. Cottell, his secretary, had died shortly after the fleet left São Tiago, and no one was named to replace him.[12] Consequently, Drake's financial records had to be reconstructed after he came home. Drake claimed expenses of £60,400 in getting the fleet ready to sail. The auditors finally agreed to allow £57,000.[13]

This was an enormous sum. A few years later Drake equipped a larger fleet at half the cost.[14] No doubt there were investors who thought that Drake's accounts were inflated. To them the auditors said, "We are persuaded for any thing that we Can perceve, that he dealeth very liberally and truly with the adventurers, and beareth him selfe a very great loss thearin."[15]

Many men were still unpaid, and Francis Knollys objected strongly to the accounting. As a consequence he was put under arrest for a few days.[16] Carleill was still looking for payment in May 1587. Frobisher and others were still unpaid in 1588.[17]

The total value of the captured ordnance was £6,700. The treasure was valued at £43,000. Hides, iron, copper, and lead brought the total plunder to £67,000. Expenses reduced this amount to £46,000, which meant that investors received only fifteen shillings for every pound invested in the voyage, a net loss of about 25 percent.[18]

This was an unpleasant fact, but it was not the whole story. The ransom collected at Santo Domingo and Cartagena was worth £45,000 to £55,000, to say nothing of the amounts collected from private citizens or the loot taken at Vigo. The churches at Vigo reported losses of nearly 7,000 ducados in stolen vestments, candle wax, and gold and silver ornaments.[19] The figures may have been inflated, but there were obviously large sums of money not included in Drake's official totals.[20] Very likely these amounts were excluded from the accounts for the same reason that the plunder from the earlier voyage was not listed in its entirety. If the amount was not recorded, it would not be easy for Spanish officials to claim reimbursement.

But Spanish officials still had good information about affairs in England. Early in November, Mendoza's London informant sent him a full report of the financial aspect of Drake's voyage:

> Concerning the return of Francis Drake from the
> Indies, I advised your lordship that he had arrived
> here and what he had brought. He captured at Santo
> Domingo, Cartagena, and other places in the surround-
> ing area, about 140 pieces of bronze artillery, some very
> good and large, and a number of iron pieces as well;
> some 16,000 or 18,000 ducados' worth of pearls, a little
> more than 150,000 ducados of gold and silver, and some
> goods that he took in Santo Domingo. He lost more
> than 800 men on the voyage. Everything he brought
> back for division among the investors in the fleet was
> valued at 48,000*l.* in the local money, but the real value
> must exceed ten or twelve thousand pounds more. Even
> so, not a single *real* has been given to anyone except the
> soldiers, who got 6*l.* each (equal to 20 Spanish escudos),
> and as a result there has been tumult and rioting among
> them, but to no effect. The rest of the proceeds were
> placed in the castle. Everything has turned out so badly
> for them that one can guess they will not return to the
> Indies to sack towns.[21]

Mendoza was not alone in having fairly full accounts of Drake's exploits. The chanceries of Europe echoed with gossip about Drake's raids in the Caribbean. As soon as reports from the islands arrived in Spain, the duke of Urbino received copies. One report said that Drake fell on Santo Domingo "with the ferocity of a demon."[22] The Venetian ambassador in Spain sent frequent reports to the doge and the Senate, with marvelous accounts of Drake's activities in the Caribbean. Government offices in Lisbon and Madrid were said to be in an uproar.[23]

Drake was no longer just a pirate, though the diplomatic correspondence continued to refer to him this way for a few more months. By 1586 Drake's raids were beginning to be seen as blows delivered by the queen of England against the king of Spain. The grand vizier of Constantinople wondered how "a woman all alone has the courage not merely to attack him, but to despoil him of so large a part of his dominions."[24] The papal secretary of state prodded the apostolic nuncios in Portugal and Spain to send more information on Drake. At one point the beleaguered nuncio of Spain wrote huffily that he reported only facts and not gossip.[25]

In fact, Queen Elizabeth's moves against Spain were increasingly ambitious. Her original decision to send Drake's fleet to the rescue of the merchant ships at Vigo was part of a cautious plan to thwart Spanish influence on the Continent. Another part was more direct, a promise of aid to the Protestant revolutionaries in the Netherlands. In fulfillment of this promise Elizabeth dispatched Leicester with 7,000 troops, and she sent financial assistance as well.[26] Philip responded by launching preparations for an invasion of England.[27]

Early in May 1586, Philip received his first news of the English raid on Santo Domingo. Later came word about the capture of Cartagena. Philip responded by ordering the marquis of Santa Cruz, captain general of the Ocean Sea, to prepare his fleet for retaliation against the English "in their own homes." The duke of Medina Sidonia was to assist him. As part of his preparations, Medina Sidonia conferred with Alvaro Flores de Quiñones, commander of the Armada of the Guard, escort for the Indies flotas. Augmenting this fleet of eight galleons with eleven armed merchantmen, Medina Sidonia dispatched Quiñones to the Caribbean at the end of May.[28] Drake was already on his way home.

Queen Elizabeth also began girding for war. Her plans naturally involved Sir Francis Drake and Sir John Hawkins. Drake had scarcely arrived home when Hawkins put to sea with five of the queen's galleons. For a time, following the unrest fomented by the Babington Plot, Hawkins sailed up and down the Channel on the lookout for Spanish invasion ships. Later he sailed for the coast of Spain, perhaps looking for the Spanish treasure fleet expected at the end of the summer. In October he was home once more, but preparing to take to sea again.[29]

Drake himself began to plan another voyage as soon as he arrived in Plymouth. Little is known about his intentions. Spanish informants thought for a time that he was going to the West Indies again. After the Babington Plot unraveled, all English ships were ordered to patrol the Channel or along the coast of Portugal or Spain.[30]

At about this time Pedro Sarmiento de Gamboa appeared in England as a prisoner of Sir Walter Raleigh. Sarmiento had been on his way back from the Strait of Magellan when he was captured by Raleigh's ships off Terceira. He was something of a curiosity in England, where he met with the queen, with Drake, and others. Elizabeth decided that Sarmiento would not be held for ransom but would be returned to Spain as a sort of unofficial emissary, carrying private messages for the king.[31]

As it turned out, Sarmiento did not reach Spain immediately. He was captured by Huguenots in France and kept in prison until the war was over.[32] Still, Mendoza was able to meet with Sarmiento in Paris and to tell the king what Elizabeth had in mind. Sarmiento thought that she wanted peace, and Mendoza thought it was a good idea to come to terms.[33] Something might have come of these diplomatic efforts if Sarmiento had reached Madrid, but probably not. Both Elizabeth and Philip were firmly set on a course that led to war.

Sarmiento, the peace negotiator, had scarcely been sent on his way when Elizabeth dispatched another representative to prepare for war. Dom Antonio was still insisting that Elizabeth help him in his quest for the crown of Portugal. Perhaps more as a show of support than anything else, Elizabeth decided to send Drake to Holland to ask her Continental allies to provide some of the necessary aid.[34] Taking a small fleet with money and reinforcements for Leicester's army, Drake and his delegation arrived in Holland on 3 November.[35] On 13 November he met with representatives of the States General. Drake told them that with ships, men, and supplies from the Netherlands he could help Dom Antonio gain the throne of Portugal. It was difficult for the members of the States General to see how this

Le vray portraict du Cappitaine Draeck, lequel a circuit toute la terre, en trois
annees, nuoirs deux mois, et 17. iours. il partit du Royaulme D'Angleterre, le 13. de
Decembre 1577. et fist son retour audict Royaulme, le 26. iour de Sept. 1580.
Paul de la Houue exud.

This engraved portrait of Drake at age forty-two is by
Paulis de la Houue from an original portrait by Jean
Rabel, published in Paris about 1586. From John
Carter Brown Library at Brown University.

distant project could further their war effort against Spain. After only a day of consideration they told Drake that the States General could not give direct help but would allow individual towns to give assistance when and as they might be able. Not a positive reply, but Elizabeth can scarcely have had much hope of aid.[36]

Back home in early December, Drake began preparing his fleet for some projected voyage, either to Portugal or to the Indies. There were reports that Drake was still dealing with Dom Antonio. As with much gossip, some details in the reports were true, some not. Drake had taken Dom Antonio to view the seven ships he had in hand. One was 400 tons, another 300 tons, a third 250 tons, and the rest ranged from 150 tons to 180 tons. The flagship had twenty-eight guns, and all were well armed with bronze ordnance. The States General had offered to supply forty ships more. With characteristic bravado, Drake promised Dom Antonio to put him on the throne or die trying.[37]

As winter progressed, it became more apparent that King Philip was preparing an invasion fleet. In consequence, Drake was given a deadline of 20 March for completion of his preparations. On 18 March, Drake signed a contract with the London merchants who would supply many of the ships. By this agreement, "whatsoever pillage shall be had by sea or land" would be divided equally, half to the crown and half to the investors.[38]

The royal contribution was made in the form of four ships of war. Drake's flagship was again the *Elizabeth Bonaventure,* 550 tons. Other royal ships were the *Golden Lion,* 550 tons; the *Rainbow,* 500 tons; and the *Dreadnaught,* 400 tons. In addition, the 50-ton *Spy* and 25-ton *Cygnet* went along to serve the larger ships. Drake contributed three or four more ships, including the 80-ton *Drake* that he had seized off the coast of Spain two years earlier, the 200-ton *Thomas,* and the 70-ton *Elizabeth.* The lord admiral sent a ship of his own, the 150-ton *White Lion.* John Hawkins sent at least one ship of his own, the 130-ton bark *Hawkins.* William Wynter may have been the owner of the 200-ton *Minion.* The London merchants had a fleet of ten ships that they had intended to send after the East India fleet. These included some large vessels, the 400-ton *Merchant Royal,* the 350-ton *Susan,* the 300-ton *Edward Bonaventure,* three others ranging from 150 to 200 tons, and several pinnaces.[39]

As usual, Elizabeth remained indecisive about dispatching the fleet. Drake received his sailing orders on 27 March and immediately left from Dover with the queen's ships, intending to rendezvous with the rest of the fleet at Plymouth. Off the Isle of Wight he met some of the merchant ships that had come from the Thames.[40] When they were all assembled in Plymouth harbor two days later, there were sixteen ships and seven pinnaces.[41]

Drake's ships drew their crews from Plymouth, but some of the local sailors refused at the last minute to go on the voyage. The usual complaints on Drake's ships were about pay and discipline. The exact disagreement in this case is unclear, but Drake's expectation that the sailors would also participate in land battles seems to have been part of the argument. When the sailors left, complaining loudly and putting their objections in writing, Drake wrote to local sheriffs and asked that the men be jailed for desertion. He then secured soldiers to replace the missing sailors.[42]

Sensitive as ever, Drake feared that the incident might become a blot on his own character. Drake wrote to London, saying that the missing men ought to be punished. "If we deserve ill, let us be punished," he said. "If we discharge our duties in doing our best, it is a hard measure to be reported ill." This was the Drake who could not endure criticism.[43]

Officials in London had advised Drake not to tarry in Plymouth but to leave as soon as the fleet was assembled. This he did, departing from Plymouth harbor on 2 April 1587. It was well he did. A few days later information arrived in London that made the authorities believe that the threat from Spain had diminished. Consequently, the Privy Council issued new orders: "You shall forbear to enter forcibly into any of the said King's ports or havens, or to offer violence to any of his towns or shipping within harbouring, or to do any act of hostility upon the land."[44] On the other hand, he might seize whatever Spanish ships he could find on the high seas, especially those going to or from the Indies. Perhaps to avoid future arguments about just how much booty there might be, he was not to offload any cargo or treasure but was to bring captured ships into port intact.[45]

As it turned out, Drake did not receive the message. A young son of Hawkins was sent in a pinnace with the dispatch, but he did not rendezvous with the fleet, supposedly because of bad weather.[46] Perhaps it was never intended that the message reach Drake, although Drake himself found it fairly simple to send reports to London. On 2 April, after his ship was well out of the harbor at Plymouth, he signed a letter to Burghley that said: "The wind commands me away. Our ship is under sail. God grant we may so live in His fear as the enemy may have cause to say that God doth fight for her Majesty as well abroad as at home."[47] These are not Drake's words, though he must have liked them. The letter was the first of a series of rhetorical excursions that typified his ghostwritten correspondence on this voyage.

Beyond the dispatch sent too late from London, no written orders appear to have been issued to Drake for this voyage. The understanding was that he would attack the ports where the Spanish fleet was being assembled, doing whatever damage he could. More than that, he was to intercept supply ships and to keep the various parts of the fleet from joining together. Should the fleet get to sea despite his efforts, he was to follow it, picking off stragglers and doing what he could to prevent a landing. If that did not keep him busy, then he was to intercept the fleets going to or from the Indies.[48]

Making good time, Drake and his fleet caught sight of Cape Finisterre on 5 April. Held up for some time by a severe storm, no doubt the same one that delayed young Hawkins, and further delayed by a severe leak in the *Dreadnaught,* the fleet arrived off the harbor at Lisbon on 16 April.[49] Here he received information from sailors on a small craft in the outer bay that a large merchant fleet, totally unprotected, was in the bay at Cádiz.[50] Because Lisbon was difficult to enter and well fortified, Drake decided to sail on to Cádiz, where he arrived on the afternoon of 19 April.[51] It was a brilliant move, one of Drake's typical last-minute decisions, unexpected by authorities in Spain.[52]

About midday, while the fleet was still some distance from Cádiz, Drake called his captains into conference. There he announced his decision to enter the port and attack as soon possible. His second in command, William Borough, objected strenuously, saying that it would be better to wait for daybreak.[53] Borough was a mature man and an experienced sailor, but Drake ignored his objections—to good effect, as it turned out.

The port of Cádiz lay on the coast south and east of San Lucar de Barrameda, where smaller ships could turn inland and ascend the Rio Guadalquivir to Seville. Cádiz was a large bay, well protected, but shallow in places and treacherous. On the day Drake arrived, Cádiz was busy, as it had been for months, filled with ships from Spanish and Mediterranean ports. Most of the ships were simply waiting at anchor while small vessels carried the goods from ship to shore. There were a few ships of war, but most were merchant ships, bringing provisions for the fleet that would soon be sent to invade England.

When Drake's sails were seen off the coast at about five that afternoon, everyone assumed that it was the squadron of Juan Martínez de Recalde,

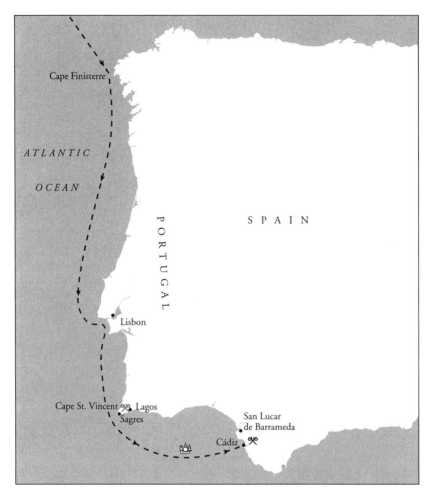

Drake's operations in Spain and Portugal, 1587

returning from the Bay of Biscay. To help preserve as long as possible the illusion of a friendly fleet, Drake's ships flew no flags.[54] As the ships drew closer to the bay, a galley and a galliot commanded by Don Pedro de Acuña came out to see just who the strangers were. The answer came when Drake's guns opened fire on the galleys and drove them back into the harbor toward Puerto de Santa María.[55] As Drake's ships came into the harbor, Acuña brought the other Spanish galleys around stern-to so that they could begin firing on the advancing English fleet. It was an unequal match, as the English guns had a much longer range. The Spanish galleys were easily driven off, and they took up a position between the seaward fort at Cádiz and the rocks called Los Puercos.[56]

Meanwhile, the fleet became involved in a battle with an armed Genoese merchantman of about 1,000 tons. This ship was quickly captured, followed by a 700-ton Biscayan galleon. That day or the next, five merchant ships loaded for the Indies were taken, as well as a galleon owned by the Marqués de Santa Cruz, commander of the armada. Once these ships were looted of their valuables, Drake had them set afire.[57]

Many of the merchant ships anchored in the harbor were without crews or sails and could not move. Taking to the small boats and pinnaces, Drake's sailors settled in among these ships and stripped them of everything that could be hauled away. Those merchant vessels that could maneuver began to cut their anchor cables and make for the inner harbor. Some were able to take shelter under the guns at Puerto Real, where they had the added protection of two galleys.[58]

During the night Acuña's galleys came out by threes and fours, firing at Drake's ships. The guns from the Cádiz forts kept up a continual barrage, but without much effect. At one point the galleys picked off a stray English pinnace and took five sailors captive. Toward dawn the Spanish ships headed for Puerto de Santa María and found the place in a ferment of somewhat disorganized defensive preparations. It was all put in order the next day when the Duke of Medina Sidonia arrived with several thousand reinforcements, including artillery, infantry, and cavalry.[59] There was no prospect of saving the ships in the harbor. All Medina Sidonia could do was prevent Drake's troops from landing and looting the towns.

Undaunted, Drake moved his fleet toward the inner harbor, looking for the vessels that had escaped the night before. This part of the bay was badly shoaled, and the *Edward Bonaventure* ran aground.[60] Seeing this, Drake transferred his troops to the boats and pinnaces and left the larger ships behind.[61] At least one of his ships ignored the danger from the shoals. The armed merchant vessel *Merchant Royal* sailed past the Puntal with Drake's pinnaces and joined in the pillage.[62]

While this was going on, Medina Sidonia was busy fortifying the bridge across the Río Sancti Petri to secure the land entrance to Cádiz. Drake's fleet was within cannon range of the Puntal, so Medina Sidonia had two large bronze guns hauled to the promontories and ordered them to fire on the fleet.[63] With Spanish troops fully in command of all the forts and the approaches to Cádiz, there was no longer any possibility of landing the troops and sacking the city.

As usual, Drake had left for the inner bay without informing his second in command. After a time Borough came into the harbor in his own pinnace, looking for the commander. No sooner had he arrived than he learned that Drake had returned to his own flagship. While Borough was gone, Medina Sidonia's heavy guns on the promontory began raking Borough's *Golden Lion*. One ball went through the hull onto the gun deck and struck off the leg of Borough's master gunner.[64]

Back on his own flagship and not the least bit worried, Drake busied himself giving instructions to the fleet. The plunder had to be divided among the ships, and some captured vessels were made ready for sea. All the rest were burned. Though Drake was unfazed, the master of the *Golden Lion* was thoroughly frightened. With his ship becalmed, Borough's master put men into boats and had them haul the stricken vessel to the entrance of the outer harbor. There Borough rejoined his ship, and there Acuña took up the fight again, assailing Borough's *Golden Lion* until other English vessels arrived to drive him off.[65]

A couple of months after the battle Borough drew a map that shows his *Golden Lion* taking the brunt of the fire from the galleys. In fact, Borough claimed his ship was the only one to do any fighting that day. "The spite the enemy had was ever chiefly against the Lion," he said, "which they attempted to show as much as they could or durst."[66]

By noon Drake was ready to leave. He had looted and burned everything in sight, including more than two dozen ships, though the exact number is uncertain. Bringing his fleet together at the mouth of the bay, Drake attempted to sail out, but the ships lost the wind. Seeing the English ships lying helpless in the bay, the Spanish floated small boats filled with barrels of burning pitch in the direction of the fleet. These were easy

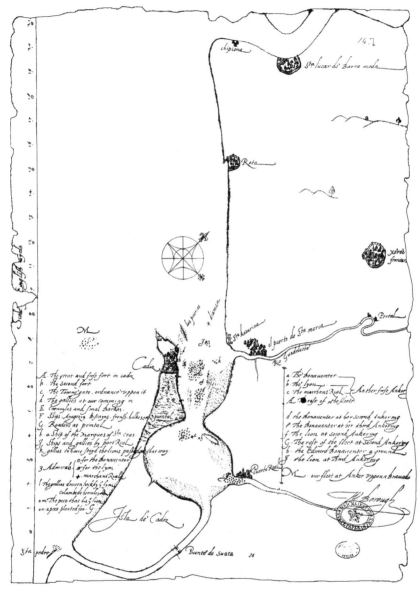

William Borough's map of the Cádiz raid. From PRO, MPF 318.

to spot and no damage was done to Drake's ships. Finally, about midnight, the wind came up and they sailed out of the bay.[67]

Hard on their heels came Acuña and the Spanish galleys. A short distance out of the bay the fleet again lost the wind, and a brief battle ensued. Once again the galleys proved to be a poor match for the heavily armed English fighting ships. About noon the galleys rowed out of gunshot and lay there within sight of the English fleet. Drake sent a messenger to see whether they had the five English prisoners aboard. The reply was no, but if Drake wanted to wait for another day, perhaps an exchange could be arranged. Fearing a trick, Drake decided not to wait.[68]

In the raid on Cádiz, Drake had resupplied his fleet, loading the ships with huge supplies of wine, oil, biscuit, and dried fruits. Four of the Spanish ships, loaded with provisions, were added to his fleet, with two or three dozen more left at Cádiz, burned to the waterline. The Spanish authorities estimated their loss at 172,000 ducats. Besides the ships burned and sunk, the cargoes were a huge loss. A Biscayan ship of 700 tons was filled with iron. A Portuguese ship carried 3,000 fanegas—about 4,800 bushels—of wheat. Not all were bringing goods for the Armada. Several were headed for Brazil or cities in Italy.[69] This was a great victory, not in a pitched battle, where Drake had little sea experience, but in a surprise attack, where he was a master.

As usual, Drake looked for information as well as loot. During his thirty or so hours in Cádiz, Drake had managed to learn the whereabouts of Recalde's Biscayan squadron. This group of armed merchant ships had been cruising off Cabo San Vicente in order to provide an armed escort for the returning Indies fleet. In recent days the ships had been ordered back to Lisbon, where Santa Cruz was assembling his fleet. Hoping to intercept Recalde, Drake headed north from Cádiz and sailed past Cabo San Vicente.[70] He was too late. The Biscayan fleet was already inside the harbor at Lisbon.[71]

Determined to get some use out of the troops that were still crowded onto his ships, Drake called his captains together on 29 April and announced a plan to land at Sagres, to the south. William Borough objected in writing.[72] The traditional command structure in the English navy included a council of captains to advise the commander, who was morally obligated to follow their best advice.[73] In his letter Borough said that Drake's new plan was rash and poorly conceived. More than this, he thought that Drake's method of command was an affront to experienced captains.[74]

Drake was furious. Seething for two days, he conferred with his captain, Thomas Fenner, and his chaplain, Philip Nichols. Following the procedure used with Knollys, Drake worked with these two friends to compile a list of charges against Borough. Then, still in a rage, he summoned Borough to the flagship. There, in the presence of Fenner and Nichols, Drake charged Borough with insubordination and removed him from his command.[75] Thoroughly shaken, Borough wrote a letter of apology, but it was not enough. The former captain was suddenly a passenger on his own ship.[76]

The argument with Borough underscores a serious defect in Drake's character. Always suspicious, always wary of a plot, Drake became even more anxious under the burden and isolation of sea command. Corbett considered it an emotional problem; the execution of Doughty had "permanently warped Drake's judgement."[77] But it was more than that. Drake needed a scapegoat, someone like Doughty and Knollys, to serve as an object of general ridicule and scorn.

Still refining his plans, Drake decided to land instead at Lagos, on the Algarve coast. On 4 May, Drake led his fleet into the harbor at Lagos and put 1,000 soldiers ashore.[78] A Spanish cavalry patrol shadowed their moves until they reached the walls of the town, some five miles distant from the landing. Lagos was heavily manned and fortified, and fire from the Spanish guns inflicted heavy casualties on Drake's troops. Drake could do little in reply, except to fire on the cavalry units nipping at the heels of his army. Finally, Drake recalled the soldiers, loaded them back on his ships, and sailed out of the harbor.[79]

Retracing his path a bit, Drake landed 800 men next morning at the village of Sagres, where they burned the huts and boats of the fishermen. The nearby fort made no resistance, and it was captured. A mile farther, on the cape, the castle of Sagres proved to be more difficult. The garrison held a hundred men with six or seven guns of various sizes, defending a place where their families were packed inside. Drake's plan of attack was simple.

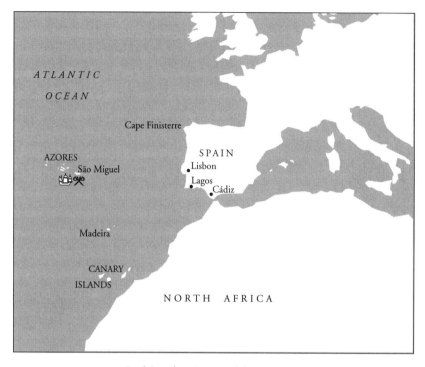

Drake's raids in Spain and the Azores, 1587

He set fire to the castle gate, then bombarded the place for two hours. The commander soon surrendered.[80]

On the next day Drake marched his men to a nearby monastery from which the monks had fled. According to a Spanish report, Drake's army ransacked the place, destroying images, and finally setting the buildings on fire: "They committed their usual feasts and drunkenness, their diabolical rampages and obscenities. They stole everything they found and then set the place on fire, having first committed a thousand excesses and diabolical desecrations on the images of the saints, like wicked heretics."[81] Drake himself was not actively involved. He and the gentlemen returned to the ships, giving the men free rein to do what they wished.[82] It was the standard routine for Drake. A raid was not complete unless the church was desecrated. The fleet remained in the harbor until 9 May, refitting his ships and taking on wood and water.[83]

From here Drake sailed to the outer harbor of Lisbon, arriving on 10 May. With no very clear plan in mind, Drake anchored his fleet near Cascaes and waited to see what would happen. Soon Santa Cruz came down the river with seven galleys, blocking the entrance but not attempting an open battle. Drake sent a message asking Santa Cruz whether he had English prisoners to exchange and received a negative reply. Unable to attack the city, Drake sailed out of the harbor on 11 May and for the next two weeks cruised about Cabo San Vicente.[84]

The port at Sagres served once more as a place to take on wood and water. A few galleys happened to come near, but Drake easily chased them off. The English fleet captured a number of stray trading vessels, though just how many is unclear. Fenner said that they took forty-seven caravels and barks and fifty or sixty fishing boats.[85] Borough reported that between 27 April and 26 May the fleet captured "about 28 or 30 ships and barks."[86] Drake told Walsingham that it was several times that number: "It hath pleased God that we have taken forts, ships, barks, carvels, and divers other vessels more than a hundred, most laden, some with oars for galleys, planks and timber for ships and pinnaces, hoops and pipe-staves for cask, with many other provisions for this great army."[87] All of this was burned. Drake was no doubt correct in judging that the hoops and staves were the most important goods he had taken, as the Armada could not go forward without barrels for water and provisions. Sensitive about relations with Dom Antonio, Drake had some misgivings about the destruction of the fishing nets and the fishing boats. These all belonged to the Portuguese fishermen in the area, and though Drake made a point of telling them how sorry he was, the fishermen were doubtless not appeased.[88]

Early in May, Drake sent Captain Robert Cross back to London with two prize ships and some reports. On 17 May, Drake wrote again, reporting continued success and asking for several more ships. His purpose, he said, was to stay at Cabo San Vicente until ordered to do otherwise.[89] A few days later some undefined illness struck the fleet, and the plans began to change. In an effort to keep the disease from spreading, Drake loaded some of the sick men into a small boat, and on 20 May he sent them back to England, with a request that the ship be returned if at all possible.[90] A day or so later Drake was on his way to the Azores, where he seemingly had news of the arrival of a huge ship from the Indies.[91] This switch from warfare to piracy was perfectly natural for Drake, who always had profits in mind, for himself and for his partners.

With the disease now beginning to look like plague and spreading to all the ships, Drake's men were reluctant to extend their voyage. They grumbled, but Drake insisted. Less than a day into the voyage, a storm struck, and most of the merchant ships took this as an excuse to leave. When the storm abated on 22 May, the *Golden Lion* could be seen heading north as well. The men on the ship, forty-six of them sick, had given the captain a written demand to return home. Offering little or no resistance, Captain John Marchant, who had replaced Borough, simply abandoned the ship and returned to the flagship. Borough, relieved of his command, nonetheless advised the men to return to the fleet.[92] They did not. By 5 June the *Golden Lion* was back in Dover, and Borough was writing his own account of events to the lord high admiral.[93] The queen was not amused. Borough and the mutineers were clapped into prison to await Drake's return.[94] Drake, for his part, immediately convened a court, which found Borough guilty of desertion. Drake immediately pronounced the sentence of death.[95]

With a fleet reduced to nine ships, Drake sailed to the Azores, looking for new spoils. He wrote to Walsingham on 2 June that his men were very ill and supplies were short, but they were still looking for a rich prize: "I assure your honour our sickness is very much, both of our soldiers and mariners. God mitigate it. Attending to his goodwill and pleasure, we are not yet thoroughly resolved what service we shall next take in hand. And for that there is as yet no supplies come out of England, it causeth our men to droop and desire much to go for England. But if God will bless us with some little comfortable dew from heaven, some crowns or some reasonable boo[ty] for our soldiers and mariners, all will take good heart again, although they were half dead."[96]

On the morning of 8 June the fleet came within sight of São Miguel, and by nightfall the lookout had spotted the sails of a large ship lying in the lee of the island. Next morning, with a fresh breeze astern, Drake made directly for the ship and was pleased to see it coming out to meet him. As he drew closer he noticed her flag, a red cross, being raised and lowered. The ship wanted Drake to identify himself, but he refrained until within cannon range. Then Drake ran up the flags of England as well as his battle streamers and pennants.[97]

Surrounding the beleaguered ship, Drake fired at her from every direction. There was answering fire from the other vessel, but it was no contest. In a short time, several of its crewmen were dead, others injured, and the hull was pierced in several places. Two of Drake's smaller vessels drew in under the hawse holes, and some of his ships prepared to come in close for boarding. At this point the captain surrendered, and Drake went aboard to see what the prize might be.[98]

The ship was the *San Felipe,* the king's own ship, coming from the East Indies. The cargo included chests of china, bales of velvet and silk, a small amount of gold and jewels, and a number of black slaves. These last were put into a small boat with the crew and allowed to return to São Miguel. The *San Felipe* was taken with the rest of the fleet back to Plymouth, where they arrived on 26 June.[99] There is little indication in the English sources about the health of Drake's crew. Borough reported many dead on his own ship and said that all of Drake's ships were stricken with the plague.[100] A Spanish prisoner also testified that most of the men aboard Drake's ship were ill, including Drake himself.[101] Still, the English had managed to muster enough healthy men to bring home a prize.

Arriving in Plymouth, Drake was joined aboard the *San Felipe* by his wife and servants. Perhaps he was ill, but more likely he simply wanted to guard the king's ship until he had arranged with the queen about disposition of the contents; such, at least, were the reports that reached Spain.[102]

Many of the merchant ships were already home before Drake returned to Plymouth. After hearing reports from their captains, the investors grumbled that some of Drake's plunder was unaccounted for.[103] One of Mendoza's English informants said that 300,000 ducats in cash had been taken from the *San Felipe,* but that amount never appeared in the inventories.[104] In October, Burghley was still wondering how to force Drake to "yield up his account for this last voyage," a prospect that seemed dim, for there was still no full accounting for the plunder from Cartagena.[105] The inventory to that time was a list of trinkets in a small casket. There were "six forks of gold"; a dozen golden hafts for knives; six gold chains, one of them made in an S shape; plus rings, beads, and bracelets. There were some pomanders, a small flask of musk, some ambergris, and a few stones of various sorts. Drake took it all to London as a present for the queen.[106]

Shortly after he arrived in London, Drake again took up the matter of Borough, but whether by his own initiative or Borough's is not clear. A court was convened, and on 25 July at Theobald's, Lord Burghley's house, Drake read from his diary the charges and the evidence against Borough.[107] In addition to insubordination, he now charged Borough with cowardice and desertion.[108] The charges were largely based on Drake's interpretation of Borough's actions at Cádiz. In this version of events, Drake said that Borough had come aboard his ship "in trembling sort" on the morning after they entered Cádiz and urged Drake to move out of the harbor.[109] Borough's *Golden Lion* had not gone off to fight the galleys, Drake said, but rather to desert. Later, after Drake decided to go to the Azores, the commander said, Borough encouraged the men on the *Golden Lion* to mutiny.[110]

Speaking in his own defense, Borough described his considerable efforts at Cádiz, battling the Spanish galleys while the other ships were off looting. He also managed a fairly credible reply to the other charges. On the record, the charges seem inconsequential, and the defenses adequate, if exaggerated. The most serious charge was that of abetting mutiny. As it turned out, Borough himself commanded the *Golden Lion* on the way home, a clear enough indication that he had had some role in the mutiny.[111]

In the end Borough was cleared of the charges. Two of Drake's captains, Platt and Spindelow, had visited the imprisoned sailors in the Marshalsea and forced them to give perjured testimony. When this came out, the case began to fall apart.[112] Finally, Borough reminded the court of Drake's own shortcomings. Specifically, he said that Drake deserted John Hawkins at San Juan de Ulúa, forcing Hawkins to leave a hundred men on shore, where they were captured by the Spanish colonial authorities:

> Sir Frauncis Drake, in urginge this matter so vehe-
> mently agaynst me beinge able sufficiently to cleere my
> self from beinge privie or abettinge to the comynge
> awaye of the Lyon, doth altogether forgett how he
> demeaned him self towarde his Master and Admyrall
> Mr John Hawkins, at the port of St John de Loo in the
> Weste Indyas, when contrary to his saide Admyrals
> comaund he came awaye and left his sayd master in
> greate extremytie, wheruppon he was forced to set at
> shoare in that contrye to seek their adventurs 100 of his
> men; which matter if it had been soe followed agaynst
> him: (for that he colde noe wayes exchuse it) might
> iustly have procured that to himself which nowe most
> uniustly, bloddely, and malitiously by all devises what
> soever he hath soughte and still seekethe agaynst me.[113]

Borough also reminded the court of the Doughty execution. From the time he was relieved of his command until the time he went back to England, Borough said he lived in constant expectation that the "the Admyrall would have executed uppon me his bludthirstie desier as he did uppon Dowtey." Once the mutiny occurred, said Borough, his death was a certainty, as Drake had shown by his court martial.[114]

Borough was lucky enough to be defending himself at a time when Elizabeth was once again eager to appease the king of Spain. In spite of Drake's demonstrated success against the Spanish galleys, Elizabeth's ships were not yet ready to take on the Armada that Philip had in preparation. Consequently, the orders sent to Drake in March were pulled out of the files and read to the Spanish representative in England. In a long letter of apology, Lord Burghley insisted that "unwittingly, yea unwillingly, to her Majesty those actions were committed by Sir Fras. Drake, for the which her Majesty is as yet greatly offended with him."[115]

On the voyage to Spain and Portugal, Francis Drake began to pay serious attention to the record that he was leaving behind him. The death of his secretary during the West Indies campaign made it possible for Drake to choose a new aide to help with his letters. Very likely the secretarial services were performed by one or both of his two close friends, the chaplain Philip Nichols and Thomas Fenner, the captain of his flagship. Drake was a pious man, but he was not an educated person. His earlier communications were brief and simple, and done in an almost indecipherable hand.[116] One historian put it this way: "Drake was not a very elegant penman."[117] He could have added that Drake lacked eloquence as well.

The Drake letters of 1587 were completely different. They were filled with invocations of the deity, prayers for the queen and for Burghley, and requests for their prayers for his fleet. Corbett felt that many of these letters were done in Drake's own hand. This may be doubted. It is clear that the letter to Walsingham on 2 April contains Drake's own sentiments but not his own words. "The wind commands me away" is not a phrase from Drake's tongue or pen, and none of the pious expressions come from Drake.[118]

True, Drake did mention the name of God now and then in his own letters, as was the practice in those days, but he made no extended reference to the deity. Look at two examples. In a letter to Burghley written in the summer of 1586, Drake said: "I will make it most aparent unto your ho[nour] that it escaped us but twelve owers the foole treasure which the King of Spayn had out of the yndyes this last year, the cause best knowen to God." He ended the letter with the observation that upon his return to London "I shall give your ho[nour] somthing to understand I hope in god to your Lordship's good likeng."[119]

Compare these simple references with the elaborate invocations in the letter to Walsingham on 2 April, quoted earlier, and in another letter written a few weeks later. Speaking of the Armada, Drake said: "When they come they shal be but the sonnes of morttal men, and for the most part enemyes to the truth and upholders of balles or dagon's Image, which hath alredye fallen before the arke of our god with his hands and armes and head stroken off." This is pretty potent imagery for a man who was used to plain speaking. Later in the same letter the writer inserted a long paragraph about defending the church and the nation against the forces of evil, a passage that could easily have graced a Sunday sermon of the time.

Other references in the letter are equally foreign to Drake's way of speaking and writing. For example, Drake may have heard of Hannibal and Scipio, but he would not have been able to write about them. A postscript added to the letter in Drake's own hand employs Drake's own rude vocabulary to refer to Walsingham's wife as "your yoeke partener."[120] It is certainly significant that the only Drake letters with sophisticated theological digressions and references to figures from Roman history were those written while he was in the company of Philip Nichols and Thomas Fenner.

A good case in point is a letter to John Foxe dated 27 April 1587, which is usually considered to contain some of Drake's most heartfelt religious sentiments. The original letter is unknown and may no longer exist, but there are several manuscript copies, all slightly different.[121] One of the best known copies begins with the salutation, "To the Reverend father in God John Fox my very good friend." The letter itself is a report of the attack on Cádiz, not a particularly inspiring religious subject, but the first and last sentences and the postscript express religious sentiments that are worth quoting:

> Mr fox where as we have had of late such happy suxces
> against the Spanniards, I doe assure my self that you
> have faithfully remembered us in your good prayers . . .
> where fore I: shall desire you to continue a faithfull
> remembrance of us in your praiers that our part [*sic*]
> service may take that Effect as god may bee Glorified,
> his Church our Queen and Country preserved, the
> Ennymies of the truth soe vanquished that wee may
> have continuall peace in Israel, from abourd hir
> Majesties good shipp called the Elizabeth Boneadven-
> ture, in very great hast 27 of Aprill 1587.
>   Your loving and faithfull sonne in
>   Christ Jesus, francis Crake [*sic*]
>   Our Enemies are many but our protector comman-
> deth the whole world. Lett us all pray continually, and
> our Lord Jesus will hear us in good time Mercifully.[122]

A manuscript of about 1611 attributed to Simeon Foxe contains the statement that "Francis Drake was one of the military men who was glad to be a close friend" of John Foxe.[123] Nothing else is known about the relationship between Drake and Foxe. One authority has called the 1611 memoir "untrustworthy and spurious."[124]

The same might well be said about the letter. It first appeared in a small book by Thomas Greepe, *The true and perfect Newes of the woorthy and valiaunt exploytes performed and doone by that valiant Knight Syr Frauncis Drake,* which was rushed into print as soon as Drake returned to England.[125] The letter may have been composed by Philip Nichols for his own signature.[126] It certainly sounds more like a letter from a minister of the gospel to a colleague than a letter from an admiral to a friend. When the fleet arrived in England in the summer of 1587, Drake and Nichols learned that John Foxe had just died. Someone, perhaps Nichols, then gave the letter to Greepe, who added it to his news-ballad with an attribution to Drake.[127] With its brief summary of the action at Cádiz the new letter also allowed Greepe to extend the title of his work to cover Drake's attacks *Not onely at Sancto Domingo, and Carthagena, but also nowe at Cales, and uppon the Coast of Spayne.*

Though officially out of favor, Drake had the good sense to continue his practice of showering the queen with rich gifts. Thus he could still remain in London and visit with the queen, even while Burghley wrote that he was in disgrace.[128] No one believed it, certainly not King Philip. Mendoza sent regular dispatches recounting the preparations carried on in England so that Drake might go out with a new fleet to prey once more on Spanish ships and possessions. It was clear than in any armed conflict between England and Spain, Francis Drake would be an important leader. No longer was Drake called a pirate in the conversations in European chanceries. Drake had managed to apply his piratical experience to naval purposes in two stunning raids on Cádiz and Sagres. Suddenly foreign gossips had to change their descriptions. Drake the pirate became a "captain general" of the English navy.[129]

II

Defeat of the Spanish Armada

IN THE COURSE OF HIS abruptly canceled raid on Cádiz and the coast of Portugal, Drake gathered sufficient information to show that the Spanish government was seriously embarked on preparations for an invasion. After the raid on Cádiz, he wrote to Walsingham: "I assure your honour the like preparation was never heard of nor known, as the King of Spain hath and daily maketh to invade England." He thought Spain would soon be able to put 40,000 men in the field and keep them supplied for a year. England should begin arming. "All possible preparations for defence are very expedient to be made." Before sending the letter, Drake had additional information about the fleet that was coming through the Strait of Gibraltar to rendezvous with the ships assembling in Lisbon. "I dare not a'most write unto your honour of the great forces we hear the King of Spain hath out in the Straits. Prepare in England strongly, and most by sea. Stop him now, and stop him ever. Look well to the coast of Sussex."[1]

Despite his clear message to authorities at home, Drake seems not to have fully understood his own position. The sole reason for his presence at Cabo de San Vicente was to block the strait and prevent Andalusian ships from joining the Spanish fleet at Lisbon.[2] Spanish officials knew what he was up to, and they were surprised when he finally turned away from the strait: "Drake is sailing off Cabo de San Vicente. They say he has split his fleet. He has eyes for the Indies, taking prizes. He intended to keep the Andalusian and Lisbon fleets from joining."[3]

In this light, Drake's decision to go after the Indies ship in the Azores might be seen as rash and self-serving if the practice were not so common in the English maritime service. So long as merchant investors were recruited to participate, fleet commanders would always have an eye for profits. Drake had learned his trade with the Hawkins family, who always looked on government service as a way to personal enrichment. Following their example, Drake always made his ventures a blend of patriotism and profit, and it was usually difficult to determine which was the more important.

Profits in the fall of 1587 were considerably different from those a year earlier. Spanish reports held that the booty taken in the *San Felipe* was worth a million ducats, most of it coming from the pockets of private individuals and only 200,000 ducats belonging to the king.[4] The total was equivalent to more than £250,000, but the English reports showed only £114,000 shared among the investors. There were additional profits from the Cádiz raid.[5] Once again the exact amount may never be known, though it was an impressive sum, much more than the plunder from the voyage to the West Indies.

While Drake was away from England a new fleet had been assembled, some thirty ships, and there were rumors that Drake would be sent to sea once more. Publicly he declared his eagerness to go, though privately he expressed reservations. The Marqués de Santa Cruz would surely have his fleet at sea looking for him, Drake told the Privy Council.[6] It was not a good time to go. In this judgment Drake was certainly correct. Santa Cruz had his forty-ship fleet at sea on 11 August, heading for the Azores. He was too late to protect the *San Felipe,* but two other ships from the Indies were expected any day.[7]

Most of the new English fleet was stationed at Plymouth, where the main danger was. A few of the rest were at Southampton, and others were at the mouth of the Thames. Frobisher had seven of the queen's ships in the Channel cruising about the Netherlands coast.[8] Drake was kept at court, conferring with the queen and the Council. There were plans to improve the fortifications at Plymouth and Portsmouth as well as at Dover and the rest of the Cinque Ports.[9]

For a time it seemed that Drake's raid on Cádiz might halt Spanish preparations for an invasion. Certainly he did manage to disrupt the plan for an invasion in 1587. Annoyed at first, then embarrassed, Philip suggested that Santa Cruz might be well advised to put an end to Drake's interference. After considerable delay, Santa Cruz took his fleet on a fruitless search for Drake, perhaps not realizing that the English commander had

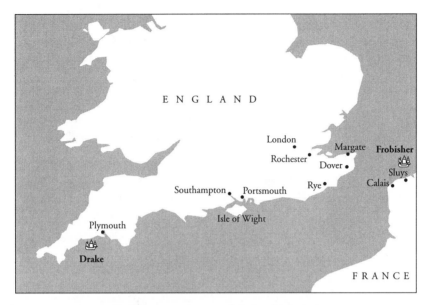

English ports on the route of the Spanish Armada

gone back to England. When Santa Cruz returned to Lisbon in October, his own ships were badly battered and in need of refit, and the preparation of the Armada had to be resumed.[10]

From the start the Spanish invasion plans were badly handled. The duke of Parma proposed to send an invasion force of 30,000 men, taken from his own army in Flanders. He would muster the force in secret and transport them to England in shallow-draft vessels that could navigate the rivers of Flanders. The landing would be made on the coast between Margate and Dover. A fleet from Spain might be useful, but largely to draw attention from Parma's force. Sailing after nightfall and landing at dawn the next day, his army would march on London, which might be occupied in two or three days.[11]

A separate plan submitted by Santa Cruz envisioned an army of 60,000 men invading England in a great fleet of 800 ships. Operating perhaps from a local port, the fleet would establish Spanish supremacy in the Channel and along the route between Spain and England. Philip's initial choice was for a small-scale invasion of Ireland, together with an expanded naval force to guard the route to the Indies.[12] Spanish plans changed from time to time, as events in England and Europe unfolded. Expectations of a Catholic uprising in England, a rebellion in Scotland, or a welcome in Ireland caused Philip and his advisers to alter their strategic thinking.[13]

In the plan that finally emerged the Armada would cover the Channel crossing of Parma's army, then carry out its own operations while keeping open the option of a landing in Scotland or elsewhere. A major element in the plan was the capture by Parma's army of Sluys, near Calais, in August 1587. Despite its limitations as a port, Sluys was seen as a place for the Armada to rendezvous with Parma's fleet. His preparations had become public knowledge from the first, and a secret invasion was no longer a possibility, if it ever had been.[14] By December 1587, the Dutch at Antwerp and elsewhere were promising Queen Elizabeth that they could attack Parma's invasion barges and prevent their leaving the coast.[15]

Once he realized this, Parma became reluctant to proceed. Finally it was decided that the Spanish fleet would first secure the control of the landing area between Dover and Margate, then take up a position off Margate or in the Thames estuary. This was a somewhat dubious plan, for it left unanswered just how the Armada would assist in the embarkation of Parma's army and how it might guard the invasion ships as they crossed the Channel. It was never made clear how or whether the Armada might enter the shallow waters of the Flanders coast and guard Parma's invasion army at the point of embarkation. In the same way, it was never decided how or whether Parma's shallow-draft fleet might make its own way past the threatening Dutch gunboats along the coast.[16] With a divided command, coordination was essential for the success of the plan. But there was no definite plan for coordinating the movements of the huge Armada with the operations of Parma's giant invasion force.[17]

England's own defensive plans were in similar disarray. The main reliance was on local militia units, organized by county, to supplement a tiny corps of regular troops, the Queen's Guard. The local forces would be alerted by a series of beacons. These were braziers mounted on poles. Each beacon was attended by a watchman and was visible from one or more other beacons. Thus an alarm could be given easily enough, though the response from that point onward was a bit problematic.[18] Militia members no doubt planned to wait until it was necessary to defend their own homes, while the authorities likely envisioned their marching to whatever place they might be needed.

A plan to defend England finally began to take shape in December, when Lord Charles Howard of Effingham was appointed as commander-in-chief. Howard was to guard the Channel with eighteen of the queen's ships, heavily armed and manned. Drake, without a formal title, was to go to Plymouth, where he would have thirty-six armed ships—seven of the queen's galleons and twenty-nine armed merchant ships.[19] Enactment of the plan lagged, and it was the middle of January before Drake left London for Plymouth, accompanying the lord admiral as far as Rochester.[20] The royal ships assigned to Drake were at Queenborough, including the *Revenge,* 400 tons; the *Hope,* 500 tons; the *Nonpareil,* 400 tons; the *Swiftsure,* 300 tons; and the *Aid,* 200 tons.[21] Some of these were familiar ships that Drake had sailed with before. The final strategy was still under discussion, but there was no longer any serious thought of allowing Spanish troops to land before engaging them in battle.

This was not necessarily bad news for the Spanish Armada. Spanish fleet superiority lay in grappling and boarding. Spanish fighting ships carried large numbers of soldiers ready for hand-to-hand combat. English ships, on the other hand, relied on heavy firepower from guns that had greater range than did comparable Spanish artillery. English master gunners also had developed a tactic of positioning their artillery to fire low, striking enemy ships in the hull, close to the waterline. So English fighting ships preferred to fight their enemies at as great a distance as possible, pounding their targets with heavy artillery. Spanish commanders wanted close combat, where their soldiers could swarm over the other ships and capture them in hand-to-hand fighting.[22]

Drake's original hope appears to have been to sail immediately and engage the Spanish ships close to home. According to Spanish informants, Drake had demanded and gotten "an unlimited commission." He would sail when and where he pleased, land men if he chose to do so, and "burn and sack Spanish towns" if the opportunity should arise. If this was true,

Drake may have had some idea of coordinating his moves with those of other pirates who were hovering off Cabo de San Vicente, copying what Drake himself had done a few months earlier.[23] There is some indication that Drake had a hand in the work of these pirates. At the very least he had his own pinnaces on the Spanish coast.[24] Two Spanish sailors taken prisoner by the pirate John Naunton later reported that one of the pinnaces that Drake burned at Cádiz had belonged to Naunton and that Drake reimbursed Naunton for the loss out of the plunder he had taken in the port.[25]

The queen's ships were not ready for wartime service and would not be for some considerable time. At Queenborough, Lord Howard had his own ships drawn ashore one by one, then scraped and tallowed.[26] As soon as Drake had his assigned ships in Plymouth, he delivered them to his cousin William Hawkins for refit. On 17 February, Hawkins wrote to his brother the treasurer of the navy, reporting his progress with Drake's fleet. Work on the *Hope* and the *Nonpareil* was well along. Both were graved and tallowed, but the *Revenge* was still being careened. This procedure involved putting the ship aground, burning the furze off the bottom, then covering the hull anew with a mixture of tallow and pitch. An important problem was pitch, which as usual was in short supply.[27]

Even with a royal appointment and a royal commission, which he got on 15 March, Drake was still not allowed to go to sea. The council ordered him to assemble provisions for a two-month voyage, 24 April to 24 June, but failed to provide funds to implement the orders.[28] This permission was as always subject to royal whim. When news reached England about the illness of the Marqués de Santa Cruz, Elizabeth once again began to entertain the thought that everything might be settled without war, and Drake was ordered to keep his ships at Plymouth.[29] This placed a great strain on the people of Plymouth, and the other ports, who were required to support the fleet. Wartime trade disruptions had brought economic stagnation to the port, and the presence of the fleet made things just that much more difficult.[30]

The death of Santa Cruz in early February meant that Philip had to look for another commander. It also meant that the Armada could not sail until the new commander had the fleet organized and equipped to his own liking. Philip's immediate choice was the Duke of Medina Sidonia, a gentleman reluctant to accept the post, partly because he lacked his predecessor's extensive experience in maritime affairs. On the other hand, the new appointee was rich, well-connected, and an able administrator. He hated to go to sea, because he suffered from rheumatism.[31] But duty was a powerful palliative.

Parma was having troubles as well. At the end of January he wrote a long letter to the king, saying that the invasion fleet was not such a good idea after all. His ships were nothing but unarmed barges, he said. With their new fleet the English would be able to sink Parma's ships at will before they could ever cross the Channel. In fact, three or four ships' boats could chase them all off the sea. The main thrust of Parma's argument was that he could not embark his troops without the protection of the Armada.[32]

Drake saw this point just as clearly, and in March he wrote to the Privy Council with his views on the subject. The document is not in his own hand and only partly in his own words, yet it is a fairly cogent statement of Drake's strategic thinking. In his opinion the best way to fight the Armada was to attack just as the fleet left port.

The introductory paragraph is interesting only because it shows a self-effacement that Drake did not have. No doubt his secretary advised that he should assume this humble stance if he expected anyone to read his letter:

> Right honorable, and my verie good Lordes; understandinge by your good Lordships Lettres, her Majestys goode inclynacon for the speedye sendinge of theis forces here, unto the seas for the defence of thenemye, and that of her Majestys greate favor, and your Lordships good opynyon, you have made choice of me (althoughe the leaste of many) to be as an Actor in so greate a cause; I am moste humblie to beseeche my moste gracious Soveraigne and your good Lordships to heare my poore opynyon, with favor, and So to Judge of it accordinge to your greate wisdomes.[33]

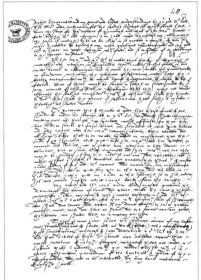

Drake's letter to the Privy Council, suggesting strategy to be used against the Spanish Armada.
PRO SP 12/209/40, fol. 58–v.

Drake saw clearly that Parma could not bring his invasion fleet to En-
gland without the help of the Armada under preparation in Spain. This
Armada clearly would come with invasion in mind, and Drake felt that the
Spanish fleet ought to be kept as far away as possible:

> If her Majestie, and your LLordships thinke, that the
> King of Spaigne meanethe any invasyon in Englande,
> then doubtlesse, his force is, and wilbe greate in Spaigne,
> and thereon he will make his groundworke, or founda-
> tion, whereby the prynce of Parma maye have the better
> entraunce, which in myne owne Judgemente, is moste to
> be feared, But if there maye be suche a staye or stoppe
> made, by any meanes, of this Fleete in Spaigne, that they
> maye not come throughe the seas, as conquerors (which I
> assure my selfe, they thincke to doe) then shall the prince
> of Parma, have suche a checke therebye, as were meett.[34]

He understood that Spain wanted to gain a psychological advantage by striking the first blow. There was only one practical way to prevent this, to increase the size and armament of Drake's fleet and send it to sea. This would increase public confidence in the government and in the state religion. After all, the people of Spain were "God's enemies" as well as England's:

> To prevente this, I thinke it goode, that theise forces
> here, should be made as stronge, as to your Honours'
> wisdomes shalbe thoughte convenyentt, and that for two
> speciall causes: Firste, for that they are like, to strike the
> firste blowe, and secondlie, it will putt great and goode
> hartes, into her Majesties lovinge subiects, bothe abroade
> and at home; For that they wilbe perswaded in con-
> scyence, that the Lorde of all strengthes, will putt into
> her Majestie, and her people, coraige, and boldnes, not
> to feare any invasyon in her owne Countrie, but to seeke
> Gods enemyes and her Majesties, where they maye be
> founde: For the Lorde is one our side, whereby we maye
> assure our selves, our nombers are greater than theirs. I
> muste crave pardone of your good Lordships, againe and
> againe, for, my conscience hath caused me, to putt my
> pen to the paper, and as, God in his goodnes, hathe putt
> my hande to the ploughe, so in his mercy he will never
> suffer me, to turne backe from the truthe.[35]

The key to success would be to give Drake a fleet of fifty ships and send him to raid the Spanish coast—the sooner, the better:

> My verie good Lordships, nexte under Gods mightie
> protection, the advantaige and gaine of tyme and place,
> wilbe the onlie & cheife meane, for our goode, wherein
> I most humblie beseech your good Lordships to perse-
> ver, as you have began, for that with feiftie saile of ship-
> pinge, we shall doe more good uppon their owne

Coaste, then a greate manye more, will doe here at
home, and the sooner we are gone, the better we shalbe
able to ympeache them.[36]

There were advantages beyond an improvement in morale among the
people in England. A victory close to the Spanish mainland would weaken
the determination of the Spanish forces. Drake had evidence from a ship
he had sent to spy on the Spanish coast that Spain was equipping her own
vessels with English flags. Drake thought this intolerable and was eager to
put a stop to it:

There is come home synce the sendinge awaie of my
laste messenger, one bark (whome I sente out as an Espi-
all,) who confyrmeth those intelligencs, whereof I have
advertized yor Lordships by him: and that divers of
those Biskaines' are abroade uppon that coaste, wearinge
Englishe flagges, whereof there are made in Lisbone
three hundreth, with the redde Crosse, which is so
greate presumpcon, proceedinge of the hautynes &
pride of the Spayniarde, and not to be tollerated, by
any true naturall Englishe harte.[37]

Finally, Drake told the Privy Council that the strength of the English
fleet was in its guns. The Council had to supply more powder and shot,
much more:

I have herein enclosed, sente this note unto your Lordships to consider if our proporcione, in powlder, shotte
and other munycion, under the hande of the Surveyors
clerke of the ordynaunce; the which proporcion in
powlder and shotte, for our greate ordynaunce in her
Majesties shippes, is but for one daie and halfes servyce,
if it be begonne & contynewed, as the service maye
requyer; and but five lastes of powlder for xxiiii saile of
the marchaunte shippes, which will scante be suffytyent
for one daies service, as divers occasyons maye be offred:

Good my Lords I beseeche you, to consider deeplie of
this, for it importeth but the losse of all.[38]

As usual, Drake made good use of spies and informants. He was always
impulsive, but he seldom took any aggressive action without information
about his opponents:

I have staied this messenger somewhat the longer, for
the hearinge of this Ducheman, who came latelie out of
Lisbone; and hath delivered theise advertisements,
herein enclosed, under his hande the 28th of this
Marche, before my selfe and divers Justics.[39]

Like all field commanders, Drake felt the officials in London were holding back supplies that he needed for his ships:

I have sente unto yor good Lordships the note of suche
powlder and munytyon, as are delivered unto us for this
great service, which in truthe I Judge to be iuste a thirde
parte, of that which is needefull; For if we should wante
it when we shall have moste neede thereof, it wilbe too
late to sende to the Tower for it; I assure your Honours:
it neither is or shalbe spente in vaine. And thus restinge
at your Honours' farther direcion, I humblie take my
leave of your good Lordships, From Plymowth this
xxxth of marche 1588:
    Yor good Lordships verie readie
    to be comaunded:
    Fra: Drake[40]

Not everyone agreed with Drake's assessment. At first Hawkins thought
that a half-dozen ships could patrol the Spanish coast to gather information. The rest of the fleet should stay close to home, for no one knew when
the Armada would be ready to sail, and there was a real danger to England
if the Armada should arrive unopposed. Eventually Hawkins changed his
mind, as did most of the other experienced officers. Late in June, Lord

Howard informed Walsingham that not only Drake but also Hawkins, Frobisher, and others as well thought that it would be best to attack the Spanish fleet on their own coast and in their own ports.[41]

For several weeks after leaving Queenborough, Drake remained in port at Plymouth, cooling his heels, feeding his soldiers and sailors, and waiting for a reply to his letter to the Privy Council. Mendoza, as usual, reported what gossip he heard about Drake's fleet. The soldiers were discouraged, and some were mutinous because they had not been paid.[42] Desertions were numerous.[43] Those remaining were becoming careless. An exploding cannon on Drake's flagship, the *Revenge,* killed thirty-five men and wounded seven more.[44] At length Drake received orders to go to sea, leaving half his fleet in Plymouth and taking the rest to attack the Spanish fleet in the port of Lisbon.[45]

This was not quite what Drake had proposed in his letter to the Privy Council, but his reply gives us another indication of his grasp of the tactical situation. First, Drake addressed his letter to the queen, his "Most gracyous soverayne," rather than to Walsingham, who had written to him. Nothing at all should be done, he said, until there was better information about the enemy. Perhaps more important, Drake needed time at sea with his men and his ships. He was always suspicious of the people who served under him, and he wanted time to test their own ability and the loyalty of his own officers and men:

> Trewly, this poynt is hardly to be answered as yeat, for
> two specyal causes: the first, for that our intellengencs
> are as yeat uncertayne, the second is the resolucyon of
> our own people, which I shall better understand when I
> have them at sea. the last insample at Calles [Cádiz] is
> not of dyvers yeat forgotten: for one flying nowe, as
> borrowghes dyd then, will put the wholle in peril.[46]

These were not the only necessities. Drake also needed more ships if he was to have a chance against the huge Armada being assembled in Lisbon. Once reinforced, his fleet could sail toward Spain, engage the Armada as it left port, and prevent its arrival off the coast of England:

If your majestie will geve present order for our proced-
ing to the sea: and send to the strenghing of this fleet
here foer more of your majesties good ships, and thos 16
saill of shipes with ther penaces, which ar preparing in
London, then shall your majestie stand asured, with
gods assistance, that yf the flett come out of Lysborne,
as long as we have victuall to live withal uppon that
cost, they shalle be fought with, and I hope through the
goodnes, of our mercyful god, in such sort as shall hyn-
der his quyett pasage into yngland.[47]

Besides good ships, Drake's great need was for good men. He thought
the men in his fleet were good men, with perhaps a few exceptions:

I assure your Majesty, I have not in my liffe time known
better men, and possessed with gall[anter] minds then
your majesties people are for the most part.[48]

He warned that speed was essential for victory. The Armada would surely
leave port very soon, and the English fleet would have to be ready:

The advantage of tyme and place in all marciall
accyons is half a victory, which being lost is irrecover-
able. Wherefore if your Majestie will command
me a way with thos shipes, which are here alredye,
and the rest to follow with all possible expedycyon,
I hold it in my poor opynyon the surest and best
course; and that they bring with them victuall suffy-
cyent for them selves and us, to the intent the service
be not utterly lost for want thereof.[49]

Economy was always on the queen's mind, but not usually on Drake's.
This time, though, he foresaw that food and supplies would be essential
for a successful voyage:

For an ynglysheman, being farre from his country, and
seing a present want of victuall to insue, and perceaving

no benefitt to be looked for, but only blowes, will hard-
lye be brought to stay. . . . Here may the wholl servic
and honor be lost for the sparing of a few crownes.[50]

Walsingham had asked what sort of fleet would be required. Drake was
almost afraid to reply, because the total would be so great:

Touching my poor opynyon how strong your Majesties
fleet should be, to encounter this great forc of the
enemy, god increac your most excellent majesties forces
both by sea and land dayly for this I surly think: ther was
never any force so stronge as there is now redye or making readye agaynst your Majesty and trew relygyon.[51]

Not a direct answer, this, but at least it was an indication that Drake
thought it was best to keep adding as many ships to the fleet as possible.
He ended with a prayer. This invocation and the other prayers scattered
through this letter indicate that Drake was very likely still served by the
same chaplain-secretary who had accompanied him on the recent West Indies trip:

Thus in all humble duty I continewelly will pray to the
All myghtye to bless and geve you victorye over all his
and your enemeyes.
    From Plimoth this xiiith of Aprell 1588.
    Your Majesties most
    loyall
    Fra: Dra[ke][52]

Drake's proposal to intercept the Spanish Armada along the coast of
Portugal finally began to make sense to the queen and council. His other
request, for an independent command, did not. The final decision must
have surprised everyone. Lord Admiral Howard was ordered to take his
fleet to Plymouth, leaving forty ships under Lord Henry Seymour to guard
the coast where Parma's army was expected to land. Just how the decision
was reached is a bit of a mystery.

Drake was summoned to London about the middle of May, and there he learned what the plan would be.[53] The reason for his presence was the very real fear that he would refuse to serve as Lord Howard's second in command. This was settled when it became clear that there was no alternative. The queen and her council no doubt had serious conversations with Drake, and we can guess that he was told to accept the new role in good grace.

He likely was asked to consider the realities. Even though Howard was nominal commander of the English navy, Spanish authorities always considered Drake to be the real leader of the fleet. They could not imagine a naval battle that did not have Drake as the major opponent. It was equally unthinkable for England to send a fleet to sea without Drake, for the Spanish considered him to be an implacable foe. On the other hand, many English officers were reluctant to serve under Drake, apparently because he was considered overbearing and capricious.[54]

The visit to London had the desired effect. Drake left London by post on 21 May and was back in Plymouth on 23 May when the signal came that Howard's fleet was approaching.[55] Drake immediately took his own ships out of the harbor to form an honor guard for the lord admiral, thirty ships in ranks of three. Howard's flagship carried both the admiral's flag and that of the vice admiral. As commander of the fleet in Plymouth, Drake also flew the admiral's flag. As Howard's ship came near, Drake lowered his own flag to indicate submission to the authority of the new commander. At the same time, Howard lowered the vice admiral's flag from his own mast and sent it by pinnace to Drake in the *Revenge*. It was a marvelous ritual, with all the crews assembled on deck and cheering, and with accompanying flourishes from trumpets and drums.[56]

Drake and Howard hit it off well from the start. Expecting the worst, the lord admiral was most attentive to his vice admiral. The two men attended church together on Whit Sunday, prayed together, and received the sacrament together.[57] Pleased with the relationship, Howard wrote to Walsingham. "I must not omit to let you know how lovingly and kindly Sir Francis Drake beareth himself," wrote Howard, "and also how dutifully to her Majesty's service and unto me, being in the place I am in." This was a man who had expected trouble and had not found it. "I pray you that he may receive thanks," continued the Lord Admiral, "by some private letter from you."[58] Drake repaid the compliment, telling Burghley, "I finde my Lord Admirall so well affectede for all honorable services in this accion as it dothe assure all his followers of good successe and hope of victorie."[59]

Howard was a man of great charm, good humor, and considered judgment. On 24 and 25 May he called his captains into council to determine just what their course of action should be. Drake naturally favored an attack on the Armada near the coast of Spain. Other officers argued that it would be better to wait until the Armada approached the English coast, when it would be in waters unfamiliar to the Spanish captains. Ultimately Drake's opinion prevailed.[60] A couple of weeks later Howard wrote to Walsingham that he had originally been opposed to Drake's plan but had become convinced that it was the correct move. "I confesse my error at that time," he noted, "but I did and will yield ever unto them of greater experience."[61]

This agreement was a vindication of Drake's arguments favoring an attack near Lisbon, but it came too late. Medina Sidonia was already on his way down the Tagus with his fleet, heading for the coast of England. In an impressive ceremony on the feast of Saint Mark, the cardinal archbishop of Lisbon blessed the royal banner, which carried the inscription "Exurge Domine et vindica causam tuum," and delivered it to the fleet.[62] Ominously, the winds then became contrary and kept the fleet bottled up in the bay for another month. Finally, at the end of May the ships cleared the cape and sailed away.[63]

Gale-force winds still hampered progress of the Armada, blowing the ships farther and farther south until it seemed that they might round Cabo de San Vicente. Finally they were able to head north, but progress was agonizingly slow. After three weeks at sea Medina Sidonia ordered the fleet into port at La Coruña for reorganization and repairs. Even this proved difficult, as another storm scattered the ships, driving them to take refuge in various ports along the coast of Galicia, Asturias, and Vizcaya.[64]

The same storm created similar difficulties for Howard and Drake. Leaving port on 30 May, the English fleet was badly buffeted by the wind.

In the end, the fleet was unable to reach the coast of Spain, returning to Plymouth on 6 June. The only positive outcome of this brief voyage was an encounter with "a hulke which came from St. Lucar sixe weekes paste." The sailors on board advised Drake and Howard that the Armada had left Lisbon and was at sea with perhaps 150 or 200 ships.[65]

Two weeks later, on 19 June, the fleet sailed once more from Plymouth. This time the ships were driven back to port in only two days. Once safely back in Plymouth Sound, Howard and Drake were informed that a few ships of the Armada had been sighted, scattered by the storm and heading for La Coruña. Losing no time, the fleet put to sea for a third time, on 24 June, and very nearly reached the coast of Spain. At this point, the wind changed once more, and it was feared that the Spanish fleet would be able to use it to reach the coast of England. Consequently, the English headed again for Plymouth, arriving on 12 July.[66]

Still trying to evaluate the spotty information being received about the Spanish fleet, Howard and Drake kept their ships at Plymouth for a few days of refitting. Suddenly, on 19 July the news arrived that the Armada had been spotted off the Lizard, the southernmost tip of Cornwall, heading toward Plymouth.[67] This was wonderful luck for Medina Sidonia, because his ships would be able to grapple with the English vessels in the harbor, where they could not maneuver for position. It was the worst sort of luck for Howard, for the wind and the tide were both against him, and he would not be able to sail for several hours.[68]

A wonderful story has been told and retold about Drake's equanimity during this time of stress. When word arrived that the Spanish Armada had been sighted, the captains of the fleet were supposedly playing bowls on the Hoe at Plymouth, where there was a good view of the harbor and the fleet. Rather than going immediately to his ship, Drake said that there was sufficient time to finish the game, and then to finish the Spaniards.[69] His exact words vary from one telling to the next, primarily because no eyewitness account of the incident has ever been found.

The earliest source is a pamphlet published in 1624 by Thomas Scott, an English clergyman. It was a fictional account of discussions by Spanish noblemen, one of whom said that the Armada arrived off the shore at Ply-

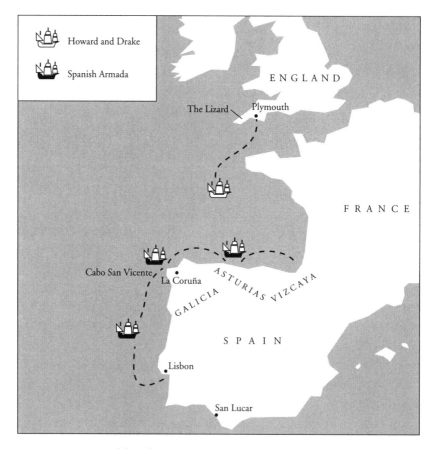

English and Spanish fleet movements, May and June 1588

mouth "while their Commanders and Captaines were at bowles upon the hoe of Plimouth."[70] Whether there was any factual basis for the story is uncertain. A century passed before Drake's name was connected with the game of bowls, and the direct quotation is even later. The story may be true, though one doubter has observed that bowling on public ground was forbidden at that time.[71]

In spite of some slight disparity in numbers, the fleets were approximately equal in effective strength. Howard and Seymour had about 120 ships between them, while the Armada had assembled about 130. Many of the English ships were small coasters. Fewer than two dozen could be considered major ships of war. Of the total English fleet, Howard had about 90 ships at Plymouth. Nineteen were queen's ships and the rest armed merchantmen. Of the 30 ships in Seymour's fleet, about half were royal navy ships.[72] Similarly, Philip had only about 23 fighting galleons and galleasses, the latter a heavily armed ship that supposedly combined the maneuverability of a galley with the armament of a galleon.[73] Some of the merchant ships proved to be effective in battle, but only a few. The urcas and hulks in the Spanish fleet were simply transports, carrying men and supplies for the invasion.[74]

The Armada commanders had the advantage of experience. At Lepanto in 1571 and again in the Azores campaign of 1582–83, Spanish commanders had worked with fleets of considerable size and armament. Their great disadvantage was the lack of a central naval command. The Armada was not so much a fleet as a collection of provincial squadrons drawn from Portugal, Castile, Andalusia, Guipúzcoa, Vizcaya, and Levant. In addition, there were special units for hulks, pinnaces, galleasses, and galleys.[75]

Having been ordered to head straight for the Channel and to avoid fighting before then, Medina Sidonia gave only passing consideration to an attack on Plymouth.[76] Instead, he lay off the Lizard, sending out patrol vessels and assembling his fleet for an advance toward the Isle of Wight. Exactly what he intended to do at Wight is not clear, though it had been suggested as a possible assembly point for the Armada and a rendezvous with Parma's invasion fleet.[77]

While Medina Sidonia dawdled off the Lizard, Howard and Drake were busy warping their ships out of the harbor. In the face of contrary winds and currents it was necessary for each ship to send out a small boat to drop the anchor as far ahead as possible. The ship was then drawn forward on the anchor cable and the whole process repeated. By the afternoon of 20 July the English fleet had fifty-four ships out of the harbor as far as the Eddystone, where they could see the Armada but could not be seen themselves. It was hard work, and it was not over. Around midnight one of the Spanish scouts returned with the information that the enemy ships were commanded by Howard and Drake. All that night the English ships worked their way westward. About 2 A.M. on Sunday, 21 July (31 July by

Spanish calculation), the wind began to shift, and by dawn Howard and Drake saw they had gained the wind of the enemy.[78]

Battle order for the Armada on 21 July consisted of an arc of ships with tips projecting to envelop the enemy. The flagship and the heavier galleasses were massed in the center, ahead of the line of the arc, with a small reserve line to the rear. The idea was to bear down upon the enemy, isolate one or two ships, and come close enough to grapple. When Medina Sidonia discovered the main body of the English fleet at his rear, he raised his battle flag and ordered the Armada to come about. Howard brought his fleet forward in oblique lines, one group under his command, the other under Drake. As a formal opening of the battle, Howard on the *Ark Royal* sent his pinnace the *Disdain* to fire a challenging shot at what he took to be the Spanish flagship, *San Martín.* In fact it was the *Rata Encoronada,* commanded by Alonso de Leyva.[79]

While Howard and his ships traded shots with the *Rata,* Drake in the *Revenge* headed for the right wing of the Spanish arc, where Juan Martínez de Recalde commanded in the *San Juan de Portugal.* This became the center of the battle, with the *Revenge* pressing so hard on the *San Juan* that it seemed for a time to invite the close fighting that the Spanish wanted. Noting the heavy fighting between Drake and Recalde, Medina Sidonia brought his *San Martín* into the fight. But the English would not be drawn in close. Medina Sidonia spent some time trying to recover the weather gauge, but finally had to break off and order his fleet to continue sailing up the Channel.[80]

The fight had lasted two or three hours, with very little damage inflicted on either side, except for substantial weakening of Recalde's foremast. Each fleet came away with new respect for the adversary. Expecting the underpowered artillery that they had encountered at Cádiz, the English commanders were impressed with the number and size of the heavy guns with which the Armada had been equipped. The Spanish, meanwhile, were astonished at the firepower and maneuverability of the English ships.[81]

The most serious Spanish losses occurred as the Armada turned about. At five in the evening an explosion reverberated through the fleet. The *San Salvador,* almiranta of the Guipúzcoa squadron, had blown up. The story spread that the explosion was caused by sabotage: a German artilleryman, angry at what he took to be mistreatment by the Spanish officers, had supposedly set a match to a barrel of gunpowder. Everything above decks was destroyed, and many men were killed or horribly burned.[82] Seeing the damage, Medina Sidonia ordered the survivors taken off the ship and had the hulk set adrift.[83]

While the *San Salvador* was still burning, another ship came to grief. Attempting to come about, the *Nuestra Señora del Rosario* of Don Pedro de Valdés collided with the *Santa Catalina* and lost its bowsprit. As a result, the foremast was loosened and came crashing down against the main yard. While the strong westerly winds continued to drive the Armada eastward, the *Rosario* began to fall astern. Rather than call the fleet back to save the straggler, Medina Sidonia ordered a few ships to stay and try to take her in tow.[84] It is difficult now to understand why Medina Sidonia felt obliged to abandon the *Rosario*. For several hours he had been skirmishing with the English ships, trying to force one of them to come to grips with his fleet. Here was an opportunity that he simply failed to recognize.

At the same time it was an opportunity that Drake recognized very clearly. Called by Howard into council, Drake and the other captains were ordered to follow the Armada at a distance, waiting for the rest of the English ships to emerge from Plymouth harbor and come up with the fleet. In the meeting Drake was given two assignments. First, he was to send a caravel to Seymour, off the coast of Dover, to inform him of the arrival of the Spanish fleet.[85] Second, he was to lead the pursuit, his stern lantern acting as a marker for the rest of the fleet. Defying these clear orders, Drake had the lantern extinguished and sailed off in the darkness to capture the *Rosario*.[86]

With Drake's *Revenge* nowhere in sight, the English fleet was left leaderless. Howard in the *Ark Royal* followed the Spanish fleet, together with the *Bear* or the *Mary Rose*. The rest of the English ships remained behind, waiting for some signal to advance.[87] Drake, meanwhile, came up to the *Rosario,* and after dawn Valdés sent emissaries to ask Drake about terms.[88] Drake invited him to come aboard the *Revenge* and there talked to the Spanish commander through an interpreter. Drake told Valdés to surren-

The capture of the Nuestra Señora del Rosario,
from a set of seventeenth-century playing cards. From
National Maritime Museum, London. A8121.

der or be put back aboard his own ship to fight. Thoroughly demoralized
by the Armada's abandonment, Valdés took a brief time to reflect, then surrendered.[89] It was Monday, 22 July, the second day of the running battle.

While not exactly cowardice, the surrender must still be seen as a surprising development. Valdés had nearly 350 men on board his heavily armed
galleon. The ship was rated at 1,150 tons, and armament included forty-six
great guns, 114 quintals of powder, and 2,300 rounds of shot. To surrender
without firing a shot must be seen as the act of a man not terribly eager to
fight.[90] In his defense it ought to be noted that many in the Spanish fleet
thought that he had been abandoned without reason. The reaction in some

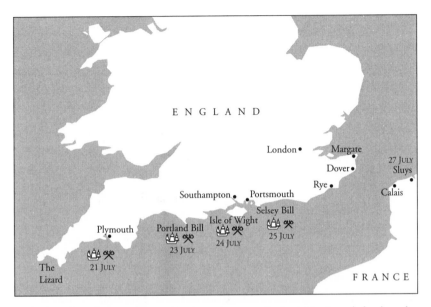

The dates shown here are those used in sixteenth-century England. The Armada battles took place from 30 July to 10 August according to the Gregorian calendar used in Spain.

parts of the fleet was so severe that Medina Sidonia took special steps to enforce discipline. A dispatch boat was sent through the fleet, carrying an executioner and announcing that any captain who left his station without orders would be hanged.

Drake's own conduct is equally difficult to understand. With specific orders to stay ahead of the fleet and serve as a beacon for the rest, Drake abandoned his post. Instead he hunted out the *Rosario* and lay off about 500 yards, waiting for dawn. Once morning came, he demanded and got the surrender of the ship. In his own defense Drake insisted that it was all an accident. He had gone off to investigate some suspicious-looking ships, found that they were innocent German merchantmen, and then lay to, waiting for daylight.[91] As dawn broke—and much to his surprise—there was the *Rosario,* two or three cables away.[92]

The *Rosario* was one of the pay ships of the Armada. How much she carried is unclear, though most sources confirm a total of 50,000 gold ducats.[93] Valdés said in his testimony that there were 20,000 ducats, which may be an error on the part of the secretary.[94] Drake delivered 25,300 ducats to Howard in September.[95] There was much talk of theft by Spanish sailors before the surrender and by English sailors afterward.[96] Frobisher and others thought that Drake had kept a great deal for himself, perhaps as much as 15,000 ducats.[97] One of the sailors on the *Revenge* said that Drake paid a bonus of £2,000 to two of the officers of the fleet, plus smaller amounts to others.[98] George Hewes said that "the Lord Admirall & Sir Francis Drake & others were authorised by the late Q[ueen] to bestowe some of the same treasure upon the commanders gent[lemen] & others that were in that voyadge." Of this unspecified amount Hewes "had a parte."[99] Lady Elizabeth Fuller Eliott-Drake reported having seen a record of a payment of £110 to the crew of the *Revenge* after the capture of the ship.[100] With the treasure and the important prisoners removed, the *Rosario* was taken to Torbay, escorted by the *Roebuck*. While Howard was no doubt surprised by the performance of his vice admiral, he took no action to censure Drake, probably thinking that he was acting very much as he had always done.

Unaware of the surrender of Valdés, but no doubt having anticipated some such development, Medina Sidonia spent most of the morning revising the battle formation for the Armada. Still formed in the shape of a crescent, the right and left wings of the fleet became a rearguard of forty-three of the strongest galleons and galleasses. Medina Sidonia and the rest of the fleet composed the vanguard.[101] Once these arrangements were completed, the Spanish commander sent a message to Parma, warning him that they were approaching the Channel and asking for pilots to guide them along the Flemish coast.[102]

It was late Monday evening before Drake and the stragglers caught up with Howard, who with a few other ships was trailing close behind the Spanish fleet.[103] The other captains found that the admiral had not been idle. The *San Salvador,* heavily damaged by fire the day before, had been abandoned by the Spanish crew, who went aboard other ships in the Armada. Howard sent John Hawkins and Lord Thomas Howard in the skiff *Victory* to inspect the stricken vessel. Though the superstructure was gone, the hull was still sound, as was much of the cargo of powder and shot.

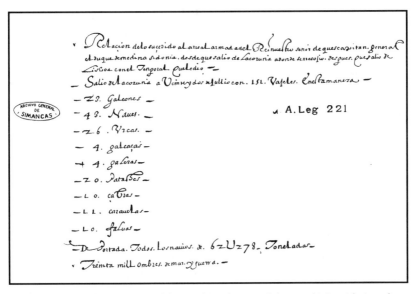

Pedro Coco Calderón's estimate of the numbers of men and ships in the Spanish Armada.
AGS Guerra Marina 221, fol. 190, 1°. Ministerio de Educación y Cultura de España, Archivo
General de Simancas.

Many wounded men, horribly burned, for the most part, had been abandoned with the ship. All of the wounded seem to have been left aboard a bit longer while the vessel was towed into Weymouth the following day.[104]

The fleet lay becalmed that night, but on Tuesday morning, 23 July, the wind came up from the northeast, giving the Armada the weather gauge. As the English fleet moved toward shore, the Spanish came down to intercept them. Several Spanish ships moved in close to grapple, and the *Regazona* came very close to the *Ark Royal,* which immediately moved to leeward and out to sea. The *Nonpareil,* the *Elizabeth Jonas,* and the *Victory* then came up to assist the *Ark Royal,* but help proved to be unnecessary as the Spanish ships were forced south by the Portland Race tidal current and fell astern of the English vessels.[105]

Meanwhile, several other English ships were being threatened off Portland Bill. When these vessels were separated from the main fleet, several Spanish galleasses moved in to attack. The battle lasted for about an hour and a half, but again the Spanish were unable to get close enough to board the English ships. At length the wind shifted once more, and Howard moved in with his larger galleons. Medina Sidonia in the *San Martin* then moved in to grapple with Howard in the *Ark Royal*, but the heavier fire and the superior maneuverability of the English ship once more drove the Spanish off. When the wind shifted again to give the English ships the weather gauge, the Spanish vessels broke off the fight and sailed east.[106]

As dawn broke on Wednesday, 24 July, the English could see that an armed Spanish merchant vessel, the *Gran Grifón,* straggled behind the rest. Catching the light morning wind, the English galleons pursued the wallowing ship. One heavily armed ship, unnamed in the reports, came swiftly across the beam of the *Gran Grifón* and loosed a broadside at her. Turning about, the English galleon then came across her stern and again raked the ship with heavy fire. Not wanting another *Rosario,* Medina Sidonia quickly dispatched his galleasses to take the *Grifón* in tow. The Spanish admiral then tried to engage the English vessels in a general battle, but they withdrew out of range.[107]

It was a stunning move at very close range by a daring sea captain. English tradition, following Corbett, has identified the ship as Drake's *Revenge,* but it is also possible to identify his ship with more certainty.[108] The Spanish relief forces took the attacker under heavy fire and managed to destroy the *entena del arbol mayor*—either the main topmast or the main yard.[109] In the survey of the Queen's ships made in October 1588, the mainmast of the *Revenge* had to be replaced because it was "decayed and perished with shot."[110] The loss to the *Revenge* was not severe, but temporary repairs would take Drake out of action for a time.

While inflicting little real damage on either side, the heavy fire from the guns had cost them both an enormous amount of powder and shot. As a result Howard sent orders to have the powder and shot removed from the two prizes and parceled out among the ships of the fleet. The English commander was also becoming aware of the tactical differences between his own disorganized fleet and the highly disciplined Spanish Armada. While the fleet was reassembling, Howard took the opportunity to organize it into four attack squadrons. The four commanders were Howard himself, Sir Francis Drake, John Hawkins, and Martin Frobisher.[111]

Medina Sidonia had also taken the opportunity to regroup his own fleet.[112] Then, following another council with his captains, he seems to have decided to pause in the anchorage off the Isle of Wight until some word was received from Parma concerning the date and place for a meeting. In order to improve his own tactical mobility, he rearranged the rearguard of the Armada in two squadrons, adding Leyva's vanguard to the rearguard previously commanded by Recalde. With the rearguard sailing in a crescent formation and his own ships in an arc, English accounts described the new Armada formation as a roundel. Having accomplished this reorganization, Medina Sidonia then proceeded with his Armada toward the eastern entrance of the Solent, the channel between Wight and the mainland.[113]

On Thursday morning, 25 July (4 August in the Spanish accounts), Hawkins with his newly designated squadron sighted the Portuguese galleon *San Luis* and the Andalusian hulk *Duquesa Santa Ana* becalmed and lying somewhat to the rear of the rest of the Armada. With small boats he began to tow his galleons into firing range, responding to one more attempt by Medina Sidonia to draw the English ships into a close fight.[114] Once the English ships opened fire, three Spanish galleasses headed for the two threatened vessels. There was a furious exchange of gunfire, but the English ships never came within grappling distance.[115] The English ships thought they had inflicted heavy losses on the Spanish ships. In fact, the galleasses were able to take the *San Luis* and *Santa Ana* in tow, and none of the ships was badly damaged.[116]

While this was going on, Frobisher had used the currents to work his squadron around the landward end of the Armada. Medina Sidonia engaged the *Triumph* in a gun duel and for a time thought he had the ship disabled. The Spanish ships were closing in for boarding when the wind came up a bit, and Frobisher managed to pull away. Two Spanish vessels gave chase, while Frobisher sailed clear around the Armada. He was too fast for them and managed to escape with very little damage.[117]

During this day's fighting Drake's *Revenge* was not reported anywhere. Most historians have followed Corbett in saying that the silence in the records comes from the fact that Drake was working his way around the seaward flank of the Armada. Anticipating an afternoon change in the wind, Drake had placed his squadron in position to drive the Spanish fleet onto the Owers, rocks south of Selsey Bill.[118] This interpretation depends upon several assumptions. First, Corbett assumed that the English squadrons were arranged with Frobisher on the landward side, followed by Howard, Hawkins, and finally Drake on the seaward end.[119] A second assumption was that the Spanish galleon *San Mateo* was on the seaward wing of the Armada rather than near the center. A third was that the attack on the *San Mateo* was made by Drake rather than Howard.[120]

Using a broader range of Spanish sources, Peter Pierson has reconstructed the day's battle in a different way. His conclusion is that Drake was not mentioned in Spanish or English accounts of the day's fighting because he was not there. Instead, he was very likely taking time out to repair his mainmast and rigging, perhaps even going to a nearby port for this purpose. Rather than Drake's *Revenge,* the attacking ship was Howard's *Ark Royal.* Howard's attack very nearly penetrated the Spanish center, forcing Medina Sidonia to retreat to the east and abandon his attempt to enter the Solent.[121] Having accomplished this, the English fleet broke off the battle, intending to save their powder and shot for the expected fight near Dover.[122]

For the next two days there was no fighting. Howard took "men, powder, shot, victuals, and ships" from forts along the coast. While shadowing the Armada, he used the respite to call his principal officers into council, where he conferred the order of knighthood on Hawkins and Frobisher as a reward for their service the previous day.[123]

Medina Sidonia was in a quandary. He had sent messengers to Parma on numerous occasions but had received no response. He had not the slightest idea what Parma was doing or where they would meet. Having failed to find a haven at the Isle of Wight, he headed instead for Calais, where he could anchor and arrange a rendezvous with Parma. Some of his men were doubtful about the whole affair and beginning to think it ought to be abandoned. Medina Sidonia asked Parma to send some fighting vessels and to embark his men in preparation for the Channel crossing.[124] When Parma finally replied, it was to say that he could not be ready for another week.[125]

The anchorage was hazardous, but a move farther up the Channel was more so, for the winds could easily drive the Armada into the North Sea.[126]

On Saturday, 27 July (6 August in Spanish accounts), both fleets reached Calais. The armada sighted the French coast about ten in the morning and anchored off Calais at about 6 P.M. The English fleet, reinforced by Seymour's squadron, reached Calais Cliffs at about the same time. The English fleet now numbered about 140 ships. Realizing that the Armada was in a serious predicament, Howard sent for Sir William Wynter, who commanded one of the newly arrived ships.[127]

By his own account, Wynter suggested that the Armada was in a position where fire ships would be very effective.[128] Howard was delighted with the idea, which promised to disperse the Spanish fleet at the cost of only a few expendable English vessels. The Spanish fleet was crowded into an open roadstead, with the treacherous Flemish shoals to the leeward. At a council of war on Sunday morning, 28 July, the English captains accepted Wynter's suggestion and determined to send eight burning ships bearing down on the Spanish fleet.[129]

Eight merchant vessels, one of them Drake's *Thomas,* were packed with combustibles, and their guns were loaded, ready to fire when the flames reached the touchholes.[130] As it turned out, there was no chance for secrecy. Medina Sidonia was aware of the "Hellburners of Antwerp" that had put fear into Parma's soldiers three years earlier, and he warned his captains to set out boats to take fire ships in tow and move them out of the way. The English sailors were also careless, setting two of the ships alight before they left the fleet and thus notifying the Spanish vessels that the attack was coming. In spite of this warning, several of the English fire ships got through the Spanish picket boats. Medina Sidonia ordered his captains to move out of the way, and in something approaching panic, the Spanish ships simply cut their mooring lines and sailed off.[131]

Every one of the fire ships drifted ashore without exploding or setting fire to an Armada vessel. Even so, they accomplished their purpose. The high winds and strong tides gripped the Spanish ships and forced them out of the anchorage. A few ships were able to turn about and reenter the anchorage, but most drifted off in the direction of Dunkirk. In the confusion the flag galleass *San Lorenzo* suffered a damaged rudder and mainmast and was forced to head for shore. Caught in a falling tide, the *San Lorenzo* ran aground at the entrance to Calais, where the English fleet promptly pounced on the luckless ship. With the ship heeled over to one side the guns were useless, and an English boarding party sacked the vessel.[132]

On Monday morning, 29 July, Medina Sidonia found himself out of the roadstead, a few miles off Calais, with four ships in his company and the English fleet bearing down for the attack. He fired a signal cannon to call his other ships to assist, and most of the fighting ships then turned about.[133] Drake in the *Revenge* brought his squadron up to the *San Martín* and fired the first shots of the Battle of Gravelines.[134] For nine hours the battle raged, as the fleets drifted between Gravelines and Ostend. Other ships soon closed in, firing so heavily that it was impossible to see more than one or two ships at a time through the smoke. Eventually as many as thirty-two of the Armada's fighting ships managed to join the formation against a somewhat larger number of English ships. Fighting was done at such a close range that men could shout and curse at one another between the ships.[135]

In the course of the battle the Spanish and English ships felt for the first time the real effect of the enemy artillery. The Spanish flagship *San Martín* took more than a hundred hits in her hull, masts, and sails, with several shots below the waterline that caused serious leaks. Two Spanish galleons, *San Felipe* and *San Mateo,* hoping to grapple with the enemy, worked their way past the battle line and into a nest of English ships. The *San Felipe* had five guns put out of action, decks very nearly destroyed, pumps broken, and rigging in shreds. Nevertheless, her captain broke out the grappling hooks and challenged the English sailors to come alongside for a fair fight. When they would not, his crew shouted out that they were "Cowards" and "Lutheran chickens" and drove the English ships away with musket fire.[136]

The *San Mateo* was surrounded by English galleons and riddled with English shot. The recoil from her own cannons very nearly finished the work of the English gunners, threatening to pull the hull apart. Unable to keep up with the Armada, the *San Mateo* and the *San Felipe* were beached

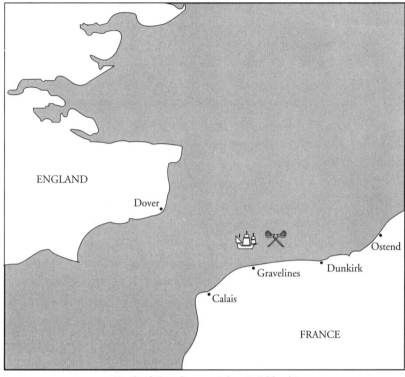

Battle of Gravelines, 29 July 1588 (old style)

by their commanders between Nieuwpoort and Ostend. A third Spanish ship, the *María Juan,* was badly damaged during the fighting. While relief ships came up to take off the survivors, the vessel suddenly sank, with the loss of most of the crew.[137] These are the known casualties, but other ships may have been sunk or driven ashore.[138]

It is not clear which of the English ships inflicted the most damage. In Pierson's reconstruction of the battle, the *San Mateo* and the *San Felipe* were surrounded by elements of Frobisher's, Seymour's, and Drake's squadrons. For reasons that are not entirely clear, Drake remained in the fight only for the first hour or so, then withdrew. Frobisher, still fuming about the *Rosario,* said that Drake was either "a cowardly knave or a traitor." He was not sure which, but added, "the one I will swear."[139] Cowardice was not a possibility, despite Frobisher's fulminations. Drake may have gone off to look for prizes, as some have suggested, but another explanation may serve.[140]

In the course of the battle Drake's *Revenge* took several hits, including two shots through the hull where the Captain's cabin was located. In an incident that seems to have been told by Drake himself, "two gentlemen" were in the cabin when a cannon ball destroyed the bed that one of the men was lying on, though "without his taking the least hurt." Later, when the Earl of Northumberland and Sir Charles Blount were in the cabin, another shot went through "from one side to the other without doing any harm other than scrape the foot, taking off the toes of one who was there with them."[141]

The interesting part of this story is that two of the men were named and two were not. The unnamed "gentlemen" were almost certainly the Spanish prisoners whom Drake had taken from the *Rosario* a week earlier. They were still on the *Revenge* because Drake expected to collect ransom from their families in Spain. When Drake took the *Revenge* out of the battle, he likely did so in order to deliver his captives to a place of safety. For Drake the whole point of battle was to gain material advantage from his enemy, at times by taking treasure from the king's ships, at other times by holding the king's subjects for ransom. To lose one or the other would, in Drake's mind, mean losing the battle.

Drake was surely aware of Frobisher's criticisms, but there was little he could do to counter them. A year or so later Petruccio Ubaldino's account of the battle was issued in an English edition, giving Drake a very minor role in the whole Armada campaign. Drake thereupon insisted that Ubaldino compose a revised version that included more about his own part in the various battles. The resulting narrative still assigned Drake a distinctly minor role in the fighting. The only significant addition made by Ubaldino was the story of the cannon shot piercing the cabin of Drake's ship. This seems like an unimportant event, but its inclusion is evidence that Drake thought the incident explained his own role at Gravelines.[142]

The Spanish prisoners were Pedro de Valdés, commander of the ship *Nuestra Señora de Rosario,* as well as Don Alonso de Zayas of Laja and Don Vasco de Mendoza y de Silva of Jérez de los Cavalleros, both of whom were infantry captains.[143] Drake wanted to keep the prisoners himself, but the queen had other plans. She ordered the Privy Council to have them brought to London, and the Council dispatched Richard Drake of Esher to carry the message to his distant kinsman.

Before this news arrived, Drake had orders from Howard to land his prisoners in England. Exactly when he did this is not clear. On the "last of July 1588" he wrote to Walsingham, saying that the lord admiral had ordered him to send the men ashore. Drake was worried about losing the credit for the prisoners, no doubt because of the ransom involved. "If they should be given from me unto any other," he wrote, "it would be some grief to my friends."[144] As it turned out, Richard Drake was allowed to keep Valdés at Esher. After both Richard and Francis Drake were dead, their descendants argued about the arrangements. Richard's heirs said that the queen had appointed him to be responsible for the Spanish prisoner. Thomas Drake said that his brother had had full charge of the prisoner but had paid Richard Drake to house and entertain him. One of the servants at the Herbar reported that Francis Drake had contributed £4 per week for his upkeep.[145] Beyond this, he later submitted claims for payments of £112 to Tristam Gorges and Captain Thomas Cely for taking the Spanish prisoners ashore, plus another £50 to Tristam Gorges for taking Valdés to London.[146] These payments reinforce the suspicion that Drake took money secretly from the *Rosario* and that he may have had some sort of private agreement with Valdés as well.[147]

Drake was positively elated with the outcome at Gravelines. "God hath geven us so good a daye," he wrote to Walsingham that evening. The English fleet had managed to force the Armada close to the shoals. "I hope in god the prince of parma; and the duke of Medonya, shall not shake hands this Fewe dayes," he continued. "When so ever they shall meet, I beleve nether of them will greatly reioce of this dayes Servis."[148]

Throughout the night of 29 July the English fleet followed the Spanish ships, which were driven by the wind toward the shoals. At one point Medina Sidonia ordered the galleasses to turn about and attack the English. This forced them to stand off a bit and gave the Armada more room to maneuver. About the middle of the morning on Tuesday, 30 July, the

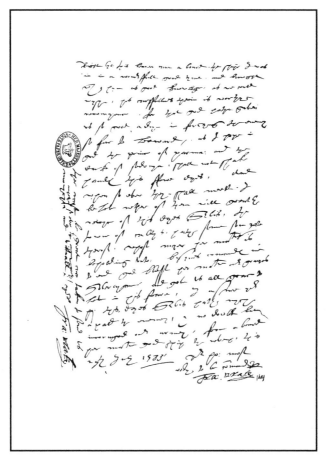

*The letter of 29 July 1588, written in Drake's nearly indecipherable
hand. PRO SP 12/213/65, fol. 150.*

wind shifted southward and allowed the Armada to head north once
more.[149]

During a council that day Medina Sidonia and his captains discussed
their next move. It was clear that they would have either to find a port in
which to refit the fleet or return to Spain. The decision was somewhere in
between. If they encountered winds favorable for a return to Calais, they
would go there. Otherwise, they would sail north, round Scotland and Ireland, and return to Spain. With this decision made, Medina Sidonia made

one more attempt at bringing the English fleet into a close battle. On 31 July 1588 he turned his flagship about and ordered signal guns fired so that the rest of his ships would do the same. Perhaps a dozen responded. He fired another and still another with the same result.[150]

As it turned out, the English ships held back, having insufficient ammunition for another fight, but Medina Sidonia was in a rage. Finally able to gather the Armada once more, he convened a court martial and sentenced twenty captains to hang. Only one was actually executed, but the other captains had a lesson in obedience. Two days later, with the wind still driving the Armada north, the English fleet broke off and headed for home.[151] The Armada continued on its course around Scotland.[152]

This was the end of the invasion attempt. Although the Armada was badly battered, it was generally in no worse shape than the English fleet. The important point, however, was that the opportunity for an invasion of England no longer existed. Because Parma had not been ready to join forces with Medina Sidonia, the whole Spanish effort came to nothing. The real destruction of the Armada came in the ensuing weeks. Battered by storms, many ships were driven ashore as they rounded the coasts of Scotland and Ireland. Only about half of the ships that had sailed to England actually made port again in Spain.

The main body of the English fleet headed for home on 2 August (12 August by Spanish calculation), leaving some pinnaces to shadow the fleet as far as Fair Isle. The fleet then returned to the Thames for victuals and repairs—just in time. Supplies were exhausted. Disease was decimating the ranks, and men were dying by the thousands.[153] On 22 August, Howard wrote to the Privy Council from Dover that in some vessels so many men were sick that the ships could not weigh anchors.[154] "The infection is grown very great," he wrote to the queen. "Those that come in fresh are soonest infected; they sicken one day and die the next."[155]

A week later Drake received word that there was perhaps one more service he could do for his queen. An attack on the treasure fleet was what she had in mind.[156] Though Drake remained a favorite of the queen, there is no evidence that he had a large role in the Armada battles. The information available now shows that Howard, Frobisher, and Hawkins fought valiantly, but there is little about Drake. In fact, we would not even know that Drake was vice admiral if he had not insisted that Ubaldino put this title in his Armada manuscript. To the Spanish navy and especially to the Spanish king, Drake personified the navy of England.[157] To English sea captains of his day Drake was something else.

12

Expedition to Lisbon

ONCE OFFICIALS IN LONDON BEGAN to grasp the dimensions of the Spanish disaster, they realized that the coast of Spain would be undefended until the Armada made its way back to Lisbon. Immediate action was required, but plans were formulated slowly and executed even more slowly. During the fall months there were several proposals to take advantage of this new situation. At first the queen thought of sending Francis Drake to capture the treasure fleet returning from the Indies. He had tried and failed before to do just that, but conditions seemed good for another attempt. The crown could certainly use the money. The fleet had been assembled at an enormous cost, and fresh demands on the treasury continued to arrive each day.[1] Hundreds of men were deathly sick and needed hospital care. Great numbers died every day. Others were healthy but had to be paid before they could be sent home.[2]

To save money most of the army was discharged and ships from the fleet were put into dock.[3] Only a few were kept active for use in the new operation. None was really ready to go to sea. Before any new project was undertaken, the ships required refitting.[4] They had been at sea for months, and all of them needed to be careened and caulked. Sails, spars, and rigging had to be mended. Damage from Spanish artillery needed to be repaired.[5] Most of all, the ships all needed to be cleaned thoroughly and fumigated to get rid of whatever was causing the disease that had decimated the crews. But all this would take time, and the opportunity for attacking before the Armada's return might well be lost.

Toward the end of August, Walsingham asked Howard whether it might be possible to send a few ships to the Azores to intercept the Indies fleet on its way home. After discussing the matter with Drake, who was himself ill, Howard replied that the ships could not be refitted quickly or sent out in secret. The navy was not in any condition for battle, he wrote, and if all the captains knew the destination, how could the plan be kept secret? It was as though the people in London were unaware of the battles that the fleet had fought in recent weeks. Perhaps they thought the Azores were very close to England. "This is not as if a man would send but over to the coast of France, I do assure you," he wrote, echoing his conversations with Drake. Perhaps it would be better for Drake himself to explain things in person. "I thought it good therefore to send with all speed Sir Francis . . . to inform you rightly of all."[6]

Drake went to London and discussed many possibilities with the authorities. Dom Antonio still wanted to return to Portugal, so Drake talked with him at some length about this. The local gossips were busy reporting all the discussions. Some thought that Drake would go to hunt down stragglers from the Armada. Others expected him to take Dom Antonio to Portugal.[7] Among the possibilities discussed in late September were a raid on Seville and Lisbon to burn the ships there, the capture of Lisbon, and occupation of the Azores.[8] "So many rumors are current," wrote Mendoza's agent in London, "that it is impossible to know how much to believe."[9]

Money, as usual was the great problem. After negotiating with the Sharif of Morocco, Dom Antonio had reason to believe that men and money might be made available to assist with an attempt to put him on the throne of Portugal.[10] Dom Antonio thus became part of England's plan. Even with this promise of assistance, the crown lacked the money to finance another expedition of any considerable size. As usual in such situations, a joint venture evolved. Drake and an old associate from Ireland, John Norris, proposed to raise money privately if the queen would contribute six of her own ships and £20,000 in cash. She was also to encourage Londoners and others to contribute twenty additional ships, and she was to contribute 6,000 or 8,000 soldiers, plus arms and guns of various sorts. In return for all this, the private investors would contribute £40,000 and would attempt to raise additional support in the United Provinces of the Low Countries.[11]

The negotiations resulted in a joint royal commission, authorizing Sir John Norris and Sir Francis Drake to raise and equip an armed force and to enroll private investors who would be able to divide profits that might be made. No enemy was named in the document, but the description was thorough: "And with the same men, provisions, and furniture shipped and embarked do we authorise you jointly and severally, both in your own persons and by such others also whom ye or either of you shall depute, by sea and land to invade and destroy the powers, forces, and the preparations for all such forces made and to be made by all manner of persons and their adherents that have this last year both by sea and by land with their hostile and warly powers and armadas sought and attempted the invasion of our realm of England."[12]

As the work on the expedition progressed, news arrived in London that the survivors of the Armada had begun to arrive in Spanish ports, and the objectives of the expedition began to change. Some forty ships had taken shelter in the port of Santander, while another dozen went to San Sebastián. These ports were far removed from the proposed objectives of Lisbon and the Azores and equally far from the route of the Indies fleet. Elizabeth retained her interest in destroying the ships in these ports, but the private investors and Dom Antonio kept their eyes on Lisbon and the Azores.[13]

Elizabeth probably did not much care whether Dom Antonio was ever placed on the Portuguese throne, and he was not invited to participate in the planning sessions. In spite of this official snub, both Norris and Drake were careful to keep Dom Antonio well informed, and he may very well have made private arrangements with them.[14] He certainly made commitments to the Queen.

First, Dom Antonio promised that he would not enter into any sort of treaty with King Philip without her consent. In addition, he promised to be her ally in any war against Philip. He granted free use of any Portuguese ports to English ships and promised that English merchants could live and trade with complete freedom in Portugal and its possessions. He promised that all English people living in Portugal would be free to practice their religion "in their houses," which is more than was allowed to Spanish subjects in England.[15] All this was academic, of course, for Portugal and its possessions were in the determined grip of the Spanish crown.

Dom Antonio, pretender to the throne of Portugal. Reprinted from
Prince, *Danmonii Orientales Illustres, vol. 1, opp. p. 273.*
Huntington Library 313163, extraillustrated.

Drake invested at least £2,000 of his own money in the enterprise, perhaps more. Norris had also planned to invest in the commercial aspects of
the expedition, but it is not clear that he actually did so. Many of the private investors had significant interests in overseas trade. Sir George Barnes
of the Muscovy Company had been interested in earlier voyages to
Guinea and in Fenton's voyage of 1582. Sir Edward Osborne and Richard
Stapers had been involved in earlier attempts to establish trade with India.
Others, like Robert Flick, hoped to renew their former trade with Portuguese merchants.[16]

With all the preparations for this new command, Drake was spending
more time in London than ever before, and his wife was there as well. No

doubt she accompanied him on many other occasions, but the records are silent about this. In any case, their social life was very active during these days. Don Pedro Valdés proved to be a marvelously popular guest for Richard Drake, attracting visitors from far and near. Drake and Howard visited frequently, as did "many other commanders in the warres and many others of higher and lower degree."[17] Don Pedro must have spoken passable English, for he helped Richard Percyvall compile the first Spanish-English dictionary.[18] At any rate, Elizabeth Drake loved to talk with him. One of the men who served in Drake's house in London said, "My Lady Drake wyfe to Sir Francis did oftentymes lie a long while together at the said Ric[hard] D[rake's] howse at those tymes that the said Don Pedro laie there."[19]

The relationship between Richard Drake and Francis Drake is not clear, though Samuel Pomfret of Esher later recalled that Francis called Richard "his very good cozen" and said that he planned to leave some part of his estate to Richard's son, who was also named Francis.[20] Whether the two had any agreement about the maintenance of the Spanish prisoner is not clear. Thomas Drake later said that Richard Drake had taken charge of Valdés as Drake's agent and that the ransom that Valdés later paid to Richard Drake should have gone to Francis Drake.[21] The queen seems to have considered Valdés to be Francis Drake's prisoner. One day when the queen was strolling with Francis Drake in Saint James Park, they saw Valdés walking further on. The queen turned to Drake and said, "Drake, God give thee ioy of this prisoner," an apparent reference to Drake's hope for ransom.[22] Even so, it is clear that Richard Drake kept the ransom money, which likely means that Francis Drake already had his reward from the treasure carried in the ship.[23]

Because Francis and Elizabeth Drake were spending so much time in London they needed suitable quarters. On 6 November 1588 Drake purchased a long lease on a fine house called the Herbar, close to the river in the parish of Saint Mary Bothaw.[24] A decade and a half later the chronicler John Stow described the neighborhood: "Downe lower have ye Elbow lane. . . . On the East side of this downgate streete, is the great olde house before spoken of, called the Erber, near to the Church of saint Marie Bothaw. . . . It was lately new builded by sir Thomas Pulliam Maior, and was afterward inhabited by sir Francis Drake that famous mariner."[25] The Herbar had once served as a royal residence. Later, but before Drake sailed on his trip around the world, the house was leased to Antonio de Guaras, the merchant who then had charge of Spain's diplomatic affairs in London. The next lessor, Sir Thomas Pulliam, had renovated the building thoroughly, so it probably was very grand when the Drakes occupied it. There were gardens, cellars, outbuildings, and other appurtenances. It was an expensive place, £26 3s 4p annual rent.[26]

About this time Sir John Norris went to the United Provinces to arrange for troops and transports. In a strange bargaining maneuver he took with him 1,500 English troops to add to those engaged in lifting the siege of Bergen-op-Zoom. These were supposed to be used for an immediate lifting of the siege, whereupon it was thought that the grateful Dutch would offer to pay for the use of the troops when they returned to the Norris-Drake expedition. The Dutch refused to do so.[27] Norris also asked the Dutch to provide 2,000 infantrymen and 600 horsemen from the 7,000 men commanded by Lord Willoughby and provided under the Treaty of 1585.[28] Surprisingly, the States General agreed to most of this, giving Norris 2,000 infantry and 200 horse from the force at Bergen-op-Zoom and another 1,000 from those in Ostend. In addition he was to be allowed ten companies of Dutch infantry and eight or ten warships, along with a couple of dozen vessels to transport the troops and supplies.[29]

The arrangements were made with nearly total misunderstanding on each side. This was probably the fault of Norris, who must have misinformed the queen. She wrote to Willoughby that the States General had agreed to release the English troops and to make up for their absence by providing their own replacement garrisons.[30] The Dutch replied that they had made no such agreement and demanded that certain minimum numbers of English troops remain in Bergen and Ostend, as provided in the treaty.[31] By this time Norris had returned to England, and negotiations were handled by Willoughby, who seems to have allowed the States General to think that the queen had refused to meet their conditions. As a result, the promised Dutch warships and guns and most of the Dutch troops and transports were not provided.[32]

Over a period of several months the small fleet of galleons originally proposed to intercept the Indies treasure ships had become an armed invasion of Portugal, with the intention of capturing Lisbon, putting Dom Antonio back on the throne, then sailing on to the Azores. Elizabeth was not pleased with the addition of Dom Antonio, for his plans were not necessarily hers. On the other hand, both Drake and Norris saw genuine military and commercial advantages in making Dom Antonio an important part of the expedition.[33]

In notes containing his reply to proposals put in writing by Norris and Drake, Dom Antonio promised to repay them for their costs in raising the expedition and "to reimburse the said knights and in addition recompense them according to their deserts and the royal liberality always displayed by our predecessors." He agreed to pay the troops, beginning ten days after landing and continuing for three or four months, which was the time limit for the soldiers coming from the United Provinces. He placed limitations on pillage of Portuguese towns but agreed that in other Spanish possessions "the soldiers shall be permitted the utmost freedom according to military usage and custom." The exceptions were "churches and other places of devotion" and "the honour and modesty of women."[34]

In January the Sharif of Morocco offered to provide money, troops, provisions, and the use of his ports in return for a promise from the invaders to attack Spanish territory inside the Strait of Gibraltar. This plan was as unattractive to the queen as the invasion of Portugal. In reply she welcomed the offer of victuals and simply ignored the rest of the proposal.

The queen's own plans called for the destruction of the Armada ships that had returned to Spanish ports around the Bay of Biscay. On 23 February she issued orders to Drake and Norris defining her aims. First, they were to "distress the King of Spain's ships." Secondly, they were to capture the Azores and use them as a base to "intercept the convoys of treasure that doth yearly pass that way." The queen was aware of the plan to put Dom Antonio back on the throne of Portugal, but she thought it unlikely to succeed. For this reason she ordered that priority be given to the destruction of the Spanish fleet: "Before you attempt any thinge either in Portugall or in the said Islands; our express pleasure and comaundment is, that you first shall distress the shippes of warre in Guipuscoa, Biscay, and Galizia and in any other places that appertayne either to the kinge of Spayne or his subiects."[35]

A huge fleet was necessary to transport the 12,000 troops that Drake and Norris hoped to assemble for the campaign, and some port had to be found to use as a base. The problem found a miraculous solution just before the main part of the expedition reached Plymouth. While Drake and Norris were puzzling out some way to fit all their men on so few transports, a fleet of Dutch vessels sailed past Dover and was immediately pressed into use.[36]

Just how many men and ships there were in the expedition is not certain. Before leaving Plymouth, Norris and Drake reported an armed force of 115 companies in 14 regiments, which may have numbered nearly 19,000 officers and men.[37] When the expedition returned in failure, they reported a total force of 13,324 men.[38] In addition to this there were more than a hundred ships, plus numerous smaller vessels.[39]

Expenses far exceeded the original estimates. By the time the fleet reached Plymouth on 19 March, the joint commanders had spent more than £96,000. As an emergency measure they began to issue reserve rations to feed the sailors and soldiers, at the same time sending a request to the queen for more money. In the end Elizabeth, who had originally promised £20,000, provided nearly £50,000.[40]

Shortly before the fleet left Plymouth, the young Earl of Essex, the current favorite of Elizabeth, was itching to join the expedition. Unable to gain the queen's permission, he fled from London and concealed himself on board the *Swiftsure,* where Sir Roger Williams was captain. Williams had served as deputy to Norris, and the queen was certain that he had conspired with Essex, perhaps with the knowledge or approval of Norris and Drake. Angry about the whole affair, she ordered Norris and Drake to put Williams under arrest and to send Essex back to London.[41] Drake and Norris pretended to know nothing about Essex, and Walsingham suppressed the order.[42] The whole episode illustrates the increasing divergence between the queen's objectives and the plans of Norris and Drake. Elizabeth was beginning to entertain serious doubts about the wisdom of the entire operation, but she continued to assume that the fleet would go first to Santander and only later to Lisbon.

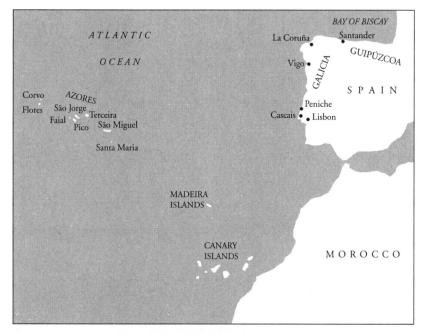

Expedition of Drake and Norris, 1589

Drake and Norris had other plans. On 6 April they wrote to the Privy Council, saying that they had learned that a large fleet was gathered in the ports of Galicia and Portugal, especially at La Coruña—almost always called the Groyne by the English, who were forever on the lookout for a near-equivalent English sound for foreign words. This would be their first stop. They asked that additional supplies be forwarded to them at "Cape Finisterre or the Isles of Bayon."[43]

The expedition sailed from Plymouth on 18 April 1589, with Drake as sea commander and Norris commander of the land forces.[44] The fleet included six ships belonging to the queen. Drake's ship was the *Revenge*, repaired and renovated following the damage of the Armada battles. Norris was commander of the *Nonpareil.* Thomas Fenner was commander of the *Dreadnought* and deputy to Francis Drake. Sir Roger Williams commanded the *Swiftsure,* and Sir Edward Norris commanded the *Foresight.* Following the experience of the Armada campaign, the fleet was divided into five squadrons of sixteen or eighteen ships apiece. Each of the captains commanded one of these squadrons.[45] A sixth ship, *Aid,* was commanded by William Fenner, who served as "rear admiral of the army" but had no additional ships under his command.[46] These six captains served as the council, which was to be consulted "in all matters of importance."[47]

There were other familiar ships and other familiar faces in the expedition. The chaplain was Philip Nichols, presumably Drake's confidant from earlier voyages. The evidence is compelling that he was the same "Mr Nicholes, Preacher of god," chaplain of the fleet, who had entered into discussion with various London divines regarding the moral propriety of aiding the Papist, Dom Antonio.[48] Equally familiar were the names of Wynter and Drake and Hawkins and Norris, all of whom appeared in the lists of officers.[49]

Leaving Plymouth, the fleet sailed straight for La Coruña, reaching the town in five days. La Coruña was divided into two parts. There was a small upper town with a fine fortification, situated atop a high rocky promontory linked to the mainland by a narrow strip of sand. The lower town spread over this neck of sand, with the harbor situated to the south and west.

The harbor did not shelter the 200 ships that Drake expected to find. In fact, it was almost entirely deserted. There were two large merchant vessels, a couple of galleys, a ship loaded with pikes and firearms, and a single galleon, the *San Juan,* which had served as vice admiral of the Armada. Lack of wind kept the English fleet out of the harbor until the next day.[50]

Late in the afternoon of 24 April the first English troops landed inside the bay, about two miles from the town. Within a few hours there were 7,000 English soldiers on the peninsula, but the darkness and a sudden rain prevented them from advancing during the night. The next morning guns were brought up and fired at the lower town. Neither the galleon nor the galleys were able to provide covering fire for the defenders, perhaps because they were not fully manned. With these ships out of the way, the English forces then landed an additional 2,000 troops, attacking the town from the harbor. The fortress brought some guns to bear on the attacking army, but the lower town fell with a loss to the English force of about 20 men. Spanish losses amounted to some 500 soldiers, most of whom "had

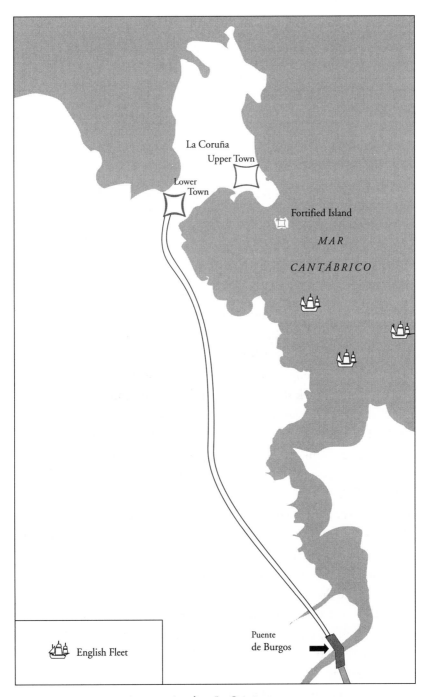

La Coruña
Upper Town

Lower
Town

Fortified Island

MAR

CANTÁBRICO

English Fleet

Puente
de Burgos

Attack on La Coruña

their throats cut" after "falling into the hands of the common soldiers."[51] A few others were taken prisoners.

The upper town was a different matter. The walls were high and the fortifications strong. Norris landed some additional guns, but his gun crews proved to be inexperienced, and they accomplished little. During the assault on the upper town Drake led a diversionary attack on a fortified island under the walls of the main fort. Repeating an exercise that had become familiar in the West Indies campaign, he took 300 men in pinnaces and landed on the island. But the Spanish soldiers proved to be much more stubborn in their defense than the militia at Cartagena, and he was driven off with the loss of 30 men.[52]

An attempt to set a mine under one of the towers was poorly done, and the force of the explosion blew back toward the besiegers. But on 3 May one of the cannons made a breach in the wall, and another mine brought one side of the tower crashing down. The assault troops then ran forward, only to be crushed under debris when another part of the tower fell on them. Still other troops attempted to climb over the rubble before the breach, causing a rock slide that buried the men behind them. When the dust cleared it was obvious that only the top portion of the wall had come down. Half the wall was still standing. Some of Drake's troops were involved in the assault on the wall, apparently led by Captain Anthony Sampson. These soldiers almost lost Drake's ensign in the retreat after the wall collapsed.[53]

These reversals so discouraged the soldiers that the attack on the upper town was not renewed. Other troops had been sent to raid the countryside, and they brought back reports of a relief force of several thousand men marching toward La Coruña. Leaving Drake behind with five regiments to guard the artillery emplacements, Norris immediately took to the field. His 7,000 troops met the Spanish near their encampment at the Puente de Burgos, a narrow bridge about 200 yards long. After a forty-five-minute battle Norris and his troops put the Spanish to flight and captured their baggage.[54]

The two commanders had very little to show for their two-week stay in La Coruña. The galleon had been destroyed by the sailors, who feared that it would fall into enemy hands. The captured arms included "150 brass pieces and a shipload of Spanish pikes, muskets, and calivers." In addition they captured a large quantity of biscuit, dried fish, powdered beef, and other provisions, which helped to make up for the short supplies with which they had left home.[55] Less useful was the huge supply of wine, which the soldiers were drinking like water. The slaughter of the unfortunate captives taken in the lower town was blamed on the wine. When disease spread through the ships, the wine was blamed for that as well.[56]

One deficiency could not be blamed on the wine. That was the lack of siege guns. The queen had originally promised to provide them, then changed her mind, perhaps thinking that the lack of guns would dissuade the leaders from trying to take Lisbon. Captain Anthony Wingfield, who was field commander for the troops under Sir Edward Norris, wrote, "The foure cannons and other pieces of batterie promised to the iourney and not performed might have made Her Maiestie Mistres of the Groyne."[57]

Two days later, on 8 May 1589, the men boarded the ships once more, and the fleet sailed out of the harbor. Essex and Sir Roger Williams, who had sailed with a few ships from Falmouth harbor, managed to join the main fleet near Bayona on 13 May. The fleet then continued to Peniche, a town some forty-five miles north of Lisbon, because Drake had heard that a rich merchant ship from the Indies was harbored there. The ship had gone by the time they arrived, but the decision was made to march from this place toward Lisbon.[58] On 16 May they landed the troops at Peniche, which was defended by a garrison of about 5,000 Spanish soldiers. Eager to show his own ability as a soldier, Essex led the first troops ashore.[59]

After two days of hard fighting, the Spanish garrison abandoned the town of Peniche, and a day later the soldiers in the castle capitulated. The retreat gave the English army command of a bridgehead in Portugal, but the delay at Peniche and the subsequent march to Lisbon ended any hope of a surprise attack on the capital. In fact, Spanish authorities knew that the English were contemplating an invasion by way of Peniche at least two months before the attack actually took place. One of the several informers in the entourage of Dom Antonio had written to Ambassador Mendoza in March

A TRVE
Coppie of a Dif-
courſe written by a Gentleman,
employed in the late Voyage of
Spaine and *Portingale :*

Sent to his particular friend, and
*by him publiſhed, for the better ſatisfacti-
on of all ſuch, as hauing been ſedu-
ced by particular report, haue entred into conceipts tending to the diſ-
credit of the enterpriſe, and
Actors of the
ſame.*

AT LONDON
Printed for Thomas Woodcok,
*dwelling in Paules Churchyard, at
the ſigne of the blacke Beare.*
1 5 8 9.

Anthony Wingfield's account of the 1589 expedition.

to tell him about contingency plans for a Peniche landing followed by a march to Lisbon.[60] Apparently unconcerned about the element of surprise, the English marched off for Lisbon on 18 May. Drake stood on the brow of a hill, watching the troops march by and shouting his best wishes to each commander as he passed. Drake's regiment marched overland with the rest of the troops, while Drake himself took the fleet out of the road and headed for the Tagus River, promising to rejoin the troops nearer Lisbon.[61]

The overland march of the English army was mostly unopposed, the Spanish forces falling back as the English advanced. Still, it was slow work. Many of the men were sick, no one had made advance provision for a baggage train, and the summer heat was more intense than anything the English soldiers had experienced before. Provisions again were in short supply, and Dom Antonio had forbidden the troops to take food from the Portuguese people.

Captain Fenner, who went with the overland party, described the suffering of the men in spare but graphic prose: "Divers of our men fainted by the waye with heat & dyed for want of food & divers moare saved that would have dyed by that honouorable gentleman the earll of essex who commaunded all his stoffe to be cast outt of his carrages & to be laden with those men & gentlemen that fainted."[62] After the first day of short rations, the officers confronted Dom Antonio; "after some expostulations," he agreed to allow them to seize whatever local food supplies they might need.[63]

A few brief skirmishes occurred along the road. On the fourth night Drake's regiment bivouacked in a village near Lores. In the darkness some Spanish soldiers approached, calling out "Viva el rey Don Antonio!" Thinking that they were friends, the English soldiers let them pass. Once inside the lines the Spanish "fell to cut their throats," and killed more than a dozen men before being driven off. It was the same everywhere. People called out "Viva el rey Don Antonio" as the English army passed by, but there was no organized support for the pretender. In fact there was almost no indication of enthusiasm anywhere. As they entered the outskirts of Lisbon on the evening of 23 May, a few beggars cheered for Dom Antonio, but the streets were otherwise deserted.[64] The town itself was heavily fortified and held by a strong garrison. In the harbor were twelve galleys to give added support to the batteries on the walls and to bring supplies from across the river.[65]

The next day more English troops approached the town, intending to occupy the church of San Antonio, which abutted the town wall and might provide a covered base for undermining the fortifications. Seeing what they were up to, the Spanish commander sent his own soldiers to occupy the church, just managing to secure the place before the English soldiers arrived. A strong Spanish detachment then came out of the fortified part of town, marching down the streets and firing as they approached the English advance party. A vicious fight ensued, with heavy losses among the English soldiers, who were tired from six days' march and sick as well. The whole advance party might have been lost had not Norris come forward with the rest of the troops and driven the Spanish soldiers back inside their gates.[66]

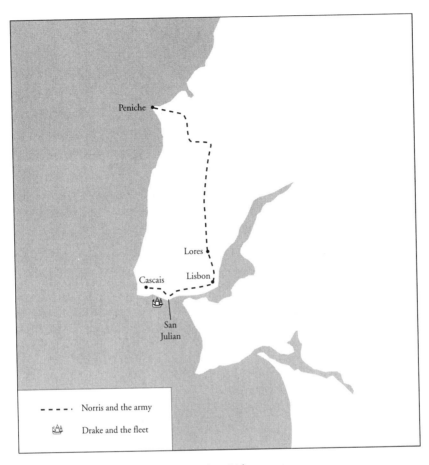

Attack on Lisbon

After this there was not much activity in Lisbon. Dom Antonio sent out messengers on all sides, trying to gather supporters. A few friars came across the river to greet him, promising that others would follow, but no more came. The garrison and the townspeople remained secure behind the walls of Lisbon, firing at the English soldiers, who stationed themselves in houses nearby. With control of the river in Spanish hands, there was no shortage of supplies for the garrison, which received shipments every day from across the way. The English soldiers, short of powder and shot and weakened by wounds and disease, lacked the resources to mount a successful assault on the place. After fruitless arguments with Dom Antonio, who kept predicting the immediate arrival of reinforcements, Norris finally decided to retreat to Cascais.[67]

On the morning of 26 May the English troops began withdrawing from Lisbon. The regiments marched away in good order from the outskirts of town, but some Spanish in the river began to fire at them, and troops of Spanish horse and foot picked off everyone who straggled behind. Lacking a proper baggage train, Norris was unable to bring away the sick and wounded. Those who could not make it under their own power were abandoned at the roadside or left in the houses facing the walls of Lisbon.[68]

From the time Drake had bid them all goodbye eight days earlier, there was no communication between the two commanders. Drake's ships reached Cascais on 20 May, and his troops occupied the town with no trouble the following day. For the next day or so his fleet rounded up stray merchant ships and doubtless spent some time plundering these.[69]

Several strong forts around the castle San Julian guarded the entrance to the Tagus River. For some reason Drake seems to have made no effort to pass the forts or to secure information about the road to Lisbon. Instead he waited at Cascais, and on 25 May he finally received word that Norris was in the outskirts of Lisbon. He reported later that he had intended to move up the river on 27 May and would have done so had not Norris reached Cascais on the evening before.[70]

For the next few days the army and the fleet remained in Cascais, in the forlorn hope that supplies might arrive from England or that Portuguese soldiers might suddenly appear to support Dom Antonio. Neither of these things happened. Envoys sent to the Sharif of Morocco returned with good wishes but no assistance.[71]

On 3 June the captains met in council and decided to leave for the Azores. Two days were required to embark the troops, and another day or so passed before the wind was right for sailing out of the harbor. While they were waiting to get out of the harbor, fifty or sixty hulks arrived from Danzig, Stettin, Rostock, Lübeck, and Hamburg. These ships carried a varied supply of stores for repairing the Armada ships—masts and spars, cables and copper, wax and other materials. The greatest part of the cargo, however, was grain to supplement the poor Andalusian harvest. These vessels were added to the English fleet, and the Dutch ships seized off Dover were allowed to go home.[72]

The wind finally changed on 8 June. Just as the fleet prepared to sail away, word arrived that Essex was to return immediately and that the queen was angry and would send no more aid.[73] Several ships and a small garrison had been left at Peniche to guard the place in case the army was forced to retreat in that direction. A half-dozen ships were dispatched to bring these troops away. These messengers discovered that the English commander of Peniche had already departed. The Spanish took the guns he left behind and killed the abandoned troops.[74]

On 9 June the dozen galleys that had sailed from the river at Lisbon appeared off Cascais, reinforced by nine more from Andalusia. With the English ships scattered across the bay and immobilized by the lack of wind, the galleys moved in to attack. First they picked off three small vessels that were separated from the rest of the fleet. Then William Hawkins's ship *William* appeared, also isolated, and that was captured as well. After another ship or two were captured, a wind came up and allowed the remaining English ships to sail slowly away.[75]

Strangely enough, Drake made no attempt to draw his fleet into the divisions that had been organized before they left Plymouth. This was a perfect chance to employ the tactics that Howard had found so helpful in the Channel, but Drake made no effort to do so. Drake and his captains never practiced squadron maneuvers, and Ralph Lane, the muster-master for the expedition, implied that Drake did not understand the need to do so. In Lane's opinion only divine intervention had saved the fleet from the attack by the galleys.[76]

For several days the wind drove the ships to the north, and some kept going, all the way to England. On 18 June, most of the remaining ships were off the islands of Bayona. Without much discussion the commanders decided to move the fleet upriver and to attack Vigo the next morning. There were only 2,000 men in the landing force, but it was enough. The streets were barricaded, but the town was deserted. When the inhabitants heard that the English army was coming, they scooped up their belongings and abandoned the place. For the rest of the day the army plundered Vigo and the surrounding countryside, though there was little enough to plunder, aside from the usual good supply of wine. On 21 June the troops set fire to the town, then went back to their ships.[77]

Realizing that the army was too weak to resume the campaign, Drake and Norris decided to select the twenty best ships and to man them with the remaining healthy soldiers and sailors. Drake would take this force to the Azores and try to waylay the Indies fleet. Norris, meanwhile, would return to England with the other ships and men. This was quickly accomplished, and on 22 June, Drake sailed off, leaving Norris in the river at Vigo with the remaining thirty-three ships of the fleet. Once out of the river, Drake found himself sailing into a great storm. Over the next day or so he reconsidered his situation and headed for Plymouth. When Norris arrived there on 2 or 3 July, he found Drake in the harbor waiting for him.[78]

News was slow to arrive in England, so the queen was not immediately aware of the extent of the disaster. At first she wrote to welcome Norris and Drake and to congratulate them on the success of the voyage.[79] Then she became aware that dozens of ships had been destroyed or damaged and thousands of men lost to wounds and disease, with nothing to show for the effort. The queen was particularly irate that Drake and Norris had made no attempt to attack Santander or to destroy the Spanish fleet.[80]

The queen was not the only person angry at Norris and Drake. Ralph Lane said that both were arrogant men, "ii soe overweenynge spyryttes contempninge to be advysed and desdaygnynge to aske advyse" from their senior officers.[81] Lane and others who participated in the expedition charged Drake with incompetence or cowardice or both because of his failure to reinforce the army during the attack on Lisbon.[82] This was bad enough, but some men accused Drake of lying later to cover his failure in the Lisbon operation. At first Lane hesitated to criticize Drake: "A counsell of warre woulde never have admitted so longe a marche, as between Pinechia & Lisbon uppon a bare promise of the other Generall his cominge aboute with the shippes, the not performaunce whereof, was evear to be excused by manye reasonable surmises (how untrewe soever) thoughe all we at the lande throughe defaulte thereof, had beine cut in peeces."[83]

Ralph Lane supported this view, though timidly at first. "If wee had not wanted powlder and match, wee had not retired from Lisbourne before Sir France Drakes passinge of Sainct Julyans with the fleete."[84] Later, he blamed the army's failure to take Lisbon more directly on Drake: "We marched towardes Lysboane and uppon a bare warde gyven us by Sir Francis Drake that hee wulde withoute all fayll passe St. Gulians and meete us with the fleete at Lysboane; Th[e] army to have thruste ytselfe most valleantely into the suburbes of the said town; And in the ende of 3 dayes, findinge that he came not and ourselves in wante of Powder and matche to mayntayne a fight halfe a day against the Ennemy."[85]

Dom Antonio did not understand why Drake had failed to come up the river but assumed that he had orders from the queen. "Otherwise," said Dom Antonio, "I am sure Sir Francis would not have failed to do so, for he is full of valour and determined to place me in Lisbon, as also was General Norris."[86] According to one later anonymous commentator, Drake said that he could not go upriver because the channel was too shallow for his ships, and in any case the guns at San Julian would have destroyed any ships that tried to get past.[87] Francis Bacon found "foure great Disfavours of the Voyage" in his analysis of the campaign. One of them was "the Disappointment of the Fleet that was directed to come up the River of Lisbone."[88] Nearly everyone felt that too much time had been wasted in the fruitless siege of La Coruña. And though no one said so at the time, Drake never really tried to intercept the West Indies fleet, which was the original plan and one that surely had some appeal for Drake.

For a time it seemed as if part of the expenses might be paid off from the cargoes seized at Lisbon. Commissioners came to Plymouth and the other ports to take inventory and sell the goods, only to find that the seamen and soldiers had already looted the ships: "It appeareth likewyse, that all those shipps weare taken and brought to Plymouth by the than Generalls Sir John Norris and Sir Francis Drake. But we find by Mr. Ashleys certificat that two-thirds parts of all the lading weare spoiled and imbecilled by the men of warr and marriners at the sea, before they weare brought into Plymouth, and that the one half of that third remayning was purloyned and scattered since the arrival of the shipes in that haven, so that nothing was left aboard the ships but that which was too cumbersome or heavy to carry away."[89] Many of the captains deliberately took their ships and prizes to different ports so that they could loot the cargoes without worry. Norris himself was found to have taken some of the cargo. Nothing was ever alleged against Drake, who had considerable experience from previous voyages and knew how to evade royal audits.

What really annoyed the queen was the idea that Drake and Norris had violated their solemn obligations. "You did sundry times so far forth promise," she wrote at the end of May, "as with oaths to assure us and some of our Council that your first and principal action should be to take and distress the King of Spain's navy and ships in ports where they lay." She recalled every word. "If ye did not ye affirmed that ye were content to be reputed as traitors."[90] This was strong stuff, but there was more to come.

On 27 July the Privy Council ordered Norris and Drake to come to London and bring their records with them.[91] On 23 October they were made to answer several charges "of not having performed the effect of such instructions as they receaved from her Majestie." The first three were general charges, that they had never intended to go to Santander in the first place; that they had had a second opportunity to go there after the attack on La Coruña and had again failed to do so; and finally that they had landed in Portugal without first receiving assurances that the local people were prepared to support Dom Antonio.[92]

The answers were somewhat disingenuous. To the first charge they offered to swear "by theire several oathes" that they had intended to attack the Spanish fleet in Santander, even though "the place of St Anderas was not mentioned in their enstructions." Only a contrary wind had prevented their sailing against the Spanish fleet. After the attack on La Coruña their captains advised against going to Santander because "there was no safe harborough upon that coaste where such a fleet might ryde in safety before the Army should have landed (the wynde being westerly)."[93]

The Lisbon question was a little more complicated. There were "special . . . instructions" to destroy the fleet at Lisbon, and this could not be done without landing the troops. Beyond that, it was impossible to gauge the support for Dom Antonio without landing and asking the local people:

"To the third, they alleage they have a speciall article in theire instructions whereby they wer directed to attempt the destruction of the shippes at Lisbone, which the Generalls founde not performable unless they might have theire forces as well at land as at sea, according to theire opinions delivered to the Lords of the Councell before theire departure out of Englande neyther was there any means to try what party Don Antonio had but onely by landing theire forces. Before which landing they never received any advice out of the countrey."[94]

The fourth charge concerned Drake alone, and he was required to answer it alone. "Sir Francis Drake did not according to his promise repaire with the fleete from Penechia to Lisbone for the dystressing of such shippinge of the enemy as lay within the river aboute Lisbone the wynde servinge well for that purpose at his first arryvall at Cascais, as is testified by sondry of the masters." This was the most serious charge, because the captains who served under Drake supported the allegations. In reply Drake asserted that he first sent agents ashore to determine where the English army was. Then he summoned his captains and determined that the men were too sick to man the ships. Nonetheless, he ordered two-thirds of the ships to be ready on 27 May to sail up to Lisbon. This became unnecessary when Norris came down to Cascais:

> To the fourthe Sir Fra: Drake answeareth that before his
> going up the river toward Lisbone he thought it meete
> to understande in what state our army stood which he
> atteyned unto by setting certeyne Portingalls ashoare at
> Cascais where him selfe also thought fitt to lande as
> required thereunto by the inhabitants of the towne,
> thereby to fynde the enclinacon of the people and what
> partie might be founde for Don Antonio, according to
> the enstructions which done he called a councell of the
> captaynes and masters to advise and resolve for the man-
> ner of his going up to Lisbone. And albeyt he founde by
> their severall reports testified under their hands to be
> showed that the sicknes and weaknes of the marynes an

soldiors was so extreame as they were not abell to handle
the tackle of theire shippes, and that the sea captaynes
and masters were all of opinion as appeareth under
their hands likewise that it was most dangerous for
sondry good reasons to have passed upp with the fleete
yet neverthelesse the said Sir Frauncis, desirous to have
performed as much as in him lay gave order that twoe
third parts of the best shipps of the navy and best
manned should bringe them selves into the further
channell ready to take the first good wynde which came
the very next day being the xxvii at southwest and the
other third parts to stay behinde at Cascais for guard of
the towne and the flyboates which had accordingly proceeded had not Sir John Norreys returned to Cascais
with the Army.[95]

It was a weak reply, incomplete in some places, contradictory in others.
When did his agents go ashore? When did he find out that the army was
attacking Lisbon? If the men were too weak to man the ships, how could
two-thirds of them be taken to Lisbon? The questions were never answered, and the matter was pressed no further.

For a decade Drake's reputation for valor and daring had been, if anything, greater in Europe than in England. After the fiasco in Portugal he
discovered how fickle were his admirers. According to Richard Verstegan,
people were saying that "though the English soldiers fought bravely, their
leaders were craven and the expedition came to nought." He added, "The
proud Drake was mobbed on his return to Plymouth by the women whom
he had made widows."[96] There is no evidence that Drake was really
mobbed in Plymouth, but the quotation shows something of what European gossips were saying.

The expedition to Spain and Portugal should have cleared up any lingering doubt about Drake's ability to command a fleet in battle. If he understood the demands of the position, which is not entirely clear, he cer-

tainly did not demonstrate the patience or the personality of a good commander. He was stubborn and impulsive. He did not lack personal bravery, but he also did not see any reason to risk himself or his ships when
there was no hope of personal gain. At heart Drake was still a pirate. He
understood the capture of lightly defended towns, especially when he
could hold them for ransom. He knew how to surprise merchant vessels
and how to attack lightly armed treasure ships, both of which could yield
enormous booty. But he had no interest in a sustained battle with a large
army, where there was no hope for plunder or ransom.

IV

A PIRATE'S LEGACY

13

The Last Voyage

AT ABOUT THE TIME THAT Norris and Drake appeared in London to defend their conduct in the peninsular expedition, Richard Hakluyt was ready to publish his monumental collection of reports and documents on English voyages of discovery. The title page, already set in type, announced that the contents would include English voyages "in the South Sea to *Chili, Peru, Xalisco,* the Gulfe of *California, Nova Albion* upon the backside of Canada" and other places purportedly visited by Sir Francis Drake. But the book as issued did not include anything about Drake's voyage around the world, and that omission has been the subject of great controversy ever since.

Hakluyt said something about the exclusion in his introduction. He had already prepared a text, he said, "wherein I must confesse to have taken more than ordinary paines, meaning to have inserted it in this work." But he did not use the text, and he explained why in more than ordinarily obtuse Elizabethan prose: "Being of late (contrary to my expectation) seriously delt withall, not to anticipate or prevent another mans paines and charge in drawing all the services of that worthie Knight into one volume, I have yeelded unto those my friends which pressed me in the matter, referring the further knowledge of his proceedinges, to those intended discourses."[1] What, exactly, does this mean? Drake scholars have puzzled about it for four centuries, trying to determine who Hakluyt's "another man" was and whether someone was really writing a biographical study that drew "all the services of that worthie Knight into one volume."

Almost certainly the other author was Philip Nichols, the chaplain who went with Drake on the West Indies voyage of 1586–87 and may have been with him in the Iberian campaign as well.[2] Drake and Nichols were good friends, and Nichols had the ability to write a long narrative, while Drake did not. Drake admitted this in an open letter that he addressed to the queen. This letter, dated 1 January 1592, was used as an introduction for Nichols's book about the earlier West Indies voyage. In it Drake complained that attempts to publish accounts of his exploits "hitherto have been silenced."[3] Apparently they were still silenced in 1592–93, for the Nichols book was not published until well into the next century.

The work originally undertaken by Nichols probably was a book or a series of books recounting all of Drake's voyages, including his recent expedition to Spain and Portugal. Drake wanted something published to clear his name and restore his reputation. Even though much of Drake's open letter to the queen was probably written by Nichols, we can hear Drake's own words in at least one sentence. "I have thought it necessary myself," he said, "as in a card to prick the principal points of the counsel taken, attempts made and success had, during the whole course of my employment in these services against the Spaniard."[4]

The book by Nichols, *Sir Francis Drake Revived,* finally appeared in 1626. Containing some very brief and inexact remarks about Drake's early life, this work was intended to be the first part of the complete Drake biography, or at least as much as Francis Drake wanted us to know. The second part was published in 1628 under the title *The World Encompassed by Sir Francis Drake.* The third part was never completed, and the first two parts were not published during Drake's lifetime.

If Nichols had not started his work on the Drake biography before 1589, he was almost certainly put to work on it as soon as Drake returned from the peninsular expedition. From the little that is known about Nichols's life it appears that he had the time to do this writing after Drake returned from Lisbon that summer of 1589. Nichols studied and taught at Cambridge University from 1569 to 1583.[5] After that he was involved with Drake in the voyage to the West Indies and the expedition to Cádiz. He may have been the Mr. Nicholes who was fleet chaplain on the most recent expedition to Lisbon and the Spanish coast, and perhaps he was with Drake on the *Revenge* during the Armada battles.

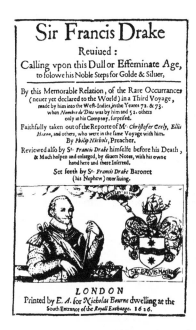

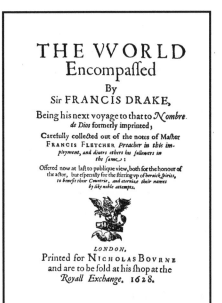

Two volumes published by Drake's nephew from manuscripts prepared by Philip Nichols.

For his story of the earlier voyage to the West Indies, Nichols made use of notes and journals kept by men who went with Drake on the voyage. The title page of *Sir Francis Drake Revived* informs us that it was taken from reminiscences of Christopher Ceely, Ellis Hixon, and other men who were on the voyage with Drake. There were even a few additions made by Drake, for the title page refers to "divers Notes, with his owne hand here and there Inserted." Nichols probably finished the manuscript by late 1591, when he accepted an appointment as rector of Falmouth, near Plymouth. After a few months at Falmouth, Nichols moved to Wembworthy, and he later had other more important ecclesiastical posts in Devon.[6] No doubt the last thing he wrote for the book was the open letter to the queen, which Francis Drake signed on 1 January 1592. Drake was almost certainly still out of favor with the queen at this time, so permission to publish was not granted.

The second volume was not so far along. Nichols may just have begun to take it in hand when he and Drake sought permission to print the first volume. Rejection of the first volume may have discouraged Nichols from finishing work on the second. All of this is conjecture; it is impossible to know with certainty.[7] In any case, the manuscript of the second book remained incomplete, and Drake's nephew Francis had to rewrite it extensively before he published it in 1628.[8] After failing to secure permission to publish the first volume, Nichols was perhaps discouraged from starting work on a third volume, which would logically have included the West Indies voyage of 1586–87, the battles with the Spanish Armada, and the expedition to Spain and Portugal.

Out of favor he may have been, but Drake was not in seclusion. He and Elizabeth stayed in London until the end of December, then went to stay with his wife's family at Coombe Sydenham in Somersetshire. This was not an entirely pleasant visit, for Drake had hurt his back, and the pain would not go away. Back pain sufferers will sympathize with his description of the symptoms: "Beinge touched with some greif before cominge out of london with a straine I tooke in quenching the Fire I found my travaile soe muche increase the paine as I had much to do to recover Sir George Sydenhams house where I have ever since contynued and in my chamber for the most parte. . . . I do yet find little ease, for that my payne not tareing in one place is fallen more into my leggs and maketh me verie unable to stande without muche greif."[9]

Back pains come and go, and Drake eventually got over this one. By late April the Privy Council had word that the Spanish government had preparations in hand for another naval assault on the English coast. The closest and most likely places for an attack were in Devon and Cornwall, and Plymouth was the best port in the area. The council wrote to Drake on 23 April 1590, telling him to confer with the earl of Bath and the mayor of Plymouth and find out what was necessary to put the defenses in order. The council was especially interested in learning "how and by what meanes they may sett their shippes on fire if they come in to the porte of Plimouth."[10]

The news reached Plymouth that an invasion was imminent—so certain that many people decided to gather up their belongings and leave. Amid this ridiculous panic, Drake and his wife came to stay in town for a while, thus calming most of the panic-stricken people. This visit may be reflected in a notation in the Plymouth municipal records: "5£ for a supper for Drake and his lady and other Justices"—justices of the peace who had charge of local militia musters.[11] As a result of this affair, Drake, the mayor, and the rest of the masters and townsmen petitioned the council for a new fort to defend the entrance to Plymouth harbor.[12]

Some additional armaments were added to the old castle, very likely with Drake's advice and assistance. Four iron cannons and seven brass pieces were added to the defenses, and the gun platforms were newly timbered. The roof on one tower of the castle was sheathed with lead to make it more fire resistant. A new gate was built and installed and ordered to be shut every night. The fortifications on Saint Nicholas Island were also strengthened.[13]

Rebuilding the fortification was a long-term project, requiring a great deal of money—£5,000, according to one estimate. To provide the funds the town was authorized to levy a tax on the pilchard fishery.[14] It was not an easy tax to collect. The Cornish fishermen began landing their catch at Cawsan Bay, thus evading the tax. At one point Drake and several others were sent there by the Privy Council to enforce the order, but problems remained.[15] In the end Drake and other landowners were required to contribute their own funds to help meet the cost of construction.[16]

In November 1590 Drake became acting deputy lieutenant for the district and as such was ordered to confer with the earl of Bath regarding measures to be taken to counter new Spanish advances against France and new threats to Devon and Cornwall. Sir John Hawkins was ordered to take navy ships under his command to Plymouth, and Drake was directed to assist him in refitting the ships there. He was also told to send out a pinnace to scout the coast of Normandy and report back. Finally, he was instructed to ensure that the harbor defenses, especially the provisions for making fire ships, were ready.[17] He complained about the great expense that he had incurred in all these preparations and was invited to submit a bill.[18]

During these months, while Drake was traveling between London and Plymouth on official business, hostilities seemed to be on the point of renewal, and all of Drake's old comrades were at sea capturing foreign ships "by waye of reprysall." John Hawkins was out with six galleons, and others were taking similar action.[19] He and his friends were not greatly concerned with nationality. If a cargo was rich and the ship foreign, it was likely to be seized. Many neutral merchants complained to the Privy Council, and as a result Drake was named "Commyssyoner for the Causes of Reprysall" to settle disputes between the captains and the merchants who owned the ships and cargoes. This was closely akin to putting the fox among the chickens.[20]

These were boom years for English pirates. Queen Elizabeth and her ministers had managed to organize the West Country pirates into a body of adventurers with a "peculiar legal status."[21] For some years the High Court of Admiralty, where Drake's friend Julius Caesar sat as judge, issued letters of reprisal, a hundred or more every year.[22] These documents allowed captains to seize cargoes belonging to Spanish merchants or other traders from hostile countries. There were rules, of course, one of which was that the cargoes had to be inventoried by royal officials, for piracy was not only an instrument of war but a means of taxation as well.[23] Drake had spent most of his life as a pirate, and even when he was on official expeditions, he never lost an opportunity for taking a foreign ship as a prize. No doubt this explains his appointment as commissioner.[24]

Among the dozens of prize ships and cargoes that appeared in Plymouth during Drake's term as commissioner, one or two were marvelously rich. Late in 1590 a certain Captain Davies brought back a "Venetian Argosey" filled with expensive goods. Drake and his friends made an inventory as they were ordered to do, but somehow they forgot to mention the arrival of the ship to Sir John Gilbert, who was vice admiral of Devon. In making the inventory, they somehow allowed Davies to keep 200 bags of pepper, a barrel of mace, and "divers juells and other thinges of great value." After many letters back and forth, Drake and his associates managed to put their hands on 135 bags of pepper, 62 chests and 3 butts of sugar, and 63 elephant tusks, not the sorts of goods it would be easy to overlook. Some Devon men, found with the pepper in their warehouses, had it rebagged and newly labeled and refused to surrender it to the authorities. Disputes were still continuing in 1593.[25]

A short time after the appointment was made, John Hawkins and Martin Frobisher came to Plymouth with a Dutch ship full of the scarlet dye cochineal. Upon appeal by the owners, Drake ordered Hawkins and Frobisher to return the cargo. This was done, but as soon as the ship left port on its way to London, Hawkins seized the ship and cargo again and brought them back to Plymouth. This was too much. Drake and his confederates were ordered by the Privy Council to give the cargo back once more.[26]

One of the most valuable ships taken during this time was a Portuguese carrack named the *Madre de Dios,* said to be the largest ship afloat.[27] This ship was crammed full of gold, diamonds, rubies, jewels, silks, musk, ambergris, and pepper from the East Indies. Following the time-honored custom among unpaid pirate crews, the seamen plundered the vessel thoroughly before it reached Dartmouth. The prize was so rich that various special commissioners were sent to help with the inventory. Sir Walter Raleigh was even released from jail to give a hand.[28] The seamen removed everything they could carry, and merchants came from London to purchase their booty.[29] After all this the commissioners still counted £150,000 as the value of the cargo.[30]

During the early 1590s Francis Drake seems to have spent most of his time in Plymouth and at his house at Buckland. From time to time he was called to London on official business. At least once he was able to combine personal business with a favor for the queen. A certain Edmund Nevill, imprisoned in the Tower, claimed a title of nobility. In support of this case Nevill tried to gain possession of the manor of Clavering and other lands that the queen held "by the attayndor of Margarett Countesse of Salisburie." While he was in jail Nevill was in no position to press his case against the queen, so he brought "an action of trespasse in her Majesty's Benche against a servante of Sir Francis Drake, knighte, for the tryinge of the tytle" to his house in London, which was only a small part of the property involved in the case. The details were very involved, and the Privy Council suggested that the simplest solution would be to allow Nevill to proceed with a suit involving only the house to which Drake held the lease. To this, they said, Sir Francis Drake was "not unwilling."[31] The decision in the case seemingly was against Nevill and for Drake, who quickly sold the lease on the property to Alderman John Banninge.

With Plymouth viewing the pilchard fishery tax as a source of income, it was only natural that fishermen should decide to go elsewhere and avoid paying Plymouth taxes. Drake and John Gilbert accused four Cornwall fishermen of evading council orders, and in December 1590 they were all summoned before the council for a hearing. As a result, the previous orders were rescinded and new arrangements made. This time there was a commission of six, three from Devon and three from Cornwall, with Drake as one of the commissioners for Devon. Even so, when the pilchard season opened once more in 1591, the dispute flared up anew. There was really no way to resolve the dispute to everyone's satisfaction. In August 1593 Drake wrote to the Privy Council, complaining that the pilchard tax was still impossible to collect. The official response was a "placard" announcing "to al the Customers of the portes that no entries shal from henceforth be taken until the impozicions be dulie paied."[32]

There was a reason for the construction of new fortifications at Plymouth. War with Spain continued. One of the Spanish prisoners who was released in early 1592 reported to his king that Drake had been called to London to confer with the queen about measures to be taken to assist the French king. Several ships were to be fitted out and sent to the coast near Rouen.[33]

Additional steps were taken to ensure that the justices of the peace were men of unquestionable loyalty. In October 1592 the Privy Council ordered Drake and other deputy lieutenants to administer oaths of allegiance to all JPs, especially requiring them to take the oath of supremacy. This was a move to flush out any Catholics who might be serving as justices. In addition to taking the oaths, all justices had to attend a church where the Book of Common Prayer was used. No one could be a JP unless every member of his family attended such services.[34] Drake and the others took their oaths at Exeter castle on 24 November 1592.[35]

When parliament met on 19 February, Drake was there once more as a member for Plymouth. The main purpose of the parliamentary session was finance. Specifically, the queen wanted to fit out a new fleet for renewing the war against Spain. Sir Robert Cecil urged the members to approve three subsidies in support of the fleet, and Drake naturally spoke in favor of the measure. A brief summary of his speech has been preserved, one of the shortest in the session, and the only parliamentary speech by Drake that seems to have been recorded: "He described the k. of Spaynes strength and his crueltie where hee came, and wished a ffranke ayde to bee yeilded to withstand him, and hee agreed to the three subsidies."[36] After several members spoke on the subject, a committee was named to consider the bill. Drake was appointed to serve on the committee and was no doubt active in that capacity. On 2 March Sir George Cary described the reason for Drake's interest: "The Spaniard already hath sent seven thousand Pistolets of Gold into Scotland to corrupt the Nobility, and to the King twenty thousand crowns now lately were dispatched out of France into Scotland for the levying of three thousand, which the Scottish Lords have promised; and the King of Spain will levy thirty thousand more and give them all Pay. Her Majesty is determined to send Sir Francis Drake to Sea to encounter them with a great Navy."[37]

As before, Drake served on various other parliamentary committees. One of the first such appointments was made on 22 February, when he was named to the "Committee for the Liberties and Priviledges of the Members of the House and Their Servants." The immediate purpose of the committee was the resolution of a dispute about the election of Richard Hutton, but there were other disputes as well during the session.[38]

Somewhat more interesting was a committee convened after Cecil spoke of the need to provide relief for the poor and to assist sick and wounded soldiers and sailors. This might have seemed like a proposal that none could oppose, but many members thought that such aid would encourage rogues and louts who loafed about the countryside. In the end each member was required to contribute to a relief fund, with members of the Privy Council contributing thirty shillings, knights twenty shillings, and burgesses five shillings. Extremely disappointed at the outcome, Cecil withdrew the proposal, but a committee was named to oversee the "dispensing of the contribution of both Houses collected toward the relief of poor maimed Souldiers," and Drake was a member of the committee.[39]

In addition to some brief remarks about the subsidies, Drake also spoke on "the first Bill exhibited against recusants," but his words were not put on the record.[40] Drake was probably not an important parliamentary leader. He was named to some committees with a nautical interest, including one to consider "An Act for the avoiding of deceit used in making and selling twice laid Cordage" and another to consider "Salted Fish and salted Herrings."[41]

After the session ended on 10 April, Drake returned to Buckland, accompanied by visitors. Richard Drake of Esher had been acting as jailer-host for Don Pedro de Valdés, who was ransomed in February 1593 after nearly five years in rather luxurious captivity. His ransom amounted to £3,550, more than half of which was paid by Edward Winter, an English merchant held in Spanish captivity. The ransom paid by Valdés was small compared with the £2,500 demanded by Richard Drake for his upkeep.[42] Because Francis Drake had contributed at least a thousand toward the maintenance of Valdés, it seems likely that a good part of this sum, if not all, went to him.[43] None of this is very clear, despite lengthy argument about it after Drake's death.

Two of the parties to the argument were Richard Drake and his son Francis, who were Francis Drake's guests at Buckland that spring. Francis and Elizabeth Drake had no heirs, and Richard seemingly took this opportunity to broach the idea that his own son should be a principal heir. The matter was left undecided, though Richard and his son came away with the impression that their suggestion was well received.[44]

While he was in London, Drake completed negotiations to sell his house there. On 28 May 1593 Alderman John Banning paid Drake £1,300 for the remaining portion of his seventy-one-year lease.[45] No doubt Drake had several reasons for selling the place. He had used the house only intermittently, because his presence was required in Plymouth for long stretches of time. With Don Pedro de Valdés gone, Elizabeth Drake's interest in visiting London may have diminished. One likely reason for the sale is that Drake needed cash to support a new expedition against the Spanish Indies.

The plan made in 1593 never became effective, though a warrant was issued to allow Drake to take three of the queen's ships and twenty merchant ships on his expedition.[46] From the very beginning this new expedition involved another joint command, Francis Drake and John Hawkins. Almost as soon as the warrant was issued, hostilities in France grew more involved, and the West Indies plans were suspended for a few months. Frobisher, Norris, and other English captains took English ships and soldiers to raise the Spanish siege of Brest. This was finally accomplished in a furious assault on the Spanish position. The English troops won the day but lost Frobisher, who was mortally wounded in the attack. This ended for a time the Spanish threat to France and improved England's naval position as well. In 1594 the plan to send Drake and Hawkins to Panama was renewed.[47]

So much of the planning was done without adequate record keeping that it is impossible to know all the details. The capture of Panama was part of the original plan, though it is difficult to imagine that Drake and Hawkins intended to hold it permanently.[48] A large land army would be required to take Panama, and the Earl of Essex used his influence to help recruit proper commanders for the force.[49]

There was no way to pay for such an army except by making the expedition a joint-stock venture. The queen contributed £30,000.[50] Drake and Hawkins each invested £10,000. Soldiers and sailors were promised shares of the plunder instead of salaries, and it proved difficult to attract men in this way. Private ship owners received shares for their own vessels, but the total amount invested by all parties was probably not much more than £60,000.[51]

In addition to her cash investment, the queen also contributed six of her own ships. The assignment of the ships to the expedition was officially performed in her commission to Hawkins and Drake, dated 29 January 1594 (1595 by the current calendar). The *Garland,* at 660 tons, became the flagship of Sir John Hawkins. The *Defiance,* at 550 tons, was Drake's flagship. The other royal ships were the *Hope,* the *Bonaventure,* the *Adventure,* and the *Foresight.*[52]

By the time the commission was issued it appeared that voluntary enlistments would not be sufficient to support the new expedition. For this reason the commanders were given the authority to impress sailors, carpenters, gunners, soldiers, "and other artificers and seafaringe men as shalle be suffi-ciente to furnishe all the shippes."[53] In the end some 2,500 men accompa-nied the expedition to the Indies, about a thousand of them soldiers.[54]

As in the previous expeditions, all of the preparations for this new voy-age to the Indies were reported in detail to King Philip. One of the first re-ports sent home by Don Pedro de Valdés after his release from captivity was information about Drake's preparations to take a new fleet to the In-dies. According to Valdés, Drake planned to capture Puerto Rico and to establish a base there for further attacks on Havana and San Juan de Ulúa. The plans continued to change as the time for departure came closer. Just before Valdés departed for Brussels he heard that Drake and Hawkins planned to occupy the island of Curaçao. From this place they hoped to command the route between Nombre de Dios and Cartagena and to be able to attack the Spanish fleets coming from New Spain and Tierra Firme.[55] In the face of the Spanish threat to Brittany this plan was aban-doned for a time. The new plan formulated in the winter of 1594 envi-sioned a march across the isthmus to capture Panama. News of the prepa-rations reached Spain early in the new year, and a warning was issued to the governors of Santo Domingo, Havana, and Panama.[56]

This was part of a renewed Spanish determination to take whatever steps might be necessary to defend the Indies. There was a new mood in Spain, reflected in an expanded military presence in the Spanish colonies. Drake's raids of the mid 1580s had caused great embarrassment to the Spanish crown and had helped to convince officials that additional money had to be spent on the defense of the colonies. As early as 1587 there were discussions about building and maintaining a special fleet to defend the Indies from Drake and his fellow pirates.[57] The destruction of the ships in the port of Cádiz brought similar demands for renewal of the fortifications in that port.[58] Re-sponding to these demands, Spanish officials began building and equipping defensive installations in all the places that pirates liked to attack.

They also began to carry the war to the shores of England. By the time Drake's new fleet was ready, a Spanish raiding party had already descended on Cornwall, burning Penzance and other towns. Rumor had it that an-other fleet would soon invade Ireland, and still another would come to

England the following year. In the face of this threat Elizabeth ordered Drake and Hawkins to return home within six months. Before they left European waters the two commanders were to try to intercept the Spanish treasure fleet heading home from the West Indies. In the meantime, they were to determine whether a Spanish fleet was in fact headed for Ireland and if so to destroy it. Obviously, Elizabeth had little confidence in their plan for taking Panama, and she told them, "Your own delays hath made your journey now so notorious (yea in particular to the Spaniard)."[59]

Drake and Hawkins immediately fired off messages of protest, and the order was rescinded. What changed the queen's mind was the news, conveyed by Drake and Hawkins, that a Spanish treasure galleon had taken refuge in the harbor at San Juan de Puerto Rico, dismasted and rudderless. The partners argued that they should take this ship before going to Panama. "It lieth in our way," they said, "and will no way impeach us."[60]

This was Drake the pirate speaking—older, slower, but still interested in seeing what plunder he could take. In 1591 and again perhaps in 1594 Drake posed for paintings by Marcus Gheeraerts the Younger. These portraits show a portly man with a gray beard and a receding hairline. He was a man in his fifties, no longer fit, too old to lead troops in the field. If there was a fire of impetuosity and adventure in his eye, the artist did not capture it. John Hawkins was even older, slower, and less robust. Neither man had ever shown a capacity for sharing authority.

The officers and men of the expedition were puzzled about the joint command. They saw that their leaders were men of conflicting temperaments, both used to giving orders and being obeyed. Thomas Maynarde, a land captain who sailed on the *Foresight,* described their incompatibility in a classic verbal portrait:

> Sir Fra[ncis] Drake was named generall. . . . A man of
> great spirit and fitt to undertake matters, In my poore
> oppinion better able to conduct forces and discreetly to
> governe in conductinge them to places where service
> was to be done, then to comande in the execution
> thereof. But assuredly his very name was a greate terror

Thomas Maynarde's description of Drake and Hawkins. BL Add. MS 5,209, fols. 2v-3.

to the enemie in all those partes. . . . But . . . his selfe-
willed and peremptorie comand was doubted. And that
caused her maiestie (as should seeme) to joyne Sir John
Haukins in equal comission. A man ould and Warie
entringe into matters with so laden a foote that the others meate woulde be eaten before his spit could come to
the fire, men of so different natures and dispositions
that what the one desireth the other would commonly
oppose against.[61]

If any joint command ever had a chance for success, this was not the one.
Still, Drake employed some of his usual measures in preparing for the trip.
Always reluctant to sail anywhere without pilots who knew the local har-
bors, Drake somehow managed to recruit two Portuguese pilots from the
Azores who knew how to navigate in the West Indies.[62]

Drake's will is dated simply "The   daye of August." PRO Prob. 11,
vol. 87, f. 2d.

Before leaving Plymouth Francis Drake had a will written out. Under the terms of the marriage agreement, Elizabeth Drake had a life interest in Buckland, so he left her the household goods and furniture as well, except the silver, which would have to be sold to pay his debts. His brother Thomas received a house in Plymouth, and others received lesser things. For some reason he did not date or sign the will. Instead, he bundled up all the papers and took them on the voyage, apparently hoping to delay making final decisions about the disposition of his property.[63]

On 28 August 1595 the fleet left Plymouth harbor. There were two squadrons of twenty-seven ships in all. Taking the usual route south to the Canaries, the two commanders called their first conference on 3 September when they were off Cabo San Vicente. Drake, having skimped on expenditures as usual, sailed without sufficient victuals for all the men in his fleet. He asked Hawkins to relieve him of some of his men, and Hawkins refused. There were bitter recriminations, and in a later meeting Drake suggested that they attack either one of the Madeiras or Gran Canaria to get more supplies, as well as plunder. No doubt Hawkins could see the old impulsive Drake at work here, and he again refused to deviate from the original plans. After additional argument, during which Drake said that he would go to the Canaries alone if necessary, Hawkins finally relented.

On 25 September the fleet was at Las Palmas on the island of Gran Canaria. Intending to land his troops from the pinnaces, Drake first fussed around in the bay for several hours, placing markers where the boats should go ashore. When the troops finally tried to go ashore, they found the surf too high. Defenders on shore were entrenched in preparation to oppose his landing, and artillery fire spread confusion among his boats. In the face of this opposition he abandoned the attempt. Four men were lost in the action.[64]

The following day Drake took his fleet to the other side of the island, and during the next two days all of the ships took on water. On 28 October the captain of one of the shore parties took his men to a nearby hill, presumably for a better view. There the soldiers were set upon by shepherds, armed only with staves, who killed several Englishmen, wounded the rest, and took the survivors into custody. One of the prisoners was the surgeon from the ship *Solomon.* He revealed the whole plan of the voyage to his captors, though it was already well known from other information sent out of England.[65] This was not an auspicious beginning. The Spanish authorities immediately dispatched a fast ship to warn the treasure fleet in Puerto Rico. Other vessels were sent to Spain carrying the same warning, and after some delay a fleet was dispatched from Lisbon to intercept the English ships.[66]

After the dismal interlude at Gran Canaria, Drake and Hawkins took their fleet directly to the West Indies. They reached the Lesser Antilles on 26 October and came to anchor at Guadalupe three days later. The next day lookouts on two small English barks, the *Delight* and the *Francis,* which had lagged behind the rest of the ships, saw the fleet of Don Pedro

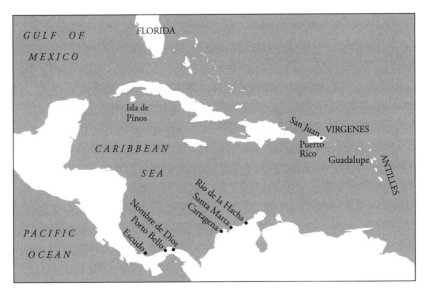

Drake and Hawkins in the West Indies, 1595–96

Tello de Guzman in the distance and mistook the Spanish ships for the English fleet.[67] Once they realized their error, it was too late. The Spanish ships gave chase and captured the *Francis.* Though the other ship escaped, the crew was taken off the *Francis,* and the little ship was left "driving in the sea."[68]

Tello de Guzman quickly determined that the destination of the fleet was Puerto Rico, and he hastened there to give the warning. The crew of the *Delight* witnessed the capture of the *Francis* and sailed off to warn Drake and Hawkins. There are two versions of what happened after this. According to Maynarde, Drake suggested that they immediately sail for San Juan and try to capture the port before the news arrived. Hawkins demurred, saying that it would be better to spend a few days putting the fleet in order. Maynarde said that Drake did not dispute the decision because Hawkins was ill and he did not wish to disturb him further.[69]

The other version comes from Spanish prisoners captured by Drake and later released. Their information came from other members of Drake's expedition, who said that Drake wanted to capture the fragatas before Tello could reach Puerto Rico. Hawkins, they said, "did not want to go after the

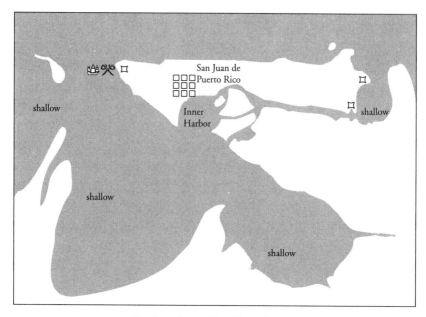

San Juan, Puerto Rico, November 1595

fragatas from Guadalupe, though he knew that they had captured the ship and were headed for Puerto Rico."[70]

In fact, both versions may be mistaken. The English fleet was in no condition for a fight. All the guns were stowed belowdecks, and it was probably not possible to get them mounted while trying to pursue Tello's fragatas. Whether Drake and Hawkins agreed on this matter or not, it is clear that they spent ten days in Guadalupe, bringing the guns up on deck and preparing their pinnaces for the attack on San Juan.[71] During this time, on 3 November, Tello reached the island with the news of Drake's arrival, and the military authorities began a storm of preparations. San Juan was situated on an island at the mouth of the bay. During the previous decade extensive work had been carried out to protect the entrance to the harbor. The fortifications were far from complete, but work had progressed sufficiently that with everyone mobilized the island people could put up a stout defense.[72]

Drake and Hawkins were also preparing for war. The pinnaces were launched on 3 November, and the next day the soldiers and seamen boarded the ships once more. On the fifth of the month the fleet set sail but was becalmed within sight of land. Next morning the wind blew up a gale, and the fleet had good sailing for the next three days. On the afternoon of 8 November they anchored "in a sounde in the Virgines northe northeaste from Santa Cruse." Next morning bright and early the men were mustered on shore and then reboarded. Here the captains were called into conference, after which they set sail once more. On Monday morning the eleventh they anchored off Puerto Rico, where John Hawkins died.[73]

While standing at anchor off the northern shore of San Juan, the ships suddenly came under heavy fire from the shore guns. This was an unfortified part of the island, but when the Spanish commander saw the English ships at anchor, he had guns pulled into position and began bombarding the English ships. Aboard the *Defiance,* Drake and his officers were eating supper. One or two shots came through the cabin, killing Drake's friend Brute Brown and badly wounding Sir Nicholas Clifford, who died that night of his wounds.[74] According to a story told much later Drake himself had a miraculous escape. The stool on which he sat was shot from under him, just as he was raising a cup of beer.[75] This was taken as a sign to leave for a better anchorage, which they did.

Faced with this fierce resistance, the captains were called together on Friday, 13 November, to suggest a new course of action. Their decision was to mount an immediate attack on the fragatas in the harbor. That night Drake led his ships under the guns of Morro castle, sailing into the harbor with thirty pinnaces and small boats. The men, the guns, and the ships battled fiercely for an hour or more. Cannon fire from the fort lit the harbor with flashes of light, while Drake's men hurled fire bombs at the anchored Spanish ships. As each vessel caught fire, the crews quickly put out the blaze. Finally one Spanish ship burst into flames, and the fire could not be stopped. The flames gave the gunners on shore clear targets, and they finally drove the English ships from the harbor.[76]

Losses were great on both sides. The anonymous author of the Munich log said that the Spanish gunners "killede many of our men." The Spanish admitted about forty men dead and many wounded but claimed to have killed at least two hundred English soldiers and sailors. If the English losses were not that great, they were serious.[77] In a meeting on the morning of 14 November, one of Drake's officers, Thomas Baskerville, advised him that another attack like the one the night before "would hazard the whole action." Drake agreed, saying, "I will bringe thee to twenty places foure more wealthye and easier to bee gotten."[78] Sir John Hawkins and Sir Nicholas Clifford were buried at sea on 14 November while the fleet was anchored off Puerto Rico. They next day the English set sail for the western end of the island.[79]

Not satisfied to leave without having the last word, Drake sent a letter to the Spanish commander, Pedro Xuarez:

> Colonel Governor of Puerto Rico.
>
> Understanding your lordship to be the principal gentleman and soldier, I write this brief letter, so that you may understand that I have always and on all occasions dealt with the Spanish nation with much honor and clemency, granting liberty to all its people, not to just a few, but to many. For example, at the time that our men set fire to the fragatas, they rescued some Spanish from the fury of the fire, doing them no harm after their capture, but treating them in the best tradition of warfare.
>
> From them I have learned that the capitana of Don Pedro Tello captured a small vessel from our armada, with twenty-five or more Englishmen, treating them well, according the best usages of war. I accept this as the usual arrangement, but if it should turn out otherwise, I will do what I have never found in myself to do. Still, as there are soldiers and gentlemen in that city, I do not doubt that our people will be treated well and freed according to the best principles of war. This I hope and pray.

I remain always at the service of your excellency,
except in the current matter.

From the capitana of the Holy Majesty, the Queen of
England, my Lady, on 23 November 1595, English style.

Francis Drake[80]

In a very roundabout way, Drake was asking for good treatment for the
English who were in Spanish hands, promising the same treatment for his
own prisoners and implying that he was willing to free the Spanish sailors
in exchange for his own. He was also continuing his practice of polishing
the image of piracy that dogged the reports of his actions.

Surprise was no longer possible anywhere in the Caribbean. Drake left
Puerto Rico on 15 November. The next day the Spanish messengers arrived
at Cartagena with the news. A week later the word of his arrival reached
Panama.[81] Nevertheless, Drake took his time on the crossing. On 19 November he anchored his fleet in Bahía San Germán, at the southwest tip of
Puerto Rico. Going ashore, the men spent the next four days repairing the
ships and building four additional pinnaces.[82]

The fleet left San Germán on the afternoon of 24 November and four
days later had a landfall at Curaçao. On 30 November the ships anchored
under Cabo de la Vela, and the next day they were at Rio de la Hacha.[83]
Anchoring in the bay, Drake saw a town not much different from the one
he had seen in 1568. It was a poor place of about fifty houses. Warned in
advance, the citizens had gone, taking their valuables with them. Perhaps
hoping that something would turn up, Drake decided to remain here for
a bit, demanding a ransom before he would leave. He could hardly have
hoped for much in such a town, but it was also a good place to rest the
men and refit the ships. With the help of some cooperative citizens and a
few slaves his men scoured the countryside, locating some caches of buried
goods and a few pearls from the local pearl fishery. The citizens finally
agreed to pay a small ransom in pearls, but the amount delivered was not
what had been agreed upon. The governor told Drake that all of their negotiations had only been a means of delaying him until help might arrive.
He refused to pay any more, and that was the end of it. Drake then told

his men to set fire to anything within reach that would burn, and on the night of 19 November they left.[84]

The next day they were in the small settlement of Santa Marta, which was deserted. They looted the place and a day later set fire to the buildings and sailed away. Cartagena was the next logical stop for the raiders, but Drake knew that it would be well guarded and did not stop there. His next destination was the Isthmus, the original goal of the luckless expedition.[85]

The fleet anchored in the harbor at Nombre de Dios on 27 December 1595. As with all the other towns, this place was abandoned and stripped of all valuables. Some of his men rummaged around in a guardhouse and found a bar of gold and a few pieces of silver, but that was all. It was an insignificant town, important only because the road for Panama started there. Baskerville, with fewer than a thousand men, set off on 29 December along the mule road to Panama. The plan was that he would take the town, then Drake would bring boatloads of reinforcements and supplies up the Chagres River to Cruces.[86]

It was a terrible plan. In the rainy season the river was high and easily navigable, but Baskerville's men found the muddy hills impassable. After two days of miserable marching, the army came to Capira Pass, which was held by about fifty Spanish troops behind a barricade of tree trunks and branches. Hesitant to attack, Baskerville waited until the morning of 31 December, when the Spanish troops were reinforced by another sixty men. There was a battle, short and brutal, after which Baskerville retreated to Nombre de Dios.[87]

Back with the fleet, Baskerville decided that his men were too exhausted and his force too weak for another attempt to capture Panama. There was nothing to be done. Drake took the men aboard the ships and set fire to Nombre de Dios. On 5 January they set sail, heading west toward Honduras and Nicaragua.[88] Just where Drake intended to go is unclear. He told Maynarde that "God hath many things in store for us, and I knowe many meanes to do her maiestie good service, and to make us ritch." But Maynarde also reported that Drake was extremely depressed. "Since our returne from Panama he never caried mirth nor ioy in his face."[89]

On 9 January they stopped at Escudo Island for rest and refitting. Four more pinnaces were built, and two that were badly damaged were burned. Sickness was always a problem on these expeditions, and a deadly fever ran through the fleet, making everyone ill. Drake himself contracted the disease, a bloody dysentery. He put the fleet to sea once more on 24 January, though he was already very sick. For two days the ships worked back and forth, trying to catch the wind. On 27 January they turned eastward, heading for Porto Bello. Drake's condition was much worse, and perhaps he hoped that a stay ashore would bring improvement.[90]

Several of the captains visited Drake during the day. Thomas Drake, who commanded the *Hope,* later said that he found Drake's aide, Jonas Bodenham, hovering at the bedside and urging Drake to sign two special documents for him.[91] One would have absolved Bodenham of any debts; the other would have named him executor.[92] Rather than do this, Drake dictated and signed a codicil to his will, naming his brother Thomas his heir and executor: "I Francis Drake of Buckland monachorum in the Countie of Devon knighte, Generall of her majesties Fleete now in service for the west Indies being perfect of mynde and memorie, thankes bee therefore unto godd, although sicke in body, do make and ordaine my last will and testament in manner and forme followinge; Viz first I comend my soule to Jesus Christe my savior and redemer in whose righteousnes I am made assured of everlastinge felicitie and my bodie to the earth to be entombed at the discression of my executor."[93] Thomas Drake was named his executor, and Thomas and other friends and relatives received property not specified in the will that Drake had written in August. While the poor man was hovering at the point of death, his family and retainers engaged in some unseemly behavior. Thomas Drake said later that Jonas Bodenham tried to trick his master into signing part of the estate to him. Bodenham said that Thomas "did fall a rifflinge & gatheringe togeather of all such chestes . . . before the breath was out of his said brothers bodye."[94] It was obvious that Thomas Drake and Jonas Bodenham would never be close friends. Hoping to avert trouble between his brother and his trusted aide, Francis Drake told Jonas to give his hand to Thomas as a gesture of reconciliation.[95] That done, he had himself dressed, perhaps in his armor, as one account has it, then took to his bed again. He died at about 4 A.M. on 28 January 1596.[96]

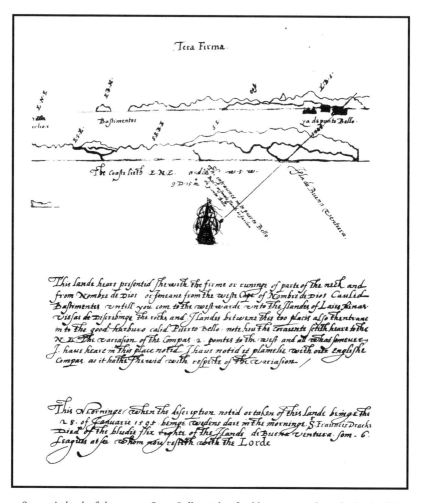

Seaman's sketch of the coast at Porto Bello, with a final laconic note about the death of Sir Francis Drake. From Bibliothèque Nationale, Paris, MS Anglais 51.

The fleet sailed on into the harbor at Porto Bello. Baskerville took command of the fleet and had Drake's body sealed in a lead coffin. In spite of his clear request the day before to be buried on land, Drake was taken aboard ship once more and buried at sea, about a league from the land. A story published much later said that there was an impressive ceremony for his burial at sea, and perhaps there was: "His corps being laid into a Cophin of Lead, he was let downe into the Sea, the Trumpets in dolefull manner echoing out this lamentation for so great a losse, and all the Cannons in the fleet were discharged according to the custome of all Sea Funeral obsequies."97

After this, the captains met in council to decide what course to take from that point onward. Everyone knew that they would have to answer for the disastrous outcome of the voyage, so careful notes were taken. Ransom had been the whole reason for staying so long in port, but the Spanish settlers were in no mood to pay. Simply to show that they had made an effort, the English captains decided to stay at Porto Bello for a few more days to see whether a ransom could be collected. If this did not work, they would abandon the "Supfluous" prisoners and black slaves, those who had been promised freedom in exchange for their help.98

These were the easy decisions. It was more difficult to decide where to go next. Santa Marta and Honduras were both included in the original list of places to attack. After considerable debate they decided to go to Santa Marta for three or four days if that could be done without "great difficultie." Then they would sail to Jamaica, which seemed the most likely place to obtain victuals. If they could resupply the ships in Jamaica, the captains agreed to make one more try at a raid in Honduras. Otherwise, they would return to England.99

Nothing went right. Off the Isla de Pinos they met a small Spanish fleet and fought inconclusively for several hours. Following this battle the English fleet scattered, the commanders taking the exercise as the "great difficultie" that would excuse them from any further stay in the Indies. Each ship made its own way home, and most of the vessels reached England in April and May.100

The whole voyage had been a disaster, and after the death of the commanders, discipline was nonexistent. The trifling amount of booty that had been taken in the various raids was pilfered by the soldiers and seamen before the ships reached port. Even had he lived, it seems doubtful that Francis Drake could have saved the voyage. The Indies were no longer undefended, and the new Spanish fleet had ships and commanders of great daring. More than this, Drake's luck had finally run out.

14

The Drake Legend

During the sixteenth century the maritime region of south Devon spawned dozens of English seafarers who made a fair living from commercial voyages. For many of them this was not enough, and they turned to piracy for added income. The best of them managed to get away with it because they coordinated their depredations with English foreign policy. Francis Drake grew up around Plymouth, where many such men made their homes. He was trained by the Hawkins family, one of the leading families of merchant-pirates. The education was practical, the skills, those a seaman and merchant might use. Formal schooling was not involved, so Drake never acquired the ability to compose a written memoir. Thus there is no way now to know his inmost thoughts, and that is a problem for historians.

There are additional problems with the evidence from Drake's associates. Only a few of his contemporaries took the time to write about the man, and those who did seem not to have known him well. The only reliable basis now for assessing his character is the scant evidence derived from a view of his relationships with other people. From this sort of information it is possible to see that Drake was charming enough to be a welcome companion to the queen but ruthless enough to cheat his brother's widow and to execute a close friend. Most of those who served with Drake in combat saw a man who was absolutely fearless, but they also understood that he had no talent for planning and conducting an extended military or naval campaign. For Drake the mark of success was to amass great wealth, preferably by taking it from someone else. That was the purpose of warfare, and that was success as he understood it.

Francis Drake was a good seaman, and he knew how to handle small ships, but he lacked the patience and organizational ability to control a large fleet. His understanding of ocean navigation was sufficiently broad to make him reluctant to go anywhere without good maps and the help of experienced pilots who knew the local waters. Discipline was usually good on his ships because he tolerated no misbehavior. But he had a streak of paranoia that appeared after a few weeks at sea and made him imagine that the other officers and men were plotting to do him harm. This was a fatal flaw, so serious that after his one brilliantly successful voyage, the queen was reluctant to trust him with solitary command.

Born to a clerical father, he developed that indifference to religious ritual that often characterizes children of such families. His years with the Hawkins family showed him that success could come without a firm religious commitment, and Drake himself was not noticeably devout. The daily religious observances on board his ships served largely as a means to maintain discipline, though he sometimes used religion to impress other people. He liked to put on a religious show for his Spanish prisoners, for example, and he usually had a cleric aboard ship to handle his correspondence and to lace his letters with references to the deity. In private he was crude and profane. Once he staged a parody of a religious service to "excommunicate" the Reverend Francis Fletcher. If Francis Drake possessed any sort of devout inner life, the evidence has not yet appeared.

Nor did he have a well-developed moral sense. He procured a female slave for the use of his men, and when the unfortunate girl became pregnant, he abandoned her on a deserted island. Like his Devon neighbors, Drake cheerfully evaded customs regulations whenever possible. He had little notion of personal loyalty. After a successful raid he saw no reason to divide the spoils with his seamen or his partners unless circumstances forced him to do so. Somewhat cold in his personal relations, Drake had no children and no close friends, except for his brother Thomas, who was also his heir.

During his lifetime Drake was known as a master pirate, though his reputation rested largely on one astonishingly successful raid through the Spanish ports in the Pacific. He was never able to repeat this stunning achievement, though he tried repeatedly. Although the queen enjoyed his company, she understood his shortcomings in leadership, and she refused to trust him with an important command. Drake tried several times to show the queen and her councillors that he had the skills of a great military leader, but he was never quite able to bring it off.

Even though English authorities steadfastly refused to put him in command of a naval fleet, Spanish officials continued to think of Drake as the embodiment of English military might. In a sense his reputation was created by Spanish settlers in the New World. Embarrassed at their own ineffectual response to Drake's raids, the citizens of the towns along the Spanish Main reported to the crown that Drake was a man of such agile mind and such great military ability that only the greatest show of force would be sufficient to withstand him. To emphasize the threat he posed to Spanish society, the reports also said that Drake was a *gran luterano,* a threat to the soul as well as the body.

The citizens of Santo Domingo were among the most vociferous in this regard. After Drake's raid in February 1586, the dean and chapter of the cathedral reported to the king that Drake's raid was almost a religious war and that the citizens were helpless to resist him.[1] A government official insisted that Drake fought so fiercely that if he and his men had been at the gates of Seville, the citizens would have fled in panic.[2] Reports like these forced Philip II to divert funds from his European projects and spend them on defense in the Indies.[3] When the Spanish king sent his great Armada to invade England, Elizabeth refused to trust Drake with an independent command, but the Spanish still thought of the English fleet as Drake's fleet. For Spain, Drake was the personification of English sea power. Drake's reputation, in short, was created by his enemies rather than by his friends.

In fact, when Drake died in 1596 his reputation at home was in eclipse, but Spain rejoiced at the passing of a powerful foe. The Spanish dramatist and cleric Lope de Vega celebrated the event in 1598 with his epic poem *La Dragontea,* publicizing ever more widely many of the tales current in Spain about the aptly named "dragon" who had once preyed on Spain and the Church. A few years later Antonio de Herrera included a long section about Drake's exploits in his *Historia general del mundo,* and Bartolomé Leonardo de Argensola repeated much of the same material in his own *Conquista de las Islas Molucas.*[4] Both Argensola and Herrera emphasized the astonishing ease with which Francis Drake had once sailed through Spanish seas.

Both works were in print for several years before the general histories of Edmund Howes and William Camden were published in England. Howes and Camden dwelt at length upon the Drake theme but saw him as just one of many brave, daring, and resourceful English seamen. Camden's work was first published in Latin and did not come out in an English edition until 1625, just before Francis Drake's nephew and namesake joined with Philip Nichols to issue two other books in a successful attempt to restore Drake's faltering reputation.[5] The book that Nichols completed, *Sir Francis Drake Revived,* was followed quickly by *The World Encompassed by Sir Francis Drake,* which was extensively revised by the younger Francis Drake.[6] These volumes covered Francis Drake's early raids on the Spanish Main and his voyage around the world. The first title caught the public imagination, and the book became a basic work in England, where it was reprinted four times during the next quarter-century. Following this initial success, another author, Nathaniel Crouch, added considerable material and republished the work in 1681 under the title *The English Hero: or, Sir Francis Drake Reviv'd.*[7] Crouch's work appeared in many editions, under slightly varying titles, during the next hundred years. Answering the charges leveled by earlier critics, Nichols, Drake, and Crouch portrayed their hero as a patriot, whose unfortunate forays into piracy were more than offset by a zealous devotion to English Protestantism.

This was the central problem in Drake's rehabilitation. There is no way to avoid the fact that Drake's greatest success was based on piracy. Henry Holland began tracing an outline of a possible Drake biography in 1620, when he included Francis Drake in his *Herwologia,* a book of English heroes, complete with full-page portraits of all the subjects.[8] Ending his work with a poetical epitaph, Holland intimated that Drake might some day rise from his watery grave to defend the world against a resurgent Roman Catholicism.

This portrait of Francis Drake, "the Golden Warrior"
(Miles Auratus), is from Holland's Herωologia
Anglica *(1620), 106. Huntington Library.*

Holland's work was not widely circulated, partly because it was written in Latin. Thomas Fuller included a similar but somewhat longer English text in his 1642 book, *The Holy State and the Profane State.* In this new work Fuller proclaimed Francis Drake to be the very model of a Christian sailor, and a Protestant hero to boot. In Fuller's account, Drake agonized at first over the acts of piracy but finally decided on good moral advice that piracy was justified because the robberies were against England's Catholic enemies.[9] With rare exceptions, this has remained the theme of Drake biography ever since.

An early attempt to set Drake's record straight was made by George William Anderson. His 1781 work, *A New, Authentic, and Complete Collection of Voyages Round the World,* used manuscript collections in the British Museum to show that Drake's heroism was heavily tinged with villainy.[10] Anderson was clearly the first Drake biographer to use these sources critically, but his work has been ignored almost completely by both the biographers and the bibliographers of Drake.[11]

Victorian England embellished the Drake legend, placing him in a newly enlarged pantheon of English heroes. In an age when the British Empire covered the world and the British navy controlled the sea routes to these distant parts, it seemed useful to recount that it all started with Francis Drake. There were novels and plays and poems by dozens of authors, reaching a sort of culmination in the work of Sir Henry Newbolt. His 1895 poem "Drake's Drum" has reminded English boys for a century that when they go to sea in warships they do so in company with Drake and his sailors.

Most modern biographies use as their starting point the 1898 biography of Drake by Julian Corbett. A respected naval historian, Corbett was also a friend of the Drake family, particularly of Lady Elizabeth Fuller Eliott-Drake, who allowed Corbett to use certain family papers. In return Corbett contributed both information and advice for Lady Elizabeth's own study of the Drake family. The two-volume works of Corbett and Eliott-Drake have set the tone for many of Drake's twentieth-century biographers. To Corbett and his followers Drake was not only a great seaman, a leader of men, and a Protestant gentleman, but a fine naval strategist and the real founder of the English navy. Elements of this interpretation, widely accepted for many years, still have a great appeal for English historians. In 1938 James A. Williamson modified the Corbett interpretation with his own study of *The Age of Drake*. In Williamson's view the navy had two fathers. John Hawkins gave the navy an efficient system of administration, and Francis Drake originated the tradition of undivided command responsibility.

Both ideas have been subject to recent revision, most notably in 1967, when Kenneth R. Andrews published *Drake's Voyages*. Andrews showed that though both Drake and Hawkins were important figures in Elizabethan maritime expansion, they were scarcely founders of a true naval tradition. Citing the final voyage, Andrews concluded that Drake in particular was a poor choice as founder of a tradition of absolute authority for the naval commander. In spite of the work of Andrews and others, new Drake biographies appear every year or two, confidently asserting that

*John Hawkins. Reprinted from
Holland,* Herωologia Anglica *(1620), 101.
Huntington Library.*

Francis Drake had an important role in founding the English navy and explaining his piracy as the patriotic conduct of an intensely religious man.

The Drake myth started when his victims complained to the Spanish king that they could not be expected to defend themselves all alone in the New World. To make their point, they described Drake as a man of terrifying stature, an enemy of their king and their church. As their dozens of reports reached the Spanish court, the name of Francis Drake came to represent the English enemy, and stories of his exploits circulated through the diplomatic circles of Europe.

Response was different in England, where chroniclers originally viewed Drake as one of a group of adventurous seamen, but not necessarily a national hero. Some years after Drake's death, in response to comments at home and abroad, his nephew began trying to refurbish his reputation by publishing a sympathetic version of Drake's exploits. Revised and amplified, this work became the basis for a new type of patriotic book with Drake no longer a pirate but a hero, defending God and queen against a threatening Spain.

That sort of biography no doubt served a national purpose, but history ought to say what the man was really like. Francis Drake was a rogue, an able seaman, and a pirate. Drake was a commoner who made himself rich and in the process became a friend of the queen, who tried to turn him into a gentleman. This is the Drake who emerges from the historical record, an interesting fellow but not the Francis Drake of patriotic myth.

APPENDIX I
EDMUND DRAKE

IN MODERN BIOGRAPHIES MOST OF the information about the father of Francis Drake has come from the Elizabethan chroniclers William Camden and John Stow, whose details were only partly factual. When Julian Corbett published his biography of Francis Drake in 1898, he set the standard for others to follow. Corbett described Edmund Drake as a fiery Protestant preacher who was forced to flee from Devon by Catholic fundamentalists opposed to the changes he advocated. Taking refuge for a while on an island in Plymouth harbor, the Drake family soon left for Kent. There Edmund found work reading prayers to sailors of the fleet, while his wife and children sheltered in the hull of an abandoned ship. Persecuted for his Puritan beliefs, Edmund nonetheless managed to instill a passionate religious fervor in his oldest son, Francis.[1]

This story is almost wholly imaginary. Edmund Drake was neither a Puritan nor a preacher, and he had little to do with the education of his son Francis. Devon Catholics did rebel in 1548 and 1549, but there was no uprising in Tavistock, where John, Lord Russell, kept a firm hold on his newly acquired estates and tenants.[2] In any case, Edmund Drake was already out of the area before the uprising took place. On the other hand, John and Margerie, the grandparents of Francis Drake, remained in Tavistock, along with other family members, including their son Robert and his family.[3] If the family of Edmund Drake ever lived in the hull of a ship in the royal dockyards or anywhere else, that evidence has not survived.[4]

The fault does not lie entirely with the chroniclers. John Stow had most of the basic facts straight. Stow wrote that Francis Drake's father was the vicar of Upchurch, a village in Kent.[5] William Camden was a little less factual. Claiming to have information from Drake himself, Camden said that Edmund Drake was vicar of Upnore.[6] There was no church in Upnore, so this is clearly a mistake for Upchurch.[7] Both Stow and Camden seem to

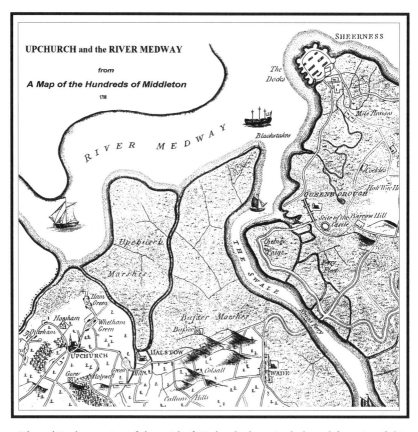

Edmund Drake was vicar of the parish of Upchurch, shown in the lower left portion of this eighteenth-century map. Reprinted from Hasted, "Map."

have known Francis Drake personally, and both men said his father Edmund was vicar of a church in Kent.[8]

In this they were correct. Edmund Drake was in fact curate and vicar of Upchurch in Kent from 1559 to 1566. In 1553 he had been a curate in the same parish.[9] How Edmund Drake came to be a curate and vicar are not clear, for church records from this period are incomplete. A manuscript note perhaps written after 1595 by Drake's friend and biographer Petruccio Ubaldino says flatly: "His father was a priest."[10] This is confirmed by the church records, which give Edmund Drake the priestly title *dominus* and confer on him the full duties and powers of the priesthood.

Not a university graduate, Edmund Drake was nevertheless a "learned" man—learned in English rather than Latin.[11] Even so, he knew enough Latin to keep his parish records in that language, something his predecessor did not do and his successor was not able to do.[12] When Archbishop Parker appointed Edmund Drake as vicar in 1561, he gave him the full "cure of souls," a post for which only an ordained priest was eligible.[13]

It is unclear whether Edmund Drake was a monastic or a secular priest. After Henry VIII closed the religious houses in the 1530s and 1540s, most of the former religious remained celibate, though some married after they left the religious life.[14] Edmund Drake probably married before 1540, when his son Francis was born. When he first became a curate at Upchurch, in September 1553, he was probably still a married man, for his son Thomas was born only a few years later. When Queen Mary came to the English throne, Edmund Drake may have given up his wife and family in order to resume his priestly duties, as did John Townsley, another married priest of Edmund's acquaintance. When Queen Mary's new church authorities began to enforce the laws against priestly marriage, both Townsley and Drake lost their appointments, both apparently for this very reason. Townsley thereupon separated from his wife and did the required penance. He was later made vicar of Upchurch.[15] What Edmund Drake did is not apparent in the records, but in 1561 he was listed as an unmarried priest.[16]

John Townsley was still vicar of Upchurch in 1559, when Edmund Drake was reappointed as curate. Formerly a monk at Boxley Abbey, Townsley had married after the abbey was closed.[17] As a monk he was called John Rede, but he began using his family name again when the monastery was dissolved.[18] This illustrates one of the great problems in identifying men listed in sixteenth-century English church records. Many men took different surnames when they entered religious life, and it is often impossible to discover their secular names.[19] John Townsley held parish appointments under both names.[20] A brief notation in one of these documents is the only record that makes the fact clear.[21] If Edmund Drake was once a member of a religious order under another name, it might not be possible now to find the record.

In any case, Edmund Drake continued to associate with priests and former priests. Once, in fact, he and two confederates, William Master and John Hawking, at least one of whom was a priest, received royal pardons for several serious crimes (see Chapter 1). There is no certain evidence to explain their crimes against the prosperous landowners John Harte and Roger Langiford, but the religious connection may be the key.

The various administrative and liturgical changes made by Henry VIII following the suppression of the monasteries brought only superficial change to the mode of worship followed by the great majority of people in Tavistock and the rest of rural Devon. And dispossessed members of the clergy, both pensioned and unpensioned, continued to find employment in the parish, as the church warden accounts show. But serious change began under Edward VI. In 1547 local authorities began to take the first steps in confiscating the chantries and thereby eliminating a major source of income upon which many priests depended for a living.[22]

The disruption was compounded in April 1548, when William Body began the systematic removal of statues and other popish decorations from the churches of Cornwall.[23] Even more drastic changes were in the wind. Rumors began to circulate about a new prayer book that would completely revise the order of worship, the vestments, the prayers, perhaps even the basic elements of faith. It is not too difficult to imagine that the wealthy gentlemen John Harte and Roger Langiford were on the profit-making side of these changes, while the unbeneficed priests, William Master, John Hart, and Edmund Drake were among the dispossessed.[24] Certainly, there was some sort of serious turmoil in Tavistock at this time, and the authorities feared the sort of general uprising that had occurred in many of the parishes of Cornwall. When one of the ringleaders of Cornwall was executed at Plymouth, a messenger was dispatched to Tavistock to display part of the poor wretch's quartered body as a warning to the local people.[25]

The crimes of Edmund Drake and his colleagues took place in 1548, so they were likely still out of the territory, fugitives from justice, in 1549 when the rebellion actually came to Devon. Under other circumstances they might not have had to flee. A priest who broke the law could ordinarily claim benefit of clergy and have his case heard by ecclesiastical authorities, but highway robbery was an exception to the rule. Consequently,

these three criminal clerics had to ask for a royal pardon, and in due course
it was granted. Following the practice used with other *clerici convicti,* they
were listed in the pardon document by their secular occupations.[26]

There is no record of Edmund Drake's marriage. Protestant reformers in
Devon later said that it was a common scandal that priests lived more or
less openly with women.[27] No doubt this is an exaggeration, but it happened nonetheless, even with priests who held benefices. For unbeneficed
priests, working at secular occupations, the temptation to ignore the vow
of celibacy must have been great. Throughout the reign of Henry VIII,
English law did not allow clerical marriage, though there was a general
tendency to ignore the statute during the later years of his reign. Even
Matthew Parker, who became Elizabeth's first archbishop of Canterbury in
1559, showed his contempt for the law well before it was changed. In 1540
he became affianced to Margaret, daughter of Robert Harlston, and in
1547 they were married. The bill to end clerical celibacy was discussed in
parliament at the end of 1548 and passed in February 1549.[28] Like Parker,
Edmund Drake may have been one of those who anticipated the change
in the law and married before it was really permissible to do so. Whether
this is the case or not, his son Francis was clearly born before the law was
changed.

The name of Edmund's wife is not known. On very slender evidence
some modern authors say she was the daughter of Richard Myllwaye.[29]
Clement Myllwaye and others in the Myllwaye family were prominent
members of the parish at Upchurch, where Edmund was curate and later
vicar.[30] No doubt the two men were well acquainted. In 1560 Clement
Myllwaye leased the rectory of Upchurch, thus providing Edmund with a
cash income.[31] Clement also was witness to the parish transcripts submitted by Edmund Drake.[32] In 1565 he was one of the two witnesses to Edmund's will. These facts indicate an association of some sort between Edmund Drake and Clement Myllwaye, but the only indication of a closer
relationship is a phrase in Edmund's will referring to "my father Melwaye,"
presumably the witness Clement Myllwaye. In one line of his will Edmund referred to Richard Saywell, the other witness, but he gave his chair
and cushion to "Richard Melwaye." This name may very well be an error,

either for Richard Saywell or for Clement Myllwaye, since there is no evidence of a Richard Myllwaye in Upchurch. At the point of death when he wrote the will the day before he died, Edmund Drake asked that it be recopied. This was not done, and the reference to "my father Melwaye" is the only evidence that Myllwaye is the family name of Francis Drake's mother.[33]

On equally slim evidence other writers have said that the mother of Francis Drake was either the daughter or the cousin of Sir John Hawkins.[34] Nuño de Silva, who knew Drake from the voyage along the coast of South America, said that he was "a son and relative" of the Hawkins family.[35]

The best evidence about the family of Francis Drake comes from his cousin John Drake, testifying at a Spanish tribunal in Lima in 1587. John Drake identified his paternal uncles as John, Edmund, and another John. The first two were deceased, the other still living. He also had "two or three aunts," also deceased, whose names he could not remember "except that one was called Ana."[36]

Both the Drakes and the Myllwayes were yeomen. This is what the chronicler Camden meant when he said that the Drakes were *loco mediocri*.[37] They were a family of freemen without a claim to nobility.[38] The same could have been said of the Myllwaye and Hawkins families.[39] If Edmund Drake married into the Myllwaye or the Hawkins family, he would have been marrying in his own social group.

There is some evidence about Edmund Drake's religious beliefs, but nothing to show that he was a Puritan or even a preacher. In fact, the records show that his beliefs were fairly orthodox and that he was not authorized to preach. His theology closely matched that of Matthew Parker. Archbishop Parker held that the core of Christian belief was contained in Saint Paul's statement that "Jesus Christ came into the world to save sinners." He came not to judge men or to teach them about justification by faith, but to save them. This is the key to Archbishop Parker's theology, a statement easily accepted by other priests, who repeated it in their wills.[40] It was echoed by Edmund Drake in his own will: "I doe believe assuredlye that I am redeamed by the bluod of Christ as a Lamb undefyled and wythout spott."[41]

In most respects Edmund Drake was a model vicar, poor but pious. Parish priests were supposed to "keep hospitality" by giving 2½ percent of their income each year to the poor of the parish.[42] Following the practice of most of the poorly paid vicars, Edmund Drake did not keep hospitality.[43] Nor did he preach, a privilege denied to priests who lacked a university degree. Instead, they were to hire a licensed preacher four times each year to provide theologically acceptable sermons for their parishioners. Because Edmund Drake was too poor to keep this rule, his parishioners went without sermons. At each Sunday service priests were supposed to read a homily from among those published in 1547 and 1563; Edmund Drake did this. He also provided the required copies of the Bible and the *Paraphrases* of Erasmus, along with other books and pamphlets. He said the communion service as provided in the *Book of Common Prayer,* and he baptized, married, and buried a few members of his parish every year. He maintained his residence in Upchurch, as he was supposed to do.[44] During the six years or so Edmund Drake was in Upchurch, only one complaint was ever made against him. In March 1563 the episcopal visitor made a note concerning Upchurch, "It is presented that they have not their sermons but the homelies [are] redd."[45]

The moral standard set in Edmund Drake's parish was neither strict nor lax but somewhere in between. Two people were charged with public immorality in 1560, and others were accused of similar acts in 1562. In April 1563 the people of the parish were admonished by the archdeacon for not sending their children to catechism lessons, a warning that was no doubt made at the urging of the vicar himself.[46]

The records show Edmund Drake as a good priest. He was a man who believed in the basic tenets of his faith, a man who tried to minister to his parishioners, but above all a man who tried to get along. His marriage was probably a mistake, for clerical duties disrupted his personal life and gave him little opportunity to be a husband or a father to his children. This is particularly true of Francis Drake, who never lived for any considerable length of time in his father's house or otherwise came under his father's religious influence.

Appendix 11
The Institution of Edmund Drake as Vicar of Upchurch

Institution in the Vicarage of Upchurch [marginal note].

On the twenty-fifth day of the previously written month of January [1560–61] at Lambeth the Most Reverend [archbishop] admitted Edmund Drakes, cleric, as vicar perpetual of the parish church of Upchurch in the diocese of Canterbury, made vacant by the death of the last immediate vicar of the same place; to which, having been presented by the Warden and Associates of the College of All Souls of the Faithful Departed of Oxford as the said perpetual vicar, he was instituted in the same by Edward Orwell, notary public, our procurator, etc. with the rights and perquisites; he committed to him in the Lord the care, etc. [and rule of souls], always reserving the archepiscopal rights, dignity, and honor and [that of the Metropolitan] Church of Christ of Canterbury in all things. He received from the same Edward [Edmund] in the name of the procurator, etc. the oath of legitimate obedience, etc., according to the statutory form, etc.; and [he received from the same Edmund the oath of] continuous residence, etc.; and the care, etc. [of the same souls] was accepted [by the same Edmund].[47]

APPENDIX III
EDMUND DRAKE'S PARDON, 1548

EDWARD THE SIXTH, BY THE grace of God King of England, France, and Ireland, defender of the faith and supreme head on earth of the English and Irish church, to our beloved and faithful counselor Richard Rich, knight, our lord high chancellor of England, greeting. We command you to take in hand our seal of England, which is in your custody, and cause our patent to be issued in the following form: The King, to all to whom, etc., greeting: Whereas Edmund Drake, lately of Tavistock in the county of Devon, sherman, and John Hawking, lately of the same village and county, tailour, also called John Harte, having been indicted for as much as the same men on the twenty-fifth day of April of the second year of our reign by force and arms, to wit, staves, swords, and knives, at Tavistock in the previously named county, having come upon one horse of the value of three pounds from the goods and chattels of the said [*sic*] John Harte, feloniously seized it and carried it away, contrary to our peace and the dignity of our crown. And also whereas William Master, lately of Tavistock in the aforementioned county, cordiner, and Edmund Drake, lately of Tavistock, previously mentioned, sherman, stand similarly indicted that on the sixteenth day of April in the second year of our reign by force and arms, to wit, staves and swords, at Petertavy in the aforementioned county in the Via Regis called Le Cross Lane, made verbal insult to a certain Roger Langifforde, then and there being in the peace of our God, and so maltreated him that he feared for his life; and also, finding twenty-one shillings seven pence in good and legal money and English coin from the goods and chattels of the said Roger, in a purse which lay then and there upon the body of the very same Roger, seeing it, they feloniously seized it from the said Roger Langifford and carried it away, contrary to our peace, our crown, and our dignity as explained more fully in the aforesaid indictment. Know ye that we, by our special grace and clear understanding and individual motion, though with the advice and consent of our most distinguished uncle, Edward duke of Somerset, governor of our royal person, our crown, and our domain, and protector during our minority, and [with the advice and consent] of our other counselors, pardon, free, and release, and by these presents we do pardon, free, and release the aforesaid Edmund Drake, lately of Tavistock in the county of Devon, sherman, John Hawking, lately of the same town and county, tailour, also called John Harte, and William Master, lately of Tavistock in the aforementioned county, cordiner, and any other names or surnames whatsoever or additional names or surnames under which the same Edmund, John, and William might be felt guilty or might be accused or any of them might be felt guilty or might be accused: each and every felony and robbery whatsoever perpetrated by the said Edmund, John, or William or any of them, prior to the twentieth day of the month of October preceding the present date, even though the same Edmund, John, and William and any of them, may have been indicted, summoned, arrested, banished, jailed, condemned, convicted, attainted, or face the possibility of indictment, accusation, arrest, banishment, imprisonment, condemnation, conviction, attainder in the future, and also for all and every indictment, presentation, penalty of death and execution of the same by reason of the matters mentioned previously returned, performed, adjudged, and held against the said Edmund, John, and William or any of them, and that might be returned, performed, adjudged, and held against the said Edmund, John, and William or any of them in the future by reason of the matters previously mentioned or any of them whatsoever. Moreover by these presents we grant them our enduring peace, in such a way that each of them stands justified before us in our curia, lest anyone dare to speak against them or any one of them concerning the previously mentioned matters or concerning anything previously mentioned. Moreover, in our abounding grace, we grant pardon, freedom, and release to the same Edmund, John, and William and to each one of them for the forfeiture of all and any one of their terraces and tenements, goods and chattels whatsoever, on previous occasions forfeited or surrendered to us and imposed on their lands and tenements, goods and chattels. Moreover, by these presents we grant and restore not only the very same lands and tenements, goods and chattels, but also all and every legal right, both royal and personal, for their recovery and for the restoration of any loss whatsoever, withholding from the same Edmund, John, and William and each of them only so much of our gift as is expressly mentioned, etc. In testimony whereof our private seal has been affixed at our Palace of Westminster, the 18th day of December in the Second year of our reign.{rubric}

E {rubric} Clerke[48]

APPENDIX IV
FRANCIS DRAKE'S DATE OF BIRTH

THERE IS A MASS OF general evidence regarding the date of birth for Francis Drake, but only a few statements by people who knew him well. Nuño de Silva, a close associate for several months in 1579, said that Drake was then thirty-eight years old, give or take two years.[49] Francisco de Zárate, who had been with Drake for a briefer span of time that year, said that he was perhaps thirty-five years old.[50] Both of these estimates place his birth date in the early 1540s.

Nicholas Hilliard painted a miniature portrait of Drake, dating it 1581 and reckoning that as his subject's forty-second year.[51] Diego Hidalgo Montemayor interviewed Drake's interpreter and numerous officials who had talked with Drake at Cartagena in March 1586, then wrote in May 1586 that Drake was by his own account forty-six years old.[52] Both these sources agree that he was born about 1540.

Other inscribed pictures giving much less exact information point to a birth date no earlier than 1539. A portrait credited to Abraham Janssen bears a date of 1594 and a statement that Drake was then fifty-two.[53] There is some reason to believe that this is not an original portrait but rather a copy of a portrait, dated 1591, by Marcus Gheerarts, which has no age inscription.[54] Countering this informed guess, another authority suggests that the "1591" portrait is really a copy of the 1594 portrait.[55] Either way, the birth dates seem to fall between 1539 and 1542.

Several undated illustrations evidently published during Drake's lifetime also display his age. A map engraved by Nicola van Sype about 1591 bears a portrait of Drake at age forty-one.[56] An engraved portrait generally credited to Jodocus Hondius is undated and gives Drake's age as forty-two.[57] One engraving published in Amsterdam by Cornelis Claesz about 1592 depicts Drake at the age of forty-three.[58] Two similar engravings evidently derived from the same original are labeled pictures of Drake in his forty-third year. These are said to be the work of Thomas de Leu and Paulis de la Houue, based on an unknown painting by the French artist Jean Rabel. Because Rabel is not known to have been in England or Drake then in France, most authorities think that Rabel copied an English original, perhaps the one sent by the French ambassador in 1586.[59] In spite of various attempts to date these pictures, none can be used to determine the exact year of Drake's birth.[60] The engravings do suggest, though, a date no earlier than 1539 or later than 1543.

One early printed source gives a more precisely datable statement about his age. This is the assertion printed by Edmund Howes in 1615 that Francis Drake was fifty-five years old when he died, on 28 January 1595 by the Julian calendar.[61] This points to 1540 as the year of birth.

The Howes book is a continuation of the earlier *Annales* of John Stow, who died in 1607. Stow may have known Drake and may have known when he was born, but he did not publish it in any of his own editions. There is no indication that Howes knew Francis Drake, but most of his statements about Drake are made with such precision that they seem to be based on exact information, and there is an almost irresistible urge to believe them.

From a review of all the sources, it appears that the best are Nuño de Silva and Nicholas Hilliard, both of whom knew Drake personally. They agree that he was born about 1540. Diego Hidalgo Montemayor and John Stow/Edmund Howes appear to have had their information from reliable sources. Hidalgo says that Francis Drake was forty-six in March of 1586. Howes says that Francis Drake was fifty-five in January 1595. Taken together, these two sources point to a birthday in February or March 1540. The other more general evidence points to dates between 1539 and 1543. The obvious conclusion is that Francis Drake was born between 1539 and 1543, most likely in February or March of 1540.[62]

APPENDIX V
THE PIRATE LETTER OF FEBRUARY 1571

CARTA DE UNOS COSARIOS YNGLESES digo su copia de la original que enbiaron a esta ciudad de el nombre de dios con unos dos hombres que habian tomado por prisioneros andando por esta costa de tierra firme. y se envia por mi el factor Christoval de salinas a su magestad y en su real consejo de las yndias.

[Archival note: Cosarios]

Arraes y los otros de esta fregata maravillamonos porque asi huyeron de nosotros y despues no quisieron venir a habrar sobre nuestra bandera de pas y conosiendonos y por prueva de dias passados. no hasemos mal a nadi sobre nuestra bandera de pas sino habrar quisieramos con vosotros. y pues con cortesia no quieren venir a hablar con nosotros sin mal y daño, anse hallar su fregata perdida por sus mismas culpas. y qualquier que con cortesia viniere a hablar con nosotros no haremos malo sobre la vandera y quien no hara echa la culpa en si. y no piensen que tubimos miedo de los navios ni de otros. que con la ayuda de dios a de costar sus vidas antes que provechan sobre nos. y ya por prueva ven que feria mejor que hubieran venidos a hablar con nos pues que en la fregata no tenian al valor de quatro reales de plata. fecha de ingleses piadosos no aviendo cause al contrario pues si lo ay feremos diabiles mas que de hombres.[63]

APPENDIX VI
NUNCUPATIVE WILL OF JOHN DRAKE

IN THE NAME OF GOD amen anno 1573 John Drake late of plymouth in the countie of Devon maryner being on a voyage to the Indese sodenlie stroken with a gunne shott and nere his death and being then at that instant which was about the ix^th or x^th daie of June last past in anno domini 1573 in good and perfect memorie was demaunded by two or three of other mariners in the same shipe at that present tyme whether he had made his testament left at eny place—whoe answered them that he had made none at all / wherefore saied he I doe nowe nomynate and apoint my brother Francis Drake to be my full and whole executor of suche goods as I have / excepting myne adventure of xxx^li which I have in this shippe called the paschoe of Plymouth the which xxx^li with the proffitt of the same adventure cominge I give unto Alice Drake my wief, and I shall desier my brother Francis to see it trulie paied and consented to my saied wief, and because my wief is a yonge woman I have made my saied brother executor to the extent that he maie be an ayde and helper unto my saied wief (as I trust he will) Theie witnesses John Crockit John Prouse.

Proved at London on the twelfth day of February 1573 by the procurator of Francis Drake, nominated as executor of the said will, to whom the commissary gave the administration of all and each of the goods, rights, and credits, etc.

[Marginal note] Declared null and invalid by the definitive sentence given on the feast of Saint Catherine, 1575, as appears from the acts

Sentence of nullity on the will of John Drake recently of Plymouth, deceased.

In the Name of God Amen. The worth and circumstances as well as the faults of a certain pending testamentary document having been heard, seen, and understood and fully and completely discussed by us William Drury, doctor of laws in the Prerogative Court of Canterbury, properly and legitimately appointed as chief guardian or commissary, of the alleged will of John Drake, deceased, recently during his lifetime a resident of Plymouth, Diocese of Exeter, Province of Canterbury, this particular affair was brought before us as a suit between Alicia Cotton, alias Drake, widow of the said deceased, as party of the first part, and Francis Drake, appointed as executor of the purported will of the said deceased, the party against whom this action is undertaken; for some time, it was argued, disputed, and contested on one side and another, and it still stands undecided, brought before us in judgment by the aforesaid parties proceeding duly and lawfully through their procurators, duly and lawfully present. And on the part of the aforesaid Alice Cotton, alias Drake, to pronounce sentence and let justice be done on her part and indeed justice on the part of the aforesaid Francis Drake justice on his part. And the respective claim and petition having been earnestly examined by us in a complete and thorough fashion, held and performed and diligently searched out in this matter for the first time, and the provisions of the law having been observed by us in this part, it should be advanced to our final definitive sentence or our final decree in this matter—we expected to be proceeding and we do proceed in the manner that follows:

SINCE by properly taken legal actions, tried, alleged, advanced, tested evenhandedly, and publicly discussed in the matter held under consideration, we ascertained and clearly discovered on the part of the said Francis Drake his intent in his particular allegation and purported will, whose wording, howsoever formed, constructed, and presented, was selected and composed for this purpose, we hold and we are of the opinion that it is in no way founded or proven but in every aspect of its proof it is deficient and it fails.

THEREFORE, We William Drury, doctor of laws, guardian and commissary aforesaid, having first called upon and considered the name of Christ, keeping only God before our eyes, and with the counsel of men learned in the law, with whom in this matter we have discussed the will of the said John Drake, deceased, otherwise having been placed before us on the part of the said Francis Drake—having been presented and defended in such a way that it can in no way have been done or made but, inasmuch as no will has previously been made by him, he appears to us to have departed from this life and to have died intestate, [and] we [so] pronounce, declare, and decree. Moreover, we revoke the administration of goods, rights, and credits of the said deceased, alias the same Francis Drake, granted by the authority of the said court; and we announce, determine, and declare before all men that such letters of administration granted for this purpose have been and are null and invalid, and have lacked, lack, and ought to lack legal effect; and we commit the administration of all and every one of the goods, rights, and credits of the same John Drake, deceased, as though he had died intestate, to the said Alice Cotton, alias Drake, survivor of the said deceased, in the person of her administrator, duly and legitimately appointed; and we condemn the aforenamed Francis Drake in the legitimate payments already made and being made on the part of and by the part of the said Alice Cotton, alias Drake, in this matter, through this our definitive sentence and this our final decree, which we make and promulgate in this document; but we have reserved and do reserve the enumeration or rather the control of expenditures to ourselves or to other competent judges in this matter.

William Drury

Let it be entered: Let the aforesaid definitive sentence by the said Master William Drewrie, commissary *in loco* of the Consistorial See, be carried out and promulgated, on the juridical day after the Feast of Saint Catherine, Monday the twenty-eighth day of November, in the year of Our Lord one thousand five hundred seventy-five. It was adjudicated in court on a petition of Master Saye, notary public, procurator of Alice Cotton, alias Drake, in the presence of Master John Jurent, notary public, procurator of Francis Drake, upon whose definitive sentence Dominus Magister Say demanded judgement; Anthony Latrum, notary public then present for his own settlement, *unum vel plura intra publica ac testes partibus tunc ibidem* Master Henry Jones, Robert Forth, and John Lloyd, doctors of laws, John Lewes, George Harrison, Christopher Smith, and William Bulham, notaries public, as witnesses.[64]

APPENDIX VII

CORTE BESCHRYVINGHE VAN DIE SEER HEERLIICKE VOYAGIE, DIE CAPITEYN DRAECK INDE ZUIDERSCHE ZEE.

THIS *Brief Description of the Wonderful Voyage of Captain Drake into the South Sea* is the broadside text now attached to the Hondius map, *Vera Totius Expeditionis Nauticae,* in the British Library map department (M.T. 6.a.2.). Although neither the text nor the map carries the name of the publisher, both were very likely done by the Amsterdam printer Cornelis Claesz. As Paul Valkema Blouw of Amsterdam showed me, it is possible to make this identification with more than usual certainty because of the peculiar typefaces used on both sheets. Although some fonts are found in the works of other printers, all of them seem to appear only in the work of Claesz. In fact, it is even possible to derive a fairly close publication date for both map and text in the same way. Some of the typefaces appear in works printed by Claesz as early as 1585, when Claesz published a work "first printed at London by Christopher Barker."[65] All the Germanic typefaces appear together for the first time in an undated work that was published in 1595.[66] The ornamental letter *A* that begins the text was first used by Claesz in a work issued in 1596.[67] Other letters from that font, though, were used by Claesz earlier. The initial letter *C* used in the Cavendish account that also accompanies the Hondius map, for example, was first used by Claesz in an earlier version of the Cavendish story that he issued in late 1588 or early 1589.[68]

Rodney W. Shirley, whose book on printed world maps is now the standard reference work, says that a separate pamphlet edition of the map text appeared in Amsterdam in 1596. Helen Wallis says the same, but I have not been able to find a copy.[69] Even so, the evidence seems to point to 1595 or 1596 as the publication date for the broadside text.

Publication details for the map have also been the subject of scholarly debate. Antoine DeSmet, a Belgian cartographic historian, followed Nordenskiöld in setting the date of publication at 1590.[70] Henry Wagner thought that the map was published in 1593 or 1594, in either London or Amsterdam.[71] Dr. Wallis, who is the former curator of the map department in the British Library, is of the opinion that the map might have been printed twice, once in London in 1590 and again in the Netherlands in 1595.[72] But the evidence for a London publication is weak—two engravings pasted on the back of a copy of the map in the Royal Geographical Society, marked "fecit Londini."[73] Wallis also cites a 1636 biographical sketch of Hondius, which states that he published a map of the Drake voyage during his stay in London. Although this is certainly true, the map in question is probably a much smaller map, published in 1589.[74]

By 1589 Claesz was well established as a printer of maps. His map of Holland, published in that year, employs some of the typefaces used on the broadside text. Others appeared in ensuing years, and all were gathered together in an atlas of the Netherlands published by Hondius about 1600.[75] Because he was in the business of publishing maps, Claesz obviously had the equipment and the experience to publish the Hondius broadside map. Thus it seems likely that both the Hondius map and the Dutch text were published in Amsterdam about 1595 or 1596 in the print shop of Cornelis Claesz.

A note appearing at about the middle of the text identifies the routes shown on the map, thus demonstrating clearly that the map and the text are companion pieces. The Dutch original and an English translation appear below:

Nota
   Also hier de verclaringe van Sir Draeck eyndicht, so
volcht nu t'verhael van Mr. Thomas Cavendish, de prin-
cipale materien van beyde voyagien, ghetogen zijnde
uyt hetghene dat de Ghedeputeerde der Majesteyt van
Engelants Druckers daer van degruckt hebben, en omte
doen verstaen vvat vvegl dat Draeck en Candish elck
besonder gheseylt hebben, so is inde Caerte geteijckent

een omloopendelinie aldus . . . . . beteeckenende de passagien van Draeck, en een ander aldus————
aenvvyfende de passagien van Candish. Oock is te verstaen dat een *Legue* vveynich differeert van een myle,
vvant 17½ *Legues,* maken ghelijck 15, mylen eenen
gradus.

Note

The description of Sir Drake ends here, while the
story of Mr. Thomas Cavendish begins. The principal
material for both voyages is taken from that which
the Deputy of Her English Majesty's Printers have
printed. To understand the way Drake and Cavendish
each have sailed, a line is inscribed on the map in this
manner . . . . . signifying the route of Drake, and
another line in this manner————marking the
route of Cavendish. It should also be understood that
one league is different from one mile; 17½ leagues
make about 15 miles and one degree.

Appendix VIII
Drake's Letter to John Wynter

La carta que scrivio al capitan francisco díaz ingles que entro en el mar de sul por el estrecho de magallanes desde su navio nombrado gama dorado con el navio nombrado San Joan de [ ] que avia robado sus compañeros y que si era el que quedava atras.

Señor Viter, si dios fuere servido que encuentre con St Joan entonces le ruego que se aya bien con el conforme a la palabra que le tiene dada, y si a.V.m. le faltare alguna cosa de las que lleva Sant Joan entonces pague las a.V.m. dobladas de llas nuestras q.V.m. trae, y mandara.V.M. que ninguno de sus soldados le haga mal ni hieran, y la determinaçion que entre nosotros quedo para tornar a nuestra tierra se cuplire dios queriendo aunque tengo mucha dubda de que esta carta vaya a.V.m. por los Spañoles yo quedo siempre rogando continuamente a nuestro señor que nos torne a ambos ydos y a todo el mundo para salvar y condenar al qual le doy graçias siempre amen esto que yo scrivo no solo lo hago para el señor Viter sino tambien para el señor Caoche y al señor Anton con todos los demas Vuestros amigos a los quales encomiendo lo que nos compraren Aunque yo tengo sperança en dios que no nos adedar mas travajos y nos a de ayudar en nuestras tribulaçiones y yo os ruego por las entrañas de Jesu Xpo que si dios permitiere que tengais algunas tribulaciones que no desespereis de la grande misericordia de dios que el avra por hecho que el guardara hasta tornar otra vez a dar la vida destas mas mercedes y muestra su misericordia y honrra y poder y imperio para siempre hazer amen.

con treinta [tristeza]   que tengo el
corazon muy afligido

         francisco diaz.[76]

NOTES

Introduction

1. Whiting, *Blind Devotion of the People*, 145–47, 259–61.

2. A brief account of the surrender is found in Finberg, *Tavistock Abbey*, 266–67. A less accessible but more detailed account is Radford, "Tavistock Abbey."

3. The original document is in the Public Record Office [hereafter PRO], E322, no. 236.

4. See the terms of surrender for the monks of Saint Mary of Biddlesden and the equally insulting terms of the surrender document for the Grey Friars of Bedford in Woodward, *Dissolution of the Monasteries*, 118–120.

5. PRO E322, no. 236, bears the signatures of the abbot, the prior, and twenty monks. The signatures were transcribed and published in PRO, *Eighth Report*, Appendix II, p. 44. As might be expected, there are discrepancies between the listed signatures and the pension list. See Feinberg, *Tavistock Abbey*, p. 267, n. 4; and Snell, *Suppression of the Religious Foundations*, 140.

6. The pension payments are listed in Snell, *Suppression of the Religious Foundations*, 140; and in Hodgett, "Unpensioned Ex-Religious."

7. Finberg, *Tavistock Abbey*, 250–251, 270–73.

I.
From Tavistock to Plymouth

1. Finberg, *Tavistock Abbey*, 40–52, 250–51, 270–73.

2. Devon Record Office [hereafter DRO], Exeter, England, Bedford Settled Estate Collection, W 1258/M, D 53/14/3, dated 10 September 21 Edward IV (1481). See also the undated summary of abbey lands, c. 17–21 Edward IV, in DRO, W1258M, D84, Box 21–50, fols. ii, ii verso, xxvi; and the comments on the documents in Alexander, "Crowndale." Also see Finberg, *Tavistock Abbey*, 94, 250–51, 272.

3. On Drake family prosperity see Archivo General de Indias [hereafter AGI], Patronato 266, ramo 49, fol. 1, testimony of John Drake, 24 March 1584. This John Drake was the younger cousin of Francis Drake and son of Edmund's brother Robert. Young John is quoted as saying that the Drakes "were noble people" *(eran gente noble),* which is not literally true. William Camden, claiming firsthand information from Francis Drake, said he was born *loco mediocri,* a freeman but not noble. See his *Rerum Anglicarum,* 301. Robert Drake was not listed in the Lay Subsidy Rolls for Tavistock, though there is a fairly consistent listing for Richard Drake. Extracts of the rolls in question may be found in DRO, Eliott-Drake Collection, 346M/F574 and 346M/F575.

4. On Simon's passing the lease to John, see Alexander, "Crowndale."

5. Stoate, *Devon Lay Subsidy Rolls, 1524–27,* 151.

6. Stoate, *Devon Lay Subsidy Rolls, 1543–45,* 137.

7. DRO, Bedford Settled Estate Papers, Indenture dated 8 June 1732, L 1258 M/L/E 2/48/5.

8. DRO, Bedford Settled Estate Papers, Indenture dated 29 June 1753, L 1258 M/L/E 2/48/6. It is clear that the boundaries changed somewhat over the years; see DRO, Bedford Settled Estate Papers, Survey of the Manor of Hurdwick, T 1258 M/E 38.

9. DRO, Bedford Settled Estate Papers, T 1258 M/E 36b, vol. 1, part 2, pp. 241–42.

10. The man in question was Edward Atkins Bray. The noted historian of Tavistock, Gerry Woodcock, has informed me that "Edward Atkins Bray was Vicar of Tavistock from 1812 to his death in 1857. He had been born in 1778, the son of the Duke of Bedford's Tavistock Agent. The Brays were a dynasty of high ranking local officials. He would have had easy access to Bedford estate documents. He also was a trained lawyer, having been called to the bar before ordination." Personal correspondence, 13 December 1992.

11. Lewis, *Scenery of the Rivers Tamar and Tavy,* view no. 18, last sheet. The subscribers to the book included Sir Trayton F. Eliott-Drake, a descendant of Francis Drake. Unsatisfactory as the engraving is, we owe a debt to Lewis for publishing it. When Alfred John Kemp visited the place a few years later, the ruins had already been pulled down. *Notices of Tavistock and Its Abbey,* folio. See also Bray, *Description of Devonshire,* 2:166–68. Anna Bray was the wife of Edward Atkins Bray and a writer of some distinction. See Woodcock, "Mrs Bray."

12. Alexander, "Crowndale," 281. In a later article Alexander reported having seen a map in the Bedford Estate Papers, marked to show the building where Francis Drake was said to have been born. See "Early Life of Francis Drake." He erroneously dated the map as "between 1750 and 1760," but Lady Radford, evidently citing her own research on the same map, gave accurate dates, 1760–70. See the interview in the *Western Morning News* (Plymouth), 26 August 1926, Drake clipping files, Westcountry Studies Library (hereafter WSL), Exeter. Both of these Devon historians must have completed their research near the turn of the century. Subsequent erasures have removed this and other details from the map. The mark was not there when Lady Eliott-Drake did her research, and I have not been able to detect any trace of such a mark in my own inspections. Eliott-Drake, *Family and Heirs,* 1:10.

13. Gilbert Aislabie, "A Plan of the West Part or Division of the Parish of Tavistock, containing the Manors of Hurdwick, Ogbear, and Morwell; also of the Manor of Ottery, in the Parish of Lamerton [belonging] to His Grace the Most Noble John, Duke of Bedford, [drawn] between the Years 1760 and 1770," Bedford Settled Estate Papers, Devon Record Office, T 1258 M/E5, M/E6, M/E7.

14. Mercer, *English Vernacular Houses,* 39–40. My conjectural view of the Drake birthplace is based on the eighteenth-century Bedford Estate map, the 1823 engraving, and the longhouse view shown by Mercer.

15. All this depended on local custom and available bathing facilities. For the practice in monasteries see Gasquet, *English Monastic Life,* 104. For conclusions based on sixteenth-century books of manners see Furnivall, *Early English Meals and Manners,* especially pp. lxiii–lxiv.

16. Youings, *Sixteenth-Century England,* 138, notes that the late 1530s were years of abundance.

17. Furnivall, *Early English Meals and Manners.* There is similar evidence in Hurstfield and Smith, *Elizabethan People, State, and Society,* 27–28, 50.

18. Keppel-Jones and Wans, *Drake of Crowndale,* 5.

19. DRO, Russell Estate Collection, Woburn Abbey, D53/29/1 and D53/29/2.

20. Youings, *Tuckers Hall Exeter,* 4. For Edmund Drake as shearman see PRO, London (hereafter PRO), C82/893 5079, dated 18 December 1548, and C66/808 4720, dated 21 December 1548.

21. "Il padre era prete," says the unsigned biographical note, written some time after 1595, perhaps by Francis Drake's Anglo-Italian friend Petruccio Ubaldino. "La Vita del Cavaliere Drake," BL Sloane MS 3962, fol. 39v. For more about Edmund Drake see Appendix 1.

22. This conclusion is based on two sources that seem reliable. The first was Diego Hidalgo Montemayor, who interviewed numerous officials who had talked with Drake at Cartagena in March 1586. Writing in May 1586, Hidalgo reported that all the people he questioned were well informed and known to be reliable. He then wrote that of all the men in the English armada "los más viejos no pasan de quarenta años, ecepto el dicho Francisco Draque, que vino por General, y confesó havia quarenta y seis años [the oldest had not forty years, except for this very Francis Drake, who had become the general and admitted that he was forty-six]." The report, titled "Relación que envió Diego Hidalgo de Montemayor, juez de comisión de la Real Audiencia del Nuevo Reyno de Granada, a la misma Audiencia, de la toma de Cartagena por el Ynglés, y de las cosas sucedidas en ella el mes de Abril del año 1586, 6 May 1586," was transcribed by Gonzalez de Palencia in *Discurso de el Capitán Francisco Draque,* 300. Hidalgo also had much of his information from Drake's interpreter, Jonas, but whether that includes information about his age is unclear (307). A slightly different version of the same document was translated and condensed by Wright in *Further English Voyages to Spanish America,* 129–36. The second source is Howes, *Annales,* 808. For more about Francis Drake's date of birth, see Appendix 2.

23. Chambers, *Faculty Office Registers,* 8. He was included later in a list of ex-religious who had some sort of stipendiary positions in local parishes; cf. "Lists Relating to Persons Ejected from Religious Houses," 17:144, where he is shown assistant to John Peryn, former abbott of Tavistock, who served as vicar of the Tavistock parish. On Master reading the bederoll see DRO, Tavistock Parish Records, 482 A/PW16, Churchwardens Accounts. The bederoll was a list of benefactors whose names were read from the pulpit after Sunday Mass and on Christmas and Michaelmas. Parishioners were asked to pray for their souls.

24. Zell, "Economic Problems of the Parochial Clergy," 23, 27. Zell found a number of unbeneficed priests in Lancashire who worked as farmers and one who was a sheep merchant; further, "several turned to fraud for a living."

25. DRO, Churchwardens Accounts, Tavistock Parish, 1536–37, MS 482 A/PW 16; 1538–39, MS 482 A/PW 17; 1544, MS 482 A/PW 18; 1556, MS 482 A/PW 21. Some of these records were transcribed very carelessly by Worth in *Tavistock Parish Records.*

26. See the entry for John Harte in DRO, Register of Bishop John Vesey, Bishops Registers, vol. 14, fols. 183v–85.

27. DRO, Register of Bishop John Vesey, Bishops Registers, vol. 14, fols. 170–v, 172v.

28. DRO, Tavistock Parish Records, Lease from John Harte to Peter Leer, 20 October 1543.

29. DRO, Russell Estate Papers, 123 M/TP 217, deed to lands in Peter Tavy, 4 October 1543. The Lay Subsidy Roll of 1545 listed Roger Langisford at £16, the highest rating in Peter Tavy.

30. Camden, *Rerum Anglicarum,* 301. The original phrase reads, "ex lege *Sex Articulorum,* ab Henrico Octavo contra Protestantes lata in questionem vocatus, solum vertit, & in Cantium se subduxit." The English translations relied on by Corbett and others omit the word *solum,* "alone."

31. Canterbury Cathedral Archives, Canterbury, England (hereafter CCA), Archidiaconal Visitations, 1550–55, MS Z-3-6, fol. 56v; 11 December 1559, MS Z-3-5, fols. 149, 175v; 1560–62, MS Z-3-7, fols. 24, 36v, 69, 109, 143. Archdeacon's Transcripts, MS A-434, Parish of Upchurch.

32. Howes, *Annales,* 807.

33. AGI Patronato 266, ramo 54, fol. 1.

34. Wrightson, *English Society,* 110–13.

35. See the letter from William Hawkins (the younger) to William Cecil, 20 January 1568, reprinted in Lewis, *Hawkins Dynasty,* 59–60. Lady Eliott Drake said Edmund's mother was perhaps a Hawkins. See her *Family and Heirs,* 1:13. John Drake, nephew of Francis Drake, lived with his own maternal grandmother (the mother of Edmund Drake) from the age of six months until he was eight years old. See his testimony dated 8 January 1587, AGI Patronato 266, ramo 49, fol. 2v.

36. In any case, Francis Drake did not live at Upchurch with his father. Even his youngest brother Thomas lived with another family, that of Thomas Baker in London. See the will of Edmund Drake, Kent Archives Office, Maidstone, Archdeaconry Court (Canterbury), Probate Records, 16/43-D.

37. John Hawkins was born about 1532, his brother William about 1519. William Hawkins the father lived until about 1553 or 1554. See Williamson, *Hawkins of Plymouth,* 20, 36–38.

38. William Hawkins still owned property in Tavistock in 1549. See his lease of 6 April 1549 to William Sharke, listed in Worth, *Tavistock Parish Records,* 87.

39. Williamson, *Hawkins of Plymouth,* 18–40.

40. CCA, Libri cleri, Z-3-6, fol. 56v.

41. Williamson, *Hawkins of Plymouth,* 36.

42. See the 1568 testimony of Pedro Soler, MS LIII-5, Museo Canario de las Palmas, quoted in Rumeu de Armas, *Los viajes de John Hawkins,* 73–77.

2.

Learning to Be a Pirate

1. Howes, *Annales,* 807.

2. Williamson, *Sir John Hawkins,* 68–69.

3. In the original edition of his Hawkins biography, Williamson asserted that the Hawkins family never became involved in real piracy; see *Sir John Hawkins,* 26. Some

years later he took pains to explain that the term *privateer* was not really used in Tudor times, though he thought it best described the respectable manner in which the Hawkins family carried on the business. Not everyone agrees. The British naval historian Michael Oppenheim considers Hawkins and his Devon associates to be representatives of the same pirate tradition that flourished elsewhere in sixteenth-century England and Europe. *Maritime History of Devon,* 28–32.

4. "Certificate of Commissioners for Ports and Havens in County Kent of the number of persons, houses, landing places, ships, and boats in the county," 18 March 1865, BL Stowe MS 570, fols. 216–19v. "Certificate of the Mooste Reverende Father in god Matthewe Archbishop of Caunterbury touching the nombre and state of the churches parrishes and hamlects within the dioces of Canterbury," 4 July 1563, BL Harley MS 594, fol. 74v.

5. Camden, *Rerum Anglicarum,* 301.

6. See his biography of Sir Francis Drake in the *Dictionary of National Biography.*

7. Corbett, *Drake and the Tudor Navy,* 1:82.

8. "Morens illi naviculam testamento legaverit. E qua cum pauxillum nummorum corrasisset." Camden, *Annales,* 302.

9. Williamson, *Hawkins of Plymouth,* 40–46.

10. Howes, *Annales,* 807.

11. Williamson, *Hawkins of Plymouth,* 44–45.

12. Rumeu de Armas, *Viajes de John Hawkins,* 72–78. The Spanish documents quoted by Rumeu de Armas are the primary sources of information about Lovell. For no apparent reason, Rumeu de Armas refers to the man as Lowell throughout his book.

13. Museo Canario de las Palmas, Inquisición, LIII-5, Proceso de Pedro Soler, Segunda declaración de Mateo de Torres, 23 June 1568, reproduced in Rumeu de Armas, *Viajes de John Hawkins,* 385–86.

14. Rumeu de Armas, *Viajes de John Hawkins,* 75–76. Williamson does not mention the incident, either in his *Hawkins of Plymouth* or in *Sir John Hawkins.*

15. "Otra vez que estuvo en Thenerife avia siete años le vido oyr misa." As was the custom in Spanish courts, the statement of the witness was written by the notary in the third person, but as close to the actual words as possible. Testimony of Mateo de Torres, 21 June 1568, Museo Canario de las Palmas, Inquisición, LXII-5, fol. 52v, reproduced in Rumeu de Armas, *Viajes de John Hawkins,* 434–35.

16. "Juan Achin yba a la iglesia y oía misa y en sus palabras parecía catolico y en tal reputación era comunmente tenido." Rumeu de Armas, *Viajes de John Hawkins,* 77.

17. Guzman de Silva to the king, 21 July 1567, Archivo General de Simancas (hereafter AGS), Secretaría General de Estado, leg. 819, fol. 107, segundo. Each "folio" in these deciphered documents can occupy several foolscap pages, with successive pages marked 2°, 3°, and so on. The documents have been reproduced with general accuracy in the *Colección de documentos inéditos para la historia de España,* 89:516. Hereafter CDIE.

18. Williamson, *Hawkins of Plymouth,* 42, maintains that sixteenth-century Englishmen saw nothing wrong with slavery, though he admitted that Frenchmen opposed it; see his *Sir John Hawkins,* 83. Kenneth R. Andrews called Williamson's defense of Hawkins "not only facile but baseless." See his *Drake's Voyages,* 16–17.

19. Rumeu de Armas, *Viajes de John Hawkins,* 82.

20. Hakluyt, *Principall Navigations,* 522. Williamson, *Hawkins of Plymouth,* 49.

21. In listing the *Swallow* as a 100-ton vessel, Hakluyt mistakes the ship for its later namesake. See his *Principall Navigations,* 522. In any case, tonnage descriptions vary widely in Tudor records, often because of a difference between the merchant system of measuring capacity and the admiralty system of "ton and tonnage," the latter of which could add a third to the measurement. See Dietz, "Royal Bounty," 77:7. This difference can easily be seen in the various tonnages listed for the *Salomon.* Hakluyt lists it as 120 tons in his *Principall Navigations,* 522, but the bounty records consulted by Dietz list it as 160, exactly one-third higher (77:14). I have opted for the "7. score" listed by John Sparke.

22. Silva to the king, 21 July 1567, AGS, Estado 819, fol. 107, 2°.

23. Hakluyt, *Principall Navigations,* 522. Williamson, *Hawkins of Plymouth,* 50–51. The Portuguese merchants were Francisco Espindola and Tristan de la Vega, trader and shipowner, respectively. See the letter from Licentiate Echegoyan to the king, 28 July 1563, AGI Santo Domingo 71, tomo 1, fols. 271–73. There is a condensed translation of this letter in Wright, *Spanish Documents Concerning English Voyages,* 65. In a note on page 61, Wright gives the name of Vega, the shipowner.

24. Rumeu de Armas, *Viajes de John Hawkins,* 126–30. On the date of Hawkins's return see Hakluyt, *Principall Navigations,* 522. Hakluyt says the arrival occurred in September, but Williamson cites correspondence that appears to show he arrived in August. See *Sir John Hawkins,* 86.

25. Lorenzo Bernaldez to the king, c. August 1563, AGI Santo Domingo 71, tomo 2, fols. 280–82. See also the testimony of Gaspar de Campo, 5 October 1565, AGI Patronato 265, ramo 8, fols. 1–5.

26. Howes, *Annales,* 807. As noted previously, it is not possible to reconcile all the dates and times in the various accounts. In this case, Howes says that at age twenty-two Drake was "made captain of the Judith at San Juan de Ulloa," apparently referring to the 1568 trip. Howes is confused. Drake was captain of the Judith some months before arrival at San Juan de Ulloa in 1568, and he was almost certainly older than twenty-two. On the other hand, he was quite likely in the Indies at that age, just as he surely was on several other occasions.

27. John Sparke, "The Voyage Made by the Worshipful M. John Haukins Esquire," in Hakluyt, *Principall Navigations,* 523–43. Williamson refuses to accept the characterization of Hawkins as a pirate. See his *Sir John Hawkins,* 83. Andrews, *Drake's Voyages,* 16–17, reviews the evidence and concludes that Williamson did not give it "a fair reading." Andrews also rejects the argument that Hawkins's show of force was a face-saving move for the benefit of Spanish officials (18).

28. Sparke, "Voyage," 536. The involvement of French and English pirates in the West Indies hide trade is explained at great length in Hoffman, *The Spanish Crown and the Defense of the Caribbean,* 110–22.

29. Laudonnière, *L'Histoire notable de la Floride,* fols. 94–97. As it turned out, Laudonnière did not use the ship but stripped it of fittings and abandoned it when he left Florida some weeks later. Williamson is probably mistaken in saying that the ship was the *Tiger.* He is certainly wrong in calling the sale a gift, as is apparent from a careful reading of

Laudonnière's original text. See Williamson, *Hawkins of Plymouth*, 85. There is a translation of the portion dealing with Hawkins's visit in Hakluyt, *Principall Navigations*, 544–45. It is possible that the pilot who guided the fleet so skillfully to the Rio de Mayo is also the one who missed the port of Santa Cruz in Cuba and thus deprived Hawkins of the chance to purchase a load of cowhides. See Sparke, "Voyage," 536. Because Sparke reported that Hawkins gave Laudonnière a ship of "fifty tunnes" (540), Williamson and others have assumed that the ship was the *Tiger*. This leads to the unlikely assumption that the Hawkins brothers had two ships simultaneously named *Swallow*. More likely the 30-ton *Swallow* was sold to Laudonnière, then replaced after this voyage with a 100-ton ship of the same name. In fact, the records show a bounty paid on a new *Swallow* at Plymouth in 1564. Dietz, "Royal Bounty," 77:14.

30. The Spanish view of events is summarized in Rumeu de Armas, *Viajes de John Hawkins*, 37–69. For another view see Williamson, *Hawkins of Plymouth*, 68–86. Both rely heavily on the account by John Sparke in Hakluyt, *Principall Navigations*, 523–43. In addition Rumeu de Armas has also consulted a great number of original Spanish documents, while Williamson has done the same with English materials.

31. Morgan Tillert (Miguel Morgan) described some of the changes in the Communion rite in his testimony before the Mexican Inquisition. Originally AGN Inquisición, tomo 175, the document strayed somehow from the Mexican archives. George R. G. Conway located it in a private collection in Mexico City, made photostats, translations, and transcripts, and deposited them in the Library of Congress and elsewhere. See Tillert's testimony of 10 January 1573, Library of Congress, G. R. G. Conway Collection, vol. 26, pp. 31–33. Portions of his testimony also appear in AGN, *Corsarios Franceses e Ingleses*, 236–49. Widely used in Europe in Medieval days, Holy Bread was ordinary bread contributed by members of the parish, blessed by the priest, and then distributed at the end of Mass. Not consecrated, it was considered as a reminder of Christ's miraculous multiplication of loaves, but the people no doubt connected it with the Eucharist. Holy Bread was received every Sunday and holy day, while the Eucharist was usually received perhaps four times each year. Rubin, *Corpus Christi*, 73. The brief prayer of blessing was a regular part of the Missal. See Legg, *Missale ad usum ecclesie Westmonasteriensis*, vol. 2, column 524.

32. See the testimony of Morgan Tillert (Miguel Morgan), 10 January 1573, *Corsarios Franceses e Ingleses*, 329–30.

33. See, for example, the testimony of William Collins (Guillermo Calens), 17 November 1572, AGN Inquisición, tomo 52, exp. 3, fol. 69–v. Morgan Tillert (Miguel Morgan) said that a man was sent around with a whip to force men to attend religious services. See his testimony of 9 December 1572 in AGN Inquisición, tomo 52, exp. 1, fols. 77–79. See also the testimony of William Collins, who said that the punishment for missing religious service was twenty-four hours' imprisonment in the chain locker; 15 November 1572, AGN Inquisición, tomo 52, exp. 3, fol. 69.

34. "De la dicha nao salieron algunos yngleses de la gente comun del navio para comprar aves y otras cosas que avian menester y que dellos confeso este deponiente uno y que otras vido oyr misa y que de la gente prinsipal no salio ninguno porque se temian, y que oydo dezir que ay muchos luteranos en Inglaterra y que tanbien ay catolicos." Testimony

of Mateo de Torres, 21 June 1568, Museo Canario de las Palmas, Inquisición, 62–5, fol. 52v, transcribed in Rumeu de Armas, *Viajes de John Hawkins,* 434–35.

35. On the negotiations see Guzman de Silva to the king, 11 February 1566, AGI Patronato 265, ramo 9, fol. 1–v.

36. Diego Ruiz de Vallejo is authority for the statement that Lovell was considered to be a relative of John Hawkins: "El capitan dezian ser deudo de Juan anchines." See his testimony of 21 April 1568, AGI Santo Domingo 78, no. 62, fol. 1v.

37. Williamson thinks that Hawkins may have transferred his interest in the ships to his brother William. *Hawkins of Plymouth,* 94.

38. Williamson, *Sir John Hawkins,* 122–23, citing Plymouth Port Book, PRO E 190/1010/18, 9 November 1566.

39. Both are listed as 160 tons in the bounty records consulted by Dietz, "Royal Bounty," 77:7, 14; but the *Swallow* is listed elsewhere as 120 and 140 tons. Hakluyt, *Principall Navigations,* 522–23.

40. The *Pascoe* was listed in 1571 under the command of Francis Drake. "The Numbre of Shippes and vessells and the masters names being within all the Portes and Creekes as with in the Realme of England, and tradinge the ware of merchandize as appearith by the Customes Accomptes, from the Feaste of St. Michaell Tharchangel anno 1571 unto the same Feaste anno 1572, Collected by Thomas Colbin Surveior of the Port of London," PRO SP Elizabeth, Domestic Addendum, SP 15/22, fol. 21v. The *Pascoe* is described in Nichols, *Sir Francis Drake Revived,* 2, as a 70-ton ship. For the *Swallow* see Dietz, "Royal Bounty," 77:14.

41. Testimony of Morgan Tillert (Miguel Morgan), 7 February 1573, AGN Inquisición, tomo 55, exp. 1, fols. 25v–26.

42. AHN, Inquisición 1824, ramo 1. Testimony of Juan de Arcaya, 1 July 1568, transcribed in Rumeu de Armas, *Viajes de John Hawkins,* 428.

43. "Se lo dezia Frances Drac, Ingles gran luterano que venia en el navio y le convertia en su ley . . . y que en qualquiera de las dos leyes de la de Roma o de la de Ingalaterr recivia dios el bien que se hazia y que la verdadera y mejor ley era la de Ingalaterra . . . cada dia el enseñava y tratava dello." Testimony of Morgan Tillert (Miguel Morgan), 14 January 1574, AGN Inquisición, tomo 75, fol. 115–v, photostat in the George R. G. Conway Collection, Library of Congress.

44. "En diez y ocho del dicho mes de maio surgio en este puerto joan de lober corsario yngles con otras quatro naos y ciertos bateles. [On 18 May the English pirate John Lovell anchored in this port with another four ships and a few boats.]" Letter from Diego Herrero and others to the king, 8 January 1568, AGI Santo Domingo 202, ramo 1, no. 15, fol. 1v. This letter is transcribed in Rumeu de Armas, *Viajes de John Hawkins,* 418.

45. Testimony of Diego Ruiz de Vallejo, 21 April 1568, AGI Santo Domingo 78, no. 62, fol. 1v.

46. Ibid.

47. "Los unos a los otros se encubren." Ibid.

48. "Tenemos gran escrupulo de consçiencia, nosotros los oficiales de vuestra magestad por los juramentos que les hazemos tomar. pues dello no se puede averiguar otra cosa sino que crehemos que se perjuran. [We, your royal officials, have a great problem of con-

science in forcing them to testify under oath. It is not possible to say anything but that we think they only perjure themselves.]" Ibid.

49. Several *cedulas* or decrees had been issued on this matter. Two laws dated at Valladolid on 16 April 1550 declared all unmanifested goods and slaves forfeit; a third dated at Toledo on 22 September 1560 forbade anyone, native or foreigner, to go to the Indies without a license. *Recopilación de leyes de los reinos,* Libro ix, titulo 26, leyes 1 and 2 (vol. 3, fol. 84v); Libro viii, titulo 17, ley 1 (vol. 4, fol. 1).

50. Baltasar de Castellanos and others to the king, 23 June 1567, AGI Santo Domingo 202, ramo 1, no. 13, fol. 2. The reference to his abandonment of the slaves is in AGI Santo Domingo 202, ramo 1, no. 14, 10 July 1567, fol. 2. Both letters are transcribed in Rumeu de Armas, *Viajes de John Hawkins,* 416.

51. "Vuestro general le embio a desir que viniese a tierra que se queria ver con el." Diego Herrero and others to the king, 8 January 1568, AGI Santo Domingo 202, ramo 1, no. 15, fol. 1–v. The letter is transcribed in Rumeu de Armas, *Viajes de John Hawkins,* 422–23.

52. Ibid.

53. "Echo en tierra algo lexos del pueblo noventa e seys esclavos que de viejos e flacos y enfermos se le morian." Ibid.

54. Diego Herrero and others to the king, 8 January 1568, AGI Santo Domingo 202, ramo 1, no. 15, fols. 1v–2.

55. Williamson thinks that Lovell was somehow tricked into bringing the slaves ashore and that the Spanish colonists treacherously refused to pay for them. He cites in proof a later reference in a manuscript attributed to Valentine Ver or Veerd (Beard?). *Sir John Hawkins,* 125, 144, 520. The manuscript is in the British Library, Cotton, Otho E VIII, fol. 32. The attribution to Valentine Veerd is based partly on the similarity of this passage to statements in Veerd's testimony before a Spanish notary on 5 October 1568, AGI Patronato 265, no. 11, fols. 1–3. In both of Veerd's stories, the slaves of 1567 are of almost no interest to Hawkins. But Veerd's Spanish testimony establishes that Hawkins followed a familiar pattern in his relations with the people of Rio de la Hacha. Hawkins asked for permission to trade sixty slaves. This was refused. He then seized the town, destroyed part of it, and took a quantity of money and jewels. When he left, he gave the townspeople sixty slaves in payment "for the damage he had done to the town."

56. The losses also involved battles at San Juan de Ulúa, as will be seen. Nichols, *Sir Francis Drake Revived,* 2.

57. "Ansi se fue y atraveso a la ysla española donde dizen que hizo mucho estrago y daño." Diego Herrero and others to the king, 8 January 1568, AGI Santo Domingo 202, ramo 1, fol. 1v.

58. BL Cotton, Otho E VIII, fol. 32. The word *deputies* was supplied by Williamson, who has edited and transcribed the supposed Valentine Veerd manuscript in his *Sir John Hawkins,* 520.

59. Nichols, *Sir Francis Drake Revived,* 2.

60. The estimated date of Drake's arrival is based on the statement by John Mun that he returned to Plymouth about a month before the new Hawkins fleet left for the Indies, 2 October 1567. AGN Inquisición, tomo 55, exp. 3, fol. 89. This is also cited by Conway in Tomson, *An Englishman and the Mexican Inquisition,* 159. The will of Edmund Drake,

dated 26 December 1566, is in the Kent Archives Office, Maidstone, PRC 16/43–D, Probate Records Canterbury, Archdeaconry Court. The burial took place the next day, 27 December; Bishop's Transcripts, Upchurch, Canterbury Cathedral Archives.

61. At the end of the first sheet a notation partly scratched out gave Clement "Melwaye" and Richard "Sawell" twelve pence each. A second page was then added to the will, giving the chair and cushion to "Richard Melwaye." PRC 16/43–D, Kent Records Office, Maidstone.

The enrolled copy of the will states that Thomas "in minore etate existit." See the copy in the Canterbury Diocese, Archdeaconry Register, vol. 39, fols. 315–16. A very indifferent transcription of the will can be found in Eliott-Drake, *Family and Heirs,* 1:18–19. There are other transcripts in the Devon Record Office, the Kent Record Office, and elsewhere. None of these is a faithful copy of the original, which admittedly is difficult to read and understand, as it was composed when Edmund Drake was at the point of death.

62. See the statement of Doña Gregoria Perez to Rodrigo Vazquez, "como viejo, que le reduzen a la leche del pecho, la quiere por mantenimiento, y remoçar se con ella [just as an old man resumes feeding at the breast, he needs it for sustenance and for rejuvenation]." Quoted in Perez, *Relaciones de Antonio Perez,* 86–87. On nursing as a profession see Fildes, "The English Wet-Nurse," 32:166.

63. PRC 16/43–D, Kent Record Office, Maidstone. There is no way to be certain about the spelling of the name, which varies in Tudor documents. See Marc'hadour, "More's First Wife," 109:3, 7.

64. See the notation in CCA, Archdeacon's Visitation Register for 1553, MS Z-3-6, fol. 56v, which seems to imply a presentment for marriage. The reappointment of John Townsely following his penance is in CCA, Sede Vacante Register N, fol. 82v. There is no such entry for Edmund Drake.

65. PRC 16/43–D, Kent Record Office, Maidstone. This follows the meaning of the phrase "new set" given in the *Oxford English Dictionary,* to follow an entirely new course of behavior. As William Tyndale put it in his introduction to the epistle, "Be a new creature and live a new life." See Tyndale, "Prologue," *The Byble,* fol. lxvi. In this edition the Old and the New Testament are separately paginated. Lady Elizabeth Eliott-Drake followed the erroneous transcript of the will in the Eliott-Drake Papers, reading "wiffe" [wife] as "wyesh" [wish]. See her *Family and Heirs,* 1:19, and the transcript of the will, DRO 346M/F589. The enrolled copy of the will in the Canterbury Diocese Archdeaconry Register, fols. 315–16, spells the word "wyef" [wife].

66. This advice is taken directly from Luther's own prologue to the Epistle to the Romans, which Tyndale adopted and augmented with a few paragraphs of his own. Tyndale, "Prologue," *New Testament,* fol. lxvi. This appears in Taverner's Bible but is separately paginated and has its own title page.

67. Youings, *Sixteenth-Century England,* 376.

68. Eliott-Drake, *Family and Heirs,* 1:21.

69. BL Cotton MSS, Otho E, VIII, fol. 17. The names have been given in various forms. According to the Spanish ambassador, they were Anton Luís (also known as Pedro Vasquez Francisco), Diego Home, and a third man named Caldera. Guzman de Silva to the king, 9 August 1567, AGS Estado 819, fol. 62; and 27 September 1567, AGS Estado

819, fol. 199. The latter manuscript bears two dates, September 27 and September 28, the first appearing twice.

70. BL Cotton MSS, Otho E. VIII, fol. 18v.

71. Guzman de Silva told the king of Spain that the fleet left on 1 October 1567. See his letter of 13 October 1567, AGS Estado 819, fol. 207. Miles Phillips, who wrote fifteen years later, said that the date was 2 October. See his account in Hakluyt, *Principall Navigations,* 562.

72. On the tonnage of the *Swallow* see Dietz, "Royal Bounty," 77:14.

73. Robert Barrett said that fifty slaves were brought from England, and it seems reasonable to assume that they were left over from Lovell's cargo. See his testimony of 8 October 1568, AGI Patronato 265, ramo 11, fol. 16.

74. BL Cotton MSS, Otho E. VIII, fol. 18v. As usual, the sources differ in listing tonnage for the ships. The Spanish ambassador in London said the two largest ships belonging to the queen were 800 tons and 300 tons, respectively. Of the four ships in Plymouth, one was 150 tons, one 100 tons, and one 80 tons. See the letter from Guzman de Silva to the king, 12 August 1567, CDIE, 527.

75. BL Cotton MSS, Otho E. VIII, fol. 19–v.

76. "Ansimismo en la dicha nao capitana venian Herrinunam y frances Drach y Niculas Anteni." Testimony of Morgan Tillert (Miguel Morgan), 9 December 1572, AGN Inquisición, tomo 55, exp. 1, fol. 22–v. The Spanish notaries attempted to write English surnames phonetically in these documents; thus Harry Newman came out as "Herrinumam." See AGN Inquisición, tomo 56, exp. 3, fol. 129.

77. The letter to the queen, dated 1 January 1592 (1593 in the Gregorian calendar system), appears in Nichols, *Sir Francis Drake Revived,* introductory pages.

78. For the original edition of Hortop's memoirs, with no reference to Francis Drake, see Hortop, *Rare Travails.* By the time Hakluyt issued his own revised and enlarged *Principall Navigations,* the story by Hortop had been changed to include three references to Drake. See Hakluyt, *Third and Last Volume,* 487–88, 490.

79. Miles Phillips, "A Discourse Written by Miles Phillips Englishman," in Hakluyt, *Principall Navigations,* 562.

80. BL Cotton MSS, Otho E. VIII, fols. 18v–19v. John Hawkins, "The 3. Unfortunate voyage," in Hakluyt, *Principall Navigations,* 553.

81. Testimony of Juan de Valverde, 16 May 1568, Museo Canaria de las Palmas, Inquisición 62–5, fol. 48v. Transcribed in Rumeu de Armas, *Viajes de John Hawkins,* 429–31.

82. Testimony of Juan de Venero, 7 May 1568, and of Juan de Valverde, 16 May 1568, Museo Canario de las Palmas, Inquisición 62–5, fol. 48–v. Transcribed in Rumeu de Armas, *Viajes de John Hawkins,* 429–31.

83. BL Cotton MSS, Otho E. VIII, fols. 20v–21.

84. Pedro de Soler, *Interrogatorio de preguntas para los testigos,* Museo Canario de las Palmas, quoted in Rumeu de Armas, *Viajes de John Hawkins,* 217–18.

85. There is a minor uncertainty about the exact sequence of events. The Cotton manuscript says that the ships left Santa Cruz for Adeje (Adessia) and remained there for a day before receiving word that the three ships were at Gomera; Hawkins then sent the *Judith*

to tell them he was on his way. BL Cotton MSS, Otho E. VIII, fol. 21v. On the other hand, Thomas Bennett (Tomas Venito) said that Hawkins sent the *Judith* to Gomera to see whether the others had arrived; when she did not return in three days, he took that as a sign that they were indeed at Gomera. See Bennett's testimony of 18 September 1568, AGI Patronato 265, ramo 12, fol. 3v. Job Hortop is authority for the statement that the ships were supposed to meet in Tenerife. See *Rare Travailes,* first page of text.

86. Testimony of Juan de Venero, 7 May 1568; Juan de Valverde, 16 May 1568; and Josepe Prieto, 25 May 1568, Museo Canario de Las Palmas, Inquisición LXII-5, fol. 48v. Transcribed in Rumeu de Armas, *Viajes de John Hawkins,* 429–33.

87. Testimony of Robert Barrett, 6 October 1568, AGI Patronato 265, ramo 11, fol. 15v.

88. Testimony of Juan de Venero, 7 May 1568, Museo Canario de las Palmas, Inquisición LXII-5, fol. 48, transcribed in Rumeu de Armas, *Viajes de John Hawkins,* 428.

89. Testimony of Thomas Bennett (Tomas Venito), 18 September 1568, AGI Patronato 265, ramo 12, fol. 3v. Roger Armour (Armar) later said that William Bennett (Venit) was punished by Hawkins at Santa Cruz for profaning a crucifix. See his testimony in AGN Inquisición, tomo 52, exp. 3, fol. 90v. Perhaps Thomas and William are different men.

90. This is the conclusion of Rumeu de Armas, *Viajes de John Hawkins,* 24, 214, 223–24. His reasoning is circuitous but convincing. Baltasar Zamora, a local merchant, reported later that "un hermano de la condesa de Soria (Feria) . . . fué a missa en la dicha isla [a brother of the Condesa de Feria went to Mass on that island]." The only man on the voyage known to be a relative of the condesa (Lady Jane Dormer) was George Fitzwilliam. Museo Canario de Las Palmas, Inquisición 70-15, quoted in *Viajes de John Hawkins,* 224.

91. Williamson, *Hawkins of Plymouth,* 180, 184.

92. BL Cotton MSS, Otho E. VIII, fol. 22–v. Testimony of William Saunders (Guillermo Sanda), 19 October 1568, AGI Patronato 265, ramo 12, fol. 11.

93. One English witness later said the French and Portuguese ships were taken at Cabo Verde, but others disagreed with his account. Testimony by Thomas Bennett (Tomas Venito), 18 September 1568, and by William Saunders (Guillermo Sanda), 19 October 1568, AGI Patronato 265, ramo 12, fols. 9–14v. BL Cotton MSS, Otho E. VIII, fols. 22–23v. William Collins said that four of the ships had "licenses from the admiral of France to rob on the seas," but the other two did not. See the testimony of William Collins (Guillermo Calens), 20 November 1572, AGN Inquisición, tomo 52, exp. 3, fols. 73–75.

94. Hortop, "Travailes," in Hakluyt, *Third and Last Volume,* 487. See also the testimony of Rodrigo Caro, 23 July 1572, AGI Patronato 267, ramo 54, fols. 1v–3.

95. Phillips, "Discourse," 563. Testimony of Valentine Veerd, 5 October 1568, and of Robert Barrett, 8 October 1568, AGI Patronato 265, ramo 11, fols. 1–3, 15–18v.

96. Hortop, "Travails," 487.

97. BL Cotton MSS, Otho E. VIII, fols. 27–28v.

98. Hortop, "Travailes," 488.

99. Hawkins, "Unfortunate Voyage," and Phillips, "Discourse," 553, 563.

100. Testimony of Robert Barrett, 8 October 1568, AGI Patronato 265, ramo 11, fol. 16; and of William Saunders (called Guillermo Sanda or Santa in the manuscript), 19 October 1568, AGI Patronato 265, ramo 12, fols. 9–14v.

101. Testimony of Thomas Bennett (Tomas Venito), 18 September 1568, AGI Patronato 265, ramo 12, fols. 2–9.

102. Hortop, "Travailes," 488.

103. BL Cotton MSS, Otho E. VIII, fol. 29.

104. There is a record of some of the furnishings left on the flagship by Hawkins in the "Relación del suceso acaecido entre el general inglés Juan de Aquins," AGI Patronato 265, ramo 11, transcribed in Rumeu de Armas, *Viajes de John Hawkins,* 484. See also the testimony of William Collins (Guillermo Calens), 20 November 1572, AGN Inquisición, tomo 52, fols. 68–74. Low was twenty-four in 1572, though the friars where he lived thought he was no more than seven or eight years old. His testimony is in AGN Inquisición, tomo 56, exp. 5, fols. 73 ff.

105. Testimony of Morgan Tillert (Miguel Morgan), 10 January 1573, 7 February 1573, and 2 March 1573; testimony of William Collins (Guillermo Calens), 17 November 1572, AGN Inquisición, tomo 52, exp. 3, fols. 68–80; tomo 55, exp. 1.

106. Testimony of Morgan Tillert (Miguel Morgan), 7 February 1573, AGN Inquisición, tomo 55, fols. 25–27.

107. Testimony of William Collins (Guillermo Calens), 19 November 1572, AGN Inquisición, tomo 52, exp. 3, fols. 73–75.

108. BL Cotton MSS, Otho E. VIII, fol. 29–v.

109. BL Cotton MSS, Otho E. VIII, fols. 30v–32. Spanish records show the arrival as 14 April; see the letter from Diego Ruiz de Vallejo to the king, 21 April 1568, transcribed in Rumeu de Armas, *Viajes de John Hawkins,* 426.

110. BL Cotton MSS, Otho E. VIII, fols. 30v–32.

111. Hortop, "Travailes," 489. Testimony of William Collins (Guillermo Calens), AGN Inquisición, tomo 52, exp. 3, fol. 75.

112. Castellanos to the king, 26 September 1568, AGI Santo Domingo 206, ramo 1, no. 19, fol. 1. This letter is transcribed in Rumeu de Armas, *Viajes de John Hawkins,* 438.

113. BL Cotton MSS, Otho E. VIII, fol. 32.

114. Hawkins, "Unfortunate Voyage," and Phillips, "Discourse," 553–54, 563.

115. Castellanos to the king, 26 September 1568, AGI Santo Domingo 206, ramo 1, no. 19, fol. 1v.

116. Testimony of Robert Barrett, 8 October 1568, AGI Patronato 265, ramo 11, fols. 16–17.

117. Hawkins, "Unfortunate Voyage," and Phillips, "Discourse," 553, 563; BL Cotton MSS, Otho E. VIII, fols. 32v–35v.

118. Testimony of Robert Barrett, 8 October 1568, AGI Patronato 265, ramo 11, fol. 17. BL Cotton MSS Otho E. VIII, fols. 37–38v; testimony of Juan Berquito, 8 September 1568, AGI Patronato 265, ramo 12, fol. 7–v; letter from Martin de Alas to the king, 30 September 1568, AGI Santa Fe 62, transcribed in Rumeu de Armas, *Viajes de John Hawkins,* 441–43.

119. BL Cotton MSS, Otho E. VIII, fols. 38v–39; testimony of Francisco Maldonado, 27 September 1568, AGI Justicia 1000, translated in Wright, *Spanish Documents Concerning English Voyages,* 135; testimony of Robert Barrett, 28 October 1568, AGI Patronato 265, ramo 11, fol. 17v.

120. English sailors were astonished at the lack of protection. See the accounts by Henry Hawkes, "A Relation of the Commodities of Nova Hispania and of the Inhabitants"; John Hawkins, "Unfortunate Voyage"; and Robert Tomson, "The Voyage of Robert Tomson Marchant, into Nova Hispania in the yeere 1555," in Hakluyt, *Principall Navigations,* 545, 554, 586.

121. BL Cotton MSS, Otho E. VIII, fols. 39v–40; Luis Zegri to the king, 18 September 1568, AGI Patronato 265, ramo 12, fol. 3; testimony of Antonio Delgadillo, 28 September 1568, AGI Justicia 1000, transcribed in Rumeu de Armas, *Viajes de John Hawkins,* 475–77.

122. Martín Enríquez to John Hawkins, 18 September 1568, AGI Indiferente General 858, transcribed in Rumeu de Armas, *Viajes de John Hawkins,* 287–88; testimony of Francisco de Bustamante, 30 September 1568, AGI Justicia 1000, translated in Wright, *Spanish Documents Concerning English Voyages,* 149.

123. Testimony of Robert Barrett, 8 October 1568, AGI Patronato 265, ramo 11, fols. 17–18; testimony of Martín Enríquez, 27 September 1568, and of Juan de Ubilla, 29 September 1568, AGI Justicia 1000, transcribed in Rumeu de Armas, *Viajes de John Hawkins,* 474, 480–81; testimony of Francisco Maldonaldo, 27 September 1568, and of Francisco de Bustamante, 30 September 1568, AGI Justicia 1000, transcribed in Wright, *Spanish Documents Concerning English Voyages,* 136–37, 150–52.

124. Hortop, "Travailes," 490; Hawkins, "Unfortunate Voyage," 556.

125. The number of ships at various stages of the voyage is unclear. According to English sources Hawkins left the African coast with nine vessels, left one (the Portuguese ship) at Cartagena, and parted from the *William and John* in the storm off the coast of Cuba. The Spanish reports usually credit him with ten ships on his arrival in Borburata and seven at San Juan de Ulúa. BL Cotton MSS, Otho E. VIII, fol. 32v. Testimony of Robert Barrett, 8 October 1568, AGI Patronato 265, ramo 11, fols. 17–18. Testimony of Diego Ruiz de Vallejo to the king, 21 April 1568, AGI Santo Domingo 78, no. 62, fol. 1v. Testimony of Antonio Delgadillo, 28 September 1568, transcribed in Rumeu de Armas, *Viajes de John Hawkins,* 425, 458, 477. Testimony of Francisco Maldonado, 27 September 1568, AGI Justicia 1000, translated in Wright, *Spanish Documents Concerning English Voyages,* 137.

126. Testimony of Francisco de Bustamante, 30 September 1568, AGI Justicia 1000, translated in Wright, *Spanish Documents Concerning English Voyages,* 151. "Relación del suceso entre Juan de Aquins y la armada de la Nueva España en el puerto de San Juan de lua," 1568, AGI Patronato 265, ramo 12, no. 3, fols. 1–2v. Testimony of Francisco Maldonado, c. 27 September 1568, AGI Justicia 1000, transcribed in Arróniz, *La batalla naval,* 69–70.

127. "Los que tenian poco quisieron ayudar a los que tenian algo par salbar lo segun paresçe pusieron lo en cobo para si." Luis Zegri to the Audiencia y Chancilleria de Nueva España, 18 September 1568, AGI Patronato 265, ramo 12, no. 4, fol. 6.

128. Hortop gives the total as 96, Hawkins as 100, and Phillips as 114. Hortop, "Travailes," 490; Hawkins, "Unfortunate Voyage," 456; Phillips, "Discourse," 468. On Drake's damaged reputation see the statement of William Borough, c. 1587, BL Lansdowne MS 52, no. 39, fol. 108v. This document is transcribed with modern spelling and punctuation in Corbett, *Papers Relating to the Navy,* 152.

3.
Raids on the Spanish Main

1. Hawkins, "Unfortunate Voyage," 556–57.

2. Ibid.; John Hawkins to William Cecil, 25 January 1568 (1569), PRO SP Domestic, 12/49/40, fol. 83–v; John Hawkins, "A Not of the places aryved at and tymes in the way," PRO SP Domestic, 12/49/40.1, fol. 85v; William Hawkins to William Cecil, 20 January 1568 (1569), PRO SP Domestic, Elizabeth, 12/49/36, fol. 75. These have been transcribed in Arber, *English Garner,* 5:211–12. Spanish authorities took thirty-two folio pages of testimony about this incident, including that of Alonso Sanchez, 23 February 1569, "Informacion sobre el navio cosario que estaba en la villa de ponte vedra y vigo," AGI Patronato 265, ramo 13, fols 7v–9. See also the Fugger newsletter of 21 January 1569 in Klarwill, *Fugger-Zeitungen ungedruchte Briefe,* 8–9.

3. Two letters from William Hawkins to William Cecil, dated 20 and 22 January 1568 (1569), PRO SP Domestic, Elizabeth, 12/49/36 and 12/49/37, fols. 75, 77.

4. William Hawkins to William Cecil, 20 and 22 January 1568 (1569), PRO SP Domestic, Elizabeth, 12/49/36 and 12/49/37, fols. 75, 77.

5. William Hawkins to William Cecil, 20, 22, 25, and 27 January 1568 (1569), PRO SP Domestic, 12/49, nos. 36, 37, 40, and 42, fols. 75, 77, 79, 88. On John Hawkins's mule train to London see Guerau de Spes to the king, 14 February 1569, AGS Estado 821, fol. 12.

6. "Sir John Hawkins, Voyage, 1568," March and April 1569, PRO SP Domestic, vol. 53, transcribed in Arber, *English Garner,* 226–48.

7. "Aquins dizen que traxo xxviii. mil pesos en oro y una arquilla de perlas." Guerau de Spes to the king, 12 March 1569 and 2 April 1569, AGS Estado 821, fols. 25–26, 38. At first De Spes had reported that the booty would not be enough to pay costs. See his letter of 14 February 1569, AGS Estado 821, fol. 12.

8. Testimony of Antonio Texera, 15 October 1568, AGI Patronato 265, ramo 12, no. 2, fol. 5. The equivalent values are taken from the testimony of William Fowler, 23 March 1569, PRO SP Domestic, vol. 53, in Arber, *English Garner,* 5:226–30.

9. Nichols, *Sir Francis Drake Revived,* 2.

10. Rumeu de Armas, *Viajes de John Hawkins,* 328–33; Williamson, *Sir John Hawkins,* 243–53.

11. Hawkins, "Unfortunate Voyage," 556; William Borough, c. July 1587, BL Lansdowne MS 52, no. 39, fol. 108v.

12. Among the authors who defend Drake on this point are Corbett, *Drake and the Tudor Navy,* 1:124–25, 400; and Thomson, *Sir Francis Drake,* 38. Henry Wagner considers the charge of desertion to be sound. *Drake's Voyage,* 10, 458. A. E. W. Mason thinks that the experience was a good lesson for young Drake, who thereupon determined never to be caught lacking again. *Life of Francis Drake,* 24–28.

13. Herrera, *Primera parte de la historia,* tomo 1, libro 15, capitulo 18, p. 720.

14. Corbett, *Drake and the Tudor Navy,* 1:126; Williamson, *Sir John Hawkins,* 200; Mason, *Life of Francis Drake,* 27.

15. Wright, *Spanish Documents Concerning English Voyages,* xvii–xxiv. See also the Fugger newsletter dated 7 December 1569 in Klarwill and Byrne, *Fugger News-Letters,* 7–8. Because of the early references to Drake in a position of command, Williamson cautioned

that this newsletter might be misleading: "It looks almost as if two documents of different dates had been mixed." *Sir John Hawkins,* p. 229.

16. "Aquellos Ingleses eran cossarios, y . . . no se les devia guardar la fe dada." Herrera, *Primera parte de la historia,* 719.

17. Saint Budeaux Parish Register, p. 46, Devon Record Office, West Division, Plymouth.

18. Youings, "Raleigh's Country and the Sea," 70:270. Five years later, in 1574, Morgan Tillert (Miguel Morgan) numbered Harry Newman, Francis Drake, Nicholas Anthony, and John Hawkins as "grandes lutheranos." AGN, Inquisición, tomo 52, exp. 3, fol. 77v. George R. G. Conway first identified Harry Newman as the possible brother-in-law of Francis Drake. See his marginal note in the G. R. G. Conway Collection, vol. 5, p. 119.

19. Eliott-Drake, *Family and Heirs,* 1:65; Browne, "Mary Newman's Marriage to Drake." John Sugden has extended the speculation even further, concluding that the John Bodman who married Margaret Newman in 1552 was the father of Jonas Bodenham who later became a servant of Drake. *Sir Francis Drake,* 43–44.

20. Testimony of John Drake, 8 January 1587, AGI, Patronato 266, ramo 49, fol. 1v.

21. See the *Western Morning News,* 15 February 1974, and other clippings in the Drake file, WSL.

22. Nichols, *Sir Francis Drake Revived,* 2.

23. PRO Queen's Remembrancer, Port Books, Dartmouth, 1569–1570, E190/927/4, fol. 1v. Two references by Gerau de Spes in his reports to the king of Spain seem to indicate the ships were owned by William Wynter. Gerau de Spes to the king, 25 February 1570 and 22 June 1570, in Hume, *State Papers, Elizabeth,* 2:234–36, 253–54. Documents found in the Spanish archives strongly suggest, however, that the ships belonged to Hawkins, and the Spanish ambassador simply made a mistake, saying William Wynter, rather than William Hawkins. Wright, *Spanish Documents Concerning English Voyages,* xxvi–xxvii. Williamson thought Drake might very well have been working for both Wynter and Hawkins, which is certainly possible. *Hawkins of Plymouth,* 172, 198.

24. Wright, *Spanish Documents Concerning English Voyages,* xxiv–xxv. Lacking access to original Spanish sources, Corbett confused this voyage with the 1571 trip, then concluded that the reports of depredations were exaggerated. *Drake and the Tudor Navy,* 1:147–150.

25. On the cargo of cloth see PRO, Queen's Remembrancer, Port Books, Dartmouth, 1569–1570, E190/927/4, fol. 1v.

26. Williamson, *Hawkins of Plymouth,* 49–55.

27. Klarwill and Byrne, *Fugger News-Letters,* 7. Errors in transcription, including a mistake in the date, led Professor Williamson to think the references to Drake were mistakenly taken from a message sent some years later, when Drake was better known. *Sir John Hawkins,* 229n. He must be at least partly correct, since the original contains a reference only to Hawkins and not to Drake. Österreichische Nationalbibliothek, Cod. 8949, fol. 123v.

28. Hoffman, *The Spanish Crown and the Defense of the Caribbean,* 111–31.

29. Nichols, *Sir Francis Drake Revived,* 2–3.

30. "Apunte sacado de una informacion hecha en Indias sobre los graves perjuicios q se padecian en aquellos costas y puertos con los corsarios ingleses, que por alli andaban y de

los robos q hizo el pirata Francisco Drake, 1575," AGI Patronato 266, ramo 1, fols 1–2v. There is an English summary, somewhat inexact, in Butler, *State Papers, Foreign,* 17:500–503.

31. Diego Flores de Valdés to the king, 16 March 1571, AGI, Panamá 40, no. 3, fols. 2v–3.

32. Williamson, *Age of Drake,* 118–19.

33. Bodleian Library, Ashmole MS 830, No. 18, quoted in Andrews, *Drake's Voyages,* 33.

34. Venta de Cruces was sometimes called Casa de Cruces. López de Velasco, *Geografía y descripción,* 173–76. Finished in 1574 by the *cosmografo-chronista* of the Consejo de Indias, this work is the nearest we come to a contemporary description of the topography of the Spanish possessions in the New World.

35. Cristóbal de Salinas to the king, 14 March 1571, AGI, Panama 33, no. 85; Diego Flores de Valdés to the king, 16 March 1571, AGI, Panama 40, no. 3, fol. 2v; Interrogatory prepared by García de Paz, 15 May 1571, AGI, Panama 32, no. 15, fols. 3v–9. Wright thinks the name Mandinga may be a tribal designation rather than a surname, even though it is used at various times in probable reference to the same man. *Spanish Documents Concerning English Voyages,* xl note. None of the Spanish reports of this date mentions Drake by name, though his identity is established from several later documents, including the report in AGI Patronato 266, ramo 1, fols. 1–2v; the brief translation in Butler, *State Papers, Foreign,* 17:501–3; and "A summarye relacon of the harmes and robberies done by Frauncis Drake," Ashmole MS 830, no. 18, quoted in Corbett, *Drake and the Tudor Navy,* 1:149. Sugden thinks that neither Drake nor any other English pirate took part in this raid. *Sir Francis Drake,* 48–49n.

36. Testimony of Juana de Estrada and of Luys de Soto, 1 March 1571, AGI, Patronato 267, ramo 60, no. 4, fols. 1–3.

37. AGI, Patronato 265, ramo 61, fol. 1. A transcription of the original Spanish text can be found in Appendix 5. The English copy of this letter has not been found. The translation used here was taken from Wright, *Spanish Documents Concerning English Voyages,* 11.

38. Valdés to the king, 16 March 1571; Martin Barrientos and others to the king, 25 May 1571, AGI, Panama 30, no. 12. The value of the recovered goods is based on an initial report by Valdés on 16 March that the loss was 50,000 pesos and the later report giving the loss as 20,000 pesos. Interrogatory, 15 May 1571, AGI Panama 32, no. 15, fol. 9.

39. AGI Patronato 266, ramo 1, fol. 1; Butler, *State Papers, Foreign,* 17:501.

40. Interrogatory, 15 May 1571, AGI, Panama 32, no. 15, fols. 3v–7.

41. López de Velasco, *Geografía y descripción,* 177.

42. Interrogatory, 15 May 1571, AGI, Panama 32, no. 15, fols. 8–9.

43. Ibid., fols. 7v–9; Licenciado Vera and others to the king, 21 May 1571, AGI, Panama 13, fol. 1v; Gonzalo Nuñez de Cerda to the king, 24 May 1571, AGI, Panama 11, fol. 187–v; Martin Barrientos and others to the king, 25 May 1571, AGI, Panama 30, no. 12. See also Cristóbal de Salinas to the king, 20 May 1571, AGI, Panama 40, translated in Wright, *Spanish Documents Concerning English Voyages,* 25–26.

44. Martin Barrientos and others to the king, 25 May 1571, AGI, Panama 30, no 12.

45. Gonzalo Nuñez de Cerda to the king, 24 May 1571, AGI, Panama 11, fols. 187–v.

46. Nichols, *Sir Francis Drake Revived*, 4–5; López de Velasco, *Geografía y descripción*, 177.

47. Nichols, *Sir Francis Drake Revived*, p. 5.

48. Butler, *State Papers, Foreign*, 17:501.

49. For the exchange rate see Nichols, *Sir Francis Drake Revived*, 69.

50. Nichols, *Sir Francis Drake Revived*, 5–7. Phillips, "Discourse," 562.

51. See the nuncupative will of John Drake, presented 12 February 1573 (1574), PRO, Wills, 7 Martyn, 51v–52. For Hawkins's claim see Williamson, *Hawkins of Plymouth*, 174–75; Rumeu de Armas, *Viajes de John Hawkins*, 331.

52. "The Numbre of Shippes and vessells and the masters names, being within all the Portes and Creekes with in the Realme of England, and tradinge the ware of merchandize as appearith by the Customes Accomptes, from the Feaste of St. Michaell Tharchangel anno 1571 unto the same Feaste anno 1572, Collected by Thomas Colbin Surveior of the Port of London," PRO SP Elizabeth, Domestic Addendum, SP 15/22, fol. 21v. As usual, tonnage estimates vary from one source to the next. The 1626 account by Philip Nichols gives the size of the vessel as 70 tons. *Sir Francis Drake Revived*, 3. An estimate made by John Hawkins in August 1571 lists the size as 60 tons. See the list of "Las naos pertene-scientes a Juan Aquins," AGS Estado 824, fol. 23, enclosure with "Lo que se ha tractado y assentado entre Don Gomez Suarez de Figueroa Duque de Feria, del consejo destado de Su Magestad y su Capitan de la guarda y Jorge FitzWilliams en nombre de Juan Aquins Ingles," 10 August 1571, AGS Estado 824, fols. 21–22.

53. Nichols, *Sir Francis Drake Revived*, 2–3, 44–45, 47, 70–74.

54. Ibid., 3.

55. Ibid., 4–5.

56. Ibid., 5–6.

57. Ibid., 7–9.

58. Ibid., 8.

59. López de Velasco, *Geografía y descripción*, 174.

60. Nichols, *Sir Francis Drake Revived*, 7–10.

61. Ibid., 8.

62. Ibid., 9–10.

63. Ibid., 10–11.

64. The early sixteenth-century codification is described in Stanislawski, "Early Spanish Town Planning in the New World." The later development of these regulations is described in Crouch, Garr, and Mundigo, *Spanish City Planning in North America*, 2–12, 60.

65. Testimony of García de Paz, 7 April 1573, AGI, Panamá 40, no. 36, fols. 12–15; Nichols, *Sir Francis Drake Revived*, 11–13.

66. Testimony of García de Paz, 7 April 1573, AGI, no. Panama 40, no. 36, fols. 12–15; Nichols, *Sir Francis Drake Revived*, 14–15.

67. Nichols, *Sir Francis Drake Revived*, 7, 13–14.

68. Diego Ortegón and Alvaro de Carvajal to the king, 4 May 1573, AGI, Panama 13, ramo 13, no. 49; Gerónimo Nuñez and others to the king, 24 February 1573, AGI, Panama 30, no. 14. See also the testimony of García de Paz, 9 April 1573, AGI, Panama 40, no. 36, fols. 12–15; Nichols, *Sir Francis Drake Revived*, 11–13, 16.

69. Licenciate Vera and others to the king, 12 September 1572, AGI, Panama 13, ramo 12, no. 47. Gerónimo Nuñez and others to the king, 24 February 1573, AGI, Panama 30, no. 14. See also the testimony of García de Paz, 9 April 1573, AGI, Panama 40, no. 36, fols. 12–15.

70. Nichols, *Sir Francis Drake Revived,* 15–16. Needless to say, this is a favorite story of many Drake biographers. One of the first to question it was James A. Froude, the first English biographer of Drake to make a thorough study of Spanish sources. Froude said the Nichols book was "obviously mythical, in parts demonstrably false and nowhere to be depended upon. It can be made out, however, that [Drake] did go to Nombre de Dios, that he found his way into town, and saw stores of bullion there which he would have liked to carry off but could not." *English Seamen in the Sixteenth Century,* 84. This judgment is too severe. Andrews, *Drake's Voyages,* 32–33, is correct in saying that the general outline of events is no doubt correct, despite the "misrepresentation of one or two matters."

71. López de Velasco, *Geografía y descripción,* 177.

72. Nichols, *Sir Francis Drake Revived,* 16–19.

73. Statement of Martín de Mendoza, 9 December 1572, AGI, Santa Fe 82, ramo 3, no. 20, fols. 8v–9. See also Nichols, *Sir Francis Drake Revived,* 20–21. Elsewhere Nichols says the Spanish fragatas varied in size from 10 to 120 tons (80).

74. Licenciate Vera and others to the king, 12 September 1572, AGI, Panama 13, ramo 12, no. 47.

75. Nichols, *Sir Francis Drake Revived,* 21–24.

76. Will of John Drake, filed 12 February 1573, PRO, Wills, 7 Martyn, fol. 51v–52.

77. López de Velasco, *Geografía y descripción,* 182, 199; Nichols, *Sir Francis Drake Revived,* 25–26.

78. López de Velasco, *Geografía y descripción,* 196–99; Nichols, *Sir Francis Drake Revived,* 26–29.

79. Nichols, *Sir Francis Drake Revived,* 29–34.

80. Ibid., 34–40.

81. Ibid., 40–43.

82. Will of John Drake, filed 12 February 1573 (1574), PRO Wills, 7 Martyn, fol. 51v–52; Nichols, *Sir Francis Drake Revived,* 33, 45, 77–80.

83. Nichols, *Sir Francis Drake Revived,* 46.

84. Ibid., 46–48. According to the narrative, the surgeon and his boy became sick from taking medicine rather than from the surgery.

85. Testimony of Morgan Tillert (Miguel Morgan), 9 December 1572 and 7 February 1573, AGN, Inquisición, tomo 55, exp. 1, fols. 22–26.

86. Nichols, *Sir Francis Drake Revived,* 47–49.

87. Ibid., 49–53.

88. Gerónimo Nuñez and others to the king, 24 February 1573, AGI Panama 30, no. 14; Nichols, *Sir Francis Drake Revived,* 53–57. The dates given by Nichols are off by about two weeks. Some years later, when Drake was raiding the Pacific coast, he told Nicolas Jorge that he had camped in a clump of mangrove near the orchard of María Alvarez, where he had a view of the center of Panama. Testimony of Nicolas Jorge, 8 March 1579, AGI Patronato 266, ramo 11, no 1, fols. 16v–17.

89. Nichols, *Sir Francis Drake Revived,* 57–58.

90. Gerónimo Nuñez de Cerda to Juan de Ovando, 2 May 1573, AGI, Patronato 265, ramo 22, fols. 1–2; Gerónimo Nuñez and others to the king, 24 February 1573, AGI, Panama 30, no. 14.

91. Gerónimo Nuñez de Cerda to Juan de Ovando, 2 May 1573, AGI Patronato 265, ramo 22, fols. 1–v.

92. Gerónimo Nuñez and others to the king, 24 February 1573, AGI Panama 30, no. 14; Nichols, *Sir Francis Drake Revived,* 61–65. Nichols mistakenly calls the place Venta Cruz.

93. López de Velasco, *Geografía y descripción,* 175. As Nichols heard the story, each slave had to mine three pesos of gold per day for himself and two for his women. Nichols, *Sir Francis Drake Revived,* 66–71, 74.

94. "Relacion de avisos que por cartas scritas de varias personas y en diferentes tiempos se tubieron de algunos daños q hicieron en Indias cosarios Ingleses," AGI Patronato 265, ramo 29, fol. 1. The document gives the captain's name as "Mestran," which Irene Wright considers to be a Spanish rendering of Oxenham. *Spanish Documents Concerning English Voyages,* 74n.

95. AGI, Patronato 265, ramo 29, fol. 1v; Nichols, *Sir Francis Drake Revived,* 72.

96. Ibid., 73–74.

97. Diego Calderon and others to the king, 14 May 1573, AGI Panama 11, fols. 208–v. The dates given by Nichols are in error by about four weeks. *Sir Francis Drake Revived,* 74–75.

98. Diego Calderon and others to the king, 14 May 1573, AGI, Panama 11, fols. 208–v. See also his deposition of 22 April 1574, AGI Panama 103, fols. 6–9.

99. Diego Calderon and others to the king, 14 May 1573, AGI Panama 11, fol. 208v. See also his deposition of 22 April 1574, AGI Panama 103, fols. 6–9; Nichols, *Sir Francis Drake Revived,* 77–78.

100. Nichols, *Sir Francis Drake Revived,* 78–80. The Nichols narrative has erroneous dates for the early months of 1573 and gives no dates for the period from April to August. The June date for the raid near the Rio Grande is based on the assumption that the rescue attempt was not completed until the middle or latter part of May. If Drake's ships were back at Cabo de Cativas by late June, they could have had the little ships ready for sea by early July.

101. PRO, Wills, 7 Martyn, fols. 51v–52.

102. Endorsement dated 12 February 1573 (1574), PRO, Wills, 7 Martyn, fols. 51v–52.

103. The enrolled copy of the sentence of nullity is PRO 43 Pyckering, fols. 335v–36. The section in question is worded in exactly the same way in the original copy, PRO Probate 10, box 84. "Comperimus et luculenter invenimus partem antedicti Francisci Drake intentionem suam in quadam sua allegatione et testamento penso per partem suam in hoc penso negotio utcumque facto et exhibito deductam quorum tenores pro hic lectis et insertis habemus et haberi voluimus nullo modo fundasse aut probasse sed in probatione sua hujusmodi omnis defecisse et deficere."

104. PRO Probate 10, box 84. "Prenominatum quoque Franciscus Drake in expensis legitimis ex parte et per partem prefate Alicia Cotton alias Drake in hac parte factis et fiendis condemnamus per hanc nostram sentenciam diffinitivam."

105. Nichols, *Sir Francis Drake Revived,* 33, 45.

106. PRO, Wills, 7 Martyn, fols. 51v–52.

107. Gerónimo Nuñez de Cerda to the king, 2 May 1573, AGI, Patronato 265, ramo 22, fol. 1v.

108. Butler, *State Papers, Foreign,* 17:500–503.

4.

The Successful Merchant

1. Barber, "Sir Francis Drake's Investment.," 113:106.

2. According to the testimony he gave in Lima in January 1587, John Drake was twenty-two or twenty-three years old. He lived with his grandmother for eight years, with his mother for another year and a half, and became the page of Francis Drake when he was ten years old. When they began the voyage around the world, John Drake was fourteen or fifteen years old. AGI Patronato 266, ramo 49, fols. 1–2v.

3. "The Awnsweare of the Earle of Essex to the Doubtes conceaved uppon his Platte for the reformation of Ulster." BL Add. MS 48,015, fol. 329. This manuscript is undated but replies to a query dated 2 January 1574 (1575).

4. "An estimate of wages certaine and all other charges . . . to the last of April 1575," PRO State Papers, Domestic, Elizabeth, SP 63/53, fols. 114–15.

5. Corbett, *Drake and the Tudor Navy,* 194n.

6. HMC, *Manuscripts of Lord de L'Isle and Dudley,* 1:427.

7. Bagwell, *Ireland Under the Tudors,* 2:299–301.

8. Ellis, *Tudor Ireland,* 267; Edwards, *Ireland in the Age of the Tudors,* 134; "Reduction of Rathlin," 90.

9. Ellis, *Tudor Ireland,* 267; Bagwell, *Ireland Under the Tudors,* 301.

10. "Reduction of Rathlin," 90.

11. "The Awnsweare of the Earle of Essex to the Doubtes conceaved uppon his Platte for the reformation of Ulster," BL Additional MS 48,015, fol. 329–v.

12. BL Additional MS 48,015, fol. 329.

13. PRO SP, Domestic, 63/53, fols. 114–15.

14. BL Additional MS 48,015, fol. 329v.

15. PRO SP Domestic, 63/53, fol. 114–v. Corbett, for some reason, thinks there is an error in the records and that Drake did not begin until 1 May 1575. *Drake and the Tudor Navy,* 1:194n.

16. Howes, *Annales,* 807.

17. "Francisco draq es hombre pobre que no tiene posible para eso por que no tiene mas de lo que hurto en las yndias y eso lo aya gastado en unas yslas alla hazia yrlanda." Testimony of John Butler, 20 February 1579, AGI Patronato 32, ramo 6, fol. 3v.

18. See, for example, Bernardino de Mendoza to the king, 9 January 1581, CDIE, 91:533. This can be compared with the transcript made at Simancas by James A. Froude, BL Add. MS 26,056 C, fol. 127v.

19. Drake, "Facts Not Generally Known."

20. Essex to the queen, 31 July 1575, quoted in "Reduction of Rathlin," 91.

21. Ibid.; Bagwell, *Ireland Under the Tudors,* 301.

22. Essex to the Queen, 31 July 1575, quoted in "Reduction of Rathlin," 91.

23. Essex to Walsingham, 31 July 1575, quoted in "Reduction of Rathlin," 91.

24. Bagwell, *Ireland Under the Tudors,* 303.

25. Ibid., 302.

26. The evidence of Doughty's treachery to Essex is outlined in Corbett, *Drake and the Tudor Navy,* 1:202–3. Corbett thinks that Doughty's duplicity was evident to all before Drake came to Ireland, but this opinion makes it difficult to understand the growing friendship between Drake and Doughty.

27. HMC, *Manuscripts of Lord De L'Isle and Dudley,* 427.

28. For Drake as suspect see John Cooke, "Sir Francis Drake, Anno domini 1577," BL Harley MS 540, fol. 102. Some authors interpret the passage to mean that Drake accused Doughty of being the poisoner. See, for example, Corbett, *Drake and the Tudor Navy,* 1:212. The opposite interpretation is found in Mason, *Life of Francis Drake,* 102. For allegations against Leicester see Edwards, *Ireland in the Age of the Tudors,* 135; Bagwell, *Ireland Under the Tudors,* 303.

29. Acerbo Velutelli, "Answere and replye touchinge the priviledge of currants," undated, BL Cotton MS, Vespasian F. IX, fols. 220–21.

30. Cooke, "Sir Francis Drake," fols. 108v–9.

31. The copy that exists today is in the handwriting of John Stow. Corbett, *Drake and the Tudor Navy,* 1:404.

32. Cooke, "Sir Francis Drake," fol. 109.

33. "Theis words foolowinge Thomas Doughtye spake to me in plymothe in the capteynes garden: as also abourd the pellican: & other places," undated, BL Harley MS 6221, fol. 104. While the manuscript is unsigned, there are names appended at the ends of some sections, though not this one. Corbett thinks some or all of the manuscript may be copied from the testimony given at Doughty's trial, later sent to Walsingham by Dr. David Lewes of the Admiralty Court. Corbett, *Drake and the Tudor Navy,* 1:405–6. An inexact transcript of the manuscript can be found in Vaux, *World Encompassed,* 171–73.

34. Andrews, *Drake's Voyages,* 64.

35. BL Cotton MS, Otho E. VIII, fols. 8–9. Andrews says the document was "probably made out in the spring or summer of 1577." See his book, *Drake's Voyages,* 50.

36. BL Cotton MS, Otho E. VIII, fol. 9. The missing elements of this folio have been reconstructed by Eva G. R. Taylor. Her rendering of the first few letters is "anas," from which she has elaborated a sentence describing a route through the Strait of Magellan. "More Light on Drake"; "Missing Draft Project."

37. Taylor believes that the coast in question was the imaginary *Terra Australis* shown on many of the printed world maps of the period. "Missing Draft Project."

38. Kelsey, "American Discoveries."

39. BL Cotton MS, Otho E. VIII, fol. 8; Andrews, *Drake's Voyages,* 42.

40. BL Cotton MS, Otho E. VIII, fol. 8v.

41. Andrews, "Aims of Drake's Expedition."

42. Quoted in Corbett, *Drake and the Tudor Navy,* 1:191.

43. Ibid., 1:vii, 204, 263.

44. Wagner, *Drake's Voyage*, 24–27.

45. Corbett, *Drake and the Tudor Navy*, 1:294, 298.

46. Nuttall, *New Light on Drake*, xxxvii-xxxix.

47. Taylor, "Missing Draft Project"; "More Light on Drake"; and *Tudor Geography*, 118.

48. Temple, "Appreciation of Drake's Achievement," xxiv.

49. Nuttall, *New Light on Drake*, xxxv–xxxvii; Taylor, *Tudor Geography*, 115–17.

50. Andrews, "Aims of Drake's Expedition," 740–41.

51. BL Harley MS 540, fol. 109.

52. "The determinacion of a voiage to be made with the swallow of 300 tons and the pellican of 120 tons to Alexandria tripoly constantinople &c.," June 1577, PRO SP Domestic, 12/114, item 44, fol. 84.

53. Valderrama to Antonio de Guaras, 20 August 1577, PRO SP 94/8, fol. 17. "Fco D. va a las antillas aun que hechan fama que van a tripoli pero que sin falta nenguna ellos van a donde digo si ban aran mucho daño si v. m. no pone remedio en ello para que no vaya."

54. Antonio de Guaras, draft of 14 November 1577, PRO SP 94/8, fol. 101. "Pasos que prometen traher gran tresoro, siendo la reyna que tambien entra con su parte y otros del consejo por el mucho quen esperian aver a esta empresa; importe mucho se hazer saber esto luegar a españa para que se metan estos en el fondo."

55. BL Cotton MS, Otho E. VIII, fol. 9.

56. Ibid.; BL Harley MS 540, fol. 109.

57. Strong, *Elizabethan Image*, 46; Finsten, "Women in the Renaissance: Elizabeth I." A well-known portrait of Elizabeth wearing the Pelican Pendant can be seen at the Walker Art Gallery, Liverpool.

58. It was finished before the first of February 1575. "The names of the shippes throughe the realme, above C [100] tons, and the quantitie of topmen under C ton throughe all the ports of Englande," 6 February 1576 (1575), PRO SP Domestic, 12/111, item 30, fol. 66.

59. PRO High Court of Admiralty (HCA), 25/1, part II.

60. BL Harley MS 540, fol. 95v; AGI Patronato 266, ramo 54, fols. 1–2v. Despite the various guesses about the relationship, John Drake says clearly that Francis Drake was his cousin: "Francisco Drac su primo hermano Ingles, y que comunmente llaman a este confessante sobrino del dicho capitan Francisco."

61. AGI Patronato 266, ramo 49, fol. 10v.

62. The relationship is confirmed in the indenture of 6 April 1583, Gloucestershire Record Office, D 1799/T 3, where John Wynter is identified as the eldest son of George Wynter and the nephew of William Wynter.

63. BL Harley MS 540, fols. 99v, 102v, 106.

64. Ibid., fol. 103v.

65. Wagner, *Drake's Voyage*, 293, makes this inference from a letter of Bernardino de Mendoza to the king, calendered as 10 June 1579, while Wagner thinks it should be 1578. Hume, *State Papers, Elizabeth*, 2:592, 679, 683. In my own opinion the document is dated correctly, but the reference is to Drake's departure in 1577, which the document does not make clear.

66. BL Harley MS 540, fol. 93.

67. "Voyadge of Mr. Wynter with Mr. Drake to ye strayt of Magallanas June 1579," BL Lansdowne MS 100, no. 2, fol. 18.

68. Cooke, "Sir Francis Drake," fol. 93v.

69. These were the victuals carried on the Fenton expedition a few years later. See Wagner, *Drake's Voyage*, 33.

70. PRO HCA 251/1, part II.

71. PRO State Papers, Domestic, Elizabeth, SP 12/114/44, fol. 84. This is also the tonnage given by John Drake in his 1582 testimony, AGI Patronato 266, ramo 49, fol. 1.

72. "The names of the shippes throughe the realme," 6 February 1576, PRO SP Domestic, 12/111, item 30, fol. 66.

73. Naish, "Mystery of the Tonnage."

74. Robinson, "Evidence About the Golden Hind"; Naish, "Identification of the Ashmolean Model."

75. "Declaración de Nuño de Silva piloto en su viage de Oporto a Brasil habiendo caido prisionero con las piratas ingleses," 23 May 1579, AGN, Inquisición, tomo 85, ramo 13, fol. 86. The conversion is an estimate based on the two Spanish methods for computing tonnage described by Carla R. Phillips in *Six Galleons for the King of Spain*, 60–61, 228–31.

76. San Juan de Antón, who was on board for a much shorter time, said the armament was mostly cast iron, only two guns being bronze. See his testimony of 6 March 1579, PRO SP Spanish 94/9A, fol. 75. There is a contemporary English translation on fols. 77–81 and a more modern one in Butler, *State Papers, Foreign*, 13:455–60.

77. AGN, Inquisición, tomo 85, ramo 13, fol. 86.

78. "Abuses in the Admiralty touching Her Majestys Navy exhibited by Mr. Hawkins," c. 1578, BL Lansdowne MS 113, fols. 45–47.

79. Testimony of John Drake, AGI Patronato 266, ramo 49, fol. 1. The Nuttall translation erroneously says there were twelve guns in each of the other ships. *New Light on Drake*, 24.

80. Edward Cliffe, "The voyage of M. Iohn Winter in the South sea by the Streight of Magellan in consort with M. Francis Drake," in Hakluyt, *Third and Last Volume*, 748–55; AGN, Inquisición, tomo 85, ramo 13, fol. 86.

81. Testimony of John Drake, 1587, AGI Patronato 266, ramo 54, fol. 2v. Lady Eliott-Drake mistakenly translated the statement to read "sixteen," and most historians take her statement as fact, listing the armament of the Marigold as sixteen guns. See, for example, Corbett, *Drake and the Tudor Navy*, 1:217; Sugden, *Sir Francis Drake*, 99.

82. Testimony of Edward Cliffe in Hakluyt, *Third and Last Volume*, 748; Testimony of John Drake, 1587, AGI Patronato 266, ramo 54, fol. 2v. The name *Swan* appears for the first time in the 1626 account based partly on notes by Francis Fletcher in Vaux, *World Encompassed*, p. 3. The narrative mistakenly calls the *Benedict* the *Christopher* and is probably unreliable in this matter as well.

83. Testimony of John Cooke, BL Harley MS 540, fol. 94; testimony of John Drake, 1587, AGI Patronato 266, ramo 54, fol. 2v; testimony of John Drake, 1582, AGI Patronato 266, ramo 49, fol. 1. Edward Cliffe says the *Benedict* was only 12 tons. See his account in

Hakluyt, *Third and Last Volume,* 748. "Verso" denotes a gun of small caliber and short range; there is little specific information about the armament of the fleet.

84. BL Sloane MS 61, fol. 3.

85. BL Harley MS 540, fol. 93.

86. AGI Patronato 266, ramo 49, fol. 1.

87. AGI Patronato 266, ramo 54, fol. 2v.

88. AGN, Inquisición, tomo 85, ramo 13, fol. 86.

89. See Nuttall, *New Light on Drake,* 301n, 424n. The original transcript of Silva's testimony says clearly "doçientos y setenta hombres," having been written once, scratched out, and rewritten. There is a poor reproduction of the sheet on her page 296. It is easy to imagine Silva telling his interrogators that Drake left England with about 170 men, lost a hundred at the strait, and had about seventy left when he reached Mexico, plus a few boys. See also the copy of the testimony sent to Spain, where the numerals 270 are clearly written. AHN Inquisición, libro 1048, fol. 5.

90. Andrews, "Aims of Drake's Expedition," 727.

91. Stafford to Walsingham, 16 October 1584, PRO, SP Foreign, 78/12/92, fol. 265. The wording differs considerably from that published in Butler, *State Papers, Foreign,* 19:108. The subject of the letter is not entirely clear. Possibly the letter refers to secret plans for the 1585 voyage to the West Indies.

92. Compare Holinshed, *Third Volume of Chronicles,* 1554–74, with the restored version printed in *Holinshed's Chronicles,* 905–8.

93. Hakluyt says that he was "seriously delt withall" not to publish the story of Drake's circumnavigation when his book was first printed. See the fourth-to-last paragraph of his address "To the Reader" in Hakluyt, *Principall Navigations.*

94. This had been an important consideration for the States General of the Netherlands in July 1581, when Drake asked for a license to raid Spanish shipping. Japikse, *Resolutiën der Staten-General,* 306–7. It was still a consideration in 1586 when a Latin pamphlet published in Germany called him the chief of the pirates. *De rebus Gallicis &c.,* no page numbers. Stung by these charges, Drake is supposed to have wasted a good part of his treasure in a partly futile attempt to buy the respect of influential Englishmen and thus rid himself of the stigma of piracy. Mendoza to the king, 9 January 1581, Hume, *State Papers, Elizabeth,* 3:75; *Declaration of the True Causes,* 25–26; *Elizabethae, Angliae reginae,* 79–80, 116.

95. Wagner, *Drake's Voyage,* 238–39.

96. See Drake's letter to the queen, 1 January 1592, in Nichols, *Sir Francis Drake Revived,* introductory pages; because the English year began on March 25, the date would be 1593 in the Gregorian calendar. Stow, *Annales,* 1220. The John Cooke manuscript is in the British Library, Harley MS 540, fols. 93–110. W. S. W. Vaux is authority for the belief that John Stow transcribed (and reworked?) the Cooke narrative, which is very critical of Drake. Vaux, *World Encompassed,* xiii. The 1585 quotation used by Stow is from William Borough's preface to *Discourse of the Variation of the Cumpas;* the quotation differs from one in the 1581 edition. David Quinn argues that the Drake leaves were printed at almost the same time as the original book and that almost all copies came with the Drake leaves already inserted. See Quinn, "Early Accounts of the Famous Voyage," 34, 40–42, 46. This

is clearly not the case. I have inspected many copies, including some that are supposed to be in the original binding. In each one the Drake leaves were obviously inserted after the edges were trimmed for binding, after vermin had eaten holes in the paper, and/or after the facing pages were otherwise stained or marred. There is a checklist of surviving copies of the *Principall Navigations* in Quinn, Armstrong, and Skelton, "The Primary Hakluyt Bibliography," 2:474–89. This checklist is based on the original work by Kerr, "Treatment of Drake's Circumnavigation."

97. Meteren, *Historiae unnd Abcontrafentung,* book 10, page 47. The story was unchanged in the unauthorized Latin edition, *Historia Belgica nostri potissimum temporis,* 293. See Linschoten, *Itinerario,* 105. See also the correspondence between Meteren and Hakluyt in the Algemeen Rijksarchief, Staten van Holland, Archieven van raadpension-arissen, Johan de Witt, 1653–72, no. 2687, fols 61-69. Meteren received the Francis Pretty manuscript from Hakluyt in 1595, then translated and published it under the title *Beschryvinge vande overtresselijke ende wijdtvermaerde Zee-vaerdt vanden Edelen Heer ende Meester Thomas Candish.* When Meteren published his first authorized edition, *Belgische ofte Nederlantsche historie van onsen tijden,* book 13, fol. 264-v, he used this manuscript for his account of the Cavendish voyage. (Hakluyt did not publish the Francis Pretty manuscript until 1600.) Presumably if Hakluyt's Drake story had been ready in 1595, that would also have been made available to Meteren.

98. Wagner, *Drake's Voyage,* 238–45.

99. Quinn, "Early Accounts of the Famous Voyage," 34.

100. *Corte Beschryvinghe.* This text was printed to accompany the map by Jodocus Hondius, *Vera Totius Expeditionis Nauticae.* Only one copy of the text seems to exist, pasted on the Hondius "Drake Broadside" map in the British Library map department, M.T.6.a.2. I am greatly indebted to Paul Valkema Blouw of Amsterdam for helping me to locate the early Claesz publications that contain the various typefaces used to identify the publisher of the "Drake Broadside" text. Although the Hondius map is undated, it contains much of the same Drake information found in his 1589 *Typus orbis terrarum* and in the 1592 globe he engraved for Emery Molyneux just before returning to Holland. The only copy of this globe now known to exist is at Petworth House in Sussex, England. There is a later state at the Middle Temple in London. Helen Wallis thinks the "Drake Broadside" map by Hondius might have been printed once in London in 1590 and again in the Netherlands in 1595. Wallis dates the Dutch text at 1595 or 1596. "Cartography of the Drake Voyage," 145. Experts on the Continent think the date of the map should be 1590. De Smet, "Jodocus Hondius, continuateur de Mercator,"770–71; Maritiem Museum, "Prins Hendrik," page 23, plate 23.

101. Hakluyt, *Principall Navigations,* "To the Reader," fourth paragraph from the end.

102. For those who are interested, there is a loose translation of the Dutch text in Wright, *Famous Voyage of Sir Francis Drake,* and a similar translation of a small part of the text in Aker, *Identification of Sir Francis Drake's Encampment,* 114–16.

103. Among those who treat it as original are Vaux, *World Encompassed,* 254; Nuttall, *New Light on Drake,* 256n; Wagner, *Drake's Voyage,* 338; Penzer, *World Encompassed,* 169.

104. Linschoten, *Itinerario,* 105.

105. Linschoten, *Thirde Book.*

106. BL Harley MS 540, fols. 93–110. Almost all the manuscripts were copied into this volume in the same hand, no doubt that of John Stow. See Corbett, *Drake and the Tudor Navy,* 1:404.

107. AGI Patronato 266, ramos 49 and 54.

108. See Quinn, "Early Accounts of the Famous Voyage," 38–39.

109. On the reference to Cavendish's voyage and refutation of the Dutch claim see Wagner, *Drake's Voyage,* 98. Wagner thinks that the descriptions of natives are seventeenth-century additions, perhaps made by John Conyers, who made the only copy of the manuscript now known to be extant (287). Helen Wallis thought that the only addition made by Conyers was the part referring to giants at the Strait of Magellan. "Cartography of Drake's Voyage," 127.

5.

Plymouth to Cape Horn

1. John Cooke, "Sir Francis Drake, Anno domini 1577," BL Harley MSS 540, fol. 93v. The man's surname is difficult to read and has been transcribed in various ways by various authors: Siday, Lydye, Sydye, and Syday.

2. Edward Cliffe gave the best description of this place, saying that it was near the town of Asaphi (now called Safi). See his report, "The Voyage of M. Iohn Winter into the South Sea," in Hakluyt, *Third and Last Volume,* 748.

3. Cooke, "Sir Francis Drake," fol. 93v. The nearby town, once named Mogador on the maps, is now called Essaouira.

4. Hakluyt, "Famous Voyage," in *Principall Navigations,* 643a. The twelve pages comprising this report appear following page 643 and are unnumbered, as they were not part of the original printing. For ease in reference they are referred to here by the letters *a* through *l.*

5. Cooke, "Sir Francis Drake," fol. 93v; Vaux, *World Encompassed,* 5–6. See also Fletcher, "The First Part of the Second Voiage about the World Attempted Continued and Happily Accomplished within the Tyme of 3 Yeares by Mr. Francis Drake at Her Highness Commaund," BL Sloane MS 61, fol. 2.

6. Neither Cooke nor Cliffe nor Fletcher (in his notes) mentions any attempt to rescue Fry. The only mention of such an effort is in Vaux, *World Encompassed,* 6, which is drawn only in part from Fletcher's notes.

7. Cliffe called the place Cape de Guer. "Voyage of M. Iohn Winter," 748.

8. Cliffe has the most detailed account. "Voyage of M. Iohn Winter," 748–49. See also the account by Cooke, "Sir Francis Drake," fol. 94–v. The sources differ a bit on details.

9. Cliffe, "Voyage of M. Iohn Winter," 748–49; Cooke, "Sir Francis Drake," fol. 94–v. The sources differ a bit on details. John Drake said that the English "took the fish and four *quintales* [about 400 pounds] of biscuit." AGI Patronato 266, ramo 49, fol. 1. "Le tomaron el pescado y quatro quintales de biscocho."

10. Cooke, "Sir Francis Drake," fol. 93v.

11. John Wynter, "A Declaracion made by me John Winter of the shipp taken by Francis Drake," BL Lansdowne MS 115, no. 60, fols. 175v–76.

12. AGI Patronato 266, ramo 54, fol. 3.

13. Cooke, "Sir Francis Drake, 1577," BL Harley MS 540, fol. 102v.

14. John Drake, AGI Patronato 266, ramo 54, fol. 3. Edward Cliffe said that they were unable to take on water, but this seems unlikely because they did not stop at any subsequent ports in the islands. See "Voyage of M. Iohn Winter," 749–50.

15. The name of the ship appears in admiralty documents quoted in Nuttall, *New Light on Drake*, 383, 385.

16. Cliffe, "Voyage of M. Iohn Winter," 749–50. See also the account by Cooke, "Sir Francis Drake," fol. 95–v; John Drake, AGI Patronato 266, ramo 49, fol. 3.

17. "Voyadg of Mr [] Winter with Fr Drak to the Streyt of Magallanus Jun 1579," BL Lansdowne MS 100, no. 2.

18. John Cooke, BL Harley MS 540, fols. 95–96v; John Drake, AGI Patronato 266, ramo 49, fol. 3; Cliffe, "Voyage of M. Iohn Winter," 750; Fletcher, "The First Part of the Second Voiage." The original Fletcher manuscript is unknown; this copy was made about 1677 by John Conyers.

19. "The Sense of Thomas Doughtie his Oration upon the Pellycan when he came from the price to the pellycan to Remayne." BL Harley MS 6221, fol. 99.

20. Fletcher, BL Sloane MS 61, fols. 6–7. Although he reported the accusation against Doughty, Fletcher did not believe it. Fletcher also stated that without the provisions from the captured ship they would not have been able to continue the voyage.

21. Cooke, BL Harley MS 540, fol. 96–v.

22. Ibid., 96v–97. These and other remarks need not be taken as Doughty's exact words, although Cooke did attempt later to recall the exact remarks or to get them from dependable witnesses.

23. Ibid., fol. 97; Fletcher, BL Sloane MS 61, fol. 7. These two sources differ in their timing, Fletcher seeming to imply that everything took place before the fleet left the Cape Verde Islands.

24. "Certayne Speeches used by Thomas Doutye abourd of the flybott in the heringe of me, Jhon [*sic*] Saracol," BL Harley MS 6221, fol. 101.

25. Cooke, BL Harley MS 540, fols. 96–v, 98–v.

26. Ibid., fol. 98v. The main sources for information about the Doughty affair are the Cooke and Fletcher manuscripts. Both are difficult to read, and Drake's biographers have been thrown into great confusion by them. Corbett took Fletcher's statement literally and said that Doughty really was "imprisoned" on the *Swan*. *Drake and the Tudor Navy*, 226–30. Apparently taking his cue from statements in BL Harley MS 6221, fol. 100v, Wagner also adopted this view, adding that Chester remained in command and served as "a kind of jailor" for Doughty and other gentlemen, including Francis Fletcher. *Drake's Voyage*, 51, 62–63. Actually, Harley MS 6221 is contradictory on this point, saying in another place that Chester was not the captain of the *Swan* when Doughty was on the ship (fol. 101). Helen Wallis had Doughty retaining command of the *Pelican* all the way to the coast of Brazil, despite Cooke's and Fletcher's statements to the contrary. *Sir Francis Drake*, 57–58. Sugden followed her account in his *Sir Francis Drake*, 104–5.

27. See the translation of Nuño de Silva's log in Nuttall, *New Light on Drake*, 278. This log, like the few others of the period that are still available in archives, is really a clean

copy prepared after the voyage, no doubt as part of an official report drawn from the charts and rough notes kept by the pilot during the trip.

28. Cliffe, "The Voyage of M. Iohn Winter," 751; Cooke, BL Harley MS 540, fol. 97; Silva's log in Nuttall, *New Light on Drake,* 278.

29. Silva's log in Nuttall, *New Light on Drake,* 278; Cooke, BL Harley MS 540, fol. 97–v; Cliffe, "Voyage of M. Iohn Winter," 751.

30. Cooke, BL Harley MS 540, fol. 97v.

31. Ibid., fol. 98v.

32. Drake, *World Encompassed,* 18–19.

33. Cliffe, "Voyage of M. Iohn Winter," 751; Cooke, BL Harley 540, fol. 98.

34. Cooke, BL Harley MS 540, fols. 99–100v; Cliffe, "Voyage of M. Iohn Winter," 750–51.

35. Cooke, BL Harley MS 540, fol. 100–v; Fletcher, BL Sloane MS 61, fols. 18v–24; Cliffe, "Voyage of M. Iohn Winter," 750–51. Fletcher records some highly imaginative stories about the "giants" and their disgusting personal characteristics, all of which can safely be ignored.

36. Fletcher, BL Sloane MS 61, fol. 23v.

37. Cooke, BL Harley MS 540, fols. 99v–100v; Cliffe, "Voyage of M. Iohn Winter," 751; Fletcher, BL Sloane MS 61, fol. 23v.

38. John Wynter, BL Lansdowne MS 100, no. 2, fol. 19.

39. Cooke, BL Harley MS 540, fol. 100–v.

40. Taylor, "More Light on Drake," 16:140–41; Donno, *An Elizabethan in 1582,* 46, 48.

41. The planned meeting is implied in Fletcher, BL Sloane MS 61, fol. 25.

42. Ibid.

43. See, for example, the remarks in Cooke, BL Harley MS 540, fol. 100.

44. Ibid., fol. 101; Fletcher, BL Sloane MS 61, fol. 25–v.

45. John Drake, AGI Patronato 266, ramo 54, fol. 4; Cooke, BL Harley MS 540, fol. 100–v; Fletcher summarizes the argument between Drake and Doughty very briefly, condensing events that took place over a period of several weeks into five or six sentences; BL Sloane MS 61, fol. 7–v.

46. Cooke, BL Harley MS 540, fol. 101v.

47. Ibid., fols. 101v–2.

48. Fletcher, BL Sloane MS 61, fols. 17v–18v, indicates that he was not on either the *Mary* or the *Swan,* both of which were frequently separated from the rest of the fleet.

49. Cooke, BL Harley MS 540, fol. 102v.

50. BL Harley MS 6221, fols. 100–105. As with the other manuscripts concerning the voyage, these copies were prepared at some later time. The date of preparation was probably no earlier than about 1588, judging from the inclusion of information related to the later Drake voyage to the West Indies. First is the use of the term *generall* in reference to Drake. The *Oxford English Dictionary* (2d ed.) lists *A Summarie and True Discourse of Sir Francis Drakes West Indian Voyage* (London: Richard Field, 1589) as the first use in English of *general* in reference to a naval commander. In addition, the Drake material in this manuscript is bound with other items relating to the West Indies voyage. See also Cooke, BL Harley MS 540, fols. 102–3.

51. Cooke, BL Harley MS 540, fols. 102v–3.

52. Ibid., fol. 103.

53. Ibid., fol. 103v.

54. Ibid., fols. 103v–4.

55. Ibid., fol. 104.

56. Ibid. The account assembled and published a half-century later by Drake's nephew makes the unlikely assertion that Doughty himself chose to be executed rather than be set ashore or be sent home to face an English court. Drake, *World Encompassed,* 30–31 (page 31 is misnumbered 32).

57. Cooke, BL Harley MS 540, fol. 104v. Wynter remembered it somewhat differently, saying that Drake had declined the offer with the same words he had used when Doughty asked to be put ashore in Peru: "He would not accept, sainge that if he should suffer him to lyve he could not answer yt to her majestie when he came into England." See his account, "Voyadg of Mr Wynter with Fr Drak to the Streyt of Magallanus Jun 1579," BL Lansdowne 100, no. 2, fol. 19.

58. Cooke, BL Harley MS 540, fols. 104v–6. Nuño de Silva had a somewhat different story of the execution: "Francisco Draq junto toda su gente que no quedo ninguno y poniendose el mas alto que los de mas saco unos papeles y los beso y puso sobre su cabeça y los leyo en boz alta y despues de leidos los enseño a los demas y todos los vieron y miraron y cortada la cabeça la tomo en la mano y la enseño y luego la arrojo diziendo Biva la Reyna de ynglaterra y todos alli dezian que aquellos papeles heran suyos della con cuya autoridad hazia aguello y la jornada. [Francis Drake gathered all his people without exception and, placing himself higher than the others, he took out some papers and kissed them and put them on his head. He read them in a loud voice, and after reading them he showed them to the others. They all saw them and looked at them. Having cut off [Doughty's] head, he took it in his hand and showed it to them and then threw it down, saying "Long live the queen of England." Everyone said that the papers were the ones given him by her, by whose authority he did that and made the journey.]" This account is contained in Silva's own testimony of 21 May 1581 concerning the letter of safe conduct given by Drake to San Juan de Anton. See the "Salvo conduto que dio francisco draq yngles a sant Joan de anton," AHN Inquisición, libro 1048, fol. 96v.

59. We have already seen that Cooke took Drake's failure to produce the commission as evidence that he had no such document. Nuño de Silva, the Portuguese pilot captured by Drake earlier in the voyage, said later that Drake told him he had papers from the queen: "Publicava venir por mandado de su reyna cuyos papeles dezia traer por donde gover-nava." It seems clear from this that Silva did not see the papers. "Suma de la confesion de Nuño de Silva Portugues piloto en 23 de mayo de 1579 años açerca del viage de francisco draq Yngles cosario y robos que hizo en el mar del sur aviendo pasado el estrecho de mag-allanes," Madrid, Archivo Historico Nacional (AHN), libro 1048, fol. 8. (This volume was formerly part of the collection of the Archivo General de Simancas.) Francisco de Zárate, who probably could not read English, said that Drake showed him the *provissiones* or "instructions" that he had from the queen. See his testimony of 16 April 1579 in AGI Patronato 266 ramo 19, fol. 2. There are quotations from this document in Wagner, *Drake's Voyage,* 377; and Nuttall, *New Light on Drake,* 209. San Juan de Anton said that

Drake claimed to have a letter from the queen, allowing him to take prizes in her name. The copy of the document in PRO SP, Foreign, Spain, 1/23, calls this a *carta de merced*. Both Wagner (*Drake's Voyage*, 366) and Butler (*State Papers, Foreign*, 13:458–59) translate the phrase as a "letter of marque," while Nuttall (*New Light on Drake*, 171) describes it more broadly as "an authorization from the Queen." Regardless of this, various statements in Anton's testimony make it fairly clear that he did not read or understand English and that he did not in fact see such a document.

60. Andrews, *Drake's Voyages*, 68; Wallis, *Sir Francis Drake*, 101.

61. Diary of Richard Madox, 12 September 1582, in Donno, *An Elizabethan in 1582*, 184.

62. Donno, *An Elizabethan in 1582*, 140–41.

63. Wynter, "A Declaracion made by me," fol. 175.

64. Cooke, BL Harley MS 540, fol. 106v.

65. In the 1559 Book of Common Prayer the formulary for the Visitation of the Sick describes the use of private confession and absolution, very much like that of the Roman Catholic Church. Booty, *Book of Common Prayer*, 50–51, 303. In addition, many priests continued to hear confessions and grant absolution to people who were not satisfied with the general confession and absolution provided in the morning and evening prayers and the Holy Communion ritual. Davies, *Worship and Theology*, 217–19.

66. Morgan Tillert (Miguel Morgan), testimony given on 14 January 1574. Library of Congress, G. R. G. Conway Collection, vol. 5, fol. 115, photostat obtained by Conway from original document in L. H. Parry Collection, Mexico City.

67. Cooke, BL Harley MS 540, fol. 106v.

68. Fletcher, BL Sloane MS 61, fol. 29.

69. Cooke, BL Harley MS 540, fols. 107v–8.

70. Ibid., fol. 109.

71. Ibid., fol. 109–v.

72. Fletcher is probably mistaken in saying that Bright became captain of the ship (BL Sloane MS 61, fols. 31, 34). No doubt John Thomas was reappointed captain, as John Drake testified, 8 January 1587, AGI Patronato 266, ramo 54, fol. 5.

73. According to Cooke the threat was specifically that he would hang thirty men. BL Harley MS 540, fol. 110. Wynter later said that he had fifty men aboard the ship. BL Lansdowne MS 100, No. 2, fol. 19v.

74. John Cooke, BL Harley MS 540, fol. 110.

75. San Juan de Anton, a Spanish captain who was taken captive by Drake a short time later, said that Drake "era muy temido de su gente." AGI Patronato 266, ramo 10, fol. 8v. Eva G. R. Taylor describes this document as a "news-letter" and suggests that the copy in the Public Record Office (SP 94/9A, fols. 73–76v) was sent to London by one of the various English merchants working in Seville. "More Light on Drake," 14:142–44. The accompanying English translation said that Drake was "greatlie feared and revered among his men, that he had a guarde about his person." SP 94/9A, fol. 79. According to Wagner, the simple Spanish statement can and perhaps should be interpreted to mean that Drake was afraid of his men and they of him. *Drake's Voyage*, 365. The version published in Butler, *State Papers, Foreign*, 13:458, changed "feared" to "beloved," the sort of change Taylor thought might be expected in a public document. See "More Light on Drake," 16:144.

76. Cooke, BL Harley MS 540, fol. 101; Cliffe, "Voyage of M. Iohn Winter," 752; Fletcher, BL Sloane MS 61, fol. 30.

77. Cooke, BL Harley MS 540, fol. 110–v.

78. This was not a result of momentary forgetfulness. Wynter called Drake's ship *pelicane* or *pellycan* a half-dozen times in his report. BL Lansdowne MS 100, No. 2, fols. 18–19v.

79. Fletcher, BL Sloane MS 61, fol. 36.

80. The Fletcher MS has this description of the prayers after the Communion service of 17 August: "This Gratious Exercise ended with prayer to God for her Most Excellent Majesty, her Honorable councell and the Church & the common weale of England." Drake, *World Encompassed,* has the ceremony on 20 August: "Which ceremonies being ended, . . . with prayers and giving thankes for her majesty, and most honorable counsell, with the whole body of the commonweale, and church of God, we continued our course" (34).

81. Drake, *World Encompassed,* 34.

82. AGS, Guerra Marina 121, ramo 34, fol. 7. The name used by Silva is a little confusing, with a feminine noun and a masculine adjective.

83. Sarmiento de Gamboa, *Viajes al Estrecho de Magallanes,* 1:193.

84. Meteren, *Historia uund Abcontrafentungh,* vol. 2, book 10, p. 47. For a discussion of the confused publication history of Emanuel van Meteren's books see Heyden, "Emanuel van Meteren's History."

85. Stow, *Annales,* 1176–77.

86. Linschoten, *Itinerario,* 110.

87. Linschoten, *Discours of Voyages,* 422. According to "The Epistle Dedicatorie" at the beginning of the volume, Richard Hakluyt brought the Dutch edition to the publisher, recommended a translator, and further recommended the publication of the work.

88. Hakluyt, *Third and Last Volume,* 748.

89. Strong, *Elizabethan Image,* 46.

90. The phrase in quotation marks is from Derek Wilson, *World Encompassed,* 234.

91. Fletcher BL Sloane MS 61, fol. 29v.

92. Drake, *World Encompassed,* 35–36.

93. Cooke, BL Harley 540, fol. 110.

94. Hakluyt, "Famous Voyage," in *Principall Navigations,* 643e.

95. AGI Patronato 266, ramo 49, fol. 1v.

96. AGI Patronato 266, ramo 54, fol. 4.

97. N. H., "The worthy and famous voyage of Master Thomas Cavendish made round about the globe of the earth, in the space of two yeares and lesse then two monethes, begun in the yeere 1586," in Hakluyt, *Principall Navigations,* 809. On the provenance of the maps used by Cavendish see testimony of Tomás Hernández, 17 May 1587, AGI Lima 31, no 27, fol. 8v.

98. Biblioteca Nazionale Centrale, Florence, Portolano 30. This map covers the Atlantic coast. Another view of the strait appears on the west coast map, which is in the Algemeen Rijksarchief, The Hague, VEL 733. On this copy the islands are unnamed.

99. N. H., "Worthy and famous voyage." Several years later when Hakluyt published

the account of Thomas Fuller, he mentioned a third island called Elizabeth. However, the 1588 statement of N. H. is very definite concerning the name and number of the islands that he saw. The name Elizabeth is very likely Hakluyt's editorial addition to the Fuller manuscript.

100. Wynter, BL Lansdowne 100, No. 2, fol. 19.

101. Cliffe, "Voyage of M. Iohn Winter," 752.

102. Wynter, BL Lansdowne 100, No. 2, fol. 20.

103. Purchas, *His Pilgrimes,* 4:1187. The story is a marginal note to the account of Peter Carder's adventures. In the account that John Wynter wrote in June 1579 he said he had carved her majesty's name on the highest mountain in the strait. If this was intended to be an act of possession, Wynter did not say so in the report he wrote at that time. BL Lansdowne 100, no. 2, fol. 19v.

104. Wynter began his return journey on 11 November and had probably reached this same island on the nineteenth. BL Landsowne 100, No. 2, fol. 20v.

105. Fletcher, BL Sloane MS 61, fol. 34.

106. "The Log Book of Francisco Albo," in *First Voyage Round the World,* p. 219.

107. "Relacion del viaje al estrecho de Magallanes escrito por Juan Ladrillero," in Medina, *Colección de documentos ineditos para la historia de Chile,* 28:239–71.

108. The cartographer Bartolomé Olives, for example, had a copy of the Ladrillero *derrotero,* or collection of sea charts, in his workshop at Messina in 1562. Almagia, *Planisferi Nautiche e Affini,* 72–73.

109. López de Velasco, *Geografía y Descripción,* 275.

110. Österreichische Nationalbibliothek, Vienna, KL 99,416. Pedro Sarmiento de Gamboa told the king of Spain in 1583 that Sancho Gutiérrez did a poor job of revising the coastlines because he was old and sick. See his "Relación de lo sucedido a la Armada Real de Su Majestad en este viaje del Estrecho de Magallanes," in *Viajes al Estrecho de Magallanes,* 1:199–200.

111. Biblioteca Apostolica Vaticana, Urbinates Latini 283, atlante nautico, Tav. X. "Es de notar . . . la nueva descripción que traxo el S.D. García este año de 1562 de toda la Costa de Chile asta el Estrecho y paresce conformanse con el derrotero del mismo Magallanes por gran ventura vino a nuestras manos donde situs esta Costa Parte al Huest suduest y parte a la quarta del Huest 4ª al suduest y assi la descrivimos aqui hasta tener mas entra relaçion no variando las formas de los Puertos ni sus alturas de como asta aqui an andando."

112. *Novus Totius Terrarum,* 1564; *Novus Orbis Terrarum,* 1570.

113. Wagner, *Drake's Voyage,* 36–37.

114. The distance given in Hakluyt is 200 leagues. See his *Principall Navigations,* 643e.

115. For 30 September as the date of the *Marigold's* disappearance see Wynter's account, written less than a year later, "Voyadg of Mr. Winter with Mr. Drake to the streyt of Magallanas June 1579," Lansdowne MS 100, no. 2. Nuño de Silva said in his first account that the little ship disappeared on 24 September. "Relación del viage del navio que dió el piloto Nuño de Silva delante su excelencia a veynte de mayo de 79," Archivo General de Simancas (AGS), Guerra Antigua, leg. 121, no. 34, fol. 2. Three days later, perhaps after consulting his notes, he said that the event occurred on 28 September. "Suma de la confe-

sión del piloto, 23 de maio 1579," AGN Inquisición, tomo 85, no. 13, fol. 85. Cliffe, who was with Wynter, agrees that the *Marigold* disappeared "the last of September . . . a very foule night." "Voyage of M. Iohn Winter," 752.

116. On the time before landfall see Fletcher, BL Sloane MS 61, fol. 34-v. John Drake said on 8 January 1587 that Drake and his crew "did not know whether the ship was lost nor what it had done." AGI Patronato 266, ramo 54, fol. 5. In a briefer statement made some three years earlier, he said that the little ship was lost in foul weather ("mal tiempo"). Ibid., ramo 49, fol. 1v.

117. Richard Madox heard a rumor in March 1582 that the ship had returned to England. See Donno, *An Elizabethan in 1582*, 95. Thomas Cavendish, passing through the straits in 1587, reported seeing the wrecked remains of the ship on the north shore at the east end of the strait. He called it John Thomas, after the common usage of the time, referring to a ship by the name of its captain or owner. Purchas, *His Pilgrimes*, 1:59.

118. On the *Elizabeth*'s position see Wynter, Lansdowne MS 100, no. 2; on the *Pelican* see AGS, Guerra Marina, leg. 121, fol. 2.

119. BL Lansdowne MS 100, No. 2.

120. Ibid.

121. San Juan de Anton, PRO, SP 94, vol. 1, p. 74. A transcript of the Spanish original from the AGI may be found in BL Add. 44,894, fol. 130.

122. Cooke, BL Harley MS 540, fol. 110v.

123. Wynter, Lansdowne MS 100, no. 2.

124. Letter from Bernardino de Mendoza to the king of Spain, 20 June 1578, in CDIE, 91:262–63.

125. "Tambien he oydo que de las siete naos que di relación en el avisso que a vuestra merced le di para su magestad que fueron para passar el Estrecho de Magallanes que yba por capitan de ellas frances drac se han buelto dos a ynglatierra con poco provecho pobres y gastados segun tengo entendido y han seguido muy mal reccividos deziendo que si fueran hombres que no dexaran de hazer como hizieron los otros de los siete los çinco passaron por el estrecho de magallanes y estos dos dexaron de passar por temor y assi se han buelto de los demas no saven hasta agora sino que se entraron por El Estrecho. [I have also heard that of the seven ships (of which I gave your mercy a report in the dispatch for his majesty) that went to pass the Strait of Magellan with Francis Drake as captain, two have returned to England, as I understand, with poor results and badly worn. They have been ill received. People say that if they were men like those in the other five ships, they would not have quit. Those two declined to continue because they were afraid and so they turned back. As of now they know nothing about the others except that they went through the strait.]" Gabriel de Aranguibel to Miguel Mendivil, 12 December 1579, AGS Guerra Marina 91, fol. 145.

126. John Drake's testimony in AGI Patronato 266, ramo 49, fol 1v.

127. Testimony of San Juan de Anton, 1 March 1579, AGI Patronato 266, ramo 10.

128. Cliffe, "Voyage of M. Iohn Winter," 757; Cooke, BL Harley 540, fol. 110v.

129. Purchas, *His Pilgrimes*, 4:1187–90.

130. Sugden, *Sir Francis Drake*, 117–18n. Pedro Sarmiento de Gamboa says he was told by Juan Griego that Drake had lost two ships and three pinnaces in the storm. See

"Sumaria relación," AGI Patronato 33, no. 3, ramo 68, transcribed in *Viajes al Estrecho de Magallanes,* 2:73–167.

131. Among those who label Wynter a deserter are Corbett, *Drake and the Tudor Navy,* 253–54; Wagner, *Drake's Voyage,* 82.

132. Taylor, "More Light on Drake,"16:139.

133. John Drake implies that the people on the *Pelican* saw the *Elizabeth* entering the mouth of the strait. AGI Patronato 266. ramo 54, fol. 5. His suspicion seems to be confirmed by the remark in "Famous Voyage" that "Winter . . . as then we supposed was put by a storme into the streights againe." Hakluyt, *Principall Navigations,* 643e.

134. AGS Guerra Marina, leg. 121, no. 34, fol. 2.

135. AGI Patronato 266, ramo 54, fol. 5.

136. Accounts of the Magellan voyage had been available in English editions for some time. Eva G. R. Taylor thinks Drake's information about Magellan came from the "handy octavo volume, *A History of Travayle,* published by Richard Willes" in 1577. "Francis Drake and the Pacific," 1:362. The achievements of Andrés de Urdaneta were also known in England, including his earlier voyage through the Strait of Magellan and on around the world. Richard Willes, "Certaine other reasons, or arguments to proove a passage by the Northwest," in Hakluyt, *Principall Navigations,* 612.

137. Mendoza to the king, 20 April 1582, CDIE, 92:347–49. In this letter Mendoza said that he was repeating and enlarging upon information that he had first sent to the king immediately after Wynter's return in 1579.

138. The phrase is "rodeando este archipielago." Herrera, *Descripción de las Indias occidentales,* 67.

139. The original report is summarized in Bernardino de Mendoza to the king, 20 April 1582, CDIE, 92:347–49.

140. Mendoza to the king, 20 April 1582, CDIE, 92:347–49. It is not clear what part of the story was current in 1579 and what was added after Drake's return. What is clear in all this is that Mendoza was a great gossip and assumed, rightly, that the king would want to know everything he heard about Drake, true or not.

141. Luke Ward, "The voyage intended toward China, wherein M. Edward Fenton was appointed Generall," in Hakluyt, *Principall Navigations,* 662–63; Donno, *An Elizabethan in 1582,* 262.

142. See the Madox diary entry for 25 November 1582 in Donno, *An Elizabethan in 1582,* 239.

143. Ibid., 239–40.

144. The Spanish understanding of the Magellan discoveries was described by Juan Bautista Gesio, "Informe sobre el estrecho de Magallanes," 27 August 1579, AGI Patronato 1-1-2/33, ramo 7, no. 2, copy in the Pastells Collection, microfilm reel 28, fols. 100–102v.

145. "La relación que Andrés de Urdaneta haze a vuestra magestad de la armada que vuestra magestad mandó para la especería con el comendador Loaísa," AGI Patronato 39, ramo 1, fol. 32v. The original manuscript reads: "La otra caravela de francisco doçes corrió fuera del estrecho la costa hazia el sur hasta çinquenta e çinco grados e dixeron despues quando tornaron que les parecía que hera alli acabamiento de tierra."

146. Santa Cruz, *Islario general,* 1:551–54.

147. Barros Arana, *Historia Jeneral de Chile,* 1:417–19, 2:193–207. Luis Galdames puts a somewhat different interpretation on events in his *History of Chile,* 54–55. The report of Juan Fernández de Ladrillero is in "Descripción de la costa del mar occeano [*sic*] desde el sur de Valdivia hasta el Estrecho de Magallanes inclusive," Patronato 1–1–2/33, ramo 1, no. 1, fols. 71–93v; microfilm reel 28, Pastells Collection, Vatican Film Library, Saint Louis University.

148. Good examples of these world maps are the Nuño García de Toreno planisphere of 1525 in the Biblioteca Medicea Laurenziana, Florence, and the Diego de Ribero planisphere of 1529 in the Biblioteca Apostolica Vaticana, Rome (Borgiano III) which were among the first to show the discoveries of the Magellan expedition; the Sancho Gutiérrez planisphere of 1555 and later in the Österreichische Nationalbibliothek, Vienna (K.I. 99.416), which was revised to show the results of the expeditions from Chile to the straits; and the Andreas Homem planisphere of 1559 in the Bibliothèque Nationale, Paris (Rés. Ge.CC. 2719).

149. Wagner, *Drake's Voyage,* 95–98.

150. Purchas, *Hakluytus Posthumus,* vol. 3, book 3, p. 461.

151. Fletcher, BL Sloane MS 61, fol. 39. The reference here is to the island south of the strait and not the one later said to have been discovered by Drake on Saint Bartholomew's Day.

152. *Vera descriptio expeditionis nauticae, Francisco Draci Angli,* Paul Mellon Collection, Yale Center for British Art.

153. Van Sype, *La Herdike Enterprinse;* Kraus, *Sir Francis Drake,* 212, accepts the date assigned by the Newberry Library, 1581. Wallis, "Cartography of the Drake Voyage," 143, dates the map 1582–83 or even later. Rodney W. Shirley accepts a ca. 1583 date. *Mapping of the World,* 171.

154. Van Sype, *La Herdike Interprinse.* The only known copy of this state of the map is in the Huntington Library, bound in [Walter Bigges,] *Expeditio Francisci Draki Equitis Angli in Indias Occidentales A. M. D. LXXXV* (Leyden: Franciscus Raphelengius, 1588), Huntington Library rare book 9074. The map plainly was not intended for this book, as it does not fit the contents, nor does the printing match that on the other maps in the book, which are all in Latin.

155. Helen Wallis identified the engraver in her "Cartography of Drake's Voyage," 139.

156. Hondius, *Typus orbis terrarum.*

157. The broadside text is *Corte Beschryvinghe van die seer heerliicke voyagie, die Capteyn Draeck inde Zuydersche Zee.* Helen Wallis notes the existence of a pamphlet edition dated 1596, in her "Cartography of Drake's Voyage," 145. The map is Hondius, *Vera Totius Expeditionis Nauticae* [Amsterdam: Cornelis Claesz, 1595],. The Amsterdam bibliographer Paul Valkema Blouw helped me locate copies of Claesz publications in the Universiteitsbibliotheek van Amsterdam that contain all of the typefaces used in the map and broadside. All the fonts except the two large initial letters appear in books and pamphlets published by Claesz between 1588 and 1592. His shop seems not to have had the type for the initial letters until 1596, however, when he used one of them in the work entitled *VVarachtighe tydinghe vande schoone aenghevanghene victorie die Godt de Scheeps Armada uyt Enghelandt naer*

Spaengien afghevaren verleent heeft over de Armade des Conincks van Spaengien. Failing to note that the broadside contained an explanatory key to the routes of Drake and Cavendish, I previously dated the pamphlet in error at 1592 and said that it may have been intended to accompany the Dutch edition of the van Sype map. See Kelsey, "Did Francis Drake Really Visit California?" 21:451. I am glad to be able to correct these two misperceptions.

158. This portion of the Martines atlas is depicted in Wieder, *De Reis van Mahu,* opp. p. 26.

159. Such information was circulating widely at the time. See the letter from the Conde de Coruña to the king, 1 November 1582, AGS Guerra Marina 119, fol. 124. The count had read the relación given by Silva to the Inquisición and was disgusted that the interrogators lacked the imagination to ask him about the strait. "En ella no dixo mas particularidad de que era estrecho, ni se le preguntó por no ymaginarse entonçes."

160. AGI Patronato 1-1-2/33, ramo 7, fol. 102, microfilm reel 28, Pastells Collection, Saint Louis University.

161. Mercator to Ortelius, 12 December 1580, in Kraus, *Sir Francis Drake,* 86–88.

162. Voisin, *Les trois mondes,* fol. 36–v.

163. Corbett, *Drake and the Tudor Navy,* 1:404; Wallis, *Sir Francis Drake,* 68; Sugden, *Sir Francis Drake,* 98–119.

164. Quinn, in fact, thinks the manuscript was taken from Fletcher in 1580 and not returned. "Early Accounts of the Famous Voyage," 38–39.

165. Wagner, *Drake's Voyage,* 289–90.

166. The translation is from Wagner, *Drake's Voyage,* 418.

167. Fletcher, BL Sloane 61, fol 38v.

168. Quinn, "Early Accounts of the Famous Voyage," 38–39.

169. The plagiarism is described at some length in Benson, *Ferdinand Magellan,* 249–54.

170. "Trae tres libros suyos de navegacion uno en françes otro en yngles y el otro hera el descubrimiento de Magallanes no se save en que lengua." Nuño de Silva, AHN Inquisición, libro 1048, fol. 5v.

171. Cliffe said: "I have seen men in England taller than . . . any of them." "Voyage of M. Iohn Winter," 751. Wynter said the same. BL Lansdowne MS 100, No. 2.

172. Fletcher, BL Sloane MS 61, fol. 37v.

173. Vaux, *World Encompassed,* 45.

174. Hawkins, *Observations,* fol. 95.

175. *Relation of a Wonderfull Voiage,* 24.

176. Fletcher, BL Sloane MS 61, fols. 34–37.

177. Benito Díaz Bravo said that Drake told him of reaching such an island; but he added that Drake also said the people of that place had only one eye, one foot, and one hand. See the Testimony of Benito Díaz Bravo, 7 March 1579, AGI Patronato 2-5-2/21, quoted in Wagner, *Drake's Voyage,* 356.

178. Ward, "Voyage intended toward China," 662–63.

179. Wagner, *Drake's Voyage,* 84–86, 96–97.

180. Taylor, "Drake and the Pacific," 1:363.

6.

Cape Horn to Guatulco

1. Nuño de Silva said that some months later, when Drake left the port of Guatulco, he took eighty persons, of whom eight were boys ("saco del puerto de guatulco 80. personas y los ocho heran muchachos"). AHN Inquisición, libro 1048, fol. 5. The manuscript in the Mexican archives has it a little differently, saying he had "fewer than eighty souls, and eight of them were boys" (menos de ochenta personas y los ocho eran muchachos). AGN Inquisición, tomo 85, no. 13, fol. 86. This is the number quoted by Nuttall in *New Light on Drake*, 302, though Wagner evidently found a copy in Seville that gave the total as eighty-eight. *Drake's Voyage*, 348. Silva also said the crew originally numbered 270 men (dozientos y setenta hombres), which Mrs. Nuttall calls a clerical error (301); the copy in Madrid has the number written out as 270. AHN Inquisición, libro 1048, fol. 5. John Drake said in 1584 that there were only about fifty left in the crew when they sailed north from the Strait of Magellan. AGI Patronato 266, ramo 49, fol. 1v.

2. BL Lansdowne 100, No. 2.

3. AGN Inquisición, tomo 85, no. 13, fol. 86.

4. BL Lansdowne 100, No. 2.

5. AGI Patronato 266, ramo 54, fol. 5.

6. Testimony of Juan Griego, quoted in Sarmiento de Gamboa, "Relación," no. 2–33, fol. 3; Silva's log, November 1578, in Nuttall, *New Light on Drake*, 286–87. Because this document was probably compiled from notes some time after the voyage, the dates and the sequence of events are sometimes at variance with those given by other witnesses.

7. López de Velasco, *Geografía y descripción*, 269, 273.

8. It was a small island, about fifteen miles long and eight miles wide, with a population of about a thousand Indians, "all warlike," to quote a Spanish commentator of the time. López de Velasco, *Geografía y descripción*, 273. The Fletcher manuscript gives the population as two thousand, one of the many exaggerations and additions in this document. BL Sloane MS 61, fol. 40.

9. Drake, *World Encompassed*, 48.

10. Testimony of Nuño de Silva, AGS Guerra Marina 121, ramo 34, fol. 2v.

11. Nuño de Silva says that one died of his wounds; see his log, 26 November 1587, in Nuttall, *New Light on Drake*, 287. John Drake says that two died of their wounds. See his testimony in AGI Patronato 266, ramo 54, fol. 5v. Ten of the men are identified by name in "A Discourse of Sir Frances Drakes jorney," BL Harley MS 280, fol. 83. Corbett identified the author as Will Legge, whose complaints against Drake appear in various places throughout the manuscript. *Drake and the Tudor Navy*, 407. This identification seems correct, though Wagner disagreed. See his *Drake's Voyage*, 244.

12. AGI Patronato 266, ramo 54, fol. 5v; "A Discourse of Sir Frances Drakes jorney," BL Harley MS 280, fol. 83. There is a long account of the death by torture of these two captives in the Fletcher manuscript, but it is clearly imaginary. BL Sloane MS 61, fol. 40v. The editor was more nearly correct in saying the place was rich in gold and silver (fol. 41v).

13. Silva's log, 16 November 1578, in Nuttall, *New Light on Drake*, 287.

14. Several sources have printed lists that compare the latitude readings in Drake sources. See, for example, Wagner, *Drake's Voyage,* 476.

15. López de Velasco, *Geografía y Descripción,* 265–66.

16. Ibid., 266.

17. Silva, AGS Guerra Marina 121, ramo 34, fol. 3; John Drake, AGI Patronato 266, fol. 2. AGI Patronato 266, ramo 54, fol. 5v. There are some elaborate details of dealings with the Indians in Drake, *World Encompassed,* 49–51.

18. Testimony of Juan Pascual, 5 March and 13 May 1580, in Nuttall, *New Light on Drake,* 325, 334–35, 339. The phrases quoted by Pascual were very simple. Drake later found it necessary to have a special interpreter, however, and to use his services to ask a very simple question. James Baron said that at the time of the capture of a ship belonging to Don Pedro de Valdés in 1588, "The said Sir Francis Drake did will his owne interpreter to ask the said Don Pedro in the spanyshe tongue whether he would yeelde unto him or noe." Drake Family Papers, Devon Record Office, 346 M/F534, typescript.

19. John Drake, AGI Patronato 266, ramo 49, fol 2. Griego, in Sarmiento de Gamboa, "Relación," no. 2–33, fol. 3, said the ship arrived at noon.

20. Sarmiento de Gamboa, "Relación," no. 2–33, fol. 4v.

21. Juan Griego, who was pilot of the ship, said that there were five Spaniards and two blacks. His testimony is quoted at length in Sarmiento de Gamboa, "Relación," no. 2–33, fol. 3. On the other hand, John Drake, who was also there, said there were eleven Spanish seamen. AGI Patronato 266, ramo 49, fol. N. The Hakluyt account said there were eight Spanish sailors and three blacks, which agrees with the total given by John Drake. *Principall Navigations,* 643e.

22. John Drake, AGI Patronato 266, ramo 54, fol. 5v.

23. BL Harley MS 280, fol. 83.

24. Griego, quoted in Sarmiento de Gamboa, "Relación," no. 2–33, fol. 3.

25. BL Harley MS 280, fol. 83.

26. Silva, AGN Inquisición, tomo 85, fol. 87. AHN Inquisición, libro 1048, fol. 5v.

27. Griego, quoted in Sarmiento de Gamboa, "Relación," no. 2–33, fol. 3v.

28. Silva, AGN Inquisición, tomo 85, fol. 91; libro 1048, fol. 6.

29. John Drake, Patronato 266, ramo 49, fol. 2.

30. Griego, quoted in Sarmiento de Gamboa, "Relación," no. 2–33, fol. 3–v.

31. BL Lansdowne MS 30, no 10. The original of this manuscript is part of the Ashmole collection (MS 830, no. 17, fol. 63) in the Bodleian Library at Oxford. Nuttall, *New Light on Drake,* 411–12.

32. BL Harley MS 280, fols. 81, 83.

33. John Drake, AGI Patronato 266, ramo 54, fol. 5v.

34. Silva, AGS Guerra Marina 121, ramo 34, fol. 3v.

35. Griego, quoted in Sarmiento de Gamboa, "Relación," no. 2–33, fol. 3v. Silva said that there were 200 Spanish soldiers, half on foot and half on horseback. AGS Guerra Marina 121, ramo 34, fol. 3v. Sarmiento de Gamboa's information is doubtless more reliable. The unknown English witness said there were 300 men on horse and 200 men on foot (BL Harley MS 280, fol. 84), a ridiculous figure since the whole Spanish population of the region was less than a hundred souls. López de Velasco, *Geografía y Descripción,* 266.

36. BL Harley MS 280, fol. 84.

37. Griego, quoted in Sarmiento de Gamboa, "Relación," no. 2–33, fol. 3v.

38. On the shore party's success see Silva's log, in Nuttall, *New Light on Drake,* 288.

39. Silva, AGS Guerra Marina 121, ramo 34, fol. 3v.

40. John Drake, AGI Patronato 266, ramo 54, fol. 5v.

41. AGN Inquisición, tomo 85, no. 13, fol. 85; Silva's log, in Nuttall, *New Light on Drake,* 289.

42. Griego, quoted in Sarmiento de Gamboa, "Relación," no. 2–33, fol. 3v; Silva, AGS Guerra Marina 121, ramo 34, fol. 3v.

43. Silva's log, in Nuttall, *New Light on Drake,* 289–90.

44. Ibid., 290; AGN Inquisición, tomo 85, no 13, fol. 86.

45. Griego, quoted in Sarmiento de Gamboa, "Relación," no. 2–33, fol. 3v.

46. Silva's log, in Nuttall, *New Light on Drake,* 289.

47. Both John Drake and Silva agree on the total of eighteen guns. AGI Patronato 266, ramo 49, fol. 1; AGN Inquisición, tomo 85, no. 13, fol. 86. Nuttall has "thirteen" bronze guns, but the Spanish original definitely says *tres* and not *trece.* AGN Inquisición, tomo 85, no. 13, fol. 86; AHN Inquisición, libro 1048, fol. 5v.

48. Testimony of San Juan de Anton, 6 March 1579, PRO, State Papers, Foreign, Spain, 94, vol. 1, fol 75. This is a contemporary copy with an indifferent English translation by one of Walsingham's secretaries in fols. 77–82v.

49. López de Velasco, *Geografía y Descripción,* 259–60, 265–66, 272.

50. According to Henry Wagner this island was later called Santa María or Constitution. See his *Drake's Voyage,* 105.

51. Silva, AGS Guerra Marina 121, ramo 34, fols. 3v–4.

52. Griego, quoted in Sarmiento de Gamboa, "Relación," no. 2–33, fol. 4.

53. Ibid. See also Silva's testimony in AGS Guerra Marina 121, ramo 34, fol. 4; John Drake, AGI Patronato 266, ramo 54, fol. 5v. When Drake's *World Encompassed* was published a half-century later, this little Indian village of a few small huts became "a great towne . . . over whom 2. Spaniards held the government" (55).

54. Griego, quoted in Sarmiento de Gamboa, "Relación," no. 2–33, fol. 4.

55. Silva, AGS Guerra Marina 121, ramo 34, fol. 4.

56. Griego, quoted in Sarmiento de Gamboa, "Relación," no. 2–33, fol. 4; Silva, AGS Guerra Marina 121, ramo 34, fol. 4. In his testimony given in 1587 John Drake said that both men taken captive at Tarapacá were *corsos,* and because of this it is often said that the man with the silver was a Corsican. However, on two occasions, a few lines earlier, John Drake said that both men were *Españoles.* AGI Patronato 266, ramo 54, fol. 6. In the statement of Nuño de Silva, cited above, one of the two men is said to have been a *correo,* or courier. Possibly the word *corso* in John Drake's testimony is an error for *correo.* On the other hand, another manuscript copy of Silva's testimony says that one of the men was a *corço.* AHN Inquisición, libro 1048, fol. 5v. This may have been a reference to Felipe Corso, one of the ship owners.

57. Juan Griego, who ought to have known, said that there were thirty-three bars of silver. See his testimony quoted in Sarmiento de Gamboa, "Relación," no. 2–33, fol. 4. Nuño de Silva said that there were thirty-seven bars of silver. AGS Guerra Marina 121, ramo 34,

fol. 4. John Drake said there were "nearly 40 bars" of silver. AGI Patronato 266, ramo 54, fol. 6. The unknown English chronicler said, "At Arica, the 57 slabs of silver we found lying open uppon ther wares, piled one over another three barrs hye." BL Harley MS 280, fol. 81.

58. AGI Patronato 266, ramo 54, fol. 6. See also Silva, AGS Guerra Marina 121, ramo 34, 4–v; Griego, quoted in Sarmiento de Gamboa, "Relación," no. 2–33, fol. 4v.

59. Griego, quoted in Sarmiento de Gamboa, "Relación," no. 2–33, fol. 4.

60. AGI Patronato 266, ramo 54, fol. 6. See also Silva, AGS Guerra Marina 121, ramo 34, fol. 4.

61. AGN Inquisición, tomo 85, no. 13, fol. 85.

62. Silva, AGS Guerra Marina 121, ramo 34, fol. 4–v. Testimony of Nicolas Jorje, AGI Patronato 266, ramo 11. Contradicting the explicit testimony of Silva and Jorje, John Drake says that they left the ship of Felipe Corso in the harbor at Arica; his testimony was given nearly a decade later, however, while the others testified within weeks of the events. AGI Patronato 266, ramo 54, fol. 6. The testimony of Juan Griego, quoted in Sarmiento de Gamboa, "Relación," no. 2–33, fol. 4, is equivocal on this point.

63. Griego, quoted in Sarmiento de Gamboa, "Relación," no. 2–33, fol. 4.

64. López de Velasco, *Geografía y Descripción*, 247–48.

65. The witnesses do not agree on this point, some saying that the warning was given by a courier sent overland. See Jorje, 28 March 1579, AGI Patronato 266, ramo 11, no. 1, fols. 13v–14; and of San Juan de Anton, ibid., ramo 10, no 1, fol. 2–v.

66. Griego, quoted in Sarmiento de Gamboa, "Relación," no. 2–33, fol. 4.

67. Jorje, 28 March 1579, AGI Patronato 266, ramo 11, fol. 13v, translated in Wagner, *Drake's Voyage*, 350–51.

68. Testimony of Benito Díaz Bravo, 18 March 1579, AGI Patronato 266, ramo 11.

69. John Drake, AGI Patronato 266, ramo 54, fol. 6. Silva, AGS Guerra Marina 121, ramo 34, fol. 4v.

70. Jorje, 28 March 1579, AGI Patronato 266, ramo 11, no 1, fols. 13v–14.

71. Silva, AGS Guerra Marina 121, ramo 34, fol. 4v; Jorje, 28 March 1579, AGI Patronato 266, ramo 11, no. 1, fol. 15.

72. John Drake, AGI Patronato 266, ramo 54, fol. 6v.

73. López de Velasco, *Geografía y Descripción*, 237.

74. John Drake, AGI Patronato 266, ramo 54, fol. 6v.

75. Sarmiento de Gamboa, "Relación," no. 2–33, fol. 1v, says that the owner was Alonso Ruiz Baptista, although most authors give the name as Alonso Rodríguez Baptista. In any case, the second name was not necessarily the surname in sixteenth-century Spanish usage, and the man was usually known as Alonso Baptista. On this point see Jorje, AGI Patronato 266, ramo 11, no. 1, fol. 15.

76. Silva, AGS Guerra Marina 121, ramo 34, fol. 4v.

77. Ibid., fol. 5; Jorje, 28 March 1579, AGI Patronato 266, ramo 11, no 1, fol. 14.

78. Jorje, 28 March 1579 in AGI Patronato 266, ramo 11, no. 1, fol. 14v.

79. John Drake, AGI Patronato 266, ramo 54, fol. 6v.

80. Ibid.

81. On the seizure of goods see Jorje, 28 March 1579, AGI Patronato 266, ramo 11, no. 1, fol. 14v.

82. Nuño de Silva said there were two ships. AGS Guerra Marina 121, ramo 34, fol. 5. John Drake said in 1584 that there were "three ships" and in 1587 that there were "two or three ships and a pinnace." AGI Patronato 266, ramo 49, fol. 2v; ramo 54, fol. 7.

83. John Drake, AGI Patronato 266, ramo 54, fol. 7; Silva, AGS Guerra Marina 121, ramo 34, fol. 5.

84. Sarmiento de Gamboa, "Relación," no. 2–33, fols. 1–v, 5v, 7–v, 12.

85. Ibid., fol. 5.

86. Silva, AGS Guerra Marina 121, ramo 34, fol. 5v.

87. López de Velasco, *Geografía y Descripción,* 224. None of the witnesses gave statements that allow a date to be fixed exactly. The date of 24 February is based on the statement by Sarmiento de Gamboa that when he arrived in Paita on 10 March, he was told that Drake had been there fourteen days earlier. See "Relación," no. 2–33, fol. 5.

88. Silva, AGS Guerra Marina 121, ramo 34, fol. 5v.

89. On the seizure of Rodríguez see his testimony of 13 April 1579 in AGI Patronato 266, ramo 11, no. 1, fol. 27–v. On setting the ship adrift see John Drake, AGI Patronato 266, ramo 54, fol. 7.

90. Testimony of Gaspar de Montalvo, AGI Patronato 266, ramo 40.

91. Silva, AGS Guerra Marina 121, ramo 34, fol. 5v.

92. A story in circulation in Guayaquil held that Drake had taken a captive in the mouth of the Guayaquil River, tried to force the man to guide him into the port, and hanged or stabbed him when he would not do so. See the testimony of Benito Díaz Bravo, 3 April 1578 (the date appears this way in the manuscript, no doubt an error for 1579), AGI Patronato 266, ramo 11, no. 1, fol. 19. Several other men testified to versions of the same story. Francisco Jácome, ibid., fol. 22; and Juan Pérez Medina, ibid., fol. 23. Medina said he did not believe the story applied to Drake but to some other English pirates.

93. López de Velasco, *Geografía y Descripción,* 226.

94. John Drake, AGI Patronato 266, ramo 54, fol. 7; Díaz Bravo, 3 April 1578 (1579), AGI Patronato 266, ramo 11, no. 1, fols. 17–19v.

95. For friars as passengers see Silva, AGS Guerra Marina 121, ramo 34, fol. 6.

96. John Drake, Patronato 266, ramo 49, fol. 2v. BL Harley MS 280, fol. 85. AGI Patronato 266, ramo 54, fol. 7.

97. BL Harley MS 280, fol. 85.

98. Díaz Bravo, 3 April 1578 (1579), AGI Patronato 266, ramo 11, no. 1, fol. 18v.

99. Ibid., fol. 18.

100. John Drake, AGI Patronato 266, ramo 54, fol. 7; Francisco Jácome, 3 April 1579, AGI Patronato 266, ramo 11, no. 1, fol. 21–v.

101. Silva, AGS Guerra Marina 121, ramo 34, fol 6. Nuttall considered this to be the same incident as the torture of the ship's clerk. *New Light on Drake,* 306. But Silva repeated the story later, stating that this man actually took the gold and omitting any account of his survival. AGN Inquisición 85, no. 13, fol. 87; AHN Inquisición, libro 1048, fol. 6. The other accounts do not mention him, but Silva said that he was "un moço mestizo"—a mulatto servant—and the witnesses did not always think it necessary to mention what happened to black men and women.

102. Díaz Bravo, 3 April 1578 (1579), AGI Patronato 266, ramo 11, no. 1, fol. 18.

103. John Drake says that the ship was three leagues distant—about seven or eight miles—when they saw it. AGI Patronato 266, ramo 54, fol. 7.

104. Ibid., fol. 7–v.

105. Ibid., fol. 7v.

106. "Yngles man amayna." "Que vinagrera es esa para amaymar benid abordo a amay-nar." Testimony of San Juan de Anton, quoted in Sarmiento de Gamboa, "Relación," no. 2–33, fol. 8. Here as in other places, some of the original Spanish has been poorly transcribed. The actual subject of the sentence is *vinagrera* or "cruet." As Nuttall indicates, this makes no sense, and she thinks the term is a copyist's error for *Inglaterra*. This makes sense, as the words would look very much alike in the handwriting of the time. Nuttall, *New Light on Drake,* 157. Wagner translates *vinagrera* as "tub," suggesting that it was probably a common term for a smelly old ship. *Drake's Voyage,* 361. This also makes sense; the reader may choose.

107. John Drake, AGI Patronato 266, ramo 54, fol. 7v. Anton himself did not mention the wound, nor did the clerk of his ship, Domingo de Liçarça. See their testimony ibid., ramo 10 (Anton); ibid., ramo 11, no. 1, fols. 23–27 (Liçarça); and Sarmiento de Gamboa, "Relación," no. 2–33, fol. 8.

108. Anton, quoted in Sarmiento de Gamboa, "Relación," no. 2–33, fol. 7–v.

109. Liçarça, 9 April 1579, AGI Patronato 266, ramo 11, no. 1, fol. 26.

110. For the food, ibid., fols. 24v–25. For the ship fittings see San Juan de Anton, quoted in Sarmiento de Gamboa, "Relación," no. 2–33, fol. 8.

111. Anton, quoted in Sarmiento de Gamboa, "Relación," no. 2–33, fol. 9v.

112. BL Harley MS 280, fol. 83.

113. Silva, AGS Guerra Marina 121, ramo 34, fol. 6.

114. Nuttall, *New Light on Drake,* 377–78. San Juan is an unusual form for a Spanish name, even in an era when Spanish practice was less rigid than it is today. In addition, Antón would be the likelier Spanish spelling. Without the expressed accent, stress falls on the first syllable, resulting in a pronunciation much closer to Hampton.

115. "San Juan de Anton, A Discourse of the voyage made by Mr. francis Drake to the streighte of Magellanus: And so to the Seas of Sur. In A[nn]o 1577 and 1578," BL Lansdowne 122, no. 4, fols. 22–28v. For Taylor's opinion about the translation see "More Light on Drake," 16:142–44.

116. Taylor, "More Light on Drake," 16:142–45.

117. For the official name see Liçarça, 9 April 1579, AGI Patronato 266, ramo 11, no. 1, fol. 23v. For the nickname see BL Harley MS 280, fols. 84–86.

118. Nuttall, *New Light on Drake,* 165.

119. BL Harley MS 280, fol. 86.

120. Hakluyt, "Famous Voyage," 2:643d.

121. For *La Plata* see Silva, AGS Guerra Marina 121, ramo 34, fol. 6. For *La Nao Rica* see AGN Inquisición 85, no. 13, fols. 85v, 87v.

122. Quoted in Nuttall, *New Light on Drake,* 293.

123. Custodio Rodríguez, AGI Patronato 266, ramo 11, no. 1, fol. 29–v; Benito Díaz Bravo, ibid., fol. 18v.

124. Testimony of San Juan de Anton, 6 March 1579, PRO SP Spanish 94/9a, fol. 75v. Anton repeated the charge that Silva was the one who had run off with a great quantity of the king's gold and silver some fifteen or twenty years earlier.

125. Rodríguez, 13 April 1579, AGI Patronato 266, ramo 11, no. 1, fol. 28.

126. Anton gave two separate lists of these gifts. One is in PRO SP Spanish 94/9A, fol. 75–v; the other is in Sarmiento de Gamboa, "Relación," no. 2–33, fol. 9.

127. Among those who credits the Hakluyt copy as being from the original is Wagner, *Drake's Voyage,* 119, 485.

128. Silva, AGS Guerra Marina 121, ramo 34, fol. 7–v. The Spanish text, carelessly copied by the notary from the original, is reproduced in the Appendix.

129. That translation was retranslated into English in Nuttall, *New Light on Drake,* 16–17. Her Spanish transcript may be seen in BL Add. MS 44,894, fols. 38–39. The Spanish original from which she took her copy is AGI Patronato 266, ramo 35, fol. 1–v. Still another copy can be found in AHN Inquisición, libro 1048, fol. 95–v.

130. See the interrogation of Butler in AGI Patronato 266, ramo 35, fol. 2.

131. Anton, AGI Patronato 266, ramo 10; there is an identical contemporary Spanish copy in PRO SP Spanish 94/9A, 75v. See also Custodio Rodríguez, AGI Patronato 266, ramo 11, no 1, fols. 28v–29.

132. "Ellos juntos a los dichos gigantes parecian muchachos." Domingo de Liçarça, 9 April 1579, AGI Patronato 266, ramo 11, no. 1, fol. 25v.

133. Anton, quoted in Sarmiento de Gamboa, "Relación," no. 2–33, fol. 9v; Anton, PRO SP Spanish 94/9A, fol. 75.

134. Silva, AGN Inquisición 85, fol. 87v; Anton, quoted in Sarmiento de Gamboa "Relación," no. 2–33, fol. 9v; John Drake, AGI Patronato 266, ramo 54, fol. 7v.

135. In his log Nuño de Silva says they arrived on 16 March; in Nuttall, *New Light on Drake,* 293. The prisoners were pretty clear that it was the twentieth. See, for example, the testimony of several prisoners taken on 8 May 1579, in AGI Patronato 266, ramo 22. A statement by Alonso Sánchez Colchero seems to indicate that he was taken prisoner on 13 March, but that was simply the Spanish method of counting weeks. See his testimony dated 15 April 1579, in AGI Patronato 266, ramo 16, no 1, fols. 1–2.

136. Testimony of Giusepe de Parraces, 8 May 1579, AGI Patronato 266, ramo 22, fols. 2v–3; Diego de Messa, ibid., fol. 4v; Alonso Sánchez Colchero, 15 April 1579, AGI Patronato 266, ramo 16, no. 1, fols. 1–2.

137. Cornieles Lambert, 8 May 1579, AGI Patronato 266, ramo 22, fol. 1–v; Giusepe de Paraces, ibid., fols. 2v–3; Francisco de Zárate to Martin Enríquez, 15 April 1579, ibid., ramo 19; John Drake, ibid., ramo 54, fol. 7v.

138. Messa, 8 May 1579, AGI Patronato 266, ramo 22, fol. 4.

139. Parraces, 8 May 1579, AGI Patronato 266, ramo 22, fol. 3.

140. Messa, 8 May 1579, AGI Patronato 266, ramo 22, fol. 4–v.

141. Parraces, 8 May 1579, AGI Patronato 266, ramo 22, fol. 3–v; Sánchez Colchero, 15 April 1579, ibid., ramo 16, no. 1, fols. 1–2. Cornieles Lambert said that Drake had given the pilot a hundred pesos (ramo 22).

142. Sánchez Colchero, 15 April 1579, AGI Patronato 266, ramo 16, no. 1, fols 1–2. Nuño de Silva says in his log that it was 24 March. Nuttall, *New Light on Drake,* 293.

143. Parraces, 8 May 1579, AGI Patronato 266, ramo 22, fol. 3–v; Messa, ibid., fol. 4–v.

144. Cornieles Lambert, 8 May 1579, AGI Patronato 266, ramo 22, fols. 1v–2.

145. Kelsey, "Finding the Way Home," 17:160–63.

146. Parraces, 8 May 1579, AGI Patronato 266, ramo 22, fol. 3; Cornieles Lambert, ibid., fol. 4.

147. Sánchez Colchero, 15 April 1579, AGI Patronato 266, ramo 16, no. 1, fols. 1–2.

148. Zárate to Enríquez, 16 April 1579, AGI Patronato 266, ramo 19, fol. 1.

149. Ibid.

150. "Yo soy muy amigo de que me traten verdad porque de lo contrario me amovi no." Ibid.

151. Ibid.

152. "Yo viera como se avian de cumplir las palabras de los cavalleros." Ibid.

153. Ibid.

154. Ibid., fols. 1v–2.

155. Ibid., fol. 1v.

156. BL Harley MS 280, fol 86.

157. Zárate to Enríquez, 16 April 1579, AGI Patronato 266, ramo 19, fols. 1v–2.

158. "Las postreras palabras que me dixo fue pedirme encarecidamente que yo dixese a algunos Yngleses que vivian en Lima como le avia topado a seis de abril y que yva bueno." Ibid., fol. 1v.

159. Pascual, 13 May 1580, quoted in Nuttall, *New Light on Drake,* 334–36; Sánchez Colchero, 15 April 1579, AGI Patronato 266, ramo 16, no. 1, fol. **N.**

160. BL Harley MS 280, fol. 86v.

161. On the length of the journey see Parraces, 8 May 1579, AGI Patronato 266, ramo 22, fol. 3v.

162. On Indian population see López de Velasco, *Geografía y Descripción,* 120. On Spanish population see testimony of Bernardino López, 15 May 1580, in Nuttall, *New Light on Drake,* 343.

163. BL Harley MS 280, fol. 86v.

164. Gaspar de Vargas to Martin Enríquez, 13 April 1579, AGI Patronato 266, ramo 14, no 1, fol. 1–v.

165. Testimony of Bernardino López, in Nuttall, *New Light on Drake,* 343.

166. BL Harley MS 280, fol. 87; testimony of Francisco Gómez Rengifo, in Nuttall, *New Light on Drake,* 350–53.

167. Gómez Rengifo, quoted in Nuttall, *New Light on Drake,* 352; Simon de Miranda, ibid., 349.

168. Pascual, quoted in Nuttall, *New Light on Drake,* 336–37; Gómez Rengifo, ibid., 354–56.

169. Gómez Rengifo, quoted in Nuttall, *New Light on Drake,* 356–57.

170. Pascual, quoted in Nuttall, *New Light on Drake,* 337.

171. Silva, AGN Inquisición 85, no. 13, fol. 92.

172. Anton, quoted in Sarmiento de Gamboa, "Relación," no. 2–33, fol. 9–v.

173. Valverde to the king, [May] 1579, AGI Patronato 266, ramo 37, no. 2, fol. 1.

174. Pascual, quoted in Nuttall, *New Light on Drake,* 338–39.

175. Zárate to Enríquez, 16 April 1579, AGI Patronato 266, ramo 19, fol. 2.

176. Pascual, quoted in Nuttall, *New Light on Drake,* 339.

177. Ibid., 325, 336; Gómez Rengifo, ibid., 354–55.

178. Gómez Rengifo, ibid., 357.

7.
Guatulco to the Pacific and Home

1. Pascual, quoted in Nuttall, *New Light on Drake,* 339.

2. Nuño de Silva, "Relaçión que dió un portugués a quien el ingles dexo en guatulco," AGI Patronato 266, ramo 17, no. 1, fol. 3.

3. Martin Enríquez to Luis de Toledo, 24 May 1579, AGI Patronato 266, ramo 17, no. 1, fol. IV.

4. AGN Inquisición 85, no. 13, fol. 93.

5. Gastaldi, *La universale descrittione del mondo.* This description of the world was intended to accompany a map, *Cosmographia universalis et exactissima iuxta postremam neotericoriam traditionem.*

6. Juan Fernández de Ladrillero, "Apreciable declaración," in Museo Naval, *Colección por Fernández de Navarrete,* vol. 15, fol. 179–v. Sarmiento de Gamboa certainly believed that there was such a strait. See "Relación," no. 2–33, fol. 13; CDIE, 94:455–56.

7. AGN Inquisición 85, no 13, fol. 93.

8. Enríquez to Toledo, 21 May 1579, AGI Patronato 266, ramo 17, no. 3, fols. 1–3.

9. Andrés de Urdaneta to the king, undated, *Colección de documentos inéditos, América y Oceanía,* ser. 2, 2:119–38.

10. Sarmiento de Gamboa, "Relación," no. 2–33, fols. IIv–12; CDIE, 94:455. Interestingly enough, Sarmiento de Gamboa mistook the meaning of the evidence and thought that Drake would surely find the northern strait and return to England that way.

11. The best description of these expeditions is in Wagner, *Spanish Voyages.*

12. Kelsey, *Juan Rodríguez Cabrillo,* 103, 115–22, 150.

13. No copy of this map survives today, not even the copy that Drake took from Colchero. This was surrendered to the queen shortly after Drake's return, and no one has seen it since. Mendoza to the king, in Hume, *State Papers, Elizabeth,* 3:55. The word for map *(carta)* is here translated as "letter." The confusion is explained by Helen Wallis in "The Cartography of Drake's Voyage," *Sir Francis Drake,* 121–22, 161n3. Lancelot Voisin, sieur de la Popelinière, also reported Elizabeth's secrecy order. See *Les trois mondes,* fol. 36–v.

14. AGI Patronato 266, ramo 49, fol. 49.

15. Ibid., ramo 54, fol. 8.

16. BL Harley MS 280, fol. 87–v.

17. The letter is reproduced in Kraus, *Sir Francis Drake,* 86–88.

18. Stafford to Walsingham, 16 October 1584, Butler, *State Papers, Foreign,* 19:108. As noted earlier, the letter may refer to the secrecy surrounding Drake's plans for the 1585 voyage to the West Indies. The published transcription of the letter differs from the original, which can be found in PRO SP Foreign 78/12/92, fol. 265.

19. Wagner, *Sir Francis Drake,* 238–39.

20. See Drake's letter to the Queen in Philip Nichols, *Sir Francis Drake Revived* (London: 1626), introductory pages.

21. Stow, *Annales,* 1220. The quotation is from Borough's preface to *Discourse of the Variation of the Cumpas.* This quotation differs from one that appeared in the 1581 edition, which makes it possible to date Stow's story as originating some time after 1585.

22. Cooke, BL Harley MS 540, fols. 93–110.

23. Meteren, *Historiae unnd Abcontrafentung,* book 10, page 47. The story was unchanged in the unauthorized Latin edition, *Historia Belgica nostri potissimum temporis, Belgii sub quatuor Burgundis & totidem Austriacis principibus coniunctionem & gubernationem breviter: turbas autem, bella et mutationes tempore Regis Philippi, Caroli V, Caesaris filii ad annum usque 1598, plenius complectens, conscripta: Senatui, populo Belgico, posterisq inscripta A. E. Meterano Belga,* 293.

24. Linschoten, *Itinerario,* 105.

25. See the correspondence between Meteren and Hakluyt in the Algemeen Rijksarchief, Staten van Holland, Archieven van raadpensionarissen, Johan de Witt, 1653–72, no. 2687, fols. 61–69. Meteren received the Francis Pretty manuscript from Hakluyt in 1595, then translated and published it under the title *Beschryvinge vande overtresselijke ende wijdtvermaerde Zee-vaerdt vanden Edelen Heer ende Meester Thomas Candish, met drie schepen uytghevaren den 21. Julij 1586, ende met een schip wederom ghekeert in Pleymouth, den 9. September 1588.* When Meteren published the first authorized edition of his own work, *Belgische ofte Nederlantsche historie van onsen tijden,* he used this manuscript for his account of the Cavendish voyage. (Hakluyt did not publish the Francis Pretty manuscript until 1600.) Presumably if Hakluyt's Drake story had been ready in 1595, that would also have been made available to Meteren.

26. Wagner, *Sir Francis Drake,* 238–45.

27. Quinn, "Early Accounts of the Famous Voyage," 34–38.

28. *Corte Beschryvinghe.* This text is now found pasted at the edges of the "Drake Broadside" map in the British Library.

29. This is the "Drake Broadside" map in the British Library map department, M.T. 6.a.2. The fact that map and text belong together is clear from the explanation of the map symbols found in the center panel of text.

30. Van Sype, *La Herdike Enterprinse,* copy in Newberry Library, Map Department, Ayer *133 D7 H55 1581.

31. Van Sype, *La Herdike Interprinse,* copy in the Huntington Library, San Marino, bound in Bigges, *Expeditio Francisci Draki.* This is the only known copy of this state of the map, although another (later) state can be found in the New York Public Library.

32. Described in Mendoza to the king, 16 October 1580, BL Add. MS 28,420, fol. 30; ibid., 20 April 1582, CDIE, 92:347–49.

33. Anton, quoted in Sarmiento de Gamboa, "Relación," no. 2–33, fol. 9v; CDIE, 94:449–50.

34. AGN Inquisición 85, no. 13, fol. 86v.

35. Purchas, *His Pilgrimes,* vol. 3, book 3, p. 461. Helen Wallis has suggested that the map "probably perished in the fire which destroyed the Palace of Whitehall in January 1698." See "Cartography of Drake's Voyage."

36. On concealment of the map from the Spanish see Mendoza to the king, 20 April 1582, CDIE, 92:347–49.

37. John Drake, AGI Patronato 266, ramo 49, fol. 3.

38. Herrera, *Segunda parte de la historia,* 386.

39. See Sarmiento de Gamboa to the king, 15 September 1590, AGI Patronato 33, no. 3, ramo 68, fol. 73; Argensola, *Conquista de las Islas Malucas,* 105–6, 136.

40. "Draeck noemde dit Eylandt Nova Albion." BL, map department, M.T. 6.a.2. There is a loose translation of the Dutch text in Wright, *Famous Voyage of Sir Francis Drake.* A small part of the text is also translated in Raymond Aker's study, *Identification of Sir Francis Drake's Encampment,* 114–16.

41. Bry, "Descriptio primi itineris," 13. Bry, "Additamentum," 15. In the German edition, the section dealing with Drake was actually printed in 1600.

42. AGI Patronato 266, ramo 54, fol. 8.

43. Meteren, *Belgische ofte Nederlantsche historie,* book 10, fols. 174v–75. Meteren's basic Drake story was written about 1593, but the information about the latitude did not appear in the earlier unauthorized German (1593–96) and Latin (1598) editions, which were both defective in many ways. The text for the Dutch edition was probably corrected in 1596 or 1597, when it was approved for publication. Meteren made numerous corrections in this and later editions (including the addition of many later exploits by Drake and a corrected version of the Cavendish voyage around the world), but he was satisfied with his account of the Drake circumnavigation and never changed it again. The California coast is delineated on the 1559 world map of Andreas Homem, "Universa ac navigabilis totius terrarum orbis descriptio," which was copied from the Spanish *padrón general,* the official collection of navigational charts and maps in Seville. The Homem map was apparently commissioned by the Spanish king as a gift for the king of France. Cortesao and Texeira da Mota, *Portugaliae Monumenta Cartographica,* 2:67–72, plates 187–91. Homem's work was well known to Hakluyt, who called him "the prince of the Cosmographers of this age." Letter from Hakluyt to Walter Raleigh, 30 December 1586, in Taylor, *Writings of the Hakluyts,* 2:355.

44. Zárate Salmerón, "Relaciones de Nuevo Mexico," 197–99. There is a translation in Milich, *Relaciones,* 96–97. An earlier translation can be found in *Land of Sunshine* (February 1900), 12:184–85. It ought to be noted that, according to this account, the pilot had brought Drake through the Strait of Anian, from the North Sea to the South, then had wandered for some 500 leagues before seeing an arm of the Gulf of California, which he took to be the same strait. It is not clear how much of this story is attributable to Governor Rodrigo del Rio, how much to Antonio de la Ascención, and how much to Jerónimo de Zárate Salmerón, not to mention the original N. de Morera or Morena (both forms appear in the story). Zárate certainly wanted to believe that the Gulf of California (Mar Rojo) was the Strait of Anian, and this concept is planted here and there in his report.

45. Contemporary maps of the harbor appear in Basil Ringrose, "South Sea Waggoner," 9944, National Maritime Museum, Greenwich, England. Thirteen other copies are known, including HM 918 at the Huntington Library, and Codex Hack at the John Carter Brown Library.

46. The view of Acapulco bay is found in the Vingboons Atlas, VELH 619–18, Algemeen

Rijksarchief, The Hague. Vingboons copied it about 1650 from Adriaen Boot's original, which was destroyed at Middleburg during the war. The Atlas has been published in facsimile with brief remarks on Adriaen Boot and his work. See Bracht, *Vingboons-Atlas*, p. 5.

47. For a discussion of the various theories concerning the inset map see Hanna, *Lost Harbor*, 271–95. Some enhancements of the "Portus Novae Albionis" inset appear in the drawings used to illustrate comments by Raymond Aker of the Drake Navigator's Guild in "The Francis Drake Controversy," where two rock formations have become "a stranded log" and "a driftwood stump." Also see Hanna, *Lost Harbor*, 272; and Aker and Von der Porten, *Discovering Portus Novae Albionis*, 16.

48. See the Madox diary entry for 13 October 1582 in Donno, *An Elizabethan in 1582*, 208.

49. AGI Patronato 266, ramo 54, fol. 8.

50. Meteren, *Belgische ofte Nederlandische Historiie*, book 10, fols. 174v–75.

51. Hakluyt, *Principall Navigations*, 643g; Hakluyt, *Third and Last Volume*, 440, 737.

52. Drake, *World Encompassed*, 64.

53. Kelsey, *Juan Rodríguez Cabrillo*, 150–160.

54. Wagner, *Spanish Voyages*, 121–24.

55. In one of the earliest such maps available, Ringrose, "South Sea Waggoner," fol. 4v, "El Puerto de MonteRey" is "a very good port and greate succor for China ships." This description echoes the words, quoted in the text, of Padre Antonio de la Ascención, 21 March 1603, transcribed in Wagner, *Spanish Voyages*, 246. Sebastián Vizcaino called it "ample for any class of ships whatever." See his testimony of 29 December 1602, quoted in Holmes, *From New Spain by Sea*, 179.

56. See the Madox diary entry for 13 October 1582 in Donno, *An Elizabethan in 1582*, 208.

57. AGI Patronato 266, ramo 54, fol. 8.

58. For the early geographical usage of the word California see the c. 1579 letter of Licenciado Valverde in AGI Patronato 266, ramo 37; and the letter from Santiago de Vera to the king, 26 June 1588, AGI Filipinas 6, ramo 3, no. 69, fol. 1. See also the explanation of Abbad y Lasierra, *Descripción de las costas de California*, 110. The later extension of the meaning to include other areas is explained in Portillo, *Descubrimientos y exploraciones*, 117–19.

59. Quoted from the journal of Francis Pretty, excerpted in Mathes, *Capture of the Santa Ana*, 23.

60. Hakluyt, *Principall Navigations*, 643h; *Corte Beschryvinghe*; Bry, "Additamentum," 14.

61. Drake, *World Encompassed*, 71–74.

62. See the Madox diary entry for 13 October 1582 in Donno, *An Elizabethan in 1582*, 208.

63. Heizer, "Francis Drake and the California Indians."

64. Ibid., 63, 67, 71, 76–77.

65. Ibid., 23–26; Callaghan, *Bodega Miwok Dictionary*.

66. García-Pelayo y Gross and Durand, *Diccionario Moderno Español-Inglés*.

67. Von der Porten, "The Drake Puzzle Solved." See also his earlier studies, *Drake and Cermeño in California* and *Porcelains and Terra Cottas*; see also Von der Porten and Shangraw, *The Drake and Cermeño Expeditions*. The argument takes an interesting circu-

lar course in Pijl-Ketel, *The Ceramic Load of the "Witte Leeuw,"* 50, where the heretofore undated ceramics from Drakes Bay are used to identify similar pieces from the cargo of the *Witte Leeuw,* sunk more than thirty years later.

68. See, for example, Beals and Steele, "Chinese Porcelains."

69. The most recent scientific tests were reported by Helen V. Michel and Frank Asaro in their report *Chemical Study of the Plate of Brass,* p. 23, which states: "The Plate of Brass . . . was made in the XVIII to the XX centuries. The most probable period is the late XIX and early XX centuries." The whole controversy is reviewed by James D. Hart in *The Plate of Brass Reexamined.*

70. Hakluyt, *Principall Navigations,* 643i.

71. BL Harley MS 280, fol. 87.

72. See *Corte Beschryvingh.*

73. Drake, *World Encompassed,* 80.

74. BL Harley MS 280, fol. 87.

75. Hakluyt, *Principall Navigations,* 643i.

76. Drake, *World Encompassed,* 80.

77. Hakluyt, *Principall Navigations,* 643i.

78. California State Historical Resources Commission, "Francis Drake in California Hearings," p. 3. Interestingly enough, the Drake Navigators Guild does not care for this testimony. See Aker and Von der Porten, *Discovering Portus Albionis,* 29–30, which describes the meeting without ever mentioning Benson or his remarks. Thomas Cavendish saw conies at Aguada Segura. Mathes, *Capture of the Santa Ana,* 25.

79. Hakluyt, *Principall Navigations,* 643h.

80. Wagner, *Sir Francis Drake,* 169.

81. California State Historical Resources Commission, "Francis Drake in California Hearings," p. 3.

82. Hakluyt, *Principall Navigations,* 643g; Meteren, *Belgische ofte Nederlantsche historie,* fol. 174v.

83. Drake, *World Encompassed,* 64.

84. Davidson, *Francis Drake on the Northwest Coast of America,* 82–83.

85. Kelsey, *Juan Rodríguez Cabrillo,* 155–60; Kelsey, "Finding the Way Home," 17:159–60.

86. Henry Wagner thinks that Colchero told Drake that Cabrillo had not touched land at any place farther north than 36°. Perhaps so, though it seems likely that he landed in many more places than those listed in the brief narrative now known as Cabrillo's log. Wagner, *Sir Francis Drake,* 149.

87. On abandoning the ship see John Drake, AGI Patronato 266, ramo 54, fol. 8.

88. Testimony of Corneiles Lambert and Giusepe de Parraces, AGI Patronato 266, ramo 22, fols. 2, 3.

89. The stories are summarized in Hanna, *Lost Harbor,* 54–65.

90. John Drake, AGI Patronato 266, ramo 49, fol. 3v.

91. BL Harley MS 280, fol. 87.

92. Hakluyt, *Principall Navigations,* 643g.

93. Drake, *World Encompassed,* 82.

94. Kelsey, "Finding the Way Home," 17:155–61.

95. John Drake, AGI Patronato 266, ramo 54, fol. 8.

96. This is taken from the description of William A. Lessa, who analyzed the ethnographical and historical information in the various accounts in arriving at his conclusions. See *Drake's Island of Thieves,* 251–52.

97. Hakluyt, *Principall Navigations,* 643i.

98. John Drake, AGI Patronato 266, ramo 49, fol. 3; ibid., ramo 54, fol. 8.

99. In his first account John Drake said that twenty were killed. AGI Patronato 266, ramo 49, fol. 3. There was no mention of this in the second account. In Drake, *World Encompassed,* the story changed completely. The cannon was fired "not to hurt them but to affright them" (83).

100. John Drake, AGI Patronato 266, ramo 49, fol. 3; ibid., ramo 54, fol. 8.

101. John Drake, AGI Patronato 266, ramo 49, fol. 3; ibid. ramo 54, fol. 8; Hakluyt, *Principall Navigations,* 643g.

102. AGI Patronato 266, ramo 54, fol. 8v.

103. Hakluyt, *Principall Navigations,* 643g.

104. Drake, *World Encompassed,* 84.

105. Lessa, *Drake's Island of Thieves,* 179–204, 256–57.

106. Wagner, *Sir Francis Drake,* 175–76. See Lessa, *Drake's Island of Thieves,* 268, for a list of current place-name equivalents.

107. John Drake, AGI Patronato 266, ramo 54, fol. 8v; Francisco de Dueñas, "Relación y sucesso del viaje que hizo francisco dueñas a maluco por horden del governador de las Filipinas el año de 1582," c. May 1582, AGI Patronato 46, ramo 14, fols. 10v–11v. The letter from Dueñas appears in folios 8–16 of this rather long legajo. There is a translation, probably by Irene A. Wright, in Wagner, *Sir Francis Drake,* 175.

108. Hakluyt, *Principall Navigations,* 643i.

109. John Drake, AGI Patronato 266, ramo 54, fol. 8v. Hakluyt, *Principall Navigations,* 643i, is authority for the stop at Motir.

110. John Drake, AGI Patronato 266, ramo 49, fol. 10; ibid., ramo 54, fol. 8v. The stop in Ternate is mentioned in a single sentence in the account of the unknown Englishman. "They had sight of one of the Iles of Molucca, called Trenate, where they took in about vi. toon of cloves." BL Harley MS 280, fol. 87.

111. John Drake, AGI Patronato 266, ramo 49, fol. 3v.

112. Ibid., ramo 54, fol. 8v.

113. Hakluyt, *Principall Navigations,* 643j.

114. Ibid.

115. Argensola, *Conquista de las Islas Malucas,* 106.

116. AGI, Patronato 46, ramo 14, fols. 10v–11v. Translated in Wagner, *Sir Francis Drake,* 180.

117. John Drake, AGI Patronato 266, ramo 49, fol. 3v; ibid., ramo 54, fol. 9; BL Harley MS 280, fol. 87v.

118. BL Harley MS 280, fols. 84, 87v.

119. John Drake, AGI Patronato 266, ramo 49, fol. 3v.

120. BL Harley MS 280, fol. 87v.

121. Ibid., fol. 86v.

122. John Drake, AGI Patronato 266, ramo 49, fol. 3v.

123. Camden, *Rerum Anglicarum,* 308. The translation is from Darcie, *The Famous Empress Elizabeth,* 428.

124. BL Harley MS 280, fols. 86v, 87v; Vaux, *World Encompassed,* 184.

125. The sources are contradictory on this matter. John Drake said that they threw eight cannons and ten tons of cloves overboard. AGI Patronato 266, ramo 49, fol. 4. The anonymous author says it was two cannons and three tons of cloves. BL Harley MS 280, fol. 87v.

126. BL Harley MS 280, fol. 88; John Drake, AGI Patronato 266, ramo 54, fol. 9–v.

127. BL Harley MS 280, fol. 81v.

128. Ibid. In the manuscript this remark has been crossed out, but it is still possible to read it.

129. Hakluyt, *Principall Navigations,* 643k; John Drake, AGI Patronato 266, ramo 54, fol. 9–v.

130. Hakluyt, *Principall Navigations,* 643l.

131. John Drake said in his first account that they stayed fifteen days; in the second it was a month. AGI Patronato 266, ramo 49, fol. 3v; ibid., ramo 54, fol. 9v.

132. BL Harley MS 280, fol. 87v.

133. Wagner, *Sir Francis Drake,* 190–91.

134. John Drake, AGI Patronato 266, ramo 54, fol. 9v; Hakluyt, *Principall Navigations,* 643l.

135. John Drake, AGI Patronato 266, ramo 49, fol. 3v.

136. Quoted in the diary of Richard Madox, 16 September 1582, in Donno, *An Elizabethan in 1582,* 200.

137. John Drake, AGI Patronato 266, ramo 49, fol. 3v.

138. Ibid., ramo 54, fol. 9v.

139. BL Harley MS 280, fol. 87v.

140. Ibid.

141. Pedro de Rada to Gomez de Santillan, 29 July and 17 August 1580, AGI Patronato 266, ramo 41.

142. John Drake, AGI Patronato 266, ramo 54, fol. 9v.

143. *Corte Beschryvinghe,* end of column 3, "Drake Broadside" map, BL map department M.T. 6.a.2.

144. Drake, *World Encompassed,* 108.

8.

Honors and Riches

1. On the return of goods see "A declaracyon made by Mr John Winter of a shippe taken by Francis Drake captayne and generall of fyve shippes and barks bound for the parts of America for discovery and other causes of trade of merchaundyes necessary and requisite," PRO SP 139/24, fols. 71–73v. See also the certification by Anne Wynter and others, dated 6 April 1583, declaring that they knew that John Wynter had been "acquited and discharged from all mysdemeanures of pyracyes" that had been "supposed againste him by

the Portingalles that hadd bynne comytted in the tyme while the saide John Wynter was upon the seas in companie with Fraunce Drake." Gloucester Record Office, D 1799/T3.

2. Letter of Antonio de Guaras, 20 September 1577, CDIE, 91:165.

3. Mendoza to the king, 11 June 1578, CDIE, 91:248; Corbett, *Drake and the Tudor Navy*, 215.

4. Mendoza to the king, 31 March 1578, CDIE, 91:208.

5. His report in BL Lansdowne MS 100, no. 2, fols. 71–73v, bears the date 2 June 1579.

6. Mendoza to the king, 10 June 1579, AGI Patronato 265, ramo 28.

7. Mendoza to the king, 20 June 1579, CDIE, 91:262.

8. King to Mendoza, 10 August 1579, CDIE, 91:400–401.

9. Mendoza to the king, 5 September 1579, CDIE, 91:420–21.

10. Mendoza to Zayas, 13 September 1579, CDIE, 91:424–25.

11. Mendoza to the king, 29 September 1579, CDIE 91:432.

12. Mendoza to the king, 28 December 1579, CDIE, 91:445.

13. Ibid., 91:434.

14. Mendoza to the king, 20 February 1580, CDIE, 91:452–53.

15. Williamson, *Age of Drake*, 196–210.

16. Mendoza to the king, 16 October 1580, BL Add. MS 28,420, fol. 28v; 23 October 1580, BL Add. MS 26,056, fol. 121.

17. King to Mendoza, 14 November 1580, in Hume, *State Papers, Elizabeth*, 3:65. There is fairly extensive documentation on Zubiaur in Spanish archives, but nothing to show that he actually recovered any of the money. See, for example, the letter from the Prior y Consules de Sevilla to the king, 18 August 1581, AGS Guerra Marina 116, fols. 108–11, which contains extracts of correspondence between the king and Mendoza and other information regarding Zubiaur's unsuccessful efforts to gain reimbursement. See also AGI Patronato 266, ramo 43, fols. 1–3v, for correspondence between Zubiaur and the *prior y consules* of Seville.

18. Mendoza to the king, 20 February 1580, CDIE, 91:452–53.

19. Mendoza to the king, 29 September 1579, CDIE, 91:432.

20. Mendoza to the king, 20 February 1580, CDIE 91:452–53.

21. Mendoza to the king, 29 September 1580, citing his letter of 28 September; transcribed in González Palencia, *Discurso de el Capitán Francisco Draque*, 346. See also king to Mendoza, 14 November 1580, in Hume, *State Papers, Elizabeth*, 3:65.

22. Drake, *World Encompassed*, 65.

23. Mendoza to the king, 16 October 1580, BL Add. 28,420, fols. 30–31v.

24. John Drake, AGI Patronato 266, ramo 54, fol. 10.

25. Ibid.

26. Ibid.

27. Mendoza to the king, 23 October 1580, AGS Estado 833, fol. 24.

28. John Drake, AGI Patronato 266, ramo 54, fol. 10.

29. Mendoza to the king, 16 October 1580, BL Add. MS 28,420, fol. 30.

30. Ibid.

31. Queen to Tremayne, 22 October 1580, PRO SP, vol. 143, no 30.

32. The main source for information on these events is the correspondence of the Span-

ish ambassador. In his first letter Mendoza said that Drake landed the treasure first, then went to London. Mendoza to the king, 16 October 1580, BL Add. MS 28,420, fol. 30. A week later, though, Mendoza reported that Drake had first discussed matters with the queen, then put the treasure in storage. Mendoza to the king, 23 October 1580, CDIE, 91:514–15. The events described in the first letter seem more reasonable than the second.

33. Tremayne to Walsingham, 8 November 1580, PRO SP 12/144/17, fols. 40–41.

34. Mendoza to the king, 16 October 1580, BL Add. MS 28,420, fol 30.

35. Mendoza to the king, 23 October 1580, BL Add. MS 26,056, fol. 121.

36. Queen to Tremayne, 24 October 1580, PRO SP 12/143/30, fol. 83. The manuscript also has the date 22 October on the reverse side.

37. On the crew's pay see John Drake, AGI Patronato 266, ramo 54, fol. 10.

38. "Confiesan que trae xx toneladas deste pais, de plata que es dos mill libras cada uno, y cinco caxas de oro de longitud de pie y medio y gran cantidad de perlas de mucho preçio algunas." Mendoza to the king, 30 October 1580, AGS Estado 833, fol. 35.

39. "The regester of Suche tressur as is dellevered unto Xtofer hanes to be safly con-ducted and dellevered in to the tower with the number of peces and what the containe in waight," PRO SP 12/144/17, fol. 42.

40. "Golde bullion receved in Ingotts and Cakes remaining in iiii sevall bags," PRO SP 12/144/60, fol. 124v.

41. "A briefe Note of all such Silver Bullion as was brought into the Towre by Sir Francis Drake Knight and laid in the Vaute under the Jewel-House, as also what hath been taken out, and what remaineth," 26 December 1585, in Murdin, *Burghley State Papers,* 2:539–40.

42. Mendoza to the king, 9 January 1581, BL Add. MS 26,056.C, fol. 127–v.

43. Mendoza to the king, 23 October 1580, BL Add. MS 26,056.C, fol. 123; letter of Robert Persons, 17 November 1580, in *Letters and Memorials of Father Persons,* 1:53, 60. Neither source specified whether the estimates were in pesos.

44. Kingsford, *Survey of London,* 1:231.

45. On the visits see Mendoza to the king, 23 October 1580, BL Add. MS 26,056.C, fol. 120.

46. Mendoza to the king, 15 January 1581, BL Add. MS 26,056.C, fol. 131. BL Harley MS 280, fol. 84.

47. On Drake's selective and calculated generosity see Mendoza to the king, 9 January 1581, AGS Estado 835, fol. 164; Camden, *Rerum Anglicarum,* 308–9.

48. Mendoza to the king, 15 January 1581, BL Add. MS 26,056.C, fol. 131.

49. "No las quiso tomar diziendo que no sabia con que consciencia podia aceptar cosa que le ofresiese draques haviendo sido robado todo quanto traya." Mendoza to the king, 9 January 1581, AGS Estado 835, fol. 164.

50. Mendoza to the king, 1 March 1582, BL Add. MS 26,056.C, fol. 208.

51. The English summary is found in BL Lansdowne MS 30, no. 10, fols. 26–29.

52. PRO SP Dom. 12/144/17.II, fol. 43.

53. Wallis, *Sir Francis Drake,* 101; Corbett, *Drake and the Tudor Navy,* 320, citing Sir Edward Coke in the debate on martial law in the House of Commons, 1628.

54. Mendoza to the king, 9 January 1581, AGS Estado 835, fol. 164.

55. Mendoza to the king, 6 April 1581, AGS Estado 835, fol. 167. This was transcribed by Froude in BL Add. MS 26,056.C, fol. 138.

56. The word is difficult to read in the original manuscript, AGS Estado 835, fol. 167. The printed copy of the letter in CDIE, 91:562 has *rana*. The transcription made by Froude says *vana*. Mendoza to the king, 6 April 1581, BL Add. MS 26,056.C, fol 138.

57. Mendoza to the king, 11 April 1581, AGS Estado 835, fol. 180.

58. Camden, *Rerum Anglicarum*, 308.

59. Most people around the court knew of her plan to knight Drake. Mendoza reported it to the king in his letter of 9 January 1581, BL Add. MS 26,056.C fol. 127.

60. It was often said that Drake was forced to use straw purchasers because Grenville would not willingly sell to someone with his reputation. Joyce Youings effectively put this notion to rest in "Drake, Grenville, and Buckland Abbey."

61. Devon Record Office (hereafter DRO), Drake MS, 277/1, Royal Letters Patent licensing Sir Richard Grenefeild to alienate to John Hele and Christopher Harrys the ex-monastery of Buckland with messauges and lands called Calderparke, Barneparke, le Conygarth medowe, Wyndmyll parke, le longe parke, and other lands in the parish of Buckland, 1 December 1580.

62. "She gave him the title of 'Sir' because of the land he purchased" (Diole el titulo de S[eño]r para las tierras que ha comprado). Mendoza to the king, 6 April 1581, BL Add. MS 26,056.C, fol. 138.

63. DRO, Drake MS, 277/2, Indenture of sale of Buckland by Sir Richard Grenefylde of Bideford, knight, to John Hele of Plymouth and Christopher Harrys of Plymstock, 19 December 1580.

64. On the date of possession see DRO, Drake MS, 277/5, Indenture of final concord between Hele and Harris, plaintiffs, and Grenville and his wife, deforciants, concerning the sale of Buckland, Trinity Term 1581.

65. DRO, Drake MS, 2/9, assignment from Sir Francis Drake to Edmond Tremayne, John Hele, and Christopher Harrys of the remainder of his interest in two tenements or dwelling places in Plymouth, 10 August 1581. The documents describe Plymouth as the place "wherein he now dwells," a phrase that does not necessarily exclude Buckland.

66. Barber, "Sir Francis Drake's Investment,"113:107.

67. DRO, Drake MS, 277/6.

68. DRO, Drake MS, 277/8.

69. Youings, "Drake, Grenville, and Buckland Abbey," 112:97. Professor Youings thinks the transaction was really a mortgage in which the lender had the option to determine whether the borrower might be allowed to redeem the property (96).

70. Snell, *Suppression of the Religious Foundations,* 168.

71. Aslet, "Buckland Abbey."

72. Youings suggests a date of 1568. "Drake, Grenville, and Buckland Abbey," 112:97. Aslet thinks the date might have been close to 1574. "Buckland Abbey."

73. Gill, "Drake's Home, Buckland Abbey," 94. The date is actually written in Latin: •ANNO•DOMINI•M•CCCCC•LXXVI•

74. Ibid., 97.

75. Aslet, "Buckland Abbey." The National Trust now believes that "the oak panelling may be contemporary with Drake's occupation of Buckland." See the National Trust leaflet entitled "Buckland Abbey" [1988].

76. Drake, "Drake: The Arms of his Surname," 15:490–93.

77. Prince, *Damnoni Orientales Illustres,* 1:245. See also Drake, "Arms of Drake."

78. Mendoza to the king, 11 May 1586, in Hume, *State Papers, Elizabeth,* 3:378.

79. Letter of Arthur J. Jewers in *Western Antiquary* (June 1891), 10:165.

80. AGI Patronato 266, ramo 19, fol. 1.

81. AGN Inquisición 85, no. 13, fol. 93.

82. Bodleian Library, "Litterae Patentes Armorum," Ashmolean MS 834, part I, fol. 38v. A copy in BL Stowe 699, fol. 96, lacks the reference to a dragon. Local people think that the globe-and-ship device was popular in Plymouth before Drake used it. Something similar to this was found incised on a stone windowsill in Saint Andrew's Church when that building was restored after the Second World War. See G. W. Copeland, "The 'Drake Sketch' at St. Andrew's.".

83. Bodleian Library, "Litterae Patentes Armorum," Ashmolean MS 834, part I, fol. 44. A note on the document says: "This draught tooke none effect, it was never used." Perhaps because of Drake's own interference in the matter, there has been considerable dispute over the exact nature of the arms and crest to which Drake was entitled and the arms and crest he used. Corbett made an effort to determine the facts in the matter (*Drake and the Tudor Navy,* 1:61–2, 1:410–15) and concluded, with some misgivings, that Francis Drake was probably entitled to use the arms of the Drakes of Ashe. A more recent statement by the Garter King of Arms, Sir Anthony Wagner, takes a different view but stops short of saying that Sir Francis was not entitled to those arms. *Drake in England,* 13–16.

84. Jewers letter in *Western Antiquary,* 10:164–65.

85. Wagner, *Drake in England,* 15.

86. Eliott-Drake, *Family and Heirs,* 1:54.

87. Ditmas, *Legend of Drake's Drum,* 5–11.

88. These banners have a reasonably long history. One of the earliest detailed descriptions was written by Whitmarsh in "Drake Relics." Whitmarsh was convinced that they appeared sufficiently old to be the originals.

89. "Chair of Francis Drake."

90. Eliott-Drake, *Family and Heirs,* 1:51–52.

91. National Portrait Gallery, 4851.

92. Edmond, *Hilliard and Oliver,* 73–74.

93. Eliott-Drake, *Family and Heirs,* 31. Sugden thinks the probable date is too early for a painting of Drake. See "Drake: A Note on His Portraiture." Wagner confines himself to admitting that the portrait "certainly bears some likeness to Drake." See his *Drake's Voyage,* 207–8, 508.

94. Van Sype, *La Herdike Enterprise.*

95. *Corte Beschryvinghe.*

96. Wagner, *Drake's Voyage,* 509; Mendoza to the king, 26 September 1586, in Hume, *State Papers, Elizabeth,* 3:626.

97. National Maritime Museum, BHC 2622.

98. *Western Morning News,* 8 July 1932, p. 7.

99. Gratwicke, "Coat-of-Arms-Mystery."

100. Rodríguez-Salgado, *Armada,* 226–27.

101. Sugden, "Drake: A Note on His Portraiture."

102. Silva, AGN Inquisición 85, no. 13, fol. 86.

103. "Mas grueso que delgado." García Fernández de Torrequemada to the king, 1 February 1587, AGI Santo Domingo 80, ramo 4, no. 120, fol. 2v.

104. *Western Morning News,* 17 September 1881, clipping file, Westcountry Studies Library, Exeter (hereafter WSL).

105. According to Barber, there is no certain evidence about the location of Drake's house in Plymouth. See Barber, "Sir Francis Drake's Investment," 113:106–7. In addition to a house with a Drake historical marker on Looe Street, a dwelling on Andrew Street has also been erroneously identified as Drake's home. *Western Morning News,* 6–7 December 1929, Drake clipping file, Plymouth Public Library. For comments about this latter dwelling see James Barber's introduction, "Architectural and Documentary Evidence," in Fairclough, *St. Andrew Street,* 10, 19, 41.

106. A map drawn in 1593 says: "This forte upon the hoo of Plimouthe conteyneth in compasse .99. perches." See Robert Adams, "The platte of the forte upon the hoo of Plimouthe," PRO SP 12/245, fol. 31. Though he signed his name in Latin as "Adamo," it is clear from the accompanying correspondence that the delineator was Robert Adams. Stuart, *Lost Landscapes of Plymouth,* 81–82. The construction of the new wall is recorded in the Black Book, DRO W46, fol. 7. There is a reasonably accurate transcription of the entry in Worth, *Plymouth Municipal Records,* 18.

107. [Worth,] "Drake and the Plymouth Corporation," clipping file, WSL, Exeter.

108. Ibid.

109. R. N. Worth, "Sir Francis Drake and the Plymouth Water Supply," *Western Morning News,* 7 February 1881, clipping files, WSL.

110. Ibid.

111. Entries for 1589 and 1590 in the Black Book, DRO W46, fol. 8; Worth, *Plymouth Municipal Records,* 20, 21. See also the report of the lecture by R. N. Worth in the *Western Morning News,* 12 April 1884, clipping file, WSL.

112. Entries for 1589 and 1590 in the Black Book, DRO W46, fol. 8; Worth, *Plymouth Municipal Records,* 20–21.

113. Report of Worth's lecture.

114. Worth, "Drake and the Plymouth Water Supply."

115. Barber, "Sir Francis Drake's Investment," 113:103–4.

116. Ibid., 113:104–5.

117. On Yarcomb see Oliver, *Monasticon Diocesis Exoniensis,* 249. On Sampford Spinney see DRO, Drake Papers, T72/A17, Deed of Mortgage, 17 June 1581. This also seems to be a conditional sale contract, providing that "Jerome Mayhowe" might recover title to the property by payment of £500 on 6 January 1582. On Sherford see DRO, Drake Papers, 277/14, draft of royal letters patent, 12 January 1582.

118. Mendoza to the king, 2 June 1581, CDIE, 92:39.

119. Mendoza to the king, 27 September 1581, CDIE 92:115.

120. Mendoza to the king, 20 November 1581, CDIE 92:193.

121. Mendoza to the king, 10 November 1582, CDIE 92:429.

122. Corbett, *Drake and the Tudor Navy,* 391, quoting SP, Dom. Elizabeth, 1582, 153:50.

123. Mendoza to the king, 1 April 1582, CDIE, 92:328.

124. "The examinacon of Patricke Mason," 15 May 1582, PRO SP 12/153/48, fol. 98.

125. "The confesyon of Pattricke Mason beinge compelled unto the same the [blank] day of May 1582," PRO SP 12/153/49, fol. 100.

126. See Doughty's petition for release sent to the Privy Council, PRO SP Dom. 12/163/19, fol. 46. Notes on the back of the document indicate a date of 25 or 27 October 1583. There is no date in the body of the document.

127. PRO SP 12/144/44, fol. 90-v.

128. Mendoza to the king, 9 January 1581, CDIE, 91:534.

129. Mendoza to the king, 16 April 1581, CDIE, 91:572–73.

130. Mendoza to the king, 7 May 1581, CDIE, 92:24; Mendoza to the king, 24 June 1581, CDIE, 92:58.

131. Mendoza to the king, 4 July 1581, CDIE, 92:68.

132. Donno, *An Elizabethan in 1582,* 18–19.

133. Mendoza to the king, 12 August 1581, CDIE, 92:90.

134. Digges, *Compleat Ambassador,* 379.

135. Ibid., 388, 394, 422.

136. Mendoza to the king, 27 September 1581, CDIE, 114–15.

137. Donno, *An Elizabethan in 1582,* 20–21.

138. Ibid., 21–28.

139. Ibid., 30–33.

140. John Drake, AGI Patronato 266, ramo 54, fols. 10v–13v; Donno, *An Elizabethan in 1582,* 40–43.

141. Donno, *An Elizabethan in 1582,* 35–40.

142. DRO, West Devon Area, Plymouth, Saint Andrews Parish Register, "Burials January 1583," p. 6, microfiche.

143. DRO, West Devon Area, Plymouth, 542/1, Saint Budeaux Parish Register, fols. 46, 66, microfiche.

144. Eliott-Drake, *Family and Heirs,* 64–65.

145. Sugden, *Sir Francis Drake,* 43–44. The "probable sisters" were Maude, Margaret, Joanne, and Eleanor. Margaret married John Bodman (Bodenham?), and it is possible that they had a son named Jonas.

146. Courtney, *Parliamentary Representation of Cornwall,* 322–24. See also Hasler, *History of Parliament,* 2:54.

147. D'Ewes, *Journals of all the Parliaments,* 299.

148. See T. E. Hartley, *Proceedings in the Parliament of Elizabeth I* (Wilmington, Delaware: Michael Glazier, Inc., 1982).

149. Hasler, *History of Parliament,* 2:54.

150. D'Ewes, *Journals of the Parliaments of Elizabeth,* 333.

151. Ibid., 337.

152. Ibid., 339.

153. Ibid., 345, 352, 353, 355, 361.

154. Ibid., 333, 369; Hasler, *History of Parliament,* 1:123–25, 2:54.

155. Mendoza to the king, 13 January 1580, CDIE, 91:408.

156. D'Ewes, *Journals of the Parliaments of Elizabeth,* 368.

157. On the committee, ibid., 372.

158. Only a fragment of the house remains, the "best part" having been pulled down. Sydenham, *History of the Sydenham Family,* 352.

159. Quoted in Eliott-Drake, *Family and Heirs,* 1:68.

160. Mendoza to the king, 10 November 1582, CDIE, 92:429.

161. Andrews, *Drake's Voyages,* 90; Williamson, *Age of Drake,* 217–18; Wright, *Further English Voyages to Spanish America,* xvii–xxi.

162. Mendoza to the king, 1 April 1582, CDIE, 92:328.

163. Williamson, *Age of Drake,* 220–21.

164. Ibid., 222, 253–68.

165. Ibid., 276, citing "one of Burghley's papers"; Williamson, *Sir John Hawkins,* 411, citing BL Lansdowne MS 41, fols. 9–10.

166. Corbett, *Drake and the Tudor Navy,* 2:9–10, citing a commission issued by Drake to John Martyn "preserved at Nutwell Court."

9.

Raid on the West Indies

1. The queen's warrant of 29 July is recited in PRO, AO 1/1685/20 A, "The Declaration of the Accompte of Sir Frances Drake," transcribed in Keeler, *Drake's West Indian Voyage,* 52.

2. PRO, AO 1/1685/20A, transcribed in Keeler, *Drake's West Indian Voyage,* 52–53.

3. Testimony of Thomas Drake, 20 October 1605, Exchequer Bills, no. 225, transcribed in DRO Drake Papers 346M/F551, 1–2; Williamson, *Age of Drake,* 279. For comments on the value of the ships see Keeler, *Drake's West Indian Voyage,* p. 54n3.

4. Williamson, *Hawkins of Plymouth,* 225–26.

5. Mendoza to the king, 22 February 1585, in Hume, *State Papers, Elizabeth,* 3:531–32.

6. Mendoza to the king, 5 April 1585, in Hume, *State Papers, Elizabeth,* 3:535.

7. "The Spanish kings commission for the generall imbargment or arrest of the Englishe &c." in Hakluyt, *Second Volume,* 114 [actually 314].

8. PRO, AO 1/1685/20A, transcribed in Keeler, *Drake's West Indian Voyage,* 52–53.

9. PRO SP 12/180, fol. 22, transcribed with modern spelling and punctuation in Corbett, *Papers Relating to the Navy,* 36–38.

10. Mendoza to the king, 16 July 1585, in Hume, *State Papers, Elizabeth,* 3:542.

11. "A discourse of Syr Frauncs Drakes voiage as by gods grace he shall well performe," BL Lansdowne MS 100, fols. 98–102v. This is transcribed with modern spelling and punctuation in Corbett, *Papers Relating to the Navy,* 69–74. It is not entirely certain that the document is really an outline of Drake's plan. Much of it seems to be hypothesis based on knowledge of his actions in earlier voyages.

12. Andrews, *Drake's Voyages*, 98.

13. PRO, AO 1/1685/20A, transcribed in Keeler, *Drake's West Indian Voyage*, 54.

14. Mendoza to the king, 4 May 1585, in Hume, *State Papers, Elizabeth*, 3:537.

15. "The escape of the *Primrose* a tall ship of London from before the towne of Bilbao in Biscay," in Hakluyt, *Second Volume*, 112–14 [actually 312–314]. Others probably shared ownership of the *Primrose*. See Keeler, *Drake's West Indian Voyage*, 283.

16. Keeler, *Drake's West Indian Voyage*, 284.

17. Henry Wallop to Walsingham, 4 July 1585, in Hamilton, *State Papers, Ireland*, 2:571.

18. Corbett, *Drake and the Tudor Navy*, 2:13–19.

19. Worth, *Plymouth Municipal Records*, 18.

20. Mendoza to the king, 1 October 1585, in Hume, *State Papers, Elizabeth*, 3:550.

21. Christopher Carleill to Walsingham, 4–11 October 1585, PRO SP 12/183, fol. 22, transcribed in Corbett, *Papers Relating to the Navy*, 41–42.

22. "Record kept aboard the Ship *Tiger*," BL Cotton MS Otho E. VIII, fol. 229–v, transcribed in Keeler, *Drake's West Indian Voyage*, 70–74.

23. Unsigned and undated note, in Hume, *State Papers, Elizabeth*, 3:543.

24. "Record kept aboard the Ship *Tiger*," BL Cotton MS Otho E. VIII, fols. 229v–30, transcribed in Keeler, *Drake's West Indian Voyage*, 73–78.

25. Williamson, *Age of Drake*, 280.

26. Keeler, *Drake's West Indian Voyage*, 280–300.

27. Bigges, *Summarie and True Discourse* (1589). Keeler discussed the authorship question at length and concluded that there was no good reason to deny that Bigges was author of the original manuscript. *Drake's West Indian Voyage*, 301–9.

28. BL Cotton Otho E. VIII, fol. 235, transcribed in Keeler, *Drake's West Indian Voyage*, 106.

29. Quinn, "Early Accounts of the Famous Voyage," 44–45.

30. "Record kept aboard the Ship *Tiger*," BL Cotton MS Otho E. VIII, fol. 229, transcribed in Keeler, *Drake's West Indian Voyage*, 71–73.

31. Letter of William Borough, 5 June 1587, PRO SP Dom. 12/202/14, fol. 17–v.

32. "Relación de lo que diçen unos vecinos de Laredo que llegaron a eloy," 29 September 1585, AGS Guerra Marina 178, fol. 163.

33. "Record kept aboard the Ship *Tiger*," BL Cotton MS Otho E. VIII, fols. 230, transcribed in Keeler, *Drake's West Indian Voyage*, 75–76.

34. "Relación de lo que diçen."

35. Spanish authorities thought that Drake had taken two French ships. Gerónimo Brizeño to the king, 28 September 1585, AGS Guerra Marina 178, fol. 107.

36. "Record kept aboard the Ship *Tiger*," BL Cotton MS Otho E. VIII, fol. 230, transcribed in Keeler, *Drake's West Indian Voyage*, 77.

37. Bigges, *Summarie and True Discourse* (1589), 3.

38. Testimony of Thomas Drake, 20 October 1605, PRO Exchequer transcribed in DRO Drake Papers 346M/F551, 6–7.

39. "The Discourse and Description of the Voyage of Sir Francis Drake and Master Frobisher," BL Royal MS 7 C. xvi, fol. 166, transcribed in Keeler, *Drake's West Indian Voyage*, 181.

40. "Record kept aboard the Ship *Tiger,*" BL Cotton MS Otho E. VIII, fol. 230v, transcribed in Keeler, *Drake's West Indian Voyage,* 78–80.

41. Ibid., fol. 231, transcribed in Keeler, *Drake's West Indian Voyage,* 82–83.

42. On the dinner see Mendoza to the king, 1 March 1582, in Hume, *State Papers, Elizabeth,* 3:307

43. "Record kept aboard the Ship *Tiger,*" BL Cotton MS Otho E. VIII, fol. 231, transcribed in Keeler, *Drake's West Indian Voyage,* 82–83. The journalist on the *Primrose* said that the wine and sugar came from a French vessel just arrived from Terceira. He also recorded the capture of a "boate with certaine gentlewomen." See "The Discourse and Description of the Voyage of Sir Francis Drake," in BL Royal MS 7 C. xvi, fol. 166v, transcribed ibid., 182.

44. Newsletter, 4 October 1585, in Butler, *State Papers, Foreign,* 20:64–65.

45. BL Cotton MS Otho E. VIII, fol. 235v. Another journal said that four men were caught and beheaded. "Discourse and Description of the Voyage of Sir Francis Drake," BL Royal MS 7 C. xvi, fol 166v.

46. "The Discourse and Description of the Voyage of Sir Francis Drake and Master Frobisher," BL Royal MS 7 C. xvi, fol. 166v, transcribed in Keeler, *Drake's West Indian Voyage,* 182. Bigges, *Summarie and True Discourse* (1589) 6, later said that the Spanish claimed losses exceeding 30,000 ducats. In a letter to Mendoza, the Spanish king said that the daring of Drake's raid exceeded the damage he caused. Letter of 29 December 1585, in Hume, *State Papers, Elizabeth,* 3:553.

47. "Record kept aboard the Ship *Tiger,*" BL Cotton MS Otho E. VIII, fol. 231v, transcribed in Keeler, *Drake's West Indian Voyage,* 87. See also "The Discourse and Description of the Voyage of Sir Francis Drake," in BL Royal MS 7 C. xvi, fol. 166v, transcribed ibid., 182.

48. "Record kept aboard the Ship *Tiger,*" BL Cotton MS Otho E. VIII, fol. 232, transcribed in Keeler, *Drake's West Indian Voyage,* 89. See also "The Discourse and Description of the Voyage of Sir Francis Drake," in BL Royal MS 7 C. xvi, fols. 166v–67, transcribed ibid., 182–84.

49. Vicenzo Gradenigo to Doge and Senate, 25 October 1585, in Brown, *State Papers, Venice,* 8:123.

50. On the fleet's safe arrival see Wright, *Further English Voyages,* xxxi–xxxii. According to Wright, the Spanish fleet rendezvoused with an escort from Castille on 16 October and must have been in port a day or so later.

51. Drake to Burghley, 26 July 1586, BL Lansdowne MS 51, no. 14, fol. 27.

52. The Gregorian calendar reform became effective in Spain in October 1582. Ten days were dropped at that time, so that the day after 4 October was 15 October. Elsewhere in the Spanish Indies the change was made in 1583, though some isolated parts retained the old calendar until early 1585. See Kelsey, "Gregorian Calendar."

53. Wright, *Further English Voyages,* xxxii.

54. "Record kept aboard the Ship *Tiger,*" BL Cotton MS Otho E. VIII, fol. 232v, transcribed in Keeler, *Drake's West Indian Voyage,* 93. See also "The Discourse and Description of the Voyage of Sir Francis Drake," in BL Royal MS 7 C. xvi, fol. 167, transcribed ibid., 184. Dates in the two accounts are not in agreement.

55. At the meeting on 28 October the French captain told Drake that he had seen the fleet "20 or 22 dayes before." The *Leicester* journal, BL Harley MS 2202, fol. 57, transcribed in Keeler, *Drake's West Indian Voyage*, 127.

56. *Leicester* journal, BL Harley MS 2202, fol. 57 – v, transcribed in Keeler, *Drake's West Indian Voyage*, 128.

57. "Record kept aboard the Ship *Tiger*," BL Cotton MS Otho E. VIII, fol. 233, transcribed in Keeler, *Drake's West Indian Voyage*, 94. See also the *Leicester* journal, BL Harley MS 2202, fol. 58, transcribed ibid., 131.

58. The orders are transcribed in the *Leicester* journal, BL Harley MS 2202, fols. 57v – 58, transcribed in Keeler, *Drake's West Indian Voyage*, 130 – 31.

59. "Record kept aboard the Ship *Tiger*," BL Cotton MS Otho E. VIII, fol. 233 – v, transcribed in Keeler, *Drake's West Indian Voyage*, 95 – 96. See also the *Leicester* journal, BL Harley MS 2202, fol. 58 – v, transcribed ibid., 131 – 32; "The Discourse and Description of the Voyage of Sir Francis Drake," in BL Royal MS 7 C. xvi, fol. 167, transcribed ibid., 185.

60. "The Discourse and Description of the Voyage of Sir Francis Drake and Master Frobisher," BL Royal MS 7 C. xvi, fol. 167v, transcribed in Keeler, *Drake's West Indian Voyage*, 186.

61. "The Record kept aboard the Ship *Leicester*, BL MS Harley 2202, fol. 59, transcribed in Keeler, *Drake's West Indian Voyage*, 133 – 34.

62. The most complete description of this battle group is found in the *Leicester* journal, BL MS Harley 2202, fol. 59, transcribed in Keeler, *Drake's West Indian Voyage*, 134 – 35.

63. Bigges, *Summarie and True Discourse* (1589) 8 – 9.

64. "Record kept aboard the Ship *Tiger*," BL Cotton MS Otho E. VIII, fol. 233v, transcribed in Keeler, *Drake's West Indian Voyage*, 97 – 98. See also the *Leicester* journal, BL Harley MS 2202, fol. 60 – v, transcribed ibid., 138; "The Discourse and Description of the Voyage of Sir Francis Drake," in BL Royal MS 7 C. xvi, fols. 167v – 68v, transcribed ibid., 186 – 90.

65. The *Leicester* journal, BL Harley MS 2202, fol. 60v, transcribed in Keeler, *Drake's West Indian Voyage*, 138.

66. "The Record kept aboard the Ship *Leicester*," BL Harley MS 2202, fol. 61, transcribed in Keeler, *Drake's West Indian Voyage*, 139 – 41.

67. Ibid.

68. "The Record kept aboard the Ship *Leicester*," BL Harley MS 2202, fols. 61 – 62v, transcribed in Keeler, *Drake's West Indian Voyage*, 141 – 47.

69. Ibid.

70. "Record kept aboard the Ship *Tiger*," BL Cotton MS Otho E. VIII, fol. 233v, transcribed in Keeler, *Drake's West Indian Voyage*, 97 – 98. See also the *Leicester* journal, BL Harley MS 2202, fol. 62v, transcribed ibid., 148; "The Discourse and Description of the Voyage of Sir Francis Drake," in BL Royal MS 7 C. xvi, fol. 168 – v, transcribed ibid., 186 – 87.

71. "The Discourse and Description of the Voyage of Sir Francis Drake and Master Frobisher," BL Royal MS 7 C. xvi, fol. 168, transcribed in Keeler, *Drake's West Indian Voyage*, 187.

72. Bigges, *Summarie and True Discourse* (1589), 14.

73. Pedro Sánchez, who was a prisoner on one of the ships, confirmed that the disease was plague *(peste)*. His opinion is cited in the letter of Alonso Suarez de Toledo, 27 June 1586, AGI Santo Domingo 126, ramo 2, no. 35, fol. 1v.

74. "The Discourse and Description of the Voyage of Sir Francis Drake and Master Frobisher," BL Royal MS 7 C. xvi, fol. 169, transcribed in Keeler, *Drake's West Indian Voyage,* 191.

75. "Record kept aboard the Ship *Tiger,*" BL Cotton MS Otho E. VIII, fol. 233v, transcribed in Keeler, *Drake's West Indian Voyage,* 99.

76. Bigges, *Summarie and True Discourse* (1589), 14.

77. Letter of Tristan de Orive Salazar, 11 March 1585, AGI Patronato 266, ramo 50, no 12, fols. 1–2; see also the testimony of Alonso Bravo de Montemayor, 3 May 1586, AGI Santa Fe 89, ramo 2, no. 13, fol. 72. According to Bravo, Drake told him that he had lost five hundred men from disease, though other officers and men of the fleet said that seven hundred had perished and Bravo thought the total might be even higher.

78. "Record kept aboard the Ship *Tiger,*" BL Cotton MS Otho E. VIII, fol. 233v, transcribed in Keeler, *Drake's West Indian Voyage,* 100. There is some discrepancy in the dates given in the various sources. In this case, both the *Tiger* Journal, cited here, and the map text (see ibid., 65) agree.

79. Bigges, *Summarie and True Discourse* (1589), 14–15.

80. "The Discourse and Description of the Voyage of Sir Francis Drake and Master Frobisher," BL Royal MS 7 C. xvi, fol. 169v, transcribed in Keeler, *Drake's West Indian Voyage,* 191–93.

81. "Record kept aboard the Ship *Tiger,*" BL Cotton MS Otho E. VIII, fol. 234, transcribed in Keeler, *Drake's West Indian Voyage,* 101.

82. Cristóbal de Ovalle and others to the king, 24 February 1586, AGI Santo Domingo 51, ramo 9, no. 87, fols. 1–2.

83. Wright, *Further English Voyages to Spanish America,* xxx.

84. "Las dichas puertas no tienan mas que hasta cinquenta pies en largo de muralla y las demas es de arboleda." Licenciado Aliaga to the king, 13 January 1586, AGI Santo Domingo 51, ramo 9, no. 84, fol. 1v. See also Cristóbal de Ovalle to the king, 24 February 1586, AGI Santo Domingo 51, ramo 9, no. 87, fols. 1–2.

85. Melchor Ochoa and others to the king, 26 February 1586, AGI Santo Domingo 73, no. 108, fol. 1.

86. Alonso Rodríguez de Azebedo to Diego Fernández de Quiñones, 22 January 1586, AGI Santo Domingo 80, translated in Wright, *Further English Voyages to Spanish America,* 26. The original letter now seems to be missing from the legajo.

87. Bigges, *Summarie and True Discourse* (1589), 15–16.

88. Licenciado Aliaga to the king, 13 January 1586, AGI Santo Domingo 51, ramo 9, no. 84, fols. 1v–2.

89. Ibid.

90. Bigges, *Summarie and True Discourse* (1589), 16–17.

91. Cristóbal de Ovalle to the king, AGI Santo Domingo 51, ramo 9, no. 87, fol. 3v.

92. Licenciado Alonso Fernández de Mercado and Baltazar de Villafañe to the king, 14

January 1586, AGI Santo Domingo 80, ramo 3, no. 91. Antonio de Ovalle to the king, 21 January 1586, AGI Santo Domingo 80, ramo 3, no. 94.

93. Cristóbal de Ovalle and others to the king, 24 February 1586, AGI Santo Domingo 51, ramo 9, no. 87, fol. 3–v. See also Dean and chapter of the cathedral to the king, 19 February 1586, AGI Santo Domingo 94, no. 48, fol. 1–v. While comparable values are difficult to assess, it appears that Drake had in mind gold ducats or *pesos de oro,* each worth perhaps seven or eight shillings. For a lengthier explanation see Keeler, *Drake's West Indian Voyage,* p. 259, n. 2.

94. López de Velasco, *Geografía y Descripción,* 53, noted in the early 1570s that although the city once had a thousand citizens, the figure had recently dropped to half that number and was declining every day because trading ships did not come there any more. See also Wright, *Further English Voyages to Spanish America,* xxv–xxvi.

95. Cristóbal de Ovalle to the king, 24 February 1586, AGI Santo Domingo 51, ramo 9, no. 87, fol. 3–v. López de Velasco said "the currency in these islands is the worst in the Indies" (La moneda corriente de estas islas es la peor moneda de las Indias). *Geografía y Descripción,* 52.

96. Cristóbal de Ovalle and others to the king, 24 February 1586, AGI Santo Domingo 51, ramo 9, no. 87, fol. 3–v; dean and chapter of the cathedral to the king, 19 February 1586, AGI Santo Domingo 94, no. 48, fol. 1.

97. "The Discourse and Description of the Voyage of Sir Francis Drake and Master Frobisher," BL Royal MS 7 C. xvi, fol. 170–v, transcribed in Keeler, *Drake's West Indian Voyage,* 195–97.

98. Corbett, *Drake and the Tudor Navy,* 2:33–35. His evidence for this was an unsigned report in PRO SP Dom., 189:27, printed in *Papers Relating to the Navy,* 79–80.

99. Alonso Rodríguez de Azebedo to Diego Fernández de Quiñones, 22 January 1586, AGI Santo Domingo 80, translated in Wright, *Further English Voyages to Spanish America,* 26.

100. The author of the *Primrose* journal may have been a man named Henley, according to Keeler, *Drake's West Indian Voyage,* 5.

101. "The Discourse and Description of the Voyage of Sir Francis Drake and Master Frobisher," BL Royal MS 7 C. xvi, fol. 170, transcribed in Keeler, *Drake's West Indian Voyage,* 196.

102. Bigges, *Summarie and True Discourse* (1589), 17–18; BL Harley MS 6221, fols. 94–98v. Keeler has analyzed the printed sources and has concluded that, though the original manuscript has not yet been located, this one is "a variant of the original document." *Drake's West Indian Voyage,* 302–3.

103. González Palencia, *Discurso de el Capitán Francisco Draque,* 90–91. González supplies names for the friars, Juan de Caravia and Juan de Illanes (250). Wright searched for and failed to find any documentary evidence in Spanish archives to support the story. See *Further English Voyages to Spanish America,* xxxvii.

104. "Record kept aboard the Ship *Leicester,*" BL Harley MS 2202, fol. 64v, transcribed in Keeler, *Drake's West Indian Voyage,* 155.

105. See, for example, the report of the dean and chapter of the cathedral to the king, 19 February 1586, AGI Santo Domingo 94, no. 48, fol. 1–v.

106. Bigges, *Summarie and True Discourse* (1589), 19–20.

107. Juan Fernández to Alonso de la Torre, 16 February 1586, AGI Patronato 266, ramo 50, no. 6, fol. 1–v.

108. "Record kept aboard the Ship *Leicester,*" BL Harley MS 2202, fol. 63, transcribed in Keeler, *Drake's West Indian Voyage,* 151; dean and chapter to the king, 19 February 1586, AGI Santo Domingo 94, no. 48, fol. 1–v.

109. "Discourse and Description of the Voyage of Sir Frawncis Drake & Master Frobisher," BL Royal MS 7 C. xvi, fol. 170, transcribed in Keeler, *Drake's West Indian Voyage,* 196.

110. Knollys to Drake, 6 January 1586, BL Harley MS 2202, fol. 54–v, transcribed in Keeler, *Drake's West Indian Voyage,* 116–19; "Record kept aboard the Ship *Leicester,*" BL Harley MS 2202, fols. 63v, 65, transcribed ibid., 152, 156.

111. Letter of Tristan de Oribe Salazar, 11 March 1586, AGI Patronato 266, ramo 50, no. 12, fols. 1–2.

112. On the three small ships see "Record kept aboard the Ship *Leicester,*" BL Harley MS 2202, fol. 65, transcribed in Keeler, *Drake's West Indian Voyage,* 157.

113. Melchor Ochoa and others to the king, 26 February 1586, AGI Santo Domingo 73, no. 108, fol. 1.

114. "Record kept aboard the Ship *Leicester,*" BL Harley MS 2202, fol. 65, transcribed in Keeler, *Drake's West Indian Voyage,* 157.

115. Pedro Fernández de Busto to the king, 25 May 1586, AGI Santa Fe 37, ramo 5, no. 65, fol. 3v.

116. Licenciado Cristóbal de Ovalle and others to the king, 24 February 1586, AGI Santo Domingo 51, ramo 9, no 87, fol. 3–v.

117. Boazio map text, reprinted in Keeler, *Drake's West Indian Voyage,* 67. Deposition of Pedro Sánchez, AGI Contratación 5108, translated in Wright, *Further English Voyages to Spanish America,* 213. Sánchez said that the warning came from his pilots, no doubt the ones captured before and during the conquest of Santo Domingo.

118. "Relacion de lo que declaro Pedro yndio natural de la provincia de la Margarita, que esta preso en la ciudad de Cartagena," 16 February 1587, AGI Santa Fe 89, ramo 3, no. 35, fols. 1–3. Pedro said that he had been with Drake for twelve years, after first being captured by a French pirate: "Dixo que ha dose años que anda con francisco draque cosario yngles, y que vino a su poder porque en la margarita de donde es natural le cativo un capitan de las navios franceses, al qual se le quito el dicho francisco draque quando fue a las Indias la primera vez, para que le sirviese de lengua con los yndios, por que se sabe la lengua ynglesa."

119. Ibid., fol. 1.

120. López de Velasco, *Geografía y Descripción,* 195.

121. Pedro Vique y Manrique to the king, 8 April 1586, AGI Santa Fe 89, ramo 2, no. 14, fol. 1; deposition of Juan Liranço Ariza, 2 May 1586, AGI Santa Fe 89, ramo 2, no. 11, fol. 48.

122. Pedro Vique y Manrique to the king, 8 April 1586, AGI Santa Fe 89, ramo 2, no. 14, fol. 1; "El robo que de la ciudad de cartagena hiço francisco draq yngles," AGI Patronato 266, ramo 50, no. 3, fol. 1v.

123. Deposition of Martín González, 27 April 1586, AGI Santa Fe 89, ramo 2, no. 13, fols. 16v–17; Francisco de Avila to the king, 8 August 1586, AGI Santa Fe 89, ramo 2, no. 23, fol. 1.

124. Pedro Vique y Manrique to the king, 8 April 1586, AGI Santa Fe 89, ramo 2, no. 14, fol. 1; "The Record kept aboard the Ship *Leicester*," BL Harley MS 2202, fol. 66, transcribed in Keeler, *Drake's West Indian Voyage*, 160; deposition of Pedro Vique y Manrique, 3 May 1586, AGI Santa Fe 89, ramo 2, no. 13, fol. 57v. For some reason, Corbett was convinced that the entry was made by way of the more distant and more difficult Boca Chica. *Drake and the Tudor Navy*, 45–47.

125. "Record kept aboard the Ship *Leicester*," BL Harley MS 2202, fol. 65, transcribed in Keeler, *Drake's West Indian Voyage*, 157; "Discourse and Description of the Voyage of Sir Francis Drake & Master Frobisher," BL Royal MS 7 C. xvi, fol. 170v, transcribed ibid., 198.

126. For the estimate of 1,700 see "Record kept aboard the Ship *Tiger*," BL Cotton MS, Otho E. VIII, fol. 234, transcribed in Keeler, *Drake's West Indian Voyage*, 103.

127. Pedro Fernández de Busto to the king, 25 May 1586, AGI Santa Fe 37, ramo 5, no. 65, fol. 2; "El robo que de cartagena," AGI Patronato 266, ramo 50, no. 3, fol. 2v. Other figures were lower, but these are the estimates of the Spanish governor.

128. "Relacion de lo sucedido en cartagena de las yndias desde que se supo de la nueva de la venida del Capitan Francisdo Draq, general de la armada ynglesa," AGI Santa Fe 72, no. 67a, fol. 2v, enclosed in the letter from Luis de Guzman and Alonso de Tapía to the king, 1 June 1586.

129. "El governador tenia la Playa del desenparcadero enpuada donde muchos de los enemigos se maltrataron y murieron del." Many men died from the stakes, but the document does not say specifically that the stakes were poisoned. See the "Relación" enclosed in the letter from Luis de Guzman and Alonso de Tapía to the king, 1 June 1586, AGI Santa Fe 72, no. 67a, fol. 5.

130. "Record kept aboard the Ship *Leicester*," BL Harley MS 2202, fol. 66, transcribed in Keeler, *Drake's West Indian Voyage*, 162; "Discourse and Description of the Voyage of Sir Francis Drake & Master Frobisher," BL Royal MS 7 C. xvi, fol. 171, transcribed in Keeler, *Drake's West Indian Voyage*, 199; the "Relación" enclosed in the letter from Luis de Guzman and Alonso de Tapía to the king, 1 June 1586, AGI Santa Fe 72, no. 67a, fol. 2v.

131. "El robo que de cartagena," AGI Patronato 266, ramo 50, no. 3, fols. 2–3.

132. "Record kept aboard the Ship *Leicester*," BL Harley MS 2202, fol. 66, transcribed in Keeler, *Drake's West Indian Voyage*, 162–63.

133. Testimony of Martin González, 27 April 1586, AGI Santa Fe 89, ramo 2, no. 13, fols. 21v–22.

134. "Record kept aboard the Ship *Leicester*," BL Harley MS 2202, fol. 66, transcribed in Keeler, *Drake's West Indian Voyage*, 162–63.

135. "El robo que de cartagena," AGI Patronato 266, ramo 50, no. 3, fol. 2v. Drake or one of his men might have said it: "Retirar cavalleros que somos perdidos."

136. "Record kept aboard the Ship *Tiger*," BL Cotton MS Otho E. VIII, fol. 234–v, transcribed in Keeler, *Drake's West Indian Voyage*, 103–5; "Record kept aboard the Ship

Leicester, BL Harley MS 2202, fols. 66v–67, transcribed ibid., 163–64; Bigges, *Summarie and True Discourse* (1589), 23.

137. "Record kept aboard the Ship *Leicester,*" BL Harley MS 2202, fol. 66v, transcribed in Keeler, *Drake's West Indian Voyage,* 163; Bigges, *Summarie and True Discourse* (1589), 23.

138. Testimony of Pedro Mexía Mirabal, 30 April 1586, AGI Santa Fe 89, ramo 2, no. 13, fols. 28v–30v.

139. Testimony of Pedro Mexía Mirabal, 30 April 1586, AGI Santa Fe 89, ramo 2, no. 13, fols. 29–31.

140. Corbett, *Drake and the Tudor Navy,* 46–47.

141. Bigges, *Summarie and True Discourse* (1589), 22.

142. Letter of Tristan de Orive Salazar, 11 March 1586, AGI Patronato 266, ramo 50, no. 12, fols. 1–2.

143. Deposition of Blas González, 4 September 1586, AGI Contratación 5108, translated in Wright, *Further English Voyages to Spanish America,* 217–18.

144. On the withdrawal of the Spanish defenders see "The Discourse and Description of the Voyage of Sir Francis Drake and Master Frobisher," BL Royal MS 7 C. xvi, fol. 171, transcribed in Keeler, *Drake's West Indian Voyage,* 200.

145. Pedro Fernández de Busto to the Audiencia, 12 March 1586, AGI Patronato 266, ramo 50, no 13, fol. 2; "The Discourse and Description of the Voyage of Sir Francis Drake and Master Frobisher," BL Royal MS 7 C. xvi, fol. 171, transcribed in Keeler, *Drake's West Indian Voyage,* 200.

146. "The Discourse and Description of the Voyage of Sir Francis Drake and Master Frobisher," BL Royal MS 7 C. xvi, fol. 171, transcribed in Keeler, *Drake's West Indian Voyage,* 200.

147. "Record kept aboard the Ship *Leicester,*" BL Harley MS 2202, fols. 68, 70, transcribed in Keeler, *Drake's West Indian Voyage,* 168, 176.

148. Pedro Fernández de Busto to the king, 25 May 1586, AGI Santa Fe 37, ramo 5, no. 65, fol. 3v.

149. Pedro Fernández de Busto to the Audiencia, 12 March 1586, AGI Patronato 266, ramo 50, no 13, fol. 2–v. There is at least one English reference to a hurried, if not secret, burial. When Captain George Fortescue died aboard the ship *Bonner,* he "was throwne over board without any other solemnety." Tom Moone, on the other hand, had a funeral in the cathedral of Cartagena. "The Record kept aboard the Ship *Leicester,*" BL Harley MS 2202, fols. 69v–70, transcribed in Keeler, *Drake's West Indian Voyage,* 174, 176.

150. The figures vary between 400,000 and 500,000. See the report enclosed in the letter of Luis de Guzman and Alonso de Tapía to the king, 1 June 1586, AGI Santa Fe 72, no. 67a, fol. 3. See also Pedro Fernández de Busto to the king, 25 May 1586, AGI Santa Fe 37, ramo 5, no. 65, fols. 2v–3v.

151. "El dicho francisco draque tenia [en] su poder unas vuestras reales çedulas que se hallaron en casa del gobernador por el qual se dava aviso dela benida de los yngleses y porque en ella dezia francisco draque cosario el dicho se agravio como sino lo fuera." Diego Hidalgo Montemayor to the king, 23 May 1586, AGI Santa Fe 89, ramo 2, no. 17, fol. 3v. The paper has been badly eaten by vermin, but this part is clear.

152. Undated testimony [c. June 1586] of Pedro Sánchez, AGI Contratación 5108, trans-

lated in Wright, *Further English Voyages to Spanish America,* 214; Blas González, 4 September 1586, ibid., 218.

153. "Con banderas arrastrando caxas destempladas." Statement of Santos de Vergara, 22 March 1586, AGI Patronato 266, ramo 50, no. 14, fol. 2v.

154. Testimony of Diego Hidalgo Montemayor, 23 May 1586, AGI Santa Fe 89, ramo 2, no. 17, fol. 4.

155. "The Discourse and Description of the Voyage of Sir Francis Drake and Master Frobisher," BL Royal MS 7 C. xvi, fol. 171, transcribed in Keeler, *Drake's West Indian Voyage,* 201.

156. Diego Hidalgo Montemayor to the king, 23 May 1586, AGI Santa Fe 89, ramo 2, no. 17, fol. 4; Pedro Fernández de Busto, 25 May 1586, AGI Santa Fe 37, ramo 5, no. 65, fols. 3v–4v.

157. "Record kept aboard the Ship *Leicester,*" BL Harley MS 2202, fol. 70, transcribed in Keeler, *Drake's West Indian Voyage,* 178.

158. Bigges, "Resolution of the Land-Captains what course they thinke most expedient to bee taken. Given at Cartagena the xxvii of Februarie 1585," in Hakluyt, *Third and Last Volume,* 543–44.

159. Oppenheim, *Naval Tracts of Monson,* 1:123. Among Monson's followers is Corbett, *Drake and the Tudor Navy,* 2:52–54. As proof of Drake's intention to occupy Havana permanently, Corbett cites an anonymous paper entitled "A discourse of Sir Francis Drake's voyage, which by God's grace he shall well perform," 25 April 1586, BL MS Lansdowne 100, fols. 98[th]ff. This document is really a summary of Drake's raid up to the time of his departure from São Tiago, 4 November 1585, with some speculation about where he might go and what he might do thereafter. Corbett, *Papers Relating to the Navy,* 69–74.

160. Bigges, "Resolution of the Land-Captains." The Spanish prisoners who talked to Drake took his conversation about remaining in Cartagena as a bargaining ploy and nothing more. Letter of Tristan de Orive Salazar, 11 March 1586, AGI Patronato 266, ramo 50, no. 12, fols. 1–2.

161. Bigges, "Resolution of the Land-Captains."

162. "Record kept aboard the Ship *Leicester,*" BL Harley MS 2202, fol. 69–v, transcribed in Keeler, *Drake's West Indian Voyage,* 171–72; Bigges, "Resolution of the Land-Captaines."

163. "The Record kept aboard the Ship *Leicester,*" BL Harley MS 2202, fols. 59v, 60v, 62v, transcribed in Keeler, *Drake's West Indian Voyage,* 136–37, 138–39, 149.

164. Undated testimony [c. June 1586] of Pedro Sánchez, Contratación 5108, translated in Wright, *Further English Voyages to Spanish America,* 212.

165. "The Record kept aboard the Ship *Leicester,*" BL Harley MS 2202, fols. 63, 68, transcribed in Keeler, *Drake's West Indian Voyage,* 151, 169. There were in the Spanish Indies many *esclavos blancos,* white slaves, who were captured Turks and Moors.

166. Francisco de Avila, 8 August 1586, AGI Santa Fe 89, ramo 2, no. 23, fol. 1v.

167. Alonso Suarez de Toledo, 15 June 1586, AGI Santo Domingo 126, ramo 2, no 35, fol. 1v.

168. Francisco de Avila, 8 August 1586, AGI Santa Fe 89, ramo 2, no. 23, fol. 1v.

169. "Record kept aboard the Ship *Leicester*," BL Harley MS 2202, fol. 68v, transcribed in Keeler, *Drake's West Indian Voyage,* 170.

170. Deposition of Alonso Bravo, 3 May 1586, AGI Santa Fe 89, ramo 2, no. 13, fol. 73.

171. Dean to Alonso de la Torre, 16 February 1586, AGI Patronato 266, Ramo 50, no. 6.

172. "Con los marineros es muy mal." Statement of Santos de Vergara, 22 March 1586, AGI Patronato 266, ramo 50, no. 14, fol. 2v.

173. "Manda y rige con imperio es temido y ovedeçido de sus soldados castiga con res-oluçion. agudo ynquicio vien hablado ynclinado a liberalidad y anbiçion vanaglorioso ja[c]tansioso no muy cruel." García Fernández de Torrequemada to the king, 1 February 1587, AGI Santo Domingo 80, ramo 4, no. 120, fol. 2v.

174. Deposition of Alonso Bravo, 3 May 1586, AGI Santa Fe 89, ramo 2, no. 13, fol. 73.

175. "Entre otras cosas que le dixo le dixo [sic] que para que llamava excellencia aquel vergante del capitan siendo como era hombre baxo que por ser platico desta costa le avian encargado aquel armada." Deposition of Pedro Vique y Manrique, 3 May 1586, AGI Santa Fe 89, ramo 2, no. 13, fol. 64v.

176. "The Discourse and Description of the Voyage of Sir Francis Drake and Master Frobisher," BL Royal MS 7 C. xvi, fol. 171v, transcribed in Keeler, *Drake's West Indian Voyage,* 202.

177. Statement of Santos de Vergara, 22 March 1586, AGI Patronato 266, ramo 50, no. 14, fol. 3; letter of Tristan de Orive Salazar, 5 March 1586, AGI Patronato 266, ramo 50, no. 12, fols. 1–2.

178. "El robo que de cartagena," AGI Patronato 266, ramo 50, no. 3, fol. 4.

179. "The Discourse and Description of the Voyage of Sir Francis Drake and Master Frobisher," BL Royal MS 7 C. xvi, fol. 171v, transcribed in Keeler, *Drake's West Indian Voyage,* 202–3.

180. "Tengo por cierto que no acometeria a la havana por que yban ya muy divisos unos con otros, y en nynguna cosa se conformavan, y tres dias antes que saliesen hubo muchos requerimientos unos con otros y asi tengo por cierto que se yva a matanças y tomaria agua y carne y seguirian su viaje a yngalaterra." Pedro Fernández de Busto, 25 May 1586, AGI Santa Fe 37, ramo 5, no. 65, fol. 3v.

181. "El robo que de cartagena," AGI Patronato 266, ramo 50, no 3, fol. 4–v.

182. "Dizese que obo pasion entre francisco draque y algunos capitanes, y que les avia quitado los cargos y otros dizen que las vidas." Diego Hidalgo Montemayor, 23 May 1586, AGI Santa Fe 89, ramo 2, no. 17, fols. 4v–5.

183. "Record kept aboard the Ship *Leicester*," BL Harley MS 2202, fols. 62v, 63, 65, 70, transcribed in Keeler, *Drake's West Indian Voyage,* 149–50, 151, 156, 174–75.

184. Boazio map text, transcribed in Keeler, *Drake's West Indian Voyage,* 68.

185. The English source says two frigates, the Spanish one. See "The Discourse and Description of the Voyage of Sir Frawncis Drake & Master Frobisher," BL Royal MS 7 C. xvi, fol. 172, transcribed in Keeler, *Drake's West Indian Voyage,* 204; deposition of Pedro Sánchez, 26 June 1586, AGI Santo Domingo 126, ramo 2, no 34, fol. 1v.

186. "The Discourse and Description of the Voyage of Sir Frawncis Drake & Master Frobisher," BL Royal MS 7 C. xvi, fol. 172, transcribed in Keeler, *Drake's West Indian Voyage,* 204.

187. Undated testimony [c. June 1586] of Pedro Sánchez, Contratación 5108, translated in Wright, *Further English Voyages to Spanish America,* 213; Bigges, *Summarie and True Discourse* (1589), 29.

188. Testimony of Pedro Sánchez, quoted by Alonso Suarez de Toledo, 27 June 1586, AGI Santo Domingo 126, ramo 2, no. 35, fol. 1v.

189. Testimony of Pedro Sánchez [?], quoted by Gabriel de Luxan and Diego Fernández de Quiñones to the king, 26 June 1586, AGI Santo Domingo 126, translated in Wright, *Further English Voyages to Spanish America,* 169.

190. Undated testimony [c. June 1586] of Pedro Sánchez, AGI Contratación 5108, translated in Wright, *Further English Voyages to Spanish America,* 212. This is not quite what happened. The Privy Council (4 August 1586) determined to trade the Turks for captured Englishmen in Turkish hands. Dasent, *Acts of the Privy Council,* 14:205–6.

191. Alonso Suarez de Toledo to the king, 27 June 1586, AGI Santo Domingo 126, ramo 2, no. 35, fol. 1.

192. Ibid.

193. Pedro de Arana to the Casa de Contratación, 28 June 1586, AGI Contratación 5108, translated in Wright, *Further English Voyages to Spanish America,* 176–77; Gabriel de Luxan to the Casa de Contratación, 29 June 1586, ibid., 177–78.

194. Undated testimony [c. June 1586] of Pedro Sánchez, Contratación 5108, translated in Wright, *Further English Voyages to Spanish America,* 213; Bigges, *Summarie and True Discourse* (1589), 29.

195. Alonso Suarez de Toledo to the king, 27 June 1586, AGI Santo Domingo 126, ramo 2, no 35, fol. 1.

196. "The Discourse and Description of the Voyage of Sir Frawncis Drake & Master Frobisher," BL Royal MS 7 C. xvi, fols. 172–73, transcribed in Keeler, *Drake's West Indian Voyage,* 204–9; Bigges, *Summarie and True Discourse* (1589), 30–34.

197. Deposition of Francisco Hernández, 30 June 1586, AGI Contratación 4802, translated in Wright, *Further English Voyages to Spanish America,* 183.

198. "The Discourse and Description of the Voyage of Sir Frawncis Drake & Master Frobisher," BL Royal MS 7 C. xvi, fols. 172–73, transcribed in Keeler, *Drake's West Indian Voyage,* 204–9; Bigges, *Summarie and True Discourse* (1589), 30–34.

199. "Declaravan como avia de dexar el cosario todos los negros que llevaba en un fuerte y poblacion que los yngleses que agora a un año passaron por alli tenian hecho en el Jacan a donde avian de quedar los ducientos [sic] y cinquenta negros, y todos los navios pequenos que llevava y con solo los grandes passar a yngalaterra." Diego Fernández de Quiñones to the king, September 1586, AGI Santo Domingo 126, ramo 2, no. 55, fols. 1v–2. See also Juan de Posada to the king, 2 September 1586, AGI Santa Fe 89, translated in Wright, *Further English Voyages to Spanish America,* 206.

200. "The Discourse and Description of the Voyage of Sir Frawncis Drake & Master Frobisher," BL Royal MS 7 C. xvi, fols. 172–73, transcribed in Keeler, *Drake's West Indian Voyage,* 204–209; Bigges, *Summarie and True Discourse* (1589), 30–34.

201. Bigges, *Summarie and True Discourse* (1589), 34–36.

202. Ibid., 34–36.

203. Summary of the examination of Pedro Díaz by Pedro de Arana, 21 March 1589, AGI Santo Domingo 118, ramo 5, no. 210A, fol. iv.

204. Documents regarding the settlement at Roanoke may be found in Quinn, *Roanoke Voyages.*

205. Bigges, *Summarie and True Discourse* (1589), 34–36.

206. See the description recorded by a merchant who negotiated with Drake at Santo Domingo, García Fernández Torrequemada to the king, 1 February 1587, AGI Santo Domingo 80, ramo 4, no. 120. See also the statement of a merchant who negotiated with Drake at Cartagena, Santos de Vergara, 22 March 1586, AGI Patronato 266, ramo 50, no. 14, fol. 2v. Drake was aware of the general criticisms of his conduct and took pains to see something different published. See, for example, the paragraph of praise for his work in carrying water barrels at Cabo de San Antonio, which he apparently had appended to the Bigges manuscript account before it was published as the *Summarie and True Discourse* (1589), 19–20.

207. The various editions are described in Keeler, *Drake's West Indian Voyage,* 301–309.

208. Dasent, *Acts of the Privy Council,* 15:76–77.

209. Wright, *Further English Voyages to Spanish America,* lxv–lxvii; Keeler, *Drake's West Indian Voyage,* 41–42.

210. Rodríguez-Salgado, *Armada,* 15–16, 22; Pierson, *Commander of the Armada,* 56–61.

10.
Raid on Cádiz

1. Drake's letter to Burleigh, reporting his arrival and asking for money to pay his crews, bears the date 26 July. BL Lansdowne 51, fols. 27–28. Seemingly because the earlier versions of the *Summarie and True Discourse* gave the date as 27 or 28 July, Keeler felt that Drake's letter was written the night before the ships arrived. See *Drake's West Indian Voyage,* 274. Corbett accepts the conclusion that the letter was written in Plymouth, after Drake's arrival. See *Drake and the Tudor Navy,* 2:58.

2. On Plymouth's contribution to the fleet see letter of Thomas Forde and others, 17 March 1585, DRO, W360/6, quoted in Worth, *Plymouth Municipal Records,* 214.

3. Mendoza to the king, 13 August 1586, AGS Estado K.1564, B 57, no. 136.

4. *Expeditio Francisci Draki,* 20; *Le voyage de messire François Drake,* 22. The earlier news ballad by Thomas Greepe, *The true and perfect Newes of the woorthy and valiaunt exploytes performed and doone by that valiant Knight Syr Frauncis Drake: Not onely at Sancto Domingo, and Carthagena, but also nowe at Cales, and uppon the Coast of Spayne,* was very likely based on an early manuscript version of the *Summarie and True Discourse.* See Keeler, *Drake's West Indian Voyage,* 7. Greepe followed his source in saying the fleet came to Portsmouth.

5. Keeler, *Drake's West Indian Voyage,* 274–75, and others suggest that the changed date makes Drake's arrival in England coincide with an important date in the great battle against the Armada.

6. In a list of "Charges Since the Ships Came Home" there is an entry for "6,000*l.*

taken up and carried to Portsmouth for payment of the company." BL Lansdowne 52, fols. 92–100.

7. The number of men is given as 1,925 in Folger Library MS L.b. 344, cited in Keeler, *Drake's West Indian Voyage,* 46. The total is 1,922 according to BL Harley MS 366, fols. 146–47.

8. Drake to Burleigh, 26 July 1586, BL Lansdowne MS 51, fols. 27–28, transcribed in Corbett, *Papers Relating to the Navy,* 83–85.

9. "The Declaration of the Accompte of Sir Frances Drake knighte," PRO AO, 1/1685/20 A, transcribed in Keeler, *Drake's West Indian Voyage,* 55.

10. Mendoza's informants told him that the men had received 80 reales apiece, and the commissioners decided on 160 reales. Apparently the amount paid is the equivalent of two and a half pounds. See Mendoza's letter to the king, 20 October 1586, AGS Estado K.1564, B 57, no. 193.

11. Mendoza to the king, 20 October 1586, in Hume, *State Papers, Elizabeth,* 3:642; Dasent, *Acts of the Privy Council,* 18 September 1586, 14:224. The final accounts listed £6,000 wages for the men, the same amount Drake had requested from Burghley when he first arrived. BL Lansdowne MS 52, fol. 100.

12. Testimony of Thomas Drake, 20 October 1605, PRO Exchequer Bills, Answers, etc., transcription in DRO Drake Papers 346M/F551, 4–5.

13. BL Lansdowne MS 52, fol. 93, transcribed in Keeler, *Drake's West Indian Voyage,* 61.

14. Andrews, *Last Voyage,* 48–49.

15. BL Lansdowne MS 52, fols. 92–93, transcribed in Keeler, *Drake's West Indian Voyage,* 61.

16. Mendoza to the king, 8 November 1586, AGS Estado K.1564, B 57, no. 212.

17. Dasent, *Acts of the Privy Council,* 8 May 1587, 15:75–76; 12 May 1588, 16:63.

18. BL Lansdowne MS 52, fols. 92–93, transcribed in Keeler, *Drake's West Indian Voyage,* 61.

19. See the three letters and other documents from Pedro Bermudez to the king, dated between 9 April and 18 May 1587, AGS Guerra Marina 212, fols. 137–41.

20. Keeler has the various sums computed in detail. See *Drake's West Indian Voyage,* 243–44, 259–60.

21. "Tocante la buelta de Francisco Drack de las Indias ya avisse a vuestra señoria como llego aqui y que traxo, que tomo en santo domingo y cartagena e otras partes entorno a 140 piecas de artilleria de bronçe algunas muy buenas, y grandes, sin otro numero de pieças de fierro obra de 16 a 18 Mil ducados de perleria poco mas de 150 mil ducados de oro y plata y algunas mercaderias que tomo en santo domingo y perdio en el viage mas de 800 hombres. apreçiose todo lo que traxo para lo repartir entre las personas que hizieron la costa de la armada en 48 mil libras de esta moneda. aunque vien devia de valer mas de 10 a 12 mil libras mas. pero asta agora no andado un real a nenguna salvo a los soldados que fueron a .6.libras que son veynte escudos de españa a cada uno por lo que ha abido entre ellos muchos ruidos y alborotos pero no les ha aprovechado lo demas se metio en el castillo a los subçedido tan mal que se orche no bolvieran a las indias a saquear pueblos." "Copia de una carta traduzida de Ingles en español escrita en Londres 10 de Noviembre 1586," AGS Estado K.1564, B 57, no. 222.

22. "Con un ardor del demonio." Report from Madrid, 7 April 1586, Vatican Library, Urbinates Latini 1113, fol. 87; microfilm, Saint Louis University, Vatican Film Library (SLUV), roll 1873.

23. Vicenzo Gradenigo to doge and senate, 19 February 1586, in Brown, *State Papers, Venice,* 8:139.

24. Lorenzo Bernardo to doge and senate, 18 March 1587, in Brown, *State Papers, Venice,* 8:146.

25. "Quello chè si sà di certo delle cose di Drake si scrive nelli avisi. Qua dirò solamente alcune cose, chi si vanno discorrendo tra personi di giuditio." Nunziature di Spagna 19, fol. 197, 10 August 1587, quoted in Fish, *Guide,* 55.

26. Martin and Parker, *Spanish Armada,* 101.

27. Pierson, *Commander of the Armada,* 57–61.

28. Ibid., 59–60.

29. On Hawkins's return see Williamson, *Age of Drake,* 291–92. On his preparations to sail again see Mendoza to the king, 20 October 1586, AGS Estado K.1564, B 57, no. 194–1. The Babington Plot was one of several attempts to put Mary, Queen of Scots, on the English throne. The discovery of the plot resulted in Mary's execution.

30. Mendoza to the king, 26 September 1586, AGS Estado K.1564, B 57, no. 160–1.

31. Markham, *Voyage of Pedro Sarmiento de Gamboa,* 342–44; Morales, *Aventuras y désventuras,* 156–58.

32. Markham, *Voyage of Pedro Sarmiento de Gamboa,* 342–44; Morales, *Aventuras de Sarmiento de Gamboa,* 156–58.

33. Mendoza to the king, 28 November 1586, AGS Estado K.1564, B 57, no. 234.

34. She can scarcely have expected help when she was sending money at the same time. Translated letter dated 10 November 1586, sent by Mendoza to the king, in Hume, *State Papers, Elizabeth,* 3:656. Mendoza told the king that the negotiations were not serious. See his letter of 28 November 1586, ibid., 3:667.

35. Mendoza to the king, 8 November 1586, AGS Estado K.1564, B 57, no. 212.

36. Japikse, *Resolutiën der Staten-Generaal,* 5:247. See also Mendoza to the king, 28 November 1586, in Hume, *State Papers, Elizabeth,* 3:667.

37. Undated "Advices from England," in Hume, *State Papers, Elizabeth,* 3:372.

38. See Francis Drake's agreement with Thomas Cordell, John Watte, and others, 18 March 1586, BL Lansdowne MS 56, no 52, fol. 175, transcribed in Corbett, *Papers Relating to the Navy,* 105–6.

39. Thomas Fenner to Walsingham, 1 April 1587, PRO SP Dom. Elizabeth 200/1, transcribed in Corbett, *Papers Relating to the Navy,* 99–100. For ownership of the vessels I have relied on Keeler, *Drake's West Indian Voyage,* 282–89.

40. "True Advices from England," 9 April 1587, in Hume, *State Papers, Elizabeth,* 3:65–66. The account written later by Robert Leng said that Drake arrived in Plymouth eight days before the fleet departed. See "True Discripcion of the last voiage," 5:14.

41. Fenner to Walsingham, 1 April 1587, PRO SP Dom. Elizabeth, 200/1, transcribed in Corbett, *Papers Relating to the Navy,* 99–100.

42. Drake to Walsingham, 2 April 1587, PRO SP Dom. Elizabeth 102/2, transcribed in Corbett, *Papers Relating to the Navy,* 103–4.

43. Ibid.

44. Council to Drake, undated, PRO SP Dom. Elizabeth, 200/17, transcribed in Corbett, *Papers Relating to the Navy,* 101.

45. Ibid., 102.

46. Burghley to Andreas de Looe, 28 July 1587, PRO SP Flanders No. 32, transcribed in Corbett, *Papers Relating to the Navy,* 148.

47. Drake to Burghley, 2 April 1587, PRO SP Dom. Elizabeth, 200/2, transcribed in Corbett, *Papers Relating to the Navy,* 104.

48. Walsingham to Stafford, 21 April 1587, Butler, *State Papers, Foreign,* vol. 21, part 1, p. 279.

49. Drake to Walsingham, 27 April 1587, PRO SP Dom. Elizabeth 200/46, transcribed in Corbett, *Papers Relating to the Navy,* 107.

50. William Borough, "Articles objected with the answers to the same touching the voyage with the Lion of her Majesty," BL Lansdowne MS 52, no. 41, transcribed in Corbett, *Papers Relating to the Navy,* 154.

51. Drake to Walsingham, 27 April 1587, PRO SP Dom. Elizabeth 200/46, transcribed in Corbett, *Papers Relating to the Navy,* 107; Rodríguez Salgado, "Philip II and the 'Great Armada' of 1588," in *Armada,* 22.

52. Mendoza to the king, 19 April 1587, AGS Estado K. 1566, B 59, no. 109, in Hume, *State Papers, Elizabeth,* 4:69.

53. Borough, "Articles objected," transcribed in Corbett, *Papers Relating to the Navy,* 154.

54. "Treslado de lo que escriben de cadiz en carta de 3 de Mayo 1587," in Francisco della Rovere to the duke of Urbino, 3 May 1587, Vatican Library, Urbanites Latini 1115, fol. 133, SLUV, roll 1741. Although the evidence in Spanish sources is clear, English-language historians disagree about the flags. Rodríguez-Salgado says that Drake flew the flags of France and the Netherlands. See "Philip II and the 'Great Armada,'" in *Armada,* 22. Martin and Parker say that Drake flew no flags. See *Spanish Armada,* 130.

55. William Borough map of the attack on Cádiz, PRO MPF 318. Robert Leng said that the attack on the galleys was made by Drake's *Elizabeth Bonaventure.* See "True Discripcion of the last voiage," 5:14–15.

56. Vatican Library, Urbinates Latini 1115, fol. 133–v; Borough map, PRO MPF 318; Pierson, *Commander of the Armada,* 69.

57. "Advertisement of what passed at Cádiz," in Corbett, *Papers Relating to the Navy,* 117. This is Corbett's translation of the "Advis de ce quí est passé a Calez," in *Camden Miscellany,* 36. There is a similar account in Brown, *State Papers, Venice,* 8:274–75.

58. Borough map, PRO MPF 318; Pierson, *Commander of the Armada,* 69; Leng, "True Discripcion of the last voiage," 5:15.

59. Vatican Library, Urbinates Latini 1115, fols. 133v–34. Pierson, *Commander of the Armada,* 69–70.

60. PRO MPF 318.

61. "The Answere made by William Borough," PRO SP Dom. Elizabeth, 203/1, transcribed in Corbett, *Papers Relating to the Navy,* 173–74.

62. PRO MPF 318; Vatican Library, Urbanites Latini 1115, fol. 134. See also Corbett, *Drake and the Tudor Navy,* 79.

63. Pierson, *Commander of the Armada,* 70.

64. "The Answere made by William Borough," PRO SP Dom. Elizabeth, 203/1, transcribed in Corbett, *Papers Relating to the Navy,* 173–74.

65. Vatican Library, Urbinates Latini 1115, fol. 134.

66. "The Answere made by William Borough," PRO SP Dom. Elizabeth, 203/1, transcribed in Corbett, *Papers Relating to the Navy,* 178; Borough Map, PRO MPF 318.

67. Report enclosed in Hieronimo Lippomano to doge and senate, 9 May 1587, in Brown, *State Papers, Venice,* 8:275; Leng, "True Discripcion of the last voiage," 5:16.

68. Leng, "True Discripcion of the last voiage," 5:16; Vatican Library, Urbinates Latini 1115, fol. 134–v.

69. The Spanish reports acknowledged twenty-four ships captured or destroyed. "Relación de los Navios que francisco draque quemo y hecho a fondo en la baya de Cadiz en Abril 1587 y las naos y bastimientos que llevo," Vatican Library, Urbanites Latini 1115, fol. 129–v. Drake claimed thirty-five. See his letter to Walsingham, 27 April 1587, PRO SP Dom. Elizabeth, 200/46, transcribed in Corbett, *Papers Relating to the Navy,* 107.

70. Corbett, *Drake and the Tudor Navy,* 2:86–87.

71. Pierson, *Commander of the Armada,* 71.

72. Borough to Drake, 30 April 1587, PRO SP Dom. Elizabeth, 200/57, 202/14/2, and BL Lansdowne MS 52, no. 39, transcribed in Corbett, *Papers Relating to the Navy,* 123–30.

73. Corbett, *Papers Relating to the Navy,* 124n.

74. Borough to Drake, 30 April 1587, PRO SP Dom. Elizabeth, 200/57, 202/14/2, and BL Lansdowne MS 52, no. 39, transcribed in Corbett, *Papers Relating to the Navy,* 123–30.

75. Borough to Lord High Admiral, 5 June 1587, PRO SP Dom. Elizabeth, transcribed in Corbett, *Papers Relating to the Navy,* 143. Fenner was mentioned by name in the letter, but the chaplain was called simply "the Minister." Nichols's name, however, appears in the list of Drake's officers, PRO SP Dom. Elizabeth, 205/53, ibid., 187.

76. Borough to Drake, 2 May 1587, PRO SP Dom. Elizabeth, 202/14, and BL Lansdowne MS 42, fol. 115, transcribed in Corbett, *Papers Relating to the Navy,* 130.

77. Corbett, *Drake and the Tudor Navy,* 2:88.

78. Two different Spanish reports give the number of English troops as 2,000 men. "Relación de lo que el armada de la Reyna de Inglaterra ha hecho en el Algarve, de que es capitan general francisco Draq," Vatican Library, Urbinates Latini 1115, fol. 138; "La carta de Lisboa de 20 de Mayo 1587," ibid., fol. 137.

79. Leng, "True Discripcion of the last voiage," 5:17.

80. Thomas Fenner to Walsingham, 17 May 1587, PRO SP Dom. Elizabeth, 201/34, transcribed in Corbett, *Papers Relating to the Navy,* 136–37. Fenner and Leng imply that the nearby monastery was fortified as well. Leng, "True Discripcion of the last voiage," 5:18. The Spanish say it was simply a monastery of discalced Franciscans. Vatican Library, Urbanites Latini 1115, fols 137, 138.

81. Augustín de Horosco, "Discurso de la fundación y antiguedades de Cadiz y los demas subcesos que por ella an passado," BL Royal 14 A.III, fol. 157.

82. BL Royal 14 A.III, fol. 157.

83. Thomas Fenner to Walsingham, 17 May 1587, PRO SP Dom. Elizabeth, 201/34, transcribed in Corbett, *Papers Relating to the Navy,* 136–37; Leng, "True Discripcion of the last voiage," 5:18. See also Vatican Library, Urbinates Latini 1115, fols 137, 138.

84. Fenner to Walsingham, 17 May 1587, PRO SP Dom. Elizabeth, 201/34, transcribed in Corbett, *Papers Relating to the Navy,* 138–40.

85. Ibid., 137.

86. Borough, to the lord high admiral, 5 June 1587, PRO SP Dom. Elizabeth, 202/14, transcribed in Corbett, *Papers Relating to the Navy,* 142.

87. Drake to Walsingham, 17 May 1587, PRO SP Dom. Elizabeth, 201/33, transcribed in Corbett, *Papers Relating to the Navy,* 131.

88. Ibid.

89. Ibid.; Mendoza to the king, 20 June 1587, in Hume, *State Papers, Elizabeth,* 4:111.

90. Drake to Walsingham, 20 May 1587, PRO SP Dom. Elizabeth 210/38, transcribed in Corbett, *Papers Relating to the Navy,* 140–41.

91. Oppenheim, *Naval Tracts of Monson,* 1:137.

92. Borough's statement in BL Lansdowne MS 52, no. 39, transcribed in Corbett, *Papers Relating to the Navy,* 150.

93. Borough to the lord high admiral, 5 June 1587, PRO SP Dom. Elizabeth, 202/14, transcribed in Corbett, *Papers Relating to the Navy,* 142–45.

94. "Advices from England," 30 June 1587, in Hume, *State Papers, Elizabeth,* 4:115; Mendoza to the king, 1 July 1587, ibid., 4:118.

95. Borough's statement in BL Lansdowne MS 52, no. 39, transcribed in Corbett, *Papers Relating to the Navy,* 152.

96. Drake to Walsingham, 2 June 1587, in Wernham, *Expedition of Norris and Drake,* 178–79. Wernham thought this might be a letter from 1589 (355).

97. Leng, "True Discripcion of the last voiage," 5:21. A Spanish prisoner reported that Drake flew a "bandera de paz" or flag of truce while approaching the Spanish vessel. Miguel de Oquendo to the king, 14 August 1587, AGS Guerra Marina 200, fol. 209.

98. Leng, "True Discripcion of the last voiage," 5:21.

99. Ibid., 5:22; "A note or inventory of a small casket with divers jewels viewed by us in the Town of Saltash the 11th of July 1587," PRO SP Dom. Elizabeth 202, no. 53, transcribed in Corbett, *Papers Relating to the Navy;* "A brief inventory of such things as have been taken out of chests and 39 packages," PRO SP Dom. Elizabeth 204, no. 8, ibid., 202–6.

100. Borough, "Articles objected," transcribed in Corbett, *Papers Relating to the Navy,* 155; "Advices from England," 30 June 1587, in Hume, *State Papers, Elizabeth,* 4:115.

101. Miguel de Oquendo to the king, 14 August 1587, AGS Guerra Marina 200, fol. 209.

102. Francisco de Duarte to the king, 22 August 1587, AGS Guerra Marina 200, fol. 133.

103. Request of the Merchant Adventurers, 15 June 1587, PRO SP Dom. Elizabeth 202, no. 27, transcribed in Corbett, *Papers Relating to the Navy,* 145–46.

104. "Sampson's Advices from England," 30 July 1587, in Hume, *State Papers, Elizabeth,* 4:130.

105. Agenda for the Council, 3 October 1587, PRO SP Dom. Elizabeth 204/2, transcribed in Corbett, *Papers Relating to the Navy,* 199.

106. Report of the Carrack Prize Commission, 11 July 1587, PRO SP Dom. Elizabeth 202/53, transcribed in Corbett, *Papers Relating to the Navy,* 200–201.

107. Borough's statement in BL Lansdowne MS 52, no. 39, transcribed in Corbett, *Papers Relating to the Navy,* 152.

108. BL Lansdowne MS 52, no. 41., transcribed in Corbett, *Papers Relating to the Navy,* 153–56.

109. Further articles against Borough, 29 July 1587, PRO SP Dom. Elizabeth, 202/66, transcribed in Corbett, *Papers Relating to the Navy,* 159.

110. BL Lansdowne MS 52, no. 41., transcribed in Corbett, *Papers Relating to the Navy,* 155–56.

111. Testimony of Nicholas Blacollar, PRO SP Dom. Elizabeth, 202/67, transcribed in Corbett, *Papers Relating to the Navy,* 166.

112. "Borough's Affidavit in Reply," PRO SP 203/1, transcribed in Corbett, *Papers Relating to the Navy,* 183–84.

113. Borough's statement entitled, "Sir Francis Drake alleageth agaynst me William Borough that I am in faulte and guyltie, for the Golden Lyons comynge awaye from him at the sea with out his consente, nor faulte hee, his associats and followers, thincke to be punished by deathe, nor they urge, and persecute as they maye," BL Lansdowne MS 52, no. 39, fol. 108v.

114. Ibid., fol. 108.

115. Burghley to De Loo, 28 July 1587, Butler, *State Papers, Foreign,* vol. 21, part 3, p. 186.

116. See, for instance, the letter from Drake to Julius Caesar, 16 September 1586, BL Additional MS 12,504, fol. 303.

117. Wernham, *Expedition of Norris and Drake,* 355.

118. Drake to Walsingham, 2 April 1587, PRO SP Dom. 12/200/2, fol. 4.

119. Drake to Burghley, 26 July 1586, BL Lansdowne MS 51, no. 14, fol. 27–v.

120. Drake to Walsingham, 17 May 1587, PRO SP 12/201/33, fol. 51v.

121. Three of the copies are: Folger Library, V.a.321, fols. 39v–40; BL Harley MS 167, fol. 104; BL Harley MS 7002, fol. 8. Harley MS 167 bears a note saying: "Written by the hand of your obedient servant in the lorde William Spenser & subscribed with Sir Fr. owne hand in the port." Even so, the signature does not appear to be Drake's.

122. BL Harley MS 7002, fol. 8.

123. "Vita reverendi D. Johan. Foxis Latine a filio Scripta," BL Lansdowne MS 388, fol. 49. The phrase in the manuscript reads: "Inter militares viros Fran: Drakum consuetudine sua mire devinxerat." On the 1511 edition see Mozley, *John Foxe and His Book,* 4–6. The 1641 publication makes the quoted line to be: "Among military men Sir *Francis Drake* delighted in his company." See "The Life of John Fox," in Fox, *Second Volume of the Ecclesiastical History,* vol. 2, facing page 1 of text.

124. Mozley, *John Fox and His Book,* 1.

125. Greepe, *True and Perfecte Newes.*

126. The copy published by Greepe bears the notation, "Wrytten by the hands of M. Pynner." Ibid., no page numbers.

127. This was not the first time Drake was given credit for the work of another writer. George Peckham did the same thing in 1583, when he published a promotional pamphlet

attributing some introductory verses to various men whom he hoped to attract as sub-scribers to a colonizing project. See *True Reporte of the late discoveries and possession.* In a 1940 publication David Quinn recognized that the alleged poets were nothing more than "names attached to the laudatory poems" of Peckham. More recently he implied that Drake actually wrote the poem bearing his name. See his remarks in *Voyages and Colonis-ing Enterprises,* 1:90–92. See also Quinn's more recent *Drake as Seen by His Contempo-raries,* 13, 32. John Cummins says the poem is "attributable to Drake." See his *Francis Drake,* v.

128. On Drake's visit with the queen see Mendoza to the king, 16 July 1587, in Hume, *State Papers, Elizabeth,* 4:124.

129. "Relación de lo que el armada de la Reyna de Inglaterra ha hecho en el Algarve, de que es capitan general francisco Draq," Vatican Library, Urbinates Latini 1115, fol. 138.

11.
Defeat of the Spanish Armada

1. Drake to Walsingham, 27 April 1587, PRO SP Dom. Elizabeth 200/46, transcribed in Corbett, *Papers Relating to the Navy,* 108–9.

2. Walsingham to Stafford, SP, Foreign, France, vol. 88, transcribed in Corbett, *Papers Relating to the Navy,* 106–7. Borough to Drake, 30 April 1587, PRO SP Dom. Elizabeth, 202/2, ibid., 126–27.

3. "El Drach se anda al cabo de St. Vicente. Dizen tiene repartida su Armada, y tiene ojos a las de Indias, y haze presas, y desinava no dexar juntar las armadas de Andalusia y Lisbona." News letter from Madrid, 27 July 1587, Vatican Library, Urbanites Latini, 1115, fol. 149, SLUV, roll 1741.

4. News letter from Madrid, 27 July 1587, Vatican Library, Urbinates Latini, 1115, fol. 153–v, SLUV, roll 1741. The gossip in Madrid at the end of August was that Drake "returned to his house with more than two million. He did not bring the half from the Indies last year" (fol. 156).

5. PRO SP Dom. Elizabeth 204/3, cited in Corbett, *Drake and the Tudor Navy,* 2:103.

6. "The New Confidant's Advices from England," 12 August 1587, translated in Hume, *State Papers, Elizabeth,* 4:126.

7. News letter from Madrid, 27 July 1587, Vatican Library, Urbinates Latini, 1115, fols. 150, 153–v, SLUV, roll 1741.

8. Mendoza to the king, 2 October 1587, in Hume, *State Papers, Elizabeth,* 4:148.

9. Mendoza to the king, 24 October 1587, in Hume, *State Papers, Elizabeth,* 4:157.

10. Rodríguez-Salgado, "Philip II and the Great Armada," in *Armada,* 22–23.

11. Ibid., 19.

12. Ibid., 17–22.

13. Fernández-Armesto, *Spanish Armada,* 83–85.

14. Rodríguez-Salgado, "Philip II and the Great Armada," in *Armada,* 25–28; Fernández-Armesto, *Spanish Armada,* 87–88.

15. Mendoza to the king, 27 December 1587, in Hume, *State Papers, Elizabeth,* 4:183.

16. Martin and Parker, *Spanish Armada,* 140.

17. Rodríguez-Salgado, "Philip II and the Great Armada," in *Armada,* 27–28.

18. Fernández-Armesto, *Spanish Armada,* 89–92.

19. Ubaldino, "Comentario della Impresa," 88–89; Mendoza to the king, 27 December 1587, in Hume, *State Papers, Elizabeth,* 4:179–80, 183–84.

20. Mendoza to the king, 16 January 1588, AGS Estado K.1567, B 60, no. 12.

21. "The names of her Majestey's shippes that went from Quinborough towarde Plymouth under the charge of Sir Francis Drake to ioyne with the rest of his forces appointed by her hignes to impeache the Spanishe forces from invadinge," BL Stowe MS 570, fol. 246.

22. "Instrucción de lo que vos Don Juan Alonso de Guzman el Bueno, Duque de Medina Sidonia, mi primo, mi Capitan general del mar Océano y de la costa de Andalucía, habeis de hacer con la Armada que sacais del rio y puerto de Lisboa" in Fernández Duro, *Armada invencible,* 2:9–10; Fernández-Armesto, *Spanish Armada,* 140–41.

23. "Dandole la Reyna comision absoluta de combatir o no sin limitacion en el hazello ni poner gente en tierra o no quemar o saquear villages de España." Mendoza to the king, 6 January 1588, AGS Estado K.1567, B 60, no. 12.

24. Ubaldino, "Comentario della Impresa," 85.

25. The pirate is Juan Nanton in the Spanish original. Letter of Francisco de Valverde and Pedro de Santa Cruz, 27 February 1588, AGS Estado K.1567, B 60, no. 28.

26. Corbett, *Drake and the Tudor Navy,* 2:127.

27. William Hawkins to John Hawkins, 17 February 1587 (1588), PRO SP Dom. 12/208/72, fol. 162.

28. Ubaldino, "Comentario della Impresa," 85. For Drake's commission, see Patent Rolls, 30 Elizabeth, part 13, m. 1. A copy of the royal letters patent on display at Buckland is from the collection of the Plymouth City Museum, Accession 277/15. There is also a photographic copy in DRO 346 M/Z29.

29. "Avisos de Londres de 11 de Marzo estilo nuevo en portugues," AGS Estado K.1568, B 61, no. 21.

30. Mendoza to the king, 25 February 1588, AGS Estado K.1567, B 60, no. 25. This letter is erroneously dated 1587 on the front of the folio but correctly dated at the end.

31. King to Medina Sidonia, 3 June 1582; and Medina Sidonia to Juan de Idiáquez, 16 February 1588, quoted in Maura Gamazo, *El designio de Felipe II,* 121, 241–44. The first letter speaks of general concerns about Medina Sidonia's health. In the second he says specifically, "Yo no me hallo con salud para embarcarme, porque tengo experiencia de lo poco que he andado en la mar; que me mata, porque tengo muchas reumas." Rodríguez-Salgado agrees that it was rheumatism and not seasickness that made Medina Sidonia reluctant to go to sea. See her remarks in the review of Petruccio Ubaldino's *La disfatta della flotta spagnola.* I am indebted to Geoffrey Parker for advising me that the correct reading of the remark is *me mata* rather than *me mareo,* as Maura's text has it.

32. Duke of Parma to the king, 31 January 1588, AGS Estado 594, fol. 16, 1°, copy in BL Add. MS 26,056 C. fol. 376, translated in Hume, *State Papers, Elizabeth,* 4:199.

33. PRO SP 12/209/40, fol. 58.

34. Ibid.

35. Ibid.

36. Ibid.

37. Ibid.

38. Ibid., fol. 58v.

39. Ibid.

40. Ibid.

41. Howard to Walsingham, 14 June 1588, PRO SP 211/18, in Laughton, *Defeat of the Spanish Armada,* 1:200.

42. "Les advis de londres datez le 10 de maii nouvelle compte," AGS Estado K.1568, B 61, no. 30.

43. "De Londres par l'res du premier d'Avril 15[88]," AGS Estado K.1567, B 60, no. 46A.

44. Mendoza to the king, 5 April 1588, AGS Estado K.1567, B 60, no. 53.

45. The "orders" Drake received are not known, but they are described in Ubaldino, "Comentario della Impresa," 85–86. No doubt they included instructions to attack the Armada but asking whether Drake thought it might be possible to do so inside the port of Lisbon rather than waiting outside. On this and other points Ubaldino's narrative is very difficult to follow, but he wrote it at the express request of Francis Drake, from whom he apparently had correspondence and other information.

46. Drake to the queen, 13 April 1588, PRO SP 12/209/89, fol. 134.

47. Ibid.

48. Ibid., fol. 134–v.

49. Ibid., fol. 134v.

50. Ibid.

51. Ibid., fol. 135.

52. Ibid.

53. "Avisos de Londres en Portugues," 17 May 1588, AGS Estado K.1568, B 61, no. 44. Other evidence for Drake's presence at court is found in the Nutwell Court Account Book, undated, but between 28 April and 12 May, cited in Corbett, *Drake and the Tudor Navy,* 139–40.

54. Ubaldino, "Comentario della Impresa," 86; Williamson points out that the subordinate officers were jealous and surly. *Age of Drake,* 308–9.

55. On Drake's departure see "Avisos de Londres de 21 de mayo estilo nuevo en Portugues," 21 May 1588, AGS Estado K.1568, B 61, no. 44.

56. Ubaldino, "Comentario della Impresa," 87.

57. Ibid.

58. Howard to Walsingham, 14 June 1588, PRO SP Domestic 211/26, transcribed in Laughton, *Defeat of the Spanish Armada,* 202.

59. Drake to Burghley, 6 June 1588, in HMC, *Manuscripts of the Marquis of Bath,* 2:28.

60. Ubaldino, "Comentario della Impresa," 87.

61. Howard to Walsingham, 24 June 1588, PRO SP Domestic 211/18, transcribed in Laughton, *Defeat of the Spanish Armada,* 1:200.

62. Fernández Duro, *Armada Invencible,* 2:41.

63. Rodríguez-Salgado, *Armada,* 30.

64. Ibid., 30–32.

65. Drake to Burghley, 6 June 1588, HMC, *Manuscripts of the Marquis of Bath,* 2:28.

66. Ubaldino, "Comentario della Impresa," 88.

67. Ibid.

68. Waters, *Elizabethan Navy and the Armada,* 28.

69. Corbett, *Drake and the Tudor Navy,* 2:177.

70. Scott, *Second Part of Vox Populi,* 6. The "Second Part" is an apparent reference to an earlier pamphlet called *Vox Populi,* whose publication annoyed the English government sufficiently that Scott was exiled to the Netherlands.

71. The origin and development of the story is reviewed in Bracken, *History of Plymouth,* 92–93. See also Bracken, "Drake's Game of Bowls"; and Burrows, "Drake's Game of Bowls," both articles in the clipping file, WSL.

72. Waters, *Elizabethan Navy and the Armada,* 28; Adams, *Armada Campaign of 1588,* 18.

73. Adams, *Armada Campaign of 1588,* 14; Fernández-Armesto, *Spanish Armada,* 18.

74. Adams, *Armada Campaign of 1588,* 14; Waters, *Elizabethan Navy and the Armada,* 28.

75. Barkham, "Rival Fleets," 154–55; Adams, *Armada Campaign of 1588,* 14.

76. "Instrucción de lo que vos Don Alonso de Guzman el Bueno habeas de hacer," 1 April 1588, in Fernández Duro, *Armada invencible,* 2:7

77. Pierson, *Commander of the Armada,* 129–30; King to Medina Sidonia, 1 April 1588, in Fernández Duro, *Armada invencible,* 2:14.

78. Rodríguez-Salgado and Friel, "Battle at Sea," 237.

79. Pierson, *Commander of the Armada,* 135–41.

80. Ibid., 141.

81. Rodríguez-Salgado and Friel, "Battle at Sea," 237.

82. Pedro Coco Calderón, "Relacion de lo suçedido a la real armada del Rei nuestro señor de que es capitan general el duque de medina sidonia, desde que salio de la coruña a donde se recojio despues que salio de Lisboa con el Tenporalque le dio," AGS Guerra Marina 221, fol. 190. 1° verso. The translation in Hume, *State Papers, Elizabeth,* 4:441–50, bears the date 24 September 1588, but the original manuscript is undated.

83. Ubaldino, "Comentario della Impresa," 88; Rodríguez-Salgado and Friel, "Battle at Sea," 238.

84. Pierson, *Commander of the Armada,* 135–41.

85. Drake to Seymour, 21 July 1588, PRO SP Domestic 212/82, in Laughton, *Defeat of the Spanish Armada,* 1:289.

86. Rodríguez-Salgado and Friel, "Battle at Sea," 238.

87. Howard, "A Relation of Proceedings," August 1588, BL Cotton Julius F. x., transcribed in Laughton, *Defeat of the Spanish Armada,* 1:18, also reprinted in Usherwood, *Great Enterprise,* 114; Rodríguez-Salgado and Friel, "Battle at Sea," 238. Usherwood presents the documents in his volume with modernized orthography, capitalization, and syntax.

88. Ubaldino, "Comentario della Impresa," 89–90.

89. Deposition of James Baron, 7 October 1605, PRO E133/47/3, typescript copy in DRO Drake Papers 346M/F534, 3 pp.

90. Barkham, "Rival Fleets," 154; Fernández-Armesto, *Spanish Armada,* 174–75.

91. "Hans Buttber's Account of the Armada," 3 and 4 August 1588, in Klarwill and Byrne, *Fugger News-Letters,* 168.

92. Martin and Parker, *Spanish Armada,* 169.

93. See the testimony of Juan Gaietan, 12 August 1588, PRO SP 12/214/18, fols. 59–60v.

94. Examination of Pedro de Valdés, 4 August 1588, PRO SP 12/214/22, fol. 65v.

95. Howard to Walsingham, 27 August 1588, PRO SP 12/215/59, fol. 104; Drake's endorsement, with listing of amount of treasure, PRO SP 12/215/59i, fol. 105.

96. Deposition of George Hewes, 10 February 1606, PRO E 133/47/4. There is a transcription in DRO Drake Papers 346M/F555, 27.

97. Deposition of Matthew Starke, "A note of certaine speaches spoken by Sir Martyn Frobisher," 11 August 1588, PRO SP 12/214/63; also PRO SP 12/214/64, fols. 139–40v, 141–42.

98. Deposition of Evan Owen, 1605, PRO E 133/47/4.

99. Deposition of George Hewes, 10 February 1606, PRO E 133/47/4, transcribed in DRO Drake Papers, 346M/F555, 29.

100. Eliott-Drake, *Family and Heirs,* 1:93.

101. Medina Sidonia to Hugo de Moncada, 2 August 1588, in Hume, *State Papers, Elizabeth,* 4:359.

102. Rodríguez-Salgado and Friel, "Battle at Sea," 238.

103. Howard, "Relation of Proceedings," 1:8.

104. Ubaldino, "Comentario della Impresa," 92.

105. Howard, "Relation of Proceedings," 1:10; Rodríguez-Salgado and Friel, "Battle at Sea," 239.

106. Howard, "Relation of Proceedings," 1:10; Rodríguez-Salgado and Friel, "Battle at Sea," 239.

107. Martin and Parker, *Spanish Armada,* 176.

108. For the traditional identification see Corbett, *Drake and the Tudor Navy,* 2:247.

109. "Relacion de lo subcedido a la Armada de su Magestad desde los 22 de Jullio hasta 21 de Agosto de 1588," Vatican Library, Urbinates Latini 1115, fol. 228; Pierson, *Commander of the Armada,* 151, 271.

110. Laughton, *Defeat of the Spanish Armada,* 2:252.

111. Howard, "Relation of Proceedings," 1:12; Rodríguez-Salgado and Friel, "Battle at Sea," 239.

112. Medina Sidonia to Hugo de Moncada, 2 August 1588, in Hume, *State Papers, Elizabeth,* 4:359.

113. Pierson, *Commander of the Armada,* 145; Martin and Parker, *Spanish Armada,* 176–77.

114. Pierson, *Commander of the Armada,* 151–52.

115. Jorge Manrique to the king, 11 August 1588, in Hume, *State Papers, Elizabeth,* 4:374; "Aviso de las armadas de Roan," 11 August 1588, AGS Estado K.1567, B 60, no. 102.

116. Martin and Parker, *Spanish Armada,* 177; Rodríguez-Salgado and Friel, *Armada,* 239.

117. Pierson, *Commander of the Armada,* 153.

118. Corbett, *Drake and the Tudor Navy,* 235–41.

119. Ibid., 236.

120. Pierson, *Commander of the Armada,* 271. See also Howarth, *Voyage of the Armada,* 147, which questions Corbett's interpretation of the day's events.

121. Pierson, *Commander of the Armada*, 153–55, 271.

122. Howard, "Relation of Proceedings," 1:14.

123. Ibid., 1:15.

124. Pierson, *Commander of the Armada*, 156–59.

125. Martin and Parker, *Spanish Armada*, 181.

126. "Relacion de lo subcedido," fol. 229; Rodríguez-Salgado and Friel, "Battle at Sea," 240.

127. Rodríguez-Salgado and Friel, "Battle at Sea," 240.

128. Wynter to Walsingham, 10 August 1588, PRO SP 12/214/7.

129. Martin and Parker, *Spanish Armada*, 186.

130. On inclusion of the *Thomas* see Corbett, *Drake and the Tudor Navy*, 251.

131. Pierson, *Commander of the Armada*, 162.

132. Martin and Parker, *Spanish Armada*, 187–88; Pierson, *Commander of the Armada*, 162.

133. "Relacion de lo subcedido," fols. 229v–30.

134. Ubaldino, "Comentario della Impresa," 96.

135. Pierson, *Commander of the Armada*, 164; Martin and Parker, *Spanish Armada*, 187–88.

136. "Tras esto el maestre de campo mando disparar la mosqueteria y arcabuseria. Lo que por los enemigos visto se retiraron. Y los nuestros llamandoles covardes y intimando con palabras feas su poco animo llamandolas de gallinas Luteranos." Pedro Coco Calderón, "Relación," AGS Guerra Marina 221, fol. 190, 3°-v.

137. Ibid.

138. Martin and Parker, *Spanish Armada*, 192–93; Pierson, *Commander of the Armada*, 165; Rodríguez-Salgado and Friel, "Battle at Sea," 14.

139. Deposition of Mathew Starke, "A note of certaine speaches spoken by Sir Martyn Frobisher," 11 August 1588, PRO SP Domestic, 12/214/63 and 64, fols. 139–40v, 141–42.

140. Fernández-Armesto thought it "possible that Drake was acting with discretion rather than valour." See his *Spanish Armada*, 191.

141. Ubaldino, "Comentario della Impresa," 96.

142. Compare the manuscript prepared for Drake (BL Royal 14. A. xi., 16v–17) with the one published in 1590 by Ryther, *Discourse*, which omits this story.

143. Valdés to the king, 21 August 1588, PRO SP 12/215/36, translated in Laughton, *Defeat of the Spanish Armada*, 2:136.

144. Drake to Walsingham, last of July 1588, PRO SP 12/213/73, in Laughton, *Defeat of the Spanish Armada*, 1:364.

145. Testimony of Simon Wood, 9 November 1605, PRO E 133/47/3, 1605, quoted in Martin, *Spanish Armada Prisoners*, 82. Other details of the treatment accorded Valdés during his captivity can be found ibid., 79–87.

146. "Accompte of sundrye Monyes disboursed by Sir Francis Drake," November 1587 to September 1588, Plymouth City Museum, PCM 1971.5

147. Martin, *Spanish Armada Prisoners*, 34–35.

148. Drake to Walsingham, 29 July 1588, PRO SP 12/213/65, fol. 150.

149. "Relacion de lo subcedido," fols. 230v–31; Pierson, *Commander of the Armada*, 165.

150. "Relacion de lo subcedido," fol. 231; Pierson, *Commander of the Armada,* 167.

151. To justify his decision Howard had his principal captains cosign a memorandum signifying their agreement to end the pursuit. 1 August 1588, BL Add. 33,740, fol. 6, in Laughton, *Defeat of the Spanish Armada,* 2:94.

152. "Relacion de lo subcedido," fol. 231; Pierson, *Commander of the Armada,* 167.

153. Rodger, *Armada in the Public Records,* 24.

154. Howard to Burghley, 20 August 1588, PRO SP 12/214/66, in Laughton, *Defeat of the Spanish Armada,* 2:96–97.

155. Howard to Elizabeth, 22 August 1588, transcribed in Usherwood, *Great Enterprise,* 144.

156. Howard to Walsingham, 27 August 1588, transcribed in Usherwood, *Great Enterprise,* 149–50.

157. In his correspondence Philip always referred to Drake as the commander of the English navy. See for example his letter to Medina Sidonia, 1 April 1588, National Maritime Museum, PHB 1A, fols. 438–40v.

12.

Expedition to Lisbon

1. Fernández-Armesto, *Spanish Armada,* 223–27; Martin and Parker, *Spanish Armada,* 253–54.

2. Howard to Walsingham, 9 August 1588, transcribed in Usherwood, *Great Enterprise,* 142; Howard to Privy Council, 22 August 1588, ibid., 144–45.

3. Martin and Parker, *Spanish Armada,* 253.

4. Hawkins to Burghley, 28 August 1588, transcribed in Usherwood, *Great Enterprise,* 151–52; Howard to Walsingham, 27 August 1588, PRO SP 12/215/59, fol. 1e.

5. Hawkins to Burghley, 4 September 1588, PRO SP 216/3, transcribed in Wernham, *Expedition of Norris and Drake,* 5–6.

6. Howard to Walsingham, 27 August 1588, PRO SP 12/215/59, fol. 104.

7. "De Londres a 25 de Septiembre estilo viejo 1588," AGS Estado K. 1568, B 61, no. 115.

8. Notes by Burghley, 20 September 1588, PRO SP 216/33, transcribed in Wernham, *Expedition of Norris and Drake,* 11.

9. "Se dizen otras muchas cossas y tan varias que no se save a que dar credito." "De Londres a 25 de Septiembre estilo viejo 1588," AGS Estado K. 1568, B 61, no. 115.

10. Walsingham to Henry Roberts, 5 August 1588, transcribed in Wernham, *Expedition of Norris and Drake,* 6; Elizabeth to Mulay Ahmad of Morocco, 10 September 1588, BL Harley MS 296, fol. 203, ibid., 7–8.

11. Memorandum of c. 17 September 1588, PRO SP 217/79, transcribed in Wernham, *Expedition of Norris and Drake,* 8–10; note of John Norris, 19 September 1588, PRO SP 216/32, ibid., 10; note by Burghley, 20 September 1588, PRO SP 216/33, ibid., 11.

12. Commission from Elizabeth to John Norris and Francis Drake, 11 October 1588, Patent Roll, 30 Elizabeth, part IV, transcribed in Wernham, *Expedition of Norris and Drake,* 12–14.

13. Wernham, *Expedition of Norris and Drake,* xviii.

14. On Norris and Drake as sources of information for Dom Antonio see "Avissos de Inglaterra de 5 de Noviembre 1588 traduzidos de Ingles," AGS Estado K.1568, B 61, no. 127B.

15. Dom Antonio to Burghley, 23 October 1588, in Strype, *Annals of the Reformation,* vol. 3, part 2, pp. 43–45.

16. Wernham, *Expedition of Norris and Drake,* xix.

17. Testimony of Evan Owen, 8 November 1605, PRO Exchequer 133/47/3, transcribed in DRO, Drake Papers, 346M/F555, 5.

18. Percyvall, *Bibliotheca Hispanica,* introduction.

19. Testimony of Evan Owen, 9 November 1605, PRO Exchequer 133/47/4, transcribed in DRO, Drake Papers, 346M/F555, 22.

20. Testimony of Samuel Pomfret, 6 November 1605, PRO E 133/47/4, transcription in DRO Drake Papers 346M/F555, 3–4. Although Richard's son may have been named after his father's friend, it seems unlikely, for he was born about 1577, before Drake became famous. See the testimony of the younger Francis Drake, 23 November 1604, PRO Exchequer, transcription in DRO Drake Papers 346M/F552, 17.

21. Testimony of Thomas Drake, 1604, PRO Exchequer, transcription in DRO Drake Papers 346M/F552, 5.

22. Testimony of Simon Wood, 9 November 1606, PRO E133/47/4, transcribed in DRO Drake Papers 346M/F555, 16.

23. Both Thomas Drake and the younger Francis Drake admit in their 1604 testimony that Richard kept the ransom. PRO Exchequer, transcription in DRO Drake Papers 346M/F552, 5, 14

24. Details of the lease are recited in the document of sale, dated 28 May 1593, reproduced in Kraus, *Sir Francis Drake,* opp. p. 171.

25. Kingsford, *Stow's Survey,* 1:231.

26. See the indenture of sale in Kraus, *Sir Francis Drake,* opp. p. 171, and the accompanying explanatory text.

27. PRO Acts of the Privy Council 26, fols. 291–92, 29 September 1588, transcribed in Wernham, *Expedition of Norris and Drake,* 35; PRO Acts of the Privy Council 26, fol. 297, ibid., 36; Willoughby to the Privy Council, 28 October 1588, PRO SP Holland 27, fol. 196, ibid., 36; Norris to Walsingham, 29 October 1588, PRO SP Holland 27, fol. 212, ibid., 37.

28. Norris to Walsingham, 29 October 1588, PRO SP Holland 27, fol. 212, transcribed in Wernham, *Expedition of Norris and Drake,* 37; Norris to Walsingham, 10 November 1588 ibid., 38–39.

29. States General to Norris, 16 December 1588, in Japikse, *Resolutiën der Staten-General,* 6:88–90.

30. Queen to Willoughby, 22 December 1588, PRO SP Holland 29, fol. 113, transcribed in Wernham, *Expedition of Norris and Drake,* 47.

31. States general to Willoughby, 20 January 1589, PRO SP Holland 30, fol. 83, transcribed in Wernham, *Expedition of Norris and Drake,* 66–68.

32. Wernham, *Expedition of Norris and Drake,* xxvi.

33. Dom Antonio to Norris and Drake, February 1589, PRO SP Portugal 2, fol. 68, transcribed in Wernham, *Expedition of Norris and Drake,* 92.

34. Ibid., 91–98.

35. "Instructions for Sir John Norris and Sir Francis Drake, appointed to have the chiefe charge of the Armye that is to goe upon the Coaste of Spayne," 23 February 1588 (1589), BL Egerton 2541, fols. 5–9v.

36. Drake to Walsingham, 20 March 1588, PRO SP Dom. Elizabeth, 223/24, transcribed in Wernham, *Expedition of Norris and Drake,* 110–11.

37. "The list of principal officers of the army, note of how many companies there be and how many ships," 8 April 1589, PRO SP Dom. Elizabeth, 123/74, transcribed in Wernham, *Expedition of Norris and Drake,* 345–46.

38. "An estimate of the strength of the Portugal army," 2 September 1589, BL Lansdowne 60, fol. 2, transcribed in Wernham, *Expedition of Norris and Drake,* 347–50.

39. "The list of principal officers of the army, note of how many companies there be and how many ships," 8 April 1589, PRO SP Dom. Elizabeth, 123/74, transcribed in Wernham, *Expedition of Norris and Drake,* 345–46. The estimate in this document is 180 ships, but a list in September counted only 102. See also BL Lansdowne 60, fol. 12, ibid., 338–41. One Spanish source estimated the force at 160 ships and 30,000 men. "Lo que se entiende de la armada ynglesa por aviso tenido de françia de persona confidente," undated, AGS Guerra Marina 245, fol. 47. The same information is contained in a letter from Juan Pérez de Ubilla to Hernando Hurtado de Mendoza, 16 February 1589, AGS Guerra Marina 245, fol. 49. Four months later Mendoza's spy, Miles Sauri (Sawyer?), reported the same 30,000 men and more than a hundred ships. His undated report is included in the letter from Hernando Hurtado de Mendoza to the king, 5 April 1589, AGS Guerra Marina 247, fols. 45–46.

40. Wernham, *Expedition of Norris and Drake,* xxxii-xxxiii.

41. Queen to Norris and Drake, 7 April 1589, PRO SP Dom. Elizabeth 223/68, transcribed in Wernham, *Expedition of Norris and Drake,* 134–35; queen to Norris and Drake, 4 May 1589, PRO Dom. Elizabeth 224/10, ibid., 136–37.

42. Walsingham to Thomas Windebank, 2 May 1589, PRO SP Dom. Elizabeth 224/6, transcribed in Wernham, *Expedition of Norris and Drake,* 135–36.

43. Norris and Drake to Privy Council, 6 April 1589, PRO SP 223/64, transcribed in Wernham, *Expedition of Norris and Drake,* 141–42.

44. "Advices from London," 15 May 1589, in Hume, *State Papers, Elizabeth,* 4:538.

45. "Names of the ships and captains in the fleet," 9 April 1589, PRO SP Dom. Elizabeth 223/76, transcribed in Wernham, *Expedition of Norris and Drake,* 336–38; Corbett, *Drake and the Tudor Navy,* 303.

46. On Fenner's title see William Fenner to Anthony Bacon, 1589, Lambeth Palace Library MS 47, fols. 235–38, photocopy in Huntington Library.

47. "Instructions for Sir John Norris and Sir Francis Drake," 23 February 1588 [1589], PRO SP Dom. Elizabeth 222/89, transcribed in Wernham, *Expedition of Norris and Drake,* 87.

48. "A Brief report of a disputacion held amongst certaine ministers of the churches of London touching the viage which should be taken in hande for the restoring of the king of Portingal into his kingdom vi November 1588," Cambridge University Library, Hh.6.10, fols. 1–59, The first two items are letters, one to Norris and Drake, the other to Nichols.

49. Corbett, *Drake and the Tudor Navy,* 303.

50. Fenner to Burghley, 6 May 1589, PRO SP Dom. Elizabeth 224/13, transcribed in Wernham, *Expedition of Norris and Drake,* 143.

51. Wingfield, *True Coppie,* 17. This copy is the second issue, containing on page 27 an additional note to the effect that the Earl of Essex was always in the van of the march through Portugal.

52. Ibid., 20.

53. Ibid., 20–21. There is additional information in John Evesham, "The voyage of Portugal, with all the good and bad fortunes thereof," BL Harley 167, fols. 113 ff., transcribed in Wernham, *Expedition of Norris and Drake,* 229.

54. Norris and Drake to the Privy Council, 7 May 1589, BL Cotton MS Galba D. IV, fols. 199–201, transcribed in Lodge, *Illustrations of British History,* 2:389–95.

55. Ibid. The estimate of the number of brass pieces is probably an error, but it is interesting to see how creatively they were treated in the reports. The Earl of Sussex gave the number as "fifty or threescore." See his letter to Walsingham, 16 May 1589, PRO SP Dom. Elizabeth 224/44, transcribed in Wernham, *Expedition of Norris and Drake,* 159. Fenner said that there were forty-eight brass pieces. See his letter to Anthony Bacon, dated 1589, Lambeth Palace Library MS 647, fol. 236. John Evesham said that all but seven or eight of them were melted in a fire. See his "Voyage of Portugal," BL Harley MS 167, fol. 113, ibid., 228.

56. Wingfield, *True Coppie,* 9, 17.

57. Ibid., 22.

58. Tomaso Contarini to doge and senate, 3 June 1589, in Brown, *State Papers, Venice,* 8:441–42.

59. Wingfield, *True Coppie,* 27–28.

60. "Avisos que ha venido a dar david traducidos de Portugues," AGS Estado K.1569, B 62, no. 4.

61. Wingfield, *True Coppie,* 28.

62. Fenner to Bacon, 1589, Lambeth Palace Library MS 647, fol. 236. Photocopy at the Huntington Library.

63. Wingfield, *True Coppie,* 29.

64. Wingfield gives the date of the English arrival as 25 May, no doubt a typographical error. *True Coppie,* 30.

65. Ibid., 30–31.

66. Ibid., 31–32.

67. Ibid., 32–35.

68. Ibid., 38–39.

69. John Evesham, "The Voyage of Portugal," BL Harley MS 167, fol. 113, transcribed in Wernham, *Expedition of Norris and Drake,* 233.

70. Wingfield, *True Coppie,* 33–34.

71. Ibid., 42–43.

72. Ibid., 41–42.

73. Queen to Norris and Drake, 20 May 1589, PRO SP Dom. Elizabeth 224/53, transcribed in Wernham, *Expedition of Norris and Drake,* 164–68.

74. Wingfield, *True Coppie,* 42.

75. Ibid., 43.

76. Lane to Walsingham, 27 July 1589, PRO SP Dom. Elizabeth 225/42, transcribed in Wernham, *Expedition of Norris and Drake,* 219.

77. Wingfield, *True Coppie,* 43–45.

78. Ibid., 46.

79. Queen to Norris and Drake, 7 July 1589, PRO SP Dom. Elizabeth 225/15, transcribed in Wernham, *Expedition of Norris and Drake,* 200–201.

80. Queen to Norris and Drake, 20 May 1589, PRO SP Dom. Elizabeth 224/53, transcribed in Wernham, *Expedition of Norris and Drake,* 165; "Matters to charge Sir John Norris and Sir Francis Drake," 23 October 1589, PRO SP Dom. Elizabeth, 227/35, ibid., 291.

81. Lane to Walsingham, 27 July 1589, PRO SP Dom. 12/225/42, fol. 65.

82. Ibid. See also the unsigned letter, called "An Advertisement to the Right honorable the Lord Highe Treasurer of Englande," 15 February 1591, PRO SP Dom. 12/238/45, fols. 62–63v. A milder criticism can be found in Roger Williams, "A Brief Discourse of the War," in Evans, *Works of Sir Roger Williams,* 12–14.

83. "An Advertisement to the Right honorable the Lord Highe Treasurer of Englande," 15 February 1591, PRO SP Dom. 12/238/45, fols. 62–63v.

84. "The copie of a letter wrytten by Mr Ralphe Lane of the proceedings of their Portugall voyage," BL Stowe MS 159, fol. 371v.

85. Lane to Walsingham, 27 July 1589, PRO SP Dom. 12/225/42, fol. 65.

86. "Naon faltara don Francisco d'entrar por que lhe sobeja valor e sobejava voluntad de me por en lisboa que tamben sobejava ao geral noris." Dom Antonio to Antonio de Escobar, c. August 1589, AGS Estado K.1569, B 62, no. 92. The translation is from Hume, *State Papers, Elizabeth,* 4:554.

87. Commonplace book, c. 1625, Folger Shakespeare Library, MS X.d. 393, fol. 7v.

88. Bacon, "Considerations Touching a Warre with Spaine," 51–52.

89. Aubrey and Caesar to the Privy Council, 16 February 1593, PRO SP Dom. 12/247/65, fol. 96–v.

90. Queen to Norris and Drake, 20 May 1589, PRO SP Dom. Elizabeth 224/53, transcribed in Wernham, *Expedition of Norris and Drake,* 165.

91. Privy Council to Norris and Drake, 27 July 1589, in Dasent, *Acts of the Privy Council,* 17:450–51.

92. "The Answears of Sir John Norris and Sir Francis Drake to the articles obiected against them," 23 October 1589, PRO SP 12/227/35, fol. 47.

93. "Matters to charge Sir John Norris and Sir Francis Drake concerning their proceedings in the late voyage of Portugal," 23 October 1589, PRO SP 12/227/35, fol. 47.

94. Ibid.

95. Ibid.

96. Richard Verstegen, *A Declaration of the true causes of the great troubles* (Antwerp, 1592), 31, quoted in Clancy, *Papist Pamphleteer,* 34.

13.

The Last Voyage

1. Hakluyt, *Principall Navigations,* in introductory section headed "To the Reader."

2. On the identification of "another man" see Quinn, "Early Accounts of the Famous Voyage," in Thrower, *Sir Francis Drake and the Famous Voyage,* 36, 44–45.

3. Drake to the Queen, 1 January 1592, in Nichols, *Sir Francis Drake Revived,* introductory pages.

4. Ibid.

5. Quinn, "Early Accounts of the Famous Voyage," in Thrower, *Sir Francis Drake and the Famous Voyage,* 44.

6. Ibid., 45.

7. On the matter of Nichols's involvement with the second or Fletcher volume, I have relied on Quinn, "Early Accounts," 46.

8. Wagner says that the Fletcher manuscript on which much of the volume was based was so filled with animosity toward Drake that "no publisher would have cared to issue the book." See *Drake's Voyage,* 291.

9. Drake to Julius Caesar, 23 January 1589 (1590), BL Additional MS 12,507, fols. 17–18v.

10. Dasent, *Acts of the Privy Council,* 19:79.

11. Worth, *Plymouth Municipal Records,* 130. For more on the JP system see Youings, "Bowmen, Billmen, and Hackbutters."

12. Drake et al. to privy council, 3 May 1590, BL Lansdowne 65, no. 12, fols 40–41v.

13. Worth, *Plymouth Municipal Records,* 20.

14. Risk, "Rise of Plymouth."

15. Privy Council to Sir John Gilbert, Sir Francis Drake, et al., 7 September 1590, in Dasent, *Acts of the Privy Council,* 19:422–23.

16. Risk, "Rise of Plymouth," 30:354; Dasent, *Acts of the Privy Council,* 23:351–55, 24:479.

17. Dasent, *Acts of the Privy Council,* 20:51–55.

18. Privy Council to Drake, 16 November 1590, in Dasent, *Acts of the Privy Council,* 20:79–80.

19. Richard Burley to Alonso de Baçan, 2 July 1590, AGS Guerra Marina 287, fol. 94.

20. Privy Council to Drake, 16 November 1590, in Dasent, *Acts of the Privy Council,* 20:79–80.

21. Andrews, "Elizabethan Privateering," 13.

22. In 1581 Julius Caesar was appointed "justice of the peace in all causes of piracy" for the whole country. He became judge of the admiralty in 1584. Lodge, *Life of Sir Julius Caesar,* 11.

23. Andrews, "Elizabethan Privateering," 13–15.

24. Privy Council to Drake, 16 November 1590, in Dasent, *Acts of the Privy Council,* 20:79–80.

25. Dasent, *Acts of the Privy Council,* 20:77, 148, 295; 21:39–40, 230–31, 348–49; 24:346–47, 356–57.

26. Privy Council to Drake et al., 20 November 1590, in Dasent, *Acts of the Privy Council,* 20:82–83.

27. Corbett, *Drake and the Tudor Navy,* 2:368.

28. Andrews, "Elizabethan Privateering," 16.

29. Dasent, *Acts of the Privy Council,* 23:181–82.

30. Corbett, *Drake and the Tudor Navy,* 367–68. In the Bath MSS the total is listed as £97,000. HMC, *Calendar of the Marquis of Bath,* 2:41.

31. Dasent, *Acts of the Privy Council,* 22:207–8, 454–55.

32. Ibid., 20:107–8, 140–42; 21:433, 461; 24:479.

33. "Memoria que yo gonçalo gonçalez del castillo vecino de granada hiçe para su magestad de algunas cosas que he visto y oydo en ynglaterra en el tiempo que estado en ella prisionero," 9 March 1592, AGS Estado K.1592, B 81, no. 73.

34. Dasent, *Acts of the Privy Council,* 23:253–57.

35. DRO Quarter Session Records, 1592–1600, 29–31.

36. "Parliamentarie Journall, Anno 35, Reg. Eliz., Anno Domini 1592," Inner Temple Library, Petyt MS 538, 20:96. D'Ewes printed a slightly different version of the speech: "Sir Francis Drake described the King of Spains strength and cruelty where he came, and wished a frank aid yielded to withstand him; and he agreed to three subsidies." See *Journals,* 1:492.

37. D'Ewes, *Journals,* 1:484. The discussions can be found ibid., 1:474, 478, 481, 486.

38. Ibid., 1:471.

39. Ibid., 1:499, 507, 513.

40. Ibid., 1:477; Davies, *Catalogue,* 791.

41. D'Ewes, *Journals,* 1:487, 519.

42. Martin, *Spanish Armada Prisoners,* 84–86.

43. Simon and Margaret Wood testified that Drake contributed £4 per week for food and drink for Valdés. PRO Exchequer 133/47/3. There is a typed transcript of this testimony in DRO 346M/F555, 13–14. There is also testimony to the effect that Richard Drake was given as much as £1,500 of the ransom money. DRO 346M/F552, 14.

44. Testimony of Samuel Pomfret, 6 November 1605, DRO 346M/F555, 3–4; Eliott-Drake, *Family and Heirs,* 1:119–20.

45. The lease is reproduced in facsimile in Kraus, *Sir Francis Drake,* facing p. 171. According to Lady Elizabeth Eliott-Drake, the house "stood on ground now occupied by Cannon Street Station." *Family and Heirs,* 1:106.

46. Diary of Burghley, January 1592 (1593), in Murdin, *Burghley State Papers,* 800.

47. Corbett, *Drake and the Tudor Navy,* 371–76.

48. Oppenheim, *Naval Tracts of Monson,* 1:203.

49. Andrews, *Drake's Voyages,* 159.

50. Ibid.

51. Queen to Drake and Hawkins, 29 January 1594, Inner Temple Library, MS 538, 6:97.

52. Ibid.

53. Ibid.

54. "The voyage truely discoursed, made by sir Francis Drake, and sir John Hawkins, chiefly pretended for some speciall service on the Islands and maine of the West Indies," in Hakluyt, *Third and Last Volume,* 583; Andrews, *Drake's Voyages,* 164.

55. Valdés to the king, 19 March 1593, BL Add. MS 28,420, fol. 87–v.

56. Andrews, *Drake's Voyages,* 163.

57. Medina Sidonia to Antonio de Guevara, 7 June 1587, AGS Guerra Marina 198, fol. 92; 11 June 1587, fol. 93; and 3 June 1587, fol. 95.

58. "Consulta a su magestad por algunas particulares de Cadiz movidas por la venida de francisco draque," c. 1587, AGS Guerra Marina 208, fol. 89.

59. Queen to Drake and Hawkins, 11 August 1595, PRO SP Dom. Elizabeth, 253/76, transcribed in Andrews, *Drake's Voyages,* 160.

60. Drake and Hawkins to the queen, 16 August 1595, Hatfield MS, 35.30, transcribed in Andrews, *Drake's Voyages,* 162.

61. Thomas Maynarde, "Sir Francis Drake his Voyage, 1595," BL Add. MS 5,209, fols. 2v–3. For Maynarde's ship assignment see Corbett, *Drake and the Tudor Navy,* 426.

62. "The voyage truely discoursed," in Hakluyt, *Third and Last Volume,* 590.

63. PRO Prob. 11, vol. 87, f. 2d. There were lawsuits over the provisions of the will. These are discussed in Eliott-Drake, *Family and Heirs,* 1:136–48.

64. Untitled logbook, 1595–1596, Bayerische Staatsbibliothek, Munich, codex angl. 2, fol. 8v. This manuscript was transcribed somewhat carelessly by Thomas, "Logbook eines Schiffes." See also "The voyage truely discoursed," in Hakluyt, *Third and Last Volume,* 583.

65. Untitled logbook, 1595–1596, fol. 8v–9; "The voyage truely discoursed," in Hakluyt, *Third and Last Volume,* 584.

66. Andrews, *Drake's Voyages,* 168.

67. On the identity of the two English ships see untitled logbook, 1595–1596, fol. 10v; "The voyage truely discoursed," in Hakluyt, *Third and Last Volume,* 584.

68. "Relacion del Viage que hizieron las cinco Fragatas de Armada de su Magestad, yendo por Cabo dellas Don Pedro Tello de Guzman, este presente Año de Noventa y cinco," facsimile in Kraus, *Sir Francis Drake,* 174; "The voyage truely discoursed," in Hakluyt, *Third and Last Volume,* 584.

69. Maynarde, "Sir Francis Drake his Voyage, 1595," BL Add. MS 5,209.

70. "De Juan Aquines que no quiso que vinieran tras las fragatas de la isla de guadalupe, luego que supo que le habian cojido el navio y venia a Puerto-Rico." See Tapia y Rivera, "Relacion," 411.

71. Untitled logbook, 1595–1596, fol. 11; "The voyage truely discoursed," in Hakluyt, *Third and Last Volume,* 584.

72. Andrews, *Drake's Voyages,* 169–70.

73. Untitled logbook, 1595–1596, fol. 11; "The voyage truely discoursed," in Hakluyt, *Third and Last Volume,* 584.

74. Untitled logbook, 1595–1596, fol. 11v; "The voyage truely discoursed," in Hakluyt, *Third and Last Volume,* 585; Corbett, *Drake and the Tudor Navy,* 393.

75. *Full Relation,* 50.

76. Ibid., 51; "The voyage truely discoursed," in Hakluyt, *Third and Last Volume,* 585–86.

77. *Full Relation,* 51; "The voyage truely discoursed," in Hakluyt, *Third and Last Volume,* 585–86.

78. Maynarde, "Sir Francis Drake his Voyage, 1595," BL Add. MS 5,209, fol. 13v.

79. Untitled logbook, 1595–1596, fol. 11v; "The voyage truely discoursed," in Hakluyt, *Third and Last Volume,* 586.

80. "Por ellos he sabido como la capitana de Don Pedro Tello prendió un navichuelo de nuestra armada adonde habia viente y cinco ingleses ó mas, haciendo con ellos buen tratamiento y guerra limpia, quedo en el propio ser que solia, mas habiendo otra cosa, forzosamente haré lo que jamas en mi cupo; mas como hay en esa ciudad soldados y caballeros no dudo del buen suceso de nuestra jente dándoles libertad por virtud de buena guerra lo cual espero y ansiaré lo propio, en todo quedo al servicio de V. SSa. salvo la causa que hay de por medio.-De la capitana de la Sacra Magestad de la Reina de Ingalaterra, mi Señora, á 23 de Noviembre de 1595, estilo de Ingalaterra.-Francisco Draque." The letter is quoted in "Relacion de lo sucedido en S. Juan de Puerto-Rico de las Indias, con la armada inglesa, del cargo de Francisco Draque y Juan Aquines, a los 23 de Noviembre de 1595 años," in Tapia y Rivera, *Biblioteca Historica de Puerto-Rico,* 410.

81. Andrews, *Drake's Voyages,* 172.

82. Untitled logbook, 1595–1596, fol. 12; "The voyage truely discoursed," in Hakluyt, *Third and Last Volume,* 587; Maynarde, "Sir Francis Drake his Voyage, 1595," BL Add. MS 5,209.

83. Untitled logbook, 1595–1596, fol. 12v; "The voyage truely discoursed," in Hakluyt, *Third and Last Volume,* 587; Maynarde, "Sir Francis Drake his Voyage, 1595," BL Add. MS 5,209.

84. Untitled logbook, 1595–1596, fol. 12v; "The voyage truely discoursed," in Hakluyt, *Third and Last Volume,* 586.

85. Untitled logbook, 1595–1596, fol. 13; "The voyage truely discoursed," in Hakluyt, *Third and Last Volume,* 587.

86. *Full Relation,* 56–57; "The voyage truely discoursed," in Hakluyt, *Third and Last Volume,* 587.

87. *Full Relation,* 56–57.

88. Untitled logbook, 1595–1596, fol. 13; "The voyage truely discoursed," in Hakluyt, *Third and Last Volume,* 587.

89. Maynarde, "Sir Francis Drake his Voyage, 1595," BL Add. MS 5,209, fol. 26–v.

90. Untitled logbook, 1595–1596, fol. 13–v; "The voyage truely discoursed," in Hakluyt, *Third and Last Volume,* 587.

91. Thomas Drake assumed command of the *Hope* on 7 December, after the previous commander, Captain Yorke, died of the general illness that afflicted the fleet. "The voyage truely discoursed," in Hakluyt, *Third and Last Volume,* 586.

92. The dispute with Bodenham later developed into a very sordid lawsuit that continued until Thomas died. For a discussion of the details see Eliott-Drake, *Family and Heirs,* 1:142–45.

93. PRO Prob. 11, vol. 87, f. 2d. Drake's original will, written the previous August, was undated and not signed until the codicil was written. On 28 June 1596 the Prerogative Court of Canterbury held that the will and codicil were both valid. Transcripts of these are available in various places, including the Drake Papers, DRO.

94. Quoted in the "Replicacion of Thomas Drake Complaynaunt to the answere of Jonas Bodenham," transcription in DRO Drake Papers 346M/F554, 7.

95. Testimony of Thomas Drake, 2 February 1597, transcription in DRO Drake Papers 346M/F555.

96. "The voyage truely discoursed," in Hakluyt, *Third and Last Volume,* 588. Gregorian calendar date.

97. *A Full Relation,* 34–36.

98. "A Court holden at Porte Bella 6 febr[uary] 1595 wherein all the capteins at land and sea and all the mariners were assembled," BL Add. 38,091, fol. 1.

99. Ibid.

100. "The voyage truely discoursed," in Hakluyt, *Third and Last Volume,* 588–90.

14.
The Drake Legend

1. Dean and chapter of the cathedral of Santo Domingo to the king, 16 February 1586, AGI Santo Domingo 94, no 48, fol. 1.

2. García Fernández de Torrequemada to the king, 1 February 1586, AGI Santo Domingo 80, ramo 4, no. 120, fol. 1v.

3. Wright, *Further English Voyages to Spanish America,* lxvii.

4. Herrera, *Primera parte de la historia general del mundo, de XVII. años del tiempo del señor rey don Felipe II. el Prudente, desde el año MDLIIII hasta el de MDLXX* (Valladolid: Juan Godinez de Millis, 1606), 719–20; Argensola, *Conquista de las Islas Malucas al Rey Felipe III. Nuestro Señor* (Madrid: Alonso Martin, 1609), 106, 136. There is additional material on Drake in the second and third volumes of Herrera's history. See, for example, *Segunda parte de la historia general del mundo . . .* (Valladolid: Juan Godinez de Millis, 1606), 384; and *Tercera parte de la historia general del mundo . . .* (Madrid: Alonso Martin de Balvoa, 1612), 598.

5. Darcie, *Annales,* 417–29.

6. Nichols, *Sir Francis Drake Revived* (London: Nicholas Bourne, 1626); Drake, *The World Encompassed by Sir Francis Drake* (London: Nicholas Bourne, 1628). The first volume no doubt took its title from another foreign publication, the eleven-page *Franciscus Dracus Redivivus,* published in Amsterdam by Johann Clausen in 1596.

7. R[obert] B[urton], *The English Hero: or, Sir Francis Drake Reviv'd. Being a full Account of the dangerous Voyages, Admirable adventures, Notable Discoveries, and Magnanimous Atchievements of that Valiant and Renowned Commander* (London: A. Bettsworth and A. Hitch, [1681]). Crouch used the name Robert Burton as a pseudonym. The volume may have appeared earlier, though this is the earliest copy I have seen.

8. [Holland,] *Herωologia Anglica. hoc est clarissimorum et doctissimorum, aliquot Anglorum, que Florverunt ab anno Christi .M.D.C.XX.* (Arnhem: Crispinus Passeus, 1620), 107–10.

9. Fuller, *The Holy State,* 132–41.

10. Anderson, "A New, Authentic, and Complete Account of a Voyage Round the World, Undertaken and Performed by Sir Francis Drake, in the Pelican, Having under His Command the Elizabeth, Marygold, Swan, and Christopher Frigates: Performed in the Years 1577, 1578, 1579, and 1580," in *A New, Authentic, and Complete Collection of Voy-*

ages Round the World, Undertaken and Performed by Royal Authority (London: Alex Hogg, 1784), 371–98.

11. Anderson's lone dissenting voice gets a brief recognition in Cummins, *Francis Drake,* 292.

Appendixes

1. In his own work Corbett simply suggested the possibility that events such as these had taken place. *Drake and the Tudor Navy,* 1:66–69, 392–94. Later authors converted the scenario into fact. See, for example, Eliott-Drake, *Family and Heirs,* 1:13–16; Thomson, *Sir Francis Drake,* 13–14; Sugden, *Sir Francis Drake,* 4–8.

2. The point was first made by J. J. Alexander in "Edmund Drake's Flight from Tavistock."

3. AGI Patronato 266, ramo 49, fol. 1. John Drake kept the lease on Crowndale until his death in 1566, whereupon the lease passed to his widow, Margery. Finberg, *Tavistock Abbey,* 250–51. John Drake seems to have been at least a moderately faithful Catholic, helping restore the rood screen and other church ornaments during the reign of Philip and Mary. See DRO, Tavistock Parish, Churchwardens Accounts for 1556, 482 A/PW 21.

4. The story about living in an old ship is interesting but no doubt apocryphal. The earliest version, so far as I know, was written by Antonio de Herrera. According to Herrera, Drake's "father was a caballero, who was hiding with his wife in a ship during the time of the persecution of Catholics by Edward, king of England, and his mother gave birth to him there." *Tercera parte de la historia,* 598. A different version appeared in 1628 in *Sir Francis Drake Revived,* written by Philip Nichols and others and perhaps taken from Herrera's account.

5. During the 1580s John Stow transcribed and perhaps edited a manuscript of Drake's round-the-world voyage written by John Cooke. At the end of this account he placed a note that the father of Sir Francis Drake was the vicar of Upchurch in Kent. British Library, Harley MS 540, fol. 110v. Although Stow did not sign the manuscript, several authorities have identified the handwriting as his. See Vaux, *World Encompassed,* xiii; Corbett, *Drake and the Tudor Navy,* 1:393. Whether the note was from Cooke or from Stow is unclear, as is its exact date. David B. Quinn thinks that it was written before 1592, when Stow's *Annales* first appeared. A likely date is about 1585, when one of the sources quoted by Stow in his 1592 account of Drake was published. See Quinn, "Early Accounts of the Famous Voyage," 47. See also Stow, *Annales,* 1176–79; and Borough's preface to *Discourse of the Variation of the Cumpas,* which is the source of the quotation used by Stow.

6. "Vicarius Ecclesiae Upnorae," is what the original edition says. Camden, *Rerum Anglicarum,* 301. Camden also said that Francis Drake was born in Plymouth. *Britannia sive florentissimorum,* 133–34. So much for firsthand information.

7. In Camden's earlier work on the towns of Britain, *Britannia,* Upnore appears as one of the major Kentish towns, while Upchurch is omitted.

8. Corbett, *Drake and the Tudor Navy,* 1:393, is wrong in giving Stow as the source for the statement that Edmund Drake was a sailor. This statement is from Edmond Howes, who took over the work on the *Annales* after the death of John Stow in 1605. In 1615

Howes published his first revision of Stow's work, *The Annales or Generall Chronicle of England, Begun First by Maister John Stow and after Him Continued and Augmented with Matters Forreyne and Domestique, Auncient and Moderne unto the Ende of this Present Yere 1614 by Edmund Howes* (London: Thomas Adams, 1615), 807–8. It is not clear where Howes got his information about Drake, though it is clear that much of it is erroneous.

9. Canterbury Cathedral Archives, Canterbury, England (hereafter CCA), Archdiaconal Visitations, 1550–55, MS Z-3-6, fol. 56v; 11 December 1559, MS Z-3-5, fols. 149, 175v; 1560–62, MS Z-3-7, fols. 24, 36v, 69, 109, 143. Archdeacon's Transcripts, MS A-434, Parish of Upchurch.

10. "Il padre era prete," says the undated note. See "La Vita del Cavaliere Drake," BL Sloane MS 3962, fol. 39v.

11. State of Learning of the Clergy, Diocese of Canterbury, 1560–61, MS 580 Corpus Christi College Library, Cambridge. This report was compiled as a result of an episcopal letter from Queen Elizabeth's new archbishop of Canterbury, Matthew Parker. Undated MS in the Registrum Matthei Parker, fol. 260, Lambeth Palace Library, London.

12. CCA, Bishops Transcripts, Parish of Upchurch, 1560–68, MS A 434, fols. 1–7.

13. See the Registrum Matthei Parker, fol. 347v, Lambeth Palace Library, London.

14. Baskerville, *English Monks,* 263.

15. See the notation regarding the bill of presentment in CCA, Archdeacon's Visitation Register for 1553, MS Z-3-6, fol. 56v. The reappointment of John Townsley is in CCA, Sede Vacante Register N, fol. 82v.

16. MS 580 Corpus Christi College Library, Cambridge.

17. Archdeacon's Visitation Register, fols. 43, 115, Canterbury Cathedral Archives.

18. On Townsley's name change see the authorizations to take a benefice and discontinue wearing the monastic habit, 10 February 30 Henry VIII (1539), Abstracts from the Faculty Office Register, Canterbury Archives, Dunkin Collection, Add. MS 39,401, vol. 76, fol. 106, British Library.

19. Baskerville, "Dispossessed Religious of Gloucestershire." David Knowles thinks that the new surnames were "names of provenance," taken from the hamlet where the monks originated. He also notes a tendency to take a new Christian name. *Religious Orders in England,* vol. 2, *The End of the Middle Ages,* 231–32.

20. For a time at Upchurch Townsley was vicar under the name Townsley and curate under the name Rede. See CCA, Archdeacon's Visitation Record for 22 April 1555 and 12 September 1555, MS Z-3-6, fols. 145v, 148.

21. Registrum Matthei Parker, vol. 1, fol. 230, Lambeth Palace Library.

22. Hoskins, *New Survey of England,* 233.

23. Sturt, *Revolt in the West,* 13–15.

24. One John Hart, for example, was accused of retaining rents belonging to the church at Broadclyst. Whiting, *The Blind Devotion of the People,* 97.

25. The date for this event is usually given as 1549, but Frances Rose-Troupe, who wrote the basic text on the subject, seems to date it a year earlier. *Western Rebellion of 1549,* 90. For an analysis of the work of Rose-Troupe and her successors see Youings, "South-Western Rebellion of 1549."

26. See the entries in Lambeth Palace Library, Register of Matthew Parker, fols.

275–76v, where convict clerics are described as "yoman," "carpynter," "laborer," and "husbandman." Professor Youings notes similar descriptions for the leaders of the rebellion, though she does not seem to think that they could have been priests. "The South-Western Rebellion of 1549," 117–18. A short time after the pardon was issued, the former Abbot John Peryn died at Tavistock. His will lists a debt of thirty-one shillings, four pence, owed by John Drake, and some writers have suggested this was money borrowed to pay for the pardon. The will of John Peryn is quoted in Radford, "Tavistock Abbey," 140. See also Finberg, *Tavistock Abbey,* 272; Keppel-Jones and Wans, *Drake of Crowndale,* 12.

27. Philip Nichols, *A Godly New Story* (London: 1548), 24–25, 59–62, 72; quoted in Whiting, *Blind Devotion of the People,* 126–27. See also [Philip Nichols,] "An Answer to the Articles of the Commoners of Devonsheir and Cornwall," British Library, MS Royal 18 B.XI, fols. 9v–10v. Formerly attributed to Nicholas Udall and printed as *Troubles Connected with the Prayer Book of 1549,* ed. Nicholas Pocock (London: Camden Society, 1884), new series, vol. 3; the attribution to Philip Nichols appears in Scheurweghs, "On an Answer to the Articles."

28. Brook, *Life of Archbishop Parker,* 36.

29. Eliott-Drake, *Family and Heirs,* 1:11–13. Alexander, "Crowndale," 46:279.

30. Clement Myllwaye was one of the prominent parishioners listed in CCA, Archdeacon Harpesfield's Visitation of 1557, Z-3-33, fol. 54. His son Thomas Myllwaye was churchwarden in 1560; CCA, Visitation for 1562, Z-3-7, fol. 43.

31. Bodleian Library, Oxford, Upchurch Leases, MS.D.D. All Souls College, c. 156, lease number 9, 24 April 1560 (2 Eliz.).

32. CCA, Archdeacon's Transcripts, A 434, Upchurch, 1560, fol. IV.

33. The original will, dated 26 December 1566, is in the Kent Record Office, Maidstone, PRC 16/43–D. It is replete with errors and amendments, including one reference to "my sonne ~~Edmond~~ Edward."

34. Vivian, *Visitations of the County of Devon,* 299; Corbett, *Drake and the Tudor Navy,* 65.

35. AGN Inquisición, tomo 85, no. 13, "Declaración de Nuño de Silva piloto en su viage de Oporto a Brasil habiendo caido prisionero con las piratas ingleses," fol. 86.

36. AGI Patronato 266, ramo 54, fol. IV.

37. Camden, *Rerum Anglicarum,* 301.

38. Latham, *Revised Medieval Latin Word-List,* 280, 294.

39. For the Myllwayes as yeomen see Bodleian Library, Oxford, All Souls College, MS.D.D, C.71, lease of the Manor of Horsham 2 November 1563 (6 Eliz.).

40. Daeley, "Episcopal Administration of Matthew Parker," 17, 224–25.

41. Will of Edmund Drake, Kent Archives Office, Maidstone, Archdeaconry Court Canterbury, Probate Records, PRC 16/43–D.

42. Daeley, "Episcopal Administration of Matthew Parker," 39–40.

43. State of Learning of the Clergy, Diocese of Canterbury, 1561, MS 580, fol. 29, Parker Library, Corpus Christi College, Cambridge University.

44. Daeley, "Episcopal Administration of Matthew Parker," 186–220; Parker Library, Cambridge, MS 580, fol. 29.

45. CCA, Liber cleri, MS X-1-5, fols. 80v–81.

46. CCA, Act Books, MS X-1-4, fol. 132v. In 1559–60 a couple was accused of fornication; in 1562 a man was accused of bigamy but later cleared by the vicar; a woman was accused of whoredom and ordered to do public penance. CCA, Act Books, MS Y-2-24, fol. 5; MS X-1-3, fol. 147v.

47. Document translated from the Latin original in PRO, Pardons, C82/893. The patent, which contains very nearly identical wording, is in the Patent Rolls, C66, Roll 808, membrane 42.

48. Document translated from the Latin original in Lambeth Palace Library, Registrum Matthei Parker, I, fol. 347v.

49. "Llamase este ingles fran[cis]co drac hombre de 38 años dos mas o menos." AGN Inquisición, tomo 85, no. 13, fol 2. These appear to be rough notes summarizing Silva's testimony.

50. "Fran[cis]co Drac sera hombre de treynte y cinco años." Francisco de Zárate to Martín Enriquez, 16 April 1579, AGI Patronato 266, ramo 19, fol IV.

51. This portrait bears the inscription (reading clockwise) "Ano D[omi]ni : 1581 : & Etatis Suae . 42 ." It is on permanent display in the National Portrait Gallery, London.

52. Saying that all the people he questioned were well informed and known to be reliable, Diego Hidalgo reported that of all the men in the English armada "los más viejos no pasan de quarenta años, ecepto el dicho Francisco Draque, que vino por General, y confesó havia quarenta y seis años." The report, titled "Relación que envió Diego Hidalgo de Montemayor, juez de comisión de la Real Audiencia del Nuevo Reyno de Granada, a la misma Audiencia, de la toma de Cartagena por el Ynglés, y de las cosas sucedidas en ella el mes de Abril del año 1586, 6 May 1586," was transcribed by Gonzalez de Palencia in *Discurso de el Capitán Francisco Draque,* 300. Hidalgo also had much of his information from Drake's interpreter, Jonas, but whether that includes information about his age is unclear (307). A slightly different version of the same document was translated and condensed by Wright in *Further English Voyages to Spanish America,* 129–36.

53. The actual inscription is on two lines, thus: "Aetatis suae 53 / Ano 1594," which can be taken to mean: "In the fifty-third year of his age 1594." The words are just barely visible in the reproduction in Corbett, *Drake and the Tudor Navy,* vol. 1, front. For possible attributions to Abraham Janssen and to Marcus Gheerarts the Younger see Sugden, "Drake: A Note on His Portraiture," 70:308; and Sugden, *Sir Francis Drake,* 290.

54. Sugden, "Drake: A Note on His Portraiture," 70:308, credits the portrait to Gheerarts the Elder. In his later work, *Sir Francis Drake,* 290, Sugden suggests that both paintings may have been the work of Gheerarts the Younger.

55. Rodríguez-Salgado, *Armada,* 226.

56. The inscription says: "Aetat. Sue 42," presumably meaning "In the forty-second year of his age." *La Herdike Enterprinse,* Newberry Library, Map Department, Ayer *133 D7 H55 1581. The various editions and the opinions about the date are discussed in Kelsey, "Did Francis Drake Really Visit California?" 21:452.

57. The inscription reads, in part: "Ano. Aet. Sue. 43." Wagner, *Drake's Voyage,* opp. p. 9.

58. *Corte Beschryvinghe.* This text is attached to the Drake Broadside Map in the Map Room of the British Library, M.T. 6.a.2.

59. Bernardino de Mendoza to the king, 26 September 1586, in Hume, *State Papers, Elizabeth*, 3:626; Wagner, *Drake's Voyage*, 509; Sugden, "Drake: A Note on His Portraiture," 305–6. The Johns Carter Brown Library in Providence, R.I., has a separate print of the Houue engraving, done about 1586. The same picture was published in [Bigges,] *Expeditio Franciski Draki*, frontispiece.

60. Corbett, *Drake and the Tudor Navy*, 1:411–12; Alexander, "Crowndale," 281–83; Wagner, *Drake's Voyage*, 457.

61. Howes, *Annales*, 808.

62. The Gregorian calendar, promulgated in the Catholic countries of Europe after 1581, established January 1 as the beginning of the new year, rather than March 25, as it continued to be observed in England.

63. AGI, Patronato 265, ramo 61, fol. 1. The English copy of this letter has not been found. The translation that appears in Chapter 3 is taken from Wright, *Spanish Documents Concerning English Voyages*, 11.

64. English transcribed and Latin translated from the original document in PRO Probate 10, box 84.

65. *Een Verclaringhe der oorsaken bewegende de Coninginne van Enghelant, hulpe te gheven tot Bescherminghe des Benanden en verbruckten Volkes der Nederlanden Eerst ghedruckt tot London by Christoffel Barker der Coninghinlijker Majesteyte van Enghelandt .1585.* (Amsterdam: Cornelis Claesz, 1585).

66. *Groetboecxken naden Nieuwen Stijl Waer in datmen tot allen Tijden Vinden mach de hooschde ende leechde der sonnen ofi in wat graet de sonne alle dagen gaet: dit op de calculatie vanden nieuwen Almanach* (Amsterdam: Cornelis Claesz, [1595]).

67. *VVarachtighe tydinghe vande schooue aenghevanghene victorie die Godt de Scheeps Armade uyt Enghelandt naer Spaengien afghevaren verleent heeft over de Armade des Conincks van Spaengien ende eroveringe der Stadt Cadiz ofte Calis Malis, ende andere plaetsen in Andalusie, ende wes sich daer inne heeft toeghedraghen* ([Amsterdam: Cornelis Claesz, 1596]). The identification of the publisher is from Moes and Burger, *De Amsterdamsche Boekdrukkers*, 2:140.

68. *Copye Ouergeset wt de Engelsche taele in onse Nederlandische spraecke Gheschreuen aen Milore Tresorier. Van Mr. Thomas Candische Engelsche Edelman welcke in September verseden Anno 1588. Mit zijns schepen (de seplen zijnde van Damast) inghecomen is in Pleymuyt vechaesende zijn groote rijckdommen dis hy vercreghen heest: Ende in weicks maniesen hy de Werelt om is geseylt wat plaetsen hy versocht heest* (Amsterdam: Cornelis Claesz, [1589]); Moes and Burger, *De Amsterdamsche Boekdrukkers*, 2:53–54.

69. Shirley, *Mapping of the World*, 209; Wallis, *Sir Francis Drake*, 82.

70. De Smet, "Jodocus Hondius, continuateur de Mercator," 771.

71. Wagner, *Cartography of the Northwest Coast*, 1:87, 103–4.

72. Wallis, "Cartography of Drake's Voyage," 145. In an earlier study Wallis suggested Amsterdam, 1595; Wallis, *Sir Francis Drake*, 82.

73. Wallis, "Cartography of Drake's Voyage," 145; Wagner, *Cartography of the Northwest Coast*, 1:87. Wallis also cites a 1636 biographical sketch that credits Hondius with printing a map of Drake's voyage during his stay in London. Hondius actually did publish such a map, a much smaller one, a copy of which can be found in the collection of the New-

berry Library. Jodocus Hondius, *Typus Orbis Terrarum* (London: n.n., 1589), Newberry map 1F G3200 1589 HC.

74. Wallis, "Cartography of Drake's Voyage," 145; Hondius, *Typus orbis terrarum*, Newberry map 1F G3200 1589 HC.

75. Some of these maps can be seen in Oude Karten 6 to 11, Amsterdam University Library. There are also a few copies in the collection of the Maritiem Museum Rotterdam. Of most interest for comparison are the maps of *Namurcum* (O.K. 11), *Hannonia* (O.K. 10), and *Hollandt* (O.K. 6), Amsterdam University Library. For more about the atlas see Keunig, "Pieter van den Keere."

76. Nuño de Silva, AGS Guerra Marina 121, ramo 34, fol. 7–v.

BIBLIOGRAPHY

Manuscript Collections
Austria
Österreichische Nationalbibliothek, Vienna
Sancho Gutiérrez Planisphere, KL 99,416.

England
Bodleian Library, Oxford
Ashmole Manuscripts, 830, 834.

British Library, London
Additional Manuscripts, 5,209; 12,504; 26,056.C; 28,420; 38,091; 39,401; 44,894; 48,015.
Cotton Manuscripts, Titus B. V, Galba D. IV, Otho E. VIII, Titus B. VIII.
Egerton Manuscripts, 2541, 2642.
Harley Manuscripts, 167, 280, 540, 594, 6221, 7002.
Lansdowne Manuscripts, 30, 31, 51, 52, 60, 61, 65, 81, 96, 100, 115, 122, 388.
Royal Manuscripts, 7.C.16, 8.B.H, 14.A.III, 14.A.XI, 18.A, 18.B.XI.
Sloane Manuscripts, 61, 3962.
Stowe Manuscripts, 159, 699.

Cambridge University, Corpus Christi College, Parker Library
State of Learning of the Clergy, MS 580.

Cambridge University Library
MS Hh.vi.10.

Canterbury Cathedral Archives
Act Books, MSS X-1-3, X-1-4, Y-2-24.
Archdeacon's Transcripts, Parish of Upchurch, 1560–68.
Archdiaconal Visitations, 1550–55, Z-3-7, Z-3-32.
Bishop's Transcripts, Parish of Upchurch, MS A434.
Libri Cleri, MSS X-1-5, Z-3-5, Z-3-6.

Devon Record Office, Exeter
Bedford Settled Estate Collection, W 1258/M, D 53/14/3, T 1258, M/E5, M/E6, M/E7.
Eliott-Drake Collection, 346/M.
Register of Bishop John Vesey.
Russell Estate Collection, D53.
Tavistock Parish Records, 482 A, Churchwardens Accounts.

Devon Record Office, Plymouth

Black Book, W/46.
Drake Clipping Book, T/1258.
St. Andrews Parish Register.
St. Budeaux Parish Register.

Gloucestershire Record Office, Gloucester

John Wynter papers, D1799/F4, D1799/F8, D1799/T3.
Clipping files.

Inner Temple Library, London

Petyt Manuscript, 538.

Kent Record Office, Maidstone

Drake Papers, P/377.
Wills, PRC 16/43–D.

Lambeth Palace Library, London

Bacon Papers, MS 647.
Registrum Matthei Parker.
Visitation Act Book, VG 4/1.

National Maritime Museum, Greenwich

Basil Ringrose, "The South Sea Waggoner Shewing the making & bearing of all the Coasts from California to the Streights of Le Maire done from the Spanish Originals by Basil Ringrose," P.32 39.MS MS 9944.

Plymouth City Museum

Drake accounts, PCM 1971.5.

Plymouth Public Library

Clipping files.

Public Record Office, London

Borough's map of Cádiz, MPF 318.
Calendar of Pardons, C82.
Calendar of Patent Rolls, C66.
Exchequer, 133/47/3, 133/47/4, 322.
Plymouth Port Book, E 190/1010/18.
Probate 10, 11.
State Papers, Domestic, 12/49/36, 12/49/37, 12/49/40, 12/49/42, 12/111/30, 12/114/44, 12/139/24, 12/143/30, 12/144/17, 12/144/44, 12/144/60, 12/153/48, 12/153/49, 12/163/19, 12/200/2, 12/202/14, 12/201/33, 12/209/40, 12/209/89, 12/214/18, 12/214/22, 12/214/63, 12/214/64, 12/215/59, 12/225/42, 12/227/35, 12/238/45, 12/247/65, 15/22, 63/53.

State Papers, Spanish, 1/23, 94/9A.
Wills, 7 Martyn.

Westcountry Studies Library, Exeter

Clipping files.
Drake Collection.

France
Bibliothèque Nationale, Paris

Homem, Andreas. "Universa ac navigabilis totius terrarum orbis descriptio," Ge.CC.2719.

Germany
Bayerische Staatsbibliothek

Codex angl. 2.

Italy
Biblioteca Nazionale Centrale, Florence

Cavendish Map, Portolano 30.

Biblioteca Apostolica Vaticana, Vatican City

Bartolomé Olives Atlas, Urbinates Latini 283, atlante nautico, Tav. X.

Mexico
Archivo General de la Nación, Mexico City

Ramo de Inquisición, tomo 85.

Netherlands
Algemeen Rijksarchief, The Hague

Cavendish Map, Leupe Inv. 733.
Recueil Commercie, Friesland Inv. 2687.
Staten van Holland, Archieven van raadpensionarissen, Johann de Witt, 1653–72, 2687.
Vingboons Atlas, VELH 619–18.

Spain
Archivo de Indias, Seville

Lima 31.
Mexico 20.
Panama 13, 30, 40.

Patronato 32, 33, 265, 266, 267.
Santa Fe 72, 82, 89.
Santo Domingo 51, 71, 73, 80, 89, 94, 118, 126, 206, 286.

Archivo de Simancas

Estado 594, 819, 821, 824, 835, K.1564, K.1567, K.1568, K.1569. K.1592.
Guerra Marina 121, 122, 123, 198, 200, 208, 245, 247, 287.

Archivo Historico Nacional, Madrid

Inquisición 762, 1048.

Biblioteca de Francisco Zabálburu, Madrid.

Sarmiento de Gamboa, Pedro. "Relación de lo que el cosario francisco hizo y robo en la costa de chile y pirú y las diligencias que el virey don francisco de toledo hizo contra el," no. 2–33.

United States
Folger Shakespeare Library, Washington, D.C.

Mary Frear Keeler Collection.

Huntington Library, San Marino, Calif.

Ringrose, Basil. "The South Sea Waggoner Shewing the making & bearing of all the Coasts from California to the Streights of Le Maire done from the Spanish Originals by Basil Ringrose," HM 918.

John Carter Brown Library, Providence, R.I.

Codex Hack.

Library of Congress, Washington, D.C.

G. R. G. Conway Collection.
Hans P. Kraus Collection.
Arthur Stanley Riggs Papers.

Saint Louis University, Vatican Film Library.

Urbinates Latini 1049, 1053, 1054, 1060, 1113, 1115, 2512.

Books, Chapters, and Articles

Aa, A. J. Van der. *Biographisch Woordenboeck der Nederlanden.* Vol. 5. Amsterdam: B. M. Israel, 1969.
Abbad y Lasierra, Iñigo. *Descripción de las costas de California.* Ed. Sylvia Lynn Hilton. Madrid: Consejo Superior de Investigaciones Científicas, Instituto Gonzalo Fernández de Oviedo, 1981.

Adams, Simon. *The Armada Campaign of 1588.* London: Historical Association, 1988. [Pamphlet]

AGN. *See* Mexico, Archivo General de la Nación.

Aker, Raymond. "The Francis Drake Controversy: His California Anchorage, June 17–July 23, 1579." Ed. Marilyn Ziebarth, *California Historical Quarterly* 53 (Fall 1974):251–53,

———. *Report of Findings Relating to Identification of Sir Francis Drake's Encampment at Point Reyes National Seashore: A Research Report of the Drake Navigators Guild.* Point Reyes: Drake Navigators Guild, 1970.

Aker, Raymond, and Edward P. Von der Porten. *Discovering Portus Novae Albionis: Francis Drake's California Harbor.* Palo Alto: Drake Navigators Guild, 1979.

Alexander, J. J. "Crowndale." *Report and Transactions of the Devonshire Association for the Advancement of Science, Literature, and Art* 46 (July 1914):278–83.

———. "The Early Life of Francis Drake." *Devon and Cornwall Notes and Queries* 14 (January 1926–October 1927):217.

———. "Edmund Drake's Flight from Tavistock." *Devon and Cornwall Notes and Queries* 20 (January 1939):219–20.

———. "Edmund Drake's Flight from Tavistock." *Devon and Cornwall Notes and Queries* 20 (October 1939):381–82.

Almagia, Roberto. *Planisferi Nautiche e Affini dal secolo XIV al XVII existente nella Biblioteca Apostolica Vaticana.* Vatican City: Biblioteca Apostolica Vaticana, 1944.

Anderson, George W. *A New, Authentic, and Complete Collection of Voyages Round the World, Undertaken and Performed by Royal Authority.* London: for Alexander Hogg, 1781.

Andrews, Kenneth R. "The Aims of Drake's Expedition of 1577–1580." *American Historical Review* 73 (February 1968):724–41.

———. *Drake's Voyages: A Re-Assessment of their Place in England's Maritime Expansion.* London: Weidenfeld and Nicolson, 1967.

———. "Elizabethan Privateering." In *Raleigh in Exeter, 1985: Privateering and Colonisation in the Reign of Elizabeth I.* Ed. Joyce Youings. Exeter Studies in History, no. 10. Exeter: University of Exeter Press, 1985.

———. *The Last Voyage of Drake and Hawkins.* London: Hakluyt Society, 1972.

Arber, Edward, ed. *The English Garner: Ingatherings from Our History and Literature.* Birmingham, England: E. Arber, 1882.

Argensola, Leonardo de. *Conquista de las Islas Malucas al Rey Felipe III. Nuestro Señor.* Madrid: Alonso Martin, 1609.

Arróniz, Othón. *La batalla naval de San Juan de Ulúa.* Jalapa, Mexico: Universidad Veracruzana, 1982.

Aslet, Clive. "Buckland Abbey, Devon, a Property of the National Trust." *Country Life,* 28 July 1988, rpt.

Bacon, Francis. "Considerations Touching a Warre with Spaine." In *Certaine Miscellany Works of the Right Honourable Francis Lo[rd] Verulam, Viscount S[aint] Albans.* Ed. William Rawley. London: I. Haviland for Humphrey Robinson, 1629.

Bagwell, Richard. *Ireland under the Tudors: With a Succinct Account of the Earlier History.* 2 vols. London: Longmans, Green, 1885.

Barber, James. "Sir Francis Drake's Investment in Plymouth Property." *Report and Transactions of the Devonshire Association for the Advancement of Science, Literature, and Art* 113 (December 1981):103–8.

Barkham, Michael. "Rival Fleets: The Spanish Fleet, July 1588." In *Armada, 1588–1988: An International Exhibition to Commemorate the Spanish Armada.* Ed. María J. Rodríguez-Salgado, 154–63. London: Penguin, 1988.

Barros Arana, Diego. *Historia Jeneral de Chile.* Santiago, Chile: Rafael Jover, 1884.

Barros Franco, José Miguel. "Los ultimos años de Pedro Sarmiento de Gamboa." Academia Chilena de Historia *Boletin* 90 (1977–78):15–75.

Baskerville, Geoffrey. "The Dispossessed Religious of Gloucestershire." *Bristol and Gloucestershire Archaeological Society Transactions* 49 (1927):63.

———. *English Monks and the Suppression of the Monasteries.* London: Jonathan Cape, 1940.

Beals, Herbert K., and Harvey Steele. "Chinese Porcelains from Site 35-TI-1, Netarts Spit, Tillamook County, Oregon," University of Oregon *Anthropological Papers,* no. 23 (1981).

Benson, Edward F. *Ferdinand Magellan.* London: John Lane the Bodley Head, 1936.

[Bigges, Walter]. *Expeditio Franciski Draki equitis Angli in Indias occidentales A. M. D. LXXXV.* Leyden: Franciscus Raphelengien, 1588

———. *A Summarie and True Discourse of Sir Francis Drakes West Indian Voyage.* London: Richard Field, 1589.

———. *A summarie and true discourse of Sir Francis Drake's West Indian voyage.* London: Nicholas Bourne, 1652.

Booty, John A. *The Book of Common Prayer, 1559: The Elizabethan Prayer Book.* Charlottesville: University of Virginia Press for the Folger Shakespeare Library, 1976.

Borough, William. *A Discourse of the Variation of the Cumpas, or Magneticall Needle.* London: Thomas East for Richard Ballard, 1585.

Bracht, Jan van. *Vingboons-Atlas: ten geleide en beschrijving van de opgenomen kaarten.* Pamphlet issued with the *Atlas van kaarten en aanzichten van de VOC en WIC, genoemd VINGBOONS-ATLAS in het Algemeen Rijksarchief te s'Gravenhage.* Haarlem: Fibula-Van Dishoeck, 1981.

Bracken, C. W. "Drake's Game of Bowls." *Western Morning News,* 30 November 1938.

———. *A History of Plymouth and Her Neighbors.* Plymouth: Underhill, 1931.

Bray, Anna E. *A Description of Devonshire Bordering on the Tamar and the Tavy.* 3 vols. London: John Murray, 1836.

Brodsky, Vivien. "Widows in Late Elizabethan London: Remarriage, Economic Opportunity, and Family Orientations." In *The World We Have Gained: Histories of Population and Social Structure.* Ed. Lloyd Bonfield et al. Oxford: Blackwell, 1986.

Brook, V. J. K. *A Life of Archbishop Parker.* Oxford: Clarendon, 1962.

Brown, Horatio F., ed. *Calendar of State Papers and Manuscripts, Relating to English affairs, Existing in the Archives and Collections of Venice, and in Other Libraries of Northern Italy.* Vols. 8–9. London: Her Majesty's Stationery Office, 1894–97.

Browne, J. T. T. "Mary Newman's Marriage to Drake at St. Budeaux." *Western Morning News.* Undated clipping in DRO T1258, M/482A, Add. 15/PZ6.

Bry, Theodore de. "Additamentum: das ist Zuthung zwener furnemer kensen oder schif-
farten herrn Francisci Draken Ritters aus Engellandt." In *Americae achter theil.* Frankfurt am Main: Matthaeum Becker, 1599.

————. "Descriptio primi itineris sive navigationis et expeditionis a Francisco Draken
equite anglo susceptae." In *Americae Pars VIII.* Frankfurt am Main: Theodorici de Bry
P. M. relictae viudae & filiorum, 1599.

"Buckland Abbey." 1988. [Leaflet.].

Burrows, G. T. "Drake's Game of Bowls." *Western Morning News,* 24 November 1931.

Butler, Arthur J., ed. *Calendar of State Papers, Foreign Series, of the Reign of Elizabeth, and
Addenda, Preserved in the Public Record Office.* Vols. 13–21. London: Public Record
Office, 1913–21.

California State Historical Resources Commission. "Summaries of Statements Before the
State Historical Resources Commission Francis Drake in California Hearings, 21–23
October 1978." Typescript.

Callaghan, Catherine A. *Bodega Miwok Dictionary.* University of California Publications
in Linguistics 60. Berkeley: University of California, 1970.

Camden, William. *Britannia sive florentissimorum regnorum Angliae, Scotiae, Hiberniae, et
insularum adiacentum ex antiquitate chorographica descriptio.* London: George Bishop,
1594.

————. *Rerum Anglicarum Henrico VIII Edwardus VI et Maris regnantibus, Annales.* London: Officina Nortoniana, 1616.

Campbell, Linda. "Wet Nurses in Early Modern England: Some Evidence from the
Townshend Archive." *Medical History* 33 (July 1989):366.

"The Chair of Francis Drake." *Western Mining News,* 6 January 1932, p. 6.

Chambers, D. S. *Faculty Office Registers, 1534–1549: A Calendar of the First Two Registers
of the Archbishop of Canterbury's Faculty Office.* Oxford: Clarendon, 1966.

Clancy, Thomas H. *Papist Pamphleteers: The Allen-Parsons Party and the Political Thought
of the Counter-Reformation in England, 1572–1615.* Chicago: Loyola University Press,
1964.

Colección de documentos inéditos para la historia de España. Ed. José Sancho Rayon and
Francisco de Zabálbura. Vols. 89–94. Madrid: Miguel Ginesta, 1887–89.

Copeland, G. W. "The 'Drake Sketch' at St. Andrew's." Newspaper clipping dated 22
September 1949 in the Drake file, Plymouth Public Library.

*Copye ouergeset wt de Engelsche taele in onse Nederlandische spraecke Gheschreuen aen Milore
Tresorier. Van Mr. Thomas Candische Engelsche Edelman welcke in September verseden
Anno 1588. Mit zijns schepen (de seplen zijnde van Damast) inghecomen is in Pleymuyt
vechaesende zijn groote rijckdommen dis hy vercreghen heest: Ende in weicks maniesen hy
de Werelt om is geseylt wat plaetsen hy versocht heest.* Amsterdam: Cornelis Claesz, 1589(?).

Corbett, Julian S. *Drake and the Tudor Navy: with a History of the Rise of England as a
Maritime Power.* 2 vols. London: Longmans Green, 1898.

————, ed. *Papers Relating to the Navy during the Spanish War, 1585–1587.* London: Navy
Records Society, 1898, rpt. 1987.

Cortesao, Armando, and Avelino Texeira da Mota. *Portugaliae Monumenta Cartographica.*
Lisbon: Imprenta de Coimbra, 1960.

Courtney, William Prideaux. *The Parliamentary Representation of Cornwall to 1832.* London: Thomas Pettitt, 1888.

Cox, Charles J. *Churchwardens' Accounts from the Fourteenth Century to the Close of the Seventeenth Century.* London: Methuen, 1913.

Crouch, Dora P., Daniel J. Garr, and Axel I. Mundigo. *Spanish City Planning in North America.* Cambridge: MIT Press, 1982.

[Crouch, Nathaniel]. *The English Hero: or, Sir Francis Drake Reviv'd, Being a full Account of the dangerous Voyages, Admirable adventures, Notable Discoveries, and Magnanimous Atchievements of that Valiant and Renowned Commander.* London: A. Bettsworth and C. Hitch, [1681].

Cumming, Alex A. *Sir Francis Drake and the Golden Hinde.* Norwich, England: Jerrold and Sons, 1987.

Cummins, John. *Francis Drake: The Lives of a Hero.* New York: St. Martin's, 1995.

Daeley, John I. "The Episcopal Administration of Matthew Parker, Archbishop of Canterbury, 1559–1575." Ph.D. diss., University of London, 1967.

Darcie, Abraham, ed. and trans. *Annales of the True and Royall History of the Famous Empress Elizabeth.* London: Benjamin Fisher, 1625.

Dasent, John R., ed. *Acts of the Privy Council of England.* New series, vols. 13–24. Norwich: Her Majesty's Stationery Office, 1899.

Davidson, George. *Francis Drake on the Northwest Coast of America in the Year 1579.* San Francisco: Geographical Society of the Pacific, 1908.

Davies, Horton. *Worship and Theology in England from Cranmer to Hooker, 1534–1603.* Princeton: Princeton University Press, 1970.

Davies, J. Conway, ed. *Catalogue of the Manuscripts in the Library of the Honourable Society of the Inner Temple.* Oxford: Oxford University Press, 1972.

A Declaration of the True Causes of the Great Troubles Presupposed to be Intended against the Realme of England. Cologne: n.p., 1592.

De rebus Gallicis, Belgicis, Italicis, Hispanicis, Constantinopolitanis &c. recens allata. Cologne: n.p., 1586.

D'Ewes, Simonds, ed. *The Journals of all the Parliaments, during the Reign of Queen Elizabeth, Both of the House of Lords and House of Commons.* Vol. 1. London: Paul Bowes, 1682.

Dietz, Brian. "The Royal Bounty and English Merchant Shipping in the Sixteenth and Seventeenth Centuries." *Mariner's Mirror* 77 (February 1991):7.

Digges, Dudley. *The Compleat Ambassador.* London: T. Newcomb for G. Bedell and T. Collins, 1655.

Ditmas, E. M. R. *The Legend of Drake's Drum.* West Country Folklore, no. 6. Mount Durand, St. Peter Port, Guernsey: Toucan, 1973.

Donno, Elizabeth S., ed. *An Elizabethan in 1582: The Diary of Richard Madox, Fellow of All Souls.* Hakluyt Society *Works,* series 2, vol. 147. London: Hakluyt Society, 1976.

Drake, Francis. *The World Encompassed by Sir Francis Drake.* London: Nicholas Bourne, 1628.

Drake, Henry H. "Arms of Drake." *The Western Antiquary* 2 (September 1882):98.

————. "Drake: The Arms of His Surname and Family; Argent, a Waver-Dragon Gules." *Report and Transactions of the Devonshire Association for the Advancement of Science, Literature, and Art* 15 (July 1883):489–93.

————. "Facts Not Generally Known about Francis Drake and Francis Russell." *The Western Antiquary* 4 (June 1884):27.

Draper, Benjamin Poff. "Drake Bibliography, 1569–1979, with Special Reference to Francis Drake's Voyage Around the World, 1577–1580 A[nn]o D[omin]i." California State Library, California History Room, Sacramento, 1980. [Typescript.]

Dugdale, William. *Monasticon Anglicanum.* 6 vols. London: Longman, Rees, Orme, and Brown, 1821.

Edmond, Mary. *Hilliard and Oliver: The Lives and Works of Two Great Miniaturists.* London: Robert Hale, 1983.

Edwards, R. Dudley. *Ireland in the Age of the Tudors.* London: Croom Helm, 1977.

Elizabethae, Angliae reginae haeresim calvinianam propugnantis, saevissimam in Catholicos sui regni edictum, quod in alios quoq; Reipub. Christianae Principe contumelias continet indignissimas: promulgatam Londini 29. Nouemb. 1591. Augsburg: Joannes Fabrus, 1592.

Eliott-Drake, Lady Elizabeth Fuller. *The Family and Heirs of Sir Francis Drake.* 2 vols. London: Smith, Elder, 1911.

Ellis, Steven G. *Tudor Ireland: Crown, Community, and the Conflict of Cultures, 1470–1603.* London: Longman, 1985.

Evans, John X. *The Works of Sir Roger Williams.* Oxford: Clarendon, 1972.

Fairclough, G. J. *St. Andrew Street: Plymouth Excavations.* Plymouth Museum Archaeological Series, no. 2, 1976.

Fernández-Armesto, Felipe. *The Spanish Armada: The Experience of War in 1588.* Oxford: Oxford University Press, 1989.

Fernández Duro, Cesáreo. *La Armada invencible.* 2 vols. Madrid: Tipografico de los Susessores de Rivadeneyra, 1884–85.

Fildes, Valerie. "The English Wet Nurse and Her Role in Infant Care, 1538–1800." *Medical History* 32 (April 1988):142–73.

Finberg, H. P. R. *Tavistock Abbey: A Study in the Social and Economic History of Devon.* Cambridge: Cambridge University Press, 1951.

Finsten, Jill. "Women in the Renaissance: Elizabeth I." Paper read at the Huntington Library, 7 April 1989.

The First Voyage Round the World by Magellan, Translated from the Account of Pigafetta and other Contemporary Writers. Introduction and notes by Lord Stanley of Adderly. Hakluyt Society *Works,* series 1, vol. 52. London: Hakluyt Society, 1874.

Fish, Carl R. *Guide to the Materials for American History in Roman and Other Italian Archives.* Washington: Carnegie Institution of Washington, 1911.

Fox, John. *The Second Volume of the Ecclesiastical History: Containing the Acts and Monuments of Martyrs.* London: Company of Stationers, 1641.

Froude, James. *English Seamen in the Sixteenth Century.* London: Longmans, Green, 1896.

Fuller, Thomas. *The Holy State and the Profane State.* Cambridge: Roger Daniel for John Williams, 1642.

A Full Relation of another Voyage into the West Indies made by Sir Francis Drake accompanied with Sir John Hawkins, Sir Thomas Baskerfield, Sir Nicholas Clifford, and others. who set forth from Plimouth on the 28 of August 1595. London: Nicholas Bourne, 1652. [Bound in Bigges, *Summarie and True Discourse* (1652)].

Furnivall, Frederick J. *Early English Meals and Manners.* Early English Text Society, vol. 32. London: Edward Arnold, 1972.

Gairdner, James. *Letters and Papers, Foreign and Domestic, of the Reign of Henry VIII, Preserved in the Public Record Office, The British Museum, and Elsewhere in England.* Vol. 13, part 1, and vol. 17. London: Her Majesty's Stationery Office, 1892.

Galdames, Luis. *History of Chile.* Trans. and ed. Isaac Joslin Cox. New York: Russell and Russell, 1962.

García-Pelayo y Gross, Ramón, and Micheline Durand, eds. *Diccionario Moderno Español-Inglés.* New York: Larousse, 1976.

Gasquet, Cardinal. *English Monastic Life.* London: Methuen, 1924.

Gastaldi, Giacomo de. *La universale descrittione del mondo.* Venice: Matthio Pagano, 1561.

Gill, Crispin. "Drake and Plymouth." In *Sir Francis Drake and the Famous Voyage, 1577–1580.* Ed. Norman J. W. Thrower, 78–89. Berkeley: University of California Press, 1984.

―――. "Drake's Home, Buckland Abbey." In *Sir Francis Drake and the Famous Voyage, 1577–1580.* Ed. Norman J. W. Thrower, 91–98. Berkeley: University of California Press, 1984.

Gonzalez de Palencia, Angel, ed. *Discurso de el Capitán Francisco Draque que compuso Joan de Castellanos, beneficiado de Tunja.* Madrid: Instituto de Valencia de D. Juan, 1921.

Gratwicke, F. St. George. "Coat-of-Arms-Mystery: Was it Painted and Subsequently Obliterated?" *Western Morning News,* 9 July 1932, p. 8.

Great Britain, Public Record Office. *Calendar of Patent Rolls Preserved in the Public Record Office. Edward VI.* Vol. 1, 1547–48; vol. 2, 1548–49. London: His Majesty's Stationery Office, 1924.

―――. *Calendar of the Manuscripts of the Marquis of Bath Preserved at Longleat, Wiltshire.* Vol. 2. London: His Majesty's Stationery Office, 1907.

―――. *Calendar of the Manuscripts of the Most Hon. the Marquis of Salisbury, &c., &c., &c., Preserved at Hatfield House, Hertfordshire.* Part 3, *Addenda.* London: His Majesty's Stationery Office, 1915.

―――. *Eighth Report of the Deputy Keeper of the Public Records.* London: HMSO, 1847.

―――. *Report on the Manuscripts of His Grace the Duke of Portland, K.G., Preserved at Welbeck Abbey.* Vol. 9. London: His Majesty's Stationery Office, 1923.

―――. *Report on the Manuscripts of Lord de L'Isle & Dudley, Preserved at Penhurst Place.* London: His Majesty's Stationery Office, 1925.

―――. *Report on the Records of the City of Exeter.* London: His Majesty's Stationery Office, 1916.

Greaves, Richard L. *Society and Religion in Elizabethan England.* Minneapolis: University of Minnesota Press, 1981.

Greepe, Thomas. *The true and perfect Newes of the woorthy and valiaunt exploytes performed and doone by that valiant Knight Syr Frauncis Drake: Not onely at Sancto*

Domingo, and Carthagena, but also nowe at Cales, and uppon the Coast of Spayne. London: I. Charlewood for Thomas Hackett, 1587.

Groetboecxken naden Nieuwen Stijl Waer in datmen tot allen Tijden Vinden mach de hooschde ende leechde der sonnen oft in wat graet de sonne alle dagen gaet: dit op de calculatie vanden nieuwen Almanach. Amsterdam: Cornelis Claesz, 1595(?).

Hakluyt, Richard. *Principall Navigations, Voiages and Discoveries of the English Nation.* London: George Bishop and Ralph Newberie, 1589.

———. *The Second Volume of the Principall Navigations.* London: George Bishop, Ralph Newbery, and Robert Barker, 1599.

———. *Third and Last Volume of the Voyages, Navigations, Trafiques, and Discoveries of the English Nation.* London: George Bishop, Ralfe Newberie, and Robert Baker, 1600.

Hamilton, Hans Claude. *Calendar of State Papers Relating to Ireland, 1574-1585.* Vol. 2. London: Her Majesty's Stationery Office, 1860.

Hammond, George P. *Sir Francis Drake and the Finding of the Plate of Brass, on Exhibit in the Bancroft Library, University of California, Berkeley, California.* Berkeley: The Bancroft Library, c. 1970. [Leaflet.]

Hanna, Warren L. *Lost Harbor: The Controversy over Drake's California Anchorage.* Berkeley: University of California Press, 1979.

Harris, Helen J. *Drake of Tavistock: The Life and Origins of Sir Francis Drake.* Exeter: Devon Books, 1988.

Hart, James D. *The Plate of Brass Reexamined.* Berkeley: The Bancroft Library, 1977. [Leaflet.]

Hartley, T. E. *Proceedings in the Parliament of Elizabeth I.* Wilmington, Del.: Michael Glazier, 1982.

Hasler, P. W. *History of Parliament: The House of Commons, 1558–1603.* Vol. 2, *Members D-L.* London: Her Majesty's Stationery Office, 1981.

Hasted, Edward. "A Map of the Hundreds of Middleton, alias Milton, and of Tenham." History and Topographical Survey of the County of Kent. Canterbury: W. Bristow, 1798.

Hawkins, Richard. *The Observations of Sir Richard Hawkins, Knight, in His Voyage into the South Sea, Anno Domini, 1593.* London: 1622.

Heizer, Robert F. "Francis Drake and the California Indians, 1579." In *Elizabethan California,* 53–78. Ramona, Calif.: Ballena, 1974.

Herrera, Antonio de. *Descripción de las Indias occidentales.* Madrid: Imprenta Real, 1601.

———. *Primera parte de la historia general del mundo, de XVII ahos del tiempo del rey don Felipe II el Prudente, desde el aho de MDLIIII hasta el de MDLXX.* 2 vols. Valladolid: Juan Godinez de Millis, 1606.

———. *Segunda parte de la historia general del mundo, de XV ahos del tiempo del senor Rey don Felipe, el Prudente, desde el aho de MDLXXI. hasta el de MDLXXXV.* Valladolid: Juan Godinez de Millis, 1606.

———. *Tercera parte de la historia general del mundo, de XIII ahos del tiempo del sehor Rey don Felipe II el Prudente, desde el aho de 1585 hasta el de 1598 que passó a mejor vida.* Madrid: Alonso Martin de Balvoa, 1612.

Heyden, H. A. M. van der. "Emanuel van Meteren's History as Source for the Cartography of the Netherlands." *Querendo* 16 (Winter 1986):3–29.

Higham, Robert, ed. *Landscape and Townscape in the South West.* Exeter Studies in History, no. 22. Exeter: University of Exeter Press, 1989.

———. *Security and Defence in South-West England Before 1800.* Exeter Studies in History, no. 19. Exeter: University of Exeter Press, 1987.

HMC. *See* Great Britain, Historical Manuscripts Commission.

Hodgett, G. A. J. "The Unpensioned Ex-Religious in Tudor England." *Journal of Ecclesiastial History* 13 (October 1962):195–202.

Hoffman, Paul E. *The Spanish Crown and the Defense of the Caribbean, 1535–1585: Precedent, Patrimonialism, and Royal Parsimony.* Baton Rouge: Louisiana State University Press, 1980.

Holinshed, Raphaell. *The Third Volume of Chronicles.* London: John Harrison, George Bishop, Rafe Newberie, Henry Denham, and Thomas Woodcock, 1587.

Holinshed's Chronicles of England, Scotland, and Ireland. London: J. Johnson, 1807.

[Holland, Henry]. *Herwologia Anglica; hoc est clarissimorum et doctissimorum, aliquot anglorum, que florverunt ab anno Christi .M.D.C.XX.* Arnhem: Crispus Passeus, 1520.

Holmes, Maurice G. *From New Spain by Sea to the Californias, 1519-1668.* Glendale, Calif.: Arthur H. Clark, 1963.

Hortop, Job. *The Rare Travails of Job Hortop.* London: William Wright, 1591.

Hoskins, W. G. *A New Survey of England: Devon.* London: Collins, 1954.

Howarth, David. *The Voyage of the Armada: The Spanish Story.* London: Collins, 1981.

Howes, Edmond. *The Annales or Generall Chronicle of England, Begun First by Maister John Stow and after Him Continued and Augmented with Matters Forreyne and Domestique, Auncient and Moderne unto the Ende of this Present Yere 1614 by Edmund Howes.* London: Thomas Adams, 1615.

Hulsius, Levinus. *Sechster Theil, kurze warhafftige Relation unnd Beschreibung der Wunderbarsten Vier Schiffahrten so Jemals verricht worden.* Frankfurt: Imprensis Hulsianus, 1602.

Hume, Martin A. S., ed. *Calendar of Letters and State Papers Relating to English Affairs Preserved Principally in the Archives of Simancas.* Vols. 2–4, *Elizabeth, 1568–1603.* London: Her Majesty's Stationery Office, 1868–99.

Hurstfield, Joel, and Alan G. R. Smith, eds. *Elizabethan People, State and Society.* London: Edward Arnold, 1972.

Japikse, N., ed. *Resolutiën der Staten-Generaal van 1576 tot 1609.* Vol. 41 of *Rijks Geschiedkundige Publicatiën.* The Hague: Martinus Nijhoff, 1918.

Jewers, Arthur J. Letter in *Western Antiquary,* June 1891. National Trust.

Keeler, Mary Frear. *Sir Francis Drake's West Indian Voyage.* Hakluyt Society *Works,* 2d series, vol. 148. London: Hakluyt Society, 1981.

Kelsey, Harry. "American Discoveries Noted on the Planisphere of Sancho Gutiérrez." In *Early Images of the Americas.* Ed. Jerry M. Williams and Robert E. Lewis, 247–61. Tucson: University of Arizona Press, 1993.

———. "Did Francis Drake Really Visit California?" *Western Historical Quarterly* 21 (November 1990):444–62.

———. "Finding the Way Home: Spanish Exploration of the Round-Trip Route Across the Pacific Ocean." *Western Historical Quarterly* 17 (April 1986):145–64.

————. "The Gregorian Calendar in New Spain: A Problem in Sixteenth-Century Chronology." *New Mexico Historical Review* 58 (July 1983):239–52.

————. *Juan Rodríguez Cabrillo.* San Marino, Calif.: Huntington Library, 1986.

Kemp, Alfred John. *Notices of Tavistock and Its Abbey.* London: Gentlemen's Magazine, 1830.

Keppel-Jones, P. T., and J. Wans. *Drake of Crowndale: The Early Years of Sir Francis Drake.* Plymouth: Hitchings and Mason, 1986.

Kerr, Willis H. "The Treatment of Drake's Circumnavigation in Hakluyt's 'Voyages.'" Bibliographical Society of America *Papers* 34 (1940):281–302.

Keunig, J. "Pieter van den Keere." *Imago Mundi* 15 (1960):68.

Kingsford, Charles Lethbridge, ed. *A Survey of London by John Stow, Reprinted from the Text of 1603.* Oxford: Clarendon, 1908.

Klarwill, Victor. *Fugger-Zeitungen ungedruchte Briefe an dashaus Fuggeraus den jahren 1568–1605.* Vienna: Ritola Verlag, 1923.

Klarwill, Victor, and L. S. R. Byrne. *The Fugger News-Letters, Second Series.* London: John Lane the Bodley Head, 1926.

Knowles, David. *The Monastic Order in England.* 2 vols. Cambridge: Cambridge University Press, 1940.

————. *The Religious Orders in England.* 2 vols. Cambridge: Cambridge University Press, 1955.

Kraus, Hans P. *Sir Francis Drake: A Pictorial Biography.* Amsterdam: N. Israel, 1970.

Latham, R. E. *Revised Medieval Latin Word-List from British and Irish Sources.* London: Oxford University Press, 1965.

Laudonnière, René. *L'Histoire notable de la Floride situee es Indes Occidentales.* Paris: Guillaume Auuray, 1586).

Laughton, John Knox. "Francis Drake." In *Dictionary of National Biography,* 15:425–26. London: Smith, Elder, 1888.

————. *State Papers Relating to the Defeat of the Spanish Armada, Anno 1588.* 2 vols. London: Her Majesty's Stationery Office, 1894.

Legg, John W., ed. *Missale ad usum ecclesie Westmonasteriensis.* 3 vols. London: Harrison and Sons, 1891–96.

Leng, Robert. "The true Discripcion of the last voiage of tha worthy Captayne Sir Frauncis Drake." Ed. Clarence Hopper. *Camden Miscellany* 5 (1864):15–22.

Lessa, William A. *Drake's Island of Thieves: Ethnological Sleuthing.* Honolulu: University of Hawaii Press, 1975.

Lewis, Frederic Christian. *The Scenery of the Rivers Tamar and Tavy, in Forty-Seven Subjects, Exhibiting the Most interesting Views on Their Banks from the Source to the Termination of Each; Including a View of the Breakwater at Plymouth.* London: John and Arthur Arch, 1823.

Lewis, Michael. *The Hawkins Dynasty: Three Generations of a Tudor Family.* London: George Allen and Unwin, 1969.

Linschoten, Jan Huygen van. *Iohn Huygen van Linschoten: His Discours of Voyages into the East and West Indies.* London: John Wolfe, c. 1598.

————. *Itinerario, voyage ofte schipvaert van Jan Huygen van Linschoten naer oost ofte Portugaels Indien.* Amsterdam: Cornelis Claesz, 1596.

———. *The Thirde Book. The Navigation of the Portingales into the East Indies.* Trans. William Phillip. London: John Wolfe, 1598.

"Lists Relating to Persons Ejected from Religious Houses." *Devon and Cornwall Notes and Queries* 17 (January–October 1932):80–96, 143–44, 191–92, 238–40, 334–36, 381–84.

Lodge, Edmund. *Illustrations of British History, Biography, and Manners in the Reigns of Henry VIII, Edward VI, Mary, Elizabeth, and James I, in Original Papers.* London: G. Nicol, 1791.

———. *Life of Sir Julius Caesar.* London: John Hatchard and Son, 1827.

Lomas, Sophie Crawford, ed. *Calendar of State Papers, Foreign Series, in the Reign of Elizabeth Preserved in the Public Record Office.* London: His Majesty's Stationery Office, 1916.

López de Velasco, Juan. *Geografía y Descripción Universal de las Indias.* Ed. Marcos Jiménez de la Espada and María del Carmen González Muñoz. Madrid: Ediciones Atlas, 1971.

Marc'hadour, Germain. "More's First Wife. Jane? or Joan?" *Moreana* 109 (March 1992):3–7.

Maritiem Museum "Prins Hendrik." *Lof der Zeevaart: Collectie Dr. W. A. Engelbrecht.* Rotterdam: Maritiem Museum "Prins Hendrik," 1966.

Markham, Clements R., trans. and ed. *Narratives of the Voyage of Pedro Sarmiento de Gamboa to the Straits of Magellan.* Hakluyt Society *Works,* series 1, vol. 91. London: Hakluyt Society, 1895.

Martin, Colin, and Geoffrey Parker. *The Spanish Armada.* London: Penguin, 1988.

Martin, Paula. *Spanish Armada Prisoners.* Exeter Maritime Studies, no. 1. Exeter: University of Exeter Press, 1988.

Mason, A. E. W. *The Life of Francis Drake.* London: Hodder and Stoughton, 1941.

Mathes, W. Michael, trans. and ed. *The Capture of the Santa Ana, Cabo San Lucas, November, 1587.* The Baja California Travel Series, vol. 18. Los Angeles: Dawson's Book Shop, 1969.

Maura Gamazo, Gabriel. *El designio de Felipe II y el episodio de la armada invencible.* Madrid: Editorial Cultura Clásica y Moderna, 1957.

Medina, J. T., ed. *Colección de documentos inéditos para la historia de Chile desde el viaje de Magallanes hasta la batalla de Maipo, 1518–1818.* Santiago, Chile: Imprenta Elzeviriana, 1901.

Mercer, Eric. *English Vernacular Houses: A Study of Traditional Farmhouses and Cottages.* London: Her Majesty's Stationery Office, 1975.

Meteren, Emanuel van. *Belgische ofte Nederlantsche historie van onsen tijden.* Delft: Jacob Cornelisz Vennencool, 1599.

———. *Beschryvinge vande overtresselijke ende wijdtvermaerde Zee-vaerdt vanden Edelen Heer ende Meester Thomas Candish, met drie schepen uytghevaren den 21. Julij 1586, ende met een schip wederom ghekeert in Pleymouth, den 9. September 1588.* Amsterdam: Cornelis Claesz, 1598.

———. *Historia Belgica nostri potissimum temporis, Belgii sub quatuor Burgundis & totidem Austriacis principibus coniunctionem & gubernationem breviter: turbas autem, bella et mutationes tempore Regis Philippi, Caroli V, Caesaris filii ad annum usque 1598, plenius complectens, conscripta: Senatui, populo Belgico, posterisq inscripta A. E. Meterano Belga.* Cologne(?): n.p., 1598(?).

——. *Historia uund Abcontrafentungh furnemlich der Niderlandischer geschichten und kriegshendelen mit hochsten fleisz beschrieben durch Merten von Manuel.* Nuremberg: Hogenberg(?), 1593.

——. *Historiae unnd Abcontrafentung furnemblich der Niderlandischer geschichten unnd kriegshandelen, der anden theye mit hochsten fleiss beschrieben.* Nuremberg(?): Hogenberg(?), 1596.

Mexico, Archivo General de la Nación. *Corsarios Franceses e Ingleses en la inquisición de la Nueva España.* Mexico City: Imprenta Universitaria, 1943.

Michel, Helen V., and Frank Asaro. *Chemical Study of the Plate of Brass.* Lawrence Berkeley Laboratory, Energy and Environment Division, LBL-6338. Berkeley: University of California Lawrence Berkeley Laboratory, 1977.

Milich, Alicia Ronstadt, ed. *Relaciones: An Account of Things Seen and Learned by Father Jerónimo Zárate Salmerón from the Year 1538 to the Year 1626.* Albuquerque: Horn and Wallace, 1966.

Moes, E. W., and C. P. Burger Jr. *De Amsterdamsche Boekdrukkers en Uitgevers in de Zestiende Eeuw.* Amsterdam: C. L. Van Langenhuysen, 1907.

Morales, Ernesto. *Aventuras y désventuras de un navegante, Sarmiento de Gamboa.* Buenos Aires: Futuro, 1946.

Morton, Ann. *Calendar of the Patent Rolls Preserved in the Public Record Office.* Vol. 9, *Elizabeth, 1580–1582.* London: Her Majesty's Stationery Office, 1986.

Mozley, James F. *John Foxe and His Book.* London: Society for Promoting Christian Knowledge, 1940.

Murdin, William A., ed. *A Collection of State Papers Relating to Affairs in the Reign of Queen Elizabeth for the Years 1571 to 1596 Transcribed from Original Paper and Other Authentic Manuscripts Never Before Published, Left by William Cecil, Lord Burghley and Deposited in the Library at Hatfield House.* London: William Bowyer, 1759.

Naish, F. C. Prideaux. "The Identification of the Ashmolean Model." *Mariners' Mirror* 36 (April 1950):129–33.

——. "The Mystery of the Tonnage and Dimensions of the Pelican-Golden Hind." *Mariners' Mirror* 34 (January 1948):42–45.

Nichols, Philip. *Sir Francis Drake Revived.* London: Nicholas Bourne, 1626.

Nuttall, Zelia. *New Light on Drake: A Collection of Documents Relating to His Voyage of Circumnavigation, 1577–1580.* Hakluyt Society *Works*, series 2, vol. 34. London: Hakluyt Society, 1914.

Oliver, George. *Monasticon Diocesis Exoniensis, Being a Collection of Records and Instruments Illustrating the Ancient Conventual, Collegiate, and Eleemosynary Foundations in the Counties of Cornwall and Devon.* Exeter: P. A. Hannaford, 1846.

Oppenheim, Michael. *The Maritime History of Devon.* Exeter: University of Exeter, 1968.

——. *The Naval Tracts of Sir William Monson.* Navy Records Society, vol. 22. London: Navy Records Society, 1902–14.

Peckham, George. *A True Reporte of the late discoveries and possession, taken in the right of*

the Crowne of Englande, of the New found Landes: By that valiaunt and worthye Gentleman Sir Humfrey Gilbert Knight.* London: for I. C. by John Hinde, 1583.

Penzer, N. M., ed. *The World Encompassed and Analogous Contemporary Documents Concerning Sir Francis Drake's Circumnavigation of the World.* Amsterdam: Nico Israel, 1971.

Percyvall, Richard. *Bibliotheca Hispanica.* London: Richard Watkins, 1591.

Pérez, Antonio. *Relaciones de Antonio Pérez, Secretario de Estado, que fue, del Rey de España
Don Phelippe II deste nombre.* Paris: n.p., 1598.

Persons, Robert, S.J. *Letters and Memorials of Father Robert Persons, S.J.* London: Catholic
Record Society, 1942.

Phillips, Carla R. *Six Galleons for the King of Spain: Imperial Defense in the Early Seventeenth Century.* Baltimore: Johns Hopkins University Press, 1986.

Pierson, Peter. *Commander of the Armada, the Seventh Duke of Medina Sidonia.* New
Haven: Yale University Press, 1989.

———. "Elizabeth's Pirate Admiral." *MHQ: Quarterly Journal of Military History* 8
(Summer 1996):80–91.

Pijl-Ketel, Christine L. van der. *The Ceramic Load of the "Witte Leeuw," (1613).* Amsterdam: Rijksmuseum, 1982.

Portillo, Alvaro del. *Descubrimientos y exploraciones en las costas de California, 1532–1650.*
Madrid: Ediciones Rialp, 1982.

Prince, John. *Danmonii Orientales Illustres, or, The Worthies of Devon.* London: Rees and
Curtis, 1810; orig. pub. 1701.

PRO. *See* Great Britain, Public Record Office.

Purchas, Samuel. *Hakluytus Posthumus, or Purchas His Pilgrimes.* Vol. 1. London: William
Stanley for Henrie Fetherstone, 1625.

Quinn, David B. *Drake's Circumnavigation of the Globe: A Review.* Fifteenth Harte Lecture, delivered in the University of Exeter on 14 November 1980. Exeter: University of
Exeter, 1981.

———. "Early Accounts of the Famous Voyage." In *Sir Francis Drake and the Famous
Voyage, 1577–1580.* Ed. Norman J. W. Thrower, 33–48. Berkeley: University of California Press, 1984.

———. *The Roanoke Voyages, 1584–90: Documents to Illustrate the English Voyages to North
America Under the Patent Granted to Walter Raleigh in 1584.* 2 vols. London: Hakluyt
Society, 1955.

———. *Sir Francis Drake as Seen by His Contemporaries.* Providence: John Carter Brown
Library, 1996.

———. *The Voyages and Colonising Enterprises of Sir Humfrey Gilbert.* Hakluyt Society
Works, series 2, vols. 83–84. London: The Hakluyt Society, 1940.

———, ed. *The Last Voyage of Thomas Cavendish, 1591-1592.* Chicago: University of
Chicago Press for the Newberry Library, 1975.

Quinn, David B., C. E. Armstrong, and R. A. Skelton. "The Primary Hakluyt Bibliography." In *The Hakluyt Handbook.* Ed. David B. Quinn, Hakluyt Society *Works,* series 2,
vol. 145. London: The Hakluyt Society, 1974.

Radford, Mrs. G. H. "Tavistock Abbey." *Report and Transactions of the Devonshire Association for the Advancement of Science, Literature, and Art* 46 (July 1914):136–49.

Recopilación de leyes de los reinos de las Indias. 2d ed. Madrid: Antonio Babas, 1756.

"Reduction of Rathlin in 1575." *Notes and Queries.* Third series, 5 (January 1864):90–91.

Resolutiën der Staten-General van 1576 tot 1609. Vol. 5 of *Rijks Geschiedhundige Publicatiën,* Grote Serie. The Hague: Martinus Nijhoff, 1921.

Risk, J. Erskine. "The Rise of Plymouth as a Naval Port." *Report and Transactions of the Devonshire Association for the Advancement of Science, Literature, and Art* 30 (August 1898):350–61.

Robinson, Gregory. "The Evidence about the Golden Hind." *Mariners' Mirror* 35 (January 1949):62–63.

Rodger, N. A. M. *The Armada in the Public Records.* London: Her Majesty's Stationery Office, 1988.

Rodríguez-Salgado, María J. Review of Petruccio Ubaldino's *La disfatta della flotta spagnola. English Historical Review* 105 (April 1990):404.

———, ed. *Armada, 1588-1988: An International Exhibition to Commemorate the Spanish Armada.* London: Penguin, 1988.

Rodríguez-Salgado, María J., and Ian Friel. "The Battle at Sea." In *Armada, 1588–1988: An International Exhibition to Commemorate the Spanish Armada.* Ed. María J. Rodríguez-Salgado, 233–42. London: Penguin, 1988.

Rose-Troupe, Frances. *The Western Rebellion of 1549: An Account of the Insurrection in Devonshire and Cornwall against Religious Insurrection in the Reign of Edward VI.* London: Smith, Elder, 1913.

Rubin, Miri. *Corpus Christi: The Eucharist in Late Medieval Culture.* Cambridge: Cambridge University Press, 1991.

Rumeu de Armas, Antonio. *Los viajes de John Hawkins a America, 1562–1595.* Seville: Escuela de Estudios Hispano-Americanos, 1947.

Ryther, Augustine. *A Discourse concerninge the Spanishe Fleete involvinge England in the Yeere 1588 . . . written in Italian by Petruccio Ubaldino citizen of Florence.* London: A. Hatfield, 1590.

Santa Cruz, Alonso de. *Islario general de todas las islas del mundo.* Ed. Antonio Blázquez. Madrid: Imprenta del Patronato de Huérfanos de Indendencia é Intervención Militares, 1918.

Sarmiento de Gamboa, Pedro. *Viajes al Estrecho de Magallanes.* Ed. Angel Rosenblatt. 2 vols. Buenos Aires: Emecé Editores, 1950.

Scheurweghs, G. "On an Answer to the Articles of the Rebels of Cornwall and Devonshire (Royal MS. 18 B. XI)." *British Museum Quarterly* 8, no. 1 (1933–34):24–25.

Schouten, William Cornelison. *The Relation of a Wonderfull Voiage made by William Cornelison Schouten of Horne.* London: Nathaniel Newbery, 1619.

Scott, Thomas. *The Second Part of Vox Populi, or Gondomor appearing in the likeness of Matchiavell in a Spanish Parliament, wherein are discovered his treacherous & subtile Practices to the ruine as well of England as the Netherlands.* Goricum: A. Janss, 1624.

Shirley, Rodney W. *The Mapping of the World: Early Printed World Maps, 1472–1700.* London: Holland, 1983.

Smet, Antoine De. "Jodocus Hondius, continuateur de Mercator." Extrait de *La Revue Industrie,* November 1963, 770–71. Library, Maritiem Museum "Prins Hendrik."

Snell, Lawrence S. *The Suppression of the Religious Foundations of Devon and Cornwall.* Marazion: Wordens of Cornwall, 1967.

Spain, Museo Naval. *Colección de documentos y manuscritos compilados por Fernández de Navarrete.* Vol. 15. Neudeln, Lichtenstein: Kraus-Thompson, 1971.

Stanislawski, Don. "Early Spanish Town Planning in the New World." *Geographical Review* 37 (January 1947):94–105.

Stoate, T. L. *Devon Lay Subsidy Rolls, 1524–27.* Bristol: T. L. Stoate, 1979.

———. *Devon Lay Subsidy Rolls, 1543–45.* Bristol: T. L. Stoate, 1986.

Stow, John. *Annales of England, Faithfully Collected out of the Most Authenticall Authors, Records, and other Monuments of Antiquities, from the First Inhabitants untill the Present Yeere, 1592.* London: Ralph Newbery, 1592.

Strong, Roy. *The Elizabethan Image: Painting in England, 1540–1620.* London: Tate Gallery, 1969.

Stuart, Elisabeth. *Lost Landscapes of Plymouth: Maps, Charts, and Plans to 1800.* Wolfeboro Falls, N.H.: Alan Sutton, 1991.

Sturt, John. *Revolt in the West: The Western Rebellion of 1549.* Exeter: Devon Books, 1987.

Strype, John. *Annals of the Reformation and establishment of religion, and other various occurrences in the Church of England, during the first twelve years of Queen Elizabeth's happy reign. . . . Compiled faithfully out of papers of state, authentick records, publick registers, private letters and other manuscripts.* London: T. Edlin, 1725–31.

Sugden, John. *Sir Francis Drake.* Barrie and Jenkins, 1990.

———. "Sir Francis Drake: A Note on His Portraiture." *Mariner's Mirror* 70 (August 1984):305–8.

Sydenham, G. F. *The History of the Sydenham Family, Collected from Family Documents, Pedigrees, Deeds, and Copious Memoranda.* Ed. A. T. Cameron. East Molesey, Surrey: E. Dwelly, 1928.

Tapia y Rivera, Alejandro, ed. "Relacion de lo sucedido en S. Juan de Puerto-Rico de las Indias, con la armada inglesa, del cargo de Francisco Draque y Juan Aquines, a los 23 de Noviembre de 1595 años." In *Biblioteca Historica de Puerto-Rico.* Madrid: Imprenta Márquez, 1854.

Taylor, Eva G. R. "Drake and the Pacific, Two Fragments." *Pacific Historical Review* 1, no. 2 (1932):360–69.

———. "The Missing Draft Project of Drake's Voyage, 1577–1580." *Geographical Journal* 75 (January 1930):46–47.

———. "More Light on Drake." *Mariner's Mirror* 16 (April 1930):134–51.

———. *The Original Writings and Correspondence of the Two Richard Hakluyts.* London: The Hakluyt Society, 1935.

———. *Tudor Geography, 1485–1583.* London: Methuen, 1930.

Temple, Richard C. "An Appreciation of Drake's Achievement." In *The World Encompassed and Analogous Contemporary Documents Concerning Sir Francis Drake's Circumnavigation of the World.* Ed. N. M. Penzer, xiii-lxv. Amsterdam: Nico Israel, 1971.

Thomas, Georg Martin, ed. "Logbuch eines Schiffes von der dritten Expedition Franz Drake's 28. August 1595–10. Mai 1596." In *Die Entdeckung Amerikas, nach den Ältesten*

Quellen Geschichtlich Dargestellt. Ed. Friedrich Kunstmann, 101–22. Munich: A. Asher, 1859.

Thomson, George Malcolm. *Sir Francis Drake.* London: Book Club Associates, 1972.

Thrower, Norman J. W. *Sir Francis Drake and the Famous Voyage, 1577-1580.* Berkeley: University of California Press, 1984.

Tomson, Robert. *An Englishman and the Mexican Inquisition, 1556-1560.* Ed. G. R. G. Conway. Mexico City: G. R. G. Conway, 1927.

Tyndale, William. "A Prologue upon the Epystle of Saynt Paul to the Romaynes." In *The Byble.* London: John Day, 1551.

———. "A Prologue upon the Epystle of Saynt Paule to the Romaynes." In *New Testament.* London: John Day, 1551.

Ubaldino, Petruccio, "Comentario della Impresa Fatta Contra il Regno D'Inghilterra del Re Catholica L'Anno 1588." BL Royal 14. A. XI. Trans. in D. W. Waters, *The Elizabethan Navy and the Armada of Spain.* National Maritime Museum *Monographs and Reports,* No. 17 (1975):69–100.

Udall, Nicholas (?). *Troubles Connected with the Prayer Book of 1549.* Ed. Nicholas Pocock. Camden Society Publications, New Series, vol. 3. London: Camden Society, 1884.

Unwin, Rayner. *The Defeat of John Hawkins: A Biography of His Third Slaving Voyage.* London: Allen and Unwin, 1961.

Usherwood, Stephen. *The Great Enterprise: The History of the Spanish Armada as Revealed in Contemporary Documents.* London: The Folio Society, 1978.

Valor Ecclesiasticus, Temp. Hen. VIII, Auctoritate Regia Institutus. London: Record Commission, 1831.

Vaux, W. S. W., ed. *The World Encompassed by Sir Francis Drake, Being his Next Voyage to That to Nombre de Dios, Collated with an Unpublished Manuscript of Francis Fletcher, Chaplain to the Expedition.* Hakluyt Society *Works,* series 1, vol. 16. London: Hakluyt Society, 1854.

Veer, Gerrit de. *Reizen van Willem Barents, Jacob Van Heemskerck, Jan Cornelisz. Rijp en Anderen naar het Noorden (1594-1597).* Vol. 2. The Hague: Martinus Nijhoff, 1917.

Een Verclaringhe der oorsaken bewegende de Coninginne van Enghelant, hulpe te gheven tot Bescherminghe des Benanden en verbruckten Volkes der Nederlanden Eerst ghedruckt tot London by Christoffel Barker der Coninghinlijker Majesteyte van Enghelandt .1585. Amsterdam: Cornelis Claesz, 1585.

Vivian, J. L. *Visitations of the County of Devon, Comprising the Heralds, Visitations of 1531, 1564, and 1620.* Exeter: Henry S. Eland, 1895.

Voisin, Lancelot. *Les trois mondes.* Paris: Pierre L'Huillier, 1582.

Von der Porten, Edward P. *Drake and Cermeño in California: Sixteenth-Century Chinese Ceramics.* Point Reyes, Calif.: Drake Navigators Guild, 1973.

———. "The Drake Puzzle Solved." *Pacific Discovery.* 37 (July-September 1984):22–26.

———. *The Porcelains and Terra Cottas of Drakes Bay.* Point Reyes, Calif.: Drake Navigators Guild, 1968.

Von der Porten, Edward P., and Clarence Shangraw. *The Drake and Cermeño Expeditions: Chinese Porcelains at Drake's Bay, California.* Santa Rosa and Palo Alto, Calif.: Santa Rosa Junior College and Drake Navigators Guild, 1981.

Le voyage de messire François Drake chevalier, aux Indes Occidentales. Leyden: Raphe-lengien, 1588.

Wagner, Anthony. *Drake in England: Genealogical Researches with Particular Reference to the Drakes of Essex from Medieval Times.* Concord: New Hampshire Historical Society, 1963.

Wagner, Henry R. *Cartography of the Northwest Coast of America to the Year 1800.* Berkeley: California Historical Society, 1937.

———. *Sir Francis Drake's Voyage Around the World: Its Aims and Achievements.* San Francisco: John Howell, 1926.

———. *Spanish Voyages to the Northwest Coast of America in the Sixteenth Century.* San Francisco: California Historical Society, 1929.

Wallis, Helen. "The Cartography of Drake's Voyage." In *Sir Francis Drake and the Famous Voyage, 1577–1580.* Ed. Norman J. W. Thrower, 121–63. Berkeley: University of California Press, 1984.

———. *Sir Francis Drake: An Exhibition to Commemorate Francis Drake's Voyage Around the World, 1577–1580.* London: British Library, 1977.

———. *The Voyage of Sir Francis Drake Mapped in Silver and Gold.* Friends of the Bancroft Library Keepsake, no. 27. Berkeley: Friends of the Bancroft Library, 1979.

VVarachtighe tydinghe vande schoone aenghevanghene victorie die Godt de Scheeps Armade uyt Enghelandt naer Spaengien afghevaren verleent heeft over de Armade des Conincks van Spaengien ende eroveringe der Stadt Cadiz ofte Calis Malis, ende andere plaetsen in Andalusie, ende wes sich daer inne heeft toeghedraghen. Amsterdam(?): Cornelis Claesz, 1596(?).

Waters, D. W. *The Elizabethan Navy and the Armada of Spain.* National Maritime Museum, *Monographs and Reports,* no. 17. Greenwich, England: National Maritime Museum, 1975.

Wernham, R. B. *The Expedition of Sir John Norris and Sir Francis Drake to Spain and Portugal, 1589.* Aldershot, England: Temple Smith for the Navy Records Society, 1988.

Western Morning News (Plymouth), 26 August 1926. Drake clipping files, Westcountry Studies Library, Exeter.

Whiting, Robert. *The Blind Devotion of the People: Popular Religion and the English Reformation.* Cambridge: Cambridge University Press, 1989.

Whitmarsh, J. "Drake Relics." *Western Antiquary* 3 (March 1884):236–37.

Wieder, Frederick C. *De Reis van Mahu en de Cordes door de Straat van Magalhaes naar Zuid-Amerika en Japan, 1598–1600.* Vol. 22 of *Werken Uitgegeven door Linschoten Vereeniging.* The Hague: Martinus Nijhoff, 1924.

Williamson, James A. *The Age of Drake.* London: Adam and Charles Black, 1946.

———. *Hawkins of Plymouth: A New History of Sir John Hawkins and of the Other Members of His Family Prominent in Tudor England.* 2d ed. London: Adam and Charles Black, 1969.

———. *Sir John Hawkins, the Time and the Man.* Oxford: Clarendon, 1927.

Wilson, Derek. *The World Encompassed: Francis Drake and His Great Voyage.* New York: Harper and Row, 1977.

Wingfield, Anthony. *A True Coppie of a Discourse written by a Gentleman employed in the late Voyage of Spaine and Portingale Sent to his particular friend, and by him published, for the better satisfaction of all such, as having been seduced by particular report, have entred into conceipts tending to the discredit of the enterprise and Actors of the same.* London: Thomas Woodcock, 1589.

Woodcock, Gerry. "Mrs Bray." In *Tavistock's Yesterdays: Episodes from Her History.* 8 vols., 6:13–20. Tavistock, England: Penwell, 1990.

Woodward, G. W. O. *The Dissolution of the Monasteries.* New York: Walker, 1966.

Worth, R. N. *Calendar of the Plymouth Municipal Records.* Plymouth: Wm. Brendon & Sons, 1893.

———. *Calendar of the Tavistock Parish Records.* Plymouth: n.p., 1887.

[———]. "Sir Francis Drake and the Plymouth Corporation." *Western Morning News,* 12 April 1884.

Wright, Irene A. *Further English Voyages to Spanish America.* Hakluyt Society *Works,* series 2, vol. 99. London: Hakluyt Society, 1951.

———. *Spanish Documents Concerning English Voyages to the Caribbean, 1527–1568.* Hakluyt Society *Works,* series 2, vol. 62. London: Hakluyt Society, 1929.

Wright, Thomas. *The Famous Voyage of Sir Francis Drake.* London: H. Slater, 1742.

Wrightson, Keith. *English Society, 1580–1680.* London: Hutchinson, 1983.

Youings, Joyce. "Bowmen, Billmen, and Hackbutters: The Elizabethan Militia in the South West." In *Security and Defence in the South-West England before 1800,* 51–68. Exeter Studies in History, no. 19. Exeter: University of Exeter Press, 1987.

———. "Drake, Grenville, and Buckland Abbey." *Transactions of the Devonshire Association of Science, Literature, and Art* 112 (December 1980):95–99.

———. "Raleigh's Country and the Sea." *Proceedings of the British Academy* 75 (1989):267–90.

———. *Sixteenth-Century England.* London: Penguin, 1984.

———. "The South-Western Rebellion of 1549." *Southern History* 1 (1979):99–122.

———. *Tuckers Hall Exeter: The History of a Provincial City Company through Five Centuries.* Exeter: University of Exeter, 1968.

Zárate Salmerón, Jerónimo. "Relaciones de todas las cosas que en el Nuevo Mexico se han visto y sabido ási por mar como por tierra desde el año de 1538 hasta el de 1626 por el padre Gerónimo Zárate Salmerón." In *Documentos para servir a la historia del Nuevo Mexico 1538–1778.* C. Lección Chimalistic, no. 13. Madrid: Ediciones José Porrúa Turanzas, 1962

Zell, Michael L. "Economic Problems of the Parochial Clergy in the Sixteenth Century." In *Princes and Paupers in the English Church, 1500–1800.* Ed. Rosemary Day and Felicity Hall. Leicester: Leicester University Press.

Printed Maps and Portraits

Boazio, Baptista. *The Famous West Indian Voyage Made by the Englishe fleete of 22 shippes and Barkes wherein weare gotten the Townes of St. Iago: Sto. Domingo, Cartagena and St. Augustines the same beinge begun from Plimmouth in the Moneth of September 1585 and ended at Portesmouth in Iulie 1586 the whole course of the saide Viadge beinge plainlie described by the pricked line.* N.p., n.d.

————. Maps of Santiago, Santo Domingo, Cartagena, and Saint Augustine. In [Walter Bigges,] *Expeditio Francisci Draki equitis Angli in Indias occidentales A. M. D. LXXXV.* Leyden: Franciscus Raphelengium, 1588.

————. Maps of Santiago, Santo Domingo, Cartagena, and Saint Augustine. In Walter Bigges, *A Summarie and True Discourse of Sir Frances Drakes West Indian Voyage.* London: Richard Field, 1589.

Corte Beschryvinghe van die seer heerliicke voyagie, die Capteyn Draeck inde Zuydersche Zee. Amsterdam: Cornelis Claesz, c. 1596.

Gastaldi, Giacomo de. *Cosmographia universalis et exactissima iuxta postremam neotericoriam traditionem.* Venice: Matthio Pagano(?), 1562(?).

Hondius, Jodocus. *Typus orbis terrarum.* London(?): n.p., 1589.

————. *Vera totius expeditionis nauticae.* [Amsterdam: Cornelis Claesz, 1596.]

Houue, Paulis de la. *Franciscus Draeck Nobilissimus Eques Angliae.* Paris: n.p., 1586(?).

Sype, Nicola van. *La Herdike Enterprinse faict par le signeur Draeck davoir circuit toute la terre.* Amsterdam(?): n.p., 1581(?). Newberry Library, map department, Ayer *133 D7 H55 1581.

————. *La Herdike Interprinse Faict par le signeur Draeck davoir cirquit toute la terre.* 1582? Bound in [Walter Bigges,] *Expeditio Francisci Draki equitis Angli in Indias occidentales A. M. D. LXXXV.* Leyden: Franciscus Raphelengium, 1588. Huntington Library rare book 9074.

INDEX

Drake's name is abbreviated as FD within entries. The entry for Drake contains references to material on his private life and personal characteristics. Particulars of his seafaring activities will be found at the main entries for specific voyages and locations.